LATIN LESSONS

ADAPTED TO

ALLEN AND GREENOUGH'S LATIN GRAMMAR.

PREPARED BY

R. F. LEIGHTON, A.M.,

MASTER OF THE MELROSE HIGH SCHOOL.

BOSTON:

PUBLISHED BY GINN BROTHERS.

1874.

PREFACE.

THIS book has been prepared to accompany Allen and Greenough's Latin Grammar. In addition to exercises for elementary drill, going systematically over the entire ground of the Etymology and Syntax, it aims to furnish a sufficient quantity of interesting reading matter, on subjects suited to the capacity of the pupil, to prepare him to read the usual Latin authors with ease and profit; while the Notes are designed to supply all necessary information on the subjects of synonymes, ancient geography, Roman history, and antiquities. Questions for examination and review, with vocabularies, complete the volume.

Much care and study have been spent on the order and arrangement of the Lessons, especially in the earlier part, aiming mainly at these two things, — first, to introduce, very early in the course, a comparison of *the simpler verb-forms,* which are easier than nouns, and open the way to a much larger range of expression; and secondly, to give not bare words and their inflections, but *sentences from the start,* both questions and answers, in natural and easy succession. The first associations with any language, especially when learned by the young, ought to be such as make it as nearly as possible like a living tongue; the scientific study of it should follow, not go before, some familiar elementary knowledge of what it is in actual speech. Teachers who use this book may find it desirable, further, to save the learner from those mistakes which often cling in the memory long after the correction of them has been forgotten, by *reading the lessons with their classes* in advance: the value and importance of frequent reviews are too plain to need recommendation here. The Lessons, including considerably more than a hundred exercises, Latin and English, are so arranged that each gives practice on what has gone before; those to be written in Latin being based on the exercises in translation immediately preceding. Taken in course, they will be found an ample preparation for any of the more advanced manuals of Latin Composition.*

The Reading Lessons which follow are largely made up from modern Latin, — a few Fables of Æsop, and extracts from "Viri Romæ," — owing to the almost absolute lack in classic authors of matter at once simple in style and suitable for elementary practice. These are followed by Woodford's Epitome of the First Book of the Gallic War, which gives the main thread of the narrative in Cæsar's own words, omitting the more difficult constructions and parenthetical clauses. The Notes to this portion of the book have been prepared on the theory that it is better to give too much than too little at this stage of the course. Hence, besides very numerous references to the grammar, the full explanation of constructions, and frequent exhibition of synonymes, many details have been given of history, antiquities, etc., which will prove, if not essential at first, yet useful in the pupil's later studies. Some may prefer that he should get this information by his own research; but my own experience as a teacher convinces

* They have been expressly arranged as an introduction to the brief but very complete "Latin Composition" by Professor W. F. Allen.

me how little likely this is to be done, and how little danger there is of putting these matters within too easy reach.

Without entering into the discussion as to the best method of pronouncing Latin, I may be permitted to urge the great advantage and importance of knowing thoroughly *the phonetic value of the letters of the Roman alphabet*, and their simpler changes and combinations (as given in the first two sections of the Grammar), as a key to many of the difficulties of inflection and derivation. This is quite aside from the question of pronunciation, which must after all be governed by the prevailing usage. For the convenience of those who adopt the so-called English method, a few simple rules are given. It will be understood, of course, that they have no claim of authority or scientific value, and are a mere enumeration of accidental errors and corruptions which the Roman tongue has encountered in its blending with modern speech.

To the authors of the Latin Grammar, and to Professor Allen of the University of Wisconsin, I desire to express my obligations for the very serviceable aid which they have afforded me in the preparation of this book.

MELROSE, MASS., August, 1872.

CONTENTS.

PRONOUNS (*continued*).

RULES OF PRONUNCIATION.

I. ACCORDING TO THE "ENGLISH METHOD."

N. B. — The long or short vowel-sound indicated in these rules is wholly independent of the *quantity* of the vowels by the rules of Latin Prosody.

1. In Monosyllables, the vowel has —

a. The long sound, if it ends the syllable : as, *si, me, spe.*

b. The short sound, if followed by a consonant : as, *ăb, cum, hōc, hās;* except *post,* monosyllables in *es,* and (in plural cases) *os,* where it has the long sound : as, *rēs, hōs, ēs.*

2. An accented Penult has —

a. The long vowel-sound before a single consonant (or a mute with *l* or *r*), or, before a vowel or diphthong : as, *pă'ter, lib-er-ā'lis, dĕ'us, sa'cra, pa'tris.*

b. The short vowel-sound before two consonants (except a mute followed by *l* or *r*), or *x* : as, *reg'num, rex'i.*

3. An accented Antepenult has —

a. The long vowel-sound before a vowel : as, *ĕ'adem, hĭ'e-mis, fŭ'-e-rat.*

b. The short vowel-sound before a consonant : as, *in'su-la, i-tin'e-ris.*

Exceptions. — (*a.*) *u* before a single consonant (or a mute with *l* or *r*) has the long sound : *jŭ've-nis, lū'ri-dus, pu'tri-dus;* but before *bl,* the short sound : as in *res-pub'li-ca.*

(*b.*) *a, e, o,* before a single consonant (or a mute with *l* or *r*) followed by two vowels, the first of which is *e, i,* or *y,* have the long sound : as *impe'ri-um, do'ce-o, a'cri-a.*

4. In all unaccented syllables the vowel-sound is —

a. Long, if followed by a single consonant (or a mute with *l* or *r*) : as, *do-lo'ris;* but final syllables ending in a consonant are short, in a vowel, long : as, *con-sul* (except *es,* and in plur. cases *os* at the end of the word).

b. Short, before *x,* or any two consonants : as, *bel-lo'rum, rex-is'set.*

EXCEPTION. — Final *a* is sounded as in the last syllable of *America:* as, *men'sa;* and the vowel sounds in *tibi* and *sibi* are as in the English *lily*.

NOTE. — Compounds generally follow the same rules; but if the first part ends in a consonant, the vowel-sound is short: as, *ob'it, red'it, ab-e-rat, præ-ter'e-a, trans'i-tur* (except *post*, and final syllables in *as* and *os* of plural cases: as, *post-quam, post'e-ri, hos'ce*).

5. Diphthongs follow the same rules as the vowels which represent them in English: thus —

(*a*.) *æ* and *œ* have the sound of *e:* that is, long in *cæ'lum, a-mœ'nus;* short in *hæs'i-to, a-mœn'i-tas.*

(*b*.) In poetry *ei* may be regarded as a diphthong, as in *dein'de*, having the sound of *i* in mind: *eu, au, oi*, have, when diphthongs, the same sound as in *feud, author, coin:* as *Orpheus, Oileus, aurum; ui* is a diphthong, having the long sound of *i* in *huic, cui, hui; u* in connection with other vowels or diphthongs sometimes has the sound of *w* after *g* or *s:* as, *qui, lin'gua, sua'deo, quæ'ro.*

6. Consonants have generally the same power as in English: —

(*a*.) Thus, before *e, i, y*, and the diphthongs *æ, eu, œ, c* has the sound of *s*, and *g* of *j; ch* has always the sound of *k* as in chemist; *c, s, t* often have the sound of *sh* before *i* followed by a vowel, and before *eu* when preceded by an accented syllable, and *x* of *ksh*: as, *socius, censui, ratio, caduceus, anxius.*

NOTE. — It is to be understood that in these examples the rule is only *permissive*, and that usage varies considerably among the best authorities. In general, when the word, or the combination of letters is *distinctly foreign to us*, it may be better to retain the pure consonant sound: as in *men-ti-ē'tur, Min'cius, ca-du'ce-us, Ly'si-as, Mœ'si-a, ax-i-o'ma, noc'ti-um.*

It is very common, in English pronunciation, to slur or suppress the more difficult consonant sounds, particularly in such cases as *cn, gn, ps, pt, tm*, or *x*, at the beginning of a word; as in *Cnidus, gnotus, pseudo-, pteris, Tmolus, xylon.* But, in an accurate pronunciation of these, *as Latin or Greek words*, the full consonant sound will be retained.

Finally, there can be no correct rule to authorize the slipshod and slovenly habit of enunciation which is frequently allowed. To cultivate *a clear and vigorous utterance of unfamiliar words* is one of the incidental benefits of careful instruction in a foreign tongue.

II. ACCORDING TO THE "ROMAN METHOD."

The following are the rules adopted in the Boston Latin School, as given in "Old and New," November, 1871.

The English equivalents for the long and short sounds of the Vowels are here given —

ă as in ăh :	*dăbam.*	ā as in āh :	*nābam.*
ĕ " " fāted :	*vĕnio.*	ē " " fāne :	*vēni.*
ĭ " " fleet :	*vĭdeo.*	ī " " flee :	*vīdi.*
ŏ " " intonate :	*fŏveo.*	ō " " tōne	*fōvi.*
ŭ " " boot :	*fŭgio.*	ū " " moon :	*fūgi.*

The Diphthongs *ae* and *ai* are sounded like *ay*, the English adverb of affirmation ; *au* like *ow* in *owl ; oi* and *oe* nearly like *oi* in *oil ; eu* like *eh'oo ; ua,* when a diphthong, like *wah.*

Ui is sounded like the French *oui* or English *we.*

Y is sounded like the German *ü* or French *u.*

Of the Consonants, —

C has always the hard sound : thus *Cicero* is to be pronounced *Kee'kero.*

G " " " " "

J when used as a consonant corresponds in sound to our *Y :* thus *jam* is pronounced *yam.*

Qu has the sound of *K :**

V has a sound approximating to the English *W.*

T has always the simple sound : thus the second and third syllables of *justitia* are sounded alike.

S has always the pure sound, and not the sound of *Z* or *Sh.*

Ch has the power of *K.*

Th has the power of Θ (Greek), or of *th* in *thin.*

Z is sounded nearly like *S.*

The other consonants are supposed to have had sounds nearly identical with the present English sounds.

NOTE. — According to some of the best authorities, if the vowel of the Penult is short, *i* or *u* coming immediately before it is to be regarded as a semi-vowel, and pronounced like *y* or *w,* the accent going back to the syllable before : as, *mŭ'liĕres, mŏ'nuĕrat, fī'liŏlus.* But in compounds, the accent will not be thrown back of the radical syllable : thus, *im-pĭ'ĕtas, ab-fu'ĕrat.*

* Or more correctly as in English, according to Professor Lane : compare 'Ακουϊτανούς (Strabo) for *Aquitanos.*

DEFINITIONS.

Articles, Nouns, Adjectives, Pronouns, Verbs, Adverbs, Prepositions, Conjunctions, and Interjections are called Parts of Speech. There is no Article in Latin.

A Noun is the name of any thing: as, **homo,** *man;* **navis,** *ship.*

If a noun is the name of a person, or of a thing spoken of by its own name, as if it were a person, it is a Proper Noun; if not, it is a Common Noun. Thus in the sentence **Roma magna est urbs,** *Rome is a great city,* **Roma** is a proper, and **urbs** a common noun.

An Adjective is a word used to define a quality: as, **carus,** *dear;* **bonus,** *good.*

Comparison shows the degree of the quality: as,

Positive.	Comparative.	Superlative.
carus, *dear.*	**carior,** *dearer.*	**carissimus,** *dearest.*
bonus, *good.*	**melior,** *better.*	**optimus,** *best.*

A Pronoun is a word used instead of a noun: as, *he* for *the man.*

The First Person, **ego,** *I,* **nos,** *we,* is the person speaking; the Second Person, **tu, vos,** *you,* is the one spoken to; the Third Person, *he, she, it, they,* is that spoken of, and has no personal pronoun in Latin, Demonstratives being often used instead.

A Demonstrative denotes a particular person or thing: as, **hic,** *this,* **ille,** *that.*

A Relative refers to a person or thing before spoken of: as, **qui,** *who,* **quod,** *which.*

The person or thing referred to is called the Antecedent: as, **homo qui venit,** *the man who came.*

An Interrogative asks a question: as, **quis adest?** *who is here?* **ubinam gentium sumus?** *where in the world are we?*

A Verb is a word which tells an action or condition: as, **vēni,** *I came;* **cecĭdit,** *he fell.*

Mood denotes the manner of an action: as, **venit,** *he came* (Indicative); **venisset,** *he might have come* (Subjunctive).

Tense denotes the time of an action: as, **currit,** *he runs* (Present); **cucurrit,** *he ran* (Past).

Of Voices, the Active speaks of a person doing the action: as, **ferit,** *he strikes;* the Passive, as suffering it: as, **feritur,** *he is struck.*

A PARTICIPLE expresses the action, etc., of a verb in the form of an adjective: as, **feriens,** *striking;* **ictus,** *struck.*

An ADVERB is a word which qualifies the meaning of adjectives, verbs, or adverbs: as, **acerrime ferit,** *he strikes very hard.*

A PREPOSITION is a word which expresses the relations between other words: as, **in oppidum venit,** *he came to town;* **pro patria mori,** *to die for one's country.*

A CONJUNCTION is a word which connects other words or sentences: as, **procerus et validus,** *tall and strong.*

INTERJECTIONS are exclamations: as, **heus!** *halloo!*

GENDER is distinction as to sex, and is Masculine of male creatures: as, **rex,** *king;* Feminine of female creatures: as, **regina,** *queen;* Neuter of things: as, **solium,** *throne.*

Things without sex are Neuter in English: as, *stone, tree.* But in Latin they are frequently masculine or feminine: as, lapis, *stone* (masc.); **arbor,** *tree* (fem.). This is called Grammatical Gender.

NUMBER signifies *how many,* and is Singular when one is spoken of: as, **vir,** *man;* Plural when more than one: as, **viri,** *men.*

CASE is the form a noun takes to show its relation to other words: as, **pueri currunt,** *the boys run* (Nominative); **pueri soror,** *the boy's sister* (Genitive).

This relation is generally shown in English by prepositions; as, **gesta Romanorum,** *the deeds of the Romans;* **invidia mihi,** *envy against me.*

QUANTITY is the time taken in pronouncing a vowel or a syllable, in comparison with other syllables.

Thus in the word *strengthen,* the first syllable is long and the second short in quantity or time, though they are both called short in quality or sound; in *submit,* the first is long and the second short, in quantity, though the latter has the accent.

Quantity is reckoned much more important in Latin than in English, and often shows the difference in the meaning of words. Thus **lēvis** (long e) means *smooth;* **lĕvis** (short e), means *light;* **cecīdit** is *he fell;* **cecĭdit,** *he cut* or *felled.*

EMPHASIS is stress of voice on an important word or phrase: as, *cowards* run; but *brave men* stand.

ACCENT is stress of voice on a particular syllable: as, *the nécessary resérves.*

A PROCLITIC is a word without accent of its own, that seems to lean on the word after it; an ENCLITIC is one that seems to lean on the word before it.

Thus in the sentence, *The boys, and girls too, are here,* — *the* is a proclitic, and *too* an enclitic.

In Latin, the enclitics **que**, *and*, **ve**, *or*, **ne**, *whether*, and sometimes **cum**, *with*, are written as part of the preceding word. Thus in Latin, the sentence given above would be, **pueri puellæque adsunt.**

For Definitions in Syntax, see § 45.

LATIN LESSONS.

Before beginning these Lessons, the pupil should learn the rules of Pronunciation (Roman method), § 2, with the general rules of Quantity and Accent, §§ 3, 4; also the large type of §§ 5 – 8, particularly the general signification of the cases, § 7. The sections to which each lesson especially refers are designated at the head.

LESSON I.

FIRST DECLENSION. § 9.

Vocabulary.

aqua,	*water.*	**nauta,**	*sailor.*
stella,	*star.*	**puella,**	*girl.*
lūna,	*moon.*	**rosa,**	*rose.*
rīpa,	*river-bank.*	**agricola,**	*farmer.*
fāma,	*report.*	**victōria,**	*victory.*

Translate into English.

1. Rosa.[1] 2. Aquæ. 3. Lunā. 4. Agricolarum. 5. Puellarum. 6. Puellæ agricolarum. 7. Ripis. 8. Rosa puellæ.[2] 9. Lunam. 10. Agricolas. 11. Rosis puellarum.

[1] There is no article in Latin; the word **rosa** may mean *a rose, the rose,* or simply *rose.*

[a] The genitive in Latin often corresponds to the possessive in English; the words **rosa puellæ** may mean *the girl's rose* or *the rose of the girl.*

NOTE. — The quantity of all the long syllables will be marked in the vocabularies except where the rules of § 3 apply; those not marked, nor long by position, are short. The pupil should be required to account for the quantity of those vowels to which the rules apply. The vocabularies should be committed to memory by the pupil before beginning to translate the exercise.

RULE I. — Final **a** is short in declinable words, except in the ablative of the first declension.

LESSON II.

SUBJECT AND PREDICATE. § 49, 2.

Vocabulary.

silva,	*wood, forest.*	**magna,**	*large.*
insula,	*island.*	**parva,**	*small.*
via,	*way, road.*	**alta,**	*high* or *deep.*
fīlia,	*daughter.*	**densa,**	*thick, close.*
incola,	*inhabitant.*	**clāra,**	*clear, bright.*
casa,	*cottage.*	**longa,**	*long.*
et,	*and.*	**sed,**	*but.*
nōn,	*not.*	**plēna,**	*full.*
nova,	*new.*	**lata,**	*broad.*

sum,	*I am.*	**sumus,**	*we are.*
es,	*thou art (you are).*	**estis,**	*you are.*
est,	*he (she, it) is.*	**sunt,**	*they are.*

Translate into English.

1. Stellæ sunt claræ. 2. Puella est parva. 3. Luna et stella claræ sunt.[1] 4. Puella est nautæ filia.[2] 5. Silvæ

densæ sunt et altæ. 6. Insula longa est sed non lata. 7. Incolæ insularum nautæ[3] sunt. 8. Insula non est magna. 9. Est[4] (*it is*) casa agricolæ. 10. Est[5] (*there is*) parva insula, plena silvarum (silvis). 11. Est (*he is*) incola insulæ.

[1] When there are two subjects, the verb is plural; see § 49, 1.

[2] See § 9, 2 (*e*).

[3] Notice that the predicate after the verb *to be* is in the same case as the subject.

[4] Notice that the personal pronouns *I*, *thou*, &c., are contained in the endings of the verb; thus **est** is not merely *is*, but *he* (*she* or *it*) *is*; the nominative of the personal pronouns is rarely expressed in Latin.

[5] In English, when the subject is indefinite we use the word *there* with the verb *to be;* as, **insula est parva** may mean *the island is small*, an *island is small*, (there) *is a small island*, (it) *is a small island*, or *the island is a small* (one). Generally the same order in Latin can be followed as in English, unless we wish to give emphasis to some particular word; then that word should be placed either first or last in the sentence. Thus we can say **est insula parva**, *the island is small*, if we wish to contradict some one who has said it is not so. (See § 76.)

Translate into Latin.

1. The way is long. 2. The moon is bright. 3. The forest is large and thick. 4. The inhabitants of the island are sailors. 5. The islands are not small. 6. The inhabitants of the island are not sailors, but farmers. 7. She[1] is the daughter of the sailor. 8. The moon and stars are bright. 9. There[2] is a large island full of woods. 10. He is an inhabitant of the island. 11. We are farmers, not sailors.

[1] See Lesson II. Note 4. [2] See Lesson II. Note 5.

LESSON III.

SUBJECT AND OBJECT. § 52, 1.

Vocabulary.

ōra,	*shore.*	**aula,**	*hall.*
pecūnia,	*money.*	**rapida,**	*swift.*
terra,	*land.*	**paro,**	*prepare.*
do,[1]	*give.*	**seco,**	*cut.*
aro,	*plough.*	**voco,**	*call.*

matrōna, *married woman.*

amo,	*I love.*	**amāmus,**	*we love.*
amās,	*thou lovest.*	**amātis,**	*you love.*
amat,	*he loves.*	**amant,**	*they love.*

Translate into English.

1. Nautas vocat. 2. Incolas insularum vocamus. 3. Vocat puellam. 4. Vocant nautam. 5. Damus rosas puellis. 6. Oræ insularum plenæ sunt rosarum. 7. Agricolæ silvas secant magnas densasque.[2] 8. Aula est magna. 9. Matronæ dant rosas filiabus. 10. Puellæ sunt agricolarum filiæ. 11. Sumus nautæ.

[1] These verbs are inflected in the present tense like **amo.**
[2] The syllable **-que** added to a word means *and.*

Rule II. — Final **o** is common; but it is long in datives and ablatives; also, usually in verbs.

Translate into Latin.

1. He calls the sailors. 2. The farmers cut the high woods. 3. He calls the inhabitants of the islands. 4. The sailor ploughs the water, and the farmer ploughs the land. 5. The sailor calls (his)[1] daughter. 6. She is the daughter of the sailor. 7. They are the sailor's daugh-

ters. 8. It is a beautiful island, long but narrow, and the water is deep and swift. 9. (There) is a report of victory.

[1] Words in parenthesis are not to be translated.

LESSON IV.

QUESTIONS. § 71.

Vocabulary.

līttera,	*letter.*	**poēta,**	*poet.*
lītteræ (plur.),	*letter, epistle.*	**perfuga,**	*deserter.*
dēlecto,	*delight.*	**insidiæ** (plur.),	*snares.*
monstro,	*show.*	**umbra,**	*shade.*
Galba,	*Galba.*	**medicīna,**	*medicine.*
ancilla,	*maid-servant.*	**ægra,**	*sick.*

eram,	*I was.*	**erāmus,**	*we were.*
erās,	*thou wast.*	**erātis,**	*you were.*
erat,	*he was.*	**erant,**	*they were.*

Translate into English.

1. Vocatne[1] puellam? Vocat. 2. Nonne Galba insidias parat? 3. Agricola puellis viam monstrat. 4. Num poeta reginæ rosam dat? 5. Suntne puellæ agricolarum filiæ? Non sunt, sed nautarum. 6. Erantne copiæ Galbæ? 7. Regina erat ægra. 8. Nonne regina vocat ancillas? Non vocat. 9. Umbra silvarum agricolas delectat.

[1] A question may be asked in Latin by the particles **num, nonne,** and the syllable **-ne** added to a word. The enclitic **-ne** is used in questions asked for information merely; **nonne,** when the answer *yes,* and **num** when the answer *no* is expected. There is no word in Latin for *yes* or *no.* To answer a question, the verb may be repeated; thus, **vocatne,** *does he call?* **vocat,** *yes* (*he calls*); **non vocat,** *no* (*he does not call*).

Translate into Latin.

1. Does the sailor call (his) daughter? Yes. 2. Does the deserter give a letter to the queen? No. 3. Were they[1] the daughters of the farmer? 4. The farmer shows the way to (his) daughter. 5. Was the island long? 6. (There) is[2] the letter of the queen. 7. The moon delights the farmer. 8. Does the shade of the wood delight the poet? 9. Was he an inhabitant of the island?

[1] Use **num erant.**

[2] The verb must be plural; **littera,** sing., means a *letter* (as of the alphabet); **litteræ,** plur., a *letter*, i. e. an *epistle.*

LESSON V.

PREPOSITIONS. § 42.

Vocabulary.

fera,	*wild beast.*	**alba,**	*white.*
sto,[1]	*stand.*	**rubra,**	*red.*
nato,	*swim.*	**cōpia,**	*abundance.*
ambulo,	*walk.*	**cōpiæ** (plur.),	*forces.*
prōvincia,	*province.*	**pulchra,**	*beautiful.*
porta,[2]	*gate.*	**nigra,**	*dark.*
aquila,	*eagle.*	**volo,**	*fly.*

Translate into English.

1. Stant in[3] densa silva. 2. Ad silvam ambulamus, et stamus in nigra umbra. 3. Nonne nautæ natant in alta aqua, ad oram insulæ? 4. Silvæ in insula nigræ sunt et densæ. 5. Ambulantne ad silvam? 6. Agricola latam viam secat per silvam. 7. Nauta stat in (*on*) insulæ ora. 8. Suntne puellæ in silva? 9. In ripa sunt pulchræ puellæ, cum rosis rubris et albis.

[1] Inflect these verbs like **amo.**

[2] Syn. — **Porta** is used of a city; **janua**, of a house.

[3] All the prepositions govern either the accusative or the ablative. See § 56.

Note. — The preposition **in**, with the accusative, means *into;* with the ablative, it means *in:* **ad** and **per** are followed by the accusative; **ad** means *to;* **per**, *through:* **cum** is followed by the ablative, and means *with, in company with.*

Notice that **et** connects words which are considered independently and of equal importance, while **que** joins a word closely to another as belonging to it; thus, in **pueri puellæque ludunt,** *the boys and girls are playing*, **-que** connects the words under one proposition; while in **pueri student et puellæ ludunt,** *the boys study and the girls play*, **et** connects two distinct propositions.

Translate into Latin.

1. We swim in deep water. 2. The farmers stand in the thick woods. 3. The water is deep and dark. 4. Do the sailors stand on the shore of the island? 5. The sailor is in the water. 6. We walk through the woods towards the cottage. 7. The sailors (do) not stand on the shore, but swim to the river-bank in the deep and swift water. 8. The sailors are in the water. 9. We swim to the shore of the island.

LESSON VI.

SECOND DECLENSION. § 10.

Vocabulary.

ager, agri,	*field.*	**magister,**	*master, teacher.*
faber, fabri,	*smith.*	**gener,**	*son-in-law.*
equus,	*horse.*	**venit,**	*he (she, it) comes.*
dominus,	*master.*	**lūdus,**	*school.*
pābulum,	*fodder.*	**campus,**	*field.*

hortus,	*garden.*	**vesper,**	*evening.*
regnum,	*kingdom.*	**jānua,**	*door.*
servus,	*slave.*	**lēgātus,**	*ambassador.*
arvum,	*ploughed field.*	**vir,**	*man.*

Translate into English.

1. Magister cum pueris erat in agro. 2. Puer venit in januam. 3. Suntne servi in horto? 4. Pueri (*we boys*) in aqua natamus. 5. Puellas vocamus ex[1] via in hortum. 6. Est in agro[2] copia pabuli. 7. Dominus in arvo cum servis ambulat. 8. Gener venit ex casa. 9. Pueri parvi sunt in horto cum magistro. 10. Puer venit e densa silva, et natat in alta aqua ad parvam insulam. 11. Boni viri bonos pueros amant. 12. Vir venit cum servo in arvum. 13. Vir ambulat ab insulæ ora.

[1] The preposition **ex** (**e** before consonants) is followed by the ablative, and means *out of:* **a** (**a** before consonants, **ab** before vowels and consonants) means *from, away from;* it means *by*, when used with a passive verb to express the person by whom anything is done.

[2] Syn. — **Ager** is the *field* in general; **arvum**, the *ploughed field;* and **campus**, the *enclosed field* or *plain.*

Rule III. — Final **i** and **u** are long, also final **as, es,** and **os;** final **a, e,** and **y** are short; also **is** and **us**, but **is** and **us** are long in plural cases.

Translate into Latin.

1. He calls the boys out of the garden into[1] the road. 2. Does the master call the boys? No. 3. The slave comes into the field with (his) master. 4. The boy comes into the garden. 5. The girl comes out of the garden and walks towards (**ad**) the field. 6. He walks in the field with (his) son and daughter. 7. The boy walks away from the water. 8. The sailor comes out of the water.

9. (It) is the farmer's horse. 10. The man walks in the garden at (**ad**) evening with (his) boys.

[1] Observe the distinction between the prepositions **in** and **ex**, and **ad** and **ab**. **In** (with the accusative) and **ex** denote motion *to* and *from* the *inside* of a place; **ad** and **ab** (or **a**) denote motion *to* and *from* the outside of a place. Thus, **venit in Italiam**, when one comes *into* Italy; **ex Italia**, when one comes *out of* Italy; but **ad Italiam**, *to* Italy when there is no notion of entering into Italy conveyed; just so **ab Italia**, *away from* Italy, when it is simply expressed that he came away from Italy (which he had not entered).

LESSON VII.

ADJECTIVES: FIRST AND SECOND DECLENSION. § 16.

Vocabulary.

amplus,	*large.*	**castra** (plur.),	*camp.*
noster (nostra),	*our.*	**oppidum**,	*town.*
meus (voc. **mi**),	*my.*	**fluvius**,	*river.*
bonus,	*good.*	**lātus**,	*broad.*
līberi (plur.),	*children.*	**bellum**,	*war.*
saxum,	*rock.*	**prœlium**,	*battle.*
cælum,	*sky.*	**dōnum**,	*gift.*
mūrus,	*wall.*	**locus**,	*place.*

Translate into English.

1. Nonne dat puero donum? 2. Campus longus est et latus. 3. Dominus servusque sunt in lato campo. 4. Statne puer in ripa? 5. Equus salit (*leaps*) in aquam, natatque ad insulam parvam. 6. Multa saxa sunt inter[1] silvas. 7. Puer stat in magno fluvio. 8. Periculum est magnum. 9. Aquila volat trans magnum fluvium in silvam densam. 10. Venit (*he comes*) in castra[2]. 11. Aula est ampla. 12. Servus ambulat ex insula in campum.

[1] The preposition **inter** is followed by the accusative, and means *between* or *among;* **trans,** *across,* and **propter,** *on account of.*

[2] **Castra** (declined like the plural of **donum**) has a different meaning in the singular and plural. See § 14, 2 (*c*).

SYN.—**Murus** is any kind of a *wall;* **paries, ĕtis,** a *partition-wall inside a house;* **mœnia** (plur.), *city-walls,* a defence against the enemy.

Translate into Latin.

1. The farmer walks with (his) son towards[1] the dense forest and cuts a road. 2. The farmer's sons are in the large garden. 3. The boy comes across the large river into the town. 4. The servant comes out of the large hall with (his) master into the garden. 5. A great and high wall stands in the water. 6. The boy walks in the garden with his master's son. 7. A great and high rock stands in the water; and in the rock is a large cave. 8. My children love (their) master.

[1] Observe that when there is motion to a person or place (except names of towns) the preposition is expressed.

LESSON VIII.

CONJUNCTIONS AND ADVERBS. §§ 41 and 43.

INDICATIVE MOOD OF **Sum.** § 29.

Vocabulary.

nunc,	*now.*	**semper,**	*always.*
tunc (tum),	*then.*	**sæpe,**	*often.*
mox,	*soon.*	**nunquam,**	*never.*
ibi,	*there.*	**neque,**	*nor, and not.*
ubi,	*where.*	**cras,**	*to-morrow.*
hodiē,	*to-day.*	**heri,**	*yesterday.*
aut (or **vel**),	*either, or.*	**ubique,**	*everywhere.*
male,	*ill.*	**bene,**	*well.*

Translate into English.

1. Num puer natat in magno rapidoque fluvio? 2. In multis prœliis magno fuit in periculo. 3. Parvus puer sæpe trans latum fluvium natat. 4. Bonos pueros semper amamus. 5. Domini non semper boni erunt in (*towards*) servos. 6. Mox erimus in silva. 7. Multæ pulchræque puellæ, magnæ parvæque, in horto fuerunt ad vesperum. 8. Viri cum equis in prœlio fuerant magno cum periculo. 9. Magistri mei semper bene facileque docent (*teach*). 10. In oppido, in loco[1] alto, erat magnus murus.

[1] SYN. — **Locus** (masc. in the sing., and masc. and neut. in the plur.) means *place;* the plur. **loci** means *passages in books;* also used of *the points or grounds of an argument;* **loca**, *places.*

Translate into Latin.

1. Were the farmer's sons in the large garden? 2. The boy swims easily to the small island. 3. We were often on the banks of the deep river. 4. We shall soon be in the field. 5. The children of good (men) are not always good. 6. Our master teaches[1] well and easily. 7. The farmer walks with (his) sons, and not (his) daughters, into the garden.

[1] Use **docet.**

LESSON IX.

THE VERB **Sum.** § 29.

Vocabulary.

justus,	*just.*	**columna,**	*column.*
absum,	*be absent, distant.*	**Romānus,**	*Roman.*
adsum,	*be present, near.*	**probus,**	*upright.*
arma (plur.),	*arms.*	**attentus,**	*attentive.*

miser, misera,	*miserable.*	**crēber,**	*frequent.*
ædificium,	*building.*	**frūmentum,**	*corn.*
negōtium,	*business.*	**beātus,**	*happy.*
multus,	*many.*	**discipulus,**	*pupil.*

Translate into English.

1. Nova ædificia sunt alba. 2. Nautæ liberi parvi erant, sed boni pulchrique. 3. Mox erunt in silva. 4. Fuimus heri in oppido, ubi nunc sunt filii filiæque. 5. Semper a prœlio abero. 6. Puella ægra erat. 7. Fuistisne heri in oppido? Non fuimus, sed cras erimus. 8. Erant multi pueri heri in horto; et inter pueros filius[1] magistri. 9. Abfueritis a prœlio. 10. Magnæ copiæ Romanorum in prœlio aderant. 11. Probi este, pueri, et beati eritis. 12. Discipuli sint (sunto) attenti. 13. Estne copia[2] frumenti in agris? Non est.

[1] See § 10, 4 (*c*).

[2] **Copia,** *plenty;* **copiæ,** *forces.*

Translate into Latin.

1. The town was small, but beautiful. 2. The columns of the hall are white. 3. We were[1] yesterday in the garden, where were many boys and girls. 4. The boy comes across the wide field into the farmer's garden. 5. We have been on the bank of the deep river. 6. There had been many battles near the city. 7. The forces of the Romans were often in wars and battles. 8. Be just. 9. Be attentive, pupils.[2]

[1] The English past tense is to be translated by the imperfect when it *describes;* by the perfect (aorist) when it simply *states a fact.*

[2] Use the vocative. See § 53.

LESSON X.

FIRST CONJUGATION: ACTIVE VOICE. § 31.

Indicative and Imperative Moods.

Vocabulary.

regno,	*reign.*	**Amūlius,**	*Amulius.*
Horatius,	*Horatius.*	**lībero,**	*liberate.*
inceptum,	*undertaking.*	**dīmico,**	*fight.*
convoco,	*call together.*	**occupo,** *seize,*	*take possession of.*
secundo,	*prosper,*	**conclāmo,**	*cry out together.*
prōvoco,	*appeal,*	**simulo,**	*pretend.*
conjūro,	*plot, conspire.*	**ferrum,**	*iron, sword.*
tuus, tua, tuum,	*thy.*	**suus, -a, -um,**	*his, her, their (own).*
gaudium,	*joy.*	**avus,**	*grandfather.*

eum, *him.*

Translate into English.

1. Romani sæpe bello dimicaverunt. 2. Ferro dimicant pro sua patria. 3. Gaudium simulavistis; non beati eratis. 4. Contra populum Romanum conjurant. 5. Ad populum provocavit. 6. Agricola arvum suum arabat. 7. Conclamavit gaudio. 8. Dii nostra incepta secundant. 9. Amulius[1] Albæ regnabat, cum Romulus avum suum liberavit, Amuliumque necavit. 10. In populum Romanum conjuras. 11. Oppidum novum occupaverat in insula parva. 12. Puerum suum liberavit.

[1] See § 10, 4 (*c*).

Syn. — **Provoco** is to *appeal* to the people; **appello,** to *appeal* to one magistrate from the decisions of another.

Translate into Latin.

1. The boys pretend flight. 2. We shall fight with[1] the sword. 3. Romulus seized the kingdom of his grandfather Amulius. 4. They were fighting[2] with the sword. 5. They fought with the sword. 6. He has fought well

with the sword; and with the sword he will liberate his country. 7. Horatius appealed to the people and they[3] liberated him from danger. 8. The fields are not[4] large. 9. We call the inhabitants of the islands sailors. 10. Call the men from the fields. 11. They will not prosper our undertaking.

[1] Notice that when *with* expresses the *means* or *instrument* of the action, it must be translated by the ablative alone; when it denotes accompaniment, the preposition **cum** must be used.

[2] The teacher should carefully explain the meaning of the imperfect, the perfect, and aorist (perfect indefinite) tenses: *were fighting* is to be translated into Latin by the imperfect; *fought*, by the aorist; and *has fought*, by the perfect.

[3] Observe that **populus** is singular, and the pronoun that relates to it must be singular in Latin, and take a verb in the singular number.

[4] When *not* belongs to the verb, the **non** in Latin must precede the verb; as, **aula non est ampla**, *the hall is not large.*

LESSON XI.

THIRD DECLENSION: VOWEL STEMS. § 11, 1.

Vocabulary.

turris,	*tower.*	**latro,**	*bark.*
hostis,	*enemy.*	**volo,**	*fly.*
piscis,	*fish.*	**liber (libri),**	*book.*
cīvis,	*citizen.*	**vallis,**	*valley.*
nūbēs,	*cloud.*	**rūpes,**	*rock.*
canis,	*dog.*	**avis,**	*bird.*
clādes,	*slaughter.*	**juvenis,**	*young man.*
amīcus,	*friend.*	**nōtus,**	*known.*

Translate into English.

1. Canis latrat. 2. Nubes est nigra. 3. Nonne hostes agros vastant? 4. Amicus noster filiam suam dat in

matrimonium pulchro juveni. 5. Multæ turres altæ stant in ripa. 6. Magna erat hostium clades. 7. Hostium oppida occupat. 8. Romani trans fluvium multos agros vastaverunt. 9. Magister librum puero dat. 10. Valles hostibus notæ erant.

NOTE. — The nouns given above have **-em** in the accusative singular, and **-e** in the ablative. The genitive plural ends in **-ium**, except **canis** and **juvenis**, which have **-um**.

SYN. — **Hostis** is *a foreign enemy in war;* **inimicus**, *a private, personal enemy;* **adversarius**, *any opponent.*

Translate into Latin.

1. The dogs barked. 2. The dogs barked (were barking). 3. The dogs barked (have barked). 4. The enemy (plur.) took-possession-of[1] the town. 5. The master gives his book to the boy. 6. Birds fly from the thick wood to (**in**) the farmer's garden. 7. There are many black clouds in the sky. 8. Did you call the dog? No. 9. The slaughter of the enemy in battle was great.

[1] *Took possession of* is really a compound verb, and is to be rendered by **occupo**, governing the accusative.

LESSON XII.

THIRD DECLENSION: LIQUID STEMS. § 11, 2.

Vocabulary.

consul, ŭlis,	*consul.*	**soror, ōris,**	*sister.*
genus, ĕris,	*race, class, kind.*	**homo, ĭnis,**	*man, person.*
mare, is,	*sea.*	**Cæsar, ăris,**	*Cæsar.*
pater, tris,	*father.*	**victor, ōris,**	*victor.*

aer, aĕris,	*air.*	**scelus, ĕris,**	*crime.*
lītus, ŏris,	*shore.*	**creo,**	*choose, make.*
animal, ālis,	*animal.*	**varius, a, um,**	*various.*
sententia,	*opinion.*	**īra,**	*anger.*

Translate into English.

1. Populus Romanus Cæsarem consulem creat. 2. Sæpe sententiam mutat. 3. Varia sunt animalium genera. 4. In litore maris stant fratres cum sororibus. 5. Romulus fratrem liberavit. 6. Ira causa est multorum scelerum. 7. Bonos homines laudamus. 8. Consul Cæsarem sententiam[1] rogabat. 9. Magister venit (*comes*) cum puero parvo in hortum. 10. Dat consilium de animi sententia. 11. Copiæ ad oppidum festinabant.[2]

[1] Syn. — **Sententia,** *opinion;* **consilium,** *counsel, advice, project.*

[2] **Festino,** *hasten impatiently, hurry;* **propero,** *hasten with energy,* but without hurry or impatience.

Rule V. — In the increment of nouns and adjectives, **a** and **o** are generally long; **e, i, u,** and **y** are generally short; but **o** is short in the increment of neuter nouns. (For the meaning of increment, and exceptions, see Gr. p. 218.)

Translate into Latin.

1. Romulus will liberate (his) brother. 2. They make Cæsar consul. 3. Fishes swim in the water and birds fly in the air. 4. The boys stand upon the bank this-side-of (**citra**) the river. 5. Does the father call his children? No. 6. Many animals are in the great and broad river. 7. Did the boy swim in the water from the small island to the shore? 8. Were you absent from school yesterday? No.

LESSON XIII.

THIRD DECLENSION: MUTE STEMS. § 11, 3.

Vocabulary.

urbs, urbis,	*city.*	**pons, pontis,**	*bridge.*
lex, lēgis,	*law.*	**flūmen, ĭnis,**	*river.*
mīles, ĭtis,	*soldier.*	**(ops), opis,**	*aid*; (pl. *wealth.*)
lapis, ĭdis,	*stone.*	**comes, ĭtis,**	*companion.*
trabs, trabis,	*beam.*	**regno,**	*rule (as king).*
nōmen, ĭnis,	*name.*	**hiems, ĕmis,**	*winter.*
obses, ĭdis,	*hostage.*	**solitūdo, ĭnis,**	*wilderness.*

Translate into English.

1. Trabes sunt longæ in pontibus.[1] 2. Fratri frater fert (*bears*) opem.[2] 3. Miles lapide comitem occidit (*kills*). 4. Hostes dant obsides Romanis. 5. Vastæ tum in iis (*those*) locis solitudines erant. 6. Romulus nomen Romam novæ urbi dat. 7. Movit (*stirred*) animum juvenis comploratio sororis 8. Multæ aves sub[3] hiemem in insulam volant, vel in litore stant. 9. Romulus Romanorum rex erat. 10. Trabes novi pontis longæ sunt et validæ.

[1] For the gender, see § 11, IV., 3 (*d*).

[2] The word is not found in the nominative.

[3] *Towards.*

SYN. — **Flumen** (**fluo**, *to flow*), properly *the stream*, is used as a general term for *river*; **fluvius**, *river*; **amnis**, *a broad, deep river*; **rivus**, *a brook.*

RULE VI. — Most final syllables ending in a consonant, except **c**, are short; but monosyllabic nouns ending in a consonant are long.

Translate into Latin.

1. He gives hostages to Cæsar. 2. The beams of the long bridge are new and strong. 3. The name of the city was Rome. 4. Fishes swim in the deep river. 5. The enemies' camp was near the walls of Rome. 6. The enemy are in-the-power-of the consul. 7. Towards winter, birds migrate into distant (**longinquas**) lands. 8. We dwell now in the city, but we shall soon dwell in (our) gardens.

LESSON XIV.

ADJECTIVES: THIRD DECLENSION. § 16, 2 and 3.

Translate into English.

1. Puer est tristis. 2. Reges sunt potentes. 3. Dabit civitatem omnibus Italicis. 4. Consilium ducis audax est. 5. Rex ingentem numerum militum habet.[1] 6. Leges Romanorum erant egregiæ. 7. Naves hostium sunt celeres. 8. Tempus humanæ vitæ breve est. 9. Miles vulnus grave patienter tolerat. 10. Memoria in pueris est tenax. 11. Equites veloces ad silvam festinant. 12. Vita est breve iter. 13. Milites sunt audaces. 14. Longissimas vias incredibili celeritate confecit.[2]

[1] *Has.* [2] *He accomplished.*

SYN. — **Consilium,** *advice, counsel;* **concilium,** *an assembly, a meeting* (of part of the people). **Lex** is a *law* passed in a **comitia,** (an assembly of the whole people); **scitum,** one passed in a **concilium.**

Populus (originally the patricians) came to include the *whole people;* **plebs (pleo,** *to fill*), a *part of the people,* an inferior class until equality was established by the Licinian Laws, B. C. 367; the Roman people in their civil capacity were called *Quirites.*

Translate into Latin.

1. The boys were sad. 2. The king gives large rewards to the soldiers. 3. Lions are rapacious animals. 4. We live outside-of the city. 5. The ships of the enemy are in the river. 6. The king comes to the city with a large number of soldiers. 7. The ships of the king were swift. 8. The gods are immortal. 9. We are on-this-side-of the river. 10. We were in the power of the king. 11. The soldiers swim across the river and assault the town. 12. They are walking alongside a large river. 13. The farmer cuts a road in the thick forest. 14. We swim in deep water. 15. The sailors do not stand on the shore, but swim in the deep water from the island to the bank.

LESSON XV.

COMPARISON OF ADJECTIVES AND ADVERBS. § 17.

Translate into English.

1. Sumus potentes. 2. Estis potentiores. 3. Reges sunt potentissimi. 4. Noctes brevissimæ sunt æstate.[1] 5. Cicero erat doctissimus Romanorum. 6. Aqua est gravior aëre.[2] 7. Roma clarissima urbs Italiæ erat. 8. Remus oris lineamentis[3] erat matri simillimus. 9. Erat geminata victoria[3] ferox animus. 10. Longissime absunt. 11. In bello miserrimi sunt agricolæ. 12. Germani cum Romanis fortiter pugnaverunt. 13. Milites fortius pugnant. 14. Itinera erant difficillima. 15. Galli Italiam longe lateque vastaverunt. 16. Miles vulnus grave patienter tolerat.

[1] *In summer.* [2] See Rule 32. [3] See Rule 26.

Translate into Latin.

1. We are not all happy. 2. Not all soldiers are brave. 3. They are the most powerful of all. 4. Air is lighter than[1] water. 5. The Belgians are the bravest of all the Gauls. 6. Light is swifter than the wind. 7. The enemy were farthest distant from the city. 8. The enemy fight most bravely. 9. The journey is very difficult. 10. The swiftest animals are not always the strongest. 11. Remus was very like his brother.[2] 12. The Gauls laid waste the fields of the Romans far and wide. 13. The soldiers fight bravely. 14. The sailors often swam from the island in the deep water.

[1] See Rule 32. [2] Use the dative.

LESSON XVI.

IRREGULAR COMPARISON. § 17, 2.

Translate into English.

1. Horatius[1] erat bonus poeta, Vergilius melior, Homerus optimus. 2. Nihil[2] est melius quam sapientia.[3] 3. Sol major est quam terra. 4. Luna minor est quam terra. 5. Plurima et maxima animalia sunt in mari. 6. Homerus est veterrimus[4] omnium Græcorum poetarum. 7. Cum proximis civitatibus pacem et amicitiam confirmant. 8. Acriter pugnant. 9. Lupa sæpius ad parvulos, veluti ad catulos revertitur.[5] 10. Finitimi Belgis erant. 11. Urbs proxime aberat. 12. Tullus Hostilius proximo regi dissimilis fuit. 13. Armorum[6] peritissimus erat. 14. Venit ex loco superiore. 15. Est in citeriore Gallia.

[1] See § 10, 4 (*c*).
[2] See § 14, 1 (*c*).
[3] See Rule 32.
[4] See § 17, 1 (*a*).
[5] *Returns.*
[6] Render, *in arms;* **peritus** governs the gen.

Translate into Latin.

1. Cæsar establishes peace with the nearest states. 2. The soldiers fight fiercely. 3. He was unlike the last king. 4. He hastened from the city into Hither Gaul. 5. The enemy fight more fiercely. 6. He hastened to the nearest city. 7. We are in the last town of Gaul. 8. They fight often with the enemy. 9. The earth is larger than the moon.[1] 10. We call the children from the garden at (**ad**) evening. 11. The brave chiefs fortify many towns.

[1] Ablative. See Rule 32.

LESSON XVII.

GENITIVES IN **-ius**. § 16, 1 (*b*).

PRESENT INDICATIVE OF THE FOUR CONJUGATIONS. § 30 – 34.

Translate into English.

1. Uter nomen novæ urbi dat? 2. Statim Romani alius super alium exspirantes cadunt. 3. Cives Cæsari uni honorem dant. 4. Veniunt in unum locum. 5. Miles venit ex altera parte urbis. 6. Tota Cæsaris vita memorabilis erat. 7. Romanos spes tota deserit. 8. Alius[1] alium amat. 9. Alius aliud dictitat. 10. Uter erat in horto? 11. Fratres amant, alter alterum. 12. Alii puerum laudant, alii culpant. 13. Miles lapide comitem occidit. 14. Milites omnes periculum timent. 15. Videt (*she sees*) super fratris humeros paludamentum amici. 16. Mea unius causa venit.[2]

[1] Translate, *one likes one; another, another.*

[2] *He comes for my sake alone.*

NOTE.—The pupil need learn only the few lines of the large type at the beginning of § 30; the present tense of the different conjugations will be found under § 31, § 32, § 33, § 34, respectively.

RULE VII.—In increments of conjugation, **a**, **e**, and **o** are long; **i** and **u** are short; but **a** is short in the first increment of **do**, and **e** is short in the present and imperfect of the third conjugation. (For illustrations and exceptions see Gr. p. 219.)

EXC.—Final **is** in the second person singular, present indicative, of the fourth conjugation is long.

Translate into Latin.

1. We see many (and) strange animals in the sea. 2. Romulus gave another name to the new city. 3. Some praise Cæsar, others blame him. 4. The father with (his) daughter comes to the sea-shore. 5. To which (of the two) does he give the praise? 6. The one was pleasing to the citizens, the other was troublesome. 7. The boy sits easily on (his) horse. 8. The horses leap into the water and swim to the bank. 9. A wolf runs out of the forest into the field; the boys fear the wolf, and flee. 10. Do you see the slave with his master in the garden? No. 12. The farmer alone ploughs the field. 13. The brothers love each other. 14. Some insist (**flagitant**) on one thing, some on another. 15. Some praise one thing, some another.

LESSON XVIII.

FOURTH DECLENSION. § 12.

IMPERFECT INDICATIVE. § 31-34.

Translate into English.

1. Ad casum Romanorum conclamavit gaudio exercitus Albanus. 2. Alter fessum vulnere, fessum cursu trahebat

corpus. 3. Arma magnifica habebant. 4. Sapientes luctum et mœrorem deponunt. 5. Helvetii Cæsaris adventum exspectabant. 6. Cæsar magnum Germanorum exercitum trans Rhenum transducebat. 7. Agricola taurum cornibus tenebat. 8. Pater domus quattuor ædificat. 9. Parvi sunt pueri, sed non timent magistrum. 10. Mox erimus in portu, ubi multas naves videmus. 11. Dominus veniebat sub solis occasum ad oppidum[1] cum servis.

[1] Syn. — **Oppidum** is *a fortified town, a fortress;* **urbs,** *a city* (with reference to its buildings); **civitas,** *a state,* a community living under the same laws.

Exc. — Final **us** is long in the genitive sing., and in the plural of the fourth declension.

Translate into Latin.

1. Cæsar was coming to (his) army. 2. The soldiers were fighting with great fury. 3. The boys were playing in the broad field. 4. We see many new buildings in the small town. 5. The boy was coming across the field into the farmer's garden. 6. A farmer cultivates (his) field outside the walls of the city, and carries (his) produce (**fruges**) in a boat across the river into the town. 7. The farmer was leading (his) daughter home (**domum**) from the city. 8. The wind was rolling great waves to the shore. 9. There were many large ships in the harbor. 10. We swim from the small island in the deep water to the shore.[1]

[1] Syn. — **Ripa,** *a bank, as of a river;* **litus, ŏris,** *the shore of the sea* (the line which separates the land from the sea), *the strand;* **ora,** *the coast* (of the land).

LESSON XIX.

FIFTH DECLENSION. § 13.

FUTURE INDICATIVE. § 31 - 34.

Translate into English.

1. Spes victoriæ milites delectat. 2. Exercitus[1] in magnam planitiem veniet. 3. Sub terra est magna rerum utilium multitudo. 4. In prima acie[2] volitabat. 5. Imperator fortis exercitum educet et aciem instruet. 6. Circiter meridiem pugnabunt. 7. Romanos spes tota deserebat. 8. Laboris ultra fidem patiens[3] fuit. 9. Intra quintum ab adventu diem, uno prœlio hostes profligat. 10. Septimo die[4] Belgæ copias omnes ex castris educebant.

[1] SYN. — **Exercitus** (**exerceo**, *to exercise*), is *the drilled army;* **acies**, *the army drawn up in battle array;* and **agmen** (**ago**, *move*), *the army on the line of march.*

[2] *In the first rank or line*, i. e. *the van.*

[3] *Capable of enduring*, followed by the genitive.

[4] The time of an action is denoted by the ablative.

EXC. — Final **e** in the fifth declension is long; also **e** in the gen. and dat. sing. is long before **i**, except in **res**, **spes**, and **fides**: **e** is short in the future ending in **bĕris** and **bĕre.**

Translate into Latin.

1. The cavalry will come into the plain. 2. On the fifth day[1] Cæsar will come with a large army and immediately assault the town. 3. The lieutenant was hastening from the town and came with[2] all (his) forces to Cæsar's camp. 4. The next day Cæsar will move his camp. 5. About midday the messengers will come. 6. Will Cæsar renew the battle? No. 7. The consul about midday will lead out the army and renew the fierce

battle. 8. The soldiers will kill all the prisoners with[2] the sword.

[1] Use the ablative.
[2] Does *with* denote accompaniment or instrument?

LESSON XX.

NUMERALS. § 18.

PERFECT INDICATIVE. § 31–34.

Translate into English.

1. Proca, rex Albanorum, duos filios, Numitorem et Amulium, habuit. 2. Unum Horatium tres Curiatii circumsteterunt. 3. In legione Romana erant cohortes decem, manipuli triginta, centuriæ sexaginta. 4. Ab castris oppidum Remorum Bibrax aberat milia[1] passuum octo. 5. Romulus septem et triginta annos regnavit. 6. Viginti talenta piratæ postulaverunt. 7. Septem erant reges Romani; primus erat Romulus, secundus Numa Pompilius, tertius Tullus Hostilius, quartus Ancus Martius, quintus Tarquinius Priscus, sextus Servius Tullius, septimus Tarquinius Superbus. 8. Pater pueris binos libros[2] dabit. 9. Quota hora est? Tertia. 10. Puella reginæ litteras dedit.

[1] See § 18, 1 (*d*). [2] *Two books apiece.*

SYN. — **Littera,** *a letter of the alphabet;* **epistola** or **litteræ** (plur.), *a letter, an epistle;* **litteræ** also signifies *letters,* i. e. *literature;* **humanitas,** *refinement, culture.*

EXC. — **E** is short before **r** in the tenses in **ram, rim,** and **ro.**

Translate into Latin.

1. Cæsar will come with ten vessels. 2. The consul had sixty vessels. 3. Cæsar led out five legions from Italy. 4. A Roman legion had five thousand foot-soldiers,[1] three hundred horsemen. 5. The commander assaulted the town with an army of ten thousand men. 6. The town is six miles distant. 7. Cæsar enrolled two legions in Italy. 8. They demanded six hundred talents. 9. The master gave the boys three books apiece. 10. What (**quota**) o'clock (hour) is it? The fifth. 11. In a Roman legion there were ten cohorts, thirty maniples, sixty centuries.

[1] The number of soldiers in a legion varied at different periods.

LESSON XXI.

PERSONAL PRONOUNS. § 19.

Translate into English.

1. Nos sumus potentes, sed vos estis potentiores. 2. Tu es tristis. 3. Romulus vi[1] se defendit. 4. Venit tecum.[2] 5. Omnes homines se amant. 6. Populi favorem sibi conciliavit. 7. In me et in te et in nobis omnibus est animus immortalis. 8. Fratres[3] inter se amant. 9. Fratres inter se loquuntur.[4] 10. Tu laudas me, sed ego te culpo. 11. Trabes inter se distant binos pedes.[5] 12. Pueri in horto nobiscum ambulabunt. 13. Ego et frater ambulamus.[6] 14. Dum ego scribebam, tu legebas, et frater pingebat. 15. Tu multos exercitus duxisti, multasque urbes expugnavisti. 16. Nulla unquam respublica nec major, nec sanctior, nec bonis exemplis ditior fuit.

[1] See § 11, 3, 1.

[2] See § 19, 3 (*e*).

[3] *The brothers love each other.*

[4] Translate, *talk together.*

[5] *The beams are two feet distant* (apart) *from each other.*

[6] If there are two subjects connected by *and*, the verb is generally plural; if the subjects are of different persons, the verb takes the first person rather than the second, the second rather than the third.

Translate into Latin.

1. You are powerful, but we are more powerful. 2. He came in company with you. 3. He comes in company with us. 4. I gave (to) you this book. 5. I will praise you. 6. You have praised me. 7. The boys have loved each other. 8. We all love you. 9. The boy was walking with me in the garden yesterday. 10. I and (my) brother were walking in the king's garden in the evening.[1] 11. Cæsar has led a large army into Italy. 12. You are reading, but I am writing.

[1] *In the evening*, **vesperi.**

LESSON XXII.

DEMONSTRATIVE PRONOUNS. § 20.

Translate into English.

1. Vastæ tum in iis locis solitudines erant. 2. Eos aqua in sicco reliquit. 3. Illi acriter pugnaverunt. 4. Hic septem et triginta annos regnavit. 5. Is orabat populum. 6. Palus erat non magna inter nostrum atque hostium exercitum. 7. Ad eam sententiam cum reliquis causis hæc quoque ratio eos deduxit. 8. Ille unus me laudabat. 9. Fratres inter se amabant, alter alterum.[1] 10. Romulus et Remus urbem in iisdem locis condi-

derunt. 11. Ipse tu laudabas me. 12. Ego ipse te laudabam. 13. Ipse magister me laudavit. 14. Ille puer nimium se amat. 15. Laudabo illius[2] filium. 16. Est idem, qui[3] semper fuit. 17. Eadem dictitat. 18. Pater filiam suam et filiam ejus ad se vocavit. 19. Hæc sententia mihi placet, illa displicet.

[1] *The brothers loved one another.*

[2] For *his* or *her* (not referring to the subject), **ejus** should be used when not emphatic; **illius,** if the word is emphatic; **istius,** if very emphatic or at all sarcastic.

[3] **Qui,** *as.*

Translate into Latin.

1. I[1] gave you this book, and you gave me that. 2. The boy is in that place. 3. The soldiers are in that[2] town, and the enemy in this. 4. There was a bridge over (**in**) that river. 5. He hastened across this river into that cottage. 6. These mountains are lofty. 7. You yourself gave me this book. 8. In the same places (there) are many new buildings. 9. Those mountains are lofty; these are rugged. 10. Cæsar hastened with all his forces into the same place. 11. Romulus himself pretended flight. 12. On this side of these mountains (there) are many large rivers. 13. I myself will praise you. 14. We[3] are the same that we have always been. 15. We say the same things. 16. The Helvetians have contended with the Germans, and have kept them off from their boundaries.[4]

[1] **Ego** must be expressed, because contrast is denoted.

[2] **Ille** refers to what is remote; **hic,** to what is near. See § 20, 2 (*a* and *b*).

[3] Translate, **iidem sumus, qui,** etc.

[4] **Suis finibus,** ablative: **suis** is used because it refers to the subject.

LESSON XXIII.

RELATIVE PRONOUNS. § 21.

PLUPERFECT INDICATIVE. § 31-34.

Translate into English.

1. Dat negotium Senonibus reliquisque Gallis, qui finitimi Belgis[1] erant. 2. Hoc ex itinere magno impetu[2] Belgæ oppugnaverant. 3. Puer, qui studet, discit. 4. Cæsar tres legiones, quæ in provincia hiemabant, ex hibernis educit. 5. Nostri[3] parati in armis erant. 6. Felix est rex, quem omnes cives amant. 7. Galliæ sunt partes tres, quarum unam Belgæ incolunt. 8. Numitori, qui natu[2] major erat, regnum reliquit. 9. Multi homines ædificant domos, in quibus non habitabunt. 10. Is erit fortissimus, qui ipse suarum cupiditatum victor fuerit. 11. Nonne tu me laudas?

[1] See Rule 15.
[2] See Rule 26.
[3] *Our men.*

SYN. — **Oppugno** is *to assault;* **obsideo,** *to besiege.*

Translate into Latin.

1. That (**is**) king is fortunate whom all the citizens praise. 2. The soldiers who assaulted the town were quickly repulsed. 3. The boy whom you blamed was my brother. 4. The deserter hastened across the mountains which are in Farther Gaul, and came at evening to Cæsar's camp. 5. Many men have built houses in which they have not lived. 6. I have had boys in my school who have studied diligently and learned rapidly.

LESSON XXIV.

INTERROGATIVE PRONOUNS. § 21.

FUTURE PERFECT. § 31-34.

Translate into English.

1. Quis tibi hunc librum dedit? 2. Quis eos discipulos puniet qui non paruerunt? 3. Iccius Remus qui oppido[1] præerat, nuntios ad eum mittet. 4. Tunc Faustulus indicavit Romulo quis esset[2] ejus avus. 5. Quis naves longas ædificavit, et nautas gubernatoresque comparavit? 6. Cum hostes[3] acres qui sunt citra flumen urbem oppugnabunt. 7. Mare planum est, ex quo etiam æquor illud poetæ vocant. 8. Cum epistolam scripsero, ad te veniam.

[1] For the dative, see Rule 18.

[2] *Was*, see Rule 45.

[3] Give the synonymes.

SYN. — **Mare** is *the sea* (from root **mar**, *to wear away*) as a desolate waste, in opposition to the land; **pelagus** (**pelazo**, *to glisten*), **æquor** (**æquus**, *level*), *the expanse of the sea when calm;* **pontus** (root **po**, *to go*), *the deep sea* as the highway of nations.

Translate into Latin.

1. Who gave the business to you? Cæsar. 2. Who is the leader of the army which the enemy have sent to Italy? 3. Who gave you that book? 4. Who built that house in which you are living? 5. Whose book is this which I have found in my garden? 6. Whose boys are those whom you are teaching in your school? 7. Who of you have studied diligently? 8. Who is walking towards the city? 9. For[1] all the arts which belong to[2] culture have a certain common bond.

[1] Use **etenim**.

[2] Use **ad**.

LESSON XXV.

INDEFINITE PRONOUNS. § 21.

Translate into English.

1. Sibi quisque primum itineris locum petit. 2. Narravit quidam coram me istam fabulam. 3. Narrabit aliquis coram me illam fabulam. 4. Quamlibet (*or* quamvis) fabulam mihi narrate. 5. Pro sua quisque patria dimicat. 6. Quidam ex militibus decimæ legionis veniebat. 7. Faber est quisque fortunæ suæ. 8. Unusquisque nostrum habet animum immortalem. 9. Justitia nunquam nocet cuiquam, qui eam habet. 10. Sibi quisque[1] maxime consulit. 11. Unicuique nostrum est animus immortalis. 12. Ecquis[2] in horto est? 13. Numquis in horto est? 14. Quisnam domi est? 15. Quid fecit? Quod facinus commisit? 16. Uterque tenuit aliquod telum.

[1] *Each one* (everybody); **sibi consulit,** *consults his own interest.*

[2] **Ecquis** simply asks a question; **numquis** asks a question, but expects the answer *no.*

Syn. — **Quisque,** *each;* **uterque,** *each* (of two); **unusquisque,** *each one;* **quivīs** and **quilibet,** *any one you choose;* **aliquis** and **quispiam,** *some one* (it matters not who), neut. *something,* adj. *any;* **quidam** (plur. *some*), *a certain,* i. e. some definite person; **quisquam,** *any,* when it is denied that there are any; **quis** (after **si, ne, num, ec-**), *any.*

Note. — Observe that when the neuter is used as a *noun,* it takes the form **quid;** but when used as an *adjective,* **quod.**

Translate into Latin.

1. Some[1] soldiers are brave. 2. Cæsar sent a certain soldier to the town which he was going to assault on the morrow.[2] 3. Each one shall fight for his country with the sword. 4. Some one will tell this story. 5. Is any

one at home[3] to-day? 6. A[4] man was walking in my garden. 7. The boys are present whom you praised yesterday. 8. I will give the book to any of the scholars (you wish). 9. Is not a[4] man the maker of his own fortune?

[1] Use **aliquis.**

[2] **Postero die,** or **postridie.** [3] *At home,* **domi.**

[4] When *a* means *a certain* or *some,* it is to be translated by **aliquis** or **quispiam.**

NOTE.—*Any* is to be translated by **aliquis** or **quispiam** when it means *some;* in negative sentences, by **quisquam** or **ullus**; and when it means *any you please, any you wish,* by **quilibet** or **quivis.**

LESSON XXVI.

CORRELATIVES. § 22.

IMPERATIVE MOOD. § 31-34; 57, 7.

Translate into English.

1. Quales duces, tales erant milites. 2. Quot homines, tot sententiæ. 3. Vires semper exercete, pueri,[1] in optimis rebus. 4. Vos, viri fortissimi, urbem templaque Deorum defendite. 5. Ita sine ullo periculo tantam eorum multitudinem nostri[2] interfecerunt, quantum fuit diei[3] spatium. 6. Judex præmia ne dato neve capito. 7. Primum omnium, de his rebus bonum habetote animum, cives. 8. Ab his rebus animum tuum avoca. 9. Desilite, commilitones, nisi vultis[4] aquilam hostibus prodere. 10. Conservate fortunas vestras. 11. Clipeos hastis percutite. 12. Ne quid feceris, quod malum esse videatur.

[1] See § 10. [2] *Our men.* [3] See § 13, 2, N.

[4] *You wish to betray,* etc.

Translate into Latin.

1. As (are) the masters, so are the slaves. 2. As (is) the teacher, so are the scholars. 3. Do not admire all things which have the show of glory. 4. Do not destroy[1] the city, soldiers! 5. Carefully train your children; praise the good; punish the bad. 6. Let the master teach the boys the Latin language.

[1] **Nolite perdere.**

LESSON XXVII.

INFINITIVES AND PARTICIPLES. §§ 23, 25, 31–34.

Translate into English.

1. Cæsar in Gallia hiemare constituit. 2. Milites urbem custodire debent. 3. Mene id dicentem[1] audivisti? 4. Magister puerum vidit in horto sedentem. 5. Cæsar cupientibus[2] signum dat. 6. Scipio in Africam trajecit, Carthaginem oppugnaturus.[3] 7. Dicitur eos circum se habuisse. 8. Imperator dixit se cum sola decima legione venturum esse. 9. Difficile est urbem munire. 10. Se celeriter venturum nuntiat. 11. Quos laborantes conspexerat, his subsidia submittebat. 12. Helvetii cum proximis civitatibus pacem et amicitiam confirmare constituerunt. 13. Salutem insperantibus reddit.

[1] *When I said that*, lit. *saying that.*

[2] *To* (men) *desiring* it.

[3] *To attack*, for the purpose of attacking.

LESSON XXVIII.

PRESENT SUBJUNCTIVE. § 24, 31-34.

Translate into English.

1. Fidem servemus.[1] 2. In hortum eamus. 3. Sint tibi omnia bona. 4. Quid faciamus? Quibus pareamus? 5. Sit pauper, sit miser; at est frater meus. 6. Quis eum diligat quem metuit? 7. Dux imperat ut milites stationes suas servent.[2] 8. Veniet ut me videat.[3] 9. Oro ut Dii secundent incepta nostra. 10. Divitiacus Cæsarem obsecrat, ne quid[4] gravius in fratrem statuat. 11. Imperator tanta vi oppidum oppugnat, ut desperatio animos oppidanorum occupet. 12. Auxilium rogant ut hostium impetum sustineant.

[1] See Examples on p. 51 of the Grammar.

[2] Translate, *that the soldiers keep their stations.* Notice that primary tenses are followed in the subordinate clause by primary tenses; secondary by secondary.

[3] Translate, *in order that he may see me*, i. e. *to see me.*

[4] Indefinite pronoun: *lest he should* (i. e. that he should not) *determine anything too severe against his brother.*

LESSON XXIX.

IMPERFECT SUBJUNCTIVE. §§ 26, 27, 31-34.

Translate into English.

1. Hannibal magnum exercitum in Italiam duxit, ut cum Romanis pugnaret.[1] 2. Ariovistus, ut præter se binos[2] ad colloquium adducerent, postulavit. 3. Deos contestatus est ut ea res feliciter eveniret. 4. Imperator ex

castris exercitum duxit ut urbem expugnaret. 5. Tantus timor omnem exercitum occupavit, ut omnium animos perturbaret. 6. Cum hostibus erat pugnandum,[3] cum illi audacter tela conjicerent, et equos insuefactos incitarent. 7. Placuit Cæsari[4] ut ad Ariovistum legatos mitteret,[5] qui[6] ab eo postularent, ut aliquem locum colloquio[7] diceret.[8] 8. Cæsar in Italiam magnis itineribus contendit, ut duas ibi legiones conscriberet.

[1] Translate, *in order that he might fight*, etc., i. e. *to fight;* **duxit** is a secondary tense, and is followed by the imperfect subjunctive.

[2] *Two on each side.*

[3] *They had to fight with the enemy.*

[4] See § 51, 2 (*a*).

[5] *Should send*, i. e. *to send.*

[6] Lit., *who should demand*, etc., i. e. *to demand.* See Rule 44.

[7] *For a conference.*

[8] *Should appoint.*

LESSON XXX.

PERFECT AND PLUPERFECT SUBJUNCTIVE. § 31-34.

Translate into English.

1. Non dubito quin[1] Cæsar hostes superaverit. 2. Non dubitabam quin[2] Cæsar hostes superavisset. 3. Nemo dubitabat quin milites fortissime pugnavissent. 4. Ex captivis cognovit quo in loco hostium copiæ consedissent. 5. Eo cum venisset, majores in eum locum copiæ hostium convenerant. 6. Hostes acriter conflixerunt, ita tamen ut nostri omnibus partibus superiores fuerint, atque eos in silvas collesque compulerint. 7. Cum aliquamdiu Cæsar naves frustra exspectasset,[3] ne anni tempore a navigatione

excluderetur,[4] secunda cum solvisset[5] vigilia, prima 1 terram attigit.

[1] Translate, (*but*) *that Cæsar has*, etc.

[2] Translate, (*but*) *that Cæsar had*, etc.

[3] For **exspectavisset**, see § 30, 6 (*a*).

[4] *Should be prevented.*

[5] *Had cast loose*, i. e. the cables which fastened the vessels to the shore: we should say, *had weighed anchor.*

LESSON XXXI.

PRESENT AND IMPERFECT INDICATIVE: PASSIVE VOICE.
§ 31–34.

Translate into English.

1. Unus miles lapide vulneratur. 2. Helvetii continentur una ex parte flumine[1] Rheno; altera ex parte monte Jura; tertia ex parte lacu[2] Lemanno et flumine Rhodano. 3. Beati sunt ii, quorum vita virtute regitur. 4. Quinto die tragula a quodam milite conjicitur. 5. Vulnera gravia a[3] militibus accipiuntur. 6. Pueri a magistro docentur. 7. Epistola a regina scribitur. 8. Castellum a Labieno munitur. 9. Copiæ ad urbem revocantur. 10. Vir[4] fortis etiam ab inimicis honoratur. 11. Multi milites in prœlio vulnerabantur. 12. Dum urbs ab hostibus oppugnatur, a civibus defendebatur. 13. Bellum a Cæsare finiebatur.

[1] *By the river*, etc.

[2] See § 12, 3 (*d*).

[3] See Lesson VI. Note 1

[4] SYN. — **Homo, ĭnis**, *a man, a human being*, includes both sexes; **vir**, *a man, a distinguished man, a husband.*

LESSON XXXII.

FUTURE AND PERFECT INDICATIVE: PASSIVE VOICE. § 31-34.

Translate into English.

1. Auxilium a legato rogabitur. 2. Nuntii ad Cæsarem mittentur. 3. Fœdus a Cæsare violabitur, et præda sociis[1] dabitur. 4. Oppida ab hostibus munientur. 5. Pueri a magistro docebuntur. 6. Nuntius ab imperatore ad urbem mittetur. 7. Vix acies a Cæsare instructa est, cum hostes in unum locum confugerunt. 8. Milites nostri in prœlio vulnerati sunt. 9. Amatus est ille puer a me, a te, et ab omnibus amicis. 10. In castris Helvetiorum tabulæ repertæ sunt, literis Græcis confectæ.[2]

[1] *To the allies.* See Rule 14. [2] *Made out.*

LESSON XXXIII.

PLUPERFECT AND FUTURE PERFECT INDICATIVE: PASSIVE VOICE. § 31-34.

Translate into English.

1. Cum Cæsar in urbem intravit, omnium civium domus[1] floribus ornatæ sunt. 2. In castris Helvetiorum tabulæ repertæ sunt, literis Græcis confectæ, quibus in tabulis nominatim ratio confecta erat. 3. Exercitus Cassii ab Helvetiis pulsus erat, et sub jugum missus. 4. Pater Castici regnum in Sequanis multos annos obtinuerat et a senatu populi Romani amicus erat appellatus. 5. Puer a magistro punitus erat. 6. Duces exercitus[2] nostri in prœlio vulnerati erant. 7. Pueri a magistro moniti erant.

[1] See § 12, 2. [2] Genitive, see § 12.

SYN. — **Imperium (impero)**, *the supreme power* (the full **imperium** was the union of the military and civil authority), *an empire;* **regnum**, *the royal power, a kingdom;* **principatum**, *the chief authority.*

LESSON XXXIV.

IMPERATIVE AND INFINITIVE MOODS AND PARTICIPLES: PASSIVE VOICE. § 31-34.

Translate into English.

1. Mi fili,[1] verere parentes. 2. Milites bene exerceantur. 3. Puer probe excolitor. 4. Agri vastari non debent. 5. Helvetii cum proximis civitatibus pacem et amicitiam confirmare constituerunt. 6. Dicit puer se[2] laudatum esse. 7. Credo illos pueros laudatum iri. 8. Divitiacus flens a Cæsare hæc[3] petebat. 9. Hostes, adventu[4] Romanorum permoti, legatos ad Cæsarem de deditione mittunt. 10. Ariovistus dixit omnes Gallorum copias uno a se prœlio[5] fusas ac superatas esse. 11. Laudandus est ille puer et mihi[6] et tibi.

[1] For the voc. see § 10, 4 (*c*).
[2] *That he was praised.*
[3] *These things.*
[4] See Rule 26.
[5] *In one battle.*
[6] *By me and by thee*, see § 51, 4 (*a*).

LESSON XXXV.

SUBJUNCTIVE MOOD: PASSIVE VOICE. § 31-34.

Translate into English.

1. Milites, cum[1] imbribus tardarentur, tamen omnia superaverunt. 2. Magister curat ut nos bene educemur.[2] 3. Milites nostri pugnant ut urbs servetur. 4. Magister curat ut discipuli diligenter erudiantur. 5. Magister curabat ut discipulus bene educaretur, strenue exerceretur, probe excoleretur, diligenter erudiretur. 6. Flebat puer, quod librum amisisset.[3] 7. Non erat dubium quin

milites subito periculo territi essent.[4] 8. Non est dubium quin discipulus a me bene monitus sit. 9. Non est dubium quin urbs a militibus expugnata sit.

[1] *Although.*
[2] *Should be,* etc.
[3] *Had lost.* See § 63, 2.
[4] *Had been terrified.* See § 65, 1 (*b*).

Syn. — **Doceo,** *to teach;* **edoceo,** *to make one learn;* **perdoceo,** *to teach thoroughly;* **erudio** (e and **rudis,** *rough*) *to instruct,* lit. to bring from a rough condition; **educo,** *to educate,* whether in a physical or moral sense.

LESSON XXXVI.

FIRST CONJUGATION. § 31.

Deponent Verbs. § 35.

Translate into English.

1. Cædes manifesta expiatur. 2. Multi milites in prœlio vulnerabantur. 3. Romulus et Remus in iisdem locis educati fuerant. 4. In Gallia a potentioribus vulgo regna[1] occupabantur. 5. Remus a fratre liberatus est. 6. Agros populabantur. 7. Iis[2] insidiati sunt latrones. 8. Datur signum. 9. Tres Albani vulnerati sunt. 10. T. Labienus ex loco superiore hostes conspicatus est. 11. Cæsar suos cohortatus est. 12. Hoc in bello multa Cæsaris facta egregia narrantur. 13. Urbs a Romulo Roma vocatur. 14. Alii[3] me laudabant, alii[4] culpabant. 15. Est idem qui semper fuit.[5] 16. Iidem erimus cras, qui sumus hodie.

[1] Give the synonymes.
[2] See Rule 18.
[3] *Some.*
[4] *Others.*
[5] Lit. *He is the same* (person) *that he has always been.*

Syn. — **Vulnero,** *to wound* by a cut or thrust; **saucio,** *to wound* in any way.

Translate into Latin.

1. The soldiers were wounded. 2. The soldiers have been wounded by the enemy. 3. The city was called Rome. 4. The city was called Rome by Romulus. 5. The soldiers give the signal. 6. The signal is given by the soldiers. 7. Romulus liberates Remus. 8. Remus is liberated by Romulus. 9. The brothers were educated in those places. 10. He gives the business to his brother. 11. Do you see the road which has been cut through the forest by the enemy? 12. From that place the enemy has been seen. 13. Cæsar hastens across the river. 14. The enemy[1] hastened into Gaul and laid waste the fields. 15. You praise me. 16. Others praise you. 17. One says one thing, another another. 18. He is the same to-day that he will be to-morrow. 19. He is the same boy that runs from the thick wood across the wide field and swims in the deep water to the shores of the island.

[1] Plural.

LESSON XXXVII.

SECOND CONJUGATION. § 32.

Translate into English.

1. Proca, rex[1] Albanorum, duos filios, Numitorem et Amulium habuit. 2. Ea res animum Numitoris anxium tenebat. 3. Remus prior sex vultures vidit. 4. Horatii soror hostem lugebat. 5. Commeatu[2] nostros prohibuerunt. 6. Intra eas silvas hostes sese continebant. 7. Hostes in urbe manserunt. 8. Galli celeritate Romanorum permoti sunt. 9. Atrox[3] id visum est facinus patribus plebique. 10. Cæsar in Gallia detinebatur. 11. Ei

Cæsaris consilia non placebant. 12. Movit ferocis juvenis animum comploratio sororis in tanto publico gaudio.

[1] See Rule 1.

[2] See Rule 28.

[3] **Atrox** agrees with **facinus**, which stands in the predicate; **id** is the subject.

Translate into Latin.

1. The king has two sons. 2. Cæsar has five legions. 3. They see the city which the enemy are assaulting. 4. The enemy remained within the walls.[1] 5. Cæsar admonished the tribunes. 6. Did the enemy detain Cæsar in Gaul? 7. She mourned her brother. 8. Cæsar was detained by the Gauls. 9. Six vultures were seen by Remus. 10. The enemy were moved by the swiftness of Cæsar. 11. Cæsar has been detained in Gaul. 12. The tribunes have been admonished by Cæsar. 13. The soldiers remain around the city. 14. The enemy remained on this side of the river. 15. Remain in the city. 16. I see the forces of the enemy in the dense forest.

[1] Walls of a city; see synonymes.

LESSON XXXVIII.

THIRD CONJUGATION. § 33.

Translate into English.

1. Vix Cæsar aciem instruxerat, cum hostes in unum locum convolaverunt. 2. Numitori, qui natu[1] major erat, regnum reliquit. 3. Ille urbem muris cinxit. 4. Lupa ad vagitum accurrit. 5. Lupa matrem[2] se gessit. 6.

Faustulus, pastor regius,[3] rem animadvertit. 7. Ætas tempori[4] expositionis congruebat. 8. Respublica Romana a consulibus gerebatur. 9. Urbs muro cincta erat. 10. Lupa, ut fama traditum est, ad vagitum accurrit. 11. Deinde Romulus et Remus urbem in iisdem locis, ubi expositi educatique fuerant, condiderunt. 12. Inde duæ legiones, quæ proximæ conscriptæ erant, totum agmen claudebant.

[1] See Rule 26.
[2] In apposition with **se**: *as a mother.*
[3] **Regius** = **regis.**
[4] See Rule 18.

Translate into Latin.

1. Romulus has encompassed the city with a wall. 2. The consuls rule the republic. 3. Cæsar drew up his army in the city. 4. A wolf ran from the forest across the field. 5. He enrolled the legion in Gaul. 6. The republic was ruled by the consuls. 7. The city was founded by Romulus. 8. They were educated in these places. 9. The city has been encompassed by a wall. 10. Two legions were enrolled in Farther Gaul by Cæsar. 11. The legions which Cæsar enrolled in Hither Gaul assaulted the city. 12. Are the boys playing in the field? No; they are running towards (**ad**) the woods.

LESSON XXXIX.

FOURTH CONJUGATION. § 34.

Translate into English.

1. Romulus urbem mœnibus munivit. 2. Remus mœnia transilivit. 3. Multitudine[1] operum, quæ neque viderant ante Galli, neque audiverant, et celeritate Roma-

norum permoti, legatos ad Cæsarem de deditione mittunt. 4. Ab eo loco in fines[2] Ambianorum pervenit. 5. Cæsar bellum finivit. 6. Cæsar castra munire jubet. 7. Illi oculis eum custodiebant. 8. Solus potitus est imperio[3] Romulus. 9. Bellum a Cæsare finitum est. 10. Orta est inter eos contentio. 11. Sepibus densissimis, ut demonstravimus, prospectus impeditur.

[1] *Moved by the number of the works, which . . . . and by the quickness*, etc.; **quæ** is in the acc. plur.
[2] See Rule 37. [3] See Rule 31.

Translate into Latin.

1. They have fortified the city. 2. Cæsar came to the city. 3. He has come from the city. 4. Has Cæsar finished the war in Gaul? 5. The soldiers surround the enemy. 6. All hope deserted the Romans. 7. Cæsar led his army into their territories.[1] 8. The city has been fortified by Cæsar. 9. The war was finished by Cæsar. 10. The enemy have been surrounded by the soldiers. 11. They hastened to cross the river with all their forces, and advanced towards Cæsar's camp. 12. Come with me.[2] 13. Cæsar surrounded the city with a wall. 14. Cæsar hastened into Gaul with all the soldiers, whom he had enrolled in the city.

[1] Use the plural of **finis**. [2] See § 19, 3 (*e*).

LESSON XL.

VERBS IN -io, THIRD CONJUGATION. § 33, 2.

Translate into English.

1. Trigemini arma capiunt, et in medium inter duas acies procedunt. 2. Romulus eum interfecit. 3. Amu-

lius ipsam in vincula conjecit. 4. Parvulos, alveo impositos,[1] abjecit in Tiberim.[2] 5. Amulius Rheam Silviam, ejus filiam, Vestæ sacerdotem fecit. 6. Quare iis[3] insidiati sunt latrones, a quibus[5] **Remus** captus est. 7. Ipsa paludamentum confecerat. 8. Lapides ac tela conjiciebant. 9. Sub occasum solis destiterunt, seque in castra receperunt. 10. In[6] deditionem eos accepit. 11. Per eorum fines triduum iter fecit. 12. Milites in summo[4] colle ab hostibus conspiciebantur.

[1] **Impositos** agrees with **parvulos**; in English we should say, "He placed them in a trough *and* threw them," etc.

[2] See § 11, I. 3 (1). [3] See Rule 18.

[4] *Highest part of.* [5] *By whom = and by these.* [6] *Into = in.*

Syn. — **Vinculum (vincio,** *bind*), *anything that binds;* **catena,** *an iron chain;* **laqueus,** *a halter.*

Translate into Latin.

1. They take the city. 2. Romulus has killed his brother. 3. Remus has been taken by them. 4. They threw their weapons among the enemy. 5. They will throw their weapons within the walls. 6. The soldiers have been seen by the enemy. 7. They will be received in surrender. 8. The boys were cast into the Tiber.[1] 9. Did they bravely sustain the attack of our soldiers? 10. They sent legates to Cæsar. 11. They had sent legates to Cæsar concerning the surrender. 12. He recognized his sons. 13. He is delivered by the king to[2] Numitor. 14. They have been delivered by the king to Numitor for punishment.

[1] Acc. **Tiberim.** See above.

[2] Does *to* denote motion to a person, or is it the sign of the dative?

ADDITIONAL EXERCISES.

Translate into Latin.

1. I and my brother were walking[1] in the garden; we saw our teacher and spoke to him. 2. He teaches me the Latin language; he is kind and I shall always praise him. 3. I often walk in the fields that I may refresh[2] my mind. 4. This pupil studies well and learns rapidly; he has a tenacious memory and a good understanding. 5. He is often praised by his teacher for[3] his diligence. 6. Have you been at school to-day? No, I shall come to-morrow. 7. The boys had been playing on the broad plain; their teacher called them; they immediately ran to[4] school. 8. It is easy[5] to write, but it is not easy to write well. 9. The river flows through a lake; it is a large and beautiful lake, and is surrounded by[6] dense woods. 10. The boy is carefully trained by his teacher. 11. My pupil wrote a letter to his friend; but he did not tell what[7] he had written.[8] 12. We shall dwell in the city in the summer,[9] but in the winter we shall all depart into the country.[10]

[1] See Lesson XXI. Note 6.

[2] Present subjunctive.

[3] **Propter.**

[4] *Into;* use **in.**

[5] Use **facile,** neuter gender. See § 57, 8 (*a*).

[6] Use the ablative without a preposition. See Rule 26.

[7] Use **quæ.**

[8] Use the pluperfect subjunctive.

[9] The time *when* is denoted by the ablative.

[10] Use **ager** or **rus.** See § 55, 3.

LESSON XLI.

IRREGULAR VERBS. § 29 (*b*); § 37.

Translate into English.

1. Illi minus facile eam rem in imperio nostro consequi poterant. 2. Agros Remorum depopulati sunt, quos adire[1] poterant. 3. Vix Cæsar milites e castris educere potuerat, cum hostes impetum fecerunt. 4. Alterum deinde, priusquam tertius posset consequi, interfecit. 5. Volumus scire. 6. Idem velle et idem nolle, ea demum firma amicitia est. 7. Noluerant Germanos[2] diutius in Gallia versari. 8. Ambo rempublicam, quam tueri potuissent, impie perturbare maluerunt. 9. Non id potuit efficere. 10. Non minus commode ipsi sibi præscribere, quam ab aliis doceri poterant.

[1] "To approach"; **quos** is governed by **ad** in composition. See § 52, 1 (*d*).

[2] **Germanos** is in the accusative, the subject of **versari**: translate, *that the Germans should remain any longer in Gaul.*

Syn. — **Possum,** *I am able,* because I have sufficient power; **queo,** *I am able,* because circumstances allow me to do it.

Translate into Latin.

1. I am able to read, but not to write. 2. Cæsar was not able to defend the city. 3. You will not be able to read the book easily. 4. He has not been able to restrain his temper. 5. Do you wish to walk in the fields with me?[1] No; I prefer to remain at home.[2] 6. We shall be able to lead the soldiers from the camp. 7. They were unwilling to depart from the city. 8. They are unwilling (that)[3] the soldiers should remain in the city. 9. Do the

boys wish to play on the plain? No; they prefer to study. 10. Do you prefer to read or to write? I do not know (how) to write, but I wish to learn.

[1] **Mecum.** See § 19, 3 (*a*).

[2] Use **domi.**

[3] *That* is omitted in rendering the sentence into Latin; *soldiers* is translated by **milites**, the accusative, and *should remain*, by **versari**, the infinitive. See § 70, 2.

LESSON XLII.

IRREGULAR VERBS (continued). § 37.

Translate into English.

1. Non tulit populus[1] patris lacrimas. 2. Non omnis ager, qui seritur, fert fruges. 3. Eos tulit in casam. 4. Edimus ut vivamus;[2] non vivimus ut edamus. 5. Helvetii de finibus suis exeunt. 6. In eum magno impetu redit, et, dum Albanus exercitus inclamat Curiatiis, ut opem ferant[3] fratri, jam Horatius eum occiderat. 7. Princeps[4] ibat Horatius. 8. Milites e castris redeuntes occisi sunt. 9. Ipsi transire flumen non dubitaverunt. 10. Inita[5] æstate,[6] in interiorem Galliam Q. Pedium misit. 11. I, lictor, deliga ad palum. 12. Jussit ut abirem.[7]

[1] Give the synonymes.

[2] *May eat.* See § 64.

[3] *Should bear.* See § 70, 3 (*a*).

[4] An adjective used for an adverb, *first*, or *at the head.*

[5] See **ineo.**

[6] See Rule 35.

[7] Translate, *I should*, etc.

LESSON XLIII.

IRREGULAR VERBS (continued). § 37.

Translate into English.

1. Illud tum facile fiebat. 2. Onus, quod bene fertur, leve fit. 3. His rebus fit ut Helvetii minus facile finitimis[1] bellum inferre possint. 4. Cum esset[2] Cæsar in citeriore Gallia in hibernis, ita uti supra demonstravimus, crebri ad eum rumores afferebantur, literisque item Labieni certior fiebat,[3] omnes Belgas, quam tertiam esse Galliæ partem dixeramus, contra populum Romanum conjurare,[4] obsidesque inter se dare.[4] 5. Omnia ab his diligenter ad diem facta sunt. 6. Maxime gavisi sunt cives quod urbs servata erat. 7. Cæsar fisus est rebus[5] suis. 8. Numitoris greges infestare solitus est.

[1] *To their neighbors.* See Rule 18.

[2] *Was.* See § 62, 2 (*b*).

[3] *Was informed;* **certior** is an adjective agreeing with the subject of **fiebat.**

[4] **Belgas** is the subject, *that all the Belgians had conspired, ... were giving*, etc.

[5] Rule 16.

Translate into Latin.

1. The soldiers bore aid to their commander. 2. They will bear the wearied soldiers into the cottage. 3. The fields bear fruit. 4. Aid is borne to the enemy. 5. The soldiers have endured[1] many hardships. 6. The hardships have been endured patiently by the soldiers. 7. Many brave soldiers perished in the battle. 8. The king went to the town. 9. The soldiers perished by hunger. 10. A great part of the soldiers have perished by hunger. 11. Cæsar became consul. 12. They became unfriendly.

13. The burden will become light. 14. Endure these things, soldiers. 15. At the beginning of winter,[2] they returned to the camp. 16. The enemy are not able to cross the river. 17. They differ in many things. 18. He was unwilling to depart from them. 19. They passed by the camp. 20. The general wished to cross the river with all his forces on[3] a bridge.

[1] Use **perfero.**

[2] **Hiems** should be in the ablative, and the participle of **ineo** agrees with it.

[3] Use ablative.

LESSON XLIV.

IMPERSONAL VERBS: PERIPHRASTIC FORMS. §§ 39, 40.

Translate into English.

1. Militibus[1] non licebit (e) castris exire. 2. Placuit[2] Cæsari, ut ad Ariovistum legatos mitteret.[3] 3. Curritur. 4. Tibi licet id facere. 5. Decet te esse diligentem. 6. Mihi ire licuit. 7. Amandus est ille puer et mihi[4] et tibi. 8. Cæsar de quarta vigilia castra moturus est. 9. Imperator cum sola decima legione profecturus erat. 10. Militibus[5] simul et de navibus (erat) desiliendum, et cum hostibus erat pugnandum. 11. Præ omnibus rebus adhibenda est prudentia.

[1] *To the soldiers.* See § 51, 2 (*b*).

[2] *It pleased Cæsar*, i. e. *Cæsar determined.* See § 51, 2 (*a*).

[3] *Should send.* See § 70, 4 (*a*).

[4] *By me and by you.*

[5] *The soldiers . . . had to leap*, etc. See § 51, 4 (*a*).

Syn. — **Proficiscor,** *to set out on a journey;* **iter facere,** *to travel,* either at home or abroad; **peregrinari,** *to travel abroad.*

Prudentia (provideo, *foresee*), *foresight, practical judgment, knowledge of the law;* **sapientia (sapio,** *taste*), *good taste, discernment, knowledge of the world;* **scientia (scio,** *know*), *knowledge,* implying skill in or acquaintance with a subject.

LESSON XLV.

APPOSITION. § 46.

Translate into English.

1. Proca, rex Albanorum, duos filios, Numitorem et Amulium, habuit. 2. Rheam Silviam, ejus filiam Vestæ sacerdotem fecit. 3. Cum lupa sæpius[1] ad parvulos, veluti ad catulos, reverteretur, Faustulus, pastor regius,[2] rem animadvertit. 4. Interea Remum latrones ad Amulium regem perduxerunt. 5. Romulus rex creatus est. 6. Romulum regem populus creavit. 7. Consul veni ad te. 8. Neque ego neque tu hæc fecimus.[3] 9. Placuit[4] Cæsari, ut ad eum legatos mitteret. 10. Cum iis agunt reges, ut[5] pro sua quisque patria dimicent ferro.

[1] See § 17, 5 (*a*).
[2] *The king's shepherd;* § 50, 1 (*a*).
[3] See § 49, 1.
[4] What is the subject of **placuit?**
[5] *That they should fight with the sword, each for his country;* **quisque** is in apposition with the subject of **dimicent.**

Syn. — **Placet,** *it pleases,* i. e. it is one's will or determination; **libet,** *it pleases,* i. e. it agrees with one's inclination.

Translate into Latin.

1. Cæsar, the consul, came to the town. 2. He left the kingdom to his son Numitor. 3. The boys were led to

Romulus the king. 4. Cæsar, (when) consul, subdued Gaul. 5. He will be elected consul. 6. The boy was called Romulus. 7. Cæsar was the conqueror of the Gauls. 8. The commander, a brave man, led the army against the enemy; he fought a great battle on-this-side-of the river.

LESSON XLVI.

AGREEMENT OF ADJECTIVES. § 47.

Translate into English.

1. Vastæ tum in iis locis[1] solitudines[2] erant. 2. Romulus nomen novæ[3] urbi dat. 3. Reges sunt potentes. 4. Naves hostium sunt celeres. 5. Ita solus potitus est imperio[4] Romulus. 6. Deinde Romulus et Remus urbem in iisdem locis, ubi expositi educatique fuerant, condiderunt. 7. Cæsar, certior factus[5] ab Titurio, ad eos contendit. 8. Hi, novissimos[6] adorti, et multa milia[7] passuum prosecuti, magnam multitudinem eorum fugientium conciderunt. 9. Hostes impeditos nostri in flumine aggressi, magnum eorum numerum occiderunt. 10. Iniquum est de stipendio recusare.

[1] See § 14, 2 (*c*).
[2] See § 11, IV (*b*).
[3] See § 17, 3 (*c*) 2.
[4] See Rule 31.
[5] Lit. *having been informed.*
[6] See § 17, 3 (*c*) 2.
[7] See § 18, 1 (*d*).

Translate into Latin.

1. Powerful kings have large fields. 2. The new city has high walls. 3. Remus founded a city in the same place where he had been educated. 4. We are strong, but you are stronger. 5. You and I are powerful. 6.

You and I were informed by Cæsar. 7. They were educated in those places. 8. The journey is short. 9. The soldiers are brave. 10. We are in the power of the cruel enemy. 11. The soldiers killed a large number of the fugitives (those fleeing).

LESSON XLVII.

SYNTAX OF RELATIVES. § 48.

Translate into English.

1. Amulius parvulos abjecit in Tiberim, qui tunc forte super ripas erat effusus. 2. Cui[1] obvia fuit soror, quæ desponsa fuerat uni ex Curiatiis. 3. Soror vidit super humeros fratris paludamentum, quod ipsa confecerat. 4. Numitori, qui natu major erat, regnum reliquit. 5. Qui, adulti inter pastores, primo ludicris certaminibus vires[2] auxere. 6. Quod[3] Remus irridens transilivit. 7. Cæsar liberatus confestim Miletum, quæ urbs proxime aberat, properavit. 8. Flumen Axonam, quod est in extremis Remorum finibus, exercitum transducere maturavit. 9. Loci natura erat hæc quem locum nostri castris delegerant. 10. Multæ civitates ab eo defecerunt; quæ res multorum bellorum causa fuit.

[1] *His sister met him;* **cui** is in the dative after **obvia.** See § 51, 2 (*d*), Rem. 2.
[2] See § 11, III. 4 (*d*). [3] *This;* governed by **trans** in composition.

Translate into Latin.

1. The soldier whom you killed was my brother. 2. The men are absent whom you blame. 3. The boys are here to whom we gave the books. 4. Cæsar immediately hastened from the city and came to his army, which was

already in Farther Gaul. 5. She saw on the shoulders of her brother the cloak which she had made. 6. The army hastened across the river which was nearest. 7. The soldiers crossed the river which is in the extreme part of the territories of the enemy, and immediately assaulted the town.

LESSON XLVIII.

GENITIVE. § 50.

Translate into English.

1. Proca, rex Albanorum, duos filios, Numitorem et Amulium, habuit. 2. Interea Remum latrones ad Amulium regem perduxerunt, eum accusantes, quasi Numitoris greges infestare solitus esset.[1] 3. Princeps ibat Horatius, trium fratrum spolia præ se gerens. 4. Militis[2] est duci[3] parere. 5. Nemo militum fugit. 6. Jam aliquantum spatii ex eo loco[4] ubi pugnatum[5] est aufugerat, cum respiciens videt unum Curiatium haud procul ab se abesse. 7. Tunc summæ audaciæ facinus Cæsar edidit. 8. Amor gloriæ nos impulit. 9. Timor hostium[6] crescit. 10. Id negotii habeo. 11. Quid mihi consilii datis? 12. Armorum et equitandi peritissimus erat. 13. Inde decretum est a senatu, ut videret consul Opimius, ne quid detrimenti respublica caperet. 14. Unus ex his nuntios ad eum mittit. 15. Non de summa belli suum judicium,[7] sed imperatoris esse existimaverunt.

[1] See § 61, 1. [2] Translate, *It is* (the duty) *of a soldier*.
[3] See Rule 16. [4] See Lesson VIII. [5] See § 39.
[6] Translate this as subjective and as objective genitive.
[7] Translate, *The decision concerning the conduct of the war was theirs*, etc.

LESSON XLIX.

GENITIVE (continued). § 50.

Translate into English.

1. Laboris ultra fidem patiens erat. 2. Plena errorum sunt omnia. 3. Ille prudens rei militaris erat. 4. Romani appetentes gloriæ atque[1] avidi laudis fuerunt. 5. Reminiscere pristinæ virtutis Helvetiorum. 6. Obliviscere cædis atque incendiorum. 7. Animus meminit præteritorum. 8. C. Gracchum capitis damnaverunt. 9. Ille gratiam Cæsaris magni existimat. 10. Virtus maximi æstimatur. 11. Te fortunæ tuæ pœnitet. 12. Fratris mei me miseret. 13. Controversiarum et dissensionum obliviscimini. 14. Cæsar dicere solebat, non tam sua quam reipublicæ interesse. 15. Magni reipublicæ interest omnes copias convenire. 16. Illud mea magni interest. 17. Postridie ejus diei in fines Suessionum exercitum duxit. 18. Interest urbis. 19. Interest exercitui. 20. Inter ortum et occasum solis interest spatium unius diei. 21. Quid interest inter divitem et pauperem? Multum. 22. Abi[2] hinc cum immaturo amore ad sponsum, oblita fratrum, oblita patriæ. 23. Reus est capitis.[3] 24. Absolvunt te judices injuriarum. 25. Cujusnam criminis erat ille reus?

[1] Translate, *and also*.
[2] See **abeo**.
[3] See § 50, 4 (*b*).

SYN. — **Animus**, *the mind, the soul;* **mens**, *thought*, or *intellectual faculty;* **anima**, *the life, the vital principle.*

Translate into Latin.

1. The fields of the king are beyond the river. 2. The soldiers of the general are on-this-side-of the river. 3.

He seeks no[1] reward. 4. None of the enemy have fled. 5. Cæsar had a fleet of sixty vessels. 6. The soldiers are eager for glory. 7. Many men are desirous of contention. 8. He was skilled in war. 9. They fled some distance from that place. 10. Who of us is wise? 11. One of the tribunes fled. 12. Hatred towards the king actuated the people. 13. He is desirous of pleasure. 14. It is (the duty) of a good orator to speak candidly. 15. It is (the part) of a judge to hear patiently. 16. He remembers his plan. 17. He will forget his promise. 18. I am ashamed of my fault. 19. I am vexed and wearied at the folly of these men. 20. I repent of my folly. 21. I am weary of my life. 22. It is of great advantage. 23. It is of great advantage to me. 24. It is for the advantage of all. 25. The soldiers have forgotten their dissensions. 26. They condemned him to death. 27. They accused him of treachery. 28. Cæsar acquitted the soldier of the crime. 29. He is reminded of his duty.

[1] Lit. *nothing of reward.*

LESSON L.

DATIVE. § 51.

Translate into English.

1. Nam Remus oris lineamentis erat matri simillimus,[1] ætasque tempori expositionis congruebat. 2. Numitori, qui natu[2] major erat, regnum reliquit. 3. Eos tulit in casam, et Accæ Larentiæ conjugi dedit. 4. Iis insidiati sunt latrones. 5. Is quamvis integer, quia tribus impar erat, fugam simulavit. 6. Placuit[3] Cæsari, ut ad eum legatos mitteret. 7. Milites non mulieribus, non infanti-

bus pepercerunt. 8. Opem ferunt fratri. 9. Tum bellum Ptolemæo, Pompeii interfectori, intulit. 10. Finem labori nox attulit. 11. Hibernis Labienum præposuit. 12. Sex nobis filii sunt. 13. Cæsari erant multæ legiones et fideles amici. 14. Cæsar legiones duas castris præsidio relinquit. 15. Inde duæ legiones quæ proxime conscriptæ erant, totum agmen claudebant, præsidioque impedimentis erant. 16. Urbs hostibus erepta est. 17. Cæsari omnia uno tempore[4] erant agenda. 18. Hunc librum magister mihi præmio dedit.

[1] See § 17, 1 (*b*).
[2] See Rule 26.
[3] Subject?
[4] The ablative of time, *at one time.*

SYN.—**Infans** (**in**, *not*, **fari**, *to speak*), *an infant;* **puer**, *a boy*, from about seven to sixteen; **adolescens** (**adolesco**, *to grow*), *a youth*, from about sixteen to twenty-four; **juvenis**, *a young man* or *woman*, from about twenty-four to forty-five.

LESSON LI.

DATIVE (continued). § 51.

Translate into English.

1. Cui obvia fuit[1] soror, quæ desponsa fuerat uni ex Curiatiis. 2. His difficultatibus duæ res erant subsidio. 3. Legatus equitatum auxilio Cæsari miserat. 4. Philosophia animo medetur. 5. Populo Romano bellum indixisti. 6. Filius patri est similis. 7. Novis imperiis[2] studebant. 8. Dat negotium Senonibus reliquisque Gallis, qui finitimi Belgis erant. 9. Remi, qui proximi Galliæ ex Belgis sunt, ad eum legatos miserunt. 10.

Movit feroci juveni animum comploratio sororis in tanto gaudio publico. 11. Atrox id visum est facinus patribus plebique. 12. Pax petenda est mihi. 13. Circumdat murum urbi, *or*, Circumdat urbem muro. 14. Hoc mihi est curæ. 15. Sunt mihi multi libri. 16. Sanavit filium meum,[3] *or*, Sanavit mihi filium.[4] 17. In omnibus rebus te consulam. 18. In omni re consulam tibi.[5] 19. Seditio[6] urbi excidio fuit. 20. Mihi scribendum est.[7] 21. Cæsar Italiam Antonio devastandam[8] reliquit.

[1] Translate **cui obvia fuit**, *met him;* **obvia** is an adjective in the predicate, and agrees with **soror,** the subject of **fuit.**

[2] *Innovations* (or changes in the state of affairs), *a revolution.*

[3] *He cured my son* (not caring whose son).

[4] *He cured my son* (out of kindness to me).

[5] *For you,* i. e. *your interests.*

[6] Translate, *Sedition proved,* etc.

[7] See § 51, 4 (*a*).

[8] *To be laid waste by, &c.*

SYN.—**Medeor,** *to heal,* relates to the skill of the physician; **sano,** *to heal,* relates to the efficacy of the medicine.

Translate into Latin.

1. The boy was like his father. 2. He pretended flight, because he was unequal to three. 3. I will give the book to you. 4. Cæsar made war upon the Gauls. 5. I have six books. 6. Cæsar had many faithful friends. 7. Cæsar sent the third line for a protection to the baggage. 8. The soldiers spared the fugitives. 9. He left the kingdom to Numitor. 10. He gave the business to me. 11. The Gauls desire a revolution. 12. He placed a wall around the city. 13. They are nearest to the Belgians. 14. You have declared war against me. 15. These things must be done by me. 16. This seemed a bold deed to the people. 17. He will consult my interests. 18. It[1] is wise to prefer virtue to all things. 19. The soldiers will obey their commander. 20. This is my[2] care. 21.

They are unfriendly to me. 22. Do not trust fortune. 23. The lieutenant has sent the cavalry as an aid to Cæsar.

[1] Use the gen. **sapientis est**, etc. [2] Lit. *for a care to me.*

LESSON LII.

ACCUSATIVE AND VOCATIVE. § 52, 53.

Translate into English.

1. Interea Remum latrones ad Amulium regem perduxerunt. 2. Muta istam mentem. 3. Milites sanguinem sitiebant. 4. Agros Remorum depopulati sunt quos adire poterant. 5. Unum Horatium tres Curiatii circumsteterunt. 6. Hoc te rogamus omnes. 7. Consul Cæsarem sententiam rogabat. 8. Cæsar omnia consilia Æduos celat. 9. Pacem ab Romanis petierunt. 10. Ipsi transire flumen non dubitaverunt. 11. "En hæc," inquit, "mea ornamenta." 12. "Nolim quidem, Gracche," inquit, "mea bona tibi viritim dividere liceat."[1] 13. Dixit, "Tu quoque, fili mi!" 14. Rheam Silviam, ejus filiam, Vestæ sacerdotem fecit. 15. Romulus urbem Romam vocavit. 16. Agros plebi dividebat. 17. Quare convocati patres deliberabant quidnam faciendum esset.[2] 18. Vir ille grammaticam nos docebat. 19. Grammaticam a viro illo docebar. 20. Me miserum! omnes me rident homines. 21. Reminiscere, mi amice, veteris tuæ famæ.

[1] *I should not wish it to be in your power.* See § 57, 4 (*c*).
[2] See § 67, 2.

Syn.—**Peto,** *to beg,* **rogo,** *to ask,* are general terms for either a request or demand; **postulo,** *to demand as a right;* **flagito,** *to demand with earnestness;* **posco,** *to ask as a right, as a price or salary.*

Translate into Latin.

1. They lead Romulus to the king. 2. He shows the way to the boy. 3. Will you give me a book? 4. Who gave you that book? 5. They accused the soldier of treason.[1] 6. I will conceal my plans from you. 7. The guide shows the way to the soldier. 8. Cæsar demanded corn of the Ædui. 9. They ask Cæsar his opinion. 10. Cæsar is asked his opinion. 11. Cæsar concealed all his plans from the enemy. 12. They were not able to cross the river. 13. Remus leaped over the wall which Romulus had made. 14. The soldiers have laid waste the fields which they were able to approach. 15. The soldiers thirst for honors. 16. Who taught you music? 17. Will the soldiers cross the river?[2]

[1] See § 50, 4 (*b*). [2] See § 52, 1 (*d*).

LESSON LIII.

ABLATIVE. § 54.

Translate into English.

1. Pro sua quisque patria dimicat ferro. 2. Fœdus ictum est ea lege. 3. Datur signum, infestisque[1] armis terni juvenes, magnorum exercituum animos gerentes, concurrunt. 4. Stricto itaque[2] gladio transfigit puellam, simul eam verbis increpans: "Abi hinc cum immaturo amore ad sponsum, oblita fratrum, oblita patriæ." 5. Cæsar, honoris Divitiaci atque Æduorum causa, sese eos in fidem recepturum et conservaturum[3] dixit. 6. Nostri equites, cum funditoribus sagittariisque flumen[4] transgressi, cum hostium equitatu prœlium commiserunt. 7.

Ita solus potitus est imperio Romulus. 8. Numitori, qui natu major erat, regnum reliquit. 9. Julius Cæsar, functus consulatu, Galliam provinciam sorte obtinuit. 10. Culpa dignus est. 11. Aqua est gravior aëre.[5] 12. Sol major est quam terra. 13. Erat Cæsar excelsa statura, nigris vegetisque oculis, capite calvo. 14. Et T. Labienus, castris hostium potitus, et ex loco superiore, quæ res in nostris castris gererentur[6] conspicatus, decimam legionem subsidio nostris misit. 15. Multitudine hostium castra nostra complentur. 16. Pater Horatii orabat populum, ne se orbum liberis faceret.

[1] Translate, *with presented arms*, etc.
[2] **Itāque**, *and so*; **ităque**, *therefore*.
[3] *That he would receive them*, etc. See § 67, 1.
[4] Give the synonymes.
[5] See Rule 32.
[6] See § 67, 2.

LESSON LIV.

ABLATIVE (continued). § 54.

Translate into English.

1. Murus defensoribus nudatus est. 2. Eo de[1] media nocte Cæsar, iisdem ducibus usus, qui nuntii ab Iccio venerant, Numidas et Cretas sagittarios et funditores Baleares subsidio oppidanis mittit. 3. Hostibus spes potiundi[2] oppidi discessit. 4. Ad castra Cæsaris omnibus copiis contenderunt. 5. Opus est mihi duce. 6. Auctoritate tua nobis opus est. 7. Amulius, pulso fratre, regnavit; et, ut eum subole privaret, Rheam Silviam, ejus filiam, Vestæ sacerdotem fecit. 8. Caius Julius Cæsar, nobilissima genitus familia, annum agens sextum et decimum, patrem amisit. 9. Ære alieno oppressus, ipse dice-

bat sibi opus esse milies sestertium. 10. Provincias novis coloniis replebat. 11. Abstinent pugna. 12. Ille milibus passuum sex a Cæsaris castris consedit. 13. Eloquentia C. Gracchus nullum habebat parem. 14. Magno metu me liberabis. 15. Cæsar, exposito exercitu, ad hostes contendit. 16. Magni[3] reipublicæ intérest omnes copias convenire. 17. Ob eam causam Cæsar bonis spoliatus est. 18. Multo sanguine victoria stetit. 19. Relabente flumine, eos aqua in sicco reliquit.

[1] *Just at*, etc. [2] See § 73, 3 (*a*). [3] See § 54, 8 (*a*).

SYN. — **Sanguis**, *blood* while circulating in the body; **cruor**, *blood* when shed, *gore*.

Translate into Latin.

1. The soldiers fight bravely with the sword. 2. Cæsar preserves them for the sake of Divitiacus. 3. The enemy, having made an attack (lit. an attack having been made), put our soldiers into disorder. 4. Cæsar crosses the river with all his cavalry. 5. *When the sun had risen,*[1] the Romans saw the enemy. 6. *Having heard these things,* he led his army to the banks of the river. 7. The earth is greater than the moon. 8. Cæsar was more powerful than all (the rest of) the citizens. 9. The sun is larger and brighter than the moon. 10. Cæsar was a man of great eloquence. 11. Our camp is filled with soldiers. 12. Just at midnight Cæsar, using the same guides, set out from the town. 13. They have need of a guide. 14. Cæsar was oppressed by debt, and said that he needed ten thousand sesterces. 15. *When these things were done,* Cæsar ordered his soldiers to embark. 16. He will liberate you from great fear. 17. The king sold his country for gold. 18. The soldier values money highly.[2] 19. He reigned sixty years. 20. Is he worthy of praise?

21. The boy is unworthy of his father. 22. He returned from the city to the country.

[1] The sentences in italics are to be given in the Ablative Absolute.
[2] **Magni.**

LESSON LV.

TIME AND PLACE. § 55.

Translate into English.

1. Ut[1] primo concursu increpuere arma, horror ingens spectantes perstrinxit. 2. Inita æstate, Q. Pedium legatum misit. 3. Secunda vigilia, magno cum strepitu ac tumultu, castris egressi sunt. 4. Castra amplius milia[2] passuum octo in latitudinem patebant. 5. Ille tria passuum milia ab ipsa urbe castra posuit. 6. Turris pedes ducentos alta est. 7. Aggerem latum pedes trecentos, altum quinquaginta, exstruxerunt. 8. Consul Roma Athenas profectus est. 9. Cæsar Romam profectus est. 10. Cæsar liberatus confestim Miletum, quæ urbs proxime aberat, properavit. 11. Dixit Cæsar, "malle se ibi primum esse, quam Romæ secundum." 12. Decessit Corintho. 13. Puer ibat domum. 14. Puer redierat rus. 15. Ultima hora venit nuntius. 16. Multos annos domi nostræ vixit. 17. Miles humi jacebat. 18. Julius Cæsar, quæstor factus, in Hispaniam profectus est. 19. A Brundisio Dyrrachium inter oppositas classes gravissima hieme transmisit. 20. Hanno Carthagini vixit. 21. Alexander Babyloni mortuus est. 22. Atticus, Ciceronis amicus, multos annos Athenis vixit. 23. Delphis Apollinis oraculum erat.

[1] *When.* [2] See § 54, 5 (*c*).

SYN. — **Rus,** *the country,* opposed to the town; **patria,** *one's native country;* **regio,** *a large region,* including fields and cities.

Translate into Latin.

1. The towers were two hundred feet high. 2. The soldiers built a wall forty feet high, and six feet thick.[1] 3. Cæsar lived fifty-eight years. 4. In the summer my friends and I[2] shall depart from Rome; I shall go to Miletus, they will go to Athens. 5. In the first watch the soldiers departed from the camp with a great tumult. 6. Cæsar set out for Rome. 7. Cæsar set out from Rome. 8. Cæsar wished to be first at Rome. 9. My friends and I[2] shall go into the country at the beginning of summer. 10. My friend lived many years at Athens. 11. Your friend lived many years at my house. 12. Many apples lay on the ground. 13. I had-rather[3] dwell at Athens than at Rome. 14. Many great generals were born at Rome. 15. Some men live more[4] than one hundred years. 16. The consuls set out from Rome to Athens. 17. He lived at Rome. 18. He lived at Carthage. 19. He lived at Athens. 20. He died at Corinth. 21. The soldiers lie on the ground in summer. 22. Cæsar placed his camp ten miles from the city. 23. The legate set out from Carthage for Rome. 24. Cæsar, (when he was) made quæstor, hastened from Italy to Spain. 25. He comes into Italy. 26. He returns from the country. 27. They were with me both in peace and in war. 28. He returned from the city to the country. 29. I have lived at Athens, at Rome, and at Carthage; in the city and in the country; I have studied literature at home and abroad, but now I shall return to my villa in Italy.[5]

[1] **Latus, a, um.**

[2] In Latin, the pronoun of the first person is written before those of the second or third.

[3] **Malim.**

[4] **Amplius.** See § 54, 5 (*c*).

[5] Use the accusative.

LESSON LVI.

USE OF TENSES. § 58.

Translate into English.

1. Ego primus hanc orationem legi. 2. Hanc orationem primum legi, deinde transcripsi. 3. Hanc orationem primo libenter legi, postea magis[1] magisque mihi jejuna visa est. 4. Venit ut nos videat. 5. Scripsit ut nos moneret. 6. Scripsit ut nos moneat. 7. Dissimulat[2] metum atque spem vultu simulat. 8. Legibus[3] servimus ut liberi[4] esse possimus. 9. Audiam quid acturus sis. 10. Tunc Faustulus, necessitate compulsus, indicavit Romulo quis esset ejus avus, quæ mater. 11. Orta est inter eos contentio, uter nomen novæ urbi daret, eamque regeret. 12. Præmisit equites, qui viam[5] explorarent.[6] 13. Cognoscere non potuit quantæ essent hostium copiæ. 14. Ariovistus a Cæsare petivit, uti colloquio diem constitueret. 15. Quid ad me venistis? 16. Ariovistus conclamavit, quid ad se venissent. 17. Cæsari cum id nuntiatum esset, maturat[7] ab urbe proficisci. 18. Inde decretum est a senatu, ut videret[8] consul Opimius, ne quid[9] detrimenti[10] respublica caperet. 19. Vulpes vidit leonem retibus captum, et stans prope, ludificavit eum insolenter. 20. Leo autem dixit, "Non tu me ludificas, sed malum quod in me incidit." 21. Homines misit ut agrum ararent.

[1] Translate, *drier and drier*, etc.

[2] Syn. — **Simulo,** *pretend what does not exist;* **dissimulo,** *conceal what does exist.*

[3] Why dative?

[4] *Free.*

[5] Syn. — **Via** is the *path or road* on which one goes; **iter** (*the going*) is *the journey* in an abstract sense, or *the way that leads directly to a place;* **callis,** *a mountain-path;* **semita,** *a foot-path* or *by-way.*

[6] *To explore the way* (lit. *who should*, etc.). See § 64, 1.
[7] See § 58, 2 (*d*).
[8] See § 64, 1.
[9] Indefinite pronoun. See § 21, 2 (*d*).
[10] See § 50, 2 (*c*).

Translate into Latin.

1. I come to see you. 2. I came to see you. 3. Did Romulus give a name to the new city? Yes. 4. He asked whether[1] Romulus gave[2] a name to the new city. 5. He inquired whether you are going to Rome. 6. I will send the men to plough the field.[3] 7. I have sent the men to plough the field. 8. He came to warn us. 9. He has come to warn us. 10. What did you say? 11. He asked what you said. 12. He promised to send me a letter. 13. He promises to send me a letter. 14. He has promised to send me a letter.

[1] Use **num.**
[2] Use the subjunctive. See § 67, 2.
[3] See § 64, 2.

LESSON LVII.

CONDITIONAL SENTENCES. § 59.

Translate into English.

1. Si hoc facit, bene est. 2. Si hoc faciat, bene sit. 3. Si hoc fecisset, bene fuisset. 4. Si hoc faceret, bene esset. 5. Si id credis, erras. 6. Si me laudabis, ego te laudabo. 7. Si quid habet, dat. 8. Si quid habeat, det. 9. Si quid habuisset, dedisset. 10. Si veteris contumeliæ oblivisci volo, num recentium injuriarum memoriam deponere possum? 11. Nam si violandum[1] est jus, regnandi gratia violandum est. 12. Si te in Capitolium

faces[2] ferre vellet, obsecuturusne voluntati illius fuisses propter istam, quam jactas, familiaritatem? 13. Si hoc dicas, erres. 14. Si[3] quis a domino prehenderetur, concursu militum eripiebatur. 15. Si id faciemus, peccabimus. 16. Si pacem populus Romanus cum Helvetiis faceret, in eam partem ituros[4] ubi Cæsar eos esse voluisset; sin bello persequi perseveraret, reminisceretur[5] veteris incommodi populi Romani. 17. Si Allobrogibus[6] satisfaciant, sese cum iis pacem facturum. 18. Lupus videns pastores in tabernaculo ovem edentes, "Quantus," inquit, "tumultus esset,[7] si ego hoc fecissem."[8] 19. Musca sedebat[9] in cornu bovis et stridebat; et dixit bovi, "Si pondus meum tuum collum opprimit, abibo."[10] 20. At ille, "Neque," inquit, "sensi cum venisti, nec si manes mea[11] refert." 21. Si tibi satisfacerem, mihi ipsi satisfacerem. 22. Si quid venale habeo, id, quanti[12] æstimo, tantidem vendo. 23. Convincam, si negas.

[1] See § 40 (*a* and *b*).

[2] See **fax**; in this sentence **te** is the subject of **ferre.**

[3] Translate, *If any one was seized by his master, he was* (always) *rescued*, etc.

[4] See **eo.**

[5] Translate, *let him remember*, etc.

[6] See § 51, 2 (*b*).

[7] See Rule 46.

[8] What is the apodosis?

[9] See § 58, 3 (*a*).

[10] See **abeo.**

[11] See § 50, 4 (*d*).

[12] See § 54, 8 (*a*).

SYN. — **Erro,** *go astray from ignorance;* **vagor,** *roam about;* **palor,** *straggle.*

Translate into Latin.

1. If he should do this, it would be well. 2. If he shall do this, it will be well. 3. If I should have any money, I would give it to you. 4. If I had done this,

it would have been well. 5. If one gives me money, I (always) give it to the poor. 6. If you were studying, I should rejoice. 7. If he says this, he is-mistaken. 8. If you were here, you would think differently. 9. The mind grows weak, unless you exercise it. 10. If you would read this book, I would give it to you. 11. If this were so, I should be glad. 12. If you will remain with me, I shall give the money to you. 13. If any one attempted to cross the river, the soldiers prevented them. 14. If he had spoken the truth, he would have been praised. 15. If they should give up their vessels, the enemy promised them peace. 16. If this had been so, I should have been glad. 17. If Cæsar shall assault the town, the enemy will flee. 18. If this is so, I am glad.

LESSON LVIII.

COMPARATIVE AND CONCESSIVE CLAUSES. § 61.

Translate into English.

1. Cæsar, etsi prope exacta[1] jam æstas erat, tamen eo[2] exercitum adduxit. 2. Quanquam omnis virtus nos ad se[3] allicit, tamen justitia id maxime efficit. 3. Ut sementem feceris, ita metes. 4. Cum ea ita sint, tamen, si obsides ab iis sibi dentur, uti ea, quæ polliceantur, facturos intelligat, sese cum iis pacem esse facturum. 5. Quamvis molestus dolor sit, malum non est. 6. Vita brevis est, licet supra mille annos exeat. 7. Ut desint vires, tamen est laudanda voluntas. 8. Multi omnia recta negligunt, dummodo potentiam consequantur. 9. Patres metus cepit, velut si jam ad portas[4] hostis[4] esset. 10. Adero, dummodo sis domi. 11. Adero ego, licet absit amicus. 12. Dummodo tu adsis, adero ego. 13. Quamvis

tu adesses, non adessem ego. 14. Is, cum multa contra legem frumentariam dixisset, lege tamen lata,[5] ad frumentum cum ceteris accipiendum, venit. 15. Hoc facis, cum scias te punitum iri. 16. Omnia postposui, dummodo præceptis patris parerem. 17. In omnibus negotiis, priusquam aggrediare,[6] adhibenda[7] est præparatio diligens. 18. Non ante finitum est prœlium, quam tribunus militum interfectus est. 19. Decessit post annum quartum quam expulsus est. 20. Interfuit pugnæ[8] navali apud Salamina, quæ facta est[9] priusquam pœna[10] liberaretur. 21. Magno me metu liberabis, dummodo inter me atque te murus intersit.

[1] See **exigo.**
[2] *Thither.*
[3] See § 19, 3.
[4] Give the synonymes.
[5] See **fero.**
[6] *Before you attempt* (anything).
[7] Freely, *you must make careful preparation.*
[8] Why dative?
[9] *Which was fought.*
[10] *From his penalty.*

Translate into Latin.

1. Although the summer was passed, Cæsar led his army there. 2. Although I was present, you said that. 3. Provided I am present, you will be present. 4. Although you should kill me, yet I would say that. 5. I will be present, provided your father is at home. 6. I was present, although you were absent. 7. We will do this, although we know that we shall be punished. 8. Although you have laid waste our fields, yet if you will give hostages we will make peace with you. 9. Although the enemy fought bravely, yet they were driven from the town. 10. Cæsar promises to give corn until they reach[1] the river. 11. On the following day, Cæsar, before the enemy could recover from their alarm, led his army into the territories of the Suessiones.

[1] Use **dum veniatur.**

LESSON LIX.

TEMPORAL CLAUSES. § 62.

Translate into English.

1. Cum lupa sæpius ad parvulos, veluti ad catulos, reverteretur, Faustulus, pastor regius, rem animadvertit. 2. Tiberius Gracchus, cum esset tribunus plebis, a senatu descivit.[1] 3. Ob eam causam, Cæsar bonis[2] spoliatus, cum etiam ad mortem quæreretur, mutata veste,[3] noctu elapsus est ex urbe; et, quanquam tunc quartanæ morbo laboraret, prope per singulas noctes latebras commutare cogebatur. 4. Dum hæc geruntur, hostium copiæ conveniunt. 5. Zenonem, cum Athenis essent, audiebant. 6. Cum ad has suspiciones certissimæ res accederent, satis esse causæ arbitrabatur, quare in eum aut ipse animadverteret,[4] aut civitatem animadvertere juberet. 7. Itaque, priusquam quidquam conaretur, Divitiacum ad se vocari jubet. 8. Postquam id animum advertit,[5] copias suas Cæsar in proximum collem subducit. 9. Tempestas minatur antequam surgat. 10. Ducentis annis antequam Romam caperent, in Italiam Galli descenderunt. 11. Dum reliquæ naves convenirent, ad horam nonam exspectavit. 12. Cæsar, cum Pompeium apud Pharsalum vicisset, in Asiam trajecit. 13. Cæsar ad Pompeii castra pervenit, priusquam Pompeius sentiret. 14. Ea continebis quoad te videam. 15. Rhenus servat violentiam cursus, donec Oceano misceatur. 16. Priusquam incipias, consulto opus est. 17. Donec te videram, valde sollicitus eram. 18. Donec te vidisset, noluit abire puer.[6] 19. Donec te viderat, noluit abire puer. 20. Vulpes, videns uvas maturas alte pendentes, edere conata est. Sed multum laborans, cum attingere non posset, dissimulavit dolorem suum, dixitque, "At sunt virides, et acerbæ."

[1] Translate, *abandoned the party of the Senate.*

[2] See Rule 28.

[3] What does this ablative absolute express?

[4] See § 63, 2. Why is this subjunctive? See § 66.

[5] The phrase **animum advertit** is to be translated as a single word: *observed* (lit. *turned his mind to it*).

[6] The subjunctive in this sentence implies that the boy did go away without seeing you; while the next sentence implies that he did not go until he accomplished his object.

Translate into Latin.

1. When I am at Athens, I shall hear Zeno. 2. When I was at Athens, I heard Zeno. 3. When Cæsar was sought for to be put to death,[1] he escaped from the city by night. 4. While these things were going on at Rome, the forces of the enemy assembled. 5. Before you begin, there is need of deliberation. 6. After Cæsar perceived that, he led his forces to the nearest hill. 7. He waited until the rest of the ships assembled. 8. When Cæsar had conquered Pompey, he crossed into Asia. 9. Before they heard of my approach, I entered the city. 10. These things took place after he had entered the city. 11. I waited until he came. 12. The forces of the enemy assembled before these things took place.[2] 13. These things did not take place until he had entered the city. 14. While the senate was preparing war against Cæsar, he made himself dictator. 5. They were present before it was light. 16. When a certain old man[3] at Athens had come into the theatre, a place was nowhere given to him by his fellow-citizens; but when he came to the Lacedæmonians, who, since they were ambassadors, were seated[4] in a certain place, they all rose together.

[1] *To seek for to put to death,* **quærere ad mortem.**

[2] Use **facta sunt.**

[3] Use **quidam grandis natu.**

[4] Use pluperfect of **consideo.**

LESSON LX.

CAUSAL CLAUSES. § 63.

Translate into English.

1. Laudo te, quia tu me laudas. 2. Laudabat me, quod filium meum culparem. 3. Quoniam jam nox est, in vestra tecta discedite. 4. Quæ cum ita sint, perge. 5. Is quamvis integer, quia tribus impar erat, fugam simulavit. 6. Alterum deinde, priusquam tertius posset consequi, interfecit. 7. Cui legi cum senatus repugnaret, Cæsar rem ad populum detulit. 8. Eo frumento, quod flumine Arari navibus subvexerat, minus uti poterat, quod iter ab Arari Helvetii averterant, a quibus discedere nolebat. 9. Succenseo tibi, quia lucrum amicitiæ anteposuisti. 10. Postridie ejus diei,[1] quod omnino biduum supererat, cum exercitui frumentum metiri oporteret, et quod a Bibracte, oppido Æduorum longe maximo et copiosissimo, non amplius milibus passuum duodeviginti aberat, rei[2] frumentariæ prospiciendum existimavit: iter ab Helvetiis avertit, ac Bibracte ire contendit. 11. Hac oratione habita, mirum in modum conversæ sunt omnium mentes; summaque alacritas et cupiditas belli gerendi innata est, princepsque[3] decima legio per[4] tribunos militum ei gratias egit, quod de se optimum judicium fecisset.

[1] See § 50, 4 Rem.
[2] Translate, *he thought he must look about for corn.* [3] *First.*
[4] See § 54, 4 (*b*).

Syn.—**Succenseo,** *to be displeased with;* **irascor,** *to be angry,* but not necessarily to show it by outward emotions; **stomăchor,** *to show anger.*

Primus, *first,* so far as one appears first; **princeps,** *first,* so far as one acts first.

Quia, *because,* regularly introduces a fact; **quod,** either a fact or statement; **quoniam,** *since,* has reference to motives.

Translate into Latin.

1. You have praised me because I praised you. 2. Since it is now night, we will depart. 3. When it is night, we will depart. 4. I will praise the boy because he studies well. 5. Since these things are so, there is need of deliberation. 6. He accuses them severely because he is not assisted by them. 7. I am angry with you, that you should prefer gain to friendship. 8. I am angry with you because you (actually) did prefer gain to friendship. 9. They rejoiced because they were going to assault the city.

LESSON LXI.

FINAL CLAUSES. § 64.

Translate into English.

1. Laudas me, ut a me invicem lauderis. 2. Laudabat me, ut a me invicem laudaretur. 3. Contendit Cæsar maximis itineribus in fines Nerviorum, ut consilia eorum præveniret. 4. Venit ut portas claudat. 5. Venit ut portas clauderet. 6. Milites cohortatus est, ut fortiter castra defenderent. 7. Milites cohortatus est, quo mortem fortius obirent. 8. Homines misit ut agrum ararent. 9. Imperavit mihi ut abirem. 10. Jussit ut abirem. 11. Inde decretum est a senatu, ut videret consul Opimius, ne quid detrimenti respublica caperet. 12. Cæsar, cum adhuc in Gallia detineretur, ne imperfecto bello discederet, postulavit ut sibi liceret, quamvis absenti,[1] secundum consulatum petere. 13. Equitatum, qui sustineret hostium impetum, misit. 14. Quamobrem placuit ei, ut ad Ariovistum legatos mitteret, qui ab eo postularent, uti

aliquem locum medium colloquio diceret. 15. Constituit Cæsar pontem in flumine Rheno facere quo copias suas transduceret. 16. Venit ut videat. 17. Venit ut nos videret. 18. Romulus edixit ne quis vallum transiliret. 19. Amulius, pulso fratre, regnavit, et, ut eum subole privaret, Rheam Silviam, ejus filiam, Vestæ sacerdotem fecit. 20. Vulpes quædam cassibus capta erat, sed postea, amissa cauda, effugit. Convocavit igitur omnes vulpes, et suasit eis, ut ipsæ quoque abscinderent caudas, quippe quæ non modo indecoræ essent, sed merum inutile pondus. Sed una ex iis, "At tu," inquit, "non ita moneres, nisi ista calamitas ipsi tibi accidisset." 21. Quamobrem placuit ei, ut ad Ariovistum legatos mitteret, qui ab eo postularent, uti aliquem[2] locum medium utriusque colloquio diceret.

[1] *Although absent.*

[2] *Some place midway between both.*

Syn.—**Licet** and **concessum est**, *it is allowed*, refers to what is allowed by human law; **fas est**, *it is allowed by Divine law.*

Translate into Latin.

1. He came to close[1] the door. 2. He has come to close the door. 3. He will come to close the door. 4. He has come to see me. 5. The Helvetians determined to depart from their own territories, in order that they might obtain possession of all Gaul. 6. He encouraged the soldiers in order that[2] they might meet death more bravely. 7. He has encouraged the soldiers in order that they may meet death bravely. 8. I gave you orders to depart. 9. I have given you orders to depart. 10. He sent legates to ask for peace. 11. We have praised you, in order that we may be praised by you in turn. 12. I will strive that I may be serviceable to you. 13. I have

striven to be serviceable to you. 14. He sent the cavalry to sustain the attack of the enemy. 15. I ask you to do this. 16. I asked you to do this. 17. I will encourage him to learn. 18. I have encouraged him to learn. 19. I will strive to conquer. 20. It happened that I was not at home. 21. I am going to look at the games. 22. I went to look at the games.

[1] Observe that the English infinitive expressing a purpose (when it is equivalent to *that, in order that*) is to be translated by **ut** with the subjunctive, or some other of the forms on page 183.

[2] **Quo** is used in preference to **ut** when there is a comparative in the clause which it introduces.

LESSON LXII.

CONSECUTIVE CLAUSES. § 65.

Translate into English.

1. Eum deterruerunt, quominus domo exiret. 2. Faciam ut mei sis memor. 3. Feci ut mei esses memor. 4. Nil faciam, quominus tu id facias. 5. Vereor ne venias. 6. Vereor ut venias. 7. Vereor ne non venias. 8. Vereor ut venerit. 9. Accidit, ut illo tempore in urbe essem. 10. Sol efficit ut omnia floreant. 11. Cura ut valeas. 12. Fac ut sciam. 13. Mea[1] refert ut venias. 14. Quid obstat quominus mœnia statim oppugnemus? 15. Tantum ægrotabam, ut apud illum non possem cœnare. 16. Nemo est, qui id mihi persuadeat. 17. Flumen[2] est Arar, quod per fines Æduorum et Sequanorum in Rhodanum influit, incredibili lenitate, ita ut oculis in utram partem fluat judicari non possit. 18. Cæsar non exspectandum sibi[3] statuit, dum in Santones Helvetii pervenirent. 19. Le-

gatos miserunt qui dicerent. 20. Non dubito quin sapientissimus sis. 21. Dignus est qui audiatur. 22. Rufum Cæsar idoneum judicaverat quem mitteret. 23. Majus gaudium fuit, quam[4] quod universum homines caperent. 24. Dignus est qui laudetur. 25. Tanta vis probitati est, ut eam vel in hoste diligamus. 26. Nemo tam potens est, ut omnia quæ velit efficere possit. 27. At Numitor, considerato adolescentis vultu, haud procul erat quin nepotem agnosceret. 28. Nemo erat, qui cuperet me ex civitate pellere.

[1] See § 50, 4 (*d*). [2] Give the synonymes. [3] Why dative?
[4] Translate, *than* (what) *men could take in all at once;* § 65, 2 (*e*).

SYN. — **Timeo,** *fear*, the fear that arises for the body, from timidity; **metuo,** *fear*, is the fear of the mind arising from a consideration of circumstances; **vereor,** *reverence*, expresses a reverential or humble fear, or doubt about the happening of some event; **formido,** *dread*, of a great and lasting fear.

Translate into Latin.

1. I will deter him from going from home. 2. I deterred him from going from home. 3. The soldiers prohibited me from going to the city. 4. The soldiers have prohibited me from going to the city. 5. There was no one who did not rejoice. 6. I feared you would not come. 7. I fear he has not come. 8. I fear you will come. 9. I fear he has come. 10. What prevents us from seeing the games? 11. What prevented us from seeing the games? 12. The river was so broad that he did not cross it. 13. The fear of the soldiers was so great that he did not lead them from the camp. 14. He deserves to be heard. 15. He does not deserve to be heard. 16. He deserved to be heard. 17. He did not deserve to be heard. 18. He is a suitable person to send.[1] 19. He was a suitable person to send. 20.

There were some who departed from the city. 21. There are some who do not fear. 22. There are some who wish to see the games. 23. He gave orders to lead the soldiers out of the camp. 24. What hinders him from leading the soldiers out of the camp? 25. He is not a suitable person to lead the soldiers out of the camp. 26. There were some who led the soldiers out of the camp. 27. The enemy were so terrified that they fled. 28. The Romans fought so bravely that they defeated the enemy. 29. We cannot object[2] (to it) that others should differ from us.[3]

[1] Translate **quem mittamus**, or, **qui mittatur.**

[2] Lit. *We are not able to object.* [3] *From us,* **a nobis.**

LESSON LXIII.

INTERMEDIATE CLAUSES. § 66.

Translate into English.

1. Id quod habeo tibi dabo. 2. Id quod habebat tibi dabat. 3. Dixit puer se tibi quodcumque haberet daturum esse. 4. Jussit ut quæ venissent naves Eubœam peterent. 5. Cui obvia fuit soror, quæ desponsa fuerat uni ex Curiatiis; visoque super humeros fratris paludamento sponsi, quod ipsa confecerat, flere et crines solvere cœpit. 6. Cum tridui viam[1] processisset, nuntiatum est ei, Ariovistum[2] cum suis omnibus copiis ad occupandum Vesontionem (quod est oppidum maximum Sequanorum) contendere, triduique[3] viam a suis finibus profecisse. 7. Interim quotidie Cæsar Æduos frumentum, quod essent publice[4] polliciti,[5] flagitare.[6] 8. Postridie ejus diei præter castra Cæsaris suas copias transduxit, et milibus passuum

duobus ultra eum castra fecit,[7] eo consilio,[8] uti frumento commeatuque, qui ex Sequanis et Æduis supportaretur,[9] Cæsarem intercluderet. 9. Ubi eum[10] castris se tenere Cæsar intellexit, ne diutius commeatu prohiberetur, ultra eum locum, quo in loco Germani consederant, circiter passus sexcentos ab his castris idoneum locum delegit, acieque triplici instructa, ad eum locum venit.

1 *Journey of three days.*
2 *That Ariovistus was hastening*, etc.
3 *And had completed a journey of three days*, etc.
4 *In the name of the state.*
5 The subjunctive refers to the promise as made by the Ædui.
6 *Kept demanding.* See Rule 40.
7 *Pitched his camp.*
8 *With this design.*
9 **Supportaretur:** *was coming in;* lit. *was* (being) *brought.*
10 *That he held himself in camp.*

LESSON LXIV.

INDIRECT DISCOURSE. § 67.

Translate into English.

1. Dicit, "Rex urbem oppugnat." 2. Dicit regem urbem oppugnare. 3. Dicit, "Cupio discere." 4. Dicit se cupere discere. 5. Ad hæc Cæsar respondit; Se id quod in Nerviis fecisset, facturum. 6. Dixit se, si quid haberet, daturum esse. 7. Censeo, si hoc dicas, te errare. 8. Censebat, si hoc diceres, te errare. 9. Censebat, si hoc diceres, te erraturum esse. 10. Dicit, si quid habuisset, se daturum fuisse. 11. Is ita cum Cæsare agit; Si pacem populus Romanus cum Helvetiis faciet, in eam partem ibunt Helvetii, ubi eos esse Cæsar voluerit. 12. Is ita

cum Cæsare agit; Si pacem populus Romanus cum Helvetiis faceret, in eam partem ituros, ubi Cæsar eos esse voluisset. 13. Censebam me, cum adessem, id dicere. 14. Dicit se, quia tu se laudes, te laudare. 15. Dixit se, eo frumento, quod flumine Arari navibus subvexisset, minus uti potuisse, quod iter ab Arari Helvetii avertissent, a quibus discedere nollet. 16. Dixit se intelligere quid ageret hostis. 17. Dixit se intelligere quid egisset hostis. 18. Dixit se intellexisse quid egisset hostis. 19. Si quid mihi a Cæsare opus esset, ad eum venissem. 20. Ei legationi Ariovistus respondit; Si quid ipsi a Cæsare opus esset, sese ad eum venturum esse. 21. Dicebat se, si posset, venturum esse. 22. Si quid habet, dat. 23. Dicit, si quid habeat, se dare. 24. Si quid habeat, det. 25. Dicit, si quid habeat, se daturum esse. 26. Dixit, si quid habuisset, se daturum fuisse. 27. Ad hæc Ariovistus respondit; Jus esse belli, ut qui vicissent his quos vicissent, quemadmodum vellent, imperarent. 28. Eodem die ab exploratoribus certior[1] factus, hostes sub monte consedisse milia passuum ab ipsius castris octo, qualis esset natura montis et qualis in[2] circuitu adscensus, qui cognoscerent, misit.

[1] *Being informed.*

[2] Lit. *the ascent in a circuit.*

Syn. — **Aveo,** *long for;* **desidero,** *desire* what one has had, but now feels the loss of (hence, *regret*); **volo,** *wish;* **opto,** *prefer;* **cupio,** *desire* (general term); **gestio,** *desire,* and manifest it by gestures.

Dico, *say* (transitive form of **loqui**); **loqui,** *speak* or *talk* (opposed to **tacere,** *keep silent*); **fari,** *talk,* use articulate speech; **dicere** is to speak for the information of the hearers; **aio** expresses the assertion of the speaker (opposed to **nego**); **inquam** is used to introduce the very words of the speaker, and always comes after one or more words of the quotation.

Translate into Latin.

1. I am going to Rome. 2. The boy says, "I am going to Rome." 3. Cæsar has assaulted the city. 4. The messenger said, "Cæsar has assaulted the city." 5. The messenger said that Cæsar had assaulted the city with all his forces. 6. He thinks that you are mistaken if you say this. 7. He thinks you would be mistaken if you should say this. 8. He thinks you would have been mistaken if you had said this. 9. He thinks you would be mistaken if you had said this. 10. He says that he understands what the enemy are doing. 11. He said that he understood what the enemy had been doing. 12. He said that he praised you because you had praised him. 13. The messenger said that the forces of the enemy assembled while these things were going on. 14. He said that he feared you would not come. 15. Cæsar said that he had sent his lieutenants to do this. 16. The legate said that he was present before it was light. 17. Cæsar said that the Helvetians had departed from their territories in order that they might obtain possession of all Gaul. 18. He says that he has come to see you. 19. He said that he had come to see you. 20. Cæsar said that he had sent the cavalry to sustain the attack of the enemy. 21. Cæsar said that he feared that the general would not lead his forces out of the camp. 22. It is related that when Cæsar had conquered Pompey, he crossed into Asia. 23. Ariovistus said that he would not wage[1] war upon the Æduans,[2] if they paid the tribute yearly.[3]

[1] Use **illaturum esse.**

[2] Use the dative.

[3] Use **quotannis.**

LESSON LXV.

THE INFINITIVE IN INDIRECT DISCOURSE. § 58, 11; 57, 8.

Translate into English.

1. Putas me scribere.[1] 2. Putabo me scribere. 3. Putas me scripsisse. 4. Putabis me scripsisse. 5. Puto te scripturum esse. 6. Cum pugnaretur,[2] humi jacebat. 7. Memini eum cum pugnaretur humi jacere. 8. Dicit me cum pugnaretur humi jacuisse. 9. Dicit puer se laudatum esse (*or*, fuisse). 10. Putat puer se laudatum iri. 11. Sciebam te, si posses, venturum esse. 12. Sciebam te, si potuisses, venturum fuisse. 13. Putabat puer se laudatum[3] iri (*or*, futurum[3] esse ut laudaretur). 14. Putabit puer se laudatum iri (*or*, fore ut laudetur). 15. Putaverat puer se laudatum iri. 16. Nuntius dicit, equites tela conjicere. 17. Nuntius dixit equites tela conjicere. 18. Nuntius dixit equites tela conjecisse. 19. Nuntius dicit equites tela conjecisse. 20. Volui consulem eum esse.[4] 21. Cæsar intellegit bellum parari. 22. Cæsar intelleget bellum paratum esse. 23. Cæsar intellexit bellum paratum iri. 24. A primo tempore æstatis juri te studere memini. 25. Cæsar reperiebat initium fugæ a Dumnorige factum esse. 26. Dixit se regem vidisse. 27. Lycurgi temporibus Homerus fuisse dicitur. 28. Imperare sibi maximum est imperium. 29. Vincere scis, Hannibal, victoria[5] uti nescis. 30. Nunquam putavi fore,[6] ut supplex ad te venirem. 31. Locutus est pro his Divitiacus;[7] Galliæ totius factiones esse duas; harum alterius principatum tenere Æduos, alterius Arvernos. 32. Hi cum de potentatu[8] inter se multos annos contenderent, factum esse,[9] uti ab Arvernis Sequanisque Germani mercede[10] arcesserentur. 33. Horum[11] primo circiter millia

quindecim Rhenum transisse; posteaquam agros, cultum et copias Gallorum homines barbari adamavissent, traductos esse plures. 34. Petierunt, uti sibi concilium totius Galliæ in diem certam indicere idque Cæsaris voluntate facere liceret; sese[13] habere quasdam res, quas ex communi consensu[14] ab eo petere vellent.

[1] For the time denoted by the infinitive in indirect discourse, see § 58, 11 and *b*; thus: **putas me scribere,** *you think I am writing:* **putas me scripsisse,** *you think that I was writing, wrote, have written,* or *had written:* **putas me scripturum esse,** *you think that I will write:* when the principal verb is in a past tense, the translation of the infinitive is changed, though the relation of time is the same, thus: **putavisti me scribere,** *you thought I was writing;* **putavisti me scripsisse,** *you thought I had written.*

The pupil will notice that the imperfect tense, as well as the perfect and pluperfect, is represented in indirect discourse by the *perfect infinitive.* But after **memini,** the *present infinitive* regularly stands for the imperfect. The same construction occurs exceptionally after other verbs, but had better be avoided by beginners.

[2] Observe the imperfect: *while the fight was going on.*

[3] Observe that the future infinitive is made up of the supine and **iri**; when the verbs have no supine, **fore** or **futurum esse** must be used.

[4] See § 58, 11 Rem.

[5] See Rule 31.

[6] See § 58, 11 (*f*).

[7] **Principatum tenere,** *stood at the head.*

[8] *Superiority.*

[9] *It came to pass.*

[10] *Were invited by* (promises of) *reward.*

[11] *Of the latter.*

[12] *After that these barbarous men had grown fond of the lands .... more crossed over.*

[13] (Saying) *that they had,* etc.

[14] *In accordance with the general consent.*

Syn. — **Potestas,** *power, lawful authority, as of a magistrate;* **potentia,** *unconstitutional power, predominance;* **potentatus,** *the power of a ruler,* which is acknowledged by those subject to him; **ditio,** *power, jurisdiction.*

Translate into Latin.

1. He says, "I am writing." 2. He says that he is writing. 3. He says, "I have written." 4. He says that he has written. 5. He says, "I wrote." 6. He says that he has written. 7. He says, "While you were absent I was writing." 8. He says that while you were absent he was writing.[1] 9. He says, "I will write." 10. He says that he will write. 11. He says, "I had written." 12. He says that he had written. 13. He said that he had written before you came from the country. 14. He said, "I know." 15. He said that he knows. 16. He said, "I will come." 17. He said that he would come. 18. He says, "I will come." 19. He says that he will come if he can. 20. You ought to have done this. 21. I remember that you said this. 22. You[2] may go to the city if you wish. 23. It is difficult to do this. 24. They wish to cross the river. 25. He[3] said that the town would be taken.

[1] Use the perfect infinitive.
[2] Lit. *It is permitted to you*, etc.; see Note Gr. p. 51.
[3] Render this both ways. See § 58, 11 (*f*).

LESSON LXVI.

WISHES AND COMMANDS. § 68.

Translate into English.

1. Laudemus nomen Dei. 2. Confer[1] longissimam ætatem cum æternitate. 3. Secernant se a bonis. 4. "Nolim[2] quidem, Gracche," inquit, "mea bona tibi viritim dividere liceat; sed si facies, partem petam." 5. Utinam eas res efficere possim. 6. Utinam vera inve-

nire possim. 7. Si quid acciderit novi,[3] facies ut sciam. 8. Ne transieris Rhodanum. 9. Ineamus in urbem. 10. Eum iratus Romulus interfecit, his increpans verbis: "Sic posthac malo adficietur, quicumque transiliet mœnia mea." 11. Stricto itaque gladio, transfigit puellam, simul eam verbis increpans: "Abi hinc cum immaturo amore ad sponsum, oblita fratrum, oblita patriæ." 12. Sic eat quæcumque Romana lugebit hostem. 13. Valetudinem tuam cura diligenter. 14. Cives mei sint beati. 15. Equidem vellem,[4] ut domi esses. 16. Tunc Scipio Nasica, cum esset consobrinus Tiberii Gracchi, patriam cognationi prætulit, sublataque dextera proclamavit: "Qui rempublicam salvam esse volunt, me sequantur."

[1] See § 30, 6 (*c*).
[2] *I should be unwilling* (in some future case).
[3] See § 50, 2 (*c*).
[4] *I should* (now) *wish* (on some condition not fulfilled).

Translate into Latin.

1. Let us go to the city. 2. Let us love our country. 3. Cross not the river. 4. Would that I could[1] accomplish this. 5. Do not forget your country. 6. Would that you had been here. 7. Let all who wish to accomplish this follow me. 8. May you be happy. 9. No good[2] (man) can doubt concerning the providence of God. 10. My friends, I hope you are well.[3] 11. I hope my father is alive.[4] 12. I wish my father were alive.[5] 13. I wish my father had lived. 14. Let us imitate our ancestors. 15. Would that he had led forth with him all his forces.

[1] In some future case.
[2] **Nemo bonus.**
[3] *May you be safe.*
[4] *Would that my father may be alive.*
[5] *Would that my father was alive.*

LESSON LXVII.

SUBSTANTIVE CLAUSES. § 70.

Translate into English.

1. Accidit, ut illo tempore in urbe essem. 2. Quamobrem placuit ei, ut ad Ariovistum legatos mitteret, qui ab eo postularent, uti aliquem locum medium colloquio diceret. 3. Sol efficit, ut omnia floreant. 4. Nunquam putavi fore[1] ut supplex ad te venirem. 5. Romulus edixit ne quis vallum transiliret. 6. Eo fit, ut milites animos demittant. 7. Ubi de ejus adventu Helvetii certiores facti sunt, legatos ad eum mittunt,[2] qui dicerent,[3] sibi esse in animo, sine ullo maleficio iter per provinciam facere. 8. Aliud est docere; aliud, discere. 9. Quibus rebus cognitis, cum ad has suspiciones certissimæ res[4] accederent, quod per fines Sequanorum Helvetios transduxisset, quod obsides inter eos dandos[5] curasset, quod ea omnia non[6] modo injussu suo et civitatis sed etiam inscientibus ipsis fecisset, quod a magistratu Æduorum accusaretur, satis esse causæ[7] arbitrabatur, quare in eum aut ipse animadverteret,[8] aut civitatem animadvertere juberet. 10. Cum ab his quæreret, quæ civitates quantæque in armis essent, et quid[9] in bello possent, sic reperiebat. 11. Nolim[10] puer veniat. 12. Legem[11] brevem esse oportet, quo facilius ab imperitis teneatur.[12] 13. Thales Milesius aquam dixit esse initium[13] rerum.

[1] *That it would happen.* [2] See § 58, 2 (*d*).

[3] See Rule 44; for the tense, see § 58, 10 (*d*).

[4] *The most positive facts.*

[5] See § 73, 5 (*c*); how would it affect the sense if this verb was in the indicative?

[6] Translate, *not only without his command, and that of the state*, etc.

[7] Why genitive?

[8] See § 67, 2.

[9] *What they could* (do) *in war.*

[10] See § 70, 3 (*f*), Rem.

[11] Translate, *A law ought to be short.*

[12] *May be comprehended.*

[13] *The first principle of* (all) *things.*

LESSON LXVIII.

QUESTIONS. § 71.

Translate into English.

1. Quærit num Cæsar in urbe sit. 2. Num ita audes dicere? 3. "Nonne," inquit, "idonea dolendi causa est, quod nihildum memorabile gesserim, eam ætatem adeptus, qua Alexander jam terrarum orbem[1] subegerat?"[2] 4. Utrum Romæ an in agris hibernis mensibus manere mavis? 5. Utrum Cato an Cæsar tibi præstantior et clarior vir esse videtur? 6. Jussit eos speculari num hostes ex castris exirent. 7. Quæritur Dii utrum sint, necne. 8. Isne est quem quæro, annon? 9. Num dubium est casune an consilio factus sit mundus? 10. Cujus hic liber est? tuusne? non, sed fratris. 11. Utrum ea vestra an nostra culpa est? 12. Is, se[3] præsente de se ter sortibus consultum[4] dicebat, utrum igni statim necaretur, an in aliud tempus reservaretur.

[1] **Orbis terrarum,** rather than **terra,** when there is decided reference to other lands.

[2] See **subigo.**

[3] See Rule 35.

[4] Translate, *that it had been consulted by the lots about him three times;* sc. **esse,** what is the subject of **consultum?**

Translate into Latin.

1. Has Cæsar set out for Rome? 2. He inquired whether Cæsar had set out for Rome. 3. Is the city strongly fortified? 4. He asked whether the city was strongly

fortified. 5. Does he deserve praise? 6. It is doubtful whether he deserves praise or not. 7. Will you perform these things or not? 8. Are the soldiers obedient to their commander? 9. Do you or I deserve praise? 10. Is he a good man? 11. It is uncertain whether he is a good man or not. 12. Did you inquire how great the forces of the enemy were? 13. Is the victory due to the soldiers or to the commander? 14. He inquired whether the victory was due to the soldiers or the commander. 15. Is this book yours or not? 16. He inquired whether this book was yours or not. 17. Is that the man they seek or not? 18. He inquired whether that was the man they sought or not.

LESSON LXIX.

PARTICIPLES. § 72.

Translate into English.

1. Quo cognito,[1] Amulius ipsam in vincula conjecit, parvulos alveo impositos abjecit in Tiberim, qui tunc forte super ripas erat effusus; sed, relabente flumine, eos aqua in sicco reliquit. 2. Eos tulit in casam, et Accæ Larentiæ conjugi dedit educandos.[2] 3. Tunc Faustulus, necessitate compulsus, indicavit Romulo quis esset ejus avus quæ mater. 4. Is quamvis integer, quia tribus impar erat, fugam simulavit, ut singulos per intervalla secuturos separatim aggrederetur. 5. Terra mutata non mutat mores. 6. Milites, pilis conjectis,[3] phalangem hostium perfregerunt. 7. Vereor ut certus sis eundi. 8. Sole oriente, fugiunt tenebræ. 9. Cæsar, urbe capta,[4] discessit. 10. Rediit, belli casum de integro tentaturus.

11. Datur signum, infestisque armis terni juvenes, magnorum exercituum animos gerentes, concurrunt. 12. Quis est, qui me unquam viderit legentem? 13. Tiberius in Capitolium venit, manum ad caput referens. 14. Gracchum fugientem persecutus in eum irruit, suaque manu eum interficit. 15. Ea re commotus, in Italiam rediit, armis injuriam acceptam vindicaturus; plurimisque urbibus occupatis, Brundisium contendit, quo Pompeius consulesque confugerant. 16. Ex amissis civibus dolor fuit. 17. Homines misit agrum araturos. 18. Cum sola decima legione profecturus est. 19. Nam priusquam incipias, consulto,[5] et ubi consulueris, mature facto opus est.

[1] Translate, *when this was known*, etc. Observe that the ablative absolute expresses various circumstances of the action, of time, means, condition, manner, etc. See § 54, 10 (*b*).

[2] The participle in **-dus** here denotes a purpose. See § 72, 5 (*c*).

[3] What circumstance does this denote, — time, condition, or cause?

[4] As there is no perfect active participle, its place is supplied by the ablative absolute, or by a clause with **cum**: as, **urbe capta** = **cum urbem cepisset**, etc.

[5] Lit. *there is need of consulting*, or freely, *you need advice*. See § 72, 3 (*a*).

Translate into Latin.

1. *When this was known*, Cæsar departed. 2. Cæsar, *when he went to Britain*, took three legions. 3. He[1] *seized them and* took them to Rome. 4. Cæsar, *having subdued*[2] *the Gauls*, marched to Rome. 5. He assists others *without robbing himself*.[3] 6. *He placed them in* a skiff and threw them into the Tiber. 7. Cæsar returned to Italy *to avenge* his injuries by arms. 8. He goes away *without your perceiving it*.[4] 9. I come *to aid* you. 10. *Receiving his commission*, he departed to Rome. 11. Are you certain of

going? 12. *When I had spoken,* you went away. 13. *Because the king was killed* they threw their arms away. 14. The soldiers avenged *the death of their* commander.[5] 15. The soldiers, *by hurling their javelins,* broke the phalanx of the enemy. 16. *Having called together their chiefs,* he accuses them severely. 17. There was grief *at the loss of the citizens.*[6] 18. Cæsar was disturbed by this affair, and returned to Italy *to avenge* his injuries. 19. This happened one hundred years before the *founding of the city.* 20. Did you hear me *when I said that?* 21. I saw my friend sitting in the garden yesterday. 22. Cæsar *is going to set forth* from the camp with five legions.

[1] Lit. *He took them seized to Rome.*

[2] Observe that the ablative absolute can be used only when the subject of the subordinate clause is different from that of the principal clause (except in such phrases as **se invito**, *against his will,* used in indirect discourse, and a few others not to be imitated).

[3] Lit. *not robbing himself,* **se non spolians.**

[4] Lit. *you not perceiving it,* **te non sentiente.**

[5] Lit. *their commander killed,* **cæsum imperatorem.**

[6] Lit. *on account of the citizens having been lost,* **ex amissis civibus.**

LESSON LXX.

GERUND AND GERUNDIVE. § 73.

Translate into English.

1. In ambulando mecum cogito. 2. Hic mihi[1] non dormiendum est. 3. Discimus docendo. 4. In libris tuis legendis hos tres dies cum multa voluptate exegi. 5. Cupido urbis condendæ[2] Romulum cepit. 6. Proficiscendum mihi erat illo ipso die. 7. Hostes in spem vene-

rant potiendorum castrorum.[3] 8. Cæsar loquendi finem facit. 9. Gracchum idem furor, qui fratrem Tiberium invasit; seu vindicandæ fraternæ necis, seu comparandæ regiæ potentiæ causa, vix tribunatum adeptus est, cum pessima cœpit[4] inire consilia; maximas largitiones fecit, ærarium effudit, legem de frumento plebi dividendo tulit. 10. Julius Cæsar in captanda plebis gratia, et ambiendis honoribus, patrimonium effudit. 11. Longissimas vias incredibili celeritate confecit, ita ut persæpe nuntios de se præveniret, neque eum morabantur flumina, quæ vel nando vel innixus inflatis utribus trajiciebat. 12. Ars pueros educandi difficilis est.[3] 13. Bellum suscepit reipublicæ delendæ causa. 14. Homines misit ad agrum arandum. 15. Homines misit agri arandi causa. 16. Oppidum magnam ad ducendum bellum dabat facultatem. 17. Ager colendus est, ut fruges ferat. 18. Cæsari omnia uno tempore erant agenda: vexillum proponendum (quod erat insigne, cum ad arma concurri oporteret), signum tuba dandum, ab opere revocandi milites, qui paulo longius aggeris petendi causa[5] processerant arcessendi, acies instruenda, milites cohortandi, signum dandum. 19. Optimus quisque agendi quam loquendi studiosior est. 20. Militibus simul et de navibus (erat) desiliendum, et cum hostibus erat pugnandum. 21. Multi in equis parandis[6] adhibent[7] curam, in amicis eligendis negligentes.

[1] See § 51, 4 (*a*).

[2] Or, **urbem condendi.**

[3] What would the construction be if the gerund had been used?

[4] See § 38 (*a*).

[5] Translate, *for the sake of seeking materials for a mound.*

[6] *In getting.*

[7] *Take pains.*

Translate into Latin.

1. The mind is nourished by learning and thinking. 2. While drinking we conversed about many things. 3. He is desirous of hearing. 4. He is desirous of hearing Plato. 5. They undertook the war for the sake of destroying the republic. 6. He came here for the sake of seeing his friends. 7. He crossed the river by swimming. 8. Gracchus obtained the tribuneship for the sake of avenging his brother's death. 9. I am not fitted for advising you. 10. I must write a letter. 11. Virtue must be cultivated. 12. The field must be ploughed. 13. We must set out immediately. 14. What must we do, friends? 15. He was desirous of possessing the camp. 16. Ambassadors came to seek peace. 17. We must not believe all men. 18. I must write. 19. We are desirous of seeing and hearing many things. 20. The mind is nourished by reading books. 21. We learn to write by writing, to speak by speaking. 22. We must leap from the walls and fight with the enemy. 23. You must fight for liberty. 24. Every[1] kind of elegance of speech is made more refined[2] by a knowledge of literature. 25. We[3] must not only get wisdom, but enjoy it.

[1] Every kind of elegance, **omnis elegantia.** [2] Use **expolitur.**
[3] Lit. *Wisdom not only must be prepared for us,* etc.

LESSON LXXI.

SUPINE. § 74.

Translate into English.

1. Ibat spectatum ludos. 2. Id facile dictu est. 3. Dignus est auditu. 4. Oratores Romam veniunt pacem

petitum. 5. Legati totius fere Galliæ ad Cæsarem gratulatum convenerunt. 6. Legati venerunt injurias questum. 7. Quod optimum factu videbitur, facies. 8. Divitiacus Romam ad senatum venit, auxilium postulatum. 9. Ædui legatos ad Cæsarem mittunt rogatum auxilium. 10. Quod optimum est factu, faciam. 11. Exclusi eos, quos tu ad me salutatum miseras. 12. Quid est tam jucundum cognitu[1] atque auditu, quam[2] sapientibus sententiis gravibusque verbis ornata oratio? 13. Eamus Jovi Maximo gratulatum.

[1] *In the learning or the hearing.* [2] *As.*

Translate into Latin.

1. They sent legates to the city to seek for peace. 2. The soldiers advanced to forage. 3. They sent to inquire what they should do. 4. This is difficult to be done. 5. The men came to plough the field. 6. Many things are difficult to be done. 7. They set out for the city to see the games. 8. A true friend is difficult to be found. 9. The enemy came with a large army to assault the camp. 10. It is difficult to read this. 11. When the war with the Helvetii was finished, ambassadors from almost the whole of Gaul[1] came to congratulate Cæsar.

[1] Use the genitive.

LESSON LXXII.

THE ROMAN CALENDAR. § 84.

Translate into English.

1. Cæsar Idibus Martiis in senatum venit. 2. Natus est ante diem tertium Kalendas Martias (*or*, Natus est

a. d. iii. Kal. Mart.) 3. Supplicationes decretæ sunt in[1] a. d. iv. et iii. et pridie Idus Novembris.[2] 4. De fratre nuntii nobis venerunt ex a. d. iii. Nonas Januarias. 5. Supplicatio decreta est ad pridie Nonas Maias. 6. Imperavit mihi ut adessem in postridie Calendas Januarias (*or*, in a. d. iv. Non. Jan.). 7. Is dies erat a. d. v. Kal. Apr. 8. Spero te apud nos Græcis Kalendis[3] cenaturum. 9. Natus est a. d. ix. Kalendas Octobris.[2] 10. Obiit Kalendis Augustis. 11. Meministine me ante diem xii. Kalendas Novembris[2] dicere in senatu, fore in armis certo die, qui dies futurus esset ante diem vi. Kalendas Novembris, C. Manlium? 12. Consul comitia in a. d. iii. Nonas Sextilis[2] edixit. 13. In ante dies viii. et vii. Kalendas Octobris[2] comitiis dicta dies. 14. Venire jussi sumus ad Nonas Februarias. 15. Is dies erat pridie Idus Jan. 16. Is dies erat a. d. xi. Kal. Feb.; a. d. iii. Idus Jan.; a. d. iii. Nonas Mart.; pridie Idus Mart.; a. d. xvi. Kal. Decembris.[2] 17. Spero me circa Idus Octobris[2] Romæ futurum esse. 18. Dixi ego idem in senatu, cædem te optimatium contulisse in ante diem v. Kalendas Novembris.[2]

[1] **In ante,** *for.*

[2] Observe that the form in **is** in these dates is the *accusative plural.*

[3] *The Greek Calends,* a phrase signifying *never;* this style of reckoning not being used by the Greeks.

Translate into Latin.

1. He died on the fifth of January. 2. He was born on the fifteenth of October. 3. He was born on the sixteenth of March. 4. He came to Rome on the fifteenth of April. 5. On the first of March he entered the senate. 6. The time of the elections is appointed for the twenty-

fifth of July. 7. We came to Rome by the tenth of February. 8. The day was the tenth of July. 9. A public thanksgiving was ordered for the tenth of May. 10. Special religious services were ordered for the ninth, tenth, and eleventh of November. 11. On the second of May I will be at Rome. 12. On the first of July I will be at Athens. 13. About the beginning of June, in the consulship of M. Tullius Cicero and C. Antonius, he first began to-address-himself-to[2] single (persons). 14. We set out for Rome on the second of November, and arrived there on the tenth; on the twelfth we laid our demands before the senate; on the fifteenth we left the city. 15. On the first, second, or third of October I shall go to Rome.

[1] About the beginning of June, **circiter Kalendas Junias.**
[2] Use **appellare** (historical infinitive).

ADDITIONAL EXERCISES.

Translate into Latin.

1. The waves on the shores [of the sea] are high. 2. Volsinii, a town of the Tuscans was consumed[1] by lightning. 3. Neither you nor I have done this. 4. You and he praise the streams of the country. 5. The man said one thing[2] and the boy another. 6. Homer is called the king of poets. 7. The Sequani shuddered at the cruelty of Ariovistus. 8. Hear much,[3] speak little. 9. After his death the people repented of their judgment. 10. Cæsar kept demanding corn of the Ædui. 11. The elephant is said to live two hundred years. 12. Augustus died at Nola. 13. He wandered about the banks of the river Po

and the shores of the Adriatic Sea. 14. A good man forgets all injuries. 15. At what price does he give lessons?[4] 16. It is not lawful for any man[5] to lead an army against his country. 17. Having learned these things, Cæsar returns to the fleet. 18. What o'clock is it? 19. Is that your fault or mine? 20. He asked whether that was your fault or mine. 21. If they (shall) give hostages, Cæsar will make peace with them. 22. Can anybody do this? 23. Can somebody do this? 24. Plato lived eighty-one years. 25. Wherefore it pleased him to send[6] legates to Ariovistus, to demand[7] from him that he should appoint some place central with respect to both of them for a conference, (saying) that he wished to treat with him concerning the republic, and the highest interests of both. 26. On the 10th of April we set out for the province. 27. Is this said to have been done by night or by day? 28. The Germans have not entered a house for fourteen years. 29. It is of great consequence[8] to me[9] that I should see you. 30. On the last day of December he set sail,[10] and arrived at Athens on the 10th of January. 31. In the first of the spring the consul came to Ephesus, and, having received the troops from[11] Scipio, he held[12] a speech[13] in-presence-of[14] his soldiers (in which), after extolling their bravery, he exhorted them to undertake[15] a new war with[16] the Greeks, who had (as he said) helped Antiochus with auxiliaries.

[1] Use **concrematum est.**
[2] Use **aliud .... aliud.**
[3] Use the plural.
[4] Lit. *teach.*
[5] Use **licet nemini.**
[6] See § 64, 1.
[7] See § 64, 2 (2).
[8] See § 50, 1 (*i*).
[9] See § 50, 4 (*d*).
[10] Use **solvit.**
[11] Use **a.**
[12] Use **habuit.**
[13] Use **contionem.**
[14] Use **apud.**
[15] Use **ad** with the ger. of **accipere.**
[16] Use **cum.**

READING LESSONS.

I. FABLES.

Note. — The figures in the following sections refer to the rules in § 75 of the Grammar.

1. *The Kid and the Wolf.*

Capella,[7] stans[2] in tecto domus,[8] lupum[21] vidit[5] prætereuntem, et ludificavit. Sed lupus, "Non tu," inquit "sed locus tuus, me ludificat."

2. *The Boy bathing.*

Puer, balneum petens in fluvio, aqua pæne exstinctus est. Et videns viatorem quendam, clamavit "Subveni mihi!"[16] Sed hic exprobravit puero[14] temeritatem. Puellulus autem dixit, "Primum subveni, deinde reprehendere[38] licet."

3. *The Fox and the Lion.*

Vulpes vidit leonem retibus[26] captum, et stans prope, ludificavit eum insolenter. Leo autem, "Non tu," inquit, "me ludificas,[5] sed malum quod in me incidit."

4. *The Ass in the Lion's Skin.*

Asinus, pellem leonis[8] indutus, circum currebat, cetera animalia[21] terrens. Et cum vulpem videret, eam quoque ter-rere[38] conatus est. Sed hæc, asini vagitu[35] audito, "Scito," inquit, "me[22] quoque territam futuram fuisse nisi te vagientem audissem."[46]

5. *The Hound and the Lion.*

Canis venaticus[2] leonem vidit, et insecutus est. Cum autem leo se verteret, ac rugiret, canis metuens retrorsum fugit. Tum vulpes, conspicata, "O malum caput!" inquit; "Tene[22] leonem sectari? cujus[4] ne vocem quidem tolerare potuisti."

6. *The Wolf and the Lamb.*

Lupus insecutus est agnum. At hic in templum confugit. Lupo autem agnum invocante, et minitante pontificem eum sacrificaturum, respondit agnus, "Mallem quidem deo sacer esse quam a te trucidari."

7. *The Ant.*

Formica quæ[4] nunc est, olim homo erat. Et maxime agriculturæ[16] studens, laboribus[30] suis contentus non erat; sed semper, bonis[16] alienis[3] invidens, fruges proximorum carpebat. Jupiter autem, iratus ejus avaritiæ,[16] mutavit eum in animal quæ nunc formica[1] vocatur. Sed, forma[35] immutata, indolem non mutavit; nam etiam nunc, circumiens ad acervos frumenti, fruges alienas colligit, sibique[15] reponit.

8. *The Ant and the Dove.*

Formica quædam sitiens descendit ad fontem; sed, flumine[26] correpta, pæne est submersa. Columba autem, hoc videns, virgulam decerpsit, et in aquam injecit; super quam[4] formica ascendens, sese servavit. Tum forte auceps,[7] arundinibus collectis, proficiscitur ad columbam capiendam.[41] Quod[21] videns, formica pedem aucupis momordit. Et ille, punctu[26] dolens, arundinibus abjectis, columbam liberavit.

9. *The Cat and the Mice.*

In quadam domo multi erant mures. Quo cognito, felis intravit, et singulos[21] correptos[2] comedebat. Et mures, dum perpetuo capiuntur, in foraminibus latuerunt, nec felis eos consequi[38] potuit. Cum igitur dolo[28] opus esset, ut e latibulis allicerentur,[44] de trabe suspensa, simulavit se[22] esse mortuam. Sed quidam e muribus, videns eam, "At," inquit, "etiam si saccus esses,[46] non aggrederemur."

10. *The Farmer and the Snake.*

Agricola senex, hiemis tempore, serpentem invenit gelu rigentem, et miserescens sub veste condidit. Mox serpens, incalescens, et indolem suam recuperans, benefactorem momordit interfecitque; qui moriens dixit, "Justa patior, qui[4] animali[15] improbo vitam servaverim."[44]

11. *The Widow's Hen.*

Vidua quædam gallinam habuit, quæ singula ova quotidie peperit. At rata, si plus hordei[10] gallinæ[14] dedisset,[47] hanc bina quotidie ova parituram, ita fecit. Sed gallina, pinguis facta, ne singula quidem postea parere valebat.

12. *Stratagem of the Mice.*

Bellum quondam inter feles et mures exortum est. Et mures, semper victi, cum una convenissent, censuerunt se talia pati,[39] quod duces non haberent.[47] Duces igitur elegerunt; qui, quo[33] facilius cognosci possent,[44] cornua induti sunt. Prœlio[35] deinde facto, et muribus devictis, ceteri quidem facile effugerunt; duces autem, propter cornua, foramina[21] intrare nequiverunt, et ad unum capti sunt ac devorati.

13. *The Stag and the Lion.*

Cervus quondam sitiens venit ad fontem. Ubi inter bibendum,[41] videt imaginem suam in aqua; et miratur quidem cornua, quippe quæ longa essent[44] et pulchra; sed crura magnopere contempsit, ut macilenta atque debilia. Ita dum secum cogitat, leo subito apparet, et sectatur cervum; hic autem, fugiens, longe antecurrit. Et currens per campos latos, usque servatur; cum autem in silvestrem locum intrâsset, cornibus inter virgulta hærentibus, longius currere non potuit. Et a leone captus, moriturus dixit, "O me miserum! servatus enim per id quod contempsi, proditus sum ab eis quibus[16] maxime confidebam."

14. *Union is Strength.*

Agricola senex,[1] cum mortem sibi[18] appropinquare sentiret, filios convocavit — qui, ut fieri solet, interdum inter se discordes erant — et fascem[22] virgularum afferri jussit. Quibus allatis,[35] filios hortatur ut fascem frangerent. Quod cum facere non possent, distribuit singulas virgas; iisque celeriter fractis, docuit juvenes quam firma res esset[45] concordia, discordia quam imbecilla.

15. *The Lion's Share.*

Societatem junxerant[6] leo, juvenca, capra, ovis. Præda[35] autem, quam ceperant, in quattuor partes divisa, leo "Prima" inquit "mea est; debetur enim hæc præstantiæ meæ. Tollam quoque secundam, quam meretur robur meum. Tertiam vindicat mihi[14] egregius labor meus. Quartam qui sibi arrogare voluerit, is sciat[43] se habiturum me sibi inimicum." Quid facerent imbelles bestiæ? aut quæ sibi leonem infestum habere vellet?

16. *King Log and King Stork.*

Ranæ, dolentes propter turbatam civitatem, legatos miserunt, qui a Jove regem postularent.[44] At ille, videns earum simplicitatem, demisit trabem in paludem ubi habitabant. Primo igitur ranæ, sonitu territæ, in ima palude sese abdiderunt. Mox autem, cum viderent trabem immotam innoxiamque, paullatim ad tantum audaciæ[10] pervenêre, ut insilientes in eam ibi subsiderent. Tum, dedignantes se[22] talem habere regem, iterum ad Jovem convenêre, orantes ut sibi[19] regem alterum daret; primum enim inertem esse,[39] atque nequam. Sed Jupiter, iratus, immisit ciconiam, a qua[27] captæ sunt ac devoratæ.

II. TALES FROM ROMAN HISTORY.

1. *Romulus and Remus.*

1. Proca,[7] rex[1] Albanorum,[8] duos[2] filios,[21] Numitorem et Amulium, habuit.[5] Numitori,[19] qui[4] natu[26] major erat, regnum reliquit: sed Amulius, pulso[35] fratre, regnavit, et, ut eum subole privaret, Rheam Silviam, ejus filiam, Vestæ[8] sacerdotem[1] fecit; quæ[4] tamen Romulum[21] et Remum uno partu[26] edidit, natos deo Marte[29] creditos.[2] Quo cognito,[34] Amulius ipsam in vincula conjecit, parvulos alveo[18] impositos abjecit in

Tiberim, qui tunc forte super ripas erat effusus; sed, relabente flumine, eos aqua in sicco reliquit. Vastæ tum in iis locis solitudines erant. Lupa, ut fama traditum est, ad vagitum accurrit, infantes lingua lambit, ubera eorum ori[18] admovit, matremque[1] se gessit.

2. Cum lupa sæpius ad parvulos, veluti ad catulos, reverteretur, Faustulus, pastor regius, rem animadvertit: eos tulit in casam, et Accæ[19] Larentiæ conjugi[27] dedit educandos. Qui,[4] adulti inter pastores, primo ludicris certaminibus vires[21] auxere, deinde venando[26] saltus peragrare[38] cœperunt, tum latrones a rapina pecorum arcere. Quare iis[17] insidiati sunt latrones, a quibus Remus captus est; Romulus autem vi se defendit. Tunc Faustulus, necessitate compulsus, indicavit Romulo quis esset[45] ejus avus, quæ mater. Romulus statim, armatis pastoribus, Albam[36] properavit.

3. Interea Remum latrones ad Amulium regem perduxerunt, eum accusantes, quasi Numitoris greges infestare[38] solitus esset;[46] Remus itaque a rege[27] Numitori ad supplicium traditus est: at Numitor, considerato adolescentis vultu,[35] haud procul erat quin nepotem agnosceret.[44] Nam Remus oris[8] lineamentis[26] erat matri[15] simillimus, ætasque tempori[17] expositionis congruebat. Dum ea res animum Numitoris anxium tenebat, repente Romulus supervenit, fratrem liberavit, et, Amulio interfecto, avum Numitorem in regnum restituit.

4. Deinde Romulus et Remus urbem in iisdem locis, ubi expositi educatique fuerant, condiderunt:[6] sed orta est inter eos contentio, uter nomen novæ urbi daret,[45] eamque regeret: adhibuere auspicia. Remus prior sex vultures,[21] Romulus postea,[41] sed duodecim, vidit. Sic Romulus, augurio victor, Romam vocavit; et, ut eam prius legibus quam mœnibus muniret, edixit ne quis vallum transiliret.[44] Quod[21] Remus irridens transilivit; eum iratus Romulus interfecit, his increpans verbis: "Sic posthac malo afficietur, quicumque transiliet mœnia mea." Ita solus potitus est imperio[31] Romulus.

2. *Horatii and Curiatii.*

Erant apud Romanos trigemini Horatii, trigemini quoque apud Albanos Curiatii. Cum iis agunt reges, ut pro sua quisque patria dimicent[44] ferro. Fœdus ictum est ea lege,[26] ut unde victoria, ibi quoque imperium esset. Itaque trigemini arma capiunt, et in medium inter duas[2] acies procedunt. Consederant utrimque duo exercitus. Datur signum, infestisque armis[26] terni juvenes, magnorum exercituum[9] animos gerentes, concurrunt.

Ut primo concursu[34] increpuere arma, horror ingens spectantes[21] perstrinxit. Consertis deinde manibus, statim duo Romani alius super alium exspirantes ceciderunt: tres Albani vulnerati. Ad casum Romanorum conclamavit gaudio exercitus Albanus. Romanos jam spes tota deserebat. Unum Horatium tres Curiatii circumsteterunt: is quamvis integer, quia tribus[15] impar erat, fugam simulavit, ut singulos[21] per intervalla secuturos[2] separatim aggrederetur.[45] Jam aliquantum[23] spatii[10] ex eo loco ubi pugnatum est aufugerat, cum respiciens videt unum Curiatium haud procul ab se abesse.[38] In eum magno impetu redit, et, dum Albanus exercitus inclamat Curiatiis, ut opem ferant fratri,[19] jam Horatius eum occiderat. Alterum deinde, priusquam tertius posset consequi,[38] interfecit.

Jam singuli supererant, sed nec spe nec viribus pares. Alterius[9] erat intactum ferro corpus, et geminata victoria ferox animus. Alter fessum vulnere fessum cursu trahebat corpus. Nec illud prœlium fuit. Romanus exsultans Albanum male sustinentem arma[21] conficit, jacentemque spoliat. Romani ovantes ac gratulantes Horatium accipiunt, et domum[36] deducunt. Princeps ibat Horatius, trium fratrum[9] spolia præ se gerens. Cui[18] obvia fuit soror, quæ desponsa fuerat uni[19] ex Curiatiis, visoque super humeros fratris paludamento[35] sponsi, quod ipsa confecerat, flere[38] et crines solvere cœpit. Movit feroci juveni[14] animum comploratio sororis in tanto gaudio publico: stricto itaque gladio[35] transfigit puellam, simul eam verbis increpans: "Abi hinc cum immaturo amore ad sponsum, oblita fratrum,[12] oblita patriæ. Sic eat[43] quæcumque Romana lugebit hostem."

Atrox id[2] visum est facinus patribus[14] plebique, quare raptus est in jus Horatius, et apud judices condemnatus. Jam accesserat lictor, injiciebatque laqueum. Tum Horatius ad populum provocavit. Interea pater Horatii senex[1] proclamabat filiam[22] suam jure cæsam fuisse; et juvenem amplexus, spoliaque Curiatiorum ostentans, orabat populum, ne se orbum liberis[28] faceret. Non tulit populus patris lacrimas, juvenemque absolvit, magis admiratione virtutis quam jure causæ. Ut tamen cædes manifesta expiaretur, pater, quibusdam sacrificiis peractis,[35] transmisit per viam tigillum, et filium, capite adoperto, velut sub jugum misit: quod[4] tigillum *sororium* appellatum est.

III. LIFE OF POMPEY.

1. Gn. Pompeius, stirpis senatoriæ, bello[34] civili se[21] et patrem consilio servavit. Pompeii pater suo exercitui[16] ob avaritiam erat invisus. Itaque facta[2] est in eum conspiratio. Terentius quidam, Gn. Pompeii filii contubernalis, hunc occidendum susceperat, dum alii tabernaculum patris incenderent. Quæ res juveni Pompeio[14] cœnanti[2] nuntiata est. Ipse, nihil[24] periculo motus, solito[32] hilarius bibit, et cum Terentio eadem, qua antea, comitate[31] usus est. Deinde cubiculum ingressus clam subduxit se tentorio,[28] et firmam patri[18] circumposuit custodiam. Terentius tum destricto ense[35] ad lectum Pompeii accessit, multisque ictibus[26] stragula percussit. Orta mox seditione,[35] Pompeius se in media conjecit agmina, militesque tumultuantes precibus et lacrimis placavit, ac duci[14] reconciliavit.

2. Pompeius eodem bello[34] civili, partes Sullæ secutus, ita egit ut ab eo[27] maxime diligeretur. Annos[23] tres et viginti natus, ut Sullæ[20] auxilio[20] veniret, paterni exercitus reliquias collegit, statimque dux peritus exstitit. Illius magnus apud militem amor, magna apud omnes admiratio fuit, nullus ei[20] labor tædio,[20] nulla defatigatio molestiæ[20] erat. Cibi[12] vinique[12] temperans, somni parcus, inter milites corpus exercebat. Cum alacribus saltu,[26] cum velocibus cursu,[26] cum validis lucta[26] certabat. Tum ad Sullam iter intendit, et in eo itinere tres hostium exercitus aut fudit aut sibi adjunxit. Quem[22] ubi Sulla ad se accedere[39] audivit, egregiamque sub signis juventutem aspexit, desiliit ex equo, Pompeiumque salutavit imperatorem;[1] deinceps ei[18] venienti solebat assurgere de sella et caput aperire, quem honorem nemini nisi Pompeio tribuebat.

3. Postea Pompeius in Siciliam profectus est, ut eam[22] a Carbone, Sullæ inimico,[1] occupatam[2] reciperet.[44] Carbo comprehensus et ad Pompeium ductus est. Quem[22] Pompeius, postquam acerbe in eum invectus fuisset, ad supplicium duci[39] jussit. Longe moderatior fuit Pompeius erga Sthenium, Siculæ cujusdam civitatis principem. Cum enim in eam civitatem animadvertere decrevisset, quæ sibi[15] adversata fuerat, exclamavit Sthenius, eum[22] inique facturum,[39] si ob culpam unius omnes plecteret. Interroganti Pompeio,[14] quisnam ille unus esset?[45] "Ego," inquit Sthenius, "qui meos cives ad id induxi." Tam libera voce[26] delectatus Pompeius omnibus[16] et Sthenio[16] ipsi pepercit.

4. Transgressus inde in Africam Pompeius Jubam, Numidiæ regem,[1] qui Marii partibus[16] favebat, bello persecutus est. Intra dies quadraginta hostem oppressit, et Africam subegit adolescens quattuor et viginti annorum. Tum ei litteræ a Sulla[27] redditæ sunt, quibus jubebatur exercitum dimittere, et cum una tantum legione successorem exspectare. Id ægre tulit Pompeius; paruit tamen, et Romam[36] reversus est. Revertenti incredibilis multitudo obviam ivit. Sulla quoque lætus eum excepit, et Magni cognomine appellavit; nihilo[33]

minus Pompeio[16] triumphum petenti restitit; neque ea re a proposito deterritus est Pompeius, aususque est dicere,[38] plures solem orientem adorare quam occidentem: quo dicto innuebat Sullæ[9] potentiam minui,[39] suam vero crescere. Ea voce[35] audita, Sulla juvenis constantiam admiratus exclamavit: "*Triumphet, triumphet!*"

5. Metello[14] jam seni[1] et bellum in Hispania segnius gerenti collega[1] datus est Pompeius, ibique adversus Sertorium vario eventu dimicavit. In quodam prœlio maximum subiit periculum; cum enim vir vasta corporis magnitudine[26] impetum in eum fecisset, Pompeius manum hostis amputavit, sed multis[35] in eum concurrentibus, vulnus in femore accepit, et a suis fugientibus desertus in hostium potestate erat. At præter spem evasit; barbari enim equum ejus auro phalerisque eximiis instructum ceperant. Dum vero prædam inter se altercantes partiuntur, Pompeius illorum manus effugit. Altero prœlio[34] cum Metellus Pompeio[20] laboranti auxilio[20] venisset, fususque esset Sertorii exercitus, hic dixisse fertur: "Nisi ista anus supervenisset,[46] ego hunc puerum verberibus castigatum Romam[36] dimisissem." Metellum anum appellabat, quia is jam senex[2] ad mollem et effeminatam vitam deflexerat. Tandem, Sertorio interfecto, Pompeius Hispaniam recepit.

6. Cum piratæ maria omnia infestarent, et quasdam etiam Italiæ urbes diripuissent, ad eos opprimendos[41] cum imperio extraordinario missus est Pompeius. Nimiæ viri[8] potentiæ[18] obsistebant quidam ex optimatibus, et imprimis Quintus Catulus, qui cum in contione dixisset, esse[39] quidem præclarum virum[1] Gnæum Pompeium,[22] sed non esse uni[14] omnia tribuenda,[39] adjecissetque: "Si quid ei acciderit, quem in ejus locum substituetis?" Acclamavit universa contio: "Te ipsum, Quinte Catule." Tam honorifico civium testimonio victus, Catulus e contione discessit. Pompeius, disposito per omnes maris recessus navium præsidio, brevi terrarum orbem illa peste[28] liberavit, prædones multis locis victos fudit; eosdem in deditionem acceptos in urbibus et agris procul a mari

collocavit. Nihil hac victoria[32] celerius;[2] nam intra quadragesimum diem piratas toto mari expulit.

7. Confecto bello piratico, Gn. Pompeius contra Mithridatem profectus est, et in Asiam magna celeritate contendit. Prœlium cum rege conserere[38] cupiebat, neque opportuna dabatur pugnandi facultas, quia Mithridates interdiu castris se continebat, noctu vero haud tutum[2] erat congredi[38] cum hoste in locis ignotis. Quadam tamen nocte[34] Mithridatem Pompeius aggressus est. Luna magno fuit Romanis[20] adjumento.[20] Quam cum Romani a tergo haberent, umbræ corporum longius projectæ ad primos usque hostium ordines pertinebant; unde decepti regii milites in umbras, tamquam in propinquum hostem, tela mittebant. Victus Mithridates in Pontum profugit. Adversus eum filius Pharnaces rebellavit, quia occisis a patre[27] fratribus[35] vitæ[14] suæ ipse timebat. Mithridates a filio obsessus venenum sumpsit, quod cum tardius subiret, quia adversus venena multis antea medicaminibus corpus firmaverat, a milite Gallo volens interfectus est.

8. Pompeius deinde Tigranem, Armeniæ regem,[1] qui Mithridatis partes secutus fuerat, ad deditionem compulit; quem tamen ad genua procumbentem erexit, benignis verbis recreavit, et in regnum restituit; æque pulchrum[2] esse judicans et vincere[38] reges et facere. Tandem rebus Asiæ compositis, in Italiam rediit. Ad urbem venit non, ut plerique timuerant, armatus, sed dimisso exercitu,[35] et tertium triumphum biduo duxit. Insignis fuit multis novis inusitatisque ornamentis[24] hic triumphus: sed nihil illustrius visum, quam quod tribus triumphis tres orbis partes[7] devictæ causam præbuerunt; Pompeius enim, quod antea contigerat nemini, primum ex Africa, iterum ex Europa, tertio ex Asia triumphavit: felix opinione[26] hominum futurus, si, quem gloriæ, eundem vitæ finem habuisset, neque adversam fortunam esset expertus jam senex.[1]

9. Inita erat inter Pompeium, Cæsarem, et Crassum societas; postea vero, cum Crassus, contra Parthos profectus, prœlio fusus occisusque fuisset, orta est inter Pompeium et Cæsarem gravis dissensio, quod hic superiorem, ille vero pa-

rem ferre non poterat: inde bellum civile exarsit. Cæsar cum infesto exercitu in Italiam venit. Pompeius, relicta urbe ac deinde Italia[35] ipsa, Thessaliam petiit, et cum eo consules senatusque omnis; quem insecutus Cæsar apud Pharsalum acie fudit. Victus Pompeius ad Ptolemæum Alexandriæ regem, cui tutor a senatu datus fuerat, profugit; sed ille Pompeium[22] interfici[39] jussit. Latus Pompeii sub oculis uxoris mucrone confossum est, caput abscissum, truncus in Nilum conjectus. Dein caput velamine involutum ad Cæsarem delatum est, qui eo[35] viso lacrimas fudit, et pretiosissimis odoribus cremandum curavit.

10. Is fuit viri præstantissimi post tres consulatus et totidem triumphos vitæ exitus. Erant in Pompeio multæ ac magnæ virtutes, ac præcipue admiranda frugalitas. Cum ei ægrotanti præcepisset medicus, ut turdum ederet, negarent autem servi, eam avem usquam æstivo tempore posse reperiri, nisi apud Lucullum, qui turdos domi saginaret; vetuit Pompeius turdum inde peti, medicoque dixit: "Ergo nisi Lucullus perditus deliciis esset,[46] non viveret Pompeius?" Aliam avem, quæ parabilis esset, sibi jussit apponi.

11. Viros doctos magno in honore habebat Pompeius. Ex Syria decedens, confecto bello Mithridatico, cum Rhodum venisset, nobilissimum philosophum Posidonium cupiit audire; sed cum is diceretur tunc graviter ægrotare, quod maximis podagræ doloribus cruciaretur, voluit saltem Pompeius eum visere. Mos erat ut, cum consul ædes alicujus ingressurus esset, lictor fores virga percuteret, admonens consulem adesse; at Pompeius vetuit fores Posidonii percuti, honoris causa. Quem ut vidit et salutavit, moleste se ferre dixit, quod eum non posset audire. At ille: "Tu vero," inquit, "potes; nec committam, ut dolor corporis efficiat, ut frustra tantus vir ad me venerit." Itaque cubans graviter et copiose disseruit de hoc ipso: nihil esse bonum, nisi quod honestum esset, et nihil malum dici posse, quod turpe non esset. Cum vero dolor interdum acriter eum pungeret, sæpe dixit: "Nihil agis, dolor, quamvis sis molestus; nunquam te esse malum confitebor."

IV. LIFE OF CÆSAR.

1. C. Julius Cæsar, nobilissima genitus familia,[29] annum agens sextum et decimum, patrem amisit. Paullo[33] post Corneliam duxit uxorem, cujus cum pater Sullæ[15] esset inimicus, voluit Sulla Cæsarem compellere[38] ut eam dimitteret; neque id potuit efficere. Ob eam causam Cæsar bonis[28] spoliatus, cum etiam ad mortem quæreretur, mutata veste, noctu elapsus est ex urbe, et, quamquam tunc quartanæ morbo laborabat, prope per singulas noctes latebras commutare cogebatur; et comprehensus a Sullæ liberto, vix data pecunia[35] evasit. Postremo per propinquos et affines suos veniam impetravit, diu repugnante Sulla, qui[4] cum deprecantibus ornatissimis viris denegasset, atque illi pertinaciter contenderent, victus tandem dixit, eum, quem salvum tantopere cuperent, aliquando optimatium partibus,[20] quas simul defendissent, exitio[20] futurum, multosque in eo puero inesse[39] Marios.

2. Cæsar, mortuo Sulla et composita seditione civili, Rhodum secedere[38] statuit, ut per otium Apollonio, tunc clarissimo dicendi magistro, operam daret; sed in itinere a piratis captus est, mansitque apud eos quadraginta dies.[23] Per omne autem illud spatium ita se gessit, ut piratis[20] terrori[20] pariter ac venerationi[20] esset. Interim comites servosque dimiserat ad expediendas pecunias, quibus redimeretur. Viginti talenta piratæ postulaverant; ille vero quinquaginta daturum[39] se spopondit. Quibus numeratis, expositus est in litore. Cæsar liberatus confestim Miletum,[36] quæ urbs proxime aberat, properavit; ibique contracta classe, stantes adhuc in eodem loco prædones noctu adortus, aliquot naves, mersis aliis,[35] cepit, piratasque ad deditionem redactos eo affecit supplicio, quod[4] illis sæpe per jocum minatus erat, cum ab iis detineretur; crucibus[18] illos suffigi jussit.

3. Cæsar quæstor[1] factus in Hispaniam profectus est; cumque Alpes transiret, et ad conspectum pauperis cujusdam vici

comites ejus per jocum inter se disputarent, an illic etiam esset ambitioni[17] locus; serio dixit Cæsar, malle se ibi primum esse quam Romæ[36] secundum. Ita animus dominationis[12] avidus a prima ætate regnum concupiscebat, semperque in ore habebat hos Euripidis, Græci poetæ, versus: *Nam si violandum est jus, regnandi gratia violandum est; aliis rebus pietatem colas.*[43] Cum vero Gades,[36] quod est Hispaniæ oppidum, venisset, visa Alexandri[8] magni imagine ingemuit, et lacrimas fudit. Causam quærentibus amicis: "Nonne," inquit, "idonea dolendi causa est, quod nihildum memorabile gesserim, eam ætatem adeptus, qua[34] Alexander jam terrarum orbem subegerat?"

4. Cæsar in captanda[41] plebis gratia et ambiendis[41] honoribus patrimonium effudit; ære alieno oppressus ipse dicebat, sibi[17] opus esse millies sestertium,[10] ut haberet nihil. His artibus consulatum adeptus est, collegaque ei datus Marcus Bibulus, cui[16] Cæsaris consilia haud placebant. Inito magistratu[35] Cæsar legem agrariam tulit, hoc est, de dividendo egenis civibus[19] agro publico; cui legi[16] cum senatus repugnaret, Cæsar rem ad populum detulit. Bibulus collega in forum venit, ut legi[18] ferendæ[41] obsisteret; sed tanta commota est seditio, ut in caput consulis cophinus stercore[28] plenus effunderetur, fascesque frangerentur. Tandem Bibulus, a satellitibus Cæsaris foro[28] expulsus, domi[36] se continere per reliquum anni tempus coactus est, curiaque abstinere. Interea unus Cæsar omnia ad arbitrium in republica administravit; unde quidam homines faceti, quæ eo anno gesta sunt, non, ut mos erat, consulibus[35] Cæsare et Bibulo acta esse dicebant, sed Julio et Cæsare, unum consulem nomine et cognomine pro duobus appellantes.

5. Cæsar functus consulatu[31] Galliam provinciam accepit. Gessit autem novem annis,[34] quibus in imperio fuit, hæc fere. Galliam in provinciæ Romanæ formam redegit; Germanos, qui trans Rhenum incolunt, primus Romanorum[10] ponte fabricato aggressus maximis affecit cladibus.[26] Britannos antea ignotos vicit, iisque[16] pecunias et obsides imperavit; quo in

bello multa Cæsaris facta egregia narrantur. Inclinante in fugam exercitu, rapuit e manu militis fugientis scutum, et in primam aciem volitans pugnam restituit. In alio prœlio aquiliferum terga vertentem faucibus[26] comprehendit, in contrariam partem retraxit, dexteramque ad hostem protendens: "Quorsum tu," inquit, "abis? Illic sunt, cum quibus dimicamus." Quo facto militibus animos addidit.[19]

6. Cæsar cum adhuc in Gallia detineretur, ne imperfecto bello discederet, postulavit ut sibi liceret, quamvis absenti, iterum consulatum petere;[38] quod ei a senatu est negatum. Ea re commotus in Italiam rediit, armis injuriam acceptam vindicaturus; plurimisque urbibus[35] occupatis Brundisium contendit, quo Pompeius consulesque confugerant. Tunc summæ audaciæ facinus Cæsar edidit: a Brundisio Dyrrachium inter oppositas classes gravissima hieme[34] transiit; cessantibusque copiis, quas subsequi jusserat, cum ad eas arcessendas[41] frustra misisset, moræ[12] impatiens castris noctu egreditur, clam solus naviculam conscendit obvoluto capite, ne agnosceretur. Mare, adverso vento vehementer flante, intumescebat; in altum tamen protinus dirigi navigium jubet; cumque gubernator pæne obrutus fluctibus[26] adversæ tempestati cederet: "Quid times?" ait; "Cæsarem vehis."

7. Deinde Cæsar in Thessaliam profectus est, ubi Pompeium Pharsalico prœlio fudit, fugientem persecutus est, eumque[22] in itinere cognovit occisum fuisse. Tum bellum Ptolemæo,[18] Pompeii interfectori,[1] intulit, a quo sibi quoque insidias parari videbat; quo victo, Cæsar in Pontum transiit, Pharnacemque, Mithridatis filium, rebellantem aggressus intra quintum ab adventu diem, quattuor vero, quibus in conspectum venerat, horis, uno prœlio profligavit. Quam victoriæ celeritatem inter triumphandum notavit, inscripto inter pompæ ornamenta trium verborum titulo, *Veni, vidi, vici.* Sua deinceps Cæsarem ubique comitata est fortuna. Scipionem et Jubam, Numidiæ regem, reliquias Pompeianarum partium in Africa refoventes, devicit. Pompeii liberos in Hispania superavit. Clementer usus est victoria,[31] et omnibus,[16] qui contra se

arma tulerant, pepercit. Regressus in urbem, quinquies triumphavit.

8. Bellis civilibus confectis, Cæsar, dictator[1] in perpetuum creatus, agere insolentius cœpit. Senatum ad se venientem sedens excepit, et quemdam, ut assurgeret monentem, irato vultu[26] respexit. Cum Antonius, Cæsaris in omnibus expeditionibus comes, et tunc in consulatu collega, ei[18] in sella aurea sedenti pro rostris diadema, insigne regium, imponeret, non visus est eo facto offendi.[38] Quare conjuratum est in eum a sexaginta amplius viris,[27] Cassio et Bruto ducibus conspirationis. Cum igitur Cæsar Idibus[34] Martiis in senatum venisset, assidentem specie officii circumsteterunt, illicoque unus e conjuratis, quasi aliquid rogaturus, propius accessit, renuentique togam ab utroque humero apprehendit. Deinde clamantem, "Ista quidem vis est," Cassius vulnerat paullo infra jugulum. Cæsar Cascæ brachium arreptum graphio trajecit, conatusque prosilire aliud vulnus accepit. Cum Marcum Brutum, quem loco filii habebat, in se irruentem vidisset, dixit: "Tu quoque, fili mi!" Dein ubi animadvertit undique se strictis pugionibus peti, toga caput obvolvit, atque ita tribus et viginti plagis[26] confossus est.

9. Erat Cæsar excelsa statura,[26] nigris vegetisque oculis,[26] capite[26] calvo, quam calvitii deformitatem ægre ferebat, quod sæpe obtrectantium jocis esset obnoxia. Itaque ex omnibus honoribus sibi a senatu populoque decretis non aliud recepit aut usurpavit libentius, quam jus laureæ perpetuo gestandæ. Eum vini[11] parcissimum fuisse ne inimici quidem negarunt; unde Cato dicere solebat, unum ex omnibus Cæsarem ad evertendam rempublicam sobrium accessisse. Armorum[9] et equitandi[9] peritissimus erat; laboris ultra fidem patiens; in agmine nonnunquam equo, sæpius pedibus anteibat, capite detecto, sive sol, sive imber esset. Longissimas vias incredibili celeritate confecit, ita ut persæpe nuntios de se prævenerit, neque eum morabantur flumina, quæ vel nando[26] vel innixus inflatis utribus[18] trajiciebat.

V. LIFE OF CATO.

1. Marcus Cato, adhuc puer,[1] invictum animi robur ostendit. Cum in domo Drusi avunculi sui educaretur, Latini de civitate impetranda[41] Romam[36] venerunt. Popedius, Latinorum princeps, qui Drusi hospes erat, Catonem puerum rogavit, ut Latinos apud avunculum adjuvaret. Cato vultu constanti negavit id se facturum. Iterum deinde ac sæpius interpellatus in proposito perstitit. Tunc Popedius puerum, in excelsam ædium partem levatum, tenuit et abjecturum inde se minatus est, nisi precibus[16] obtemperaret; neque hoc metu[26] a sententia eum potuit dimovere. Tunc Popedius exclamasse[38] fertur: "Gratulemur[43] nobis, Latini, hunc esse tam parvum; si enim senator esset, ne sperare quidem jus civitatis nobis liceret."

2. Cato, cum salutandi gratia ad Sullam a pædagogo duceretur, et in atrio cruenta proscriptorum capita vidisset, Sullæ crudelitatem exsecratus est; seque[22] eodem esse animo significavit, quo puer alius nomine Cassius, qui tunc publicam scholam cum Fausto, Sullæ filio, frequentabat. Cum enim Faustus proscriptionem paternam in schola laudaret, diceretque "se, cum per ætatem posset, eandem rem esse facturum," ei[19] sodalis gravem colaphum impegit.

3. Insignis fuit, et ad imitandum præponenda, Catonis erga fratrem benevolentia. Cum enim interrogaretur, "quem omnium maxime diligeret,"[45] respondit, "fratrem." Iterum interrogatus, "quem secundum maxime diligeret," iterum, "fratrem," respondit. Quærenti[19] tertio idem responsum dedit, donec ille a percunctando desisteret.[44] Crevit cum ætate ille Catonis in fratrem amor: ab ejus latere non discedebat; ei in omnibus rebus morem gerebat. Annos[23] natus viginti nunquam sine fratre cœnaverat, nunquam in forum prodierat, nunquam iter susceperat. Diversum tamen erat utriusque ingenium: in utroque probi mores erant, sed Catonis indoles severior.

4. Cato, cum frater, qui erat tribunus militum, ad bellum

profectus esset, ne eum desereret, voluntaria stipendia fecit. Accidit postea, ut Catonis frater in Asiam[37] proficisci cogeretur, et iter faciens in morbum incideret: quod[21] ubi audivit Cato, licet tunc gravis tempestas sæviret, neque parata esset magna navis, solvit e portu Thessalonicæ exigua navicula[26] cum duobus tantum amicis tribusque servis, et, pæne haustus fluctibus, tandem præter spem incolumis evasit. At fratrem, modo defunctum vita,[31] reperit. Tunc questibus[19] et lacrimis totum se tradidit: mortui corpus quam magnificentissimo potuit funere extulit, et marmoreum tumulum exstrui curavit suis impensis.[26] Vela deinde facturus, cum suaderent amici ut fratris reliquias in alio navigio poneret,[6] animam[21] se[22] prius quam illas relicturum respondit, atque ita solvit.

5. Cato quæstor[1] in insulam Cyprum missus est ad colligendam[41] Ptolemæi regis pecuniam, a quo populus Romanus heres[1] institutus fuerat. Integerrima fide[26] eam rem administravit. Summa longe major quam quisquam sperare potuisset redacta est. Fere septem milia talentorum[10] navibus[18] imposuit Cato: atque, ut naufragii pericula vitaret, singulis vasis,[18] quibus[26] inclusa erat pecunia, corticem suberis longo funiculo[26] alligavit, ut, si forte mersum navigium esset,[46] locum amissæ pecuniæ cortex supernatans indicaret. Catoni advenienti senatus et tota ferme civitas obviam effusa est, nec erat res triumpho[15] absimilis. Actæ sunt Catoni a senatu gratiæ, præturaque illi et jus spectandi[41] ludos prætextato extra ordinem data. Quem honorem Cato noluit accipere, iniquum esse affirmans, "sibi decerni, quod nulli alii tribueretur."

6. Cum Cæsar consul legem reipublicæ[15] perniciosam tulisset, Cato solus, ceteris exterritis,[35] huic legi[18] obstitit. Iratus Cæsar Catonem[22] extrahi curia,[28] et in vincula rapi, jussit: at ille nihil de libertate linguæ remisit, sed in ipsa ad carcerem via de lege disputabat, civesque commonebat, ut talia molientibus adversarentur. Catonem[21] sequebantur mœsti patres, quorum unus, objurgatus a Cæsare quod nondum misso senatu[35] discederet, "Malo," inquit, "esse cum Catone in carcere, quam tecum in curia." Exspectabat Cæsar, dum ad

humiles preces Cato sese demitteret:[44] quod ubi frustra a se sperari intellexit, pudore victus, unum e tribunis misit qui Catonem dimitteret.[44]

7. Cato Pompeii partes bello civili secutus est, eoque victo, exercitus[10] reliquias in Africam cum ingenti itinerum difficultate perduxit. Cum vero ei summum a militibus deferretur imperium, Scipioni,[16] quod vir esset consularis, parere[38] maluit. Scipione etiam devicto, Uticam, Africæ urbem, petivit, ubi filium hortatus est, ut clementiam Cæsaris experiretur; ipse vero cœnatus deambulavit, et cubitum[42] iturus arctius diutiusque in complexu filii hæsit; deinde, ingressus cubiculum, ferro sibi ipse mortem conscivit. Cæsar, audita Catonis morte, dixit illum gloriæ[16] suæ invidisse, quod sibi[19] laudem servati Catonis eripuisset. Catonis liberos, eisque patrimonium incolume, servavit.

VI. LIFE OF CICERO.

1. Marcus Tullius Cicero, equestri genere,[29] Arpini,[36] quod est Volscorum oppidum, natus est. Ex ejus avis unus verrucam in extremo naso sitam habuit, ciceris grano[15] similem: inde cognomen Ciceronis genti inditum. Cum id Marco Tullio a nonnullis probro[20] verteretur; "Dabo operam," inquit, "ut istud cognomen nobilissimorum nominum splendorem vincat." Cum eas artes disceret, quibus ætas puerilis[2] ad humanitatem solet informari, ingenium ejus ita eluxit, ut eum æquales e schola redeuntes medium, tanquam regem, circumstantes deducerent domum:[36 n] immo eorum parentes, pueri fama commoti, in ludum litterarium ventitabant, ut eum viserent. Ea res tamen quibusdam[14] rustici et inculti ingenii[9] stomachum movebat, qui ceteros pueros graviter objurgabant, quod talem condiscipulo suo honorem tribuerent.[44]

2. Tullius Cicero adolescens eloquentiam et libertatem suam adversus Sullanos[3] ostendit. Chrysogonum quendam, Sullæ

libertum, acriter insectatus est, quod, dictatoris potentia[30] fretus, in bona civium invadebat. Ex quo, veritus invidiam, Cicero Athenas petivit, ubi Antiochum philosophum studiose audivit. Inde eloquentiæ gratia Rhodum[36] se contulit, ubi Molone,[31] rhetore tum disertissimo, magistro[1] usus est. Qui, cum Ciceronem dicentem audivisset, flevisse[39] dicitur, quod prævideret[44] per hunc Græcos a Romanis ingenii et eloquentiæ laude superatum[42] iri. Romam[36] reversus, quæstor in Sicilia fuit. Nullius vero quæstura aut gratior aut clarior fuit: cum in magna annonæ difficultate ingentem frumenti vim inde Romam mitteret, Siculos initio offendit; postea vero ubi diligentiam, justitiam et comitatem ejus experti fuerunt, majores quæstori suo honores, quam ulli unquam prætori, detulerunt.

3. Cicero, consul factus, Sergii Catilinæ conjurationem[21] singulari virtute, constantia, curaque compressit. Is nempe, indignatus quod in petitione consulatus[8] repulsam passus esset, et furore amens, cum pluribus viris nobilibus Ciceronem interficere, senatum trucidare, urbem incendere, ærarium diripere constituerat. Quæ tam atrox conjuratio a Cicerone detecta est. Catilina metu consulis Roma[36] ad exercitum, quem paraverat, profugit; socii ejus comprehensi in carcere necati sunt. Senator quidam filium supplicio mortis ipse affecit. Juvenis scilicet, ingenio, litteris et forma inter æquales conspicuus, pravo consilio amicitiam Catilinæ secutus erat, et in castra ejus properabat: quem pater ex medio itinere retractum[2] occidit, his eum verbis increpans: "Non ego te Catilinæ[15] adversus patriam, sed patriæ adversus Catilinam, genui."

4. Non ideo Catilina ab incepto destitit, sed infestis signis Romam petens, cum exercitu cæsus est. Adeo acriter dimicatum est, ut nemo hostium prœlio[18] superfuerit: quem quisque in pugnando ceperat, eum, amissa anima, tegebat locum. Ipse Catilina longe a suis[3] inter eorum, quos occiderat, cadavera cecidit,—morte pulcherrima, si pro patria sua sic occubuisset. Senatus populusque Romanus Ciceronem patriæ patrem[1]

appellavit: ea res tamen Ciceroni[15] postea invidiam creavit, adeo ut abeuntem magistratu[28] verba facere ad populum vetuerit quidam tribunus plebis, quod cives, indicta causa,[35] damnavisset,[14] sed solitum duntaxat juramentum præstare ei[16] permiserit. Tum Cicero magna voce: "Juro," inquit, "rempublicam atque urbem Romam mea[3] unius[2] opera[26] salvam esse": qua voce delectatus populus Romanus, et ipse juravit verum esse Ciceronis juramentum.

5. Paucis post annis[33] Cicero reus factus est a Clodio,[27] tribuno plebis, eadem de causa, quod nempe cives Romanos necavisset. Tunc mœstus senatus, tanquam in publico luctu, vestem mutavit. Cicero, cum posset armis[26] salutem suam defendere, maluit urbe[28] cedere, quam sua causa cædem fieri.[39] Proficiscentem omnes boni flentes prosecuti sunt. Dein Clodius edictum proposuit, ut Marco Tullio[18] igni et aqua[28] interdiceretur, et ejus domum villasque incendit. Sed vis illa diuturna non fuit; mox enim, maximo omnium ordinum studio, Cicero in patriam revocatus est. Obviam ei redeunti ab universis itum est. Domus ejus publica pecunia restituta est. Postea Cicero, Pompeii partes secutus, a Cæsare victore veniam accepit. Quo interfecto, Octavium heredem Cæsaris fovit atque ornavit, ut eum Antonio[18] rempublicam vexanti[2] opponeret; sed ab illo deinde desertus est et proditus.

6. Antonius, inita cum Octavio societate, Ciceronem jamdiu sibi[15] inimicum, proscripsit. Qua re audita, Cicero transversis itineribus fugit in villam, quæ a mari proxime aberat, indeque navem conscendit, in Macedoniam transiturus. Cum vero jam aliquoties in altum provectum venti adversi retulissent, et ipse jactationem navis pati non posset, regressus ad villam: "Moriar," inquit, "in patria sæpe servata." Mox adventantibus percussoribus, cum servi parati essent ad dimicandum fortiter, ipse lecticam,[22] qua[26] vehebatur, deponi jussit, eosque quietos pati, quod sors iniqua cogeret. Prominenti[14] ex lectica, et immotam cervicem præbenti, caput præcisum est. Manus quoque abscissæ: caput relatum est ad Antonium, ejusque jussu inter duas manus in rostris positum. Fulvia,

Antonii uxor, quæ se a Cicerone[27] læsam arbitrabatur, caput manibus[26] sumpsit, in genua imposuit, extractamque linguam acu confixit.

7. Cicero dicax erat, et facetiarum[12] amans, adeo ut ab inimicis solitus sit appellari *Scurra consularis.* Cum Lentulum, generum suum, exiguæ staturæ[9] hominem, vidisset longo gladio accinctum: "Quis," inquit, "generum meum ad gladium alligavit?" Matrona quædam, juniorem se quam erat simulans, dictitabat se triginta tantum annos habere. Cui Cicero: "Verum est," inquit, "nam hoc viginti annos[28] audio." Cæsar, altero consule mortuo[35] die Decembris ultima, Caninium consulem hora[34] septima in reliquam diei[10] partem renuntiaverat: quem cum plerique irent salutatum[42] de more: "Festinemus,"[43] inquit Cicero, "priusquam abeat magistratu." De eodem Caninio scripsit Cicero: "Fuit mirifica vigilantia[26] Caninius, qui toto suo consulatu[34] somnum non viderit."[44]

VII. LIFE OF BRUTUS.

1. Marcus Brutus, ex illa gente quæ Roma[36] Tarquinios ejecerat oriundus, Athenis[36] philosophiam, Rhodi eloquentiam, didicit. Sua eum virtus valde commendavit: ejus pater, qui Sullæ partibus[16] adversabatur, jussu Pompeii interfectus erat; unde Brutus cum eo graves gesserat simultates: bello tamen civili Pompeii causam, quod justior videretur, secutus est, et dolorem suum reipublicæ utilitati[18] posthabuit. Victo Pompeio, Brutus a Cæsare servatus est, et prætor etiam factus. Postea cum Cæsar, superbia[26] elatus, senatum contemnere, et regnum affectare cœpisset, populus, jam præsenti statu[30] haud lætus, vindicem libertatis requirebat. Subscripsere quidam primi Bruti statuæ,[18] *Utinam viveres!* Item ipsius Cæsaris statuæ: "Brutus, quia reges ejecit, primus consul factus est; hic, quia consules ejecit, postremo rex factus est." Inscrip-

tum quoque est Marci Bruti prætoris tribunali[18]: *Dormis, Brute!*

2. Marcus Brutus, cognita populi Romani voluntate, adversus Cæsarem conspiravit. Pridie quam Cæsar est occisus, Porcia, Bruti uxor, consilii[12] conscia, cultellum tonsorium, quasi unguium resecandorum[41] causa, poposcit, eoque, velut forte e manibus elapso, se ipsa vulneravit. Clamore ancillarum vocatus in cubiculum uxoris, Brutus objurgare eam cœpit, quod tonsoris officium præripere voluisset; at Porcia ei secreto dixit: "Non casu, sed de industria, mi Brute, hoc mihi[14] vulnus feci: experiri enim volui, satisne mihi animi esset[45] ad mortem oppetendam, si tibi[14] propositum ex sententia parum cessisset." Quibus verbis auditis, Brutus ad cælum manus[21] et oculos sustulisse dicitur, et exclamavisse: "Utinam dignus tali conjuge[30] maritus videri possim!"

3. Interfecto Cæsare, Antonius vestem ejus sanguinolentam ostentans, populum veluti furore quodam adversus conjuratos inflammavit. Brutus itaque in Macedoniam concessit, ibique apud urbem Philippos[1] adversus Antonium et Octavium dimicavit. Victus acie, cum in tumulum se nocte[34] recepisset, ne in hostium manus veniret, uni[19] comitum[10] latus transfodiendum præbuit. Antonius, viso Bruti cadavere, ei suum injecit purpureum paludamentum, ut in eo sepeliretur. Quod cum postea surreptum audivisset, requiri furem et ad supplicium duci jussit. Cremati corporis reliquias ad Serviliam, Bruti matrem, deportandas curavit. Non eadem fuit Octavii erga Brutum moderatio: is enim avulsum Bruti caput Romam ferri jussit, ut Caii Cæsaris statuæ[18] subjiceretur.

VIII. LIFE OF AUGUSTUS.

1. Octavius Juliæ, Caii Cæsaris sororis, nepos, patrem quadrimus amisit. A majore avunculo adoptatus, eum in Hispa-

niam profectum secutus est. Deinde ab eo Apolloniam[36] missus est, ut liberalibus studiis[16] vacaret. Audita avunculi morte, Romam rediit, nomen Cæsaris sumpsit, collectoque veteranorum exercitu, opem Decimo Bruto[19] tulit, qui ab Antonio Mutinæ[36] obsidebatur. Cum autem urbis aditu[28] prohiberetur, ut Brutum de omnibus rebus certiorem faceret, primo litteras laminis[18] plumbeis inscriptas misit, quæ per urinatorem sub aqua fluminis deferebantur. Ad id postea columbis[31] usus est: iis[18] enim diu inclusis et fame affectis litteras ad collum alligabat, easque a proximo mœnibus[15] loco emittebat. Columbæ lucis[12] cibique avidæ, summa ædificia petentes, a Bruto excipiebantur, maxime cum ille, deposito quibusdam in locis cibo, columbas illuc devolare instituisset.

2. Octavius bellum Mutinense duobus prœliis confecit, in quorum altero non ducis modo, sed militis etiam functus est munere:[31] nam aquilifero graviter vulnerato, aquilam humeris subiit, et in castra reportavit. Postea reconciliata cum Antonio gratia, junctisque cum ipso copiis, ut Caii Cæsaris necem ulcisceretur, ad urbem hostiliter accessit, inde quadringentos milites ad senatum misit, qui sibi consulatum, nomine exercitus, deposcerent.[44] Cunctante senatu, centurio legationis princeps, rejecto sagulo, ostendens gladii capulum, non dubitavit in curia dicere: "Hic faciet, si vos non feceritis." Cui respondisse[39] Ciceronem ferunt: "Si hoc modo petieritis Cæsari consulatum, auferetis." Quod dictum ei deinde exitio[20] fuit: invisus enim esse cœpit Cæsari, quod libertatis[12] esset amantior.

3. Octavius Cæsar, nondum viginti annos natus, consulatum invasit, novamque proscriptionis tabulam proposuit: quæ proscriptio Sullana[32] longe crudelior fuit: ne teneræ quidem ætati[16] pepercit. Puerum quendam, nomine Atilium, Octavius coëgit togam virilem sumere, ut tanquam vir proscriberetur. Atilius, protinus ut e Capitolio descendit, deducentibus ex more amicis, in tabulam relatus est. Desertum deinde a comitibus ne mater quidem præ metu recepit. Puer itaque fugit, et in silvis aliquamdiu delituit. Cum vero inopiam

ferre non posset, e latebris exiit, seque prætereuntibus[19] indicavit, a quibus interfectus est. Alius puer etiam impubes, cum in ludum litterarium iret, cum pædagogo, qui pro eo corpus objecerat, necatus est.

4. Octavius, inita cum Antonio societate, Marcum Brutum Cæsaris interfectorem bello persecutus est. Quod bellum, quanquam æger atque invalidus, duplici prœlio transegit, quorum[10] priore, castris[28] exutus, vix fuga[26] evasit; altero victor se gessit acerbius. In nobilissimum quemque captivum sæviit, adjecta[2] etiam supplicio[18] verborum contumelia.[35] Uni suppliciter precanti sepulturam respondit, "jam illam in volucrum atque ferarum potestate futuram." Ambo erant captivi pater et filius; cum autem Octavius nollet, nisi uni, vitam concedere, eos sortiri jussit, utri[16] parceretur. Pater, qui se pro filio ad mortem subeundam obtulerat, occisus est; nec servatus filius, qui præ dolore voluntaria occubuit nece: neque ab hoc tristi spectaculo oculos avertit Octavius, sed utrumque spectavit morientem.

5. Octavius ab Antonio iterum abalienatus est, quod is, repudiata Octavia sorore, Cleopatram Ægypti reginam duxisset uxorem: quæ mulier cum Antonio luxu et deliciis certabat. Gloriata est aliquando se centies sestertium[10] una cœna absumpturam. Antonio,[18] id fieri posse neganti, magnificam apposuit cœnam, sed non tanti sumptus[9] quanti promiserat. Irrisa igitur ab Antonio, jussit sibi afferri vas aceto[28] plenum: exspectabat Antonius quidnam esset[45] actura. Illa gemmas pretiosissimas auribus[18] appensas habebat; protinus unam detraxit, et aceto dilutam absorbuit. Alteram quoque simili modo[26] parabat absumere, nisi prohibita fuisset.

6. Octavius cum Antonio apud Actium, qui locus in Epiro est, navali prœlio dimicavit. Victum et fugientem Antonium persecutus, Ægyptum petiit; obsessaque Alexandria,[31] quo Antonius cum Cleopatra confugerat, brevi potitus est. Antonius, desperatis rebus, cum in solio regali sedisset regio diademate cinctus, necem sibi conscivit. Cleopatra vero, quam[22] Octavius magnopere cupiebat vivam comprehendi, triumpho-

que[15] servari, aspidem sibi in cophino inter ficus afferendam curavit, eamque ipsa brachio[18] applicuit: quod ubi cognovit Octavius, medicos vulneri remedia adhibere jussit. Admovit etiam Psyllos, qui venenum exsugerent,[44] sed frustra. Cleopatræ[19] mortuæ communem cum Antonio sepulturam tribuit.

7. Tandem Octavius, hostibus victis, solusque imperio[31] potitus, clementem se exhibuit. Omnia deinceps in eo plena mansuetudinis[12] et humanitatis. Multis[16] ignovit, a quibus sæpe graviter læsus fuerat, quo in numero fuit Metellus, unus ex Antonii præfectis. Cum is inter captivos senex squalidus sordidatusque processisset, agnovit eum filius ejus, qui Octavii partes secutus erat, statimque exsiliens, patrem complexus, sic Octavium allocutus est: "Pater meus hostis tibi fuit, ego miles: non magis ille pœnam, quam ego præmium, meriti sumus. Aut igitur me propter illum occidi jube, aut illum propter me vivere. Delibera, quæso, utrum sit[45] moribus[15] tuis convenientius." Octavius postquam paulum addubitavisset, misericordia motus, hominem sibi infensissimum propter filii merita servavit.

8. Octavius in Italiam rediit, Romamque triumphans ingressus est. Tum bellis toto orbe compositis, Jani gemini portas sua manu clausit, quæ tantummodo bis antea clausæ fuerant, primo sub Numa rege, iterum post primum Punicum bellum. Tunc omnes[21] præteritorum malorum oblivio cepit, populusque Romanus præsentis otii lætitia[31] perfruitus est. Octavio[19] maximi honores a senatu delati sunt. Ipse Augustus cognominatus est, et in ejus honorem mensis Sextilis eodem nomine est appellatus, quod illo mense[34] bellis[18] civilibus finis esset impositus. Equites Romani natalem ejus biduo semper celebrarunt: senatus populusque Romanus universus cognomen Patris Patriæ maximo consensu ei tribuerunt. Augustus, præ gaudio lacrimans, respondit his verbis: "Compos factus sum votorum[12] meorum; neque aliud mihi optandum est, quam ut hunc consensum vestrum ad ultimum vitæ finem videre possim."

9. Dictaturam, quam populus magna vi offerebat, Augus-

tus, genu nixus, dejectaque ab humeris toga, deprecatus est. Domini appellationem semper exhorruit, eamque sibi tribui edicto vetuit, immo de restituenda[41] republica non semel cogitavit; sed reputans et se privatum non sine periculo fore,[39] et rempublicam plurium arbitrio commissum iri, summam retinuit potestatem, id vero studuit, nequem novi status[12] pœniteret. Bene de iis etiam quos adversarios expertus erat et sentiebat et loquebatur. Legentem aliquando unum e nepotibus invenit; cumque puer territus volumen Ciceronis, quod manu tenebat, veste tegeret, Augustus librum cepit, eoque statim reddito: "Hic vir," inquit, "fili mi, doctus fuit et patriæ amans."

10. Pedibus sæpe per urbem incedebat, summaque comitate adeuntes[21] excipiebat: unde cum quidam, libellum supplicem porrigens, præ metu et reverentia nunc manum proferret, nunc retraheret; "Putasne," inquit jocans Augustus, "assem te elephanto dare"? Eum aliquando convenit veteranus miles, qui vocatus in jus periclitabatur, rogavitque ut sibi adesset. Statim Augustus unum e comitatu suo elegit advocatum, qui litigatorem commendaret. Tum veteranus exclamavit: "At non ego, te[35] periclitante bello Actiaco,[3] vicarium quæsivi, sed ipse pro te pugnavi"; simulque detexit cicatrices. Erubuit Augustus, atque ipse venit in advocationem.

11. Cum post Actiacam victoriam Augustus Romam ingrederetur, occurrit ei inter gratulantes opifex quidam corvum tenens, quem instituerat hæc dicere: *Ave, Cæsar victor, imperator.* Augustus, avem officiosam miratus, eam viginti milibus nummorum[10] emit. Socius opificis, ad quem nihil ex illa liberalitate pervenerat, affirmavit Augusto illum habere et alium corvum, quem afferri postulavit. Allatus corvus verba, quæ didicerat, expressit: *Ave, Antoni victor, imperator.* Nihil ea re exasperatus, Augustus jussit tantummodo corvorum doctorem dividere acceptam mercedem cum contubernali. Salutatus similiter a psittaco, emi eum jussit.

12. Exemplo incitatus, sutor quidam corvum instituit ad parem salutationem; sed, cum parum proficeret, sæpe ad

avem non respondentem dicebat: *Opera et impensa periit.* Tandem corvus cœpit proferre dictatam salutationem: qua audita dum transiret, Augustus respondit: "Satis domi talium salutatorum[10] habeo." Tum corvus illa etiam verba abjecit, quibus dominum querentem audire solebat: *Opera et impensa periit:* ad quod Augustus risit, atque avem emi jussit, quanti[11] nullam adhuc emerat.

13. Solebat quidam Græculus descendenti e palatio Augusto honorificum aliquod epigramma porrigere. Id cum frustra sæpe fecisset, et tamen rursum eundem facturum Augustus videret, sua manu in charta breve exaravit Græcum epigramma, et Græculo venienti ad se obviam misit. Ille legendo laudare cœpit, mirarique tam voce quam vultu gestuque. Dein cum accessit ad sellam, qua[26] Augustus vehebatur, demissa in pauperem crumenam manu, paucos denarios protulit, quos principi daret; dixitque "se plus daturum fuisse, si plus habuisset." Secuto omnium risu, Græculum Augustus vocavit, eique satis grandem pecuniæ summam numerari jussit.

14. Augustus fere nulli se invitanti negabat. Exceptus igitur a quodam cœna satis parca et pæne quotidiana, hoc tantum insusurravit: "Non putabam me tibi[15] esse tam familiarem." Cum aliquando apud Pollionem quendam cœnaret, fregit unus ex servis vas crystallinum: rapi illum protinus Pollio jussit, et, ne vulgari morte periret, abjici murænis,[19] quas ingens piscina continebat. Evasit e manibus puer, et ad pedes Cæsaris confugit, non recusans mori, sed rogans ne piscium esca fieret. Motus novitate crudelitatis, Augustus servi infelicis patrocinium suscepit: cum autem veniam a viro crudeli non impetraret, crystallina vasa ad se afferri jussit; omnia manu sua fregit; servum manumisit, piscinamque compleri præcepit.

15. Augustus in quadam villa ægrotans noctes inquietas agebat, rumpente somnum ejus crebro noctuæ cantu; qua molestia cum liberari se vehementer cupere significasset, miles quidam, aucupii[12] peritus, noctuam prehendendam curavit, vivamque Augusto attulit, spe ingentis præmii; cui Augustus

mille nummos dari jussit: at ille, minus dignum præmium existimans, dicere ausus est: "Malo ut vivat," et avem dimisit. Imperatori nec ad irascendum causa deerat, nec ad ulciscendum potestas. Hanc tamem injuriam æquo animo tulit Augustus, hominemque impunitum abire passus est.

16. Augustus amicitias non facile admisit, et admissas constanter retinuit: imprimis familiarem habuit Mæcenatem, equitem Romanum, qui ea,[2] qua apud principem valebat gratia ita semper usus est, ut prodesset omnibus[16] quibus posset, noceret nemini. Mira erat ejus ars et libertas in flectendo[41] Augusti animo, cum eum ira incitatum videret. Jus aliquando dicebat Augustus, et multos morte damnaturus videbatur. Aderat tunc Mæcenas, qui circumstantium turbam perrumpere, et ad tribunal propius accedere, conatus est: cum id frustra tentasset, in tabella scripsit hæc verba, *Surge tandem, carnifex:* eamque tabellam ad Augustum projecit; qua lecta, Augustus statim surrexit, et nemo est morte multatus.

17. Habitavit Augustus in ædibus modicis, neque laxitate neque cultu conspicuis, ac per annos amplius quadraginta in eodem cubiculo hieme et æstate mansit. Supellex quoque ejus vix privatæ elegantiæ[9] erat. Idem tamen Romam, quam pro majestate imperii non satis ornatam invenerat, adeo excoluit, ut jure sit gloriatus, "marmoream se relinquere, quam lateritiam accepisset." Raro veste alia usus est, quam confecta ab uxore,[27] sorore, filia, neptibusque. Altiuscula erant ejus calceamenta, ut procerior quam erat videretur. Cibi[9] minimi erat atque vulgaris. Secundarium panem et pisciculos minutos et ficus virides maxime appetebat.

18. Augustus non amplius quam septem horas[23] dormiebat, ac ne eas quidem continuas, sed ita ut in illo temporis spatio ter aut quater expergisceretur. Si interruptum somnum recuperare non posset, lectores arcessebat, donec resumeret. Cum audisset senatorem quendam, licet ære alieno oppressum, arcte et graviter dormire solitum, culcitam ejus magno pretio[25] emit: mirantibus dixit: "Habenda est ad somnum culcita, in qua homo qui tantum debebat dormire potuit."

19. Exercitationes campestres equorum et armorum statim post bella civilia omisit, et ad pilam primo folliculumque transiit; mox, animi laxandi causa, modo piscabatur hamo, modo talis nucibusque ludebat cum puerculis, quos facie et garrulitate amabiles undique conquirebat. Alea multum delectabatur; idque ei vitio[20] datum est. Tandem, afflicta valetudine, in Campaniam concessit, ubi remisso ad otium animo, nullo hilaritatis genere[28] abstinuit. Supremo vitæ die, petito speculo, capillum sibi comi jussit, et amicos circumstantes percontatus est, num vitæ mimum satis commode egisset;[45] adjecit et solitam clausulam: "Edite strepitum, vosque omnes cum gaudio applaudite." Obiit Nolæ[36] sextum et septuagesimum annum agens.

IX. THE HELVETIAN WAR.

FROM CÆSAR'S GALLIC WAR. Book I.

1. Gallia est omnis divisa in partes tres. Unam incolunt Belgæ, aliam Aquitani, tertiam Celtæ, qui[4] lingua[26] nostra Galli appellantur. Hi omnes lingua,[26] institutis, legibus, inter se differunt. Gallos ab Aquitanis Garumna flumen dividit, a Belgis Matrona et Sequana. Fortissimi[2] sunt Belgæ, propterea quod proximi sunt Germanis,[15] qui trans Rhenum incolunt, quibuscum continenter bellum gerunt. Helvetii quoque reliquos Gallos virtute[26] præcedunt, quod fere quotidianis prœliis cum Germanis contendunt. Una pars initium capit a flumine Rhodano; continetur Garumna flumine, oceano, finibus Belgarum. Attingit etiam flumen[1] Rhenum. Vergit ad septemtriones. Belgæ ab extremis Galliæ finibus oriuntur; pertinent ad inferiorem partem fluminis Rheni; spectant in septemtriones et orientem solem. Aquitania a Garumna flumine ad Pyrenæos montes et eam partem oceani, quæ est

ad Hispaniam, pertinet; spectat inter occasum solis et septemtriones.

2. Apud Helvetios nobilissimus[2] et ditissimus fuit Orgetorix. Is conjurationem nobilitatis fecit; et civitati[16] persuasit, ut de finibus suis cum omnibus copiis exirent. Facilius eis persuasit, quod undique, loci natura,[26] Helvetii continentur; una ex parte, flumine Rheno, latissimo atque altissimo, qui agrum Helvetium a Germanis dividit; altera ex parte, monte Jura altissimo, qui est inter Sequanos et Helvetios; tertia, lacu Lemanno, et flumine Rhodano, qui Provinciam nostram ab Helvetiis dividit. His rebus adducti, constituerunt ea quæ[4] ad proficiscendum pertinerent comparare;[38] jumentorum et carrorum quam maximum numerum coëmere; sementes quam maximas facere; cum proximis civitatibus amicitiam confirmare. In tertium annum profectionem lege confirmant. Ad eas res conficiendas[41] Orgetorix deligitur. Is legationem ad civitates suscepit. In eo itinere persuadet Castico, Sequano, ut regnum in civitate sua occuparet, quod[4] pater ante habuerat. Itemque Dumnorigi Æduo, qui maxime plebi acceptus erat, ut idem conaretur persuadet. Inter se jusjurandum dant, et totius Galliæ sese potiri posse sperant. Ea res est Helvetiis[14] enuntiata: Orgetorigem ex vinculis causam dicere coëgerunt. Damnatum pœnam sequi oportebat, ut igni[26] cremaretur. Die constituta[34] Orgetorix ad judicium omnem suam familiam, et omnes clientes obæratosque conduxit. Per eos se eripuit.

3. Cum civitas, ob eam rem incitata, armis jus suum exsequi conaretur, Orgetorix mortuus est. Post ejus mortem nihilominus Helvetii id quod constituerant facere[38] conantur. Ubi se paratos esse[39] arbitrati sunt, oppida sua omnia, vicos, privata ædificia incendunt. Trium mensium molita cibaria quemque domo efferre jubent. Erant omnino itinera duo, quibus[4] itineribus domo exire possent; unum per Sequanos, angustum et difficile, inter montem Juram et flumen Rhodanum; alterum per provinciam nostram multo facilius atque expeditius, propterea quod Rhodanus nonnullis locis vado[26]

transitur. Extremum oppidum Allobrogum est Geneva. Ex eo oppido pons ad Helvetios pertinet. Omnibus rebus[35] ad profectionem comparatis, diem dicunt, qua die ad ripam Rhodani omnes conveniant. Cæsari cum id nuntiatum esset, maturat ab urbe proficisci, et in Galliam ulteriorem contendit. Pontem jubet rescindi.[39]

4. Ubi de ejus adventu Helvetii certiores[2] facti sunt, legatos ad eum mittunt, qui[44] dicerent sibi[17] esse in animo sine ullo maleficio iter per provinciam facere. Cæsar a lacu Lemanno ad montem Juram murum fossamque perducit. Negat se posse[39] iter ulli per provinciam dare.[38] Relinquebatur una per Sequanos via, qua, Sequanis invitis, propter angustias ire non poterant. His[16] cum persuadere non possent, legatos ad Dumnorigem mittunt, ut, eo deprecatore,[35] impetrarent. Dumnorix apud Sequanos plurimum poterat, et Helvetiis[15] erat amicus, quod Orgetorigis filiam in matrimonium duxerat. Itaque rem suscipit, et a Sequanis impetrat, ut per fines suos Helvetios ire patiantur.

5. Cæsar in Italiam magnis itineribus contendit, duasque ibi legiones conscribit, et tres ex hibernis educit, et in ulteriorem Galliam, per Alpes, ire contendit. In fines Vocontiorum die septimo pervenit; inde in Allobrogum fines, ab Allobrogibus in Segusianos exercitum ducit. Hi sunt extra provinciam trans Rhodanum primi. Helvetii jam per angustias et fines Sequanorum suas copias transduxerant, et Æduorum agros populabantur. Ædui, cum se[21] defendere non possent, legatos ad Cæsarem mittunt, rogatum[42] auxilium. Eodem tempore Ambarri, consanguinei[1] Æduorum, Cæsarem certiorem faciunt, sese, depopulatis agris, non facile ab oppidis vim hostium prohibere. Item Allobroges, qui trans Rhodanum vicos possessionesque habebant, fuga[26] se ad Cæsarem recipiunt. Cæsar non exspectandum sibi statuit, dum in Santonos Helvetii pervenirent.

6. Flumen est Arar, quod per fines Æduorum et Sequanorum in Rhodanum influit, incredibili lenitate,[26] ita ut oculis in utram partem fluat judicari non possit. Id Helvetii, rati-

bus et lintribus junctis, transibant. Ubi Cæsar certior factus est tres copiarum partes Helvetios[22] transduxisse, quartam vero partem citra flumen esse, de tertia vigilia e castris profectus ad eam partem pervenit, quæ nondum transierat. Eos impeditos aggressus, magnam eorum partem concidit. Reliqui sese in proximas silvas abdiderunt. Is pagus appellabatur Tigurinus:[1] nam omnis civitas Helvetia in quattuor pagos divisa est. Hic pagus Lucium Cassium consulem interfecerat, et ejus exercitum sub jugum miserat. Ita, quæ pars calamitatem populo[18] Romano intulerat, ea princeps pœnas persolvit.

7. Hoc prœlio facto, reliquas copias Helvetiorum ut consequi posset, pontem in Arare faciendum curat, atque ita exercitum transducit. Helvetii, repentino ejus adventu commoti, legatos ad eum mittunt, cujus legationis Divico princeps fuit, qui bello[24] Cassiano dux Helvetiorum fuerat. Is ita cum Cæsare agit: Si pacem populus Romanus cum Helvetiis faceret, in eam partem ituros, ubi Cæsar eos[22] esse voluisset; sin bello persequi perseveraret, reminisceretur et veteris incommodi[12] populi Romani, et pristinæ virtutis Helvetiorum; se ita a patribus majoribusque suis didicisse, ut magis virtute quam dolo contenderent. Quare, ne committeret, ut is locus, ubi constitissent, ex calamitate populi Romani nomen caperet.

8. His Cæsar ita respondit: Sibi[14] minus dubitationis dari, quod eas res, quas commemorassent, memoria[26] teneret. Si veteris contumeliæ[12] oblivisci vellet, num recentium injuriarum memoriam deponere posse? Tamen, si obsides ab iis sibi dentur, uti ea quæ polliceantur facturos intelligat, et si Æduis de injuriis quas ipsis sociisque eorum intulerint, item si Allobrogibus satisfaciant, sese cum iis pacem facturum. Divico respondit: Ita Helvetios a majoribus suis institutos esse, uti obsides accipere, non dare consueverint; ejus rei populum Romanum esse testem. Hoc responso dato, discessit. Postero die castra ex eo loco movent. Idem facit Cæsar. Equitatum omnem præmittit, qui[44] videant, quas in partes hostes iter faciant. Qui alieno loco cum equitatu Helvetiorum

prœlium committunt, et pauci de nostris cadunt. Helvetii audacius subsistere, nonnunquam nostros lacessere cœperunt. Cæsar suos a prœlio continebat; ac satis habebat in præsentia hostem rapinis[28] prohibere. Ita dies[23] circiter quindecim iter fecerunt, uti, inter novissimum hostium agmen et nostrum primum, non amplius quinis aut senis milibus[32] passuum interesset.

9. Interim quotidie Cæsar Æduos[35] frumentum, quod[4] essent publice polliciti, flagitare. Nam, propter frigora, non modo frumenta in agris matura non erant, sed ne pabuli quidem satis magna copia suppetebat. Eo autem frumento,[31] quod flumine Arare navibus subvexerat, minus uti[38] poterat, quod iter ab Arare Helvetii averterant, a quibus discedere nolebat. Diem ex die ducere[40] Ædui; conferri, comportari, adesse dicere. Ubi se diutius duci intellexit, et diem instare, quo die frumentum[21] militibus metiri oporteret, convocatis eorum principibus, quorum magnam copiam in castris habebat, in his Divitiaco et Lisco, qui summo magistratui[18] præerat, graviter eos accusat, quod ab iis non sublevetur; præsertim cum, magna ex parte eorum precibus adductus, bellum susceperit. Tum demum Liscus proponit: esse nonnullos, quorum auctoritas apud plebem plurimum valeat; hos[22] seditiosa atque improba oratione multitudinem deterrere,[39] ne frumentum conferant. Ab iisdem nostra consilia hostibus enuntiari; hos a se coerceri non posse. Quin etiam, quod rem Cæsari enuntiarit, intellegere sese quanto id cum periculo fecerit; et, ob eam causam, quamdiu potuerit, tacuisse.

10. Cæsar hac oratione Dumnorigem,[28] Divitiaci fratrem, designari[39] sentiebat; sed quod, pluribus præsentibus, eas res[28] jactari nolebat, celeriter concilium dimittit; Liscum retinet; dicit liberius atque audacius. Eadem secreto ab aliis quærit; reperit esse vera: ipsum esse Dumnorigem summa audacia,[26] magna apud plebem propter liberalitatem gratia, cupidum novarum rerum[12]; complures annos[23] omnia Æduorum vectigalia parvo pretio redempta habere; propterea quod, illo licente, contra liceri audeat nemo. His rebus suam rem fami-

liarem auxisse, magnum numerum equitatus semper circum se habere. Favere Helvetiis[16] propter affinitatem; odisse Cæsarem et Romanos, quod eorum adventu potentia ejus deminuta, et Divitiacus frater in antiquum locum gratiæ atque honoris sit restitutus. Si quid accidat Romanis, summam in spem regni per Helvetios obtinendi venire; imperio populi Romani, non modo de regno, sed etiam de ea quam habeat gratia, desperare.

11. Cum ad has suspiciones certissimæ res accederent, satis esse causæ arbitrabatur, quare in eum aut ipse animadverteret, aut civitatem animadvertere juberet. His omnibus unum repugnabat, quod Divitiaci fratris summum in populum Romanum studium, summam in se voluntatem, egregiam fidem, justitiam, temperantiam cognoverat: nam ne ejus supplicio Divitiaci animum offenderet verebatur. Itaque, priusquam quidquam conaretur,[44] Divitiacum[22] ad se vocari jubet; simul commonefacit quæ, ipso[35] præsente, in concilio Gallorum sint dicta; et ostendit quæ separatim quisque de eo apud se dixerit. Divitiacus multis cum lacrimis obsecrare cœpit, ne quid gravius in fratrem statueret: scire[39] se,[22] illa esse vera; sese tamen et amore fraterno et existimatione vulgi commoveri. Quod si quid ei[14] a Cæsare gravius accidisset, cum ipse eum locum amicitiæ aqud eum teneret, neminem existimaturum non sua voluntate factum; qua ex re futurum, uti totius Galliæ[8] animi a se averterentur. Cæsar ejus dextram prendit; Dumnorigem ad se vocat; fratrem adhibet; quæ in eo reprehendat ostendit; monet ut in reliquum tempus omnes suspiciones vitet.

12. Eodem die, ab exploratoribus certior[2] factus hostes sub monte consedisse millia[23] passuum ab ipsius castris octo, qualis esset[45] natura montis, et qualis in circuitu adscensus, qui cognoscerent[44] misit. Renuntiatum est facilem esse. De tertia vigilia Titum Labienum, legatum, cum duobus legionibus summum jugum montis adscendere jubet. Ipse de quarta vigilia eodem itinere, quo hostes ierant, ad eos contendit; equitatumque omnem ante se mittit. Prima luce, cum sum-

mus mons a Tito Labieno teneretur, ipse ab hostium castris non longius mille et quingentis passibus abesset, neque aut ipsius adventus, aut Labieni, cognitus esset, Considius, equo admisso, ad eum accurrit; dicit montem, quem a Labieno occupari voluerit, ab hostibus[27] teneri; id se ex Gallicis armis atque insignibus cognovisse. Cæsar suas copias in proximum collem subducit, aciem instruit. Labienus, ut erat ei præceptum (ut undique uno tempore in hostes impetus fieret), monte occupato, nostros exspectabat, prœlioque abstinebat. Multo denique die, per exploratores Cæsar cognovit montem a suis teneri, et Considium, perterritum, quod[4] non vidisset pro viso renuntiâsse. Eo die, quo consuerat intervallo, hostes sequitur; et millia passuum tria ab eorum castris castra ponit.

13. Postridie ejus diei, quod omnino biduum supererat cum exercitui frumentum metiri oporteret, et quod a Bibracte, oppido Æduorum longe maximo et copiosissimo, non amplius millibus passuum duodeviginti aberat, rei frumentariæ[18] prospiciendum existimavit, ac Bibracte[36] ire contendit. Helvetii, seu quod perterritos Romanos discedere existimarent, sive quod re frumentaria[28] intercludi posse confiderent, itinere converso, nostros a novissimo agmine insequi ac lacessere cœperunt. Postquam id animum advertit, copias suas Cæsar in proximum collem subducit; equitatumque, qui sustineret hostium impetum, misit. Ipse interim in colle medio triplicem aciem instruxit. Sarcinas in unum locum conferri, et eum ab iis, qui in superiore acie constiterant, muniri jussit. Helvetii, cum omnibus suis carris secuti, impedimenta in unum locum contulerunt. Ipsi confertissima acie,[26] rejecto nostro equitatu, phalange facta, sub primam nostram aciem successerunt. Cæsar, primum suo[35] deinde omnium remotis[35] equis, ut spem fugæ tolleret, cohortatus suos, prœlium commisit. Milites, e loco superiore pilis missis, facile hostium phalangem perfregerunt. Ea desjecta, gladiis districtis in eos impetum fecerunt.

14. Gallis[20] magno erat impedimento,[20] quod, pluribus eo-

rum scutis[35] uno ictu[26] pilorum transfixis et colligatis, cum ferrum se inflexisset, neque evellere, neque, sinistra impedita, satis commode pugnare poterant. Tandem vulneribus defessi, et pedem referre, et, quod mons suberat circiter mille passuum, eo se recipere cœperunt. Capto monte, et succedentibus nostris, Boii et Tulingi, qui agmen hostium claudebant, ex itinere nostros aggressi, circumvenere; et id conspicati Helvetii, qui in montem se receperant, rursus instare et prœlium redintegrare cœperunt. Romani conversa signa bipartito intulerunt; prima et secunda acies, ut victis[16] ac submotis resisteret; tertia, ut venientes exciperet. Ita ancipiti prœlio diu atque acriter pugnatum est. Diutius cum nostrorum impetus sustinere non possent, alteri se, ut cœperant, in montem receperunt; alteri ad impedimenta et carros suos se contulerunt. Nam hoc toto prœlio, cum ab hora septima ad vesperum pugnatum sit, aversum hostem videre nemo potuit. Ad multam noctem etiam ad impedimenta pugnatum est; propterea quod pro vallo carros objecerant. Impedimentis castrisque nostri potiti sunt. Ibi Orgetorigis filia atque unus e filiis captus est. Ex eo prœlio circiter millia hominum centum et triginta superfuerunt, eaque tota nocte ierunt; in fines Lingonum die[34] quarto pervenerunt; cum, et propter vulnera militum et sepulturam occisorum, nostri eos sequi non potuissent. Cæsar ad Lingones literas nuntiosque misit, ne eos frumento neve alia re juvarent. Ipse, triduo intermisso, cum omnibus copiis eos sequi cœpit.

15. Helvetii, omnium rerum inopia adducti, legatos de deditione ad eum miserunt. Qui cum se ad pedes projecissent, suppliciterque locuti pacem petissent, atque eos in eo loco, quo tum essent, adventum suum exspectare jussisset, paruerunt. Eo postquam pervenit, obsides, arma, servos, qui ad eos perfugissent, poposcit. Helvetios in fines suos reverti jussit; et quod, omnibus frugibus amissis, domi[36] nihil erat, Allobrogibus imperavit, ut iis frumenti copiam facerent; ipsos oppida vicosque, quos incenderant, restituere jussit, quod noluit eum locum[22] vacare,[39] ne, propter bonitatem agrorum Germani in

Helvetiorum fines transirent. In castris Helvetiorum tabulæ repertæ sunt, literis Græcis confectæ, quibus in tabulis nominatim ratio confecta erat, qui numerus domo[36] exisset[45] eorum, qui arma ferre possent; et item separatim pueri, senes, mulieresque. Summa omnium fuerat ad millia trecenta sexaginta et octo. Eorum, qui domum redierunt, repertus est numerus millium centum et decem.

X. THE WAR WITH ARIOVISTUS.

1. Bello Helvetiorum confecto, totius fere Galliæ legati, principes civitatum, ad Cæsarem gratulatum convenerunt: intelligere sese, tametsi, pro veteribus Helvetiorum injuriis populi Romani, ab iis pœnas repetisset, tamen eam rem non minus ex usu terræ Galliæ quam populi Romani accidisse; propterea quod, florentissimis rebus, domos suas Helvetii reliquissent, ut toti Galliæ[18] bellum inferrent, imperioque potirentur; locumque domicilio deligerent, quem opportunissimum ac fructuosissimum judicassent; reliquasque civitates stipendiarias haberent. Petierunt, uti sibi concilium totius Galliæ in diem certam indicere liceret; sese habere quasdam res, quas ex communi consensu ab eo petere vellent. Ea re permissa, jurejurando ne quis enuntiaret inter se sanxerunt. Eo concilio dimisso, iidem principes, qui ante fuerant ad Cæsarem, reverterunt petieruntque uti sibi[14] secreto de omnium salute cum eo agere liceret. Ea re impetrata, sese omnes flentes Cæsari ad pedes projecerunt: Non minus se contendere, ne ea, quæ dixissent, enuntiarentur, quam uti ea quæ vellent impetrarent; propterea quod, si enuntiatum esset, summum in cruciatum se venturos viderent.

2. Locutus est pro his Divitiacus: Galliæ totius factiones esse duas; harum alterius principatum tenere Æduos, alterius Arvernos. Hi cum de potentatu inter se multos annos con-

tenderent, factum esse, uti ab Arvernis[27] Sequanisque Germani mercede[26] arcesserentur. Horum primo circiter millia quindecim Rhenum transisse; posteaquam agros, cultum, et copias Gallorum homines barbari adamassent, transductos esse plures. Nunc esse in Gallia ad centum et viginti millium numerum; cum his Æduos eorumque clientes semel atque iterum contendisse; pulsos, omnem nobilitatem,[21] omnem senatum, omnem equitatum amisisse. Quibus calamitatibus, qui plurimum ante in Gallia potuissent, coactos esse Sequanis obsides dare, nobilissimos civitatis, et jurejurando civitatem obstringere, sese[22] neque obsides repetituros, neque auxilium a populo Romano imploraturos, neque recusaturos quominus perpetuo sub illorum imperio essent. Unum se esse ex omni civitate Æduorum, qui adduci non potuerit, ut juraret, aut liberos suos obsides daret. Ob eam rem se[22] ex civitate profugisse, et Romam[36] venisse, auxilium postulatum.[42] Sed pejus victoribus Sequanis, quam Æduis victis accidisse; propterea quod Ariovistus, rex Germanorum, in eorum finibus consedisset, tertiamque partem agri Sequani occupavisset. Futurum esse paucis annis, uti omnes ex Galliæ finibus pellerentur, atque omnes Germani Rhenum transirent. Ariovistum autem, ut semel Gallorum copias prœlio vicerit, superbe et crudeliter imperare, obsides nobilissimi cujusque liberos poscere, et in eos omnia exempla cruciatusque edere. Hominem esse barbarum, iracundum, temerarium; non posse ejus imperia[22] diutius sustineri. Nisi si quid in populo Romano sit auxilii,[10] omnibus Gallis idem[22] esse faciendum,[39] quod[4] Helvetii fecerint, ut alias sedes, remotas a Germanis, petant; fortunamque, quæcunque accidat, experiantur. Cæsarem deterrere[38] posse,[39] ne major multitudo Germanorum Rhenum transducatur.

3. Hac oratione habita, omnes, qui[4] aderant, magno fletu auxilium a Cæsare petere cœperunt. Animadvertit Cæsar, unos Sequanos[22] nihil earum rerum[10] facere,[39] quas[21] ceteri facerent; sed tristes terram intueri. Ejus rei causa quæ esset,[45] cum ab iis sæpius quæreret, neque ullam omnino

vocem exprimere posset, idem Divitiacus respondit: Hoc esse graviorem fortunam Sequanorum quod soli ne in occulto quidem queri,[38] neque auxilium implorare,[38] auderent, absentisque Ariovisti crudelitatem, velut si adesset, horrerent. His rebus cognitis, Cæsar Gallorum animos confirmavit: magnam[22] se habere[39] spem,[21] beneficio suo adductum, Ariovistum finem injuriis facturum. Multæ res eum hortabantur, quare eam rem[22] cogitandam et suscipiendam putaret; imprimis, quod Æduos, fratres sæpenumero a senatu appellatos, in servitute videbat Germanorum teneri; quod, in tanto imperio populi Romani, turpissimum sibi et reipublicæ esse arbitrabatur. Germanos[22] Rhenum transire[39] periculosum videbat; neque sibi temperaturos existimabat, quin, ut ante Cimbri Teutonique fecissent, in provinciam, atque inde in Italiam, contenderent; quibus rebus[18] quam maturrime occurrendum putabat.

4. Quamobrem placuit ei,[14] ut ad Ariovistum legatos mitteret, qui ab eo postularent,[44] uti aliquem locum medium colloquio diceret: Velle[39] sese[22] de republica et summis utriusque rebus cum eo agere.[38] Ei legationi Ariovistus respondit: Si quid ipsi[17] a Cæsare opus esset, sese ad eum venturum fuisse; si quid ille se velit, illum ad se venire oportere; sibi autem mirum videri, quid in sua Gallia, quam bello vicisset, aut Cæsari[17] aut omnino populo[17] Romano negotii[10] esset. His responsis ad Cæsarem relatis, iterum legatos cum his mandatis mittit: Quoniam, beneficio affectus, hanc sibi populoque Romano gratiam referret, hæc esse, quæ ab eo postularet; primum, ne quam hominum multitudinem amplius trans Rhenum in Galliam transduceret; deinde obsides, quos haberet ab Æduis, redderet; neve his[14] sociisve[14] eorum bellum inferret. Si id non impetraret, sese,[22] quoniam senatus censuisset, uti, quicunque Galliam provinciam obtineret, amicos populi Romani defenderet, Æduorum injurias non neglecturum.[39]

5. Ad hæc Ariovistus respondit: Jus esse belli, ut, qui vicissent, quemadmodum vellent, imperarent; populum Ro-

manum victis,[16] non ad alterius præscriptum, sed ad suum arbitrium, imperare consuesse. Æduos[22] sibi, quoniam belli fortunam tentassent, ac superati essent, stipendiarios[1] esse factos.[39] Se[22] obsides redditurum non esse; neque bellum[21] illaturum, si stipendium quotannis penderent. Cæsar, cum vellet, congrederetur; intellecturum, quid invicti Germani, qui inter annos quatuordecim tectum non subissent, virtute possent. Eodem tempore legati ab Æduis et Treviris veniebant; Ædui questum,[42] quod Harudes, qui nuper in Galliam transportati essent, fines eorum popularentur; Treviri, pagos centum Suevorum ad ripas Rheni consedisse, qui transire conarentur. Quibus rebus Cæsar vehementer commotus maturandum sibi existimavit, ne, si nova manus cum veteribus copiis Ariovisti sese[21] conjunxisset, minus facile resisti posset. Itaque, re frumentaria comparata, magnis itineribus[26] ad Ariovistum contendit.

6. Cum tridui viam[21] processisset, nuntiatum est ei Ariovistum[22] cum omnibus copiis ad occupandum Vesontionem, quod[4] est oppidum maximum Sequanorum, contendere,[39] triduique viam a suis finibus processisse.[39] Id ne accideret, præcavendum Cæsar existimabat. Namque omnium rerum,[8] quæ ad bellum usui erant, summa erat in eo facultas; idque natura[26] loci sic muniebatur, ut magnam ad ducendum[41] bellum daret facultatem; propterea quod flumen Dubis pæne totum oppidum cingit; reliquum spatium mons continet, ita ut radices ex utraque parte ripæ fluminis contingant. Hunc murus arcem efficit, et cum oppido conjungit. Cæsar, occupato oppido, ibi præsidium collocat. Dum paucos dies rei frumentariæ causa[26] moratur, ex percunctatione[26] nostrorum vocibusque[26] Gallorum ac mercatorum, qui ingenti magnitudine[26] corporum Germanos,[22] incredibili virtute[26] atque exercitatione in armis, esse prædicabant; sæpenumero sese, cum iis congressos, ne vultum quidem atque aciem oculorum ferre potuisse; tantus subito timor exercitum occupavit, ut omnium mentes animosque perturbaret. Hic ortus est a tribunis militum reliquisque, qui, amicitiæ causa Cæsarem secuti, non

magnum in re militari usum habebant. Alius alia causa[35] illata petebant, ut discedere liceret; nonnulli, ut timoris suspicionem vitarent, remanebant. Hi, abditi in tabernaculis, aut suum fatum querebantur, aut cum familiaribus suis commune periculum miserabantur. Totis castris testamenta obsignabantur. Horum vocibus[26] etiam ii, qui[4] magnum in castris usum habebant, perturbabantur. Qui se[22] minus timidos[24] existimari volebant, non se hostem vereri, sed angustias itineris, et magnitudinem silvarum, quæ intercederent inter ipsos atque Ariovistum, dicebant. Nonnulli etiam Cæsari renuntiabant, cum castra[22] moveri ac signa ferri jussisset, non fore dicto audientes milites.

7. Hæc[21] cum animadvertisset, convocato consilio omniumque ordinum adhibitis centurionibus, vehementer eos incusavit; quod, aut quam in partem, aut quo consilio ducerentur, sibi quærendum aut cogitandum putarent: Ariovistum cupidissime populi Romani amicitiam appetisse: cur hunc temere quisquam ab officio discessurum judicaret? Sibi[16] quidem persuaderi, cognitis postulatis, eum[22] neque suam neque populi Romani gratiam repudiaturum. Quod si, furore impulsus, bellum intulisset, cur de sua virtute aut de ipsius diligentia desperarent? Factum ejus hostis periculum, cum, Cimbris et Teutonis a Caio Mario pulsis, non minorem laudem exercitus, quam imperator, meritus[38] videbatur. Factum etiam nuper in Italia servili tumultu.[34] Ex quo judicari posset, quantum haberet in se boni[10] constantia; propterea quod, quos aliquamdiu inermes timuissent, hos armatos superassent. Denique hos esse eosdem, quibuscum sæpenumero Helvetii congressi, non solum in suis sed etiam in illorum finibus, plerumque superarint, qui tamen pares esse nostro exercitu non potuerint. Si quos adversum prœlium Gallorum moveret, hos reperire posse, Ariovistum,[22] cum multos menses castris se tenuisset, desperantes[21] de pugna et dispersos subito adortum[39] magis consilio quam virtute vicisse. Qui suum timorem in angustias conferrent, facere arroganter, cum aut de officio imperatoris desperare, aut ei præscribere, viderentur.

Quod non fore dicto audientes milites dicantur, nihil[24] se[22] ea re commoveri, et proxima nocte de quarta vigilia castra moturum, ut quam primum intelligere posset, utrum apud eos officium an timor valeret. Si præterea nemo sequatur, tamen se cum sola decima legione iturum, de qua non dubitaret, sibique[17] eam prætoriam cohortem futuram.

8. Hac oratione habita, mirum in modum conversæ sunt omnium mentes, summaque cupiditas belli gerendi innata est; princepsque decima legio per tribunos ei gratias egit, quod de se optimum judicium fecisset. Deinde reliquæ legiones egerunt, uti Cæsari satisfacerent; et, itinere exquisito per Divitiacum, quod ei maximam fidem habebat, de quarta vigilia, ut dixerat, profectus est. Septimo die ab exploratoribus[27] certior factus est, Ariovisti copias a nostris millibus passuum quattuor et viginti abesse. Cognito Cæsaris adventu, Ariovistus legatos ad eum mittit: Quod antea de colloquio postulasset, id[22] fieri licere,[39] quoniam propius accessisset. Non respuit conditionem Cæsar; magnamque in spem veniebat, pro suis populique Romani in eum beneficiis, fore uti pertinacia[28] desisteret. Dies colloquio dictus est, ex eo die quintus. Interim Ariovistus postulavit, ne quem peditem Cæsar adduceret; uterque cum equitatu veniret; alia ratione se non esse venturum. Cæsar, quod neque colloquium[22] tolli volebat, neque salutem suam Gallorum equitatui committere audebat, commodissimum esse statuit, omnibus equis Gallis equitibus detractis, eo milites legionis decimæ imponere, ut præsidium quam amicissimum haberet. Planities erat magna, et in ea tumulus terrenus. Hic locus æquo fere spatio ab castris utrisque aberat. Eo ad colloquium venerunt. Legionem Cæsar passibus ducentis ab eo tumulo constituit; equites Ariovisti pari intervallo constiterunt.

9. Ariovistus, ex equis ut colloquerentur, et præter se denos ut ad colloquium adducerent, postulavit. Cæsar initio orationis beneficia commemoravit; quod rex appellatus esset a senatu; quod munera amplissima missa; quam rem et paucis contigisse et pro magnis officiis docebat. Docebat etiam, quam

veteres quamque justæ causæ necessitudinis ipsis cum Æduis intercederent; quæ senatus consulta, quamque honorifica, in eos facta essent; ut omni tempore totius Galliæ principatum tenuissent. Postulavit deinde eadem, quæ[4] legatis in mandatis dederat. Ariovistus ad postulata Cæsaris respondit: Transisse Rhenum sese[22] non sua sponte, sed arcessitum[39] a Gallis;[27] sedes habere ab ipsis concessas; obsides ipsorum voluntate datos; stipendium[21] capere jure belli; non se Gallis[18] bellum intulisse; omnes Galliæ civitates ad se oppugnandum[41] venisse; et uno prœlio superatas esse. Si iterum experiri velint, iterum paratum sese decertare; si pace uti velint, iniquum esse de stipendio recusare, quod sua voluntate ad id tempus pependerint. Amicitiam populi Romani sibi[20] præsidio[20] non detrimento esse oportere. Quod multitudinem Germanorum in Galliam transducat, id[21] se[22] sui muniendi non Galliæ impugnandæ causa facere. Se prius in Galliam venisse quam populum Romanum. Nunquam ante hoc tempus exercitum populi Romani provinciæ fines egressum. Quid sibi vellet? Cur in suas possessiones veniret? Provinciam suam hanc esse sicut illam nostram. Ut ipsi concedi non oporteret, si in nostros fines impetum faceret, sic item nos esse iniquos, qui in suo jure se interpellaremus.

10. Multa ab Cæsare[29] dicta sunt, quare negotio[28] desistere non posset: Neque suam neque populi Romani consuetudinem pati, uti optime meritos socios desereret; neque se judicare, Galliam potius esse Ariovisti quam populi Romani. Si judicium senatus[9] observari oporteret, liberam debere esse Galliam, quam bello victam suis legibus[31] uti[38] voluisset. Dum hæc in colloquio geruntur, Cæsari nuntiatum est equites Ariovisti propius tumulum accedere, et lapides[21] telaque in nostros conjicere. Cæsar loquendi finem fecit; se ad suos recipit; imperavit ne quod omnino telum in hostes rejicerent. Nam, etsi sine ullo periculo legionis delectæ prœlium fore videbat, tamen committendum non putabat, ut, pulsis hostibus, dici posset, ab se in colloquio circumventos. Posteaquam in vulgus militum elatum est, qua arrogantia Ariovistus usus Gallia

Romanis[18] interdixisset, impetumque in nostros ejus equites fecissent, multo major alacritas studiumque pugnandi exercitui[8] injectum est.

11. Biduo post Ariovistus ad Cæsarem legatos mittit, velle[39] se[22] agere[33] cum eo; uti aut iterum colloquio diem constitueret, aut ex legatis aliquem ad se mitteret. Colloquendi Cæsari causa visa non est. Legatum ex suis sese magno cum periculo ad eum missurum, et hominibus[18] feris objecturum, existimabat. Commodissimum visum est, Gaium Valerium Procillum propter fidem et propter linguæ Gallicæ scientiam, qua[31] multa jam Ariovistus utebatur, ad eum mittere, et Marcum Mettium, qui hospitio Ariovisti usus erat. Quos cum in castris conspexisset, conclamavit: Quid ad se venirent? an speculandi causa? et in catenas conjecit. Eodem die castra promovit, et milibus passuum sex a Cæsaris castris sub monte consedit. Postridie præter castra Cæsaris suas copias transduxit, et milibus passuum duobus[33] ultra eum castra fecit; eo consilio,[26] uti commeatu,[28] qui ex Sequanis et Æduis supportaretur, Cæsarem intercluderet. Dies continuos quinque Cæsar pro castris suas copias produxit, ut, si vellet Ariovistus prœlio contendere, ei potestas non deesset. Ariovistus exercitum castris continuit; equestri prœlio quotidie contendit.

12. Ubi eum[22] castris se[21] tenere[39] Cæsar intellexit, ne diutius commeatu[28] prohiberetur, ultra eum locum circiter passus sexcentos castris idoneum locum delegit; acieque triplici instructa, primam et secundam in armis esse, tertiam castra munire jussit. Eo circiter hominum numero sexdecim milia expedita Ariovistus misit; quæ copiæ nostros munitione prohiberent. Cæsar, ut ante constituerat, duas acies hostem propulsare, tertiam opus perficere jussit. Munitis castris, duas ibi legiones reliquit, quattuor reliquas in castra majora reduxit. Proximo die Cæsar e castris utrisque copias suas eduxit; paulumque a majoribus progressus, aciem instruxit, hostibusque pugnandi potestatem fecit. Ubi ne tum quidem eos prodire intellexit, circiter meridiem exercitum in castra reduxit. Tum demum Ariovistus partem suarum copi-

arum, quæ castra minora oppugnaret,[44] misit. Acriter utrinque pugnatum est. Solis occasu[34] copias Ariovistus, multis et illatis et acceptis vulneribus, in castra reduxit.

13. Cum ex captivis quæreret Cæsar, quam ob rem Ariovistus prœlio[26] non decertaret, hanc reperiebat causam; quod apud Germanos consuetudo esset, ut matres familiæ sortibus et vaticinationibus declararent, utrum prœlium committi ex usu esset, necne; eas dicere: Non esse fas Germanos superare, si ante novam lunam prœlio contendissent. Postridie Cæsar omnes alarios in conspectu hostium pro castris minoribus constituit, quod minus multitudine militum legionariorum pro hostium numero valebat. Ipse, triplici instructa acie, usque ad castra hostium accessit. Tum demum necessario Germani suas copias eduxerunt; omnemque aciem rhedis et carris circumdederunt, ne qua spes in fuga relinqueretur. Eo mulieres imposuerunt, quæ in prœlium proficiscentes milites, passis manibus, flentes implorabant, ne se Romanis traderent.

14. Cæsar singulis legionibus singulos legatos et quæstorem præfecit, uti testes[21] quisque virtutis haberet. Ipse a dextro cornu, quod eam partem[22] minime firmam hostium esse animum adverterat, prœlium commisit. Ita nostri acriter in hostes, signo dato, impetum fecerunt; itaque hostes celeriter procurrerunt, ut spatium pila in hostes conjiciendi non daretur. Rejectis pilis, gladiis pugnatum est. At Germani, celeriter phalange facta, impetus[21] gladiorum exceperunt. Reperti sunt complures nostri milites, qui in phalangas insilirent, et scuta manibus revellerent, et desuper vulnerarent. Cum hostium acies a sinistro cornu pulsa atque in fugam conversa esset, a dextro cornu vehementer multitudine suorum nostram aciem premebant. Id[21] cum animadvertisset Publius Crassus adolescens, qui equitatui[18] præerat, tertiam aciem subsidio[20] misit. Ita prœlium restitutum est, atque omnes hostes terga verterunt, neque prius fugere[38] destiterunt, quam ad flumen Rhenum, milia passuum ex eo loco circiter quinquaginta, pervenerint. Ibi perpauci, aut viribus confisi transnatare contenderunt, aut lintribus inventis sibi salutem repererunt.

In his fuit Ariovistus, qui, naviculam deligatam ad ripam nactus, ea profugit; reliquos omnes consecuti equites nostri interfecerunt.

15. Duæ Ariovisti uxores in ea fuga perierunt; duæ filiæ harum, altera occisa, altera capta est. Caius Valerius Procillus, cum a custodibus in fuga, trinis catenis[26] vinctus, traheretur, in ipsum Cæsarem hostes persequentem incidit. Quæ quidem res Cæsari non minorem quam ipsa victoria voluptatem attulit. Is, se præsente, de se ter sortibus consultum dicebat, utrum igni statim necaretur, an in aliud tempus reservaretur; sortium beneficio se esse incolumem. Item Marcus Mettius ad eum reductus est. Hoc prœlio trans Rhenum nuntiato, Suevi, qui ad ripas Rheni venerant, domum reverti cœperunt. Ubii magnum ex his numerum occiderunt. Cæsar, una æstate duobus maximis bellis confectis, maturius paulo quam tempus anni postulabat, in hiberna in Sequanos exercitum deduxit; hibernis Labienum præposuit; ipse in citeriorem Galliam ad conventus agendos profectus est.

NOTES.

I. FABLES.

1. **domus**: genitive, 4th declension, § 12, 3 (*e*); how does it differ in meaning from **domi**? — **prætereuntem** agrees with **lupum**, object of **vidit**.

2. **subvĕni** (imperative), *help*. — **puero**, etc., *reproached to the boy his rashness;* we should say, *reproached him for his rashness.*

3. **malum** (nominative), understand **me ludificat.**

4. **pellem indutus**, *having put on the skin*, § 52, 3, Remark. — **audissem** for **audivissem**, § 30, 6 (*a*).

5. **tene . . . . sectari**, *you hunt a lion?* see § 57, 8 (*g*). — **ne . . . . quidem**, *not even: whose voice even you could not endure.*

6. **pontificem sacrificaturum** sc. **esse**, *that the priest would*, etc.: see § 67, 1. — **mallem**, *would rather*, § 57, 4 (*c*).

7. **quæ**: for the gender, see § 48, 2.

8. **aucupis**: for the form, see § 11, iii, 1 (*b*).

9. **singulos correptos comedebat**, *caught and ate them, one by one:* see § 72, 3. — **dum capiuntur**, see 58, 2 (*e*): we should use a past tense in English. — **simulavit se esse mortuam**, *pretended to be dead*, § 70, 2 (*d*).

10. **justa**, *justly;* lit. *just things:* see § 41, 1 (*i*); § 47, 4 (*b*).

11. **rata hanc parituram** [**esse**], *supposing that she would lay*, § 67, 1; 72, 1 (*b*).

12. **quo**: generally used instead of **ut** with comparatives, § 64, 1 (*a*).

13. **usque**, *for a while.*

14. **ut fieri solet**, *as often happens.* — **frangerent**: for the tense, see § 58, 10 (*e*). — **quam firma res esset**, *how strong a thing is*, etc.: see § 58, 10 (*d*).

16. **in palude**, see § 56, 1 (*c*), Remark.

II. TALES FROM ROMAN HISTORY.

These extracts have been taken from *Viri Romæ*, a compilation made in the last century from Livy, Valerius Maximus, and other historical writers. The earlier tales, though very famous, are entitled to little credit as history, but contain such traditions as were current at the time of the empire.

1. **rex Albanorum.** The Albans were citizens of Alba Longa (*the long white city*), the chief city of Latium. It was situated on the Alban Lake about twenty miles southeast from Rome. It was at the head of the league of the thirty Latin cities, until supplanted by Rome. — **natu major**, lit. *greater by birth*, i. e. *older;* for the ablative of **natu** see Rule 26; how is **major** compared? what kind of a clause is **qui natu major erat**? — **regnum** (same root with **rego**, *to rule*) is the royal power. — **pulso fratre**, lit. *his brother having been expelled*, or, *when he had expelled his brother;* for the case of **fratre**, see Rule 35. Notice that the noun in the ablative absolute denotes a different person or thing from the subject of the sentence. — **ut eum subole privaret**, this is a final clause depending on **fecit**, and denotes the purpose of the action. Why is **privaret** in the *imperfect* tense? — **ejus** refers to **Numitor**; if **Amulius** had been referred to, **suam** would have been used. — **Vestæ.** The priestesses of Vesta, called the Vestal Virgins, kept alive the sacred fire of Vesta, the divinity of the Hearth. They were six in number, and were never to be married so long as they remained in this service. — **quæ**, i. e. **Rhea Silvia**: translate, *but she:* see § 48, 4. — **quo cognito**, lit. *this being known;* this ablative absolute denotes time: render, *when this was known.* — **Tiberim.** The Tiber rises in the Apennines, and after a course of about two hundred and fifty miles, empties into the Tuscan Sea by two mouths near the town of Ostia, which derives its name from being near the mouth (**ostium**) of the Tiber. Rome was situated about eighteen miles from the mouth of the Tiber. For the termination of the accusative in **-im**, see § 11, i. 3, 1. — **impositos**, etc.: render, *placed the little ones in a skiff* (and) *threw them into the Tiber.* — **relabente flumine**, *when the river fell again.* — **in sicco**, *on dry land.* — What is the plural of **locus**? — **solitudines** (from **solus**, *alone*): for the gender, see § 11, iv. 1 (*b*). — **ubera eorum ori admovit**, *suckled them.* — **matremque se gessit**, *acted as their mother.*

2. **sæpius**, *quite often.* — **pastor regius**, *the king's shepherd*, § 50, 1 (*a*). — **reverteretur**: for the mood, see § 62, 2 (*b*). The clause introduces a reason for Faustulus noticing the fact. — **(eos) conjugi**

dedit educandos, *gave them to his wife to be brought up* (to bring up). The gerundive agrees with **eos**, and expresses a purpose passively: see § 72, 5 (*c*). — **vires**, see § 11, III. 4 (*d*). — **venando,** *in hunting:* see § 73, 3 (*d*). — **primo . . . . deinde . . . . tum,** mark a threefold division of a subject. — **cœperunt**, see § 38, 1 (*a*). — Why is **a** expressed before **quibus**? — What kind of a pronoun is **quis**? The clause **quis esset ejus avus,** *who was his grandfather,* contains an indirect question, Rule 45; the direct question would be, **quis est ejus avus,** *who is his grandfather?* Is this clause subject or object? — **armatis pastoribus,** *having armed the shepherds.* — **Albam,** see Rule 36. — Is **properavit** in the historical perfect (aorist) or the perfect definite?

3. **accusantes,** *accusing him as if he was accustomed to molest,* etc., i. e. *of being in the habit of molesting,* etc. — **a rege,** i. e. *by Amulius, who was now king.* — **haud . . . . agnosceret,** *was not far from recognizing,* etc.: see § 65, 1 (*b*). — **lineamentis,** § 54, 7 (*a*). — **simillimus,** *very like:* see § 17, 1 (*b*). — **animum Numitoris,** etc., *kept the mind of Numitor anxious;* **anxium** agrees with **animum.** — **condiderunt,** why plural? see § 49, 1. — **contentio,** what gender? — **uter,** *which of the two;* this is an indirect question depending on the verb implied in **contentio.** — **adhibuere auspicia: auspicia** (**avis** and **specio**) means divination by means of birds; **augurium** (**avis,** and an old verb **gurio** from which comes our word *garrulous*) had nearly the same meaning. — **prior,** § 17, 3, an adjective agreeing with **Remus,** where we should use an adverb; in place of the ordinal adverbs, **prius, primo, posterius,** the corresponding adjectives are often used, § 47, 6. — **Romam,** etc., *he called* (the city) *Rome.* — **ut . . . . muniret,** *that he might fortify it by laws sooner than by walls;* **antequam** and **priusquam** are often separated. Why is **muniret** in the imperfect subjunctive? what is the object of **edixit**? — **ne quis,** *that no one:* when a purpose is expressed, **ne quis** is used instead of **ut nemo,** *that no one;* **ne ullus** for **ut nullus,** *that none;* **ne unquam** for **ut nunquam,** *that never;* **ne usquam** for **ut nusquam,** *that nowhere.* — **vallum,** *earthen rampart.* — **quod,** *this;* it relates to the clause **edixit,** etc. — **sic . . . . mea,** *whoever shall leap over my walls shall be thus affected with evil;* the subject of **afficietur** is understood, the *antecedent* of **quicumque; afficietur, transiliet,** see § 59, 1 (*a*). — **solus**: for the inflection, see § 16, 1 (*b*).

On the death of Romulus, Numa Pompilius was elected king. He is said to have been the author of the religious institutions of Rome; he instituted the pontiffs who had the general superintendence of religion, and the augurs who consulted the will of the gods. Numa was succeeded by Tullus Hostilius during whose reign a war broke out between Rome and Alba Longa.

1. **erant**, *there were;* **trigemini** is the subject. — **cum iis agunt reges**, *the kings treat with these.* — **ut . . . . ferro**, *that they should fight with the sword each for his own country;* **quisque** is in apposition with **fratres**; sometimes the verb agrees with **quisque** instead of the proper subject-word; why subjunctive? why present tense? — **ea lege**, *on these terms.* — **ut unde . . . .** lit. *that whence victory* (should be), *there it also should empire be;* **unde** is a relative adverb, and has **ibi** for its antecedent. — Why is **esset** subjunctive? — **ităque**, *therefore;* **ita-que**, *and so.* — **infestis armis**, *with presented arms.* — **terni**: this distributive numeral implies, *three on each side.* — **animos**, *the courage.*

2. **ut**, *when.* — **concursu**, § 54, 10. — **consertis manibus**, *with their hands woven together,* i. e. in hand-to-hand conflict. — **alius super alium**, *one upon the other.* — **ad casum**, *at the disaster.* — **gaudio**, why ablative? — **exercitus** (**exerceo**, *to exercise*) is the drilled army; **agmen** (*to lead*), an army on the line of march; **acies**, an army drawn up in line of battle. — **deserebat**, *was on the point of deserting.* — **tota**: for inflection, see § 16, 1 (*b*): give the English derivative. — **Horatium**: for vocative of names in **ius**, see § 10, 4 (*c*). — **circumsteterunt**, see § 52, 1 (*d*). — **integer** (**in**, *not*, **tango**, *to touch*), *unhurt.* — **tribus**, why dative? — **secuturos**, *when they should follow:* see § 72, 4 (*a*). — **aggrederetur**, why *imperfect* subjunctive? — **aliquantum spatii**, *some* (of) *distance*, Rule 10. — **pugnatum est**, *they fought* (lit. *it was fought*, or, *the fighting took place*). — **non**, *not*, is the usual negative; **ne** is used in wishes, prohibitions, and purposes; **haud** is used with adjectives and adverbs, and in the phrase **haud nescio an**. — **loco** has in the plural **loci** and **loca**: see § 14, 2 (*c*). — **ut**, what kind of a conjunction? why is it followed by the *present* subjunctive? — **opem**, the nom. of this word is not used. — **posset**, see § 62, 2, 3 (*c*).

3. **singuli**, *one on each side.* — **supererant**, see **supersum**. — **alterius** limits **corpus** and **animus**. — **fessum** agrees with **corpus**. — **bellum** (from **duellum, duo**), *war;* **prœlium**, *an engagement, action;* **pugna** (root **pug**, whence **pugno**), *any kind of a contest or battle;* **acies**, *a pitched battle.* — **sustinentem**, a participle agreeing with **eum** understood: translate, *kills him while he can scarcely hold up his arms.* — **jacentem**, *as he lies prostrate.* — **domum**, Rule 36. — **princeps**: in the place of the ordinal adverbs, **prius, primum, posterius**, the corresponding adjectives are often used when they belong to a noun in the sentence. — **cui**, dative after **obvia**, see § 51, 2, *his sister met him.* — **quæ**, see § 48. — **uni**, why dative? — **ex Curiatiis** for **Curiatiorum**, see § 52, 2, Rem. — **viso**, what does this participle denote? — **paludamento**, why ablative? This was the military cloak worn by officers; the **sagum** was worn by the common soldiers. — **juveni**, see § 51, 7 (*a*). — **comploratio**, rule for the gender?

— **abi**, from **abeo.** — **oblita** agrees with **tu**, the subject of **abi.** — **eat,** *let her perish.* — **hostis,** *a foreign enemy in war;* **inimicus,** *a private personal enemy;* **adversarius,** *any opponent.*

4. **atrox** agrees with **facinus.**—**in jus,** *for trial.*—**lictor.** The lictors were the attendants who walked before the king (afterwards the higher magistrates). Their duties were to arrest the guilty, and punish them by beheading or scourging; they carried the **fasces,** —axes bound in a bundle of rods; the axes, as symbols of beheading and scourging. — **provocavit: provoco** was to appeal to the people for life; **appello,** *to appeal* to a magistrate. — **interea** and **interim** both mean *in the mean time;* **interea** refers to an event continuing during the *whole* of the time, **interim** to one occurring at some time in the interval. — **jure,** *rightfully.* — Distinguish between the meaning of **ne, non, haud.** — To whom does **se** refer? — **peractis,** see **perago;** *when certain sacrifices had been performed;* **transmisit per viam,** *placed over the road.*

III. LIFE OF POMPEY.

1. **suo exercitui,** *to his army.* — **bello civili,** i. e. the war between Marius and Sulla, B. C. 83-82. — distinguish between **ităque** and **itaque,** see § 4, 2 (*c*). — **facta est: fio,** in the sense of *to be made* is used as the passive of **facio.** — **conspiratio:** for the gender, see § 11, IV. (*b*). — **quidam,** see Lesson XXV. — **contubernalis,** *a tent-mate.* It was the custom for young men of rank, who wished to learn the art of war, to accompany a general on his campaign; these were called **contubernales.** — **eum occidendum,** *to kill him;* the participle in **-dus** may be translated in three ways: (1), like the present infinitive active or passive, see § 72, 5 (*c*); (2), see § 40, (*b*); (3), see § 73, 2. — **incenderent,** see 62, (*b*) & (*c*). — **quæ,** see § 48, 4. — **cœnanti,** (while) *supping.* — **nihil,** *in no respect,* § 52, 3. — **solito hilarius,** *with more than his usual hilarity.* — **eadem .... usus est,** *he used the same affability as before;* **qui** after **idem** is translated *as.* — **districto ense,** *with drawn sword.* — **stragula,** *the covering of his bed.* — **suo duci,** *to their leader:* **suo** here refers not to the subject of the sentence, but to the **milites** the object of **placavit** and **reconciliavit.**

2. **partes,** *the party.* — **secutus,** see **sequor.** — **ita egit,** *so acted:* see **ago.** — **diligeretur,** see § 65, 1. — **annos .... natus,** *when he was twenty-three years old.* — **statimque .... exstitit,** *and immediately became*

a skilful leader. — **nullus . . . . tædio,** *no labor was irksome to him.* — **saltu,** *in leaping.* — **aut . . . . adjunxit,** *he either routed or joined them to himself:* see **fundo.** — **quem . . . . audivit,** *when Sulla heard that he was approaching him.* — **egregiamque . . . . aspexit,** *and saw his distinguished youth* (i. e. Pompey) *under his standard.* — **imperator,** *as imperator.* — **ei venienti,** *when he approached* (him). — **quem,** *this.* — **tribuebat,** *he was accustomed to bestow:* see § 58, 3.

3. **profectus est,** see **proficiscor.** — **ut . . . . reciperet,** *that he might retake it* (as it) *had been taken possession of,* etc. — **quem . . . . jussit,** *Pompey commanded that he should be led to punishment, after that he had sharply rebuked him:* for the construction after **jubeo,** see § 57, 8 (*d*), end; § 70, 2. — **Siculæ . . . . principem,** *the chief of a certain Sicilian city.* — **in,** *against.* — **animadvertere,** *to take measures.* — **si . . . . plecteret,** *if he punished all on account of the fault of one;* in direct discourse, **Tu inique facies, si ob culpam unius omnes plectes,** see 59, 4. — **interroganti Pompeio,** *when Pompey asked.* — **ego . . . . qui,** *it was I . . . . who.* — **libera voce,** *with his bold speech.* — **pepercit,** see **parco,** see § 30, 3 (*d*), 1.

4. **qui . . . . favebat,** *who favored the party of Marius.* — **adolescens,** (though being) *a youth.* — **a Sulla,** *by Sulla.* — **quibus,** *by whom.* — **dimittere,** *to disband.* — **cum . . . . legione,** *with only one legion.* — **id . . . . Pompeius,** *Pompey was displeased at this.* — **revertenti,** *when he returned.* — **obviam ivit,** *came out to meet him.* — **lætus,** *with joy,* lit. *joyful:* see § 47, 6. — **nihilominus . . . . restitit,** *nevertheless he opposed Pompey seeking a triumph:* see Hand-book under the word *triumph.* — **cognomen,** see § 15, 1 and 2. — **a proposito,** *from his purpose.* — **ausus est,** see § 35, 2. — **quo . . . . minui,** *by this saying he insinuated that the power of Pompey was decreasing;* for the infinitive see § 58, 11. — **triumphet,** *let him triumph:* see § 68, 1.

5. **Metello . . . . Pompeius,** *Pompey was appointed as a colleague to Metellus,* etc. — **subiit,** *he incurred.* — **vasta . . . . magnitudine,** *of great size of body.* — **fecisset,** see § 62, 2 (*b*). — **multis . . . . concurrentibus,** *when many rushed upon him.* — **fugientibus,** *who fled.* — **præter spem,** *contrary to his expectation.* — **illi . . . . caperent,** *they captured,* etc. — **illorum . . . . effugit,** *escaped from their hands.* — **laboranti,** *hard pressed.* — **fertur,** (Sertorius) *is said.* — **fusus est,** see **fundo.** — **supervenisset,** *had come up:* see § 59, 3 (*b*). — **puerum,** i. e. Pompey; he was only thirty years old when he was sent into Spain to conduct the war against Sertorius.

6. **infestarent,** see § 62, 2 (*b*). — **ad eos opprimendos,** see § 64, 2 (4). Pompey was appointed to this command in the year B. C. 67. In consequence of the Social and Civil Wars, and the absence of a fleet in

the Mediterranean Sea, the number of pirates had so increased that they often plundered the cities on the coast, and cut off all communication between Rome and the provinces. — **nimiæ viri potentiæ**, *the too great power of the man.* — **imprimis**, *especially.* — **qui cum**, *when he.* — **esse . . . . tribuenda**, *that Cneius Pompey is indeed*, etc. — **si quid**, *if anything.* — **ecquem**, *whom.* Is this the direct or indirect discourse? **brevi**, *in a short time.* — **prædones . . . . fudit**, *he conquered and routed the pirates in many places.* — **acceptos**, *when he had received.* — **fudit**, see **fundo.**

7. Give the synonymes of **proficiscor.** — Pompey was appointed in B. C. 66 to the command of the war against Mithridates in place of Lucullus. — **opportuna**, *suitable.* — **castris**, *in his camp:* see § 55, 3 (*f*). — **noctu . . . . ignotis**, *but by night it was not safe*, etc. — **luna . . . . adjumento**, *the moon was a great assistance*, etc. — **nam . . . . pertinebant**, *for since the Romans had this behind them, the shadows of their bodies being cast forward quite a distance, extended even to the front ranks of the enemy.* — **regii milites**, *the soldiers of the king.* — **Pontus**, for the boundaries: see Hand-book. — why is **a** expressed before **patre**? — **timebat**, etc., *he feared for his own life:* see § 51, 2 (3). — **quod . . . . subiret**, *and when it* (the poison) *operated too slowly.*

8. **partes**, *the party*: what does this relative clause denote? see § 63, 1 and 2. — **quem . . . . erexit**, *yet he raised him up kneeling before him.* Give the synonymes of **regnum.** — **æque pulchrum judicans**, *judging it to be equally noble.* — **rebus Asiæ compositis**, *when the affairs of Asia had been settled:* see **compono.** — **ut**, *as.* — **tertium . . . . duxit**, *he celebrated a third triumph within two days*, i. e. three triumphs in the space of two days. — **hic triumphus**, *this triumph*, i. e. this series of triumphs considered as a whole. — **quam quod**, *than because.* — **tribus triumphis**, *for three triumphs.* — **tres . . . . devictæ**, *three parts of the world being conquered.* — **quod**: what is the antecedent of **quod**? what is **contingo** compounded of? Syn. **Accidit** is used of any unexpected event; **contingit**, of what occurs by the gift of fortune, generally something favorable; **evenit**, *it turns out*, is used of what is either lucky or unlucky. — **ex**, *on account of.* — **felix opinione**, *in the estimation.* — **si . . . . habuisset**, *if he had had the same end of life as of glory.*

9. **orta est**, see **orior.** — **hic**, *the former;* **ille**, *the latter.* — **exarsit**, see § 36 (*c*). — **quem . . . . fudit**, *Cæsar followed and routed him with his army at Pharsalia:* the battle of Pharsalia was fought in B. C. 48. — **victus . . . . profugit**, *after Pompey had been conquered he fled . . . . to whom he had been appointed tutor by the senate.* — **sub oculis**, *before the eyes.* — **delatum est**, see **defero.** — **qui . . . . fudit**, *who when he saw this, shed tears.* — **illud . . . . curavit**, *he took care to have it burned*, etc.

10. **is . . . . exitus,** *such was the end of the life of a most renowned man,* etc. — **cum . . . . medicus,** *when his physician ordered him when sick.* — **negarent . . . . reperiri,** *but his servant said that that bird could not be found anywhere in the summer time.* — **nisi apud Lucullum,** *unless at the house of Lucullus.* — **aliam . . . . apponi,** *he commanded that another bird which was easy to be procured should be set before him.*

11. **Posidonium.** Posidonius was a Stoic philosopher. Why is **audire** in the infinitive? — **voluit . . . . visere,** *Pompey wished at least to call upon him;* what kind of a verb is **viso**? (See Gr. foot of p. 99.) — **quem . . . . salutavit,** *when he saw and saluted him.* — **moleste se ferre,** *that he grieved.* — **nec . . . . efficiat,** *neither will I allow that the pain of my body shall cause that,* etc. — **cum . . . . pungeret,** *but when sometimes the pain afflicted him severely.* — **nihil agis,** lit. *you accomplish nothing,* i. e. *it is of no use.* — **quamvis,** *although.*

IV. LIFE OF CÆSAR.

1. **annum . . . . decimum,** *being in his sixteenth year.* — **paulo post duxit uxorem,** *a little while after he married Cornelia;* **ducere uxorem,** *to marry,* is said of the husband only. — **cujus . . . . inimicus,** *since her father was unfriendly to Sulla:* how does **inimicus** differ from **hostis**? — **ut eam dimitteret,** *to divorce her,* lit. *that he should divorce her.* — **bonis,** *property:* see § 47, 4 (*b*). — **cum . . . . quæreretur,** *when he was even sought for in order to be put to death:* what kind of a clause is this? why imperfect subj.? on what verb does it depend? — **mutata veste:** what does this participle denote? how is the ablative absolute rendered? — **quartanæ,** supply **febris,** lit. *sick with the disease of quartan ague;* **laboret,** why subj.? — **per proximos suos,** *by means of his relations:* for the use of **per,** see § 54, 4 (*b*). — **qui . . . . denegasset,** *when he would have refused it to the distinguished men who begged for it:* **denegasset,** see § 62, 2 (*b*). — **aliquando . . . . futurum,** *will ruin* (lit. *be for a ruin*) *the party of the aristocracy,* etc.: give the synonymes of **cupio**; of **puer.**

2. Sulla died B. C. 78 — **mortuo,** see 35, 1 (*a*). — **secedere,** *to retire.* — **per otium,** *at* (his) *leisure.* — **dicendi,** *of oratory.* — **operam daret,** *might give* (his) *attention.* — SYN. **maneo,** *remain* whether for a long or short time; **commŏror,** *remain* for some time in a place, *sojourn;* **habito,** *dwell permanently.* — **se gessit,** *he conducted himself.* —

ut . . . esset: does this clause denote purpose or result? — why is esset in the impf. subj.? — Give the syn. of **interim**. — **ad . . . . pecunias**, *to get money:* for the gerundive denoting purpose, see § 64, 2. — **servus, mancipium, famulus**, all mean *a slave;* **servus**, as one politically inferior; **mancipium**, a salable commodity; **famulus**, a family possession. — SYN. **comes** (**con, eo**), *companion*, a *fellow-traveller;* **socius**, a *companion*, member of the same society; **sodalis**, a *companion* in amusement or pleasure. — **quibus redimeret**: does this relative clause denote purpose or result? — **Miletus**, a flourishing city of Ionia. — **proxime aberat**, *was at the nearest distance off.* — SYN. **pœna**, general word for *punishment;* **supplicium** (**supplico**, *kneel*), a *severe punishment* (the criminal kneeling for the blow); **cruciatus** (**crux**, *cross*), *torture*, as of one on the cross; **tormentum** (**torqueo**), a *racking torture*, to extort confession.

3. **Quæstor . . . . factus**: **fio**, in the sense of, *to be made, appointed*, is used as the passive of **facio**. — **inter se**, *together*. — **concupiscebat**, *desired earnestly, coveted;* see § 59, 3. — **in ore habebat**, lit. *had in his mouth*, i. e. kept repeating. — **colas**, see § 68, 1. — **quod**, see § 48, 2. — **memorabilis**: a partitive genitive could not be used after **nihil**, only neuter adjectives of the second declension are so used: see § 50, 2, Rem. — **orbis terrarum** must be used in preference to **terra**, when there is a decided reference to other lands.

4. **in . . . . honoribus** *in soliciting the favor of the plebeians, and in canvassing for the magistracies* (honors). — **dicebat . . . . sestertium**, lit. *he used to say that there was need to himself of* 1,000 *times* 100,000 **sestertii**, — 100,000,000 **sesterces**, or nearly $4,000,000; **sestertium**, gen. plur. used for **sestertiorum**: see § 85, 3. — **ut haberet nihil**: after he had freed himself from debt, there would be nothing left of his own. — **consulatum**: every Roman citizen who aspired to the consulship had to pass through a regular gradation of public offices, and the age in which he was eligible to each was fixed by the Lex Annalis, B. C. 179, as follows: for the Quæstorship, which was the first of the magistracies, one must be twenty-seven years of age; for the Ædileship, thirty-seven; for the Prætorship, forty; and for the Consulship, forty-three. See Hand-book, p. 84-87. — **inito . . . . tulit** (see **ineo**), *when he had entered upon the office Cæsar proposed*, etc. — **egenis civibus**, *among needy citizens*. — **ut . . . . obsisteret**, *that he might oppose the law's being enacted.* — **foro**, *from the forum.* The Forum was situated between the Capitoline and Palatine hills; it was the chief place of public business. There were other **fora**, but this was distinguished as Forum Romanum, or as Forum, being the most important. — **domi se continere**, *to remain at home.* — **curia**, *from the senate-house:* **senatus**, *the senate*, either the senators or the place where they met; **curia**, *the building where the senators assembled.* — **quidam**, *some.* — **non ut mos erat**, *not as was the*

custom; **mos,** *an established custom,* especially of a nation; **consuetūdo,** *habit,* which results in a settled usage (**mos**); **cæremonia,** *a religious ceremony.* — **consulibus Cæsare et Bibulo.** *In the consulship of Cæsar and Bibulus.* The year was generally designated at Rome in this way; the name of the consuls for the year being put in the ablative absolute with **consulibus.** This was the year B. C. 59. In this case the two names (**nomen, i. e.** Julius; **cognomen,** Cæsar) of Cæsar are used: see § 15.

5. A Consul after his term of office expired was often sent as proconsul to govern a province; by Sulla's laws a consul must remain in Italy during his term of office, and then might be sent to govern a province. Cæsar departed to his province in B. C. 58. — **gessit . . . . fere,** *during the nine years in which he was in power he accomplished in substance the following.* — **primus Romanorum,** *first of the Romans.* — **ponte fabricato,** *by constructing a bridge.* — **maximis . . . . cladibus,** *he made a great slaughter.* — **iis,** *from them.* — **quo in bello,** *in this war.* — **inclinante in fugam,** *giving way.* — Syn. **Scutum,** *any shield;* **clipeus,** *a round shield;* **parma,** similar to **clipeus,** but smaller, *a buckler;* **ancile,** *an oval shield.* — **in primam aciem,** *to the front.* — **terga vertentem,** *turning his back* (to the enemy), *fleeing.* — **illic sunt,** *there are those.* — **animos,** *courage.*

6. **adhuc,** *still.* — **ut . . . . absenti,** *that it should be permitted to him although absent;* what is the subject of **liceret**? It was a law that every candidate for the consulship should appear before the magistrate, and have his name entered on the official list of candidates before election. — **vindicaturus,** *to avenge;* see § 72, 4. — **Brundisium,** a town in Calabria, was the port from which those going from Rome to Greece or the East embarked; **Dyrrachium,** a city on the coast of Illyricum. — **cessantibus copiis,** *his forces delaying;* what does this participle denote? — **flante,** *blowing.* — **in altum,** *out into the deep sea.* — **dirigi,** *to be steered.* — **cederet,** *would yield.* Cæsar had sailed from Brundisium with only 20,000 men. Owing to the vigilance of the enemy the rest of Cæsar's army was unable to follow him. His position was thus critical; cut off from the rest of his army, and threatened by a force three times superior to his own. In his impatience he attempted to sail in a fisherman's boat across the Adriatic to Brundisium, for his reinforcements, but the storm compelled him to turn back. In a short time the remainder of the army succeeded in crossing; at the battle of Pharsalia (in Thessaly), Pompey's army was totally defeated. (B. C. 48.)

7. **fugientem,** (him) *fleeing.* — **eumque . . . . fuisse,** *and on the way he learned that he had been killed.* — Syn. **Cognosco,** *learn* (something beforehand); **agnosco,** *recognize* (something before known. — **Ptolemæo,** *against Ptolemy.* The war against Ptolemy is called the Alexandrine

war. — **quattuor .... profligavit,** *but he conquered him in one battle within four hours after he had come;* the relative **quibus** is in the ablative agreeing with its antecedent **horis.** — **inter triumphandum,** *during his triumph.* After a successful campaign, the victorious general was awarded, by a decree of the senate, the honor of a triumph. He entered the city in a chariot drawn by four horses, preceded by the captives and spoils of war, and followed by his soldiers. After passing along the **Via Sacra,** he ascended to the temple of Jupiter Capitolinus to offer sacrifice. **Pompeianarum partium,** *of the Pompeian party.* The battle was fought at Thapsus, in Africa, in B. C. 46. — **in Hispania:** the two sons of Pompey, Cneius and Sextus, had collected a large army in Spain. After a hard-fought battle Cæsar completely defeated them at Munda, (B. C. 45).

8. **cœpit,** a perfect, sometimes translated like the present, § 58, 5 (*d*), Rem. — **quendam,** for **quemdam.** — **assurgeret,** why imperfect subj.? — **ei .... sedenti,** *on him sitting in the golden chair.* — **regium,** *royal.* — **a sexaginta .... viris,** *by more than sixty men;* **amplius,** see § 54, 5. — **conjuratum est,** *a conspiracy was formed:* see § 39, (*c*). — **Idibus Martiis,** *on the Ides of March,* i. e. the 15th. — **assidentem ..... circumsteterunt,** *they stood around him sitting, under pretence of paying honor.* — **quasi .... rogaturus,** *as if to ask something.* — **clamantem,** sc. **eum,** i. e. **Cæsarem.** — **arreptum,** *which he had seized.* — **quem .... habebat,** *whom he had regarded as his son.*

9. **erat .... statura,** *Cæsar was of,* etc., see § 54, 7 (*a*). — **ægre ferebat,** *grieved* (on account); **quod .... obnoxia,** *it was often the subject for the jokes of his slanderers.* — **sibi,** *to him.* — **laureæ gestandæ,** *of wearing a crown of laurel.* — **eum .... fuisse,** *that he was.* — **inimici:** give the synonymes. — **ne** and **quidem** enclose the emphatic word as in the text; see § 76, 3 (*b*). — **ad .... rempublicam,** *to overturn the republic.* — **anteibat,** see **anteeo.** — **detectum,** *uncovered:* see **detego.** — **sive .... esset,** *whether it was sunshine or rain.* SYN. **Pluvia,** *rain* (general word); **imber,** *rain* (heavy, pouring shower); **nimbus,** *rain* (from dark clouds). — **longissimas vias.** Cæsar was noted for the rapidity of his movements; he is said to have travelled at the rate of one hundred Roman miles per day, equal to about ninety-two English miles. — **innixus .... utribus,** *resting upon inflated bags.*

V. LIFE OF CATO.

1. **domo,** what kind of a noun is **domus?** what is the meaning of the genitives **domŭs** and **domi?** — **de civitate,** i. e. *to obtain the right of citizenship:* full citizenship consisted of private and public rights: see Hand-book under **Civitas.** In how many ways can a purpose be expressed in Latin? Give the synonymes of **impetro.** — **se id facturum,** *that he would do that.* — **in excelsam . . . . levatum,** *after he had taken him to a high part of the house.* — **obtemperaret,** *should comply with.* — **hoc metu,** *by this fear,* i. e. *through fear of this.* — **exclamasse,** for **exclamavisse,** see § 30, 6 (*a*). — **gratulemur,** *let us congratulate.* SYN. **Gratulor,** *congratulate, wish one joy;* **congratulor** is used in the same sense as **gratulor,** but generally of many persons. — **hunc esse,** *that he is.* — **si . . . . esset,** *for if he were a senator.* — **ne . . . . quidem,** *not even to hope;* see § 59, 3 (*b*).

2. **in atrio:** in the **atrium** the Roman received his friends; here were the images of his household gods, and of his ancestors. About the **atrium** were the various rooms of the house. — **seque . . . . Cassius,** *and he showed that he was of the same opinion with another boy,* (lit. *of which another boy was*) *Cassius by name.* — **se . . . . facturum,** *that he . . . . would do the same thing.* — **impegit,** see **impingo.** Give the synonymes of **sodalis.**

3. **insignis . . . . benevolentia,** *the affection of Cato towards his brother was remarkable, and should be held up for imitation.* — **quærenti tertio,** *to one asking him the third time.* **ille . . . . amor,** *that remarkable affection of Cato towards his brother:* see § 20, 2 (*b*). — **ei . . . . gerebat,** *he gratified him in all things.* — **indoles,** *the natural disposition.*

4. **voluntaria . . . . fecit,** *served voluntarily as a soldier;* on what does the clause **ne eum desereret** depend? what is the subject of **accidit?** — **quod,** *this.* — **licet,** *although.* — **Thessalonicæ.** A city of Macedonia. — **cum . . . . servis,** *with only two friends and three servants.* — **præter . . . . evasit,** *contrary to his expectation he escaped unharmed.* — **defunctum vita,** *dead;* see § 54, 6 (*d*). — **totum se tradidit,** *he gave himself wholly up.* — **mortui . . . . extulit,** *he interred the body of the deceased with as magnificent funeral rites as possible.* — **vela facturus,** *being about to sail:* lit. *to make sail.* — **animam . . . . respondit,** *he replied that he would,* etc. — **solvit,** *loosed* (sc. **navem**) *the ship from her moorings.*

5. **quæstor,** *as questor:* the quæstors had charge of the finances of the state, i. e. to receive the revenues, and make the payments for the military and civil services. At first there were only two, but with the

conquests of the republic, the number was increased to forty. — **Cyprum**: give the situation of Cyprus. — **heres**, *as an heir.* — **summa .... redacta est**, *the amount brought back was far greater than any one could have hoped:* **redacta**, see **redigo**. — **singulis vasis**, *to each vessel;* **vas** in the plural is of the second declension; **vasa, orum**. — **si .... esset**, *if by chance the ship were sunk.* — **Catoni .... effusa est**, *the senate .... poured out to meet Cato on his return.* — **actæ sunt**, *were given.* — **prætura .... data**, *the prætorship was given to him, and contrary to custom the right of beholding the games, although clothed in the prætexta.* — **quem**, *this.* — **iniquum esse affirmans**, *affirming that it was unjust:* with what does **iniquum** agree?

6. **extrahi curia**, *to be dragged forth from the senate-house.* — **at .... remisit**, *but he abated nothing from the boldness of his language.* — **sed .... via**, *but even on the way to prison.* — **ut .... adversarentur**, *that they should oppose those doing such things.* — **quod .... discederet**, *because he departed from the senate, although it was not yet dismissed.* — **sese demitteret**, *condescended.* — **quod .... intellexit**, *when he saw that this was hoped for by himself in vain.* — **qui .... demitteret**; what does this relative clause denote?

7. **eoque victo**, *and when he was conquered.* — **exercitus reliquias**, *the remnants of his army.* — **cum .... imperium**, *but when the chief power was conferred upon him by the soldiers.* — **vir consularis**. One who had been a consul was called **consularis**. — **Scipione .... devicto**, *even when Scipio was conquered.* — **et .... iturus**, *and being about to go to bed.* — **dixit illum**, *he said that.* — **quod .... eripuisset**, *because he had taken from him,* etc.: for the subjunctive see § 63, 2.

VI. LIFE OF CICERO.

1. **equestri genere**, *of equestrian family.* — **Arpini**, *at Arpinum.* — **ex .... unus**, *one of his ancestors;* see § 50, 2 (*e*), Rem. — **sitam**, *placed,* see **sino**. — **inditum**, *bestowed upon.* — **cum .... verteretur**, *when this was cast as a reproach by some to Cicero;* see § 51, 5. — **dabo operam**, *I will strive.* — **vincat**, *shall surpass.* — **quibus .... informari**, *by which his boyhood was accustomed to be trained to learning.* — **ut .... domum**, *that his equals returning from school standing around him in the midst,* etc. — **pueri fama**, *by the reputation of their boy.* — **in .... ventitabant**, *kept going into the school for literature;* see § 36, (*b*). — **stomachum movebat**, *stirred the anger of.* — **tribuerent**, why subjunctive? Give the English derivatives.

2. **libertum**, *a freedman:* **libertinus** is the general word for freedman, but when used with the name of his former master the form is **libertus**; the attack was in his speech for Roscius Amerinus, delivered in B. C. 80. — **ex .... invidiam**, *fearing the ill-will of him.* — **ubi .... usus est**, *where he employed Molo .... as teacher.* — **nullius .... quæstura**, *but the quæstorship of no one:* see § 16, 1 (*b*). — **ingentem .... vim**, *a large amount of corn.* — **majores .... detulerunt**, *they conferred greater honors*, etc.

3. **Catilinæ**: the conspiracy of Catiline was crushed in the year B. C. 63. — **in petitione consulatus**, *in his canvass for the consulship.* — **cum .... constituerat**, *with many noble men he determined to kill Cicero*, etc. — **Roma**, *from Rome.* — **quem**, *him.* — **ex medio itinere**, *from the midst of his journey.* — **non .... genui**, *I did not beget thee for Catiline against thy country*, etc.: for **genui**, see **gigno.**

4. **adeo .... dimicatum**, *so fiercely did they fight*, lit. *it was fought.* — **quem .... locum**, *the place which each one held while fighting, this, his life being lost, he covered with his body.* — **inter .... cadavera**, *among the bodies of those whom he had killed.* — **cecidit**, *fell;* see **cado.** — **adeo .... plebis**, *so that a certain one of the tribunes of the plebeians forbade him when going out of office to speak to the people.* — **indicta causa**, *their cause not having been pleaded.* — **sed .... permiserit**, *but it was only permitted to him to give the accustomed oath.* — **mea unius opera**, *by the aid of me alone;* § 46, 2 (*c*); 47, 5 (*b*).

5. **reus factus est**, *was prosecuted.* — **vestem mutavit.** The senate wore mourning attire, such as a person about to be tried for a criminal offence. — **cum**, *although.* — **urbe**, *from the city.* — **sua causa**, *on his account.* — **proficiscentem**, *him departing.* — **ut .... interdiceretur**, *that Marcus Tullius should be forbidden the use of fire and water*, i. e. forbidden to obtain the bare necessities of life, and therefore obliged to go into exile; see § 51, 2 (*f*). — **obviam .... itum est**, *all went out to meet him when returning:* **ei**, see § 51, 2 (2). — **partes**, *the party.* — **veniam**, *pardon.* — **quo interfecto**, *when he was killed.* — **ut .... opponeret**, *in order that he might place him against Antony* [who was] *disturbing the republic.*

6. **transversis itineribus**, *by cross-roads.* — **quæ .... aberat**, *which was very near the sea.* — **transiturus**, *for the purpose of crossing;* see § 72, 4 (end). — **in altum provectum**, *having put out to sea.* — **retulissent**, see **referro.** — **in patria sæpe servata**, *in the country* (which I have) *often preserved.* — **mox .... percussoribus**, *presently his murderers coming nearer.* — **qua**, *in which.* — **eosque .... quod**, *that they quietly should endure what.* — **prominenti .... præcisum**, *then leaning out of the litter, and offering his neck unmoved, his head was cut off.* — **positum**, *was placed.* — **se .... læsam**, *that she had been injured by Cicero;* see

lædo. — **in genua**, *upon her knees.* — **extractam . . . . confixit**, *pierced the tongue torn out, with a needle;* **acu**, see § 12, 2.

7. **scurra consularis**, *the jesting consular.* — **accinctum**, *equipped.* — **juniorem . . . . erat**, *that she was younger than she was.* — **dictitabat . . . . habere**, *kept saying that she was only thirty years old:* what kind of a verb is **dictitabat**? how formed? — **cui**, *to her.* — **audio**, see § 58, 2 (*d*). — **altero . . . . ultima**, *the other consul having died on the last of December.* — **Caninium . . . . renuntiaverat**, *declared Caninius consul at the seventh hour for the remaining part of the day;* this was about one o'clock in the afternoon. As the new consuls entered upon office on the first of January, Caninius was consul for only a part of one day. — **salutatum**, *to salute him.* — **festinemus**, *let us hasten.* — **mirifica vigilantia**, *of remarkable vigilance;* see § 54, 7.

VII. LIFE OF BRUTUS.

1. **ex . . . . oriundus**, *descended from that family which had expelled the Tarquins from Rome.* — **Sullæ partibus**, *the party of Sulla.* — **cum . . . . simultates**, *had borne a severe grudge against him.* — **dolorem . . . . posthabuit**, *he regarded his own resentment less than the advantage of the republic.* — **regnum affectare**, *to aim at the royal power.* — **præsenti statu**, *at the present state of affairs.* — **subscripsere**, *wrote under;* perfect, third person plural. — **primi Bruti**, i. e. Lucius Junius Brutus who had expelled the Tarquins from Rome. — **hic**, i. e. Cæsar. — **tribunali**, *on the judgment-seat;* notice that neuter nouns in **e**, **al**, and **ar** have **i** in the ablative.

2. **pridie quam**, *the day before.* — **cultellum tonsorium**, *a razor;* what kind of a noun is **cultellum**? see § 44, 1 (3). — **eoque . . . . vulneravit**, *this as if by chance slipping from her hands, she wounded herself.* — **tonsoris . . . . præripere**, *to take away the duty of a barber.* The Roman barbers not only shaved and cut the hair, but also pared the nails, etc. — **de industria**, *designedly.* — **an . . . . oppetendam**, *whether there was enough courage in me to seek death;* **esset**, why subjunctive? — **maritus**, see § 46, 2. — **si . . . . cessisset**, *if your design should not turn out according to your desire.* — **mihi**, see § 51, 7 (*d*).

3. **Philippos**: Philippi took its name from its founder, Philip, the father of Alexander the Great. — **uni . . . . præbuit**, *he offered his side to be pierced by one of his companions.* — **ei**, *upon it.* — **ut**, etc., *that he might be buried in it.* — **quod . . . . audivisset**, *when he heard that this*

was afterwards stolen. — **cremati corporis,** *of the body* (after it was) *burned.* — **non .... moderatio,** *the moderation of Octavius towards Brutus was not the same.* — **is .... jussit,** *for he commanded that the head of Brutus, being torn off, should be borne to Rome;* see § 57, 8 (*d*), end.

VIII. LIFE OF AUGUSTUS.

1. **a majore avunculo.** Julius Cæsar, the brother of Julia, the grandmother of Octavianus. — **vacaret,** *he might have leisure* (to attend). —Apollonia was a city of Illyria. It was celebrated as a seat of learning, and thither the nobility of Rome repaired to study the literature and philosophy of Greece. — **Mutinæ,** *at Mutina* (Modena), a city of Cisalpine Gaul. — **cum .... prohiberetur,** *but when he was prevented from entering the city.* — **ut .... faceret,** *in order that he might inform;* **certiorem,** see Rule 2. — **quæ .... deferebantur,** *which was borne under the water of the river by a diver;* see § 54, 4 (*b*). — **ad id,** *for that purpose.* — **summa,** see § 47, 8. — **maxime .... instituisset,** *especially when he had trained the doves to fly thither,* etc.

2. **in .... munere,** *in one of which he performed the duty not only of a leader, but also of a soldier.* — **reconciliata .... gratia,** *a reconciliation being effected with Antony.* — SYN. **Ulciscor,** *revenge from a feeling of anger;* **vindico,** *avenge as an act of justice.* — **qui .... deposcerent,** *to demand the consulship for himself in the name of the army.* — **hic .... feceritis,** *he will act, if you shall not act,* see § 59, 4 (*e*). — **si .... auferetis,** *if in this manner you shall seek the consulship for Cæsar, you will obtain it;* see § 59, 4 (*c*). — **quod .... fuit,** *afterwards this speech was his ruin;* see Rule 20. — **invisus .... amantior,** *for he began to be hateful to Cæsar, because he was too fond of liberty.*

3. **invasit,** *seized upon.* — **novamque .... tabulam,** *a new proscription list.* — **Sullanā,** *than the Sullan* (proscription). — **pepercit,** see **parco,** § 30, 3 (*d*), 1 and 2. — **nomine,** see § 54, 9. — **ut .... proscriberetur,** *in order that as a man he might be proscribed.* — **protinus .... descendit,** *immediately after he descended from the capitol* (built upon the Capitoline hill). — **qui .... objecerat,** *who had exposed his body in front of him.*

4. **Societate:** this was the second triumvirate, an alliance formed between Octavianus, Antony, and Lepidus, B. C. 43. — **quod,** *this.* — **quanquam,** *although.* SYN. — **Æger,** *disordered;* either mentally or physically; **ægrotus, a, um,** *ill, unwell;* **morbidus,** *diseased;* the last

two are used of bodily sickness. — **castris exutus**, *being stripped of his camp;* Rule 28. — **altero . . . . acerbius**, *in the other, as a victor he conducted himself cruelly.* — **sæviit**, *he vented his rage.* — **adjecta . . . . contumelia**, *abusive language being added even to punishment.* — **uni . . . . respondit**, *to one suppliantly beseeching burial he replied.* — **illam**, i. e. **sepulturam.** — Syn. **Volucer** (properly an adjective), *any winged creature*, including *insects;* **avis** and **ales**, *a winged creature;* **avis** is a general word for *bird;* **alites**, are *large birds*, and in the language of the augurs, a bird whose flight was to be interpreted, as distinguished from **ocines**, *birds whose cry furnished the omen.* — **cum . . . . parceretur**, *but when Octavius was willing to grant life to one only, he commanded them to determine by lot which of the two he should spare.* — **pro filio**, *in the place of his son.* — **se . . . . obtulerat**, *offered himself.* — **præ dolore**, *on account of his grief.* — **voluntaria . . . . nece**, *by a voluntary death.* — **morientem**, (while) *dying.*

5. **repudiata**, *being divorced.* — **duxisset uxorem**, *married.* — **centies sestertium**, 100 times 100,000 sesterces, about 400,000 dollars, see § 85, 3. — **Antonio . . . . cœnam**, *she served a magnificent dinner to Antony denying that this was able to be done.* — **tanti**, *of so much.* — **quanti**, *as.* — **irrisa . . . . Antonio**, *therefore she being laughed at by Antony.* — **esset actura**: for sequence of tenses, see § 58, 10. — **auribus**, from **auris.** — **simili**; notice that the ablative retains **i**, and the gen. plur. **ium**, in all neuters ending in **e**, **al**, and **ar.**

6. **Actium**: Actium is really in Acarnania, at the entrance of the **Sinus Ambracius.** This decisive battle was fought September 2, B. C. 31. It completely crushed the republicans, and formed the commencement of the empire. Alexandria: this city was founded by Alexander the Great. — **cum**, *although.* — **necem sibi conscivit**, lit. (*procured death for himself*), *committed suicide.* — **vivam**, *alive.* — **aspidem . . . . curavit**, *took care that an asp should be brought to her in a twig basket among some figs.* — **quod**: what is the antecedent? — **medicos . . . . jussit**, *he commanded the physicians to apply remedies to the wound.* — **Psyllos**, *the Psylli*, a people of Libya, celebrated for their skill in curing the bite of the most venomous serpents by sucking out the poison without injury to themselves. — Syn. **Communico** and **participo**, *give a share of;* **impertio** and **tribuo** mean *give* or *impart*, without implying that any part is retained by the donor. — **frustra**, *in vain;* said of one who has gained nothing by his toil; **nequidquam**, *in vain;* of one who has not accomplished his purpose.

7. **clementem se exhibuit**, *proved himself merciful.* — **cum . . . . processisset**, *when he an old man, filthy and clad in ragged garments, proceeded among the captives.* — **non . . . . meriti sumus**, *he does not merit punishment more than I do reward;* see § 49, 1 (*a*). — **me . . . .**

occidi, *that I should be killed.* — **utrum,** *which of the two.* — **moribus:** observe the difference in meaning between the singular **mos,** *custom,* and the plural **mores,** *character,* from which our word *moral* is derived.

8. **Jani gemini,** *of the two-faced Janus:* Janus is represented as an ancient king of Italy. He is said to have sheltered Saturn, when pursued by Jupiter, and to have received from him the power of knowing both the past and future. Hence he is represented with two faces, one looking backward, and the other forward. — **tantummodo,** *only.* — **post .... bellum:** the first Punic war began in B. C. 264, and terminated in B. C. 241. — **delati sunt,** *were conferred.* — **ipse .... cognominatus,** *he was surnamed Augustus.* — **Sextilis:** this month was called *Sextilis,* because the Roman year originally began with March. The year was made to begin with January in B. C. 153. — **eodem nomine,** i. e. *Augustus.* — **biduo,** *for the space of two days.* — **celebrarunt,** see § 30, 6 (*a*). — **maximo consensu,** *with the greatest unanimity.* — **compos .... meorum,** *I have obtained my wishes.*

9. **dictaturam .... deprecatus,** *he begged to be free from the dictatorship.* — **genu nixus,** *kneeling.* — **non semel,** *more than once,* lit. *not once only.* — **sed .... pœniteret,** *but thinking that both as a private citizen he should not be without peril .... that no one should repent of the new state of affairs.* — **tegeret,** *was trying to hide.* — SYN. **Doctus,** *learned, accomplished;* **peritus,** *experienced, skilful;* **eruditus,** *educated.*

10. **summaque .... excipiebat,** *he received those approaching him with the greatest courtesy.* — **libellum .... porrigens,** *offering a petition.* — **putasne .... dare,** *do you suppose that you are giving.* — **eum .... miles,** *at one time a veteran soldier met him.* — **ut sibi adesset,** *that he would aid him.* — **sed .... pugnavi,** *but I myself,* etc. — **erubuit:** see § 36, (*a*). — **ipse .... advocationem,** *come himself as an advocate for him.*

11. **quem,** *which.* — **socius:** give the synonymes and English derivatives. — **ad .... pervenerat,** *to whom nothing from,* etc. — **Antoni,** see § 10, 4 (*c*). — **nihil,** lit. *in no respect,* see Rule 24. — **tantummodo,** *merely.*

12. **parum proficeret** (sc. **corvus**), *made but little progress.* — **opera .... periit,** *my labor and expense have gone for nothing.* — **satis .... habeo,** *I have enough of such saluters at home;* see § 50, 2 (*d*). — **tum .... adjecit,** *then the crow added even those words.* — **quanti** (sc. **tanti**), *for so much .... as.*

13. **Græculus,** *insignificant or paltry Greek:* the Greeks, though better educated, were despised by the Romans as a servile and cowardly race. — **honorificum .... porrigere,** *to offer a short poem as a mark of honor.* — **exaravit,** *he wrote.* — **et .... misit,** *and sent it to the Greek coming to meet him.* — **ille .... gestuque,** *he, on reading it, began to*

praise it, and to manifest his admiration by his voice as well as by his countenance and gesture. — **qua,** *in which.* — **demissa . . . . manu,** *putting his hand into his lean purse.* — **quos . . . . daret,** *to give to the prince.* — **se plus daturum,** etc.: in direct discourse, **plus darem, si plus haberem.** — **summam,** *amount* (of money).

14. **fere nulli,** *to hardly anybody.* — **exceptus . . . . insusurravit,** *therefore having been entertained by a certain one at a very frugal and ordinary dinner, he only whispered this.* — **me . . . . familiarem,** *that I was so intimate with you.* — **patrocinium suscepit,** *undertook the protection.* — **servus:** what are the synonymes?

15. **rumpente . . . . cantu,** *the frequent screeching of an owl interrupting his sleep.* — **liberari . . . . cupere,** *that earnestly desired to be free from.* — **prehendendam:** in what three ways may the participle in **dus** be translated?

16. **Augustus . . . . admisit,** *Augustus did not easily form friendships.* — **imprimis . . . . Mæcenătem,** *above all he was intimate with Mæcenas.* — **qua . . . . valebat,** *which he exercised with the prince.* — **jus . . . . Augustus,** *sometimes when Augustus was administering justice.* — **multos . . . . damnaturus,** *about to condemn many to death.* — **qua lecta,** *this being read.* Syn. — **tento,** *try by feeling, carefully to test;* **experior,** *try by experiment;* **periclitor,** *try,* facing the danger arising from the experiment.

17. **supellex . . . . erat,** *his household furniture also was scarcely of the elegance of that of private persons.* — **cibi . . . . vulgaris,** *his food was common, and very little in amount;* see 50, 1 (*c*).

18. **dormiebat,** *used to sleep.* — **audisset,** for **audivisset.** — **licet,** *although.*

19. **exercitationes campestres,** *exercises in the Campus Martius.* — **transiit,** *he resorted.* — **modo . . . . modo,** *at one time . . . . at another.* — **alea,** *in gaming.* — **id . . . . datum est,** *this was imputed as a fault to him;* what is the antecedent of **id**? — **remisso . . . . animo,** *his mind being giving up to leisure.* — **vitæ . . . . egisset,** *whether he had acted pretty well the comedy of life.* — **edite . . . . applaudite;** words of this kind were usually added at the end of the plays in the theatre; this Augustus applies to his departure from the stage of life. Augustus died in A. D. 14. Nola is in Campania, nearly east from Naples.

IX. THE HELVETIAN WAR.

C. Julius Cæsar was born in the year B. C. 102 (usual date B. C. 100), and was assassinated in the year B. C. 44, at the age of fifty-seven years and eight months. This date of his birth is consistent with the fact that he was Ædile in B. C. 65, Prætor in 62, and Consul in 59; since these offices could not be held by the **Lex Annalis** until one had entered upon the age of thirty-seven, forty, and forty-three respectively.

The Romans had already extended their power over the Greek states of the East, and had virtually subjugated all the peoples that skirted the Mediterranean sea, except the Celtic tribes of the West. Their conquest the Roman people intrusted to Cæsar. His relationship with Marius and Cinna, his refusal to divorce his wife Cornelia, his wanderings during the proscription of Sulla, his bravery at Mitylene and in Cilicia, his defence of the Latin colonies, his brilliant successes in Spain, his liberality and magnanimity, and even his vices endeared him to the people, and all eyes were turned towards him as the leader of the popular party. For a long time the Romans had felt the importance of possessing Gaul, but as yet had made no systematic effort to extend their dominion in that quarter farther than occupying the seaboard between the Alps and Pyrenees (B. C. 118). The climate of Gaul was healthy, the soil rich and fertile, and the intercourse easy by land and sea with Rome. For a long time Roman merchants and farmers had emigrated in great numbers to Gaul, and so disseminated Roman culture and civilization, that many of the tribes could transact business in the Latin language. The centre of this civilization and refinement was the old Greek city Massilia; also the resort of those who had been banished from the capital. The merchants stationed here carried on an extensive trade with the interior of Gaul, and even with Britain. They transported their produce up the Rhone and Saone, and thence by land to the Seine and Loire, or across to the Garonne, and so to the Atlantic. This intercourse produced a close connection between the tribes from the Rhone and Garonne to the Rhine and Thames. Cæsar saw how essential the possession of this country was to the Roman state, and that to its conqueror it offered the prospect of surpassing the fame of Camillus and Marius.

Cæsar's effort to gain control of the government by means of Catiline's conspiracy, while Pompey was in the East engaged in the war against Mithridates, was unsuccessful. But Pompey's variance with the senate on his return from the East gave Cæsar an opportunity of forming an alliance with him. Cæsar promised him the support of the democratic party to carry his measures in spite of the senate. He also succeeded in effecting a reconciliation between Pompey and Crassus. This was called the first triumvirate (B. C. 60). In return for these favors Cæsar was to be consul the next year (B. C. 59), and in accordance with the Sullan laws, to govern as pro-consul a province the following year. He was intrusted with the command of Cisalpine Gaul, Illyricum, and the province Narbo, or simply **Provincia**, with three legions, for the term of five years. Cæsar had now attained his object. As proconsul of Cisalpine Gaul, he could watch the progress of affairs in the capital, while the threatening movements of the tribes in Gaul opened to him the prospect of subjugating the country and training an army for the civil war impending, which he saw was inevitable between himself and Pompey.

Of the population of Gaul, the Ædui had entered into an alliance with Rome, while the Belgæ in the north and the Sequani in the south sought an alliance with the Germans. The Ædui, relying on the assistance of Rome, imposed heavy tolls on the navigation of the Saone. The Sequani complained bitterly of this, and thinking that the Roman government was too much occupied with its own contentions at home to furnish its clients assistance, determined to rid themselves of the influence of Rome, and punish the Ædui. For this purpose they invited the German prince, Ariovistus, with about 15,000 men, to their assistance. The Ædui were defeated, and forced to pay tribute to the Sequani, to give hostages, and to swear never to wage war for their recovery, or to solicit the aid of Rome. Divitiacus, the chief magistrate of his clan, alone refused to sign the treaty, and fled to Rome to ask assistance. Ariovistus now invited other tribes across the Rhine, and demanded land to settle them on; the whole frontier of Gaul from the sources of the Rhine to the ocean was threatened by the invasion of the German tribes. These tribes so pressed upon the Helvetians, who were hemmed in on the south and west by the Alps, Lake Geneva, and the Jura mountains, that they determined to abandon their country to the Germans, and seek larger and more fertile fields in the West. Cæsar, on the expiration of his consulship, had remained in the vicinity of the capital until he accomplished his political schemes. But when the news reached him that the Helvetii had abandoned their homes, and were advancing upon Geneva with the purpose of crossing the Rhone and forcing their way through the Province, he hastily made his preparations, and reached the Rhone in eight days.

The following is a brief outline of Cæsar's campaigns in Gaul (see Latin Reader): —

I. Cæsar checks the attempt of the Helvetians to colonize in Western Gaul, and forces them, after a bloody defeat, to return to their own territory. He then engages with a powerful tribe of Germans, who had made a military settlement in Eastern Gaul, and drives them, with their chief, Ariovistus, beyond the Rhine.

II. A formidable conspiracy of the northern populations of Gaul is suppressed, with the almost complete extermination of the bravest Belgian tribe, the Nervii, in a battle which seems to have been the most desperate of all Cæsar ever fought. In this campaign the coast towns of the west and northwest (Brittany) are reduced to submission.

III. After a brief conflict with the mountaineers of the Alps, who attacked the Roman armies on their march, the chief operations are the conquest of the coast tribes of Brittany (Veneti, etc.), in a warfare of curious naval engineering in the shallow tide-water inlets and among the rocky shores. During the season, the tribes of the southwest (Aquitani), a mining population, allied to the Iberians or Basques, are reduced by one of Cæsar's officers.

IV. An attack from the Germans on northern Gaul is repulsed; and Cæsar follows them, by a bridge of timber hastily built across the Rhine. Returning, he crosses to Britain in the early autumn, for a visit of exploration.

V. The partial conquest of Britain (second invasion) is followed by various movements in northern Gaul, in which the desperate condition of the Roman garrisons is relieved by the prudent and brave conduct of Labienus and Quintus Cicero.

VI. Cæsar makes a brief expedition across the Rhine against the Germans. Some general disturbances are quelled, and northern Gaul is reduced to peace.

VII. Vercingetorix, a brave and high-spirited chief of southern Gaul, effects a conspiracy of the whole country, which is at length subdued. Vercingetorix, in brilliant equipment, surrenders himself, to secure the quiet of the country, and is taken in chains to Rome, where he is afterwards put to death in Cæsar's triumph.

VIII. Slight insurrections, breaking out here and there, are easily subdued, and the subjugation of Gaul is made complete.

During the winter of the following year (B. C. 50) Cæsar employed himself in settling the conditon of the country, and conciliating the favor of the people. The territory was united with the province of Narbo until B. C. 44, when two new governorships, Gaul proper and Belgica, were formed out of it. Cæsar imposed light taxes, and left the levying of them to each community. Although he showed every consideration to the nation, and spared their national, political, and religious institutions, so far as was consistent with their subjection to Rome, yet he did not renounce the fundamental idea of his conquest, the Romanizing of Gaul. He bestowed the franchise upon a number of noble Celts, admitted several to the senate, introduced the Roman monetary system, and made the Latin the language used in official intercourse. By his wise and judicious measures the laws and institutions of Rome were thoroughly accepted by the people, and became the basis of their social and political life.

"But the fact that this great people was ruined by the Transalpine wars of Cæsar was not the most important result of that grand enterprise; far more momentous than the negative were the positive results. It hardly admits of a doubt that, if the rule of the senate had prolonged its semblance of life for some generations longer, the migration of peoples, as it is called, would have occurred four hundred years sooner than it did, and would have occurred at a time when Italian civilization had not become naturalized either in Gaul, or on the Danube, or in Africa and Spain. Inasmuch as the great general and statesman of Rome, with sure glance, perceived in the German tribes the rival antagonists of the Romano-Greek world; inasmuch as with a firm hand he established the new system of aggressive defence down even to its details, and taught men to protect the frontiers of the empire by rivers or artificial ramparts, to colonize the nearest barbarian tribes along the frontier with the view of warding off the more remote, and to recruit the Roman army by enlistment from the enemy's country; he gained for Hellenico-Italian culture the interval necessary to civilize the West just as it had already civilized the East. Ordinary men see the fruits of their actions; the seeds sown by men of genius germinate slowly. Centuries elapsed before men understood that Alexander had not merely erected an ephemeral kingdom in the East, but had carried Hellenism to Asia; centuries again elapsed before men understood that Cæsar had not merely conquered a new province for the Romans, but had laid the foundation for the Romanizing of the regions of the West. It was only a late posterity that perceived the meaning of these expeditions to England and Germany, so inconsiderable in a military point of view, and so barren of immediate results. An immense circle of peoples, whose existence and condition hitherto were known barely through the reports—mingling some truth with much fiction—of the mariner and the trader, was disclosed by this means to the Greek and Roman world. This enlargement of the historical horizon by the expedition of Cæsar beyond the Alps was as much an event in the world's history as the exploring of America by European bands. To the narrow circle of the Mediterranean states were added the peoples of Central and Northern Europe, the dwellers on the Baltic and North Seas; to the old world was added a new one, which thenceforth was influenced by the old and influenced it in turn. What the Gothic Theodoric afterwards succeeded in came very near being already carried out by Ariovistus. Had it happened, our civilization would have hardly stood in any more intimate relation to the Romano-Greek than to the Indian and Assyrian culture. That there is a bridge connecting the past glory of Hellas and Rome with the prouder fabric of modern history; that Western Europe is Romanic, and Germanic Europe classic; that the names of Themistocles and Scipio have to us a very different sound from those of Asoka and Salmanassar; that Homer and Sophocles are not merely, like the Vedas and Kalidasa, attractive to the literary botanist, but bloom for us in our gardens,—all this is the work of Cæsar; and while the creation of his great predecessor in the East has been almost wholly reduced to ruin by the tempests of the Middle Ages, the structure of Cæsar has outlasted those thousands of years which have changed religion and polity for the human race, and even shifted the centre of civilization itself; and it stands erect for what we may term perpetuity."—*Mommsen.*

1. **Gallia**: *Gaul* extended from the Pyrenees and the Gulf of Lyons on the south to the British Channel and German Ocean on the north. It was bounded on the west by the Atlantic Ocean, and on the east by

the Rhine and Italy. It was called **Transalpina** (i. e. *beyond the Alps*), to distinguish it from **Cisalpina** (i. e. *on this side of the Alps*), in northern Italy. It included France, Belgium, part of Switzerland and Holland, and the part of Germany west of the Rhine. In the division which Cæsar here makes he does not include the southeast part, called **Gallia Narbonensis,** or commonly **Provincia,** whence the modern name Provence. The Roman dominion in the **Provincia** was secured by the establishment of **Narbo Marcius,** a Roman colony on the Atax, in B. C. 118.

The most remote Roman towns towards the west and north were Lugdunum, Convenarum, Tolosa, Vienna, and Geneva. The country was well provided with roads and bridges. The commerce on the Rhone, Garonne, Loire, and Seine was considerable and lucrative, and extended even into Britain. The people were tall, of fair complexion, and sanguine temperament; fond of fighting, and easily discouraged. They were skilled in working copper and gold. Copper implements of excellent workmanship, and even now malleable, have been found in the tombs of Gaul. The Romans are said to have learned the art of tinning and silvering from them. They had attained so much skill in mining, that the miners, especially in the iron-mines on the Loire, acted an important part in sieges. There was no political union among the different clans, no leading canton for all Gaul, no tie, however loose, uniting the whole nation under one leadership. Sometimes one canton would extend its power over a weaker one, as the Suessiones in the north, the maritime cantons in the west, the two leagues in the south, one headed by the Ædui, the other by the Sequani; but the Celts as a nation lacked political unity, and the cantons, for the most part, existed independently side by side. In matters of religion they had long been centralized. The association of Druids embraced the British islands, all Gaul, and perhaps other Celtic communities. The Druids had a special head elected by the priests themselves, special privileges, as exemption from taxation and military service, and an annual council.

The Province in Cæsar's time extended from the Pyrenees to the Alps on the coast, and was bounded on the east by the Alps, on the west by the **Mons Cevenna** (Cevennes), southward from the latitude of **Lugdunum** (Lyons), and on the north (where it narrowed off) by the Rhone from the western extremity of Lake Geneva, to the junction of the Rhone and Saone. — **omnis**: Cæsar means all of Gaul, except that part which had been subdued by the Romans, in opposition to **Gallia** in the limited sense of one of the three divisions (see Hand-book). — **tres** is placed at the end of the sentence as being the significant word, indicating the number of divisions. — **unam**: supply **partem.** — **aliam,** *another* **(part)**: if Cæsar had been enumerating them in order, he would have used **alteram** or **secundam.** — **tertiam . . . . appellantur,** *the third, those who are called in our language Gauls.* — **institutis,** *in customs;* when three or more nouns stand together, the conjunctions may be omitted altogether, or used between the first and second, and second and third, etc. — **inter se,** *among themselves,* or *from one another.* — **dividunt** is to be supplied after **Matrona** et **Sequana.** — **propterea quod,** *because.* — **Germanis,** *to the Germans.* — **incolunt,** *dwell.* Give the synonymes of **bellum.** — **quŏque,** *also;* the ablative of **quisque** is **quōque.** — **virtute,** *in valor:* **virtus,** from **vir,** means *manhood.* — **una pars,** *one part,* of the main divisions of Gaul, i. e. **Gallia Celtica.** — **flumine,** etc.: notice that the connectives are omitted. — **finibus: finis,** *limit;* plur., **fines,** *limits,* often applied to what is included in those limits, *territories.* — **ad,** *towards.* — **Belgæ;** hence the modern *Belgium.* — **inferiorem partem,** *towards the mouth of the river.* — **ad,** *near to.* — **spectat inter occasum solis,** *it looks between the setting of the sun,* i. e. *it looks northwest.*

2. **apud,** *among;* **apud** with the name of a person means *at the house of;* with the name of an author, *in the writings of.* — **nobilissimus,** see § 17. — **ditissimus** from **dis.** — Note the position of the word **Orgetorix** at the end of the sentence, to give prominence to the name. SYN. **nobilis, clarus, illustris,** denote distinction; **clarus** is one celebrated for *his deeds;* **illustris,** for *his rank* or *character;* **nobilis,** for *his noble birth;* **celeber** and **inclitus,** denote *celebrity,* are generally used of things, not of persons. — **civitati,** *the state,* i. e. *the people,* all the inhabitants of a state under one government; it is here the indirect object of **persuasit,** while the clause introduced by **ut** is the direct object. — **exirent** is plural on account of the plural implied in **civitas.** — **continentur,** *are hemmed in.* — **una ex parte,** *on one side.* — **altera,** see note, § 1. — **altissimo; altus,** *high,* when reckoned from below; *deep,* when from above downward. — **Helvetium,** see **Helvetius.** — **lacu Lemanno:** now *Lake Geneva.* — **altissimo,** *very high.* The pupil should be required to describe the rivers and give the situation of the places mentioned in the text: see Hand-book. — **tertia,** sc. **ex parte.** — **adducti,** *induced.* — **pertinerent** is in the subjunctive, because it is implied that these things belonged to their departure in the opinion of the Helvetians; *which* (as the Helvetians thought) *pertained to their departure.* — **jumentorum** (from **jugo,** *to yoke*) is both pack and draught animals. — **sementes . . . . facere,** *to make as large sowings as possible;* for the force of **quam** with the verb **possum** in connection with the superlative, see § 17, 5 (*b*). — **proximus** has no positive, its place is supplied by **propinquus.** — **in . . . . confirmant,** *they fix upon their departure for the third year by law.* — **conficiendas,** *to accomplish.* In how many ways may a purpose be expressed in Latin (§ 64, 2)? what would be the construction if the gerund

were used?—**deligitur**: **deligo**, *to choose* (not to be undecided in one's choice); **eligo**, *choose*, in the sense of *selecting*. — **Sequano**, *the Sequanian*. — **ut regnum . . . . occuparet**: this clause is the direct object of **persuadet**; **persuadet** is in the historical present, and therefore followed by the imperfect subjunctive. Give the synonymes of **regnum**. — **plebi**, *to the plebeians*; see Hand-book. — **ut idem conaretur**, *that he should strive for the same thing*. — **totius**, *all*. — Synonymes. **omnis**, *all* (without exception), in opposition to **nemo**; **universi**, *all* collectively, in opposition to **singuli**; **cuncti**, *all* united together in opposition to **dispersi**; **totus**, *the whole* as made up of parts, which may be broken up; whereas **omnis** applies to each individual. — **ea res**, *this design*, lit. *this thing*. — **ut**, *when*. — **ex . . . . dicere**, *to plead his cause in chains*; lit. *out of chains*, i. e. (being) in chains. — **damnatum**, sc. **eum**, translate, *it was necessary that the punishment should follow him condemned, namely, that he should be burned*; the clause **ut igni cremaretur** explains **pœnam**; for this use of the subjunctive see § 70, 4. SYN. — **ignis**, *fire*; **flamma**, *flame*; **incendium**, *a conflagration*; **ignis** is the *cause*, **flamma**, the *effect*. — **familiam**, *household*. — **clientes**, for the relations between client and patron at Rome, see Hand-book: here the word is applied to the retainers of the Helvetian chief. — **obæratos**, **debtors**. — **per eos se eripuit**, *by their means he rescued himself*; for the force of **per**, see § 54, 4 (*b*). — **cum**, see § 62, 2.

3. **incitata**, *incensed*. — **jus suum exsequi**, *to inforce* (lit. *follow out*) *their authority*. — **nihilominus**, lit. *the less by nothing*, *nevertheless*. SYN. — **conor**, *try*, *attempt*; **molior** (**moles**), *undertake a difficult work*; **nitor**, (lit. *lean upon*); *strive*. SYN. — **ædificium** is a general word for *buildings* of all kind; **domus**, *the house* as the residence and home of the family; **ædes** also means a *dwelling-house*, composed of several apartments. — **incendo, accendo, inflammo**, all mean *to set on fire*; **incendo**, *from within*; **accendo**, *from a single point*, as *to light a lamp*; **inflammo**, *to put into a blaze*, either from within or without; **succendo**, *set on fire from beneath*; **cremo**, *destroy by burning*. — **trium mensium** (genitive), *for three months*. — **quemque**, *each one*; **domo**, *from home*; **jubent**, for the construction after **jubeo** see § 57, 8 (*d*); § 70, 2. — **quibus itineribus**: the noun to which the relative refers is sometimes repeated as in this case; this repetition of the antecedent is necessary when there are two nouns preceding, and it might be difficult to determine to which the relative referred; the relative clause denotes a consequence and takes the subjunctive, see § 65, 2. — The pupil should be required to trace this route on the map. — **alterum**, *the other* (of the two). — **nonnullis**, see § 41, 2 (*e*), Rem. — **locis**, for the omission of the preposition see § 55, 3 (*f*). — **vado transitur**, *is crossed by a ford*. — **Allobrogum**. The Allobroges dwelt on the south side of Lake Geneva next to the Helvetii, where the

Rhone flowed from the lake. — **ad Helvetios pertinet,** *extends* (across) *to the Helvetii.* The Helvetii occupied a greater part of what is now Switzerland. — **diem dicunt,** *they appoint a day;* for the repetition of the antecedent, see note above. — **conveniant,** *are to assemble:* the indicative means that they are assembling; what does this relative clause denote, purpose or result? Describe the Rhone. — **maturat,** *hastened,* the historical present; what is the object of **maturat**? — **ab urbe,** *from the city,* i. e. Rome. Cæsar had obtained previously to the expiration of his consulship (B. C. 59), the provinces Cisalpine Gaul, and Illyricum with three legions for five years; afterwards Transalpine Gaul was added with another legion. He set out from the city as pro-consul in the spring of B. C. 58. — **Galliam ulteriorem,** *Farther Gaul,* i. e. Gaul beyond the Alps, or Transalpine Gaul.

4. **certiores facti sunt,** *were informed.* — SYN. **Legatus,** *an ambassador, a lieutenant;* **orator,** *one who pleads a cause, an envoy, an orator;* **rhetor,** *one who gives lessons in rhetoric, a rhetorician.* — **qui dicerent,** *to say,* lit. *who should say,* a relative clause denoting purpose. — **sibi esse in animo,** *that it was their intention,* lit. *that it was to them in mind:* what is the subject of the verb **esse**? — **sine ullo maleficio,** *without* (doing) *any harm.* The Helvetii had two ways by which they could go from home, one through the narrow pass between Mount Jura and the banks of the Rhone; the other by the fords of the Rhone, which led directly into the province. In order to prevent the Helvetii from taking this route, he drew a line of fortifications on the southern side of the river, from Lake Geneva to the Jura mountains, a distance of about eighteen miles. — **negat se posse,** *he says he cannot;* **nego** is generally used in preference to **dico non.** — **una** is emphatic, *one only.* — **ut . . . . impetrarent,** *that he being the intercessor, they might obtain* (their request). — **plurimum poterat,** *was able to accomplish a great deal,* sc. **facere,** or more freely, *had great influence.* — **amicus,** *friendly.* — **in matrimonium duxerat,** *had married,* when speaking of a man taking a wife **ducere** (**uxorem**) was used, i. e. he *leads* her to his house; of a woman taking a husband, **nubere** was used, lit. **nubere se viro,** *to veil herself for a husband,* — an allusion to the veil worn during the marriage ceremony. — **ităque,** *therefore.* — What is the object of **impetrat**?

5. **in Italiam,** *into Italy,* i. e. into Cisalpine Gaul. — **duas legiones conscribit:** in addition to the four he already had. The Allobroges and Vocontii were both in the province. — **jam,** *by this time,* i. e. while Cæsar was absent collecting troops. — SYN. **Populor,** *to ravage* (by pillage and fire); **vasto,** *to lay waste;* **depopulor,** *utterly to ravage.* — **rogatum,** *to ask,* see § 74, 1. — **depopulatis,** for the use of the participle of the deponent verb in a passive sense see § 35, 1 (*a*) and (*g*). — **sese . . . . non facile . . . . prohibere,** *that they could not easily ward off,* etc. — **se . . . .**

recipiunt, *betook themselves.* — **non exspectandum (esse) sibi statuit,** *he thought he ought not to wait:* **sibi,** see § 51, 4.

6. **flumen est Arar,** *there is a river* (called) *Arar;* now the *Saone.* It unites with the Rhone at the city of Lugdunum (*Lyons*), about seventy miles from Lake Geneva. — **quod** agrees with **flumen,** see § 48, 2. — **incredibili . . . . possit,** *with incredible smoothness of current, so that it cannot be determined by the eyes in what direction it flows;* **lenitate,** *smoothness,* contrasted not only with the Rhone, but with the rapidity of the rivers in Italy. — **possit,** see § 65, 1. — **ratibus et lintribus junctis,** the ablative absolute to supply the place of the perfect active participle; **lintribus,** *small boats;* these were boats made of logs hollowed out. — **transibant,** *were now crossing.* — **Helvetios transduxisse,** *that the Helvetians had,* etc. In Napoleon's Cæsar, this place of crossing the Saone is said to have been at Chalons sur Saone. — **de tertia vigilia,** *just at the beginning of the third watch.* The Romans divided the night into four watches (the first beginning at sunset), each of three hours; the third watch began at midnight. — **aggressus** has the sense of a perfect active participle, see § 25, 3 (N). How does **concĭdit** differ from **concīdit**? — **is pagus,** *this canton.* — **appellabatur,** from **appello,** *name,* also *to speak to;* **voco,** *call, summon;* **nomino,** *name,* in the sense of appointing or electing; **cito,** *quote.* — **L. Cassium,** this defeat was in B. C. 107. — **consulem,** see Hand-book. — **sub jugum.** It was considered the lowest degree of military disgrace for the Roman soldiers to be obliged to pass under the yoke. The yoke was formed by placing two spears upright in the ground, and fastening a third across the top of the other two; under this the conquered army must pass in token of subjugation. — **ea . . . . persolvit,** *was the first to suffer punishment;* **princeps** is equivalent to **prima.**

7. **ut,** *in order that.* — **consequi,** *to overtake.* — **in Arăre,** *over* and *upon,* i. e. *a floating bridge.* — **faciendum,** see § 72, 5 (*c*). — why is **ejus** used, not **suo**? — **cujus . . . . fuit,** *the chief of which embassy was Divico.* — **bello Cassiano,** *in the war with Cassius,* i. e. in B. C. 107, when the consul Cassius was the commander. — **agit,** *argues, discourses.* — SYN. **Dux,** *a leader, a general;* **ductor,** *a guide;* **imperator,** *a commander* or *emperor.* — **pacem** and **bello** are placed prominently to mark them as significant words. This section is in indirect discourse, depending on **dicens** (*saying*) implied in **agit.** In direct discourse it would read: **si pacem populus Romanus cum Helvetiis faciet** (or **faciat**) **in eam partem ibimus** (or **eamus**) **ubi Cæsar eos esse constituerit.** For the use of the future indicative or present subjunctive, see § 59, 4 (*a* and *b*); **constituerit,** if the future is used in the protasis, would be in the future perfect indicative, otherwise in the perfect subjunctive. The tenses are secondary, after the historical present **agit.** — **perseveraret** has **Cæsar**

for its subject. In direct discourse, **sin bello perseveras, reminiscere et veteris incommodi**, etc. — **reminisceretur . . . . incommodi**, *he should remember both the old overthrow.* — **ne committeret**, *he should not bring it to pass;* **ne commiseris** in direct discourse. — SYN. **calamitas** (lit. a storm that broke down the *stalks* [calamos] of the corn-fields), *calamity;* **infortunium**, *misfortune*, as loss of property; **miseria**, *misery, affliction*; **infelicitas**, *ill-luck.*

8. **his**, sc. **legatis**. — **sibi . . . . dari**, *that the less doubt was given to him.* — **tenet memoria**, *held in memory; remembered.* — **veteris contumeliæ**, *former insult.* — **dentur** is in the present subjunctive, although **respondet**, the leading verb, is an historical present, see § 58, 2 (*d*). — **facturos**, sc. **Helvetios**. — **Æduis** is governed by **satisfaciant**. — **ipsis**: the dative follows the compound in **intulerint**; § 51, 2 (*d*). — **satisfaciant**, *pay damages.* The direct discourse would be: **mihi minus dubitationis datur, quod eas res, quas commemoravistis, memoria teneo. Si veteris contumeliæ oblivisci velim, num potero recentium injuriarum memoriam deponere? Tamen si obsides a vobis mihi dabuntur (dentur), uti ea, quæ pollicemini, vos esse facturos intelligam, et si Æduis de injuriis quas ipsis sociisque eorum intulistis, item si Allobrogibus satisfacietis, cum vobis pacem faciam.** — **hoc responso dato = cum hoc responsum dedisset.** — **ĭdem** neut.; the masculine is **īdem**. — **qui videant**: what does this relative clause denote, cause, purpose, etc.? — **videant** is plur., because **equitatum** implies **equites** as the subject. — **qui**, *these.* — **alieno loco**, *in an unfavorable place*, lit. *a place better for the other party;* for the omission of the preposition, § 55, 3 (*f*). — **audacius**, *still more boldly.* — **ac . . . . præsentia**, *and deemed it sufficient for the present.* — **ita**, *in such a way.* — **novissimum agmen**, the part of the army *nearest* to those pursuing, i. e. *the rear.* — **nostrum primum**, *our front.* — **non . . . . interesset**, *not more than five or six miles* (*each day*) *intervened;* **milibus**, see § 18, 1 (*d*); the distributives **quinis** and **senis** imply that this was the constant difference between the armies.

9. **interim**, give the syn. — **quotidie**, *every day*, is used of things that are daily repeated; **in singulos dies**, *daily*, of those things which from day to day are making advance. — **Æduos** and **frumentum**, see § 52, 2 (*c*). — **quod . . . . flagitare**, *kept demanding . . . . which they had promised in the name of the state;* **flagitare**, the historical infinitive, see § 57, 8 (*h*), equivalent to **flagitabat**; **polliciti essent** refers to the promise as made by the Ædui, see 66, 1 (*b*). — **frigora**, *the cold climate*, the plural is emphatic; the plural of words relating to the weather was often used as, soles, *sunbeams;* **nives**, *falls of snow.* — **non modo** followed by **sed (etiam)**, *not only . . . . but also*, places the emphasis on the last; when both sentences are negative, **non modo, [non] . . . . sed**

ne quidem (= **sed etiam non**), the second **non** in the first clause is omitted if both sentences have the same verb, and the verb is in the second clause; if both clauses have their own verb, as in the text, both negatives are used; **ne . . . . quidem**, see § 76, 3 (*b*). — **pabuli**, *green fodder.* — **suppetebat**, *was at hand.* — **autem**, *besides*, see § 76, 3 (*b*). — **quod . . . . subvexerat**, *which he had brought up the river Arar in vessels.* — **diem . . . . Ædui**, *the Ædui kept putting him* (Cæsar) *off from day to day.* — **ducere**, historical infinitive. — **conferri . . . . dicere**, *they kept saying that it was collecting, bringing together, was close by;* the subject of **conferri**, **comportari**, and **addesse** is **frumentum**; they all depend on **dicere**. — **se diutius duci**, *that he was put off too long.* — **frumentum.** The Roman soldier received no meal or bread as his monthly allowance, but merely the grain which he had to pound and make bread for himself. — **qui . . . . præerat**, *who was invested with the chief magistracy;* **qui** refers to **Liscus**. — Why is **ab** expressed before **iis**? why is **sublevetur** in the subjunctive? does it refer the charge to Cæsar as the general or as the historian? why present subjunctive? — SYN. **Demum**, *at length*, (not till now); **denique**, *finally* (in short); **tandem**, *at last* (after many efforts); **postremo**, *lastly* (last in order). — **proponit**, *set forth*, introduces the indirect discourse which follows. — **plurimum valeat**, *is very powerful;* **valeat**, what would this be in the direct discourse? — **seditiosa . . . . oratione**, *by seditious and wicked speeches.* — **ne frumentum conferant**, *from contributing the corn;* **conferant** is plural on account of the collective noun **multitudo** preceding. — **nostra** in the direct discourse would be changed to **vestra**. — **a se**, *by himself;* **a me** in the direct discourse. — **quin etiam . . . . enunciaverit**, *moreover as to his having disclosed the affair to Cæsar.* — **intellegere . . . . fecerit**, *he was well aware with how great peril he did that:* — SYN. **Intellego**, *understand* by means of reflection; **sentio**, *perceive* by the senses or by the mind. — **quamdiu potuerat**, *as long as he had been able.* — SYN. **Taceo**, *utter no word, be silent, pass over in silence;* **sileo**, *make no noise, be still.*

10. **Dumnorigem . . . . designari**, *that Dumnorix was meant.* Dumnorix led the national party among his people, as opposed to Rome, while his brother Divitiacus favored an alliance with the Romans. — **pluribus præsentibus**, lit. *more being present*, or *in the presence of so many.* — **eas res jactari**, *that these matters should be considered;* **jactari**, a frequentative from **jacio**. — Give the syns. of **concilium**. — **reperit esse vera**, *he finds* (that these statements) *things are true.* — **ipsum . . . . audacia**, *that it was Dumnoris himself, a man of the greatest audacity.* — **cupidum novarum rerum**, *desirous of a revolution.* — **complures . . . . habere**, *that he has farmed for many years all the revenues of the Ædui at a low price.* — SYN. **Vectigal**, *tithes* (**decuma**), *on agricultural*

produce; **tributum,** *an extraordinary property tax,* levied in the tribes, and paid back when the exigency was passed; **scriptura,** *rent of the pasture lands;* **portorium,** *harbor duties* originally, afterwards applied to tolls paid on transit of merchandise. The revenues among the Romans were not collected directly, but were farmed out (or leased) by the censors to contractors called **publicani,** who paid a fixed sum into the treasury, and collected the taxes for their own use; they so abused their privileges, that the name publican became to be a term of reproach. — **illo licente,** *he bidding.* — **audeat,** see § 67, 1. — **rem familiarem,** *private property.* **Dumnorix** is the subject of **favere** and **odisse.** — SYN. **Potentia,** *power* as an attribute of a person; **potestas,** *power* as of a magistrate, *power* to do anything; **ditio (dicio),** *power, jurisdiction.* — **siquid .... Romanis,** *if anything then should happen to the Romans.* — **si quid,** see § 21, 2 (*d*). — **obtinendi,** see § 73, 3 (*a*). — **imperio,** *under the government,* ablative absolute. — **de regno,** *of royal power.*

11. **certissimæ res,** *the most undoubted facts.* — **animadverteret,** *should punish him.* — **unum repugnabat,** *one consideration opposed.* — **summum .... studium,** *the great attachment towards the Roman people.* — **voluntatem,** *affection.* — **ejus** refers to Dumnorix. — **verebatur,** give the synonymes. — **itaque .... conaretur,** *therefore before he attempted anything:* for the subjunctive see § 62, 2 (*c*). — **commonefacit,** *reminds,* lit. *warns.* — **ipso præsente,** *when he himself was present,* i. e. Diviaticus. — **de eo,** *concerning him,* i. e. Dumnorix. — **apud se,** *before himself,* i. e. Cæsar. — **ne quid .... statueret,** *that he should not determine anything too severe against his brother.* — **scire .... vera** (saying), *that he knew those things were true.* — SYN. **Populus,** the *people,* originally only the patricians, came to include the plebeians; **plebs,** *common people,* opposed to the patricians; **vulgus,** *the ignorant multitude.* — **quod .... accidisset,** *because if anything too severe should be done to him by Cæsar.* — **eum locum,** *that place = so high a place.* — **apud eum,** i. e. Cæsar. — **futurum,** *it would happen,* see § 58, 11 (*f*). — **animi,** *the affections.* — **fratrem adhibet,** *he has his brother present.*

12. **exploratoribus:** SYN. **Explorator,** *a scout;* **speculator,** *a spy;* **emassarius,** *a secret agent.* — **milia passuum** = 4,854 ft., a little less than an English mile. — **qualis .... adscensus,** *what its ascent by a circuitous route.* — **qui cognoscerent, misit,** *he sent* (persons) *to ascertain;* **qui cognoscerent** denotes the purpose (see § 65, 2); the antecedent of **qui** is the object of **misit:** what is the object of **cognoscerent**? — **facilem,** sc. **ascensum.** — **eodem itinere,** *along the same route.* — **quo,** *by which.* — **prima luce,** *at daybreak.* — **summus mons,** *the summit of the mountain,* see § 47, 8. — **ipse,** *and when he himself,* sc. **cum.** — **passibus,** see § 55, 2 (*b*). — **neque .... Labieni,** *and* (when) *neither his own approach nor that of Labienus.* — **equo admisso,** *with his horse at full speed.* — **volu-**

erit in indirect discourse. — **se** is the subject of **cognovisse.** — **ex . . . . insignibus,** *by the Gallic arms and ornaments;* **insignibus,** lit. *marks of distinction.* This refers probably to the style of armor. — **subducit,** *draws off.* — **ut ei præceptum,** *as he had been instructed.* — **exspectabat,** *continued to look out:* imperfect, see § 58, 3. — **multo denique die,** *at last, when much of the day had passed.* — **pro viso,** *as seen;* lit. *for seen.* — what is the object of **renuntiasse**? — **quo consuerat intervallo,** *with the usual distance;* **intervallo** is the antecedent of **quo.**

13. **diei,** see § 50, 4 (*e*), Rem. — **metiri,** *to measure out.* — **rei . . . . existimavit,** *he thought he must look out for supplies,* sc. **sibi esse.** — **seu . . . . existimarent,** *because they believed that the Romans, being terrified, were departing;* the subjunctives **existimarent** and **confiderent** represent the idea as existing in the minds of the Helvetii. Cæsar's army was composed of four veteran legions, and two legions newly levied; the Helvetians had about 70,000, with about 20,000 auxiliaries, in all nearly 90,000. For the time denoted by the infinitive see § 58, 11; **discedere,** here is the imperfect of the infinitive. — **a novissimo agmine,** *on the rear.* — **postquam id animum advertit,** *after that Cæsar perceives this;* **id** is governed by **ad** in composition, see § 52, 1 (*d*). — **in colle medio,** *on the middle of the hill.* — **sarcinas,** *each soldier's baggage;* in this sense only used in the plural: each soldier carried besides, his personal baggage and trenching tools (**sarcinæ**), arms, saw, basket, provisions for a number of days, five stakes for fortifying the camp, — in all about sixty pounds; the **impedimenta** were the heavy baggage, tents, engines of war, etc., which were carried in wagons or on horses. — **eum,** sc. **locum.** — **in superiore acie,** *in the upper line,* i. e. those on the top of the hill, the two legions of newly levied soldiers. — **confertissima acie,** *in very close array.* — **phalange facta:** the phalanx consisted of a large body of men in solid mass, with their shields raised above their head, locked and overlapped so as to form a close fence. — **sub . . . . successerunt,** *they advanced close up to our front line.* — **primum . . . . equis,** *first his own horse.* — **pilis:** the pilum was a shaft of wood, a little more than six feet long, with a sharp iron head projecting about nine inches. — **perfregerunt,** *broke through,* see **perfringo.** — **ea disjecta,** *when this* (phalanx) *was broken apart.*

14. **Gallis . . . . impedimento,** *it was a great hindrance to the Gauls.* **pluribus eorum scutis,** *several of their shields,* see synonymes of **scutum.** — **cum . . . . inflexisset,** *when the iron* (head) *became bent.* Their shields were locked over their heads, and overlopped one another; a javelin would pierce through more than one, and bind them together. Movements of their left hands, in which the shield was held, were thus impeded. — **pedem referre,** *to retreat.* — **eo,** *thither.* — **capto monte,** *the mountain being reached.* — **succedentibus nostris,** *our men coming*

close up below. — **agmen . . . . claudebant,** *closed the enemy's line of march.* — **ex itinere,** *on the march.* — **circumvenere,** perfect tense, third person, plural. — **Romani . . . . intulerunt,** *the Romans turned, and advanced in two divisions:* the Romans indicated the movements of their armies by terms derived from the **signum,** *the standard:* thus **signa convertere,** *to turn;* **signa conferre,** *to engage;* **signa inferre,** *to advance;* it was the third line that wheeled about and advanced, while the first and second opposed the Helvetians who had been driven back. — **ut . . . . resisteret,** *that it might resist those* (who had been) *conquered and driven back:* for the subjunctive see § 64. — **ancipiti prœlio,** *in a double conflict.* — **alteri . . . . alteri,** *the one party . . . . the other party,* referring to the Helvetians, and to the Boii and Tulingi respectively. — **ab hora septima,** from one o'clock in the afternoon; the day began at sunrise, and ended at sunset; the end of the sixth hour was noon. — **pugnatum sit,** *the battle raged,* see § 62, 2 (*e*). — **aversum hostem,** *an enemy turned about.* — **nemo,** from **ne** and **homo.** — **ad multam noctem,** *till late at night.* — **pro vallo,** *for a rampart;* the **vallum** was composed of the dirt heaped up (**agger**) from the ditch (**fossa**) against the stakes (**valli**). — **captus est,** see § 47, 2. — **eaque tota nocte,** *during that whole night,* see § 55, 1 (*b*). — **nostri,** sc. **militis.** — **potuissent,** see § 62, 2 (*b*). — **literas,** *a letter.* — **ne . . . . rejuvarent,** (ordering) *that they,* etc.

15. **qui cum,** *when they.* — **suppliciter locuti,** *speaking suppliantly.* — **quo tum essent,** *where they then were;* the subjunctive is used to indicate that Cæsar did not know where they were, see § 66. — **paruerunt,** *they obeyed.* — **qui . . . . perfugissent,** *which had fled to him,* i. e. *whatever,* etc., see § 59, 1 (*a*). — **poposcit,** see § 30, 3 (*d*) 1; § 30, 5 (*d*). — **ut . . . . facerent,** lit. *that they should supply them with corn,* i. e. *to supply,* etc. — **tabulæ,** *lists.* — **literis Græcis confectæ,** *made out in Greek letters.* — **ratio confecta erat,** *an account had been kept.* — **qui numerus . . . . eorum,** *what number of them.* — **possent,** see § 66. — **summa,** *the sum.*

X. THE WAR WITH ARIOVISTUS.

1. **totius fere,** *from nearly,* etc. — **gratulatum,** *to congratulate.* — **intellegere se,** (saying) *that they knew.* — **pro . . . . populi Romani,** *for the injuries of the* (done by) *Helvetians to the Roman people;* **Helvetiorum** is subjective, and **populi Romani** objective, genitive; both depend on **injuriis.** — **ex usu . . . . accidisse,** *that this had happened no less to the*

advantage of the land of Gaul. — **judicassent,** *should judge,* see § 67, 1; for the form, see § 30, 6 (*a*). — **stipendiarias,** (as) *tributaries.* — **in diem certam,** *for a certain day.* — **indicere,** *to appoint.* — **sese . . . . vellent,** *that they had certain things which they wished to ask from him in accordance with the general consent.* — **jurejurando . . . . sanxerunt,** *they bound themselves by an oath that no one should disclose* (their deliberations): SYN. **Jusjurandum** and **juramentum** denote *a civil oath* by which one promises something; **sacramentum,** *a military oath,* by which a soldier promises not to forsake his standard. — **uti . . . . liceret,** *that it should be permitted to them to discuss with him without witnesses concerning the safety of all.* — **Cæsari,** of Cæsar, see § 51, 7 (*a*). — **non . . . . impetrarent,** (saying) *that they strove no less that those things should not be divulged which they might say, than to obtain what they wished.* — **se venturos,** *that they would come.*

2. **factiones esse duas,** *there are two* (political) *parties.* — **principatum tenere,** *stood at the head.* — **factumesse,** *it came to pass.* — why is **ab** expressed? — **Rhenum,** see § 52, 1 (*d*). Describe the Rhine. — **horum,** *of the latter.* — **ad numerum,** *to the number.* — **semel atque semel,** *again and again.* — **clientes,** i. e. the states dependent on the Ædui. — **pulsos,** sc. **Æduos,** the subject of **amisisse.** — **neque . . . . essent,** *neither should they refuse to be perpetually under their power;* **essent,** why subjunctive? **unum se esse,** *that he was the only one.* — **postulatum,** *to ask.* — **pejus . . . . accidisse,** *a worse thing had happened;* **pejus** is the subject of **accidisse.** — **futurum esse,** *it would come to pass.* — **omnes,** sc. **Galli.** — **ut semel,** *when once,* i. e. *as soon as.* — **nobilissimi cujusque,** *of each distinguished man,* see § 17, 5 (*c*). — **in eos . . . . edere,** *he gives forth upon them all* (kinds of) *examples and tortures.* — **hominem,** etc., *that he was a,* etc. — **nisi,** *unless* there is some help, etc. — **idem esse,** etc., *the same thing will be done,* etc. — **ut,** (namely) *that,* etc., what kind of a clause is this? — **fortunam,** etc., *and try whatever fortune may befall them.* — **Cæsarem,** etc., *Cæsar could not prevent a greater number of Germans being led across the Rhine.* — **Rhenum,** why accusative? Compare **major.**

3. **unos . . . . facere,** *the Sequani alone did,* etc. SYN. — **Reliqui,** *the others of whom some have been named before;* **ceteri,** *the rest* (of the same class); **alii,** *others,* different persons. — **ejus rei,** *of this conduct.* — **omnino,** etc., *to extort any reply at all.* — Is the **i** long or short in **idem**? — **hoc,** *on this account.* — **ne . . . . quidem,** see § 76, 3 (*b*). — **auderent,** see § 35, 2. — **absentis,** *even when absent.* — **confirmavit,** *cheered up,* etc. (saying). — **beneficio suo,** *by his* (former) *kindness,* i. e. **Cæsaris.** — **multæ res,** *many considerations.* — **quod . . . . teneri,** *because he saw that the Ædui, often called brothers and kinsmen,* etc. — **in tanto imperio,** *considering the great power.* — **Germanos . . . . videbat,** *he saw*

that it was perilous (to the interests of the Roman people) *for the Germans to cross the Rhine.* — **sibi temperaturos,** *that they would restrain themselves:* for the meaning of **tempero** with the dative and accusative, see § 51, 2, 3 (end). — **ut,** *as.* — **Cimbri:** the war against the Cimbri and Teutones was ended by Marius and Crassus, at the battle of Aquæ Sextiæ (B. C. 102), and near Vercellæ (B. C. 101). — Why is **fecissent** in the subjunctive? Does it refer to Cæsar's own past conviction or to others? — **quibus . . . . putabat,** *he thought he ought to meet these things as quickly as possible;* **rebus** is governed by **occurendum.** — **quam,** see § 17, 5 (*b*).

4. **placuit ei,** *it pleased him,* i. e. *he resolved.* — **qui . . . . postularent,** *to ask from him;* in how many ways may a purpose be expressed in Latin? — **uti . . . . diceret,** *that he should appoint some place midway between both for a conference.* — **summis utriusque rebus,** *the highest interest of both.* — **si . . . . esset,** *if he himself had need of anything from Cæsar;* **opus** stands in the predicate; it is used either impersonally with the ablative, or personally with the thing needed in the nominative. § 54, 1 (*d*), Rem. — **si . . . . velit,** *if he wants anything of him;* with **se** supply **facere,** *that he should do anything;* notice that **esset** is in the imperfect subjunctive, denying the want of anything from Cæsar in past time; **velit** in the present subjunctive, implying that Cæsar does now want something from him. — **quid . . . . negotii esset,** *what business there was,* etc. — **his responsis,** *this reply.* — for **iterum** in enumeration of particulars, see note on § 1. — **beneficio affectus,** *having been treated with kindness.* — **hanc . . . . referret,** *he now made such a return,* etc.; **hanc = talem.** — **hæc esse, quæ,** *that these are the things which;* this clause depends on **mittit.** — Syn. **Gratiam habere,** *to feel thankful;* **gratias agere,** *to return thanks in words;* **gratias referre,** *to show one's self thankful by acts.* — **ne quam,** *any.* — **si id non impetraret,** *if he* (Cæsar) *should not obtain that.* — Syn. **Obtineo,** *hold, occupy;* **impetro,** *obtain by entreaty;* **adipiscor,** *get, or obtain.* — **sese . . . . neglecturum,** *that he should not neglect,* etc. — **quicunque . . . . obtinebat;** the government of the Roman provinces was assigned by the senate to the consuls by lot. — Syn. **Tueor,** *defend or protect against danger,* in opposition to **negligo; defendo,** *defend,* from an actual attack, in opposition to **desero.**

5. **jus esse belli,** *it was the law of war.* — **populum . . . consuesse,** *that the Roman people was accustomed to command the conquered not according to the dictates of another,* etc. — **sibi,** *by himself.* — **stipendiarios esse factos,** *have become tributaries.* — **congrederetur,** *might meet him* (in battle); the subjunctive instead of the accusative with the infinitive. — **quid . . . . possent,** *what the invincible . . . . were able* (to do) *by their valor.* — **eodem tempore.** — Syn. **Tempus,** *time* (in general),

an epoch, an opportunity; **ævum,** *a long space of time, an age;* **tempestas,** *an entire space of time, a period, a season.* — **Ædui questum,** *the Ædui* (came) *to complain,* sc. **veniebant.** — **Treviri,** sc. **veniebant questum.** — **si . . . . conjunxisset,** *if* (this) *new body should join,* etc. — **ne . . . . minus . . . . posset,** *that he would be less easily resisted.*

6. **tridui viam,** *a march of three days,* see § 52, 1 (*b*). — What is the subject of **nuntiatum est**? — **occupandum:** is this the gerund or gerundive? — **quod,** see § 48, 2. — **contendere,** *was hastening.* — **processisse,** *had accomplished.* — **præcavendum . . . . existimabat,** *Cæsar thought that great precaution should be taken by him,* sc. **sibi esse.** — **facultas,** *abundance.* — **ad . . . . bellum,** *for protracting the war.* — **facultatem,** *means.* — **reliquum . . . . continet,** *a mountain occupies the remaining space.* — **ita . . . . contingant,** *so that the banks of the river touch the foot of the mountain on each side* (of the mountain). — **hunc . . . . efficit,** *a wall makes this* (mountain) *a citadel.* — **dum,** see § 62, 2 (*d*). — **ex percunctatione,** etc., *from the inquiries of our* (men) *and the remarks of the Gauls and merchants, who said that the Germans were,* etc.; **vocibus,** see § 14, (*a*). — **prædicabant,** see § 58, 3. — **sæpenumero . . . . potuisse,** (saying) *that they had contended with them very often, and were not able to endure even* (the expression of) *their countenance and the look of their eyes.* — SYN. **Facies** and **oculi,** *the face, the eyes* in a physical point of view; **vultus,** *the countenance, the looks.* By the face, which is unchangeable, one man is distinguished from another; by the countenance, which is changeable, the motives of the mind are indicated. — **tribunis:** there were six tribunes in each legion, and each commanded the legion in turn for two months. — **non magnum . . . . habebant,** *had no great experience in military affairs.* — **alius . . . . petebant,** *one having assigned one cause, another another, requested.* — **totis castris,** *throughout the whole camp.* — **qui,** etc., *those who wished to be considered,* etc. — **non . . . . dicebant,** *said that they did not,* etc. — **intercederent,** see § 66. — **castra moveri,** *that the camp should be moved:* for the description of the camp see Hand-book. — **non . . . . milites,** *that the soldiers would not be obedient to the order;* **milites** is the subject of **fore; dicto** is in the dative after **audientes.**

7. **omniumque . . . . centurionibus,** *the centurions of all ranks being admitted;* there were sixty centurions in each legion, and each centurion commanded a century. In this case all the centurions in the army were summoned to the council of war; ordinarily a council of war was composed of the commander-in-chief, the lieutenants, the tribunes, and the chief centurion of each legion. — **quærendum . . . . putarent,** *they thought that they should inquire into, or deliberate;* see § 51, 4 (*a*). — **Ariovistum,** (saying) *that Ariovistus.* — **ab officio,** *from his duty,* to the Roman people in return for what they had done for him. — **sibi . . . .**

persuaderi, *that he was indeed persuaded*, lit. *that it was indeed persuaded to him;* what is the subject of **persuaderi**? — **cognitis postulatis**, *when his demands*, etc. — **quod si**, *but if.* — **sua**, *their own;* **ipsius**, *his* (Cæsar's). — SYN. **Amens**, *without reason;* **demens**, *mad, infatuated;* **insanus**, *not in one's senses;* **excors**, *weak-minded;* **amentia** like **amens**, simply *without reason;* **dementia**, like **demens**; **furor**, *irritation.* — **factum**, etc., *that a trial of this enemy had been made.* — SYN. **Periculum**, lit. *a trial;* hence *risk, danger;* **discrimen**, *a distinction, difference, a turning-point.* — **servili tumultu**, *at the time of the servile insurrection;* the war with the gladiators in B. C. 73 - 71. — SYN. **Tumultus**, stronger than **bellum**, used by the Romans to denote a war *in Italy*, or *against the Gauls;* **turba**, *confusion.* — **constantia**, *a resolute spirit.* — SYN. **Supero**, lit. *rise above*, hence *to conquer* (an adversary); **vinco**, *conquer* (opposition). — **demum**, *at length, not till now;* **denique**, *finally, in short;* **tandem**, *at last*, after many efforts; **postremo**, *lastly*, in order of time. — **si quos**, *if any one.* — **castris**, *in his camp*, see § 55, 3 (*f*). — **consilio**, *by stratagem.* — **qui**, etc., *those who attributed their fear to the narrowness of the roads acted arrogantly, since they appeared either to despair of the commander's doing his duty, or to dictate to him.* — **quod . . . . dicantur**, *as to their saying that*, etc. — **nihil**, etc., *he was moved not at all by this circumstance.* — **moturum** (**esse**), *that he should move.* — **quam primum**, *as soon as possible.* — **sibique . . . . futuram**, lit. *that it should be a prætorian cohort to himself:* the prætorian cohort was the general's body-guard; it had more pay and privileges than the other soldiers.

8. **belli gerendi**, what would be the construction if the gerund were used? — **innata est**, see **innascor**: what is the force of **in**, in composition with verbs? with adjectives? see § 44, 3 (*g*). — **princeps** = **prima**. — **quod . . . . fecisset**, *because he had formed*, etc.: the subjunctive is used to express the opinion of the tribunes; see § 63, 2. — **egerunt**, *acted* in the same manner. — **itinere exquisito**, *the route having been sought out.* — **Ariovisti . . . . abesse**, *that the forces of Ariovistus were distant*, etc. — SYN. **Abesse**, *to be absent*, denotes absence as a local relation, *to be away* from a place; **deesse**, *to be wanting*, denotes absence by which a thing is rendered incomplete. — **quod**, (saying) *what.* — **id fieri licere**, *that could be accomplished;* **licere** depends on **mittit**. — **pro . . . . beneficiis**, *in consideration of his own benefits and those of the Roman people towards him* (Ariovistus). — **fore**, see § 58, 11 (*f*). — **ne quis** is used in negative clauses instead of **ut nemo**. — **alia ratione**, *on any other term.* — **equitatui**: the cavalry in Cæsar's army consisted wholly of Gauls; he was therefore afraid to trust entirely to them. — **audebat**, see § 35, 2. — **commodissimum esse statuit**, *he deemed it most expedient;* what is the subject of **esse**? — **omnibus . . . . imponere**,

all the horses having been taken from the Gallic horsemen, to place on them (eo), etc.

9. **ex equis**, *on horseback.* — **denos**, *ten apiece.* — **commemoravit**, *recounted.* — **quod**, *how that.* — **quam . . . . docebat**, *he informed him that this thing had both happened to few, and in consideration of important services.* — **quam**, etc., *how old, and how just causes of relationship*, etc. — **in eos**, *for them.* — **postulavit . . . . dederat**, *then he demanded the same things which he had given to the ambassadors as his demands.* — **habere**, *that he had.* — **obsides**, *that the hostages.* — **capere**, *that he had exacted.* — Syn. **Experior**, *try, learn by experiment;* **tento**, *try by feeling, test;* **periclitor**, *make trial of*, facing the danger arising from the experiment. — **pace uti**, *to enjoy peace.* — **quod . . . . pependerint**, *which they had paid*, etc., see p. 63, § 1. — **amicitiam . . . . oportere**, *that the friendship of the Roman people ought to be a protection, not an injury.* — **quod**, *as to.* — **id . . . . facere**, *that he did this to fortify himself*, etc., see § 64, 2 (6). — **prius . . . . quam**, *before*, separated by **tmesis**. — **fines egressum**, *passed beyond the territories.* — **quid sibi vellet?** *what did he wish for himself?* **sibi** refers to Cæsar. — **provinciam**, etc., *that this was his province just as*, etc. — **qui . . . . interpellaremus**, *since we interrupted him in his right*, see § 69, 2, 2 (*d*).

10. **neque . . . . desereret**, *neither his own nor the custom of the Roman people would permit that*, etc. — **potius esse Ariovisti**, *belonged to Ariovistus.* — **senatus**, *of the senate.* — **quam . . . . voluisset**, *since, though conquered*, (the senate) *had willed that it* (**quam**) *should enjoy its own laws.* — **prope**, see p. 92. — **imperavit . . . . rejicerent**, *he commanded that they should not throw back a single weapon upon the enemy.* — **ne quod**, from **ne quis**. — **legionis delectæ**, *to his chosen legion.* — **tamen . . . . circumventos**, *yet he did not think that the opportunity should be given that the enemy having been routed, it might be said* (by them) *that they had been surrounded by him* (Cæsar) *at the conference.* — **posteaquam**, etc., *after that it was spread abroad among the common soldiers*, see § 10, 3 (*b*). — **qua . . . . interdixisset**, *with what arrogance* (lit. *using what arrogance*) *Ariovistus had forbidden the Romans* (the use) *of Gaul.* — **interdico** is here followed by the dative and ablative, see § 51, 1 (*c*). — **multo major**, *greater by much.* — **injectum**, *was infused.*

11. **post**, an adverb. — **velle . . . . cum eo**, (saying) *that he wished to treat with him.* — **uti aut**, *or* (requesting) *that:* notice the twofold construction after **mittit legatos**; in the first case it implies *saying*, and is followed by the accusative with the infinitive; in the latter the verb *requesting* is implied, and therefore the subjunctive is required. — **ex legatis aliquem**, see § 50, 2 (*e*), Rem. — **visa non est**, *did not appear* (sufficient). — **legatum ex suis**, *a commissioner from his own men.* — **qua . . . . utebatur**, *which Ariovistus, from long habit, used with great*

ease; **qua** refers to **lingua**, and **multa** agrees with **qua.** — **qui . . . . usus erat,** *who was accustomed to enjoy the hospitality of Ariovistus;* notice the force of the imperfect. — **an . . . . causa,** *was it not to spy out;* the complete sentence would be **utrum aliud peterent, an speculandi causa venirent,** see § 71, 2 and (*d*) : also see § 64, 2 (5). — **præter,** *past.* — **eo consilio,** *with this design.* — **uti,** (namely) *that,* see § 70, 3 (*d*). — **ex . . . . Æduis,** *from the* (country of), etc. — **pro castris,** *before the camp.* — **si vellet,** *if he wished,* see § 59, 3 (*b*). — **ei . . . . deesset,** *that the opportunity might not be wanting to him.*

12. **ubi . . . . tenere,** *when . . . . that he held himself in his camp,* see § 55, 3 (*f*). — **acieque . . . . instructa,** *a triple line of battle being formed.* — **tertiam castra munire,** *the third to fortify the camp.* — **eo . . . . expedita,** *thither light-armed troops, about six thousand in number.* — **quæ copiæ,** *that these forces.* — **prohiberent,** see § 69, 2 (*a*). — **a majoribus,** sc. **castris.** — **potestas,** *an opportunity.* — **ubi . . . . intellexit,** *when he perceived that not even then they would come forth* (to fight), see § 76, 3 (*b*). — **tum demum,** *then at last;* give the synonymes. — **oppugnaret,** see § 64, 1. — **multis . . . . vulneribus,** *many wounds being given and received :* **illatis,** see **infero.** — SYN. **Accipio,** *take anything that is offered;* **recipio,** *take anything under one's protection;* **excipio,** *take what is escaping, intercept;* **suscipio,** *undertake a task;* **sumere,** *take up anything* (to use it) ; **capere,** *take anything* (to possess it).

13. **quam ob rem,** *on account of what thing,* i. e. for what reason. — **sortibus et vaticinationibus,** *from lots and auguries.* — **utrum . . . . necne,** *whether a battle could be fought advantageously, or not.* — **esset,** see § 71, 2, Rem. — **eas . . . . superare,** *they* (women) *said that it was not the will of heaven for the Germans to conquer.* — **alarios,** *auxiliaries,* generally stationed on the wings (**alæ**) of the army. — **quod . . . . valebat,** *because he was less strong in the number of legionary soldiers in proportion to the number of the enemy.* — **eo,** lit. *thither,* i. e. *on these* (chariots and wagons). — **passis manibus,** *with outstretched hand* (**passis** from **pando**): **flentes** agrees with **quæ,** subject of **implorabant.**

14. **Cæsar . . . . præfecit,** *Cæsar appointed over each legion a lieutenant, and quæstor:* for the duties of the quæstor see Hand-book. — **a dextro cornu,** *on the right wing* (of the Romans). — **minime firmam,** *least strong.* — **itaque,** *and so.* — **spatium,** *space* (of time). — **rejectis pilis,** *the javelins being thrown aside;* for the manner in which the Roman army was armed, see Hand-book. — SYN. **Gladius,** *sword* (a general word) ; **ensis,** *sword* (poetical) ; **pugio,** *a dagger or short sword* (often worn by magistrates) ; **sica,** *dagger,* (the secret weapon of the assassin). — **complures nostri milites,** *many of our soldiers,* see § 50, 2 (*e*), Rem. 3. — **miles** from **mil** (**mille**) and **eo,** in allusion to the army as arranged by Servius Tullius. — **qui . . . . insilirent,** *who leaped,* see

§ 65, 2.—**scuta**, etc., *tore off with their hands the shields* (of the enemy). —**a sinistro cornu**, *on the left wing* (of the Germans). —**a dextro cornu**, *on the right wing* (of the German army). —**perpauci**, *a very few.* —**confisi**, *relying on their strength:* see **confido**.

15. **cum .... traheretur**, *as he was being dragged along.* —**trinis catenis**, *with three chains.* —**in .... incidit**, *fell in with Cæsar himself.* —**de .... dicebat**, *he said that it had been thrice consulted by lots about him.* —**cœperunt**, *began*, see § 38, 1 (*a*). —**duobus bellis**, i. e. the Helvetian and German wars. —**maturius paulo**, *a little earlier.* —**ad conventus agendos**, *to hold the courts*, i. e. to attend to lawsuits, and all matters pertaining to the civil administration of the country. Each province was divided into districts, in which the pro-consul held a court, to which any one might apply for redress of grievances. The pro-consul himself presided at the trials, and pronounced the decision according to the views of the judges, who were generally selected from among the Roman citizens, who resided in the province. Cæsar also had another object for passing the winter in Italy, in order to watch the movements of political parties at the capital, and especially of Pompey, who now, according to the arrangement made by the triumvirs, held the chief power there.

QUESTIONS FOR REVIEW.

1. How do nouns of the first declension end? Decline *stella*. What words of this declension are masculine? What words have *abus* in the dative and ablative plural? For what purpose? What are the terminations of Greek nouns? Decline *cometes*. Decline together *stella lucida*. What cases are alike in the first declension? What declensions have no neuter nouns?

2. How do nouns of the second declension end? Which terminations are neuter? Which masculine? Decline *puer, donum, domĭnus*. Why is the accent in *domĭnus* on the antepenult? What nouns in *er* retain *e* in the oblique cases? How do *puer* and *lĭber* differ in declension? What class of nouns in *us* are feminine? What is said of *vir?* What nouns in *us* are neuter? What is the gender of *vulgus?* Decline *filius* and *deus*.

3. How are nouns of the third declension classified? Decline *mare* and *turris*. What is the regular ending of the accusative and ablative in this class of nouns? Which retain the regular form? What is the genitive plural of *canis?* Of *turris?* Decline *vis, Tiberis*.

4. Decline *honor, nomen*, and *consul*. What is the stem of *honor?* Explain the formation of the nominative singular. Decline *opus*. Explain the formation of the nominative singular.

5. Decline *urbs* and *ars*. Explain the formation of the nominative singular of *comes;* accent *comitēs*. In what does the ablative of nouns of this class end? Decline *apex*, explaining the formation of the nominative singular; also *rex, pax*, and *arx*. Decline *caro, vas, bos, nix*, and *os*.

6. What terminations of the third declension are masculine? What neuter? What nouns in *or* are feminine? What neuter? What is the gender of *juventus, pes, plebs, caro, æs, jus, rus*, and *arbor?* What terminations of the third declension are feminine? Write the declension of *miles, onus, ordo*, and *corpus*, explaining the formation of the nominative. Decline together *puer bonus* and *vox sæva*.

7. Give the accusative singular of *mare, turris*. Give the ablative singular and genitive plural of *sermo, homo, equus, cor, gens, pax*, and *arx*. [Observe that neuter nouns in *e, al*, and *ar* retain *i* in the ablative and *ium* in the genitive plural; nouns in *ns* and *rs* of only one syllable, as well as nouns in *is* and *es*, not increasing in the genitive (see § 78, 3 *a*), and

monosyllables ending in two consonants, retain *ium* in the genitive plural.] How do nouns in *as* form their genitive? Nouns in *a*? Nouns in *o*? Nouns in *do* and *go*? Give the genitive of *iter*; of *Jupiter*; of *cor*; of *litus*. How do nouns in *es* form their genitive? in *is*? in *os*? in *us*? In what does the ablative singular, the nominative, and genitive plural of vowel stems generally end? In what liquid stems? In what mute stems? Mention exceptions.

8. How do nouns of the fourth declension end? Decline *currus*, *fructus*, and *genu*. What nouns of this declension are feminine? What nouns of the fourth declension retain *u* in the dative and ablative plural? Decline *domus*. What difference of meaning have *domūs* and *domi*? What nouns have the forms of the second and fourth declension? Decline together *altus lacus*, *tristis casus*.

9. How do nouns of the fifth declension end? What is their gender? Decline *res*, *dies*, *spes*. What exceptions in gender? How many nouns belong to this declension? How many are complete? Mention those that have only the nominative vocative and accusative plural. Decline together *longa acies*.

10. Into how many classes are irregular nouns divided? Define each. Define heterogeneous; heteroclite. Give examples illustrating each. Decline together *Marcus Tullius Cicero*. Which is the personal name? Which the name of the *Gens*? What was the *agnomen*? Illustrate by example.

11. What is an Adjective? Into what classes are they divided? How are adjectives in *o* stems declined? Decline *servus*, *ater*, *tener*. Decline in the singular *solus*. What other words are declined like it? Decline *alter* in the singular. Decline *alius* in the singular and *uterque* in the plural. Decline *acer*. How many adjectives like it? Decline *felix*, *iens*, *vetus*.

12. Decline *carior*. Decline *dis*. Decline together *stella clara*, *insula longa*, *vir bonus*, *hortus parvus*, *campus longus*, *periculum magnum*, *acer*, *auriga*. When is the vocative different from the nominative? In what does the genitive plural of adjectives of the third declension generally end? In what the ablative of comparatives and participles in *ns*? How do adjectives of one termination form their ablative?

13. Give the genitive and ablative singular and plural of *filia*, *vas*, *passer*, *opus*, *alius*, *mitis*, *mare*, *juvenis*, *dies*, *acus*, *specus*, *nubes*, *difficultas*.

14. Give the rule for forming the comparative and superlative of adjectives. Compare *felix*, *audax*, *durus*, and *mitis*.

15. How are adjectives in *er* compared? What adjectives in *us* have a similar superlative? Compare *acer*, *piger*, *miser*, *pulcher*.

16. Compare *facilis*. What other adjectives are compared like this? Compare *doctus*, *gracilis*, *altus*, *potens*.

17. What irregularity have five adjectives in *ficus?* Compare *maledicus* and *benevolus.* Mention five adjectives whose comparatives are regular, but whose superlatives are irregular. Compare them. Compare *idoneus.* Give the rule for it.

18. Compare *bonus, magnus, malus, mirificus, dives, frugi,* and *dexter.* Compare seven adjectives which want the positive.

19. Compare *juvenis* and *senex.* What adjectives want the comparative? Mention three that want the superlative.

20. Decline *minor, animus ferox,* and *vulnus grave,* together. Compare *citerior.* What other adjectives are formed like this?

21. Compare the adverbs formed from *bonus, malus, altus, gravis.* Compare *diu, sæpe, satis, multum, ægre.*

22. How may the force of the comparative and superlative be increased? What is the force of *quam* before the superlative? What is the force of *quisque* with the superlative? Of *per?* Of *sub* in composition?

23. Name the principal classes of numeral adjectives. What are the cardinals? Which are not declined? Decline *duo.* What is irregular in the declension of *unus?*

24. Give the cardinals from 1 to 20.

25. Give the Latin for 12, 14, 16, 17, 18, 19. Explain the last two.

26. Give the Latin for 11, 21, 28, 49, 60, 75, 94, 100.

27. How is *mille* used?

28. What are Ordinals? Give the Latin ordinals from 1st to 10th. What are Distributives? Give them up to the 10th.

29. What are Numeral Adverbs? Give the first ten numeral adverbs.

30. Give the Roman numerals for 20, 45, 52, 67, 78, 98, 200, 500, 1,000, 5,000, 10,000, and explain the Roman method of notation.

31. What is a Pronoun? Decline *ego, tu, sui.* Give the possessive pronouns formed from these. How are they declined? Decline *meus puer, nostra domus.*

32. Which are the demonstrative pronouns? Decline *ille puer, hic vir, hoc prœlium, hæc sententia.*

33. Decline *ipse, ille* in the singular, and *is* and *idem* throughout; accent the last.

34. Decline *unus locus, tota acies.*

35. Define relative pronoun. Decline *qui* and *quis.* Write the nominative plural of *quis, aliquis,* and *siquis.* What is the difference between the forms in *quid* and *quod?* Decline *quivis.*

36. Decline together in the singular *quilibet miles, aliqua salus, quidam homo.*

37. Decline together *idem metus, hæc res, illud periculum, uterque miles.*

38. What is a Verb? (See Lessons for definitions.) What is the Subject of a verb? What is meant by the Active Voice? By the Passive

Voice? What is a transitive verb? Intransitive? What are Moods? How many? Define each. What is a Participle? What form has the participle? In what does it resemble the verb? In what an adjective? How many participles? What is the Gerundive?

39. What are Gerunds? What are Supines? How do they end? In what sense are they used? What are Tenses? What is the first division of time? Name the tenses, and define each. Name those which represent the action as not completed; those which represent it as completed. Upon what stems are the tenses formed?

40. What are the principal parts of a verb? What tenses are formed from each? Write the present indicative of *esse.* Write the imperfect subjunctive; the present imperative; the infinitives. For what are *forem, forent,* and *fore* used? What tense of *esse* has two forms?

41. Explain the compound of *esse* and *pro.* Write the present and perfect indicative.

42. Explain the composition of *potis* and *sum.* Write the present and imperfect indicative; the present and imperfect subjunctive.

43. What is the conjugation of a verb? How many conjugations? How are they distinguished? Illustrate the formation of the tenses of *voco, deleo, duco,* and *audio.* How were verbs classified into four conjugations (see Note, p. 61)?

44. Give a synopsis of tenses of the Present Stem in the active of *amo;* of the perfect stem of *moneo;* of the supine stem of *rego.* Inflect the present imperative, active and passive, of *amo* and *doceo.*

45. Give the synopsis in the active voice of *rego.* Give all the infinitives of *audio.* Give the present imperative, active and passive, of *rego* and *audio.* Give a synopsis of the active and passive of *audio.*

46. Give the participles, gerund, and supine of *amo.* Give a synopsis of the tenses from the supine stems of *amo.* Give the principal parts of *amo, moneo, rego,* and *audio* in both voices.

47. How are Deponent verbs conjugated? What is said of their participles? Conjugate *miror.* What is said of neuter deponents? What active forms have they? Give all the infinitives and participles of *sequor, vereor, potior, criminor.*

48. What are Semi-deponents? Name them. Give a synopsis of *audeo* and *fido.* What are neutral passives? Enumerate them.

49. Give the future indicative and present subjunctive of *capio.* Give the present indicative passive of *capio.* Inflect the imperative active and passive of *capio.*

50. Parse the following, and inflect the tenses to which they belong: *Amaverunt, monebuntur, monitus ero; monete, monere, amabit; monuerit, amet, ametur, moneat, mone, monere.* Explain how *vocatum iri* is formed. Is the termination *tum* variable?

51. *Regat, regunt, reget, regar, auditor, capiunt, regitor, rege, regere, capite, audias, audies, audire, audiret, rexero, moneant, monebis, rectus est, mirer, verear, mirator.*

52. Explain the forms *amasse, audieram, nosse, dic, fer, faxim, vocarier.*

53. Explain the formation of the present and perfect stem of *amo* (see § 30, 1); of *moneo;* of *rego;* of *audio:* the supine stem of *nomino;* of *terreo;* of *duco;* of *deleo;* of *fingo.*

54. What are derivative verbs? Define each class. Explain how they are formed, and of what conjugation.

55. Give the principal parts of *fateor, bibo, cerno, arcesso, vinco, vincio, cado, cædo, cedo, disco, plecto, fingo, do, peto, pello, lavo.*

56. What verbs are called Irregular? Give the present indicative and present subjunctive of *fero.* Give the imperatives, active and passive. Give the present and imperfect passive.

57. Give the present indicative and present subjunctive of *volo, nolo, malo.* Give the imperative of *nolo.* Give the imperfect of *volo, nolo, malo.* Give the infinitives.

58. Inflect the present indicative of *eo;* of *fio;* the present subjunctive; the imperfect indicative and subjunctive. Give the imperative of each.

59. Parse the following, and inflect the tenses to which they belong: *ferat, feret, ferar, fero; vis, volet, voluit; nonvultis, noles, noli; mavis, malle, mavultis; it, eam; fiunt, fies, fierem, fiat, fi.*

60. What are Defective verbs? Conjugate *cœpi, odi.* Give the parts in use of *aio, inquam.* In what sense are *odi* and *memini* used? What name do they have? What is said of the compounds of *fio?*

61. What are Impersonal verbs? What nominative usually precedes them in English? How are they classified? Conjugate *licet.*

62. How are the Periphrastic Conjugations formed? How the first periphrastic conjugation? How the second?

63. In what ways may verbs be compounded (see § 30, 6 *d*)? How are the compounds of *capio* and *teneo* formed? Of *cogo* and *dego?* Of *facio* with a preposition (see § 44, 3 *e*)?

64. Define Particles. How are Adverbs formed? Explain the formation of *care,* dearly; *fortiter,* bravely; *multum,* much; *falso,* falsely; *quo,* whither; *ibi,* there; *statim,* immediately. How are adverbs classified? Explain the distinction between *certo* and *certe; primum* and *primo.*

65. How are adverbs compared? Illustrate by examples.

66. What is a Preposition? How many take the accusative? How many the ablative? How many have either the accusative or the ablative? What is the distinction in the use of *a, ab,* and *abs?* Of *e* and *ex?* What is said of the meaning of prepositions in composition (see § 44, 3 *g*)?

67. What is a Conjunction? Into how many classes are conjunctions divided? What does the first class include? What the second? What conjunctions are Enclitics? How are *ac* and *atque* distinguished?

68. Distinguish between a Root and Stem. Explain the meaning of such derivatives as *ductor, victrix, viator, miles* (from *mil*, a thousand, and *eo*, go), *gaudium, flumen, puellula*. How are Patronymics formed? What is the termination of masculine patronymics? Of feminine? Of what declension are patronymics? How are gentile nouns formed? Explain the meaning in the terminations to the following words: *pugnax, ovile, alumnus, difficultas, lapidosus, Cannensis*.

69. Define a Sentence. How many kinds? Define each. Define Subject, Predicate, Copula, Substantive Verb, a Phrase, a Clause. How are clauses classified? What is meant by Agreement and Government in Grammar? Illustrate.

70. Define Apposition. Give the rule for the agreement of an adjective with a noun; when the nouns are of different gender; when they denote things without life.

71. Give the rule for the agreement of a relative pronoun with its antecedent. How is its case determined? How its gender? Illustrate.

72. What is the rule for the agreement of a verb? Of what number is the verb when belonging to two or more nominatives singular? When a nominative singular is joined to an ablative with *cum?* What is said of Collective nouns? Of *uterque? quisque?*

73. What is the rule for the Genitive after nouns? Explain the difference between the subjective and objective genitive. What is the rule for the genitive after partitives? What is the rule for the genitive after verbs? Of verbs of remembering? Verbs of accusing? Verbs of pity? Of *miseret*, etc.? Of *refert*, etc.? Of *egeo*, etc.?

74. What other construction is used after *refert* and *interest?* What is said of the nominatives of these verbs? What is said of *potior?* When do verbs of remembering take the accusative? How is the punishment expressed? What is said of *tanti, quanti*, etc.? Of *pridie and postridie?* What is said of the construction after *omnes?*

75. Give the general rule for the Dative. For the dative with verbs. Mention the verbs that take the dative generally without the sign *to* or *for*. Give the rule for verbs compounded with *ad, ante*, etc What is the rule for *esse*, and the dative? How may *esse* in such cases be translated? What is said of the agent after passive verbs? Of the agent with gerunds, etc.? Give the rule for the dative of Service, Nearness, Advantage, and Ethical dative.

76. What is the rule for the dative after adjectives? What is said of *dicto audiens?* Mention adjectives that are followed by either the genitive or dative? What is said of *propior* and *proximus?* Of *obvius?* Of *idem?* Of *nomen est?* Explain the following: *Est mihi cultellus; cultellus est meus; habeo cultellum; est mihi nomen Alexandro.*

77. What is the rule for the Direct Object of a verb? For the Cognate Accusative? For verbs of motion compounded with *circum* and

trans? For *delectat*, etc.? For verbs of asking, etc.? What prepositions take the accusative?

78. When the active voice takes two accusatives, which is retained after the passive voice? What is said of *peto?* Of *id temporis?* What is the Synecdochical accusative? Is this an illustration of it: *inutile ferrum cingitur?* In what ways may the accusative after many neuter verbs be explained? What interjections are followed by the accusative?

79. What is the rule for the Vocative?

80. Give the general rule for the Ablative; for the ablative of separation; for *opus* and *usus;* ablative of source; of cause; ablative after *dignus*, etc.; ablative of agent; of comparison; of means; of the ablative after *utor*, etc.; of quality; of price; of specification; for the locative ablative; for the ablative absolute.

81. What is said of compounds of *a*, *ab*, etc.? What is said of *egeo* and *indigeo?* When, after verbs denoting origin, is the preposition expressed? How is the agent sometimes expressed? What is said of *plus*, *minus*, etc.?

82. What is the rule for the time *when* and *how long?* For space? For place? What is said of *domi*, etc.? What is said of the use of prepositions before names of towns? Before names of other places?

83. Mention the prepositions that govern the accusative; those that govern the ablative. What is said of *in*, *sub*, *super*, *subter?* Of prepositions used in dates? Of the adverbs *pridie*, etc.? What prepositions often follow their nouns?

84. Name the Moods, and define each. How is the hortatory subjunctive used? The optative subjunctive? The concessive subjunctive? Define the Infinitive mood; as a subject; the complementary infinitive; with subject accusative; the historical infinitive.

85. Into what two classes are Tenses divided? Mention those of the first class; of the second class. Define the tenses of the indicative. How many tenses has the subjunctive? Give the primary tenses; the secondary. In compound sentences by what tense is the primary tense followed? Illustrate by examples. When is the perfect definite followed by a secondary tense? When is the present?

86. What time is denoted by the Infinitive? How is the infinitive translated in indirect discourse? Illustrate.

87. What is a Conditional Sentence? How are conditional sentences classified? Give the different forms of particular suppositions, and one example of each. When is the indicative used in both clauses? When the future indicative? Define general suppositions. Give examples.

88. What is an implied condition? Define and illustrate a disguised condition; condition omitted; potential subjunctive.

89. What are Temporal clauses? Mention the temporal adverbs. Give

the rule for the mood of temporal clauses; for *cum* temporal; for *antequam*, etc.; for *dum*, etc.; for *cum* causal.

90. What are Causal clauses? Give the causal particles and the rules for the mood following them.

91. What is a Final clause? Give the rule for sequence of tenses. In how many ways may a purpose be expressed in Latin? Illustrate.

92. What are Consecutive clauses? Give the rule for consecutive clauses after *ut*; after *quin*; for relative clauses; clause after *unus*, etc.; after *quam*; after *dignus*.

93. What is the rule for the mood in Intermediate clauses? Give examples in which the subjunctive and indicative are used.

94. What is meant by Direct Discourse? By Indirect? Write these sentences in Latin and give the rule: *I am writing; he says I am writing; if you should say that, you would be mistaken; he thinks that you would be mistaken if you should say that.*

95. What is an Indirect Question? What mood does the imperative take in indirect discourse?

96. Give the rule for Wishes and Commands.

97. When do Relative clauses take the indicative? When do they take the subjunctive? Classify them, and give one example of each.

98. What is a Substantive clause? How are they classified? Mention four kinds, and give examples of each.

99. How are Questions introduced? Mention the interrogative particles. Give illustrations of their use. How is a double question expressed? How is the Answer expressed in Latin?

100. What is a Participle? What is said of the time of the participle? How are the present and perfect participles used? What is said of the future participle?

101. What is a Gerund? Followed by what cases? Instead of the gerund of a transitive verb, what construction may be used? What is said of the participles of *utor*, etc.? When the participle in *dus* is used for a gerund, what is it called? What is the rule for the genitive of gerunds and gerundives? For the dative? For the accusative? For the ablative?

102. What is a Supine? By what cases are gerunds followed? What do they follow? What is the rule for the supine in *um*? In *u*?

103. What is the order of words in a Latin sentence? Where do numerals generally stand? Where demonstrative pronouns? Relative pronouns? What connectives occupy the second or third place? Where is a modifier of a noun and adjective placed? What is the position of *ne* and *quidem*? Of *inquam*? How can the subject and predicate be made emphatic?

QUESTIONS FOR GENERAL REVIEW.

104. Decline *mea filia, meus filius, bona dea.* Mark the quantity of the penultimate and final syllables.

105. What are Epicenes? What is meant by the Copula? Decline *Anchises, Æneas.*

106. Give the principal parts of *sto, duco, vinco, morior, oportet, jacio, jaceo.*

107. Decline *bonus vir, Orpheus, alta turris, Tiberis, Achilles, canis, juvenis.* Give the gender of each with the rule, and mark all the long vowels.

108. How are adjectives compared? Compare *hebes, humilis, inops, dexter, juvenis;* mark the quantity of all the penults.

109. Form adverbs from the following, and compare them: *levis, latus, audax, bonus, miser, facilis, gravis.*

110. By what case or cases are *peto, quæro, do, circumdo, postulo, læto, utor, consulo, facio, faveo, jubeo, nubo,* followed?

111. Give the participles of *conor, sequor, cædo, fateor, loquor, fido, domo, veto, sto, plico.*

112. Write the compounds formed from *con* and *ago, con* and *lego, in* and *ludo.* How is *texi* formed from *tego? nupsi* from *nubo? passus* from *patior? maximus* from *magnus?*

113. Decline and mark the quantity of the penultimate and final syllables of *caro, bos, nix, os, vis, Dido, Jupiter, iter, poema, fructus.*

114. Give the meaning of the following words in the singular and plural: *copia, sal, locus, impedimentum, littera, forum, finis, plaga, opera.*

115. Decline together *Tullia minor; Publius Cornelius Scipio Africanus; alter ille puer.*

116. Write in Latin, *we are reading; I and you are reading; you and that boy are reading; he and that boy are reading.* What is the quantity of monosyllables?

117. What are Patronymics? Form masculine and feminine patronymics from *Tantalus, Æneas, Priamus.* Mark the quantity of the penultimate syllable.

118. Enumerate the chief uses of the Genitive? What is the distinction between the use of *nostrum* and *nostri? vestrum* and *vestri?*

119. Explain the meaning of the terminations of the following words: *lumen* (from *luc-men*), *audacia, lacesso, cantillo, esurio, viator, collegium.* Mark the quantity of the final vowels.

120. What is an Intensive verb? Form one from each of the following words: *dico, jacio, clamo, habeo,* and *lego.*

121. Give all the infinitives and imperatives of the following: *capio, tollo, quæro, nosco, posco, pango, labor, juvo, veto, gero.*

122. Explain and illustrate the partitive genitive with numerals; with neuter adjectives. Would *nihil memoriabilis* be correct?

123. Give the principal parts, and explain how the perfect is formed, of the following verbs: *dico, colo, gigno, augeo, finio.*

124. Form nouns to express the male agent from *amo, audio, vinco;* the female agent from *vinco, venor, lego.*

125. Distinguish in meaning between the following with the dative and with the accusative: *consulo, metuo, caveo, tempero, moderor.*

126. How may a sentence in the active voice be converted into the passive? Apply the rule to the following: *Romulus urbem muris cinxit; Remus fratrem liberavit.*

127. What are Interjections? Mention the principal ones, with the cases that follow them. What is the quantity of final *as, es, os?*

128. Parse the following: *imitatus, vixisset, attulisset, edisceret, uteretur, scriptam esse, jussi, ausi simus, mansi.*

129. What are the derivations of *Romanus, oratio, orator,* and the meaning of the derivative terminations in each? What suffixes must be attached to a noun to express the office of a person? A collection of trees?

130. Enumerate the chief uses of the Dative case. What is the primary meaning of the dative?

131. Give the gender of the following words, with the rules under which they come, or to which they are exceptions: *magister, arbor, finis, deus, oratio, caput, dies, manus, amnis, lepus, mus, tellus, laus, palus, genu, collis, ensis, lex.*

132. Enumerate the chief uses of the accusative case. What is the rule for the accusative of time and space? In what other case are nouns denoting time and space often put? To denote a place by its distance from another, which case is used? Is a preposition ever expressed with this accusative? Explain the accusative in the following: *ferire fœdus, to strike a treaty.* What impersonal verbs are followed by the accusative?

133. Decline *veter, judicum, ordo, Paris, vimen, lapis, Lysias, Thales.*

134. Give the principal parts of the following: *rapio, facio, curro, tego, texo, tero, queror.*

135. Give the principal parts of *fero* when compounded with *ab, ad, con, dis, ex, in, ob, sub,* and explain the euphonic changes. Mark the quantity of each vowel.

136. Enumerate the chief uses of the Ablative. What is the rule for the voluntary agent after a passive verb? Of the voluntary agent after neuter verbs? What is said of the involuntary agent? What construction arises from the want of a present participle of *esse?*

137. How is the perfect stem of the third conjugation formed? When reduplicated, what vowel may the prefix take? What verbs retain their reduplication in their compounds? Illustrate with the following: *cado, do, mordeo, tundo, spondeo, sto; in* and *cado; in* and *mordeo; re-* and

spondeo; circum and *do; con* and *sto; con* and *disco; ex* and *posco; con* and *curro; ob* and *cædo.*

138. Compare the following: *adolescens, novus, egenus, dives, diligens, leviter, diu.* What is the quantity of final *is, us, ys?*

139. Decline *respublica, ambo, æs, mœnia, os, lacus, deus.*

140. Classify the tenses, and illustrate the rule for sequence of tenses by examples.

141. How is the place *to which, at which, from which,* expressed in Latin?

142. What is meant by the Locative case (or form)? With what case is it usually identical in form? Write the locative of *Karthago, Athenæ, Roma.* Explain the following: *Albæ constituerunt in urbe munita* (see § 46, 2 *b*).

143. Give examples of Inceptive and Diminutive verbs, and the rule for their formation.

144. How is the time *how long,* the time *when,* the time *within which,* an event occurs, expressed?

145. Explain the mode of reckoning time used by the Romans. Express in Latin, May 2, 7, 16; January 4, 9, 25. Give a rule for converting English dates into Latin and Latin into English.

146. What cases following *peto, in, sub, pœnitet, utor, indigeo, do, post, similis, proximus, propior?*

147. Classify Conditional sentences. Write the different forms in Latin, using the following sentence: *if he does this, it is well.* Write each form of particular suppositions after the word *dixit,* making the necessary changes to convert it into the indirect discourse.

148. Give a synopsis of the present stem in both voices of *capio, fero, audio, veho.*

149. Decline together *aula ampla, ipse tu, gravis idem senex.* When is *is* final long?

150. In a negative final or consecutive clause would you use *ne quis* or *non ullus?*

151. Explain the use of *cum* temporal and *cum* causal.

152. In final clauses, how is the tense of the subjunctive determined?

153. How is the want of a perfect active participle supplied in Latin?

154. Illustrate the use of the infinitive in indirect discourse by using the following sentences: *he says that he is writing; he says that he was writing; he says that he has written; he says that he will write; he said that he was writing,* etc.

155. Write two intermediate clauses, in one of which the subjunctive is used, and one the indicative.

156. In how many ways may a purpose be expressed in Latin? Illustrate by examples.

157. Mention the different kinds of Substantive Clauses. Explain the following: *post ejus mortem nihilo minus Helvetii id, quod constituerant, facere, conantur, ut e finibus suis exeant.*

158. Distinguish between the use of *ille, iste,* and *hic.* When is final *a* long?

159. Mention some deponent verbs whose perfect participle is used in a passive sense.

160. Decline (marking the quantity of the penultimate and final syllables) *littera, donum, nostra domus, genus, litus, scelus.*

161. How is a Wish conceived as possible expressed? How a hopeless wish? Illustrate by examples.

162. What perfect participles are used in the sense of a present? How is the place of the present passive participle supplied?

163. What is the distinction in the use of the interrogatives *quis, qui; quid, quod?*

164. What is the potential subjunctive? The optative subjunctive?

165. When do Causal sentences take the subjunctive? What are indefinite relatives? What mood do they generally take?

166. What verbs govern two accusatives?

167. Explain the use of the gerund and gerundive; examples. What is the use of the gerundive in connection with *curo, loco, trado?*

168. Give the principal parts of *venio, curro, disco, vinco, vincio, rapio.*

169. How is a Question asked in Latin? Give examples, using different interrogative particles. How is the answer expressed?

170. Give examples of the use of *ut* and *ne* after verbs of fearing.

171. Distinguish between *non nemo* and *nemo non;* translate *nemo non audiet.*

172. Decline and give the gender of *insula, hortus, sanguis, frons, vulgus, sal, lapis, templum, animal, gens, finis, nox, fides, arcus.*

173. What is meant by elision, ellipsis, arsis, hiatus, stanza, foot, metre?

174. Explain the following: *cæsural pause, cataleetic, synapheia.*

175. Mark the quantity of the vowels in the following words, to which the rules apply (give the rules): *amare, regitur, auditur, monetur, datum, juvi, tuli, didici, occido, nego, nequam.*

EXAMINATION PAPERS.

The following have been used, in past years, in examinations for admission to Harvard College.

I.

1. Give the gender of each of the following nouns, and the rule for it: *pax, pactio, manus, salus, ager, pes.*

2. Decline the following nouns, marking the quantity of the penultimate and final syllables in each form: *filius, iter, domus, dies.*

3. Decline *solus, fortis, idem, quidam.* Compare *ingens, similis, sacer.* Give the meaning of the following endings of nouns and adjectives: *-ula (cornicula), -ium (ministerium), -etum (saxetum), -icius (patricius).*

4. Give the principal parts of the verbs *fundo, veto, verto, voveo, sancio, cædo.* Give the third person singular of the present subjunctive active and of the future indicative passive of *veto, verto,* and *sancio.* Inflect the imperfect subjunctive passive of *facio,* and the future indicative active of *transeo.*

5. By what cases respectively are these words followed: *occurro, condemno, sub, fruor, doceo, noceo?*

II.

1. Write down the following words and mark the quantity of the penult, giving the rules of prosody: *tempora, responderunt, dederint, discedo, iniquus, oceanus, remanet, egi, impedit, manus, brevis, cervices, protulit, nolite, vectigal.*

2. Meaning of termination: *-etum* in *rosetum?* Of *-olus* in *filiolus?* Of *-ax* in *loquax?* Of *-mentum* in *tegumentum?*

3. Write the perfects and supines of *diligo, reperio, maneo, perfundo, indulgeo, cedo, cædo, cado, moveo, cognosco.*

4. Compare *acer, bene, magnus, similis, gravis.*

5. Give the present subjunctive and future indicative, third person singular, of *sum, cerno, eo, malo, caveo, venio.*

6. Decline *aliquis, alter, ipse.*

7. What is the Latin for *five?* for *fifth?* for *five times?* for *fifty? fiftieth? fifty times?* Write in Latin, *one man in every ten.*

III.

1. Decline *soror, vir, vis, vulnus, animal.* Give the gender of each of these nouns, with the rule. Mark the quantity of all the penultimate and final syllables you write in this section. Give the genitive plural of *gens* and *hostis,* with rules.

2. Decline *sacer, acer, alius.* Compare *similis, superus, parvus, juvenis.* Form and compare adverbs from *acer, altus.* Decline *idem, tu, aliquis.* Give the Latin numerals for *sixty, seventy, eighty, six hundred, seven hundred, eight hundred.*

3. Give the principal parts of *vinco, vincio, spondeo, domo, lacesso, caedo, audeo.* All the participles and infinitives of *adipiscor* and *fero.* The second person singular of the future indicative and of the imperfect subjunctive of *audeo, audio, fugio, eo, possum, volo.* Mark all the penultimate and final syllables you write in this section.

4. How is the price or value expressed in Latin? time in which? place where? What case or cases follow the verbs *miseret, obliviscor, ignosco, fungor, rogo,* respectively?

5. What is a spondee? An iambus? What is an heroic hexameter?

IV.

1. Decline *dens, alius, tu, si quis,* and *audax,* marking the quantity of penultimate and final syllables. Compare *audax, multus,* and *nequam.* Compare adverbs formed from *audax, bonus, miser,* and *honorificus.* Give the rule for the gender of *formido, caput, pax, fas,* and *Tiberis.*

2. Inflect the future indicative and present subjunctive of *teneo, gero, sto,* and *fio,* marking the quantity of all the syllables. Give the infinitives of *tollo* and *scribo.* Give all the participles of *haurio* and *orior.* Give the principal parts of *uro, vendo, paro, pario, pareo, memini,* and *nanciscor.*

3. What case or cases follow *fido, jubeo, memini, existimo, poenitet, contra, clam,* and the interjection *O*? By what two cases may price or value be expressed, and when is one used, and when the other? What case follows the comparative when *quam* is omitted? When is it necessary that *quam* be expressed? Give five important rules for the ablative without a preposition after verbs.

4. When is *ut* omitted before the subjunctive? Give the rules for the subjunctive in relative clauses. Translate into Latin *the plan of setting the city on fire,* using first the gerund and then the gerundive. (*Plan, concilium, to set on fire, inflammare.*)

V.

1. Decline *mare, pignus, cor, fructus.* Give the gender of these nouns, with the rules. Mark the quantity of any increments that occur in their declension.

2. Compare *humilis, niger, malus.* Give the synopsis of *morior* and *gaudeo.* Give the second person of the future indicative, and of the present imperfect and perfect subjunctive of *spero, fero, volo,* in the active voice. The same of *facio* and *audio* in the passive. Give the principal parts of *fateor, tono, peto, vincio, colo, tango.*

3. Compare *diu.* Form and compare an adverb from *brevis.* What are the meanings of the terminations of *copiosus, civilis, audacia, victrix?* What cases follow *infero, poenitet, parco, careo, fruor, tenax, fretus, in, ante, super?*

4. How is the place to which, the price, the agent of a passive verb, expressed in Latin?

5. How is a condition contrary to the fact expressed in Latin? State one case in which a relative clause requires the subjunctive. One case where the subjunctive is used in principal clauses. What is a gerundive? Give an example.

VI.

1. Decline *Penelope, mons, cubile,* and give the gender, with the rule. Mark the quantity of penults and final syllables of the above words. Decline *uterque.* Decline *acer,* and compare it. Form an adverb from it, and compare it.

2. Compare *senex* and *munificus.* Give the derivation of *filiolus, documentum, quercetum, audax, capesso,* and the meaning of the terminations. Give all the participles and infinitives of *vereor* and *caedo,* and mark the quantity of the penults. Inflect the imperatives of *fero, ordior, nolo, fateor.* Give the present and imperfect subjunctive, first person singular, of *adjuvo, eo, soleo,* and *fugio,* marking the quantity of the penults. Give the principal parts of *pario, pareo, paro, reddo, redeo, surgo,* and the compounds of *ab* and *fero.*

3. What case or cases follow *refert, irascor, circumdo?* How do the constructions of names of towns differ from those of other words? How is the degree of difference expressed in Latin? How the agent of the participle in *-dus?* What construction is used after verbs of saying? verbs of fearing? How may a purpose be expressed? How does a gerund resemble a noun? How does it resemble a verb? How does the gerundive differ from it?

VII.

1. Decline the following words, and give their genders respectively: *onus, collis, salus, gradus.* Decline *felix, quidam, senex.* Compare *parvus, beneficus.* Form and compare an adverb from *acer.*

2. Give the synopsis of *mordeo, scio,* in the active voice, and of *hortor, orior, polliceor, nolo.* Give the principal parts of *paro, pario, pareo, ulciscor, pango, tollo.*

3. What are the meanings of the derivative terminations in *acritudo, clamito, vinculum, parvulus ?*

4. What case or cases follow *moneo, prosum, rogo, in, praeter ?* What is the force of *num* in a question? Of *-ne ?* Explain the mood and tense of *mansisset* in *mansissetque utinam fortuna.* Explain the mood of *esset,* and the case of *fronde,* in *nos delubra miseri, quibus ultimus esset ille dies, velamus fronde.* Explain the mood of *polliceantur* in *ad eum legati veniunt, qui polliceantur obsides dare.*

5. What is the use of the supine in *-um ?* In *-u ?* Explain construction of *usui* and *fore* in *magno sibi usui fore arbitrabatur.* Describe the feet of two syllables. Mark the quantity of the penults and last syllables in the above extracts.

VIII.

1. Decline *filius, pectus, manus, animal.* Give the genders, and mark the quantity of all the penultimate and final syllables. Give the gender and the ablative singular and the genitive plural of *imago, mons, vis, turris, sedile.* Decline *capax, aeger,* and the comparative of *miser.* Compare *facilis, acer,* and an adverb formed from *piger.* Decline *uterque.*

2. Give the first person of the future indicative, and all tenses of the subjunctive of *possum, pario, sono, vereor, eo, soleo.* Mark quantities of penults. Give the infinitives and participles, active and passive, of *spondeo, morior, paro, quaero, queror, adipiscor.*

3. Explain the force of the derivative terminations in *longitudo, tenax, vehiculum, Priamides, clamito, vinolentus, filiolus.*

4. What is the construction in Latin of the place in which (including names of towns)? the price or value? the degree or measure of difference between objects compared? the agent of the passive voice?

5. What case or cases follow *credo, pudet, fungor, refert, aptus, avidus, dignus, in, pro, propter, doceo, condemno, circumdo ?*

6. How is a future condition with its conclusion expressed? How a condition contrary to fact? How an object clause after a verb of fearing? of commanding? of saying?

7. Translate *cave eas,* and explain the peculiarity. When can you use the gerundive for the gerund? Give an example of each. Give an example of the use of the supine.

IX.

1. Decline together in the singular *Marcus Tullius Cicero senex.* In the same way decline (both in the singular and plural), with the adjective annexed in the proper gender, *dies* (*fastus*), *flumen* (*aureus*); in the plural, *arma* (*victrix*), *dea* (*immortalis*). Mark the quantity of all the vowels in the above nouns and adjectives.

2. State the signification of the terminations *-men* (in *flumen*), *-eus* (in *aureus*), *-trix* (in *victrix*). What classes of words of the third declension form their ablative in *i* only?

3. Give the principal parts of *adjuvo, nolo, venio, paciscor, sperno, foveo, mordeo, scindo,* marking the quantity of the penultimate vowel.

4. Give synopsis of *mordeo* and *paciscor;* give all the infinitives and participles, and inflect the imperatives.

5. Give all the rules you remember for verbs that govern the dative. State the case or cases by which the price, the source, time when, and place where (including names of towns), are expressed, and give the rules.

6. Give the rule for the subjunctive in the following sentences:

Quid enim, Catilina, est quod te jam in hac urbe delectare possit?
Nunc ego mea video quid intersit.
Supplicatio decreta est his verbis quod urbem incendiis liberassem.
C. Sulpicium misi qui ex aedibus Cethegi, si quid telorum esset, efferret.
O fortunate adolescens qui Homerum præconem inveneris.

VOCABULARY.

I. LATIN AND ENGLISH.

ABBREVIATIONS.

a.	active.	*imperat.*	imperative.
abl.	ablative.	*impers.*	impersonal
acc.	accusative.	*indecl.*	indeclinable.
adj.	adjective.	*inch.*	inchoative.
adv.	adv.	*interj.*	interjection.
conj.	conjunction.	*m.*	masculine.
comp.	comparative.	*n.*	neuter.
dat.	dative.	*num.*	numeral.
def.	defective.	*part.*	participle.
dep.	deponent.	*perf.*	perfect.
dim.	diminutive.	*pl.*	plural.
f.	feminine.	*prep.*	preposition.
gen.	genitive.	*pron.*	pronoun.

The quantity of vowels that are long or short by *position*, of diphthongs, and final syllables, is not given.

The references are to the sections of ALLEN & GREENOUGH'S Latin Grammar.

ā, ăb, *prep.* with *abl.* (**a** only before consonants; **ab** before vowels and consonants), *from, by;* **ab aliquo stare,** *to stand on the side of any one.*

ăb-ăliēno, āre, āvi, ātum, *a.* (**ab; ăliēnus**), *to estrange, alienate.*

ab-do, dĕre, dĭdi, dĭtum, *a., to put away, hide, conceal.*

ab-eo, īre, īvi, *or* **ii, ĭtum,** *n.* (§ 37, 6), *to go away, depart.*

ab-jĭcio, jĭcĕre, jēcī, jectum, *a.* (**ab; jăcio**), *to throw away, give up, abandon.*

ab-scindo, scindĕre, scĭdi, scissum, *a., to tear away, deprive, separate.*

abs-ens, entis, *part.* (**ab-sum**), *absent.*

ab-sĭmĭlis, e, *adj., unlike, dissimilar.*

ab-solvo, solvĕre, solvi, sŏlūtum, *a., to unbind, acquit, discharge.*

ab-sorbeo, sorbēre, sorbui, sorptum, *a., to suck in, swallow up, devour.*

abs-que, *prep.* with *abl., without, but for, except.*

abs-tĭneo, tĭnēre, tĭnui, tentum, *a.* and *n.* (**tĕneo**), *to hold* or *keep away from, abstain, refrain.*

ab-sum, esse, fui, *n. irr., to be absent, to be wanting.*

ab-sūmo, sūmĕre, sumpsi, sumptum, *a., to take away, waste, destroy.*

āc, *see* **at-que.**

Acca Lārentia, æ, *f.*, the wife of the shepherd Faustŭlus, who reared Romŭlus and Remus.
ac-cēdo, cēdĕre, cessi, cessum, *n.* (**ad; cēdo**), *to go towards, approach, be added.*
acceptus, a, um, *part.* (**ac-cĭpio**), *agreeable, acceptable.*
ac-cĭdo, cĭdĕre, cĭdi, *no sup.*, *n.* (**ad; cădo**), *to fall upon, befall, happen.*
ac-cīdo, cīdĕre, cīdi, cīsum, *a.* (**ad; caedo**), *to cut, consume, weaken.*
ac-cingo, cingĕre, cinxi, cinctum, *a.* (**ad; cingo**), *to gird on, arm, equip.*
ac-cĭpio, cĭpĕre, cēpi, ceptum, *a.* (**ad; căpio**), *to take, receive, get, undertake.*
ac-clāmo, āre, āvi, ātum, *n.* and *a.*, *to cry out, applaud, proclaim.*
ac-curro, currĕre, cŭcurri *and* **curri, cursum,** *n.*, *to run to, hasten to.*
ac-cūso, āre, āvi, ātum, *a.* (**ad; causa**), *to accuse, blame, inform against.*
Ăcarnānia, æ, *f.*, a province of central Greece (now Carnia).
ācer, cris, cre, *adj.* (**ăcuo**), *sharp, keen, eager, active.*
ăcerbe, *adv.*, *sharply, bitterly, harshly.*
ăcerbus, a, um, *adj.*, *sharp, bitter, harsh.*
ăcervus, i, *m.*, *a heap, pile.*
ăcētum, i, *n.*, *vinegar.*
ăcĭdus, a, um, *adj.*, *sour, unpleasant.*
ăcies, ēi, *f.*, *an edge; a line of battle.*
ācrĭter, *adv.* (**ācer**), *sharply, keenly, fiercely.*
Actiăcus, a, um, *adj.* (**Actium**), *relating to Actium, of Actium.*
Actium, ii, *n.*, a promontory of Acarnānia on the Ambracian Gulf.
ăcuo, ĕre, ui, ūtum, *a.*, *to make sharp, rouse up, excite.*
ăcus, ūs, *f.* (**ăcuo** § **12**, 3, *d*), (a thing sharpened), *a needle, pin.*
ăcūtus, a, um, *part.* (**ăcuo**), *sharpened, sharp, pointed.*
ăd, *prep.* with *acc.*, *to, towards, near to, at, besides.*
ăd-ămo, āre, āvi, ātum, *a.*, *to begin to love.*
ad-do, addĕre, addĭdi, addĭtum, *a.*, *to add, join, annex to.*
ad-dŭbĭto, āre, āvi, ātum, *n.* and *a.*, *to be in doubt, to be doubtful of.*
ad-dūco, ĕre, xi, ctum, *a.*, *to lead along, bring to.*
ăd-eo, īre, īvi *or* **ii, ĭtum,** *n.* and *a.*, *to go to, approach; undergo, submit to.*
ăd-eō, *adv.* (**ad; is**), *so far, so long, so, truly, moreover.*
adf, *see* **aff.**
ăd-hĭbeo, ēre, ui, ĭtum, *a.* (**ad; hăbeo**), *to hold* or *apply to; to send for, summon, have near.*
ad-huc, *adv.* (**ad; hic**), *to this place, thus far, besides, as yet.*
ăd-ĭpiscor, ĭpisci, eptus sum, *dep.* (**ad; ăpiscor,** § **35**, 1, *h*), *to win, get, obtain.*
adĭ-tus, ūs, *m.* (**ădeo,** § **44**, 1, *c*. 2), *a going to, approach.*
ad-jĭcio, ĕre, ēci, ectum, *a.* (**ad; jăcio**), *to cast, throw, add, put on.*
adjū-mentum, i, *n.* (**adjŭvo,** § **44**, 1, *c*, 2), *help, assistance.*
ad-jungo, ĕre, xi, ctum, *a.*, *to join* or *fasten to, annex, put upon.*
ad-jŭvo, jŭvāre, jūvi, jūtum, *a.* and *n.* (§ **31**, 2), *to help, assist.*
ad-mĭnistro, āre, āvi, ātum, *a.* and *n.*, *to manage, perform, attend, wait.*
admīrā-tio, ōnis, *f.* (**admīror,** § **44**, 1, *c*, 2), *an admiring, admiration, wonder, surprise.*
ad-mīror, āri, ātus sum, *dep.*, *to admire, wonder at.*
ad-mitto, mittĕre, mīsi, missum, *a.*, *to allow, admit, commit;* **admisso equo,** *at full gallop.*

ad-mŏdum, *adv.*, *very*, *exceedingly*, *quite.*

ad-mŏneo, ēre, ui, ĭtum, *a.*, *to put in mind of*, *admonish*, *warn.*

ad-mŏveo, mŏvēre, mōvi, mōtum, *a.*, *to lead* or *move towards*, *bring near*, *apply.*

ădŏlescens, entis, *part.* (**ădŏlesco**), *growing up*, *young.* As NOUN, *common gender*, *a young man*, *a young woman* (from 15 to 30, and sometimes to 40 and later).

ădŏle-sco, ŏlescĕre, ŏlēvi, ultum, *n. inch.* (**ădŏleo**, § **36**, *a*), *to grow up*, *grow*, *increase.*

ăd-ŏpĕrio, īre, ui, tum, *a.* (§ **34**, 2), *to cover.*

ăd-opto, āre, āvi, ātum, *a.*, *to choose*, *adopt.*

ăd-ŏrior, ŏrīri, ortus sum, *dep.* (§ **35**, 1, *h*), *to rise up against; to attack*, *assault*, *begin.*

ăd-ōro, āre, āvi, ātum, *a.*, *to worship*, *respect*, *entreat*, *beg.*

ads, *see* **ass.**

ad-sum, ădesse, affui, *n.*, *to be near*, *be present*, *assist.*

ădultus, a, um, *part.* (**ădŏlesco**), *grown up.*

ad-vĕnio, vĕnīre, vēni, ventum, *n.*, *to come to*, *arrive*, *approach.*

adven-to, āre, āvi, ātum, *n.*, *intens.* (**advĕnio**, § **36**, *b*), *to come to*, *advance.*

adven-tus, ūs, *m.* (**advĕnio**, § **44**, 1, *c*, 2), *a coming to*, *drawing near*, *arrival.*

adversārius, a, um, *adj.* (**adversus**), *turned towards*, *fronting.* As NOUN, *m.*, *an opponent*, *enemy.*

adversor, āri, ātus sum, *dep.* (**adversus**), *to stand opposite to*, *resist*, *oppose*, *thwart.*

adversus, *prep.* with *acc.*, *opposite to*, *against*, *towards.*

adversus, a, um, *part.* (**adverto**), *turned towards*, *opposite*, *contrary.*

ad-verto, ĕre, ti, sum, *a.*, *to turn to* or *towards*, *to direct;* **animum advertere**, *to observe*, *attend to;* **animum advertere in aliquem**, *to punish one.*

advŏca-tio, ōnis, *f.* (**advŏco**, § **44**, 1, *c*, 2), *legal assistance*, *advocacy.*

advŏcātus, i, *m.* (one who is called), *a legal assistant*, *counsellor*, *attorney*, *advocate.*

ad-vŏco, āre, āvi, ātum, *a.*, *to call to*, *summon.*

ædes, is, *f.*, *a temple; pl.*, *a house* (§ **14**, 2, *c*).

ædĭfĭc-ium, ii, *n.* (**ædĭfĭco**, § **44**, 1, *c*, 2), *a building.*

æd-ĭ-fĭco, āre, āvi, ātum, *a.* (**ædes; făcio**), *to make a building*, *to build.*

Ædui, ōrum, *m.*, a tribe in Gaul between the **Lĭger** (modern Loire), and the **Ărar** (Saône).

æger, gra, grum, *adj.*, *sick*, *weary*, *sad.*

ægrē, *adv.* (**æger**), *with difficulty*, *scarcely.*

ægrōto, āre, āvi, ātum, *n.* (**ægrōtus**), *to be sick.* [*ill.*

ægrōtus, a, um, *adj.* (**æger**), *sick*,

Ægyptus, i, *f.*, *Egypt.*

æquā-lis, e, *adj.* (**æquo**), *equal in age*, *like*, *resembling.*

æquē, *adv.* (**æquus**), *equally*, *just so.*

æquor, ŏris, *n.* (**æquo**), *a level surface*, *the sea.*

æquus, a, um, *adj.*, *plain*, *smooth*, *level*, *equal*, *just right.*

æquo, āre, āvi, ātum, *a.* (*to make* **æquus**), *to make even*, *to equalize.*

āĕr, ĕris, *m.* (*acc.* **aĕra** and **aĕrem**), *the air*, *cloud*, *mist.*

ær-ārium, ii, *n.* (**æs**), (the place where money is kept), *treasury.*

æs, æris, *n.*, *copper*, *money*, *wages;* **æs alienum**, *debt.*

æs-tas, ātis, *f.*, *summer.*

æs-tĭmo, āre, āvi, ātum, *a.* (**æs**), *to estimate*, *value.*

æst-īvus, a, um, *adj.* (**æstas**), *of summer, summer-like.* As NOUN, **æstīva, ōrum,** *n., summer-quarters.*

ætas, ātis, *f.* (**ævum**), *age* (*time of life*).

ætern-ĭtas, ātis, *f.* (**æturnus,** § **44**, 1, *c*, 2), *eternity.*

æt-ernus, a, um, *adj.* (**ætas**), *eternal, everlasting, enduring.*

ævum, i, *n., an age* (*period*).

affecto, āre, āvi, ātum, *a.* (**affectus**), *to have a passion for any thing, to strive after, reach.*

affectus, ūs, *m.* (**affĭcio**), *love, fondness, passion.*

af-fĕro, ferre, attŭli, allātum, *a.* (**ad**; **fĕro**), *to bring, announce, procure, betake, allege.*

af-fĭcio, ĕre, fēci, fectum (**ad**; **făcio**), *a., to treat, affect, disturb, visit* (*with punishment,* &c.).

af-fīgo, ēre, ixi, ixum, *a.* (**ad**; **fīgo**), *to fasten, join, attach.*

af-fīnis, e, *adj.* (**ad**; **fīnis**), *bordering upon, adjacent to, kindred.*

affīn-ĭtas, ātis, *f.* (**affīnis,** § **44**, 1, *c*, 2), *relationship by marriage, relationship, alliance, nearness.*

af-firmo, āre, āvi, ātum, *a.* (**ad**; **firmo**), *to make strong, confirm, maintain.*

af-flīgo, ĕre, ixi, ictum, *a.* (**ad**; **flīgo**), *to strike, distress, cast down.*

ā-fŏre, *fut. inf. of* **absum,** *to be away, absent.*

Āfrĭca, æ, *f., Africa,* especially the country near Carthage.

ăger, gri, *m., a field, territory.*

agger, ĕris, *m., a heap, mound, embankment.*

ag-grĕdior, grĕdi, gressus sum, *dep.* (**ad**; **grădior**), *to go to, approach, attack.*

ag-men, ĭnis, *n.* (**ăgo,** § **44**, 1, *c*, 2), *a flock, troop, crowd, army* (*on the march*).

a-gnosco, noscĕre, nōvi, nĭtum, *a.* (**ad**; **gnosco** = **nosco**), *to recognize, own, acknowledge.*

agnus, i, *m., a lamb.*

ăgo, ĕre, ēgi, actum, *a., to act, do, lead, drive; to deal, treat, strive, endeavor.*

agr-ārius, a, um, *adj.* (**ăger**), *of fields* or *public lands.*

agr-ĭ-cŏla, æ, *m.* (**ăger**; **cŏlo**), *a cultivator of the land, a farmer.*

agrĭcul-tūra, æ, *f.* (**ăger**; **cŏlo,** § **44**, 1, *c*, 2), *agriculture, husbandry.*

āio, *def.* (§ **38**, 2, *a*), *to speak, say.*

āla, æ, *f., a wing, the wing of an army.*

ălăcer, cris, cre, *adj., lively, brisk, quick, eager, active.*

ălacr-ĭtas, ātis, *f.* (**ălăcer,** § **44**, 1, *c*, 2), *liveliness, eagerness, alacrity.*

āl-ārius, a, um, *adj.* (**āla**) *of the wing* (*of an army*).

Alba, æ, *f. Alba* (*Longa*), an ancient town of Latium, 20 miles S. E. of Rome, built by Ascănius, son of Ænēas.

Alb-ānus, a, um, *adj.* (**Alba,** § **44**, 1, *c*, 3), *of* or *belonging to Alba; Alban.*

albus, a, um, *adj., white, fair.*

ālea, æ, *f., a die* or *dice* for playing at games of chance; *hazard, venture, risk.*

āles, ālĭtis, *adj.* (**āla,** *and* **i,** *root of* **eo,** wing-going), *with wings, winged.* As NOUN, *com. gen., a bird.*

Ălexander, dri, *m.* (*Defender of men*), son of Philip and Olympia, surnamed "the Great," the founder of the Macedonian Empire (B.C. 356–323).

Ălexandrīa, æ, *f.,* the city built by Alexander the Great (B.C. 332), upon the north coast of Egypt, noted for its luxury.

ăli-ēnus, a, um, *adj.* (**ălius**), *belonging to another person* or *thing; another's, foreign, hostile;* **aes alienum,** *debt.*

ălĭquamdiu, *adv.* (**ălĭquis**; **diu**), *awhile, for a while, for some time.*

ălĭqu-ando, *adv.* (ălĭquis) (of time past, future, or present), *formerly, hereafter, now, some time, at length.*

ălĭ-quantus, a, um, *adj.* (ălius; quantus), *some, considerable.*

ălĭ-quanto, *adv.* (ălĭquantus), *considerably, not a little.*

ălĭ-quis (ălĭqui), **qua, quid** or **quod** (alius; quis), *pron. indef.* (§ **22**, 2, *d*), *some one, some, any;* **aliquĭd**, *something, somewhat.*

ălĭ-quot, *indefinite numeral adj., indecl.* (ălius; quot), *some, several, a few.*

ălĭquŏt-ies, *adv.* (ălĭquot), *several times.*

ălius, a, um, *adj., another, other* (§ **16**, 1, *b*); **ălius ... ălius**, *one . . . another.*

al-lĭcio, lĭcĕre, lexi, lectum, *a.* (ad; lăcio), *to allure, entice.*

al-lĭgo, āre, āvi, ātum, *a.* (ad; lĭgo), *to bind to, fasten, hinder, detain.*

Allŏbrŏges, um, *m.*, a Gallic people, bounded on the north and west by the **Rhŏdănus** (*Rhone*), south by the **Ĭsăra** (*Isère*), and extending eastward to the Alps.

al-lŏquor, qui, cūtus sum, *dep.* (ad; lŏquor), *to speak, address.*

almus, a, um, *adj.* (ălo), *nourishing, nutritious, benign, propitious.*

ălo, ĕre, ui, alĭtum *and* **altum**, *a., to nourish, support, feed, sustain.*

Alpes, ium, *f., the Alps;* the high mountain range between Italia, Gallia, and Helvetia.

altē, *adv.* (altus), *on high, highly, deeply.*

alter, tĕra, tĕrum, *adj.* (§ **16**, 1, *b*), *one of two, other, second;* **alter ... alter**, *one . . . the other.*

alter-cor, āri, ātus sum, *dep.* (alter), *to dispute, contend, wrangle.*

altius-cŭlus, a, um, *adj. dim.* (§ **44**, 3), (altus), *rather high.*

altus, a, um, *part.* (ălo), *high, deep.*

alveus, i, *m.* (alvus), *a channel, trough, skiff.*

alvus, i, *f., the belly, stomach.*

amb-io, īre, īvi or **ĭi, ītum**, *n. and a.* (eo), *to go about, solicit, canvass.*

ambĭ-tio, ōnis, *f.* (ambio; § **44**, 1, *c*, 2), *a canvassing, desire for honor, ambition.*

ambo, æ, o, *num. adj.* (§ **18**, 1, *b*), *both.*

ambŭlo, āre, āvi, ātum, *n., to walk.*

ā-mens, entis, *adj., mad, insane, distracted.*

ămīc-ĭtia, æ, *f.* (ămīcus; § **44**, 1, *c*, 2), *friendship.*

ăm-īcus, a, um, *adj.* (ămo), *loving, friendly, kind.*

ămīcus, i, *m., a friend.*

ā-mitto, mittĕre, mīsi, missum, *a., to let go, dismiss, lose.*

amnis, is, *m., a river* (large deep stream).

ămo, āre, āvi, ātum, *a., to love.*

ămor, ōris, *m.* (ămo; § **44**, 1, *c*, 2), *love, desire, longing.*

am-plector, plecti, plexus sum, *dep., to wind around, embrace.*

amplius, *comp. adv.* (amplē), *more, longer, further.*

amplus, a, um, *adj., great, ample, spacious, grand, large.*

am-pŭto, āre, āvi, ātum, *a., to cut around, lop off, prune.*

Ămūlius, ii, *m.*, a king of Alba, brother of Numitor, and great-uncle of Romulus.

ăn, *disjunctive interrogative particle* (§ **71**), *whether, or.*

ănas, ătis, *com. gen., a duck.*

an-ceps, cĭpĭtis, *adj.* (an; căput), *two-headed, doubtful, uncertain, critical.*

ancil-la, æ, *f., a maid-servant.*

ango, gĕre, xi, ctum *or* **xum**, *a., to press tight, choke, strangle.*

anguis, is, *m. and f., a serpent, snake.*

angust-iæ, **ārum**, *f.* (**angustus**, § **44**, 1, *c*, 2), *narrowness, a narrow pass, defile.*
angus-tus, **a**, **um**, *adj.* (**ango**), *narrow, scanty.*
ăn-ĭma, **æ**, *f.*, *air, breath, life.*
ănĭm-adverto, **tĕre**, **ti**, **sum**, *a.* (**ănĭmus**; **adverto**), *to attend to, consider, observe;* **animadvertere in aliquem**, *to punish one.*
ănĭm-al, **ālis**, *n.* (**ănĭma**), *an animal, living creature.*
ăn-ĭmus, **i**, *m.*, *the soul, mind, disposition, temper, thought.*
an-non, *conj.*, *or not.*
ann-ōna, **æ**, *f.* (**annus**), *the yearly produce, harvest, corn; the price of corn, provision.*
annus, **i**, *m.*, *a year.*
ante, *prep.* with *acc.*, *before, in front of.* As ADVERB, *before, previously.*
ante-curro, **ĕre**, *no perf.*, *no sup.*, *n.*, *to run before.*
ante-eo, **īre**, **īvi** *or* **ĭi**, *no. sup.*, *n.*, *to go before, precede, excel.*
ante . . . quam, *conj.*, *before that.*
Antiŏchus, **i**, *m.*, a Syrian king.
ant-īquus, **a**, **um**, *adj.* (**ante**), *former, ancient, old.*
Antōnius, **ĭi**, *m.*, *Marcus Antonius*, the distinguished triumvir, conquered by Octāviānus, at Actium, B.C. 31.
antrum, **i**, *n.*, *a cave, cavern, grotto.*
ănus, **ūs**, *f.*, *an old woman.*
anxius, **a**, **um**, *adj.* (**ango**), *tormented, anxious, troubled, unquiet.*
ăper, **pri**, *m.*, *a wild boar.*
ăpĕrio, **īre**, **ui**, **tum**, *a.*, *to open, unclose, show, reveal.*
ăper-tus, **a**, **um**, *part.* (**ăpĕrio**), *open, clear, free.*
ăpis, **is**, *f.*, *a bee.*
Ăpollo, **ĭnis**, *m.*, *Apollo*, son of Jupĭter and Latōna, twin brother of Diāna; god of light, poetry, music, archery, also of the healing art.
Ăpollōnia, **æ**, *f.*, a town of Macedonia.
ap-pāreo, **ēre**, **ui**, **ĭtum**, *n.* (**ad**; **pāreo**), *to appear, be visible, manifest.*
appellā-tio, **ōnis**, *f.* (**appello**, § **44**, 1, *c.* 2), *an addressing, address, appeal.*
ap-pello, **āre**, **āvi**, **ātum**, *a.* (**ad**; **pello**), *to address, speak to, call, name.*
ap-pendo, **ĕre**, **di**, **sum**, *a.* (**ad**; **pendo**), *to weigh.*
appĕt-ens, **entis**, *part.* (**appĕto**), *striving after, eager for.*
ap-plaudo, **ĕre**, **si**, **sum**, *a.* and *n.*, *to applaud; to clap the hands.*
ap-plĭco, **āre**, **āvi** *or* **ui**, **ātum** *or* **ĭtum**, *a.* and *n.* (**ad**; **plĭco**), *to join, fix, fasten, apply; to approach, draw near.*
ap-pōno, **ponĕre**, **pŏsui**, **pŏsĭtum**, *a.* (**ad**; **pōno**), *to put, place near, appoint, assign.*
ap-prĕhendo, **ĕre**, **di**, **sum**, *a.* (**ad**; **prĕhendo**), *to seize, take hold of.*
ap-prŏpinquo, **āre**, **āvi**, **ātum**, *n.* (**ad**; **prŏpinquo**), *to approach, draw nigh.*
Ăprīlis, **is**, *m.* (**ăpĕrio**), *April;* the month in which the earth OPENS itself to fertility. As ADJ., *of April.*
aptus, **a**, **um**, *adj.*, *joined, fastened, suited, fit, appropriate.*
ăpud, *prep.* with *acc.*, *with, near to, in the presence of;* **apud me**, *at my house.*
ăqua, **æ**, *f.*, *water.*
ăquĭla, **æ**, *f.*, *the eagle; the standard* of the Roman legion.
ăquĭl-ĭ-fer, **ĕri**, *m.* (**ăquĭla**; **fĕro**), *an eagle-bearer, standard-bearer.*
Ăquītānia, **æ**, *f.*, a province in Southern Gaul.
Ăquītān-us, **a**, **um**, *adj.*, *Aquitanian.*
Ărar, **ăris**, *m.*, a tributary of the Rhodănus in Gaul (now the Saône).

arbĭter, tri, *m.*, *a spectator, hearer, umpire, judge.*

arbĭtrium, ii, *n.* (**arbĭter**), *a decision, judgment; power, will.*

arbitror, āri, ātus sum, *dep.* (**arbĭter**), *to hear, observe, judge, think, suppose.*

arbor, ŏris, *f.*, *a tree.*

arc-a, æ, *f.* (**arceo**) (*the enclosing thing*), *a chest, box.*

arc-eo, ēre, ui, *no sup.*, *a.*, *to inclose, shut up, keep off, hinder, prevent.*

ar-cesso, ĕre, sīvi, sītum, *a.* (**ad; cēdo**) (TO CAUSE *to come*), *to summon, call, invite.*

arct-ē, *adv.* (**arctus**), *closely, tightly.*

arc-tus, a, um, *adj.*, *narrow, close, strait, confined.*

arcus, ūs, *m.*, *a bow, rainbow, curve, arch.*

ard-eo, ēre, arsi, arsum, *n.*, *to burn, blaze.*

ard-or, ōris, *m.* (**ardeo**, § **44**, 1, *c.* 2), *a burning; a flame, fire.*

ărē-na, æ, *f.* (**āreo**) (*the dry thing*), *sand.*

ār-eo, ēre, ui, *no sup.*, *n.*, *to be dry.*

argentum, i, *n.*, *silver, money.*

ār-ĭdus, a, um, *adj.* (**āreo**), *dry, parched.*

ăriĕs, iĕtis, *m.*, *a ram; an engine for battering down walls; a battering-ram.*

arma, ōrum, *n.*, *arms, defensive weapons.*

Ariovistus, i, *m.*, a king of the Germans.

Armĕnia, æ, *f.*, a country of Asia.

Armĕnius, a, um, *adj.*, *Armenian.*

armo, āre, āvi, ātum, *a.* (**arma**), *to furnish with weapons, to arm, equip, fit out.*

ăro, āre, āvi, ātum, *a.*, *to plough, till.*

Arpīnum, i, *n.*, a town in Latium, S. W. of Rome, the birthplace of Cicero and Marius.

ar-rĭpio, ĕre, rĭpui, reptum, *a.* (**ad; răpio**), *to snatch, catch, seize, engage in eagerly.*

arrŏga-ns, ntis, *part.* (**arrŏgo**), *assuming, presumptuous, haughty, proud.*

arrŏgan-ter, *adv.* (**arrŏgans**), *assumingly, haughtily, proudly.*

ar-rŏgo, āre, āvi, ātum, *a.* (**ad; rŏgo**), *to appropriate to one's self, to claim, assume.*

ars, artis, *f.*, *skill, ability, cleverness, invention.*

ăr-undo, ĭnis, *f.* (**ad; unda**) (*that which grows near water*), *the reed, cane.*

Arverni, ōrum, *m.*, a people of Gaul, in the present Auvergne.

ar-vum, i, *n.* (**ăro**), *cultivated land, a field.*

arx, arcis, *f.* (*for* **arc-s** *from* **arceo**), *a castle, citadel, tower.*

as, assis, *m.*, *a unit; an as;* a small coin used as the UNIT of weight, money, and measure among the Romans (§ **85**).

a-scendo, scendĕre, scendi, scensum, *n.* and *a.* (**ad; scando**), *to ascend, mount up, climb.*

ascen-sus, ūs, *m.* (**ascendo**, § **44**, 1, *c*, 2), *an ascending, ascent.*

Ascănius, ii, *m.*, a son of Æneās.

Asia, æ, *f.*, *Asia,* generally Asia Minor.

ăsĭnus, i, *m.*, *an ass.*

asper, ĕra, ĕrum, *adj.*, *rough, harsh, violent, sharp.*

a-spĭcio, ĕre, exi, ectum, *a.* (**ad; spĕcio**), *to look at, to behold, see.*

aspis, ĭdis, *f.* (§ **11**, iii. 6, *b*), *a viper, adder; a shield.*

as-sĭdeo, ēre, ēdi, essum, *n.* and *a.* (**ad; sĕdeo**), *to sit near, attend, watch; to invest, besiege.*

as-surgo, gĕre, rexi, rectum, *n.* (**ad; surgo**), *to rise up, stand up.*

ăt, *conj.*, *but, yet.*

Athēnæ, ārum, *f.*, *Athens,* the chief city of Attica.

Ātĭlius, ii, *m.*, *a Roman name.*

at-que *or* **ac,** *conj.* [in the best writers **ac** is used only before a word beginning with a consonant], *and also, and besides, and;* **simul atque**, *as soon as;* **minus ac**, *less than.*

atrium, ii, *n.* (the principal apartment of a Roman house, next to the entrance), *a hall, court.*

ātrox, **ōcis**, *adj., savage, fierce, wild, stern, cruel.*

at-tendo, **ĕre**, **di**, **tum**, *a.* (**ad; tendo**), *to attend to, consider.*

atten-tus, **a**, **um**, *part.* (**attendo**), *attentive, assiduous.*

Attĭca, **æ**, *f., Attica,* the most famous country of ancient Greece.

Attĭcus, **a**, **um**, *adj., of Attica.*

at-tingo, **ĕre**, **tĭgi**, **tactum**, *a.* and *n.* (**ad; tango**), *to touch, border upon, lie near, reach.*

au-ceps, **aucŭpis**, *m.* (**ăvis; căpio**), *a bird-catcher, fowler.*

auc-tor, **ōris**, *m.* (**augeo**, § **44**, 1, *c*, 1), *a founder, maker, author.*

auctōr-ĭtas, **ātis**, *f.* (**auctor**, § **44**, 1, *c*, 2), *authority, power, dignity, influence.*

auc-tus, **a**, **um**, *part.* (**augeo**), *enlarged, great, ample, rich.*

aucup-ium, **ii**, *n.* (**aucŭpor**, § **44**, 1, *c*, 2), *bird-catching, fowling.*

aucŭp-or, **āri**, **ātus sum**, *dep.* (**auceps**), *to go a bird-catching,* or *fowling.*

audāc-ia, **æ**, *f.* (**audax**, § **44**, 1, *c*, 2), *courage, boldness, daring, insolence.*

audāc-ĭter, *and* **audac-ter**, *adv.* (**audax**), *boldly, courageously, daringly.*

aud-ax, **ācis**, *adj.* (**audeo**, § **44**, 1, *c*, 3), *daring, bold, courageous, rash, violent.*

aud-eo, **ēre**, **ausus sum**, *semi-dep.* (§ **35**, 2), *to dare, venture.*

audi-ens, **entis**, *part.* (**audio**), *obedient to.* As NOUN, *m.* or *f., a hearer.*

aud-io, **īre**, **īvi**, *or* **ĭi**, **ītum**, *a., to hear, listen.*

au-fĕro, **ferre**, **abstŭli**, **ablātum**, *a. irregular* (**ab; fĕro**), *to carry away, remove.*

au-fŭgio, **ĕre**, **fūgi**, **fŭgĭtum**, *n.* and *a.* (**ab; fŭgio**), *to flee away; to flee from.*

augeo, **ēre**, **auxi**, **auctum**, *a., to increase, enlarge.*

au-gur, **ŭris**, *com. gen., a diviner, soothsayer.*

augŭr-ium, **ii**, *n.* (**augŭror**, § **44**, 1, *c*, 2), *divination, prophecy, soothsaying.*

augŭr-or, **āri**, **ātus sum**, *dep.* (**augur**), *to predict, foretell.*

aug-ustus, **a**, **um**, *adj.* (**augeo**), *majestic, noble, venerable.*

Augustus, **i**, *m.* (**augustus**), *Octavius Cæsar,* first Emperor of Rome, B.C. 31 to A.D. 14.

aula, **æ**, *f., a hall, court, palace.*

aura, **æ**, *f., the air*

aur-eus, **a**, **um**, *adj.* (**aurum**, § **44**, 1, *c*, 3), *golden.*

aur-is, **is**, *f.* (**audio**) (*the hearing thing*), *the ear.*

aurum, **i**, *n., gold.*

au-spex, **ĭcis**, *com. gen.* (**ăvis; spĕcio**), *a diviner, soothsayer.*

auspĭc-ium, **ii**, *n.* (**auspex**, § **44**, 1, *c*, 2), *an omen* (taken from the watching of birds), *an auspice;* **auspicia habere**, *to hold* or *take the auspices.*

auster, **tri**, *m., the south wind; the south.*

aut, *conj.* (§ **43**, 2, *a*), *or;* **aut . . . aut**, *either . . . or.*

autem, *conj.* (§ **43**, 2, *b*), *but, however, besides.*

auxĭlium, **ii**, *n.* (**augeo**), *help, aid, assistance;* **auxĭlia**, **ōrum**, *auxiliary troops.*

ăvār-ĭtia, **æ**, *f.* (**ăvārus**, § **44**, 1, *c*, 2), *an eager desire, greediness, avarice.*

ăv-ārus, **a**, **um**, *adj.* (**ăveo**), *eager, greedy, covetous.*

ā-vello, **ĕre**, **velli** *or* **vulsi**, **vulsum**, *a., to tear away, pluck off, pull apart.*

ăveo, **ēre**, *no perf., no sup., a., to long for, crave.*

ăveo, ēre, *no perf., no sup., n., to be safe, happy, well;* **ăvē** (*imperative of* **ăveo**), *hail, farewell.*
ā-verto, ĕre, ti, sum, *a., turn away from, avert, withdraw.*
ăv-ĭdus, a, um, *adj.* (**ăveo**), *eager, greedy, covetous.*
ăvis, is, *f., a bird.*
ā-vŏco, āre, āvi, ātum, *a., to call away from, call off, withdraw.*
ăv-uncŭlus, i, *m.* (**ăvus**), *a maternal uncle.*
ăvus, i, *m., a grandfather.*

B.

Băbўlon, ōnis, *f.* (§ **11**, iii. 6), the ancient capital of the Babylo-Assyrian Empire, in Mesopotamia, on the River Euphrates.
Băleāres, ium, *f., the Balearic isles,* in the Mediterranean, east of Spain.
balneum, i, *n.* (*pl.* **balneæ, ārum,** *f.*), *a bath.*
barba, æ, *f., the beard.*
barbărus, a, um, *adj., foreign, strange, barbarian;* **barbari, ōrum,** *m., foreigners, barbarians;* a name applied by the Greeks and Romans to people of other nations.
be-ātus, a, um, *adj.* (**beo**), *happy, prosperous, fortunate.*
Belgæ, ārum, *m., the Belgians,* a warlike people dwelling in the north of Gaul.
b-ellum, i, *n.* (*old form* **du-ellum**) (**duo**) (a contest between two parties), *war.*
bĕne, *adv.* (§ **17**, 4), *well, finely, prosperously;* **bĕne pugnare,** *to fight successfully.*
bĕnĕ-factor, ōris, *m.* (**bĕne; făcio**), *a benefactor.*
bĕnĕ-fĭcium, ii, *n.* (**bĕne; făcio,** § **44**, 1, *c*, 2), *kindness, favor, benefit, service.*
bĕnĕ-vŏlens, entis, *adj., wishing well, kind, obliging.*
bĕnĕvŏlent-ia, æ, *f.* (**bĕnĕvŏlens,** § **44**, 1, *c*, 2), *kindness, good-will, friendship.*
ben-ignus, a, um, *adj.* (**bŏnus**), *good, kind, friendly.*
beo, āre, āvi, ātum, *a., to make happy, bless, gladden.*
bestia, æ, *f., a beast, creature, animal.*
bĭbo, bĭbĕre, bĭbi, *no sup., a., to drink.*
Bibracte, is, *n., Bibracte,* the chief town of the Ædui.
Bibrax, actis, *n., Bibrax,* a town of Gaul, in the territory of the Remi.
Bĭbŭlus, i, *m., Marcus Calpurnius,* consul B.C. 59, colleague of Cæsar.
bĭ-duum, ŭi, *n.* (**bis; dies**), *a space of two days.*
bī-ni, æ, a, *numeral distributive adj.* (**bis**), *two each, two by two.*
bĭ-partīto, *adv.* (**bis; pars**), *in two parts, two divisions.*
bĭs, *numeral adv., twice.*
blandus, a, um, *adj., flattering, friendly, gentle, kind.*
Boii, ōrum, *m., the Boii,* a people of Gaul.
bŏn-ĭtas, ātis, *f.* (**bŏnus,** § **44**, 1, *c*, 2), *goodness, virtue, worth.*
bŏnus, a, um, *adj., good, kind, fit, prosperous, virtuous; n. pl., as noun,* **bŏna, ōrum,** *goods, property, riches.*
bōs, bŏvis, *com. gen.* (§ **11**, III. 4, *d*), *an ox, a cow.*
brăchium, ii, *n., an arm.*
brĕvi, *adv., shortly, in a short time, briefly.*
brĕvis, e, *adj., short, small, brief.*
Brĭtannia, æ, *f., Britain.*
Brĭtanni, ōrum, *m., the inhabitants of Britain, Britons.*
Brundĭsium, ii, *n., Brundisium;* an ancient town of Calabria, in S. E. Italy, nearest seaport to Greece.
Brūtus, i, *m., Lucius Junius,* a founder of the Roman Republic, B.C. 500.

Brūtus, *Marcus*, a friend of Cicero, a conspirator against Cæsar; *Decĭmus*, a fellow-conspirator with the preceding.

C.

C, *an abbreviation denoting* **Gaius** (**Caius**); *as a numeral*, **c** = **centum**.

căd-āver, ĕris, *n.* (**cădo**), *a dead body, corpse, carcass.*

cădo, cădĕre, cĕcĭdi, cāsum, *n.*, *to fall, happen, perish.* [den.

cæcus, a, um, *adj.*, *blind, dark, hid-*

cæd-es, is, *f.* (**cædo**), *slaughter, bloodshed, havoc.*

cædo, ĕre, cĕcīdi, cæsum, *a.* (**cădo**), (*to cause to fall*), *to cut down, kill, strike.*

cælum, i, *n.*, *see* **cœlum**.

Cæsar, ăris, *m.*, *C. Jūlius*, murdered by Brutus and Cassius, B.C. 44.

călăm-ĭtas, ātis, *f.*, *loss, misfortune, calamity.*

călămus, i, *m.*, *a reed, cane, stalk.*

calceā-mentum, i, *n.* (**calceo**, *to shoe*, § **44**, 1, *c*, 2), *a shoe.*

călendæ (**kal**), **ārum**, *f.*, *the first day of the month.*

căleo, ēre, ui, *no sup.*, *n.*, *to be warm, hot.*

căl-ĭdus, a, um, *adj.* (**căleo**), *warm, hot.*

call-ĭdus, a, um, *adj.* (**calleo**, *to be versed in*), *shrewd, cunning, crafty, skillful.*

căl-or, ōris, *m.* (**căleo**, § **44**, 1, *c*, 2); *warmth, heat.*

calv-ĭtium, ii, *n.* (**calvus**), *baldness.*

calvus, a, um, *adj.*, *bald.*

cămēlus, i, *m.*, *a camel.*

Campānia, æ, *f.*, *Campania*, a very fruitful province in middle Italy, of which the chief city was Capua.

camp-ester, estris, estre, *adj.* (**campus**), *of the plain, level, flat.*

campus, i, *m.*, *a plain, field, level surface;* **Campus Martius**, a grassy plain, in Rome, along the Tiber, dedicated to Mars, where elections were held, exercise and recreation taken.

Cănīnius, ii, *m.*, a Roman name.

cănis, is, *com. gen.*, *a dog* (§ **11**, 1, 3, *d*, (4).

căno, cănĕre, cĕcĭni, *no sup.*, *a.* and *n.*, *to sing, foretell, predict;* **tubicen cecinit**, *the trumpeter gave the signal.*

can-tus, ūs, *m.* (**căno**, § **44**, 1, *c*, 2), *singing, playing, song, prophecy.*

căpel-la, æ, *f.*, *dim.* (§ **44**, 1, *c*, 3), (**căper**), *a she-goat.*

căper, pri, *m.*, *a he-goat, a goat.*

căp-illus, i, *m.* (**căput**), *the hair.*

căpio, căpĕre, cēpi, captum, *a.*, *to take, lay hold of, seize; receive, contain.*

Căpĭtōlium, ii, *n.* (**căput**), *the capitol;* the citadel of Rome and the temple of Jupiter, built upon the Capitoline hill.

căpra, æ, *f.*, *a she-goat.*

cap-tīvus, a, um, *adj.* (**căpio**), *taken prisoner, captive. As* NOUN, **captivus, i**, *m.*, *a prisoner.*

cap-to, āre, āvi, ātum, *a.*, *intens.* (**căpio**, § **36**, *b*, and **44**, 2, *b*), *to strive after, catch at.*

căpŭlus, i, *m.* (**căpio**), *handle, hilt.*

căput, ĭtis, *n.*, *the head.*

Carbo, ōnis, *m.*, a Roman name.

carcer, ĕris, *m.*, *a dungeon, prison.*

carmen, ĭnis, *n.*, *a poem, song; an oracle.*

carnĭfex, fĭcis, *m.* (**caro; făcio**), *an executioner, hangman.*

căro, carnis, *f.*, *flesh.*

carpo, ĕre, si, tum, *a.*, *to pick, pluck, eat, gather.*

carrus, i, *m.*, *a two-wheeled cart; cart, wagon.*

Carthāgo (**Kar**), **ĭnis**, *f.*, *Carthage*, a celebrated city of Northern Africa.

cārus, a, um, *adj., dear, precious, esteemed.* [*shed.*

căsa, æ, *f., a hut, cottage, cabin,*

Casca, æ, *m.*, one of the conspirators against Cæsar.

cassis, ĭdis, *f., a helmet* (of metal).

Cassius, ii, *m.*, the chief conspirator against Cæsar.

castel-lum, i, *n., dim.* (**castrum,** § **44**, 1, *c*, 3), *a castle, fort.*

castīgo, āre, āvi, ātum, *a.* (**castus**), (*to make pure*), *to chastise, reprove, censure.*

castra, ōrum, *n. pl., a camp.*

castrum, i, *n., a castle, fortress.*

cā-sus, ūs, *m.* (**cădo,** § **44**, 1, *c*, 2), *a falling down; fall, chance, calamity.*

cătēna, æ, *f., a chain, a fetter.*

Cătĭlīna, æ, *m., Lucius Sergius Catilina;* a Roman who was notorious for several times attempting insurrections against his country.

Căto, ōnis, *m., Marcus Porcius Cato* (B.C. 93–45), the younger, the enemy of Cæsar, who committed suicide after the battle of Pharsalia.

cătŭlus, i, *m., dim., a young dog; whelp, puppy.*

Cătŭlus, i, *m., Quintus Catulus,* a Roman statesman.

cauda, æ, *f., the tail* (of animals).

causa (caussa), æ, *f., a cause, reason;* **causā,** *for the sake of, for the purpose of* (§ **54**, 3, *c*).

căveo, ēre, cāvi, cautum, *n.* and *a., to beware, take heed, guard against, avoid.*

căvus, a, um, *adj., hollow.*

cēdo, cēdĕre, cessi, cessum, *n.* and *a., to go, depart, yield, give up, give way, retreat.*

cĕlĕber, bris, bre, *adj., frequented, celebrated, glorious.*

cĕlĕbr-ĭtas, ātis, *f.* (**cĕlĕber,** § **44**, 1, *c*, 2), *a multitude; fame, renown.*

cĕlĕbro, āre, āvi, ātum, *a.* (**cĕlĕber**), *to frequent; celebrate, praise.*

cĕler, ĕris, ĕre, *adj., swift, fleet, quick, speedy.*

cĕlĕr-ĭtas, ātis, *f.* (**cĕler,** § **44**, 1, *c*, 2), *swiftness, quickness, speed.*

cĕlĕr-ĭter, *adv.* (**cĕler**), *swiftly quickly, speedily.*

cēlo, āre, āvi, ātum, *a.* (§ **52**, 2, *d*), *to hide, conceal.*

Celtæ, ārum, *m., the Celts;* the inhabitants of S. Gaul.

cēna (cœna), æ, *f.* (the principal meal of the Romans), *supper, dinner.*

cēno (cœno), āre, āvi, ātum, *n.* and *a.* (**cēna,** § **44**, 2, *a*, 1), *to dine, sup, take a meal.*

censeo, ēre, ui, um, *a., to estimate, value, think, believe, vote.*

centum, *adj., indecl., a hundred.*

centŭria, æ, *f.* (**centum**), *a division of one hundred; a century, company.*

centŭrio, ōnis, *m.* (**centum**), *the commander of a century; a centurion.*

cerno, cernĕre, crēvi, crētum, *a., to separate, discern, perceive, decide, resolve.*

certā-men, ĭnis, *n.* (**certo,** § **44**, 1, *c*, 2), *a contest, battle.*

certiōrem făcĕre, *to inform* (§ **52**, 2). [*surely.*

certo, *adv.* (**certus**), *certainly,*

certus, a, um, *adj.* (**cerno**), *determined, fixed, sure, certain; trusty; resolved.*

cervix, īcis, *f., the neck.*

cervus, i, *m., a stag, a deer.*

cesso, āre, āvi, ātum, *n. intens.* (**cēdo,** § **36**, *b*, and **44**, 2, *b*), *to delay, loiter, cease, linger.*

(cētĕrus), a, um, *adj.* (nominative singular masc. not found), *the other, the rest.*

ceu, *conj.* (§ **43**, 2, *e*), *as, as if, as it were, like as if.*

charta, æ, *f., paper, writing, letter.*

Chrȳsŏgŏnus, i, *m.*, a freedman of Sulla.

cĭbārĭa, ōrum, *n.* (**cĭbus**), *food, provisions, fodder.*

cĭbus, i, *m.*, *food.*
cĭcātrix, īcis, *f.*, *a scar.*
cĭcer, ĕris, *n.* (*used only in the sing.*), *the chick-pea, vetch.*
Cĭcĕro, ōnis, *m.*, *Marcus Tullius Cicero*, the greatest of Roman orators and writers (B. C. 106-43).
cĭcōnia, æ, *f.*, *a stork.*
Cimbri, ōrum, *m.*, a people of Northern Germany.
cingo, cingĕre, cinxi, cinctum, *a.*, *to gird, surround, enclose; besiege, invest.*
cĭnis, ĕris, *m.* and *f.*, *ashes.*
circā, *adv.*, and *prep. with the acc.*, *around, about.*
circĭter, *adv.*, and *prep. with the acc.*, *round about, near.*
circuĭ-tus, ūs, *m.* (**circumeo,** § **44,** 1, *c*, 2), *a going around in a circle; a circuit, compass.*
circum, *adv.*, and *prep. with acc.*, *around, about, near.*
circum-do, dăre, dĕdi, dătum, *a.* (§ **51, 1,** *c*), *to put around, to surround with, encompass;* **circumdăre murum urbi** or **urbem muro,** *to put a wall round the city*, or *to surround the city with a wall.*
circum-eo, īre, īvi, or **ii, ĭtum,** *n.* and *a.*, *to go round, surround, encompass, solicit, deceive.*
circum-pōno, pōnĕre, pŏsui, pŏsĭtum, *a.*, *to put* or *place around.*
circum-sto, stāre, stĕti, *no. sup.*, *n.* and *a.*, *to stand around; to surround, beset, besiege.*
cis, *prep.* with *acc.*, *on this side.*
cĭtĕrior, us, *adj.* (§ **17,** 3), *on this side, hither;* **Gallia citerior,** *hither Gaul*, i.e., *this side of the Alps.*
cĭto, *adv.*, *quickly, speedily, soon*, (*comp.* **cĭtius,** *sup.* **cĭtissĭmē**).
cĭtra, *prep.* and *adv.*, *on this side; before, within.*
cīvĭcus, a, um, *adj.* (**cīvis**), *belonging to citizens, civic.*
cīv-īlis, e, *adj.* (**cīvis,** § **44,** 1, *c*, 3), *belonging to citizens, civil, courteous.*
cīvis, is, *com. gen.*, *a citizen.*
cīv-ĭtas, ātis, *f.* (**cīvis,** § **44,** 1, *c*, 2), *citizenship; a city, state; freedom of the city.*
clādes, is, *f.*, *disaster, slaughter.*
clam, *adv.* and *prep.* (§ **56,** 2, *c*), *secretly; without the knowledge of.*
clāmo, āre, āvi, ātum, *n.* and *a.*, *to cry out, call, proclaim.*
clām-or, ōris, *m.* (**clamo,** § **44,** 1, *c*, 2), *a shout, applause, clamor.*
clārus, a, um, *adj.*, *clear, bright; plain; famous, illustrious.*
classis, is, *f.*, *a fleet.*
claudo, ĕre, si, sum, *a.*, *to shut, close, surround, finish.*
claudus, a, um, *adj.*, *lame.*
claus-ŭla, æ, *f.* (**claudo**), *a conclusion, end, clause.*
clāvis, is, *f.*, *a key.*
clēmens, entis, *adj.*, *merciful, mild, gentle.*
clēmen-ter, *adv.* (**clēmens**), *mildly, gently, calmly.*
clēment-ia, æ, *f.* (**clēmens,** § **44,** 1, *c*, 2), *mercy, mildness, kindness.*
Cleŏpātra, æ, *f.*, Queen of Egypt, conquered at Actium by Augustus.
cliens, entis, *com. gen.* (**clueo**), *a client, follower, retainer* (one attached to a patron, and protected by him).
clĭpeum, i, *n.*, *a shield* (of circular form, made of metal).
clĭpeus, i, *m.*, *a shield* (of circular form, made of metal).
Clōdius, ii, *m.*, the enemy of Cicero, killed by Milo.
cœlum (**cælum**), **i,** *n.*, *pl.* **cœli, ōrum,** *m.* (§ **14,** 2, *b*), *the sky.*
cŏ-ĕmo, ĕmĕre, ēmi, emptum, *a.* (**con; ĕmo**), *to purchase together, to buy up.*
cœna, *see* **cēna.**
cœn-ātus, a, um, *adj.* (**cœna,** § **44,** 1, *c*, 3), (provided with supper), *having dined.*

cœn-ĭto, **āre**, *no perf.*, *no sup.*, *n. frequentative* (**cœno**, § **36**, *b*, and § **44**, 2, *b*), *to dine often* or *much*, *to dine*.

cœno, *see* **cēna**.

cœpi, **cœpisse**, *a.* and *n.*, *def.* (§ **38**, 1, *a*), *to begin*, *undertake*.

co-erceo, **ēre**, **ui**, **ĭtum**, *a.* (**con**; **arceo**), *to enclose wholly*, *surround*, *encompass; restrain*, *confine*, *repress*.

cō-gĭto, **āre**, **āvi**, **ātum**, *a.* (**con**; **ăgĭto**), *to think*, *reflect upon*, *consider*, *meditate; to devise*, *intend*, *design*.

cognāt-io, **ōnis**, *f.* (**cognātus**, § **44**, 1, *c*, 2), *blood-relationship*, *kindred; connection*, *resemblance*.

co-gnātus, **a**, **um**, *adj.* (**con**; **gnascor** = **nascor**), *connected by birth*.

co-gnōmen, **ĭnis**, *n.* (§ **15**, **con**; **gnōmen** = **nōmen**), *a surname*.

cognōmĭno, **āre**, *no perf.*, **ātum**, *a.* (**cognōmen**), *to surname*.

co-gnosco, **gnoscĕre**, **gnōvi**, **gnĭtum**, *a.* (**con**; **gnosco** = **nosco**), *to examine*, *find out*, *know*.

cō-go, **cōgĕre**, **coēgi**, **coactum**, *a.* (**con**; **ăgo**), *to drive together*, *collect*, *force*, *compel*.

cŏhors, **ortis**, *f.*, *a cohort* (a company of 600 soldiers).

cŏ-hortor, **āri**, **ātus sum**, *dep.* (**con**; **hortor**), *to exhort*, *encourage*, *animate*, *admonish*.

coiens, **euntis**, *part.* (**coeo**), *meeting*, *assembling*.

cŏlăphus, **i**, *m.*, *a cuff*, *blow*.

col-lēga, **æ**, *m.* (**con**; **lĕgo**), *associate*, *colleague*, *companion*.

col-lĭgo, **lĭgĕre**, **lēgi**, **lectum**, *a.* (**con**; **lĕgo**), *to collect together*, *assemble*, *gather*.

col-lĭgo, **āre**, **āvi**, **ātum**, *a.* (**con**; **lĭgo**), *to bind together*, *fasten*, *combine; to restrain*, *stop*.

collis, **is**, *m.*, *high ground*, *a hill*.

col-lŏco, **āre**, **āvi**, **ātum**, *a.* (**con**; **lŏco**), *to place together; to settle in a place; to give a woman in marriage*.

collŏqu-ium, **ii**, *n.* (**collŏquor**, § **44**, 1, *c*, 2), (a talking together) *a conference*, *discourse*.

collum, **i**, *n.*, *the neck*.

cŏlo, **cŏlĕre**, **cŏlui**, **cultum**, *a.* and *n.*, *to till*, *cultivate*, *cherish*, *honor*, *worship; to dwell*.

cŏlōn-ia, **æ**, *f.*, (**colōnus**, § **44**, 1, *c*, 2), *a colony*, *a settlement*.

cŏl-ōnus, **i**, *m.* (**cŏlo**), *a husbandman*, *farmer*.

cŏlumba, **æ**, *f.*, *a dove*, *pigeon*.

cŏm-ĕdo, **ĕdĕre** *or* **esse**, **ēdi**, **ēsum** *or* **estum**, *a.* (**con**; **ĕdo**), *to eat up*, *consume*, *devour*.

cŏmes, **ĭtis**, *com. gen.* (**con**; **eo**), *a companion*, *associate*.

cōm-ĭtas, **ātis**, *f.* (**cōmis**, *kind*, § **44**, 1, *c*, 2), *courteousness*, *affability*, *gentleness*, *mildness*.

cŏmĭtā-tus, **ūs**, *m.* (**cŏmĭtor**, § **44**, 1, *c*, 2), *a retinue*, *escort*, *company*, *troop*, *crowd*.

cŏmĭtĭa, **ōrum**, *n. pl.* (**con**; **eo**), *the Comitia;* assembly of the Romans for electing magistrates.

cŏmĭtor, **āri**, **ātus sum**, *dep.* (**cŏmes**), *to accompany*, *follow*, *attend*.

commeā-tus, **ūs**, *m.* (**commeo**, § **44**, 1, *c*, 2), *provisions*, *supplies*.

com-mĕmŏro, **āre**, **āvi**, **ātum**, *a.* (**con**; **mĕmŏro**), *to call to mind*, *recount*, *relate*, *mention*.

com-mendo, **āre**, **āvi**, **ātum**, *a.* (**con**; **mando**), *to intrust*, *recommend*, *commit*.

com-meo, **āre**, **āvi**, **ātum**, *n.* (**con**; **meo**), *to go to and fro*, *visit often*, *resort*.

com-mīlĭto, **ōnis**, *m.* (**con**; **mīles**), *a fellow-soldier*.

com-mitto, **mittĕre**, **mīsi**, **missum**, *a.* (**con**; **mitto**), *to connect*, *join*, *set together*, *commit*, *perpetrate*, *intrust;* **pugnam** or **prœlium committere**, *to join battle;* **committere ut**, *to bring it about*, *cause that*.

commŏdē, *adv.* (**commŏdus**), *duly, properly, fitly, well.*

com-mŏdus, a, um, *adj.* (**con ; mŏdus**), *fit, advantageous, serviceable.*

commŏnĕ-făcio, făcĕre, fēci, factum, *a.* (§ **37**, 7), *to put in mind, inform, remind.*

com-mŏneo, mŏnēre, mŏnui, mŏnĭtum, *a.* (**con ; mŏneo**), *to remind, warn.*

com-mŏveo, mŏvēre, mōvi, mōtum, *a.* (**con; mŏveo**), *to move violently, shake, stir, disturb, agitate, excite;* **bellum commovere**, *to stir up war.*

com-mūnis, e, *adj.* (**con; mūnus**), *common, general.*

com-mūto, āre, āvi, ātum, *a.* (**con; mūto**), *to exchange, alter.*

cŏ-mo, cōmĕre, compsi, comptum, *a.* (**con; ĕmo**), *to comb, arrange, braid, dress.*

com-păro, āre, āvi, ātum, *a.* (**con; păro**), *to put together, unite; prepare, collect, compare.*

com-pello, pellĕre, pŭli, pulsum, *a., to drive together, to assemble, gather, constrain, force, impel.*

com-plector, cti, xus sum, *dep.* (**con; plecto**), *to encompass, surround, embrace, clasp; comprehend.*

com-pleo, plēre, plēvi, plētum, *a.* (**con; pleo**), *to fill full, fill up, satisfy, complete, finish.*

complōrā-tio, ōnis, *f.* (**comploro**, § **44**, 1, *c*, 2), *a loud weeping, lamentation.*

com-plōro, āre, āvi, ātum, *a.* (**con; plōro**), *to lament loudly.*

com-plūres, a *or* **ia**, *adj., several together, very many.*

com-pōno, pōnĕre, pŏsui, pŏsĭtum, *a.* (**con; pōno**), *to put together* or *in order; to settle,* **componere bellum**, *to finish a war by treaty.*

com-porto, āre, āvi, ātum, *a.* (**con; porto**), *to bring together, collect.*

com-pos, ŏtis, *adj.* (**con; pŏtis**), *partaking of, possessing;* **compos animi**, *of sane mind.*

com-prĕhendo, ĕre, di, sum, *a.* (**con; prehendo**), *to catch hold of, seize, arrest; to perceive, observe; to contain.*

com-prĭmo, prĭmĕre, pressi, pressum, *a.* (**con; prĕmo**), *to press together, compress, restrain, hinder.*

con-cēdo, cēdĕre, cessi, cessum, *n.* and *a., to depart, retire, withdraw; allow, grant; submit.*

con-cīdo, cīdĕre, cīdi, cīsum, *a.* (**con; cædo**), *to cut to pieces, destroy, kill.*

concĭlio, āre, āvi, ātum, *a.* (**concĭlium**), *to call together, unite; gain over, make friendly, procure the favor of, win, gain, procure, reconcile.*

con-cĭlium, ii, *n.* (**con; călo**, *to call*, § **44**, 1, *c*, 2), *a meeting, assembly, council.*

concio (contio), ōnis, *f., a meeting; a speech; a place for speaking.*

con-clāmo, āre, āvi, ātum, *a.* and *n., to shout, exclaim, cry out.*

concord-ia, æ, *f.* (**concors**, § **44**, 1, *c*, 2), *harmony, unanimity.*

con-cŭpi-sco, cŭpiscĕre, cŭpīvi or **cŭpii, cŭpītum**, *a. inch.* (**con; cŭpio**, § **44, 2, b**), *to be very desirous of, strive after, long for.*

con-curro, currĕre, curri or **cŭcurri, cursum**, *n., to run together, assemble, dash together, fight.*

concur-sus, ūs, *m.* (**concurro**, § **44**, 1, *c*, 2), *a concourse, assembly, attack, charge, onset.*

con-demno, āre, āvi, ātum, *a.* (**con ; damno**), *to sentence, condemn, blame, disapprove.*

con-discĭpŭlus, i, m., *a schoolfellow.*

cond-ĭtio, ōnis, *f.* (**condo**, § **44**,

1, *c*, 2), *a state*, *condition*, *situation*, *rank*, *agreement*, *compact; proposal*, *terms*.
con-do, **dĕre**, **dĭdi**, **dĭtum**, *a.*, *to bring together; to found*, *establish*, *store up*, *hide*, *bury*.
con-dūco, **dūcĕre**, **duxi**, **ductum**, *a.* and *n.*, *to lead together*, *hire*, *collect; to profit*.
confero, **conferre**, **contŭli**, **collātum**, *a.*, *to bring together*, *collect*, *compare*, *contribute;* **se conferre**, *to go;* **collatis viribus**, *with united forces*.
confertus, **a**, **um**, *part.* (**confercio**, *to cram together*), *close*, *crowded*, *crammed*.
confestim, *adv.* (**confĕro**), *immediately*, *speedily*.
con-fĭcio, **fĭcĕre**, **fēci**, **fectum**, *a.* (**con**; **făcio**), *to prepare; complete*, *finish*, *accomplish*, *make out*, *produce*.
con-fīdo, **fīdĕre**, **fīsus sum**, *n.* and *a.* (§ **35**, 2), *to trust confidently*, *confide; to believe certainly*.
con-fīgo, **fīgĕre**, **fixi**, **fixum**, *a.*, *to join; to pierce through*.
con-firmo, **āre**, **āvi**, **ātum**, *a.*, *to make firm*, *establish*, *strengthen*.
con-fĭteor, **fĭtēri**, **fessus sum**, *dep.* (**con**; **făteor**), *to confess*, *own*, *concede*, *allow*.
con-flīgo, **flīgĕre**, **flixi**, **flictum**, *a.* and *n.*, *to strike; to contend*, *struggle*, *fight*.
con-fŏdio, **fŏdĕre**, **fōdi**, **fossum**, *a.*, *to dig; to pierce through*, *stab*.
con-fŭgio, **fŭgĕre**, **fūgi**, *no sup.*, *n.*, *to flee for refuge*.
con-grĕdior, **grĕdi**, **gressus sum**, *dep.* (**con**; **grădior**), *to meet*, *encounter*, *contend*, *fight*.
con-gruo, **gruĕre**, **grui**, *no sup.*, *n.*, *to agree with*, *fit*, *coincide*, *come together*, *meet*.
con-jĭcio, **jĭcĕre**, **jēci**, **jectum**, *a.* (**con**; **jăcio**), *to throw together*, *throw*, *hurl;* **in fugam conjicere**, *to put to flight*.
con-jungo, **gĕre**, **xi**, **ctum**, *a.*, *to join together*, *connect*, *unite*, *couple*.
conjūrā-tus, **i**, *m.* (**conjūro**), *a conspirator*.
con-jūro, **āre**, **āvi**, **ātum**, *a.*, *to swear together*, *conspire;* **in aliquem conjurare**, *to conspire against one*.
conjux (**conjunx**), **ŭgis**, *com. gen.* (**conjungo**), *a wife*, *husband*, *a betrothed*.
cōnor, **āri**, **ātus sum**, *dep.*, *to undertake*, *attempt*, *endeavor*, *try*.
con-quīro, **quīrĕre**, **quīsīvi**, **quīsītum**, *a.* (**con**; **quæro**), *to search out carefully*, *inquire*, *seek*.
con-sanguĭn-eus, **a**, **um**, *adj.* (**con**; **sanguis**, § **44**, 1, *c*, 3), *related by blood*, *related*, *kindred*.
con-scendo, **dĕre**, **di**, **sum**, *a.* and *n.* (**con**; **scando**), *to mount*, *ascend*, *climb*, *embark*.
con-scisco, **sciscĕre**, **scīvi**, **scītum**, *a.*, *to approve*, *assert*, *accept;* **mortem sibi consciscere**, *to commit suicide*.
con-scius, **a**, **um**, *adj.* (**con**; **scio**), *knowing* or *conscious of*, *privy to*, *aware of*.
conscius, **ii**, *m.*, *an accomplice*.
con-scrībo, **bĕre**, **psi**, **ptum**, *to enlist*, *register*, *enroll*, *inscribe*, *compose*, *write*.
consen-sio, **ōnis**, *f.* (**consentio**, § **44**, 1, *c*, 2), *an agreement; a combination*, *plot*.
consen-sus, **ūs**, *m.* (**consentio**, § **44**, 1, *c*, 2), *an agreement*, *unanimity*, *concord*.
con-sentio, **tīre**, **si**, **sum**, *n.* and *a.*, *to agree*, *accord*, *harmonize*, *determine in common; to vote*.
con-sĕquor, **qui**, **cūtus sum**, *dep.*, *to follow after*, *attend*, *accompany; to reach*, *overtake; to attain*.
con-sĕro, **sĕrĕre**, **sĕrui**, **sertum**, *a.*, *to join*, *unite*, *bring together;* **pugnam** *or* **prœlium conse-**

rere, *to join battle;* **manum conserere**, *to engage in a hand-to-hand conflict.*

con-servo, āre, āvi, ātum, *a., to maintain, keep, preserve.*

consīdĕro, āre, āvi, ātum, *a., to examine, contemplate, consider, ponder, observe carefully.*

Consīdius, ii, *m.*, one of Cæsar's officers.

con-sīdo, sīdĕre, sēdi, sessum, *n., to sit down together, encamp, settle.*

consĭlium, ii, *n., deliberation, advice, counsel, design, wisdom, talent;* **consilio**, *on purpose, intentionally.*

con-sisto, sistĕre, stĭti, stĭtum, *n., to stand still, halt, make a stand, stand fast, continue.*

con-sōbrīnus, i, *m.* (**sŏror**), *a cousin, relation.*

conspec-tus, ūs, *m.* (**conspĭcio**, § **44**, 1, *c*, 2), *a sight, view, glance, survey.*

con-spĭcio, spĭcĕre, spexi, spectum, *a.* (**con; spĕcio**), *to look at, behold, spy out, observe, view, descry.*

conspĭcuus, a, um, *adj.* (**conspĭcio**), *easy to see, visible, striking, distinguished, remarkable.*

conspīrā-tio, ōnis, *f.* (**conspīro**, § **44**, 1, *c*, 2), *an agreement, conspiracy.*

con-spīro, āre, āvi, ātum, *n., to agree together, plot together, conspire.*

constans, antis, *part.* (**consto**), *firm, constant, steadfast, consistent.*

constan-tia, æ, *f.* (**constans**, § **44**, 1, *c*, 2), *firmness, constancy, perseverance, harmony.*

constan-ter, *adv.* (**constans**), *firmly, steadily, constantly.*

con-stĭtuo, uĕre, ui, ūtum, *a.* (**con; stătuo**), *to place, erect, make, build; determine, resolve.*

consue-sco, escĕre, ēvi, ētum, *n. inch.* (**consueo**, § **36**, *a*, and **44**, 2, *b*), *to be accustomed, be wont.*

consue-tūdo, ĭnis, *f.* (**consuētus**, § **44**, 1, *c*, 2), *custom, habit, usage, intercourse.*

consul, ŭlis, *m., a consul;* one of the two chief magistrates of Rome, chosen yearly.

consŭl-āris, e, *adj.* (**consul**), *of the consul.*

consŭl-āris, is, *m.* (**consul**), *one who has been consul, ex-consul.*

consŭl-ātus, ūs, *m.* (**consul**), *the office of consul, consulship.*

consŭlo, ĕre, ui, tum, *n.* and *a., to deliberate, consider, reflect, advise, consult for;* **alicui consulere**, *to consult for one's interest;* **aliquem consulere**, *to consult, take advice of one.*

consul-tum, i, *n.* (**consŭlo**), *a decree, decision, resolve.*

con-temno, nĕre, psi, ptum, *a., to despise, scorn, disdain.*

con-tendo, dĕre, di, tum, *a.* and *n., to strain, strive, strive for, contend, fight; attempt, hasten.*

conten-tio, ōnis, *f.* (**contendo**, § **44**, 1, *c*, 2), *a straining, exertion, effort; dispute, strife, fight.*

conten-tus, a, um, *part.* (**contĭneo**), *contented, satisfied.*

con-testor, āri, ātus sum, *dep., to call to witness, invoke.*

contĭnens, entis, *part.* (**contĭneo**), *moderate, temperate.*

contĭnen-ter, *adv.* (**contĭnens**), *moderately; continuously, without interruption.*

con-tĭneo, tĭnēre, tĭnui, tentum, *a.* (**con; tĕneo**), *to hold in, hold, contain, comprise, keep back, restrain; confine, bound.*

con-tingo, tingĕre, tĭgi, tactum, *a.* and *n.* (**con; tango**), *to touch, take hold of, reach, border upon; impers.*, **contingit mihi**, *it is my lot.*

contĭn-uus, a, um, *adj.* (**contĭneo**), *unbroken, constant, continuous.*

contio, *see* **concio**.

contrā, *adv.*, and *prep.* with *acc.*, *over against, opposite to, on the other hand.*

con-trăho, hĕre, xi, ctum, *a.*, *to draw together, assemble, shorten, contract.*

contrā-rius, a, um, *adj.* (contra), *opposite, contrary, opposed, hostile.*

contrōvers-ia, æ, *f.* (controversus, § 44, 1, c, 2), *controversy, dispute, quarrel, debate.*

contrō-versus, a, um, *adj.* (contra; versus), *quarrelsome; questionable.*

contŭbern-ālis, is, *com. gen.* (con; tăberna), *a tent-companion, comrade, companion.*

contŭmē-lia, æ, *f.* (contŭmeo), *abuse, insult, reproach, affront, taunt, disgrace;* in *pl.*, *abusive epithets, insulting language.*

con-vĕnio, vĕnīre, vēni, ventum, *n.* and *a.*, *to come together, assemble, agree, meet, visit;* **convenire aliquem**, *to accost one;* **convĕnit**, *impers.*, *it is agreed upon.*

conven-tus, ūs, *m.* (convĕnio, § 44, 1, *c*, 2), *a coming together; an assembly, meeting, company; compact, agreement.*

con-verto, tĕre, ti, sum, *a.*, *to turn round, change, overturn; translate, turn;* **convertere in fugam**, *to put to flight.*

con-vinco, vincĕre, vīci, victum, *a.*, *to convict; convince, demonstrate.*

con-vŏco, āre, āvi, ātum, *a.*, *to call together, assemble, summon.*

con-vŏlo, āre, āvi, ātum, *n.*, *to run together.*

cŏphĭnus, i, *m.*, *a basket.*

cōpia, æ, *f.* (con; ops), *abundance; pl.*, *supplies, troops, wealth.*

cōpiōs-e, *adv.* (copiōsus), *abundantly, plentifully.*

cōpi-ōsus, a, um, *adj.* (cōpia, § 44, 1, *c*, 3), *well supplied, abounding, plentiful, copious.*

cŏr, cordis, *n.*, *the heart, soul, feeling, mind.*

cōram, *adv.*, and *prep. with abl.*, *openly; in the presence of, before.*

Cŏrinthus, i, *f.*, *Corinth*, a city of Greece.

Cornēlia, æ, *f.*, the first wife of Cæsar.

cornu, u (ūs), *n.*, *a horn; the wing of an army.*

corpus, ŏris, *n.*, *a body, corpse.*

cor-rĭpio, rĭpĕre, rĭpui, reptum, *a.* (con; răpio), *to seize, catch up, carry off; abridge, reprove.*

cortex, ĭcis, *m.* and *f.*, *bark* (of a tree).

corvus, i, *m.*, *a raven.*

crās, *adv.*, *to-morrow.*

Crassus, *m.*, *Lĭcĭnius Crassus*, the triumvir, who perished in the Parthian war, B.C. 53.

crēber, bra, brum, *adj.*, *thick, close, frequent.*

crēdo, dĕre, dĭdi, dĭtum, *n.* and *a.*, *to trust, believe, think; entrust, confide.*

crĕmo, āre, āvi, ātum, *a.*, *to burn, consume.*

creo, āre, āvi, ātum, *a.*, *to bring forth, beget, create, elect.*

Cres, ētis, *m.*, *adj.*, *a Cretan.*

Cressa, æ, *f.*, *a Cretan woman.*

cre-sco, crescĕre, crēvi, crētum, *n. inch.* (creo, § 36, *a*, and § 44, 2, *b*), *to grow, grow up, increase.*

crīmen, ĭnis, *n.*, *a charge, accusation, reproach.*

crīnis, is, *m.*, *the hair.*

crŭciā-mentum, i, *n.* (crŭcio, § 44, 1, *c*, 2), *torture, torment, pain.*

crŭciā-tus, ūs, *m.* (crŭcio, § 44, 1, c, 2), *torture, torment, anguish.*

crŭc-io, āre, āvi, ātum, *a.* (crux), *to torture, torment.*

crūdēlis, e, *adj.*, *hard-hearted, cruel, severe, fierce.*

crūdēl-ĭtas, ātis, *f.* (crūdēlis, § 44, 1, *c*, 2), *harshness, severity, cruelty, fierceness.*

cru-entus, **a**, **um**, *adj.* **(cruor)**, *bloody*, *blood-thirsty*, *cruel.*

crŭmēna, **æ**, *f.*, *a small money bag*, *purse.*

crūs, **ūris**, *n.*, *the leg* (below the knee), *shank.*

crux, **ŭcis**, *f.*, *a cross; torture*, *misery*, *trouble.*

crystallĭnus, **a**, **um**, *adj.*, *made of crystal*, *crystalline.*

crystallum, **i**, *n.*, *a crystal.*

crystallus, **i**, *m.*, *a crystal.*

cŭb-ĭcŭlum, **i**, *n.* **(cŭbo**, § **44**, 1, *c*, 2), *a bed-chamber.*

cŭbo, **āre**, **ui**, **ĭtum**, *n.*, *to lie down*, *recline.*

culcĭta, **æ**, *f.* **(calco)**, *a bed*, *cushion*, *mattress.*

culpa, **æ**, *f.*, *crime*, *fault*, *failure*, *defect*, *mischief.*

culpo, **āre**, **āvi**, **ātum**, *a.* **(culpa)**, *to censure*, *reprove*, *condemn*, *find fault with*, *blame.*

cultel-lus, **i**, *m. dim.* **(culter**, § **44**, 1, *c*, 3), *a small knife.*

culter, **tri**, *m.*, *a knife.*

cul-tus, **ūs**, *m.* **(cŏlo**, § **44**, 1, *c*, 2), *a cultivation*, *culture; dress*, *elegance*, *ornament.*

cum, *prep.* with *abl.*, *with*, *together with*, *among.*

cum (quum), *conj.*, *when*, *since*, *although*, *though;* **cum . . . tum**, *both . . . and.*

cunctor, **āri**, **ātus sum**, *dep.*, *to linger*, *loiter*, *hesitate*, *delay*, *doubt.*

cŭpĭ-dē, *adv.* **(cŭpĭdus)**, *eagerly*, *zealously*, *ardently.*

cŭpĭd-ĭtas, **ātis**, *f.* **(cŭpĭdus**, § **44**, 1, *c*, 2), *a longing*, *desire*, *passion*, *appetite*, *greediness*, *lust*, *avarice.*

cŭp-īdo, **ĭnis**, *f.* **(cŭpio)**, *desire*, *wish*, *longing*, *love*, *lust*, *passion.*

cŭp-ĭdus, **a**, **um**, *adj.* **(cŭpio)**, *eager*, *desirous*, *covetous*, *fond.*

cŭpio, **ĕre**, **īvi** *or* **ii**, **ītum**, *a.* and *n.*, *to long for a thing*, *desire*, *wish*, *covet; to favor* (with dative).

cur, *adv.*, *why? for what reason?*

cūria, **æ**, *f.* *a curia*, one of the thirty parts into which Romulus divided the Roman people; *the senate-house.*

cūra, **æ**, *f.* **(quæro)**, *trouble*, *solicitude*, *care*, *attention*, *pains.*

Cŭres, **ium**, *m.* and *f.*, the ancient chief town of the Sabines.

cūri-ātim, *adv.* **(curia)**, *by curiæ.*

Cūriātius, **ii**, *m.*, an Alban family name.

cūro, **āre**, **āvi**, **ātum**, *a.* **(cūra)**, *to care for; manage*, *govern; cure*, *heal.*

curro, **currĕre**, **cŭcurri**, **cursum**, *n.*, *to run*, *hasten.*

cur-sus, **ūs**, *m.* **(curro**, § **44**, 1, *c*, 2), *a running*, *race*, *course*, *march*, *passage*, *journey*, *voyage.*

Cȳprus, **i**, *m.*, an island of the Mediterranean.

D.

damno, **āre**, **āvi**, **ātum**, *a.* **(damnum** = damage), *to condemn*, *pass sentence on;* **damnare capitis**, *to condemn to death.*

dē, *prep.* with *abl.*, *of*, *from*, *during*, *at*, *concerning*, *about*, *down from*, *according to.*

dea, **æ**, *f.* (*dat.* and *abl. pl.*, **deabus**, § **9**, 2, *e*), *a goddess.*

de-ambŭlo, **āre**, **āvi**, **ātum**, *n.*, *to walk much*, *promenade*, *stroll.*

dē-beo, **bēre**, **bui**, **bĭtum**, *a.* **(de; hăbeo)**, *to owe*, *be bound*, *be under obligation*, *be due;* with an infinitive after it, translate it by *ought*, *must*, *&c.; impers.*, **debet**, *it behooves*, *ought.*

dē-bĭlis, **e**, *adj.* **(de; hăbĭlis)**, *weak*, *disabled*, *frail*, *crippled.*

dē-cēdo, **cēdĕre**, **cessi**, **cessum**, *n.*, *to depart*, *retire*, *cease*, *die*, *yield*, *give way.*

dĕcem, *num. adj. indecl.*, *ten.*

Dĕcem-ber, **bris**, *m.* **(dĕcem)**, the tenth month of the Roman year, reckoned from March; *December*.

december, bris, *adj.*, *of December*.

dē-cerno, cerněre, crēvi, crētum, *a.* and *n.*, *to decide, judge, determine, decree; to fight, contend.*

dē-cerpo, pěre, psi, ptum, *a.* (**de**; **carpo** = *to pluck*), *to pluck away, pull off, gather, take away, destroy.*

dē-certo, āre, āvi, ātum, *n.* and *a.*, *to fight earnestly, strive, vie; to contend for.*

děcet, děcēre, děcuit, *no sup.*, *n. impers.*, *it is seemly, becoming, fitting, suitable, proper.*

dē-cĭdo, cĭděre, cĭdi, *no sup.*, *n.* (**de**; **cădo**), *to fall down, sink, die.*

děc-ies, *num. adv.* (**děcem**), *ten times; repeatedly.*

děc-iens, *see* **decies**.

děc-ĭmus, a, um, *num. adj.*, *the tenth.*

Decĭmus Brutus, *see Brutus.*

dē-cĭpio, cĭpěre, cēpi, ceptum, *a.* (**de**; **căpio**), *to catch, ensnare, deceive, cheat.*

de-clāro, āre, āvi, ātum, *a.*, *to make manifest, to declare, announce, proclaim, show, explain.*

děc-or, ōris, *m.* (**děcet**, § **44**, 1, *c*, 2), *that which is seemly; propriety, comeliness, elegance, charms, beauty.*

dēcrē-tum, i, *n.* (**dēcerno**), *a decree, decision, ordinance.*

děc-us, ŏris, *n.* (**děcet**, § **44**, 1, *c*, 2), *that which is becoming, ornament, splendor, dignity, honor, virtue.*

dē-dignor, āri, ātus sum, *dep.*, *to reject as unworthy; to disdain, scorn, refuse.*

dēd-ĭtio, ōnis, *f.* (**dēdo**, § **44**, 1, *c*, 2), *a giving one's self up; a surrender.*

dē-do, děre, dĭdi, dĭtum, *a.*, *to give one's self up: to surrender, yield, devote, dedicate.*

dē-dūco, dūcěre, duxi, ductum, *a.*, *to lead away, withdraw, lead forth, conduct, lead: mislead, seduce; spin out, elaborate.*

dēfătīgā-tio, ōnis, *f.* (**dēfătīgo**, § **44**, 1, *c*, 2), *a wearying; weariness, fatigue, exhaustion.*

dē-fătīgo, āre, āvi, ātum, *a.*, *to weary, fatigue.*

dē-fendo, děre, di, sum, *a.*, *to ward off, avert; to defend, guard, support.*

dēfen-sor, ōris, *m.* (**dēfendo**, § **44**, 1, *c*, 1), *one who wards off; a protector, guard, defender.*

dē-fěro, ferre, tŭli, lātum, *a. irr.*, *to bear* or *bring away, carry, convey, deliver; report, announce; impeach, accuse;* **negotium deferre alicui**, *to intrust the business to any one.*

dē-fĭcio, fĭcěre, fēci, fectum, *a.* and *n.* (**de**; **făcio**), *to forsake, abandon, desert, revolt, fail, cease.*

dē-flecto, ctěre, xi, xum, *a.*, *to turn away, divert, bend.*

dē-formis, e, *adj.* (**de**; **forma**), *without form* or *beauty.*

dēform-ĭtas, ātis, *f.* (**dēformis**, § **44**, 1, *c*, 2), *lack of beauty, ugliness, hideousness.*

dē-fungor, fungi, functus sum, *dep.*, *to discharge, perform, fulfil, finish; to depart, die.*

dein, *see* **deinde**.

dein-ceps, *adv.* (**dein**; **căpio**), *one after the other, successively; in turn, thereafter, next.*

deinde, *adv.*, *then, afterward, secondly.*

de-jĭcio, jĭcěre, jēci, jectum, *a.* (**de**; **jăcio**), *to throw down, cast down, drive out, dislodge, deprive.*

dēlec-to, āre, āvi, ātum, *a. intens.* (**dēlĭcio**, § **36**, *b*, and **44**, 2, *b*), *to delight, please, amuse.*

dēlectus, a, um, *part.* (**dēlĭgo**), *chosen, select.*

dēlec-tus, ūs, *m.* (**dēlĭgo, § 44,** 1, *c*, 2), *a choosing, selection; levy.*

dēleo, lēre, lēvi, lētum, *a., to abolish, destroy, blot out, extinguish.*

dē-lībĕro, āre, āvi, ātum, *a.* (**de; lībra,** pair of scales), *to weigh well in one's mind, deliberate, consult, consider.*

dēlĭciæ, ārum, *f.* (**dēlĭcio,** to allure), *delight, pleasure, luxury; allurements, charms.*

dē-lĭgo, lĭgĕre, lēgi, lectum, *a.* (**de; lĕgo**), *to choose out, select.*

dē-lĭgo, āre, āvi, ātum, *a., to bind together, bind up, bind fast.*

dē-lĭtesco, lĭtescĕre, lĭtui, *no sup., n. inch.* (**de; lăteo, § 36,** *a.* and **44,** 2, *b*), *to hide* or *conceal one's self, lie hid, lurk.*

Delphi, ōrum, *m.*, a town in Phocis, at the foot of Mount Parnassus, noted for the Oracle of Apollo.

dēlū-brum, i, *n.* (**dēluo,** to cleanse), *a temple, shrine.*

dē-mĭnuo, mĭnuĕre, mĭnui, mĭnūtum, *a., to lessen, diminish.*

dē-mitto, mittĕre, mīsi, missum, *a., to let* or *bring down, send down, lower, dismiss.*

dēmo, mĕre, mpsi, mptum, *a.* (**de; ĕmo**), *to take away.*

dē-monstro, āre, āvi, ātum, *a., to point out, represent, describe, mention, designate.*

dēmum, *adv., at length, at last, only;* **tum demum,** *then at length.*

dēn-ārius, a, um, *adj.* (**dēni**), *consisting of,* or *containing ten.*

dēn-ārius, ii, *m.*, a Roman silver coin, equal to about sixteen cents.

dē-nĕgo, āre, āvi, ātum, *a., to deny, reject, refuse.*

dēni, æ, a, *num. distributive adj.* (**dĕcem**), *ten each, ten at a time, by tens, ten.*

dēnĭque, *adv., at last, finally.*

dens, dentis, *m., a tooth.*

densus, a, um, *adj., thick, dense, close, frequent, numerous.*

dē-pōno, pōnĕre, pŏsui, pŏsĭtum, *a., to lay aside, put down, place, set, deposit; to intrust to, to resign, give up.*

dē-pŏpŭlo, āre, āvi, ātum, *a., to lay waste, plunder, ravage.*

dē-pŏpŭlor, āri, ātus sum, *dep., to lay waste, plunder, ravage.*

dē-porto, āre, āvi, ātum, *a., to carry off; to bring home; to acquire; to banish.*

dē-posco, poscĕre, pŏposci, *no sup., a., to demand, request, require, claim.*

dēprĕcā-tor, ōris, *m.* (**dēprĕcor, § 44,** 1, *c*, 1), *an interceder, intercessor, mediator.*

dē-prĕcor, āri, ātus sum, *dep., to beseech, pray against, deprecate, beg, pray for.*

dē-prĕhendo, dĕre, di, sum, *a., to seize upon, catch, discover, find.*

dē-prĭmo, prĭmĕre, pressi, pressum, *a.* (**de; prĕmo**), *to press down, depress, sink.*

dē-rĭpio, rĭpĕre, rĭpui, reptum, *a.* (**de; răpio**), *to snatch away, tear off.*

dē-scendo, dĕre, di, sum, *n.* (**de; scando**), *to come down, descend, dismount, march down;* **descendere in certamen** *or* **aciem,** *to engage in battle.*

de-scisco, sciscĕre, scīvi *or* **scii, scītum,** *n., to withdraw, revolt from, desert.*

de-scrībo, scrībĕre, scripsi, scriptum, *a., to point out, represent, describe, allot.*

dē-sĕro, ĕre, ui, tum, *a., to desert, forsake, abandon.*

dēsīdĕr-ium, ii, *n.* (**dēsīdĕro, § 44,** 1, *c*, 2), *a longing desire* (for any thing not possessed); *grief, regret.*

dē-sīdĕro, āre, āvi, ātum, *a., to long for* (something not possessed).

dē-signo, **āre**, **āvi**, **ātum**, *a.*, *to mark out*, *signify*, *appoint*, *assign*, *choose.*

dē-sĭlio, **sĭlīre**, **sĭlui**, **sultum**, *n.* (de; sălio), *to leap down.*

dē-sĭno, **sĭnĕre**, **sīvi** *or* **sii**, **sĭtum**, *a.* and *n.*, *to leave off*, *desist*, *stop.*

dē-sisto, **sistĕre**, **stĭti**, **stĭtum**, *n.*, *to leave off*, *give over*, *desist.*

dēspērā-tio, **ōnis**, *f.* (**despēro**, § **44**, 1, *c*, 2), *hopelessness*, *despair.*

dē-spēro, **āre**, **āvi**, **ātum**, *n.* and *a.*, *to be hopeless*; *despair of.*

dē-spĭcio, **spĭcĕre**, **spexi**, **spectum**, *n.* and *a.* (de; **spĕcio**), *to look down upon*, *despise*, *disdain.*

dē-spondeo, **dēre**, **di**, **sum**, *a.*, *to promise*, *to betroth.*

dē-stringo, **stringĕre**, **strinxi**, **strictum**, *a.*, *to unsheath*, *draw* (the sword).

dē-sum, **esse**, **fui**, *n.*, *to be away*; *to fail*, *be wanting.*

dē-tĕgo, **tĕgĕre**, **texi**, **tectum**, *a.*, *to uncover*, *expose*; *discover*, *disclose*, *reveal.*

dē-terreo, **terrēre**, **terrui**, **terrĭtum**, *a.*, *to frighten off*, *deter*, *hinder*; *avert.*

dē-tĭneo, **tĭnēre**, **tĭnui**, **tentum**, *a.* (de; **tĕneo**), *to hold off*, *keep back*, *detain*, *hinder.*

dē-trăho, **trăhĕre**, **traxi**, **tractum**, *a.*, *to draw off*, *draw away*, *pull down*, *take from*, *disparage.*

dētrī-mentum, **i**, *n.* (**dētĕro**, § **44**, 1, *c*, 2), *loss*, *damage*; *defeat.*

deus, **i**, *m.* (§ **10**, 4, *f*), *a god*, *divinity*, *deity.*

dē-vasto, **āre**, *no perf.*, **ātum**, *a.*, *to lay waste*, *devastate.*

dē-vinco, **vincĕre**, **vīci**, **victum**, *a.*, *to conquer*, *vanquish.*

dē-vŏlo, **āre**, **āvi**, *no sup.*, *n.*, *to fly down*, *hasten down.*

dē-vŏro, **āre**, **āvi**, **ātum**, *a.*, *to gulp down*, *devour*, *swallow*, *consume.*

dexter, **tra**, **trum**, *and* **tĕra**, **tĕrum**, *adj.*, *to the right*, *on the right side*, *right.*

dextĕra, **æ**, *f.*, *the right hand.*

diădēma, **ătis**, *n.*, *a royal head-dress*, *diadem.*

dic, *imperat. of* **dīco** (§ **30**, 6, *c*), *say.*

dĭc-ax, **ācis**, *adj.* (**dīco**, § **44**, 1, *c*, 3), *sarcastic*, *witty*, *keen.*

dĭco, **āre**, **āvi**, **ātum**, *a.*, *to dedicate*, *consecrate.*

dīco, **dīcĕre**, **dixi**, **dictum**, *a.*, *to speak*, *say*, *call*, *name*, *appoint*, *order*, *mean*; **dicitur**, *it is said.*

dictā-tor, **ōris**, *m.* (**dicto**, § **44**, 1, *c*, 1), *dictator*; a supreme magistrate, elected by the Romans only in seasons of emergency, when his power was absolute, and lasted for six months.

dictā-tūra, **æ**, *f.* (**dicto**, § **44**, 1, *c*, 2), *the office of dictator*, *dictatorship.*

dict-ĭto, **āre**, **āvi**, **ātum**, *a. intens.* (**dicto**, § **36**, *b*, and **44**, 2, *b*), *to say* or *plead often*, *declare*, *maintain.*

dic-to, **āre**, **āvi**, **ātum**, *a. intens.* (**dīco**, § **36**, *b*, and **44**, 2, *b*), *to say often*, *dictate*, *prescribe.*

dic-tum, **i**, *n.* (**dīco**), *a saying*, *a word*, *maxim*, *jest*, *command.*

dies, **ēi**, *m.* (§ **13**, 2), *a day* of 24 hours; *day-light*; **in dies**, *daily*, with an idea of constant increase; **ad diem**, *at the appointed time.*

dif-fĕro, **differre**, **distŭli**, **dīlātum**, *a.* and *n.*, *to delay*, *put off*; *to differ*; **inter se differre**, *to differ from each other.*

diffĭcĭl-e, *adv.* (**diffĭcĭlis**), *with difficulty.*

dif-fĭcĭlis, **e**, *adj.* (**dis**; **făcĭlis**), *hard*, *difficult*, *troublesome*, *obstinate.*

diffĭcul-tas, **ātis**, *f.* (**diffĭcĭlis**, § **44**, 1, *c*, 2), *difficulty*, *trouble*, *distress*, *poverty.*

dif-fīdo, fīdĕre, fīsus sum, *n. semi-dep.* (**dis; fīdo,** § **35,** 2), *to mistrust; despair.*

dĭgĭtus, i, *m., a finger, toe.*

dignus, a, um, *adj., worthy of, deserving, becoming, proper.*

dīlĭgens, entis, *part.* (**dīlĭgo**), *careful, attentive, diligent.*

dīlĭgen-ter, *adv.* (**dīlĭgens**), *carefully, with care.*

dīlĭgen-tia, æ, *f.* (**dīlĭgens,** § **44,** 1, *c*, 2), *diligence, carefulness; economy, thrift.*

dī-lĭgo, lĭgĕre, lexi, lectum, *a.* (**di; lĕgo**), *to value highly, esteem, love.*

dī-luo, luĕre, lui, lūtum, *a., to dissolve, dilute, weaken, do away with.*

dī-mĭco, āre, āvi *or* **ui, ātum,** *n., to fight, contend.*

dī-mitto, mittĕre, mīsi, missum, *a., to send forth, send away, dismiss, put away, divorce.*

dī-mŏveo, mŏvēre, mōvi, mōtum, *a., to put asunder, separate, divide, dismiss, remove.*

dī-rĭgo, rĭgĕre, rexi, rectum, *a.* (**dis; rĕgo**), *to direct, arrange, guide.*

dī-rĭpio, rĭpĕre, rĭpui, reptum, *a.* (**dis; răpio**), *to tear in pieces, ravage, plunder, destroy.*

dī-ruo, ruĕre, rui, rŭtum, *a., to demolish, overthrow.*

dīrus, a, um, *adj., ominous, portentous, dreadful.*

dīs, dītis, *adj., see* **dīves.**

dis-cēdo, cēdĕre, cessi, cessum, *n., to go away, depart, turn aside, decamp.*

dis-cerpo, pĕre, psi, ptum, *a.* (**dis; carpo**), *to tear in pieces, disperse.*

disc-ĭpŭlus, i, *m.* (**disco**), *a learner, scholar, pupil.*

disco, discĕre, dĭdĭci, *no sup., a., to learn.*

discord-ia, æ, *f.* (**discors,** § **44,** 1, *c*, 2), *disunion, variance, discord, strife.*

dis-cors, cordis, *adj.* (**dis; cor**), *disagreeing, at variance, discordant, harsh, unlike.*

dis-crīmen, ĭnis, *n.* (**discerno,** *to separate*), *a distinction, difference; risk, danger.*

dĭs-ertus, a, um, *adj.* (**dis; ars**), *well-spoken, fluent, eloquent, accomplished, elegant.*

dis-jĭcio, jĭcĕre, jēci, jectum, *a.* (**dis; jăcio**), *to tear asunder, scatter, disperse; shatter, break down.*

di-spergo, spergĕre, spersi, spersum, *a.* (**di; spargo**), *to scatter about, disperse.*

dis-plĭceo, plĭcēre, plĭcui, plĭcĭtum, *n.* (**dis; plăceo**), *to displease.*

dis-pōno, pōnĕre, pŏsui, pŏsĭtum, *a., to set in order, arrange, dispose, distribute, station.*

dis-pŭto, āre, āvi, ātum, *a.* and *n., to examine, investigate; discuss; argue, dispute.*

dissen-sio, ōnis, *f.* (**dissentio,** § **44,** 1, *c*, 2), *difference of opinion, disagreement, variance, strife, quarrel.*

dis-sentio, sentīre, sensi, sensum, *n., to differ, disagree; to be unlike.*

dis-sĕro, sĕrĕre, sĕrui, sertum, *a.* and *n., to set asunder; to argue about, discuss; to argue.*

dis-sĭmĭlis, e, *adj., unlike, dissimilar.*

dissĭmĭl-ĭtūdo, ĭnis, *f.* (**dissĭmĭlis,** § **44,** 1, *c*, 2), *unlikeness.*

dis-sĭmŭlo, āre, āvi, ātum, *a.* (**dissĭmĭlis**), (to pretend that a thing is not what it is), *to dissemble, disguise, hide, conceal.*

dis-suadeo, dēre, si, sum, *a., to advise against, dissuade, oppose.*

di-sto, stāre, *no perf., no sup., n., to stand apart; to be separate; to differ.*

dis-trăho, trăhĕre, traxi, tractum, *a., to pull* or *tear asunder, divide, separate.*

dis-trĭbuo, trĭbuĕre, trĭbui, trĭbūtum, *a.*, *to divide, distribute.*

di-stringo, ngĕre, nxi, ctum, *a.*, *to draw asunder; to detain, hinder; to occupy, engage.*

dis-turbo, āre, āvi, ātum, *a.*, *to drive asunder, demolish, destroy; thwart, ruin.*

dĭtio, ōnis, *f.*, *dominion, authority, rule, sway, power.*

dītior, dītissimus, *comp.* and *superlative* of **dives.**

diu, *adv.* **(dies),** *by day, a long time, long ago; comp.*, **diutius;** *superlative*, **diutissime.**

diū turnus, a, um, *adj.* **(diu),** *of long duration, lasting, long.*

diūturn-ĭtas, ātis, *f.* **(diūturnus,** § **44**, 1, *c*, 2), *length of time, long duration.*

dīver-sus, a, um, *part.* **(dīverto),** *different, unlike, contrary;* **in diversa,** *in different directions, asunder.*

dīv-es, ĭtis, *adj.*, *rich* (the *nom.* and *acc.* of the *neut. pl.* do not occur; *comp.*, **divitior** *or* **ditior;** *superlative*, **divitissimus** *or* **ditissimus).**

dī-vĭdo, vĭdĕre, vīsi, vīsum, *to separate, divide, distribute, apportion, distinguish.*

Dīvĭco, ōnis, *m.*, a Helvetian leader.

dīv-īnus, a, um, *adj.* **(dīvus),** *of* or *belonging to a deity; divine, god-like.*

Dīvĭtiăcus, i, *m.*, an Æduan chief.

dīvĭt-iæ, ārum, *f.* **(dīves,** § **44**, 1, *c*, 2), *riches, wealth.*

do, dăre, dĕdi, dătum, *a.* (§ **30**, 1, note, and 2, and § **78**, 3, *c*, ex.), *to give, grant, allow, permit, bestow, present;* **finem dare,** *to put an end to;* **pœnas dare,** *to inflict punishment;* **aliquem in fugam dare,** *to put one to flight;* **in fugam se dare,** *to take to flight.*

dŏceo, ēre, ui, tum, *a.*, *to teach, instruct, inform, show, tell.*

doc-tor, ōris, *m.* **(dŏceo,** § **44**, **1**, *c*, 1), *a teacher, instructor.*

doctr-īna, æ, *f.* **(doctor),** *teaching, instruction; knowledge, learning.*

doc-tus, a, um, *part.* **(dŏceo),** *learned, skilled, versed, experienced.*

dŏleo, ēre, ui, ĭtum, *n.* and *a.*, *to feel pain, grieve, lament, be sorry; to grieve over, deplore, be sorry for.*

dŏl-or, ōris, *m.* **(dŏleo,** § **44**, 1, *c*, 2), *pain, distress, sorrow, anguish, trouble, vexation, anger.*

dŏlus, i, *m.*, *guile, fraud, deceit, deception.*

dŏm-ĭ-cĭl-ium, ii, *n.* **(dŏmus),** *a habitation, dwelling, abode.*

dŏmĭnā-tio, ōnis, *f.* **(domĭnor,** § **44**, 1, *c*, 2), *rule, dominion, lordship, tyranny, despotism.*

dŏmĭnor, āri, ātus sum, *dep.* **(dŏmĭnus),** *to be lord and master, have dominion, bear rule.*

dŏmĭnus, i, *m.* **(dŏmo),** *a master, lord, ruler, commander, chief; owner.*

dŏmo, āre, ui, ĭtum, *a.*, *to subdue, vanquish, overcome, conquer.*

dŏmus, i, *or* **ūs,** *f.* (§ **12**, 3, *e*), *a house, dwelling, abode, home, household, family, race;* **domi,** *at home.*

dōnec, *conj.*, *as long as, while; until.*

dōno, āre, āvi, ātum, *a.* **(dōnum),** *to give, present, bestow* (with *acc.* of thing and *dat.* of person, or *acc.* of person and *abl.* of thing, § **51**, 1, *c*).

dō-num, i, *n.* **(do),** *a gift, present.*

dormio, īre, īvi *or* **ii, ītum,** *n.*, *to sleep, rest, be at ease, be inactive, be careless.*

Drūsus, i, *m.*, a Roman statesman.

Dūbis, is, *m.*, a river of Gaul.

dŭbĭtā tio, ōnis, *f.* **(dŭbĭto,** § **44**, 1, *c*, 2), *a doubting; an uncertainty, doubt, hesitation.*

dŭbĭto, āre, āvi, ātum, *a.* and *n. intens.* (**duo**, through old form, **dubo**), *to doubt, hesitate.*

dŭbius, a, um, *adj.* (**duo**), *doubtful, irresolute.* As NOUN, *n., doubt;* **procul dubio**, *without doubt.*

dŭ-centi, æ, a, *num. adj.* (**duo; centum**), *two hundred.*

dūco, ducĕre, duxi, ductum, *a., to lead, conduct, draw, prolong, put off, consider, think;* **murum ducere**, *to build a wall;* **uxorem in matrimonium ducere**, *to marry* (a woman).

dulcis, e, *adj., sweet, agreeable, delightful, pleasant, charming.*

dum, *conj., while, until, so long as, provided that.*

dum-mŏdo, *conj., provided that, if only.*

Dumnŏrix, ĭgis, *m.*, an Æduan chief.

dum-taxat, *adv.* (**dum; taxo**, *to estimate*), *only, simply, merely, at least, so far.*

duo, æ, o, *num. adj., two.*

duŏ-dĕcim, *num. adj. indecl., twelve.*

duŏ-dē-vīginti, *num. adj. indecl., two from twenty, eighteen.*

dŭ-plex, ĭcis, *adj.* (**duo; plĭco**, *to fold*), *twofold, double; false, deceitful, crafty.*

dūrus, a, um, *adj., hard, harsh, rough, rude, stern, indifferent, severe, painful.*

dux, dŭcis, *com. gen.* (**dūco**), *a leader, commander, general-in-chief; guide.*

Dyrrăchium, ii, *n.*, a sea-coast town of *Illyria*, formerly called Epidamnus (now Durazzo).

E.

e, ex, *prep.* with *abl., out of, from, of;* **ex itinere**, *on the march;* **ex equo**, *on horseback.*

ĕbur, ŏris, *n., ivory.*

ĕbur-neus, a, um, *adj.* (**ebur**, § **44**, 1, *c*, 3), *of ivory, ivory.*

ec-ce, *interj., lo! behold!*

ec-qui, quæ *or* **qua, quod,** *pronominal interrogative adj., whether any? if any?*

ec-quis, quid, *pronominal interrogative substantive, whether any? any one, anybody, any thing?* **ecquid**, *as adverbial acc., why?*

ĕd-ax, ācis, *adj.* (**edo**, § **44**, 1, *c*, 3), *voracious, gluttonous; devouring, destroying.*

ē-dīco, dīcĕre, dixi, dictum, *a., to declare, publish, ordain, make known; order, appoint, establish.*

ēdic-tum, i, *n.* (**ēdīco**), *a proclamation, ordinance, edict.*

ĕdo, ĕdĕre *or* **esse, ēdi, ēsum** *or* **essum,** *a.* (§ **37**, 5), *to eat, squander, dissipate, devour, destroy.*

ē-do, dĕre, dĭdi, dĭtum, *a., to give forth, publish, declare, exhibit, cause.*

ē-dūco, dūcĕre, duxi, ductum, *a., to lead* or *draw out, lead forth, march out troops.*

ēdŭco, āre, āvi, ātum, *a., to bring up, rear, educate.*

effēmĭnā-tus, a, um, *part.* (**effēmĭno**), *womanish, effeminate.*

ef-fēmĭno, āre, āvi, ātum, *a.* (**ex; fēmĭna**), *to make womanish; to effeminate, enervate.*

ef-fĕro, efferre, extŭli, ēlātum, *a. irreg.* (**ex; fĕro**), *to bring forth, carry forth, to bear out, produce, publish, announce; exalt, elevate;* **efferri**, *to be haughty, proud.*

ef-fĭcio, fĭcĕre, fēci, fectum, *a.* (**ex; făcio**), *to bring to pass; to effect, execute, complete, make; to produce, bear, yield.*

ef-fŭgio, fŭgĕre, fūgi, *no sup., n.* and *a.* (**ex; fŭgio**), *to flee out, get away: to escape, avoid, shun.*

ef-fundo, fundĕre, fūdi, fūsum, *a.* (**ex; fundo**), *to pour out* or *forth; to drive out, cast out,* *empty, squander;* effundere se, *to spread out.*

ĕgē-nus, a, um, *adj.* (ĕgeo), *in want of, in need of, destitute, needy.*

ĕgeo, ēre, ui, *no sup., n., to be needy, suffer want; to lack, want, need.*

ĕgo, *pron., I.*

ē-grĕdior, grĕdi, gressus sum, *dep.* (ex; grădior), *to go out, go forth, leave.*

ē-grĕg-ius, a, um, *adj.* (e; grex), *excellent, eminent, surpassing, extraordinary, remarkable.*

ē-jĭcio, jĭcĕre, jēci, jectum, *a.* (e; jăcio), *to cast, thrust,* or *drive out, expel, reject, banish;* ejicere se, *to burst forth, rush out.*

ējus-mŏdi, *of that kind* (is; mŏdus).

ē-lābor, lābi, lapsus sum, *dep., n.* and *a., to slip away, escape, disappear; to escape from.*

ē-lātus, a, um, *part.* (effĕro), *exalted, lofty, high.*

ēlec-tio, ōnis, *f.* (ēlĭgo, § 44, 1, c, 2), *a choice, selection.*

ēlĕgan-ter, *adv.* (ēlĕgans), *with correct choice, tastefully, neatly, fitly.*

ēlĕgant-ia, æ, *f.* (ēlĕgans, *from* ēlĭgo, § 44, 1, c, 2), *taste, propriety, refinement, grace, elegance.*

ĕlĕphantus, i, *m., an elephant.*

ē-lĭgo, lĭgĕre, lēgi, lectum, *a.* (ex; lĕgo), *to choose* or *pick out, select.*

ēlŏquens, entis, *part.* (ēlŏquor), *eloquent.*

ēlŏquent-ia, æ, *f.* (ēlŏquens, § 44, 1, c, 2), *a being eloquent, eloquence.*

ē-lŏquor, qui, cūtus sum, *dep., to speak out, utter, declare, speak well* or *eloquently.*

ē-lūceo, lūcēre, luxi, *no sup., n., to shine out, show itself, be apparent, manifest.*

ē-mitto, mittĕre, mīsi, missum, *a., to send out* or *forth, publish;* emittere vocem, *to utter;* emittere animus, *to give up the ghost, die.*

ĕmo, ĕmĕre, ēmi, emptum, *a., to buy, purchase, gain, acquire, obtain.*

ē-mollio, īre, ii, ītum, *a., to soften; to make gentle, mild; to enervate.*

em-ptor, ōris, *m.* (ĕmo, § 44, 1, c, 1), *a buyer.*

ēn, *interj., lo! behold! see! see there!*

ē-narro, āre, āvi, ātum, *a., to explain in detail.*

ē-nervo, āre, āvi, ātum, *a.* (e; nervus), *to enervate, weaken, render effeminate.*

ĕnim, *conj., for, indeed, truly, certainly.*

ensis, is, *m., a sword.*

ē-nuntio (cio), āre, āvi, ātum, *a., to divulge, disclose; to report, tell.*

eo, īre, īvi *or* ii, ĭtum, *n. irreg., to go* (§ 37, 6).

eō, *adv.* (is), *thither; to that place, so far; therefore.* With COMPARATIVES, *by so much, so much, the;* quo . . . eo, *the . . . the.*

eōdem, *adv.* (īdem), *to the same place, the same way.*

ĕpĭgramma, ătis, *n., an inscription, epigram.*

Ēpīrus, i, *f.*, a province in the north of Greece.

ĕpistŏla, æ, *f., a letter, epistle.*

ĕpŭlæ, ārum, *f., a feast, banquet.*

ĕpŭl-or, āri, ātus, *dep.* (ĕpŭlæ), *to give an entertainment, feast, eat.*

ĕques, equĭtis, *m.* (ĕquus), *a horseman, rider;* equites, *cavalry; also the knights, the equites,* as an order in the state.

ĕque-ster, tris, tre, *adj.* (ĕques), *belonging to horsemen, equestrian.*

ĕ-quĭdem, *adv., verily, truly, indeed, at all events, certainly, by all means, of course, undoubtedly.*

ĕquĭtā-tus, **ūs**, *m.* (**ĕquĭto**, § **44**, 1, *c*, 2), *a riding; cavalry.*

ĕquĭt-o, **āre**, **āvi**, **ātum**, *n.* (**ĕques**), *to be a horseman, to ride.*

ĕquus, **i**, *m.*, *a horse, steed.*

ergā, *prep.* with *acc.*, *over against, opposite to; towards, against.*

ergō, *adv.* (§ **43**, 3, *e*), *therefore, accordingly.*

ē-rĭgo, **rĭgĕre**, **rexi**, **rectum**, *a.* (**e**; **rĕgo**), *to raise* or *set up, erect, construct; to encourage, rouse, stimulate, cheer up.*

ē-rĭpio, **rĭpĕre**, **rĭpui**, **reptum**, *a.* (**e**; **răpio**), *to snatch away, rescue;* **eripere se**, *to snatch one's self away, to flee.*

erro, **āre**, **āvi**, **ātum**, *n.*, *to wander, go astray, roam, rove.*

err-or, **ōris**, *m.* (**erro**, § **44**, 1, *c*, 2), *a wandering away; an error, mistake, deception, delusion, false notion.*

ē-rŭbesco, **rŭbescĕre**, **rŭbui**, *no sup.*, *n.* and *a.*, *to grow red; to blush; to feel ashamed; to feel ashamed about.*

ē-rŭd-io, **īre**, **īvi** *or* **ii**, **ītum**, *a.* (**e**; **rŭdis**), *to free from rudeness, cultivate, educate, instruct, train, polish.*

ērŭdī-tus, **a**, **um**, *part.* (**ērŭdio**), *learned, accomplished, experienced, skilled.*

ē-rumpo, **rumpĕre**, **rūpi**, **ruptum**, *a.* and *n.*, *to burst forth, sally forth.*

ē-ruo, **ruĕre**, **rui**, **rŭtum**, *a.*, *to cast forth, tear out; elicit, extract.*

ērup-tio, **ōnis**, *f.* (**ērumpo**, § **44**, 1, *c*, 2), *a bursting forth; a sally.*

es-ca, **æ**, *f.* (**ĕdo**), *food, bait.*

et, *conj.*, *and, also, even, too, as;* **et . . . et**, *both . . . and, not only . . . but also.*

ĕtiam, *conj.*, *and also, besides, likewise, even; certainly, yes.* With COMPARATIVES, *still;* **magis etiam**, *still more.*

et-si, *conj.*, *though, although, even if; yet, but.*

Eubœa, **æ**, *f.*, an island in the Ægēan sea, separated from Bœotia by the Eurīpus.

Eurīpĭdes, **is**, *m.*, a celebrated Athenian tragic poet.

Eurōpa, **æ**, *f.*, the continent of Europe.

ē-vādo, **dĕre**, **si**, **sum**, *n.* and *a.* *to go forth, depart, escape; turn out, end; to escape from, climb, ascend.*

ē-vello, **vellĕre**, **velli** *or* **vulsi**, **vulsum**, *a.*, *to tear out, pluck out, eradicate, erase, remove.*

ē-vĕnio, **vĕnīre**, **vēni**, **ventum**, *n.*, *to come out, come forth; to come to pass, happen; to result, turn out.*

ēven-tum, **i**, *n.* (**ēvĕnio**), *an occurrence, event; issue, consequence, result.*

ēven-tus, **ūs**, *m.* (**ēvĕnio**, § **44**, 1, *c*, 2), *an occurrence* or *event, fortune, fate, lot; the issue, result.*

ē-verto, **tĕre**, **ti**, **sum**, *a.*, *to turn, drive* or *thrust out; to overthrow, ruin, destroy.*

ē-vīto, **āre**, **āvi**, **ātum**, *a.*, *to shun, avoid.*

ē-vŏco, **āre**, **āvi**, **ātum**, *a.*, *to call out, summon.*

ē-vŏlo, **āre**, **āvi**, **ātum**, *n.*, *to fly forth, fly up, spring out.*

ē-vŏmo, **ĕre**, **ui**, **ĭtum**, *a.*, *to vomit forth, cast out, give up.*

ēx *or* **ē** (e only before consonants), *prep.* with *abl.*, *out of, from, of.*

ex-ănĭmis, **e**, *adj.* (**ex**; **ănĭma**), *lifeless, dead.*

ex-ănĭmo, **āre**, **āvi**, **ātum**, *a.* (**ex**; **ănĭma**), *to deprive of life, kill.*

ex-ardesco, **ardescĕre**, **arsi**, **arsum**, *n. inch.* (**ardeo**, § **36**, *a*, and **44**, 2, *b*), *to blaze up; to be inflamed; to burn; to rage.*

ex-ăro, **āre**, **āvi**, **ātum**, *a.*, *to plough up; to cultivate; to write, note, set down* (something on tablets).

ex-aspĕro, āre, āvi, ātum, *a.* (asper), *to make rough, fierce* or *savage, to exasperate.*

ex-cēdo, cēdĕre, cessi, cessum, *n.* and *a.*, *to go out, depart, withdraw; to die; to exceed.*

excell-ens, entis, *part.* (excello), *high, lofty, distinguished.*

ex-cello, lĕre, lui, sum, *n.*, *to surpass, excel.*

excel-sus, a, um, *part.* (excello), *elevated, lofty, high.*

excīd-io, ōnis, *f.* (exscindo, § 44, 1, *c*, 2), *a destroying, destruction.*

excĭd-ium, ii, *n.* (exscindo, § 44, 1, *c*, 2), *overthrow, demolition.*

ex-cĭdo, cĭdĕre, cĭdi, *no sup.*, *n.* (ex; cădo), *to fall down, escape, pass away, perish.*

ex-cīdo, cīdĕre, cīdi, cīsum, *a.* (ex; cædo), *to cut off, demolish, destroy, lay waste, banish.*

ex-cio, īre, īvi *or* ii, ītum *or* ĭtum, *a.*, *to rouse, excite, stir up, call forth, send for.*

ex-cĭpio, cĭpĕre, cēpi, ceptum, *a.* (ex; căpio), *to take out; to receive, take; to catch, overtake; to succeed.*

ex-cĭto, āre, āvi, ātum, *a. intens.* (excio, § **44**, 2, *b*, and § **36**, *b*), *to rouse up, stimulate, stir up, excite, instigate.*

ex-clāmo, āre, āvi, ātum, *n.* and *a.*, *to call* or *cry out; shout aloud, exclaim.*

ex-clūdo, clūdĕre, clūsi, clūsum, *a.* (ex; claudo), *to shut out, exclude; to cut off, remove, separate; to hinder, prevent; to drive out.*

ex-cŏlo, cŏlĕre, cŏlui, cultum, *a.*, *to cultivate, till, work with great care; to improve, polish, adorn, refine, perfect; to honor.*

excŭb-iæ, ārum, *f.* (excŭbo), *a lying out on watch; a watching, keeping watch; a watch, guard.*

ex-cŭtio, cŭtĕre, cussi, cussum, *a.* (ex; quătio), *to shake off, throw away; to search, examine; to throw off, reject, discard.*

exemplum, i, *n.* (exĭmo), *a sample, pattern, copy, warning; case; precedent.*

ex-eo, īre, īvi *or* ii, ĭtum, *n. irreg.*, *to go out* or *forth; withdraw, pass, ascend.*

ex-erceo, ēre, ui, ĭtum, *a.* (ex; arceo), *to exercise, train; practise, use;* **odium exercere**, *to feel hatred;* **negotium exercere**, *to follow a business.*

exercĭtā-tio, ōnis, *f.* (exercĭto, § **44**, 1, *c*, 2), *exercise, practice.*

exerc-ĭto, āre, āvi, ātum, *a. intens.* (exerceo, § **44**, 2, *b*, and § **36**, *b*), *to exercise diligently* or *frequently.*

exerc-ĭtus, ūs, *m.* (exerceo), *a* TRAINED *body of men; an army; a multitude, host.*

ex-haurio, rīre, si, stum, *a.*, *to draw out, exhaust.*

ex-hĭbeo, ēre, ui, ĭtum, *a.* (ex; hăbeo), *to hold forth, show, exhibit, display; to maintain, support, sustain.*

ex-horreo, horrēre, *no perf.*, *no sup.*, *n.*, *to shudder at, be terrified at.*

ex-horresco, horrescĕre, horrui, *no sup.*, *inch.* (§ **36**, *a*, and § **44**, 2, *b*), *n.* and *a.*, *to tremble* or *shudder exceedingly; to be terrified; to dread.*

ex-ĭgo, ĭgĕre, ēgi, actum, *a.* (ex; ăgo), *to drive forth, expel; enforce, exact, demand; finish, complete; lead, pass;* **aliquid ab aliquo exigere**, *to demand any thing from any one;* **ultionem exigere**, *to take revenge.*

exĭg-uus, a, um, *adj.* (exĭgo), *scanty, small, little, petty, mean.*

exī-lis, e, *adj.* (exĭgo), *small, thin, slender, meagre.*

exĭm-ius, a, um, *adj.* (exĭmo),

select, distinguished, extraordinary, uncommon, excellent.

ex-ĭmo, ĭmĕre, ēmi, emptum, *a.* (**ex; ĕmo**), *to take away; free, release, deliver; remove, banish.*

existĭmā-tio, ōnis, *f.* (**existĭmo,** § **44,** 1, *c*, 2), *a judging, judgment, opinion, reputation, good name, character.*

ex-istĭmo, āre, āvi, ātum, *a.* (**ex; æstĭmo**), *to judge, consider, suppose, think, esteem.*

ex-istŭmo, *see* **existĭmo.**

exĭ-tium, ii, *n.* (**exeo,** § **44,** 1, *c*, 2), *destruction, ruin, hurt, mischief.*

exĭ-tus, ūs, *m.* (**exeo,** § **44,** 1, *c*, 2), *a going forth; departure, end, death; outlet, passage; issue, result.*

ex-ŏrior, ŏrīri, ortus sum, *dep.*, *to rise up, arise, proceed, begin, appear, become.*

ex-ōro, āre, āvi, ātum, *a.*, *to persuade by entreaty; to gain by entreaty.*

ex-pĕdio, īre, īvi *or* **ii, ītum,** *a.* (**ex; pes**) (to free the feet from), *to extricate, disengage; let loose, set free, release; bring out; obtain, prepare, arrange.*

expĕdit, *impers., it is profitable, useful.*

expĕdī-tio, ōnis, *f.* (**expĕdio,** § **44,** 1, *c*, 2), *an expedition, excursion.*

expĕdī-tus, a, um, *part.* (**expĕdio**), *unimpeded, free, easy; light-armed, without baggage.*

ex-pello, pellĕre, pŭli, pulsum, *a.*, *to drive out, eject, expel.*

experg-iscor, pergisci, perrectus sum, *dep.* (**expergo**), *to be awakened; to awake.*

expĕrī-mentum, i, *n.* (**expĕrior,** § **44,** 1, *c*, 2), *a proof, trial, experiment.*

ex-pĕrior, pĕrīri, pertus sum, *dep.* (**ex; pĕrior,** *obsolete*), *to try, prove, put to the test; attempt; experience.*

ex-pers, ertis, *adj.* (**ex; pars**), *having no part in, destitute of, devoid of.*

ex-pĕto, ĕre, īvi *or* **ii, ītum,** *a.*, *to long for, desire, seek earnestly.*

ex-pio, āre, āvi, ātum, *a.*, *to atone for, expiate.*

explōrā-tor, ōris, *m.* (**explōro,** § **44,** 1, *c*, 2), *a searcher out, scout, spy.*

ex-plōro, āre, āvi, ātum, *a.*, *to search out, examine, explore, discover, spy out, reconnoitre.*

ex-pōno, pōnĕre, pŏsui, pŏsĭtum, *a.*, *to lay* or *put out, set forth, expose; exhibit, explain; to set on shore, disembark, land.*

ex-posco, poscĕre, pŏposci, *no sup.*, *a.*, *to ask earnestly, request, entreat, implore.*

expŏs-ĭtio, ōnis, *f.* (**expōno,** § **44,** 1, *c*, 2), *a setting forth, exposition; an exhibiting, showing; a narration.*

ex-prĭmo, prĭmĕre, pressi, pressum, *a.* (**ex; prĕmo**), *to press out, force out; imitate, copy, describe, express, utter.*

ex-prŏbro, āre, āvi, ātum, *a.* (**ex; prŏbrum**), *to reproach, upbraid, charge.*

ex-prōmo, prōmĕre, prompsi, promptum, *a.*, *to show forth, discover, exhibit, display.*

ex-pugno, āre, āvi, ātum, *a.*, *to take by assault; to storm, capture, reduce; conquer, subdue.*

expul-sus, a, um, *part. of* **expello.**

ex-quīro, rĕre, sīvi, sītum, *a.* (**ex; quæro**), *to search diligently; to investigate; to inquire, to ask.*

ex-scindo, scindĕre, scĭdi, scissum, *a.*, *to cut off; to tear out, destroy.*

ex-sĕcror, āri, ātus sum, *dep.* (**ex; săcro**), *to curse, to take a solemn oath.*

exsĕqu-iæ, ārum, *f.* (**ex; sĕquor**), *a funeral procession; funeral rites, obsequies.*

ex-sĕquor, sĕqui, sĕcūtus sum, *dep., to follow out, accomplish, execute; enforce.*
ex-sĕro, ĕre, ui, tum, *a., to thrust out, reveal, show.*
ex-sĭlio, sĭlīre, sĭlui, sultum, *n.* **(ex; sălio),** *to spring forth, leap up, start up.*
exsĭl-ium, ii, *n.* **(exsul),** *banishment, exile.*
ex-sisto, sistĕre, stĭti, stĭtum, *n., to step forth, come forth, emerge, appear; to proceed, arise, become; to exist, be.*
ex-specto, āre, āvi, ātum, *a., to await, expect; to look, hope,* or *long for; to desire; to anticipate, apprehend, fear.*
ex-spīro, āre, āvi, ātum, *a.* and *n., to breathe out, exhale; to breathe one's last, expire.*
ex-stinguo, stinguĕre, stinxi, stinctum, *a., to put out, quench, extinguish; to kill, destroy;* **aqua exstinctus,** *drowned.*
ex-sto, are, *no perf., no sup., n., to stand forth; to be visible, appear, exist.*
ex-struo, ĕre, xi, ctum, *a., to heap up; to build up, raise, erect, construct.*
ex-sūgo, sūgĕre, suxi, suctum, *a., to suck out.*
ex-sul, ŭlis, *com. gen.* **(ex; sŏlum)** (one who quits, or is banished from his native soil), *an exile.*
exsŭlo, āre, āvi, ātum, *n.* **(exsul),** *to be an exile, to live in exile.*
exsul-to, āre, āvi, ātum, *n. intens.* **(exsĭlio,** § **36,** *b,* and § **44, 2,** *b*), *to spring, leap,* or *jump up; to exult, rejoice exceedingly.*
extemplo, *adv., immediately, straightway.*
ex-ter (tĕrus), ĕra, ĕrum, *adj.* **(ex),** *foreign, strange; comp.,* **extĕrior,** *outward, outer, exterior; superlative,* **extrēmus** *or* **extĭmus,** *outermost, last, extreme.*
ex-terreo, terrēre, terrui, terrĭtum, *a., to alarm, terrify.*
ex-tollo, tollĕre, *no perf., no sup., to lift up, raise up, exalt.*
extrā, *adv.* and *prep.* with *acc.* **(exter),** *on the outside, without, except; outside of, beyond, except.*
ex-trăho, trăhĕre, traxi, tractum, *a., to draw forth; to withdraw, release, extract, protract, prolong, put off.*
extra-ordĭn-ārius, a, um, *adj.* **(extra; ordo),** *out of the common order, extraordinary.*
exuo, uĕre, ui, ūtum, *a.* (§ **51, 1,** *c*), *to draw off; pull off, cast off, lay aside; to strip, despoil, deprive.*
ex-ūro, ūrĕre, ussi, ustum, *a., to burn up, consume, destroy, ravage, waste.*

F.

făba, æ, *f., a bean.*
fă-ber, bri, *m.* **(făcio),** *a carpenter, smith, artisan, workman, maker.*
fă-ber, bra, brum, *adj.* **(făcio),** *skilful, ingenious, workmanlike.*
Făbrĭcius, ii, *m.,* a Roman name.
făbrĭco, āre, āvi, ātum, *a.* **(făber),** *to frame, make, construct, build.*
făbrĭcor, āri, ātus sum, *dep., to frame, construct, build; prepare, form, fashion.*
fā-bŭla, æ, *f.* **(for),** *a story, tale, play, fable.*
făcēt-iæ, ārum, *f.* **(făcētus,** § **44, 1,** *c,* **2),** *wit, witty sayings, drollery, humor.*
făcētus, a, um, *adj., courteous, polite; elegant, fine; merry, witty, jocose, humorous.*
făci-es, ēi, *f.* **(făcio),** *form, figure, face, countenance, appearance, aspect.*
făcĭl-e, *adv.* **(făcĭlis),** *easily; certainly; readily.*

făc-ĭlis, e, *adj.* (**făcio**), *easy; courteous, affable.*

făc-ĭnus, ŏris, *n.* (**făcio**), *a deed, act, action, crime, misdeed, bad deed.*

făcio, făcĕre, fēci, factum; *passive,* **fīo, fĭĕri, factus sum,** *a., to make, do, form, produce;* **castra facere,** *to pitch camp;* **fit,** *it happens, is usual;* **fiat,** *so be it.*

fac-tio, ōnis, *f.* (**făcio,** § **44**, 1, *c*, 2), *a making; a party, faction.*

fac-tum, i, *n.* (**făcio**), *a deed, act, exploit.*

fac-tus, a, um, *part.* (**făcio**), *done, accomplished.*

făcul-tas, ātis, *f.* (**făcĭlis,** § **44**, 1, *c*, 2), *capability, power, opportunity; abundance, plenty, supply.*

fā-cundus, a, um, *adj.* (for), *fluent, eloquent.*

fallo, fallĕre, fĕfelli, falsum, *a., to deceive, cheat, escape the notice of.*

fal-sus, a, um, *part.* (**fallo**), *deceptive, feigned, spurious, false.*

fāma, æ, *f., the common talk, report, tradition; character, reputation.*

fămes, is, *f., hunger, famine,* [*poverty.*

fămĭl-ia, æ, *f.* (**fămŭlus,** a servant), *family-servants, domestics, family, household.*

fămĭli-āris, e, *adj.* (**fămĭlia**), *of* or *belonging to a house; domestic, private, intimate.*

fămĭli-āris, is, *m.* (**fămĭlia**), *a familiar friend.*

fămĭliār-ĭtas, ātis (**fămĭliāris,** § **44**, 1, *c*, 2), *intimacy, familiar intercourse, friendship.*

fămĭliār-ĭter, *adv.* (**fămĭliāris**), *on friendly terms, intimately.*

far, farris, *n.* (a species of grain), *spelt, meal.*

fas, *indecl. n.* (for), (that which is right in the sight of heaven), *divine law; right, justice, equity.*

fascis, is, *m., a bundle, parcel;* **fasces,** *pl.,* a bundle of rods and an axe carried by the lictors before a chief magistrate, with which criminals were scourged and beheaded; *the fasces.*

fā-tum, i, *n.* (for), *destiny, fate, calamity.*

fauces, ium, *f.* (found in the sing. only in the *abl.;* **fauce**), *the throat, gullet; a defile, pass.*

Faustŭlus, i, *m.,* the shepherd who brought up Romulus and Remus.

Faustus, i, *m.,* son of Sulla.

făveo, făvēre, fāvi, fautum, *n., to favor, promote, befriend, protect.*

făv-or, ōris, *m.* (**făveo,** § **44**, 1, *c*, 2), *favor, good-will, inclination, partiality.*

fax, făcis, *f., a torch, fire-brand.*

fĕbris, is, *f., a fever.*

Fĕbruārius, ii, *m., February.*

fēles or **fēlis, is,** *f., a cat.*

fēlīc-ĭtas, ātis, *f.* (**fēlix,** § **44**, 1, *c*, 2), *happiness, felicity.*

fēlīc-ĭter, *adv.* (**fēlix**), *auspiciously, favorably.*

fē-lix, īcis, *adj.* (**feo,** to produce), *fruitful; auspicious, happy, fortunate, lucky.*

fē-mĭna, æ, *f.* (**feo,** to produce), *a female, woman.*

fĕmur, ŏris *or* **ĭnis,** *n., the thigh.*

fĕra, æ, *f.* (**fĕrus**), *a wild animal, wild beast.*

fĕrē, *adv., nearly, almost, about, quite, scarcely, generally, usually.*

fermē, *adv., nearly, almost.*

fĕro, ferre, tŭli, lātum, *a. irreg.* (§ **37**, 4), *to bear, bring, endure; bring forth; tell, relate; raise, exalt;* **ferunt,** *they say;* **fertur,** *it is said;* **auxilium ferre,** *to bring aid;* **injurias ferre,** *to inflict injuries;* **ferre legem,** *to propose a law.*

fĕr-ox, ōcis, *adj.* (**fĕro**), *impetuous, courageous, bold; fierce, savage, insolent.*

ferrum, i, *n.*, *iron; sword, arms.*

fĕrus, a, um, *adj.*, *wild, uncultivated, rude, savage, cruel.*

fessus, a, um, *adj.*, *wearied, tired, fatigued, weak, feeble.*

festīno, āre, āvi, ātum, *n.* and *a.*, *to hasten, hurry, accelerate.*

fīcus, i, and ūs, *f.* and *m.*, *a fig-tree; a fig.*

fĭd-ēlis, e, *adj.* (**fĭdes**), *trusty, faithful, sincere.*

fĭd-es, ei, *f.* (**fīdo**), *trust, faith, confidence, belief, credit; promise, engagement, word.*

fīdo, fīdĕre, fīsus sum, *n., semi-dep.* (§ **35**, 2), *to trust, confide, put confidence in.*

fīdūc-ia, æ, *f.* (**fīdus**), *confidence, assurance, boldness.*

fīd-us, a, um, *adj.* (**fīdo**), *faithful, trusty, safe.*

fīgo, gĕre, xi, xum, *a.*, *to fix, fasten, settle, pierce.*

fīlia, æ, *f.* (*dat.* and *abl. plur.*, sometimes **filiabus**; § **9**, 2, *e*), *a daughter.*

fīlius, ii, *m.* (*vocative sing.*, **fili**; § **10**, 4, *c*), *a son.*

fingo, fingĕre, finxi, fictum, *a.*, *to form, shape, make; contrive, devise, invent, feign.*

fīn-io, īre, īvi *or* ii, ītum, *a.* (**fīnis**), *to limit, bound, finish, end.*

fīnis, is, *m.* and *f.*, *a boundary, limit, end*; **fines**, *pl.*, *the borders* (of a territory), *territory.*

fīn-ĭtĭmus, a, um, *adj.* (**fīnis**), *bordering upon, adjacent to, neighboring.*

fīn-ĭtĭmi, ōrum, *m.* (**fīnis**), *neighbors.*

fīo, *see* **făcio**.

firm-ĭtas, ātis, *f.* (**firmus**, § **44**, 1. *c*, 2), *firmness, solidity, durability, strength.*

firm-ĭter, *adv.* (**firmus**), *firmly, strongly.*

firm-ĭtūdo, ĭnis, *f.* (**firmus**, § **44**, 1, *c*, 2), *firmness, solidity, durability, strength.*

firmo, āre, āvi, ātum, *a.* (**firmus**), *to make firm; to strengthen, support; to fortify; to encourage.*

fir-mus, a, um, *adj.* (**fĕro**), *firm, strong, durable, steadfast.*

fīsus, a, um, *part.* (**fīdo**), *having trusted.*

fixus, a, um, *part.* (**fīgo**), *fixed, fast, immovable.*

flāgĭt-ium, ii, *n.* (**flāgĭto**), *a shameful* or *disgraceful act, shame, disgrace; rascal, scoundrel.*

flāgĭto, āre, āvi, ātum, *a.*, *to demand fiercely; to entreat, importune.*

flăgro, āre, āvi, ātum, *n.*, *to flame, blaze, burn; to be inflamed, excited.*

flāmen, ĭnis, *m.*, *a priest* (devoted to the service of some particular deity).

flamma, æ, *f.*, *a flame.*

flā-tus, ūs, *m.* (**flo**, § **44**, 1, *c*, 2), *a blowing, blast, breeze.*

flecto, flectĕre, flexi, flexum, *a.* and *n.*, *to bend, turn, direct, persuade, avoid.*

fleo, ēre, ēvi, ētum, *n.* and *a.*, *to weep, wail, lament, cry.*

flē-tus, us, *m.* (**fleo**, § **44**, 1, *c*, 2), *a weeping.*

flīgo, ĕre, *no perf.*, *no sup.*, *a.*, *to strike, strike down.*

flo, āre, āvi, ātum, *n.* and *a.*, *to blow; to blow at, blow out, blow away.*

flōre-ns, ntis, *part.* (**flōreo**), *flourishing, blooming, prosperous, fine, excellent.*

flōr-eo, ēre, ui, *no sup.*, *n.* (**flos**), *to bloom, blossom, flower; to be prosperous, to be in good repute;* **potentia florere**, *to be powerful;* **opibus florere**, *to be rich;* **bellica laude florere**, *to enjoy military renown.*

flos, flōris, *m.*, *a blossom, flower.*

fluctu-ōsus, a, um, *adj.* (**fluctus**, § **44**, 1, *c*, 3), *full of waves, billowy.*

fluctus, **ūs**, *m.* (**fluo**), *a billow, surge, wave.*

flū-men, **ĭnis**, *n.* (**fluo**; that which flows along), *a river, stream.*

fluo, **ĕre**, **xi**, **xum**, *n., to flow, overflow, stream, pour; to pass away, disappear.*

flŭv-ius, **ii**, *m.* (**fluo**), *a river, running water, stream.*

fŏcus, **i**, *m., a fire-place, hearth.*

fŏdio, **fŏdere**, **fōdi**, **fossum**, *a.* and *n., to dig, dig up; to be employed in digging.*

fœdus, **a**, **um**, *adj., foul, filthy, ugly, horrible, abominable, detestable.*

fœd-us, **ĕris**, *n.* (**fīdus**), *a league, treaty, compact, agreement.*

foll-ĭcŭlus, **i**, *m. dim.* (**follis**, § **44**, 1, *c*, 3), *a ball* (filled with air).

fons, **fontis**, *m.* (**fundo**), *a spring, fountain; source, origin, cause.*

for, **fāri**, **fātus sum**, *dep.* (§ **38**, 2, *c*), *to speak, say.*

fŏrāmen, **ĭnis**, *n., an opening, aperture, hole.*

fore, *fut. inf.* of **sum**.

fŏris, **is**, *f., a door, gate* (*gen. pl.*, **fŏrum**).

fŏris, *adv., out of doors, abroad, without.*

for-ma æ, *f.* (**fĕro**), *shape, form, beauty.*

formīca, **æ**, *f., an ant, pismire.*

formīdo, **ĭnis**, *f., fear, terror, dread.*

formīdŏl-ōsus, **a**, **um**, *adj.* (**formīdo**, § **44**, 1, *c*, 3), *dreadful, terrible, terrific; timid, fearful.*

fors, **fortis**, *f.* (**fĕro**), *chance, hap, hazard, fortune.*

fors, *adv., perchance, perhaps.*

forte, *adv.* (**fors**), *by chance, perhaps.*

for-sĭt-an, *adv., perhaps* (**fors**; **sit**; **an**).

fort-as-se, *adv.* (**forte**; **an**; **sit**), *perhaps, by chance.*

for-tis, **e**, *adj.* (**fĕro**), *strong, powerful, courageous, brave.*

fort-ĭter, *adv.* (**fortis**), *strongly, powerfully, boldly, valiantly, manfully.*

fort-ūna, **æ**, *f.* (**fors**), *chance, luck, fortune; good luck, prosperity; fate, lot.*

fŏrum, **i**, *n., a market place, public square, forum;* a long open space in Rome, between the Capitoline and Palatine hills, surrounded by porticoes and the shops of bankers.

fos-sa, **æ**, *f.* (**fŏdio**), *a ditch, trench.*

fŏveo, **fŏvēre**, **fōvi**, **fōtum**, *a., to warm, keep warm; cherish, caress, love, assist.*

frăg-ĭlis, **e**, *adj.* (**frango**), *easily broken, brittle, weak, frail.*

frango, **frangĕre**, **frēgi**, **fractum**, *a., to break, crush, subdue, weaken, wear out.*

frāter, **frātris**, *m., a brother.*

frāter-nus, **a**, **um**, *adj.* (**frāter**), *brotherly, fraternal, of a brother.*

fraudo, **āre**, **āvi**, **ātum**, *a.* (**fraus**), *to cheat, beguile, defraud.*

fraus, **fraudis**, *f., deceit, deception, guile, crime.*

frendo, **frendĕre**, *no perf.*, **frēsum** *or* **fressum**, *n.* and *a., to gnash* (with the teeth), *to crush.*

frēnum, **i**, *n.* (*pl.* sometimes **frēni**, **ōrum**), *a bit, curb, restraint.*

frĕquens, **entis**, *adj., often, frequent, common, usual; full, crowded, numerous.*

frĕquen-ter, *adv.* (**frĕquens**), *often, frequently.*

frĕquent-ia, **æ**, *f.* (**frĕquens**, § **44**, 1, *c*, 2), *an assemblage, multitude, crowd, throng.*

frĕquento, **āre**, **āvi**, **ātum**, *a.* (**frĕquens**), *to visit, frequent, resort; to crowd.*

frētus, **a**, **um**, *adj., relying* or *depending upon, trusting to.*

frīg-ĭdus, **a**, **um**, *adj.* (**frīgus**), *cold, cool.*

frīgus, ŏris, *n.*, *cold, coldness.*

frons, frondis, *f.*, *a leaf; leaves, foliage.* [*brow, front.*

frons, frontis, *f.*, *the forehead,*

fructu-ōsus, a, um, *adj.* (**fructus,** § **44,** 1, *c*, 3), *fruitful, productive, advantageous, profitable.*

fruc-tus, ūs, *m.*, *fruit, profit, advantage, income.*

frūgāl-ĭtas, ātis, *f.* (**frūgālis,** § **44,** 1, *c*, 2), *economy, temperance, thriftiness, frugality.*

frūges, um, *f. pl.* (**frux**), *fruits of the earth, crops.*

frūment-ārius, a, um, *adj.* (**frumentum**), *of corn;* **res frumentaria,** *corn, provisions.*

frū-mentum, i, *n.* (**fruor**), *corn, grain.*

frustrā, *adv.*, *without effect, in vain; without cause, groundlessly.*

fŭg-a, æ, *f.* (**fŭgio**), *a flight, exile, banishment.*

fŭgio, fŭgĕre, fūgi, fŭgĭtum, *n.* and *a.*, *to flee* or *fly; to run away; to pass away, disappear, perish; to avoid, shun, escape.*

fulg-or, ōris, *m.* (**fulgeo,** § **44,** 1, *c*, 2), *flash, glitter, gleam, brightness.*

fulgeo, fulgēre, fulsi, *no sup.*, *n.*, *to flash, lighten.*

fulg-ur, ŭris, *n.* (**fulgeo**), *lightning; brightness, splendor.*

Fulvia, æ, *f.*, wife of Clodius and of Antony.

fund-ĭtor, ōris, *m.* (**funda,** a sling), *one who slings, a slinger.*

fundo, fundĕre, fūdi, fūsum, *a.*, *to pour, shed out; to bring forth, scatter, rout;* **lacrimas fundere,** *to shed tears;* **hostes fundere,** *to rout the enemy;* **fundi,** *to be poured out, to flow.*

fungor, fungi, functus sum, *dep.*, *to perform, execute, administer, discharge, observe, do, fulfil.*

fūn-ĭcŭlus, i, *m. dim.* (**funis,** § **44,** 1, *c*, 3), *a slender rope, a cord.*

fūnis, is, *m.*, *a rope, line; cable.*

fūnus, ĕris, *n.*, *funeral rites, burial.*

fūr, fūris, *com. gen.*, *a thief, rascal.*

fŭr-or, ōris, *m.* (**furo,** § **44,** 1, *c*, 2), *rage, madness, fury.*

G.

Gādes, ium, *f.*, a colony in southern Hispania (Cadiz).

Gaius (Caius), ii, *m.*, a Roman name.

Galba, æ, *m.*, a Roman emperor; a chief of the Suessiōnes.

Galli, ōrum, *m.*, the people of Gaul.

gălea, æ, *f.*, *a helmet.*

Gallia, æ, *f.*, *Gaul.*

Gallĭc-ānus, a, um, *adj.* (**Gallĭcus**), *Gallic.*

Gall-ĭcus, a, um, *adj.* (**Gallia**), *Gallic.* [*hen.*

gall-īna, æ, *f.* (**gallus,** a cock), *a*

Gallus, i, *m.*, *a Gaul.*

Gallus, i, *m.*, a Roman name.

garrŭl-ĭtas, ātis, *f.* (**garrŭlus,** § **44,** 1, *c*, 2), *a chattering, prating, talkativeness, garrulity.*

garr-ŭlus, a, um, *adj.* (**garrio,** to chatter), *chattering, prating, babbling, talkative.*

Garumna, æ, *m.*, a river of Gaul (now *Garonne*).

gaudeo, gaudēre, gāvīsus sum, *n. semi-dep.* (§ **35,** 2), *to rejoice, be glad.*

gaud-ium, ii, *n.* (**gaudeo,** § **44,** 1, *c*. 2), *joy, gladness, delight.*

gĕl-ĭdus, a, um, *adj.* (**gĕlo,** to freeze), *icy cold, very cold.*

gĕlu, ūs, *n.*, *cold, frost, chill.*

gĕmĭnā-tus, a, um, *part.* (**gĕmĭno**), *doubled, double.*

gĕmĭno, āre, āvi, ātum, *a.* and *n.* (**gĕmĭnus**), *to double, to join; to be double.*

gĕ-mĭnus, a, um, *adj.* (**gĕno,** to bring forth), *twin, double;* **gemini fratres,** *twins.*

gemma, **æ**, *f.*, *precious stone, gem, jewel.*
gĕmo, **ĕre**, **ui**, **ĭtum**, *n.* and *a.*, *to sigh, groan, moan, lament.*
gĕner, **ĕri**, *m.*, *a son-in-law.*
Gĕnēva, **æ**, *f.*, a city of the Allobrŏges.
gĕn-ĭtus, **a**, **um**, *part.* (**gigno**), *begotten, born.*
gens, **gentis**, *f.*, *a clan, tribe, race.*
gĕnu, **ūs**, *n.*, *the knee.*
gĕnus, **ĕris**, *n.*, *birth, descent, origin, race, posterity.*
Germānus, **a**, **um**, *adj.*, *German.*
Germāni, **ōrum**, *m. pl.*, *the Germans.*
gĕro, **gĕrĕre**, **gessi**, **gestum**, *a.*, *to wear, bear, carry, do, transact, carry on;* **se gerere**, *to conduct one's self;* **bellum gerere**, *to carry on war;* **res gestæ**, *deeds, exploits;* **morem gerere**, *to humor.*
gesta, **ōrum**, *n. pl.* (**gĕro**), *deeds, exploits.*
gest-ĭto, **āre**, **āvi**, **ātum**, *a. intens.* (**gesto**, § **36**, *b*, and **44**, 2, *b*), *to carry often, carry, bear.*
ges-to, **āre**, **āvi**, **ātum**, *a. intens.* (**gĕro**, § **36**, *b*, and **44**, 2, *b*), *to bear, carry, have.*
ges-tus, **a**, **um**, *part.* of **gĕro**.
gigno, **gignĕre**, **gĕnui**, **gĕnĭtum**, *a.*, *to beget, bear, bring forth, produce.*
glăcies, **ēi**, *f.*, *ice.*
glădi-ātor, **ōris**, *m.* (**glădius**), *a swordsman, gladiator.*
glădius, **ii**, *m.*, *a sword.*
glans, **glandis**, *f.*, *an acorn, nut; an acorn-shaped ball* of lead or clay.
glōria, **æ**, *f.*, *glory, fame, renown; ambition, pride, boasting, bragging.*
glōri-or, **āri**, **ātus sum**, *dep.* (**glōria**), *to glory, boast, vaunt, pride one's self* on any thing.
glōri-ōsus, **a**, **um**, *adj.* (**glōria**, § **44**, 1, *c*, 3), *full of glory, glorious, famous, renowned; vainglorious, boasting, bragging, conceited.*
Gn. (**Cn.**), Gnæus, a Roman name.
Gracchus, **i**, *m.*, Tĭbĕrius Gracchus, tribune, B.C. 133; and his brother, Caius Gracchus, tribune, B.C. 123; both authors of popular laws, and slain by the nobility.
grădior, **grădi**, **gressus sum**, *dep.*, *to step, walk, go.*
grăd-us, **ūs**, *m.* (**grădior**), *a step, pace; station, position; step* or *round of a ladder; degree.*
Græc-ŭlus, **i**, *m. dim.* (**Græcus**, § **44**, 1, *c*, 3), *a Greekling, a poor Greek.*
Græcus, **a**, **um**, *adj.*, *Greek.*
Græcus, **i**, *m.*, *a Greek.*
grāmen, **ĭnis**, *n.*, *grass; a plant, herb.*
grāmĭn-eus, **a**, **um**, *adj.* (**grāmen**, § **44**, 1, *c*, 3), *grassy.*
grammătĭca, **æ**, *f.*, *grammar, philology, criticism.*
grandis, **e**, *adj.*, *big, large, great, full, abundant; grown-up, tall; aged, old; strong, powerful.*
grānum, **i**, *n.*, *a grain, seed, kernel.*
grăphium, **ii**, *n.*, *a writing-style.*
grātes, *pl.* (usually only in the *nom.* and *acc.*), *f.*, *thanks;* **grates agere**, *to give thanks.*
grāt-ia, **æ**, *f.* (**grātus**, § **44**, 1, *c*, 2), *favor, esteem, regard, liking, love, friendship; charm, beauty, grace; kindness, courtesy, service, obligation;* **gratiæ**, *pl.*, *thanks;* **agere gratias**, *to give thanks;* **facere gratiam**, *to grant pardon, forgive;* **gratiā**, with the *gen.* (§ **54**, 3, *c*), *for the sake of, on account of, in reference to, for the purpose of;* **ea gratia**, *for this* or *that reason, on this* or *that account;* **gratiam debere**, *to owe thanks, be under obligations to;* **gratiam reddere**, *to requite, recompense;* **in gratiam reducere**, *to reconcile.*

grātŭlā-tio, ōnis, *f.* (**grātŭlor,** § **44**, 1, *c*, 2), *a congratulation; a rejoicing, joy; a religious festival of joy and thanksgiving.*

grāt-ŭlor, āri, ātus sum, *dep.* (**grātus**), *to wish joy, congratulate; to give thanks; to thank.*

grātus, a, um, *adj.*, *beloved, dear, pleasing, agreeable; thankful, grateful.*

grăvāt-e, *adv.* (**grăvātus**), *with difficulty, unwillingly.*

grăvā-tim, *adv.* (**grăvo**), *with difficulty, unwillingly.*

grăvis, e, *adj.*, *heavy, weighty, burdensome; important, grave, severe, violent.*

grăv-ĭter, *adv.* (**grăvis**), *heavily, severely, weightily; elaborately, painfully, harshly, seriously.*

grăvo, āre, āvi, ātum, *a.* (**grăvis**), *to load, burden, weigh down, oppress.*

grăvor, āri, ātus sum, *dep.* (**grăvis**), *to take amiss, bear with reluctance.*

grĕmium, ii, *n.*, *the lap, bosom.*

gres-sus, ūs, *m.* (**grădior,** § **44**, 1, *c*, 2), *a stepping, going, step, course, way.*

grex, grĕgis, *m.*, *a flock, herd, drove; troop, band, crowd, company.*

gŭbernā-tor, ōris, *m.* (**gŭberno,** § **44**, 1, *c*. 2), *a steersman, pilot; ruler, governor.*

gŭberno, āre, āvi, ātum, *a.*, *to steer* or *pilot* a ship; *to direct, manage, govern.*

gusto, āre, āvi, ātum, *a.*, *to taste, partake of.*

gymnăsium, ii, *n.*, *a public school for gymnastic exercises.*

H.

hăbeo, hăbēre, hăbui, hăbĭtum, *a.*, *to have, hold, keep, possess; to think, consider, regard, esteem;* **bene se habere,** *to be well;* **sic habere,** *to be even so;* **haberi pro,** *to be regarded as.*

hăb-ĭlis, e, *adj.* (**hăbeo**), *suitable, fit, proper; light, nimble, swift.*

hăb-ĭto, āre, āvi, ātum, *a.* and *n. intens.* (**hăbeo,** § **36**, *b*, and **44**, 2, *b*), *to have possession of, to inhabit; to dwell, reside.*

hăb-ĭtus, ūs, *m.* (**hăbeo,** § **44**, 1, *c*, 2), *condition, plight, habit, state; dress, attire; nature, character.*

hac-tĕnus, *adv.*, *thus far, up to this time, hitherto.*

hædus, i, *m.*, *a young goat, a kid.*

hæreo, hærēre, hæsi, hæsum, *n.*, *to hold fast, hang, stick, adhere, be fixed, sit firm.*

hāmus, i, *m.*, *a hook.*

Hannĭbal, ălis, *m.*, the son of Hamilcar, leader of the Carthaginians in the second Punic War.

Hanno, ōnis, *m.*, a Carthaginian leader.

Harūdes, um, *m. pl.*, a German tribe in Gaul.

hăruspex, ĭcis, *m.*, *an inspector of entrails, interpreter of sacrifices, a soothsayer, diviner* (who foretold future events from the inspection of victims).

Hasdrŭbal, ălis, *m.*, a Carthaginian leader.

hasta, æ, *f.*, *a spear, lance, spike, javelin.*

haud, *adv.*, *not at all, by no means, not.*

haud-quāquam, *adv.*, *not at all, by no means.*

haurio, haurīre, hausi, haustum, *a.*, *to drain, empty, drink up; devour, destroy, consume, drink in, exhaust.*

hĕbes, ĕtis, *adj.*, *blunt, dull, stupid, obtuse.*

hĕbĕto, āre, āvi, ātum, *a.* (**hĕbes**), *to make blunt; to dull, impair, dim; to weaken.*

Helvētia, æ, *f.*, modern Switzerland.

Helvētii, ōrum, *m. pl.*, a people of Gallia.

Helvētius, a, um, *adj.*, *Helvetian, of the Helvetii;* **ager Helvetius,** *the territory of the Helvetii.*

herba, æ, *f.*, *grass, green blades, herbage.*

hērēd-ĭtas, ātis, *f.* (**hēres,** § **44,** 1, *c*, 2), *heirship, an inheritance.*

hēres, ēdis, *m.* and sometimes *f.*, *an heir, heiress; owner, possessor.*

hĕri *or* **hĕre,** *adv.*, *yesterday; lately.*

heu, *interj.* (an exclamation of pain or grief) *oh! ah! alas!*

hīberna, ōrum, *n. pl.*, *winter-quarters.*

hīb-ernus, a, um, *adj.* (**hiems**), *of* or *belonging to winter; wintry,*

hīc, hæc, hoc, *pron. demonstr.* (§ **20,** 2, *a*), *this, this of mine; he, she, it; the latter* opposed to **ille; hoc,** *on this account, in this way.*

hīc, *adv.*, *here, hereupon.*

hiĕmo, āre, āvi, ātum, *n.* and *a.* (**hiems**), *to pass the winter, winter; to be wintry, frozen, cold.*

hiems (mps), ĕmis, *f.*, *the winter; a storm, tempest.*

hĭlăr-e, *adv.* (**hĭlăris**), *cheerfully, gayly; joyfully, merrily.*

hĭlăris, e; -us, a, um, *adj.*, *cheerful, lively, gay, merry.*

hĭlăr-ĭtas, ātis, *f.* (**hĭlăris,** § **44,** 1, *c*, 2), *cheerfulness, gayety, good humor, mirth,*

hinc, *adv.* (**hīc**), *from this place, from here; from this time, hereafter; ago, since; hence;* **hinc . . . hinc,** *on the one hand . . . on the other.*

hĭrundo, ĭnis, *f.*, *a swallow.*

Hispānia, æ, *f.*, *Spain.* [*now.*

hŏ-diē, *adv.* (**hoc; die**), *to-day,*

Hŏmērus, i, *m.*, *Homer;* the great epic poet of Greece.

hŏmo, ĭnis, *com. gen.*, *a human being; a man* or *woman, a mortal.*

hŏnes-tas, ātis, *f.* (**honestus,** § **44,** 1, *c*, 2), *honor, reputation, character, respectability, credit; honesty, probity, integrity.*

hŏnes-tus, a, um, *adj.* (**hŏnor**), *honored, distinguished, respectable, noble, virtuous.*

hŏnor (os), ōris, *m.*, *honor, repute, respect, esteem, dignity, integrity;* **honores,** *pl.*, *offices of honor, public offices.*

hŏnōrā-tus, a, um, *part.* (**hŏnōro**), *honored, respected, respectable, distinguished.*

hŏnōrĭfĭc-e, *adv.* (**hŏnōrĭfĭcus**), *comp.* **hŏnōrĭfĭcentius,** *sup.* **hŏnōrĭfĭcentissĭmē,** *with honor* or *respect; in an honorable manner, honorably.*

hŏnōr-ĭ-fĭcus, a, um, *adj.* (**hŏnor; făcio**), *bringing honor, honorable; comp.* **hŏnōrĭfĭcentior,** *sup.* **hŏnōrĭfĭcentissĭmus.**

hŏnōro, āre, āvi, ātum, *a.* (**hŏnor**), *to honor, respect, adorn.*

hōra, æ, *f.*, *an hour; time, season.*

Hŏrātius, ii, *m.* (*a*), the name of the three brothers, in the time of Tullus Hostilius, who fought against the Alban Curiatii; (*b*) Horatius Cocles, who, in the war with Porsenna, defended a bridge single-handed.

hordeum, i, *n.*, *barley.*

horre-ndus, a, um, *part.* (**horreo**), *dreadful, terrible, fearful, terrific, horrible.*

horreo, horrēre, *no perf.*, *no sup.*, *n.* and *a.*, *to bristle; to tremble, shudder; to shudder* or *be frightened at, to dread; to look rough, dreadful, horrid.*

horreum, i, *n.*, *a store-house, barn, granary.*

horr-ĭdus, a, um, *adj.* (**horreo**), *rough, shaggy, bristly; savage, wild; unpolished, uncouth.*

horr-or, ōris, *m.* (**horreo,** § **44,** 1, *c*, 2), *a bristling; a shaking; dread, terror, horror; veneration, religious awe.*

hortā-tio, ōnis, *f.* (**hortor,** § **44,** 1, *c*, 2), *an encouragement, exhortation.*

hortā-tus, ūs, *m.* (**hortor,** § **44,** 1, *c*, 2), *an encouragement, exhortation.*

hortor, āri, ātus sum, *dep., to incite, instigate, encourage, cheer, exhort, urge.*

hortus, i, *m., a garden.*

hospes, ĭtis, *m., a sojourner, visitor, guest, friend; a stranger, foreigner.*

hospĭt-ium, ii, *n.* (**hospes**), *hospitality; a place of hospitality, lodging, inn.*

host-īlis, e, *adj.* (**hostis,** § **44,** 1, *c*, 3), *of* or *belonging to an enemy, hostile.*

hostīl-ĭter, *adv.* (**hostīlis**), *like an enemy, hostilely.*

hostis, is, *com. gen., a stranger, an enemy.*

huc, *adv.* (**hic**), *to this place, hither; hitherto, thus far;* **huc illuc** *and* **huc et illuc,** *hither and thither.*

hūjus-mŏdi, *of this kind.*

hūmān-ĭtas, ātis, *f.* (**hūmānus,** § **44,** 1, *c*, 2), *human nature, humanity, philanthropy, gentleness, kindness; liberal culture, refinement.*

hūm-ānus, a, um, *adj.* (**homo**), *pertaining to man, human, gentle, kind, courteous, civilized.*

hŭmĕrus, i, *m., the shoulder.*

hūm-ĭdus, a, um *adj.* (**hūmeo,** to be moist), *moist, humid, damp, wet.*

hŭm-ĭlis, e, *adj.* (**hŭmus**), *low, lowly, small, slight; humble, poor, insignificant; low, mean;* **humili loco natum esse,** *to be of lowly birth.*

hūmor, ōris, *m., a liquid, fluid, moisture.*

hŭmus, i, *f.* (§ **55,** 3, *d*), *the earth, ground, soil, land, country.*

I.

ĭbī, *adv., in that place, there; then, thereupon.*

ĭbīdem, *adv., in the same place, just there, there too.*

Iccius, Remus, i, *m.*, a chief of the Remi.

īco, īcĕre, īci, ictum, *a., to strike, hit, smite, stab;* **fœdus icere,** *to make* or *conclude a treaty.*

ic-tus, ūs, *m.* (**īco,** § **44,** 1, *c*, 2), *a blow, stroke, hit, stab, thrust.*

īdem, eădem, ĭdem, *pron., the same, very;* **idem qui,** *the same as.*

ĭdeo, *adv., for that reason, on that account, therefore.*

ĭdōneus, a, um, *adj., meet, proper, suitable, apt, able, capable, convenient, sufficient.*

īdus, ŭum, *f. pl., the Ides;* the fifteenth day of the months March, May, July, and October, the thirteenth day of the remaining months.

ĭgĭtur, *conj.* (§ **43,** 2, *d*), *then, thereupon; therefore, consequently.*

ignis, is, *m., fire.*

i-gnosco, gnoscĕre, gnōvi, gnōtum, *a.* (**in; gnosco** = **nosco,** with *dat.*), *to pardon, forgive, excuse, overlook.*

i-gnōtus, a, um, *adj.* (**in; gnōtus** = **nōtus**), *unknown.*

ille, a, ud, *pron. demonstr.* (§ **20,** 2, *b*), *that, that yonder;* **hic . . . ille,** *this . . . that, the one . . . the other.*

illic, *adv.* (**ille; ce**), *in that place, there.*

il-lĭco, *adv.* (**in; lŏco**), *on the spot, instantly, there.*

illuc, *adv.* (**ille**), *to that place, thither.*

il-lūdo, lūdĕre, lūsi, lūsum, *n.* (**in; lūdo**), *to play with, jest, mock, ridicule.*

il-lustris, is, *adj.* (**in; lustro,** to purify), *clear, bright, light, lustrous; famous, honorable, illustrious.*

imāgo, ĭnis, *f.*, *an image* or *likeness*, *statue*, *picture*.
imbēcillus, a, um, *adj.*, *weak*, *feeble*.
im-bellis, e, *adj.* (in; bellum), *unwarlike*, *peaceful*, *fond of peace*.
imber, bris, *m.*, *a shower*, *rainstorm*, *storm*.
imbuo, buĕre, bui, būtum, *a.*, *to wet*, *moisten*, *soak*, *steep*, *saturate; taint*, *infect*.
ĭmĭtā-tio, ōnis, *f.* (ĭmĭtor, § 44, 1, *c*, 2), *the act of imitating*, *imitation*.
ĭmĭtor, āri, ātus sum, *dep.*, *to imitate*, *copy*, *represent*.
immānis, e, *adj.*, *monstrous*, *enormous*, *huge; fierce*, *savage*, *wild*.
im-mātūrus, a, um, *adj.* (in; mātūrus), *unripe*, *immature; unseasonable*, *untimely*, *premature*.
im-mĕmor, mŏris, *adj.* (in; mĕmor), *unmindful*, *forgetful*.
im-mensus, a, um, *adj.* (in; mensus, measured), *immeasurable*, *boundless*, *immense*.
immĭnens, entis, *part.* (immĭneo), *imminent*.
im-mĭneo, ēre, *no perf.*, *no sup.*, *n.* (in; mĭneo, to project), *to hang down over*, *overhang; to be near to*, *to touch on*, *border upon; to threaten; to be intent upon*, *strive for*.
im-mĭnuo, mĭnuĕre, mĭnui, mĭnūtum, *a.* (in; mĭnuo), *to lessen*, *diminish; weaken*, *impair*.
im-mitto, mittĕre, mīsi, missum, *a.* (in; mitto), *to send into*, *to hurl against*, *discharge at;* **se immittere**, *to rush in*.
immō (īmō), *adv.*, *on the contrary; no indeed*, *by no means; yes indeed*, *certainly*, *by all means*.
im-mōbĭlis, e, *adj.* (in; mōbĭlis), *immovable*, *unmoved*.
im-mŏlo, āre, āvi, ātum, *a.* (in; mŏla), *to sacrifice*.
im-mortālis, e, *adj.* (in; mortālis), *undying*, *immortal*, *imperishable*, *eternal*, *endless*.
im-mōtus, a, um, *adj.* (in; mōtus), *unmoved*, *immovable*, *motionless*, *unshaken*, *undisturbed*.
īmo, *see* **immo**.
im-mūto, āre, āvi, ātum, *a.* (in; mūto), *to change*, *alter*.
im-par, ăris, *adj.* (in; par), *uneven*, *unequal*, *not a match for*.
im-pătiens, entis, *adj.* (in; pătiens), *not able to bear*, *not enduring*, *impatient*.
impĕdī-mentum, i, *n.* (impĕdio, § 44, 1, *c*, 2), *a hindrance*, *impediment;* **impĕdīmenta**, ōrum, *n. pl.*, *baggage*.
im-pĕdio, īre, īvi *or* ii, ītum, *a.* (in; pes), *to entangle*, *ensnare*, *shackle*, *hinder*, *embarrass*, *impede*.
impĕdī-tus, a, um, *part.* (impĕdio), *hindered*, *obstructed*, *impeded*, *encumbered*.
im-pello, pellĕre, pŭli, pulsum, *a.* (in; pello), *to push against; to drive forward*, *urge on*, *impel*, *incite*, *persuade*.
im-pendeo, pendēre, *no perf.*, *no sup.*, *n.* (in; pendeo), *to hang over*, *overhang*, *impend*.
im-pendo, pendĕre, pendi, pensum, *a.* (in; pendo), *to weigh out*, *lay out*, *expend; devote*, *employ*.
impen-sa, æ, *f.* (impendo), *outlay*, *cost*, *charge*, *expense*.
impĕrā-tor, ōris, *m.* (impĕro, § 44, 1, *c*, 1), *general*, *commander*, *leader*, *chief*, *ruler*, *master*.
impĕrā-tum, i, *n.* (impĕro), *a command*, *order*.
im-perfectus, a, um, *adj.* (in; perfectus), *unfinished*, *incomplete*, *imperfect*.
im-pĕrītus, a, um, *adj.* (in; pĕrītus), *inexperienced*, *unskilled*, *ignorant*.
impĕr-ium, ii, *n.* (impĕro, § 44, 1, *c*, 2), *a command*, *order; au-*

thority, control; dominion, empire, government.

im-pĕro, āre, āvi, ātum, *a.* (in; păro), *to command, order, enjoin; govern, rule over;* **imperare obsides alicui**, *to demand hostages from any one.*

im-pĕtro, āre, āvi, ātum, *a.* (in; pătro), *to accomplish, obtain, procure, to make a request and have it granted.*

impĕtus, ūs, *m.*, *an attack, assault, onset; violent impulse, impetuosity, violence, fury, force, eagerness, excitement.*

impi-ē, *adv.* (impius), *irreligiously, wickedly.*

im-pĭger, gra, grum, *adj.* (in; pĭger), *diligent, active, quick, energetic.*

im-pingo, pingĕre, pēgi, pactum, *a.* (in; pango), *to drive against, strike, thrust,* or *dash against.*

im-pius, a, um, *adj.* (in; pius), *irreverent, ungodly, undutiful, unpatriotic, abandoned, wicked.*

im-pleo, plēre, plēvi, plētum, *a.* (in; pleo), *to fill up; fill full; satisfy.*

im-plĭco, āre, āvi *or* ui, ātum *or* ĭtum, *a.* (in; plĭco), *to infold, involve, envelope, entwine, entangle.*

im-plōro, āre, āvi, ātum, *a.* (in; plōro), *to invoke with tears, call to one's assistance, call upon for aid; to invoke, beseech, entreat, implore.*

im-pōno, pōnĕre, pŏsui, pŏsĭtum, *a.* (in; pōno), *to put upon, lay on, impose upon;* **finem imponere**, *to make an end.*

im-pŏtens, entis, *adj.* (in; pŏtens), *powerless, weak, feeble.*

im-prīmis, *adv.* (in; prīmis), *in the first place, chiefly, especially.*

im-prĭmo, prĭmĕre, pressi, pressum, *a.* (in; prĕmo), *to press upon, impress, imprint, mark.*

im-prŏbo, āre, āvi, ātum, *a.* (in; prŏbo), *to disapprove, blame, condemn, reject.*

im-prŏbus, a, um, *adj.* (in; prŏbus), *wicked, bad.*

im-prōvīsus, a, um, *adj.* (in; prōvīsus), *not foreseen, unexpected;* **ex improviso**, *unexpectedly.*

im-prūdens, entis, *adj.* (in; prūdens), *not foreseeing, imprudent, inconsiderate.*

imprūdent-ia, æ, *f.* (imprūdens, § **44**, 1, *c*, 2), *want of foresight, imprudence, indiscretion.*

im-pūbes, ĕris *and* is, *adj.* (in; pūbes), *under the age of puberty, youthful, beardless.*

im-pŭdens, pŭdentis, *adj.* (in; pŭdens), *without shame, shameless, impudent.*

im-pugno, āre, āvi, ātum, *a.* (in; pugno), *to fight against, attack, assail, oppose.*

impūn-e, *adv.* (impūnis), *without punishment, safely.*

im-pūnītus, a, um, *adj.* (in; pūnītus), *unpunished, safe, secure.*

īmus, a, um, *adj.* (*superlative* of infĕrus), *inmost, deepest, lowest, bottom of.*

in, *prep.* with *acc.* and *abl.* (§ **56**, 1, *c*), 1. with *acc.*, *in, into, against, after, for;* **in dies**, *from day to day;* 2. with *abl.*, *in, among, upon, before, in the presence of.*

ĭnānis, e, *adj.*, *empty, void, vain.*

in-călesco, călescĕre, călui, *no sup.*, *n. inch.* (in; căleo, § **36**, *a*, and **44**, 2, *b*), *to grow warm* or *hot, to glow; to become heated.*

in-cautus, a, um, *adj.*, *incautious, heedless, inconsiderate.*

in-cēdo, cēdĕre, cessi, cessum, *n.* and *a.*, *to go, proceed, advance, march; to come to, befall, attack.*

incend-ium, ii, *n.* (incendo, § **44**, 1, *c*, 2), *a conflagration, fire, burning; ruin, destruction.*

in-cendo, dĕre, di, sum, *a.*, *to set on fire, kindle, burn; inflame, excite, provoke, rouse, irritate.*

incep-tum, **i**, *n.* (**incĭpio**), *a beginning, attempt, undertaking.*

in-certus, **a**, **um**, *adj.*, *uncertain, unsettled, unreliable, doubtful, hesitating.*

in-cesso, **cessĕre**, **cessīvi**, *or* **cessi**, *no sup.*, *a. intens.* (**in**; **cedo**, § **36**, *b*, and **44**, 2, *b*), *to fall upon, assault, assail, attack; upbraid, reproach.*

inces-sus, **ūs**, *m.* (**incēdo**, § **44**, 1, *c*, 2), *a going, walking, pace, gait; entrance, approach; invasion.*

in-cĭdo, **cĭdĕre**, **cĭdi**, **cāsum**, *n.* (**in**; **cădo**), *to fall in with, fall upon, attack, assail; to happen, occur;* **in mentionem incidere**, *to mention accidentally; impers.* **incĭdit**, *it happens*, with *dat.*

in-cĭpio, **cĭpĕre**, **cēpi**, **ceptum**, *a.* and *n.* (**in**; **căpio**), *to begin, commence, set about, undertake.*

in-cĭto, **āre**, **āvi**, **ātum**, *a.*, *to set in rapid motion; to incite, encourage, stimulate, rouse, excite, spur on; stir up, increase.*

in-cĭtus, **a**, **um**, *adj.*, *rapid, swift.*

in-clāmo, **āre**, **āvi**, **ātum**, *a.* and *n.*, *to call upon for assistance; to invoke; to cry out against, abuse, rebuke, revile, chide; to call out aloud.*

in-clīno, **āre**, **āvi**, **ātum**, *a.* and *n.*, *to bend down, incline, sink, yield, give way;* **in fugam inclinare**, *to be on the point of fleeing;* **inclinari**, *to be on the point of falling.*

in-clūdo, **dĕre**, **si sum**, *a.* (**in**; **claudo**), *to shut up, confine, include, inclose.*

in-clȳtus (**clĭtus**), **a**, **um**, *adj.* (**in**; **clueo**), *celebrated, renowned, famous, illustrious, glorious.*

incŏla, **æ**, *com. gen.* (**incŏlo**), *an inhabitant, resident.*

in-cŏlo, **cŏlĕre**, **cŏlui**, *no sup.*, *a.* and *n.*, *to dwell* or *abide in* a place, *to inhabit.*

in-cŏlŭmis, **e**, *adj.*, *unimpaired, uninjured, safe, sound.*

in-commŏdum, **i**, *n.*, *trouble, loss, misfortune, defeat.*

in-commŏdus, **a**, **um**, *adj.*, *inconvenient, unsuitable, unfit, troublesome, disagreeable.*

in-crēdĭbĭlis, **e**, *adj.* (**in**; **crēdo**), *incredible, extraordinary, unparalleled.*

incrēdĭbĭl-ĭter, *adv.* (**incrēdĭbĭlis**), *incredibly, wonderfully, extraordinarily.*

in-crĕpo, **āre**, **āvi** *or* **ui**, **ātum** *or* **ĭtum**, *n.* and *a.*, *to make a noise, rustle, rattle; to chide, rebuke, reprove; to clash.*

in-cresco, **crescĕre**, **crēvi**, *no sup.*, *n.*, *to grow in; to grow, increase, be augmented.*

in-cultus, **a**, **um**, *adj.* (**cŏlo**), *uncultivated, untilled; unpolished, neglected, rude.*

in-cumbo, **cumbĕre**, **cŭbui**, **cŭbĭtum**, *n.*, *to lean upon, recline; to apply* or *devote one's self to, pay attention to.*

in-cūria, **æ**, *f.* (**in**; **cūro**), *want of care, negligence, neglect.*

incur-sio, **ōnis**, *f.* (**incurro**, § **44**, 1, *c*, 2), *an onset, assault, attack, incursion.*

in-cūso, **āre**, **āvi**, **ātum**, *a.* (**in**; **causa**), *to accuse, blame, complain of, find fault with.*

in-cŭtio, **cŭtĕre**, **cussi**, **cussum**, *a.* (**in**; **quătio**), *to strike* or *dash against; to inspire with, inflict, excite, produce; to throw, cast, hurl.*

inde, *adv.*, *from that place, from there, thence; thereafter, thereupon, then.*

in-dĕcōrus, **a**, **um**, *adj.*, *unbecoming, unseemly, indecorous, disgraceful, shameful.*

index, **ĭcis**, *com. gen.* (**indĭco**), *an informer, betrayer, spy; sign, mark, index.*

in-dĭco, **āre**, **āvi**, **ātum**, *a.*, *to make known, point out, declare,* *disclose, reveal, indicate; accuse.*

in-dīco, dīcĕre, dixi, dictum, *a., to proclaim, publish, announce, appoint; order, enjoin.*

in-dictus, a, um, *adj., not said, unsaid, unsung.*

ind-ĭgeo, ĭgēre, ĭgui, *no sup.* (ĕgeo), *to need, want, stand in need* or *want of; to long for, desire.*

indignā-tio, ōnis, *f.* (indignor, § 44, 1, *c*, 2), *displeasure, indignation.*

indign-e, *adv.* (indignus), *unworthily, shamefully, disgracefully, dishonorably.*

indign-ĭtas, ātis, *f.* (indignus, § 44, 1, *c*, 2), *unworthiness, vileness, enormity, meanness, indignity.*

in-dignor, āri, ātus sum, *dep., to deem unworthy, to be displeased, be indignant.*

in-dignus, a, um, *adj., unworthy, undeserving, unsuitable, unbecoming, intolerable.*

in-do, dĕre, dĭdi, dĭtum, *a., to put into, impart, inspire, infuse; set over, introduce; assign, give to.*

in-dŏcĭlis, e, *adj., difficult to be taught, unteachable, not docile; unlearned, ignorant, rude.*

ind-ŏles, is, *f.* (ŏlesco, to grow), *inborn* or *native quality, nature; natural abilities, talents, genius; disposition, character.*

in-dūco, dūcĕre, duxi, ductum, *a., to lead into, conduct, bring in* or *upon, introduce, represent, exhibit, induce;* **inducere animum** *or* **in animum,** *to determine.*

in-dulgeo, dulgēre, dulsi, dultum, *n.* and *a.* (in; dulcis), *to be courteous, kind; to indulge, humor, give way to; concede, allow, grant.*

in-duo, duĕre, dui, dūtum, *a., to put on, dress in, assume, clothe;* in *pass.,* **indui vestem,** *to put on a garment* (§ **52**, 3, remark).

industria, æ, *f., diligence, activity, industry;* **de industriā,** *purposely, on purpose.*

in-eo, īre, īvi *or* **ii, ĭtum,** *a.* and *n., irreg., to go into, enter; to enter upon, begin, undertake, take part in;* **inire consilium,** *to form a plan;* **inire fœdus,** *to make a treaty;* **inire gratiam,** *to get into the good graces of.*

ĭn-ermis, e, *adj.* (in; arma), *unarmed, without weapons, defenceless.*

ĭn-ermus, a, um, *adj., see* inermis.

ĭn-ers, ertis, *adj.* (in; ars), *unskilled; inactive, idle, indolent, sluggish.*

infăcēt-e, *adv.* (infăcētus), *coarsely, rudely, unwittily, stupidly.*

in-făcētus, a, um, *adj., coarse, blunt, rude, unmannerly, not witty, stupid.*

in-fāmis, e, *adj.* (in; fāma), *of ill report, disreputable, notorious, infamous,*

in-fandus, a, um, *adj.* (not to be spoken of), *unspeakable, unutterable, unheard of, unnatural, shocking, abominable.*

in-fans, antis, *adj.* (in; for), *speechless, mute, dumb; very young, little.* AS NOUN, *com. gen., an infant, babe.*

in-fectus, a, um, *adj.* (in; făcio), *not done, undone, unperformed, unfinished; impossible, impracticable.*

in-fēlix, ĭcis, *adj., unfortunate, unhappy, miserable.*

in-fensus, a, um, *adj.* (in; fendo, obsolete), *hostile, inimical, enraged.*

infĕrior, ius, *adj.* (*comp.* of infĕrus), *lower, later, inferior.*

in-fĕro, inferre, intŭli, illātum, *a., irreg., to carry in* or *into: to bring, put,* or *throw into* or *to; to bring forward, introduce; produce, make, cause; allege; con-*

clude, infer; **inferre signa,** *to advance the standards, attack;* **inferre pedem** *or* **gradum,** *to advance, attack;* **se inferre,** *to betake one's self, repair, go;* **inferre vulnera,** *to inflict wounds upon;* **vim inferre,** *to offer violence to, lay violent hands on.*

in-fĕrus, a, um, *adj.* (*comp.* **infĕrior,** *sup.* **infĭmus** *or* **īmus**), *low, nether.* As NOUN, **infĕri, ōrum,** *m. pl.* (the inhabitants of the lower regions), *the dead.*

infesto, āre, āvi, ātum, *a.* (**infestus**), *to attack, trouble, molest, disturb, infest, injure, impair.*

in-festus, a, um, *adj.* (old *part.* of **infĕro**), *unquiet, unsafe; hostile, inimical, troublesome, dangerous.*

in-fĭcio, fĭcĕre, fēci, fectum, *a.* (in; **făcio**), *to dip into, stain, dye, color, tinge; to infect, corrupt, poison, spoil.*

infĭmus, a, um, *adj.* (*superlative* of **infĕrus**), *the lowest, last, lowest part of.*

in-fīnītus, a, um, *adj., boundless, unlimited, infinite, endless.*

in-firmus, a, um, *adj., weak, infirm, feeble, fickle.*

in-flammo, āre, āvi, ātum, *a., to set on fire, kindle, inflame, arouse, excite.*

inflā-tus, a, um, *part.* (**inflo**), *swollen, inflated, haughty, proud.*

in-flecto, flectĕre, flexi, flexum, *a., to bend, bow; to change, alter; warp, prevent; move, touch, affect.*

in-flīgo, flīgĕre, flixi, flictum, *a., to strike against, hurl at, inflict.*

in-flo, flāre, flāvi, flātum, *a., to blow into; inflate, puff up, cause to swell.*

in-fluo, fluĕre, fluxi, fluxum, *n., to flow into, flow upon, flow.*

in-formo, āre, āvi, ātum, *a., to give form to; to shape, mould, fashion; conceive, imagine; describe, represent.*

infrā, *adv.* and *prep.* with *acc., below, beneath, under, underneath.*

in-fringo, fringĕre, frēgi, fractum, *a.* (in; **frango**), *to break, check, weaken, lessen, diminish, mitigate, assuage.*

infŭla, æ, *f., a band, bandage; a fillet* (used by priests).

in-fundo, fundĕre, fūdi, fūsum, *a., to pour into, discharge; to spread upon* or *over.*

in-gĕmisco, gĕmiscĕre, *no perf., no sup., a.* and *n., to groan over, to bemoan; to groan.*

in-gĕmo, gĕmĕre, gĕmui, *no sup., a.* and *n., to groan* or *sigh over; to mourn over, lament; to mourn, lament, groan.*

in-gĕn-ium, ii, *n.* (in; **gĕno** = **gigno**, that which is inborn), *character, disposition, temper; genius, abilities, talents.*

in-gens, entis, *adj.* (in; **gens**), *vast, huge, prodigious; great mighty, strong; remarkable, distinguished.*

in-gĕro, gĕrĕre, gessi, gestum, *a., to carry* or *bring into: to hurl, cast, throw: inflict upon, utter against.*

in-grātus, a, um, *adj., unpleasant, disagreeable; ungrateful, thankless.*

in-grăvesco, ĕre, *no perf., no sup., n., to grow heavy; increase, become powerful; become troubled, wearied.*

in-grĕdior, grĕdi, gressus sum, *dep.* (in; **grădior**), *to go into, enter; engage in, apply one's self to; begin, commence; walk, advance.*

ĭn-hĭbeo, hĭbēre, hĭbui, hĭbĭtum, *a.* (in; **hăbeo**), *to keep back, restrain, curb, check.*

ĭnhŏnest-e, *adv.* (**ĭnhŏnestus**), *dishonorably.*

ĭn-hŏnestus, a, um, *adj.*, *dishonorable*, *disgraceful*, *shameful*.

ĭnĭmīc-ĭtia, æ, *f.* (ĭnĭmīcus, § 44, 1, *c*, 2), *enmity*, *hostility*.

ĭn-ĭmīcus, a, um, *adj.* (in; ămīcus), *unfriendly*, *hostile*. As NOUN, *m.*, *a* private *enemy* or *foe*.

ĭnīqu-e, *adv.* (ĭnīquus), *unequally*, *dissimilarly*; *unfitly*, *unsuitably*; *unfairly*, *unjustly*.

ĭn-īquus, a, um, *adj.* (in; æquus), *unequal*, *unfair*, *unjust*, *disadvantageous*; *unkind*, *unfriendly*.

ĭnĭtio, āre, āvi, ātum, *a.* (ĭnĭtium), *to make a beginning*; *to initiate*, *consecrate*.

ĭnĭ-tium, ii, *n.* (ineo, § 44, 1, *c*, 2), *a beginning*, *commencement*; *origin*.

in-jĭcio, jĭcĕre, jēci, jectum, *a.* (in; jăcio), *to throw* or *cast into*, *cast upon* or *against*; *infuse into*, *inspire*; **injicere metum alicui**, *to inspire one with fear*.

injūri-a, æ, *f.* (injūrius), *injury*, *wrong*, *violence*; *damage*, *insult*; *injustice*.

in-jūr-ius, a, um, *adj.* (in; jus), *injurious*, *unjust*.

in-jus-su, *m.* (used only in the *abl.*), (in; jŭbeo), *without command*.

in-justus, a, um, *adj.*, *unjust*; *harsh*, *severe*; *unlawful*, *wrong*.

in-nascor, nasci, nātus sum, *dep.*, *to be born in*; *spring up*, *arise*, *have its origin in*.

in-nītor, nīti, nīsus *or* nixus sum, *dep.*, *to lean* or *rest upon*, *support one's self by*; *to crush*, *to lean*.

in-nŏcens, entis, *adj.*, *harmless*, *inoffensive*; *blameless*, *guiltless*, *innocent*; *disinterested*, *upright*.

innŏcent-ia, æ, *f.* (innŏcens, § 44, 1, *c*, 2), *harmlessness*; *blamelessness*, *innocence*; *uprightness*, *integrity*.

in-noxius, a, um, *adj.*, *harmless*; *guiltless*, *blameless*.

in-nŭmĕrābĭlis, e, *adj.*, *countless*, *innumerable*.

in-nuo, nuĕre, nui, nūtum, *n.*, *to nod to*, *give a sign* or *intimation*, *hint*.

ĭnŏp-ia, æ, *f.* (ĭnops, § 44, 1, *c*, 2), *poverty*, *need*, *indigence*; *want*, *scarcity*, *destitution*.

ĭn-ŏpīnātus, a, um, *adj.*, *unexpected*; *off one's guard*.

ĭn-ŏpīnus, a, um, *adj.* (in; ŏpīnor), *unexpected*.

ĭn-ops, ŏpis, *adj.*, *without power*, *weak*, *needy*, *indigent*; *devoid of* (with *gen.*).

inquam, *def.* (§ 38, 2, *b*), *I say*.

in-quiētus, a, um, *adj.*, *not quiet*, *unquiet*, *restless*.

insān-ia, æ, *f.* (insānus, § 44, 1, *c*, 2), *madness*, *frenzy*, *folly*.

in-sānus, a, um, *adj.*, *mad*, *insane*; *raging*, *raving*, *frantic*, *foolish*, *silly*.

in-scendo, scendĕre, scendi, scensum, *a.* (in; scando), *to mount up into*, *to mount*; *to embark*; *get upon*.

in-sciens, entis, *adj.*, *without knowledge*, *unaware*; *ignorant*, *stupid*, *silly*.

in-scius, a, um, *adj.*, *not knowing*, *ignorant*.

in-scrībo, scrībĕre, scripsi, scriptum, *a.*, *to write upon*, *inscribe*; *exhibit*, *show*; *assign*, *ascribe*; *indicate*.

insec-tor, āri, ātus sum, *dep.* *frequentative* (insĕquor, § 36, *b*, note, and 44, 2, *b*), *to pursue*; *censure*, *blame*, *rail at*, *speak ill of*.

in-sĕquor, sĕqui, sĕcūtus sum, *dep.*, *to follow after*, *pursue*, *press upon*, *harass*; *reproach*, *reprove*, *censure*.

in-sĕro, sĕrĕre, sĕrui, sertum, *a.*, *to introduce into*, *to insert*.

in-sĕro, sĕrĕre, sēvi, sĭtum, *a.*, *to sow* or *plant in*; *implant*, *engraft*.

in-sĭdeo, sĭdēre, sēdi, sessum, *n.* and *a.* (in; sĕdeo), *to sit in*;

sit upon, settle upon; to get possession of, occupy.

insĭd-iæ, ārum, *f. pl.* **(insĭdeo),** *an ambush, ambuscade; artifice, craft, device, plot, snare;* **per insidias,** *by stratagem, craftily.*

insĭdi-or, āri, ātus sum, *dep.* **(insĭdiæ),** *to lie in wait for, watch for, expect.*

in-sīdo, sīdĕre, sēdi, sessum, *n., to settle on; sink* or *pierce into; sit down upon.*

insign-e, is, *n.* **(insignis),** *a distinctive mark; a mark, token, sign, proof; badge* (of office), *a signal; ensign, standard, flag;* in *pl.,* **insignia, ium,** *badges of honor, decorations, ornaments.*

in-signis, e, *adj.* **(in; signum),** *remarkable, eminent, distinguished, prominent, extraordinary.*

in-sĭlio, sĭlīre, sĭlui, *no sup., n.* **(in; sălio),** *to leap* or *spring into; to leap* or *spring upon.*

in-sĭnuo, āre, āvi, ātum, *a.* and *n.* **(in; sĭnus),** *to penetrate* or *enter* anywhere *by winding* or *bending; to make one's way into; to recommend one's self to; to reach, arrive at; steal into, insinuate.*

in-sisto, sistĕre, stĭti, *no sup., n., to stand, tread, step upon, press on, pursue, persevere; halt, stop, stand.*

in-sŏlens, entis, *adj.* **(in; sŏleo),** *unusual; haughty, proud, arrogant, insolent.*

insŏlen-ter, *adv.* **(insŏlens),** *unusually; haughtily, proudly, arrogantly, insolently.*

insŏlent-ia, æ, *f.* **(insŏlens,** § **44,** 1, *c,* 2), *unusualness, novelty; pride, arrogance, insolence.*

in-sŏlĭtus, a, um, *adj., unaccustomed; unusual, uncommon.*

in-spērans, ntis, *adj., not hoping, not expecting.*

in-spĭcio, spĭcĕre, spexi, spectum, *a.* **(in; spĕcio),** *to look into, examine, search; consider, contemplate, observe; weigh, ponder.*

instar, *n. indecl.,* used adverbially with *gen., like, equal to, about, worth.*

in-stĭtuo, stĭtuĕre, stĭtui, stĭtūtum, *a.* **(in; stătuo),** *to put, set, place; arrange, draw up; appoint, establish, undertake, train up, educate.*

instĭtū-tum, i, *n.* **(instĭtuo),** *custom, habit; arrangement, plan, regulation, purpose, intention, design;* in *pl., institutions, customs, usages.*

in-sto, stāre, stĭti, stātum, *n., to stand upon; assault; pursue, press upon, harass; urge, request, solicit earnestly, importune, entreat; to persevere; devote one's self to.*

in-strŭo, struĕre, struxi, structum, *a., to erect, construct, build; train, teach, instruct; set in order, arrange; equip, provide; clothe, dress, array, ornament.*

in-suē-fac-tus, a, um, *adj.* **(in; sueo; făcio),** *accustomed, habituated.*

in-suesco, suescĕre, suēvi, suētum, *n.* and *a., to become accustomed; to accustom* or *habituate* one *to* a thing.

in-suētus, a, um, *adj., unaccustomed, unused to, inexperienced in, unacquainted with.*

in-sŭla, æ, *f.* **(in; sălum,** the sea), *an island.*

in-sum, esse, fui, *irreg., to be in* or *upon, to belong to.*

in-sŭper, *adv., above, overhead; moreover, besides.*

in-sŭsurro, āre, āvi, ātum, *n.* and *a., to whisper, suggest to one, remind one.*

in-tactus, a, um, *adj.* **(in; tango),** *untouched, unharmed, uninjured, safe; pure, chaste.*

in-tĕger, gra, grum, *adj.* **(in; tango),** *untouched, unchanged;*

sound, whole, unhurt, safe; new, fresh (of troops); *blameless, pure, virtuous;* **ex integro,** *afresh.*

intel-lĕgo (lĭgo), lĕgĕre, lexi, lectum, *a.* (**inter; lĕgo**), *to perceive, discern; understand, comprehend, observe; to have an accurate knowledge of* or *skill in* a thing.

intempestīv-e, *adv.* (**intempestīvus**), *out of season, unseasonably.*

in-tempestīvus, a, um, *adj., untimely, unseasonable, inopportune, inconvenient.*

in-tempes-tus, a, um, *adj.* (**in; tempus**), *unseasonable;* **nox intempesta,** *the dead of night.*

in-tendo, tendĕre, tendi, tentum *and* **tensum,** *a., to stretch out, extend, turn toward; aim at; exert, purpose;* **intendere animum,** *to direct the thoughts;* **intendere iter** *or* **cursum,** *to direct, turn one's course, march.*

inten-tus, a, um, *part.* (**intendo**), *bent, stretched; attentive to, intent upon, vigilant, careful.*

inter, *prep.* with *acc., between, among, during, in the midst of, in the course of;* **inter se differre,** *to differ from each other;* **dare inter se,** *to interchange.*

inter-cēdo, cēdĕre, cessi, cessum, *n., to go between; to be, stand,* or *lie between, intervene; hinder, obstruct, oppose, protest* (as tribune).

inter-cĭpio, cĭpĕre, cēpi, ceptum, *a.* (**inter; căpio**), *to intercept, catch, take from, steal, carry off.*

inter-clūdo, cludĕre, clūsi, clūsum, *a.* (**inter; claudo**), *to shut off, cut off, prevent, hinder; surround.*

inter-dīco, dīcĕre, dixi, dictum, *a.* and *n., to forbid, interdict, prohibit: interfere;* **aliquid interdicere alicui,** *or* **aliquem aliquā re,** *to exclude one from, to forbid one the use of any thing;* **interdicere alicui aquā et igni,** *to forbid one the use of fire and water,* i. e., *to deprive one of civil rights, to banish.*

inter-diu, *adv., during the day, by day.*

inter-dum, *adv., sometimes, occasionally, now and then.*

inter-eā, *adv., meanwhile; notwithstanding, however.*

inter-eo, īre, īvi *or* **ii, ĭtum,** *n. irreg., to perish, die.*

inter-est, *impers.* (§ **50**, 4, *d*), *it concerns, is of interest, is important;* **interest meā,** *it is my concern;* **interest omnium,** *it is the interest of all.*

interfec-tor, ōris, *m.* (**interfĭcio,** § **44**, 1, *c*, 1), *a slayer, murderer.*

inter-fĭcio, fĭcĕre, fēci, fectum, *a.* (**inter; făcio**), *to destroy, consume; kill, slay, murder.*

intĕr-im, *adv.* (**inter; im = eum**), *in the mean time, meanwhile; sometimes; however.*

inter-ĭmo, ĭmĕre, ēmi, emptum, *a.* (**inter; ĕmo**), *to destroy, kill, slay, put to death.*

intĕrior, ius, *adj. comp.* (§ **17**, 3), *inner, interior, more hidden, more intimate.*

intĕrĭ-tus, ūs, *m.* (**intĕreo,** § **44**, 1, *c*, 2), *destruction, ruin.*

inter-jĭcio (jăcio), jĭcĕre, jēci, jectum, *a.* (**inter; jăcio**), *to place between, insert, introduce, intermix;* **anno interjecto,** *at the expiration of a year.*

inter-mitto, mittĕre, mīsi, missum, *a., to discontinue, break off, intermit, interpose.*

internĕc-io, ōnis, *f.* (**internĕco,** to kill; § **44**, 1, *c*, 2), *a massacre, carnage, utter destruction, extermination.*

inter-nuntius (nuncius), ii, *m., a messenger.*

inter-pello, āre, āvi, ātum, *a., to hinder, obstruct, interrupt, disturb; entreat, urge, importune, solicit.*

inter-pōno, **pōnĕre**, **pŏsui**, **pŏsĭtum**, *a.*, *to put* or *place between*, *interpose*, *interfere.*

interpres, **ĕtis**, *com. gen.*, *an agent*, *broker; explainer*, *translator*, *interpreter.*

interprĕtor, **āri**, **ātus sum**, *dep.* (**interpres**), *to explain*, *interpret.*

inter-regnum, **i**, *n.*, *an interreign*, *interregnum* (the time that a throne is vacant between the death of one king and the election of another).

in-terrĭtus, **a**, **um**, *adj.*, *fearless*, *undismayed.*

inter-rŏgo, **āre**, **āvi**, **ātum**, *a.*, *to question*, *interrogate*, *ask.*

inter-rumpo, **rumpĕre**, **rūpi**, **ruptum**, *a.*, *to break asunder*, *break down*, *interrupt.*

inter-sĕro, **sĕrĕre**, **sĕrui**, **sertum**, *a.*, *to intermingle*, *commingle; interpose*, *insert*, *assign.*

inter-sum, **esse**, **fui**, *n. irreg.*, *to be between*, *intervene*, *be present at*, *take part in;* **interest**, *impers.*, see **interest**.

inter-vallum, **i**, *n.*, *space between*, *interval*, *distance.*

inter-vĕnio, **vĕnīre**, **vēni**, **ventum**, *n.*, *to come between*, *intervene*, *occur*, *happen; to come in the midst of*, *arrive.*

intes-tīnus, **a**, **um**, *adj.* (**intus**), *intestine*, *civil*, *domestic.*

intĭmus, **a**, **um**, *adj.*, *superlative* (§ **17**, 3), *innermost*, *inmost.*

intrā, *adv.* and *prep.* with *acc.*, *within*, *inside*, *below*, *under* (with numerals).

in-trĕpĭdus, **a**, **um**, *adj.*, *undaunted*, *bold*, *fearless.*

intrō, *adv.*, *to the inside*, *within.*

intro, **āre**, **āvi**, **ātum**, *a.*, *to walk into*, *enter*, *penetrate.*

intrō-dūco, **dūcĕre**, **duxi**, **ductum**, *a.*, *to lead* or *bring into*, *introduce ; exhibit*, *represent.*

intro-eo, **īre**, **īvi** *or* **ii**, **ĭtum**, *n. irreg.*, *to go in*, *enter.*

introĭ-tus, **ūs**, *m.* (**introeo**, § **44**, 1, *c*, 2), *an entering*, *entrance.*

in-tueor, **tuēri**, **tuĭtus sum**, *dep.*, *to look at*, *behold*, *see*, *consider*, *contemplate.*

in-tŭmesco, **tŭmescĕre**, **tŭmui**, *no sup.*, *n.*, *to begin to swell*, *to swell* or *rise up*, *increase; to be elated*, *puffed up; be angry*, *swell with rage.*

intus, *adv.*, *within*, *inside*, *to the inside.*

ĭn-ultus, **a**, **um**, *adj.*, *unavenged*, *unpunished ; unhurt.*

ĭn-undo, **āre**, **āvi**, **ātum**, *a.*, *to overflow*, *flood*, *deluge*, *overspread*, *cover.*

ĭn-ūsĭtātus, **a**, **um**, *adj.*, *unusual*, *uncommon*, *extraordinary.*

ĭn-ūtĭlis, **e**, *adj.*, *useless*, *of no use*, *unprofitable ; powerless*, *weak.*

in-vādo, **vādĕre**, **vāsi**, **vāsum**, *n.* and *a.*, *to come upon*, *to make an attack upon*, *assail*, *invade*, *seize*, *usurp.*

in-vălĭdus, **a**, **um**, *adj.*, *not strong*, *weak*, *feeble*, *impotent; sickly*, *sick.*

in-vĕho, **vĕhĕre**, **vexi**, **vectum**, *a.*, *to carry into*, *bring into*, *carry;* in *pass.*, **invehi** (**equo**, **curra**), *to ride*, *drive; to attack; assail with words.*

in-vĕnio, **vĕnīre**, **vēni**, **ventum**, *a.*, *to come upon*, *find; invent*, *devise*, *discover; meet with.*

inven-tor, **ōris**, *m.* (**invĕnio**, § **44**, 1, *c*, 1), *a deviser*, *inventor*, *discoverer.*

inven-trix, **īcis**, *f.* (**invĕnio**, § **44**, 1, *c*, 1), *an inventress.*

in-vĭcem, *adv.* (**in**; **vĭcis**), *by turns*, *alternately*, *one another.*

in-victus, **a**, **um**, *adj.*, *unconquered*, *unsubdued; invincible*, *not to be overcome.*

in-vĭdeo, **vĭdēre**, **vīdi**, **vīsum**, *a.*, *to look spitefully at*, *regard with evil eye ; envy*, *grudge.*

invĭd-ia, **æ**, *f.* (**invĭdus**, § **44**, **1**, *c*, 2), *envy*, *jealousy*, *malice*, *grudge ; odium*, *hatred.*

invĭdĭ-ōsus, a, um, *adj.* **(invĭdia,** § **44,** 1, *c*, 3), *full of envy; detestable, hateful.*

invĭdus, a, um, *adj.* **(invĭdeo),** *envious.*

invĭdus, i, *m.* **(invĭdeo),** *an envier, one who envies.*

invī-sus, a, um, *part.* **(invĭdeo),** *hated, hateful, detestable.*

in-vīto, āre, āvi, ātum, *a., to invite, entertain, summon, allure.*

in-vītus, a, um, *adj.* **(in; vŏlo),** *unwilling, reluctant.*

in-vius, a, um, *adj.* **(in; via),** *without a road, pathless, trackless, impassable.*

in-vŏco, āre, āvi, ātum, *a., to call on* or *upon; invoke; implore, entreat.*

in-volvo, volvĕre, volvi, vŏlūtum, *a., to surround, enwrap, envelope, enclose; overwhelm, engulf.*

ipse, a, um, *pron.* (§ **20,** 2, *e*), *self, very; himself, herself, itself.*

īra, æ, *f., anger, wrath, rage, ire.*

īrācund-ia, æ, *f.* **(īrācundus,** § **44,** 1, *c*, 2), *anger, wrath, rage, fury.*

īrā-cundus, a, um, *adj.* **(īra,** § **44,** 1, *c*, 3), *prone to anger, irritable, hasty, passionate.*

īr-ascor, īrasci, īrātus sum, *dep.* **(īra),** *to be angry, be in a rage.*

īrā-tus, a, um, *part.* **(īrascor),** *angry, enraged, angered.*

ir-rĕpărābĭlis, e, *adj.* **(in; rĕpărābĭlis),** *irreparable, irrecoverable, irretrievable.*

ir-rĕvŏcābĭlis, e, *adj.* **(in; rĕvŏcābĭlis),** *irrevocable, unalterable.*

ir-rīdeo, rīdēre, rīsi, rīsum, *n.* and *a.* **(in; rīdeo),** *to laugh in ridicule; to joke, deride; mock, jeer, jest, laugh to scorn, ridicule.*

irrīs-io, ōnis, *f.* **(irrīdeo,** § **44,** 1, *c*, 2), *a deriding, mocking, mockery.*

irrīto, āre, āvi, ātum, *a., to provoke, exasperate, enrage, irritate, incite.*

ir-rĭtus, a, um, *adj.* **(in; rătus),** *undetermined; invalid, void, null; harmless; useless; vain.*

ir-rumpo, rumpĕre, rūpi, ruptum, *n.* and *a.* **(in; rumpo),** *to break in, burst in, invade, make an incursion into; interrupt; destroy.*

ir-ruo, ruĕre, rui, *no sup., n.* and *a.* **(in; ruo),** *to rush in* or *into; attack furiously, assail, assault.*

is, ea, id, *pron.* (§ **20,** 2, *d*), *this, that; he, she, it;* **is qui,** *the man who, such a one that;* **in eo esse,** *to be on the point of.*

iste, ta, tud, *pron.* (§ **20,** 2, *c*), *this of yours, that near you; this, that; that fellow* (in contempt).

ĭtă, *adv., thus, so; to such an extent;* **ita . . . ut** (*with subj.*), *in such a manner . . . that.*

Ĭtălia, æ, *f., Italy.*

Ĭtăl-ĭcus, a, um, *adj.* **Ĭtălia,** *of* or *belonging to Italy; Italian.*

Ĭtăl-us, a, um, *adj.* **(Ĭtălia),** *of* or *belonging to Italy; Italian.*

Ĭtăli, ōrum, *m., Italians.*

ĭtă-que, *conj.* (§ **4,** 2, *c*, and **43,** 2, *d*), *and thus, and so; therefore, accordingly.*

ĭtem, *adv., so, even so, just so; also; likewise.*

ĭter, ĭtĭnĕris, *n.* **(eo),** *journey, march, way, course, route;* **ex itinere,** *on the march;* **magnis itineribus,** *by forced marches.*

ĭtĕro, āre, āvi, ātum, *a.* **(ĭtĕrum),** *to do,* or *go over again, repeat; relate, tell.*

ĭtĕrum, *adv., again, a second time; next, afterwards.*

ĭt-ĭ-dem, *adv.* **(ĭtă),** *in like manner, also, moreover.*

ĭtūrus, a, um, *part.* from **eo.**

J.

jăceo, ēre, ui, ĭtum, *n., to lie, lie down, lie dead.*

jăcio, jăcĕre, jēci, jactum, *a., to throw, cast, hurl; lay, place, erect.*

jactā-tio, ōnis, *f.* (**jăcio, § 44,** 1, *c*, 2), *a throwing, hurling; tossing; boasting, ostentation.*

jact-ĭto, āre, *no perf., no sup., a. frequentative* (**jacto, § 36,** *b*, and note, and **44,** 2, *b*), *to pour forth frequently; to make a great display.*

jac-to, āre, āvi, ātum, *a. frequentative* (**jăcio, § 36,** *b*, and note, and **44,** 2, *b*), *to throw, fling, toss, cast, hurl; boast, consider, talk about.*

jăcŭl-or, āri, ātus sum, *dep.* (**jăcŭlum**), *to hurl a javelin; cast, throw, hurl.*

jăc-ŭlum, i, *n.* (**jăcio, § 44,** 1, *c*, 2), *a missile, dart, javelin.*

jam, *adv., now, already, presently, at length;* with a negative, as **jam non,** *no longer.*

jam-diū, *adv., long ago, already, for a long time.*

jam-dūdum, *adv., long ago, this long time; at once, forthwith, directly.*

jam-jam, *adv., at this very moment, already.*

jam-prīdem, *adv., a long time since, long since.*

jānua, æ, *f.* (**jānus**), *a door, gate.*

jānu-ārius, a, um, *adj.* (**jānus**), *of* or *belonging to January.* AS NOUN, *m., January.*

Jānus, i, *m.*, an ancient Latin divinity, represented with two faces, one in front, the other behind.

jējūnus, a, um, *adj., hungry, thirsty, dry; barren, sterile; mean, low, trifling.*

jŏc-or, āri, ātus sum, *dep.* (**jŏcus**), *to jest, joke.*

jŏcus, i, *m.* (in *pl.*, also **jŏca, ōrum**), *a jest, joke.*

Jŏvis, *gen.* of **Jūpĭter.**

Jŭba, æ, *m.*, a king of Numidia.

jŭbeo, jŭbēre, jussi, jussum, *a., to order, command, bid; exhort.*

jū-cundus, a, um, *adj.* (**jŭvo, § 44,** 1, *c*, 3), *pleasant, agreeable, delightful, pleasing.*

jūdex, ĭcis, *com. gen.* (**jūdĭco**), *a judge, umpire.*

jūdĭc-ium, ii, *n.* (**jūdĭco, § 44,** 1, *c*, 2), *a judgment, opinion, decision, trial, court.*

jū-dĭco, āre, āvi, ātum, *a.* (**jus; dĭco**), *to judge, decide, determine.*

jŭg-ŭlum, i, *n.*, **-us, i,** *m.* (**jungo**), *the throat.*

jŭg-um, i, *n.* (**jungo**), *a yoke; pair, team; a height,* or *summit* (of a mountain).

Jūlia, æ, *f.*, sister of Cæsar.

Jūlius, ii, *m.*, the name of a Roman *gens;* especially *Caius Julius Cæsar,* and his adopted son, *Caius Julius Cæsar Octavianus Augustus.*

Jūlius, ii, *m.*, the month of *July;* so called after Julius Cæsar.

Jūlius, a, um, *adj., of July.*

jū-mentum, i, *n.* (**jungo, § 44,** 1, *c*, 2), *a beast of burden, a draught-animal.*

jungo, jungĕre, junxi, junctum, *a., to join, unite, yoke, harness;* **societatem jungere,** *to form a partnership.*

jūnior, us, *adj., comparative* (**jŭvĕnis, § 17,** 3, *b*), *younger.*

Jū-pĭter (Jupp), Jŏvis, *m.* (**§ 11,** iii., 4, *b*), son of Saturn, brother and husband of Juno, king of gods.

Jūra, æ, *m.*, a chain of mountains extending from the Rhine to the Rhone.

jūrā-mentum, i, *n.* (**jūro, § 44,** 1, *c*, 2), *an oath.*

jūre, *abl.* of **jus,** used adverbially, *by right, justly.*

jūro, āre, āvi, ātum, *n.* and *a., to swear, take an oath, swear by, swear to.*

jūror, āri, ātus sum, *dep., to swear, take an oath.*

jus, jūris, *n., law, right, justice, authority, control.*

jusjūrandum, jurisjurandi, *n.* (**§ 14,** 2, *d*), *an oath.*

jus-sum, **i**, *n*. (**jŭbeo**), *an order, command.*

jus-sus, **ūs**, *m*. (**jŭbeo**), *an order, command.*

jus-sus, **a**, **um**, *part*. (**jŭbeo**), *commanded, ordered.*

just-ē, *adv*. (**justus**), *rightly, justly, properly, correctly.*

just-ĭtia, **æ**, *f*. (**justus**, § **44**, 1, *c*, 2), *justice, uprightness.*

jus-tus, **a**, **um**, *adj*. (**jus**), *just, upright; equitable; fair, proper, right.*

jŭven-ca, **æ**, *f*. (**jŭvĕnis**), *a young cow, heifer.*

jŭven-cus, **i**, *m*. (**jŭvĕnis**), *a young bullock, steer.*

jŭvĕnis, **is**, *adj*., *com. gen*. (§ **17**, 3, *b*), *young, youthful.*

jŭvenis, **is**, *com. gen*. (*gen. pl*., **jŭvĕnum**), *a young man* or *woman* (between 17 and 45 or 46).

jŭven-tus, **ūtis**, *f*. (**jŭvĕnis**, § **44**, 1, *c*, 2), *youth; the season of youth.*

jŭvo, **jŭvāre**, **jūvi**, **jūtum**, *a*. and *n*., *to help, aid, assist, support.*

juxtā, *prep*. with *acc*., *near to, near;* as *adv*., *near by, in like manner, alike.*

K.

Kălendæ (**Cal.**), **ārum**, *f*., *the first day of the month.*

Karthāgo (**Car.**), **ĭnis**, *f*., *Carthage;* a celebrated city of Africa.

L.

L, an abbreviation of the prænomen *Lucius.*

lāb-es, **is**, *f*. (**lābor**), *fall, downfall, ruin, stain, blemish.*

Lăbiēnus, **i**, *m*., an officer of Cæsar in Gaul, who afterwards went over to Pompey.

lābor, **lābi**, **lapsus sum**, *dep*., *to glide along, slip, fall down, slip away, escape.*

lăbor, **ōris**, *m*., *labor, toil, exertion; hardship, distress.*

lăbōr-iōsus, **a**, **um**, *adj*. (**lăbor**, § **44**, 1, *c*, 3), *laborious, toilsome, wearisome, difficult, industrious.*

lăbōro, **āre**, **āvi**, **ātum**, *n*. (**lăbor**), *to toil, labor, struggle, suffer, be hard pressed; be anxious.*

lac, **lactis**, *n*., *milk.*

Lăcĕdæmon, **ŏnis**, *f*., *Sparta;* the capital of Laconia.

lăcer, **ĕra**, **ĕrum**, *adj*., *torn, mangled, maimed.*

lăcĕro, **āre**, **āvi**, **ātum**, *a*. (**lăcer**), *to tear, mangle; waste, consume; destroy; torture, vex, pain.*

lăcesso, **essĕre**, **essīvi** *or* **essii** *or* **essi**, **essītum**, *a*., *to provoke, excite, challenge, harass, assail, attack.*

lăcio, **ĕre**, *no perf*., *no sup*., *a*., *to entice, allure.*

lăcrĭma (**cry**), **æ**, *f*., *a tear;* **lacrimas dare**, *to weep.*

lăcrĭmo (**cry**), **āre**, **āvi**, **ātum**, *n*. and *a*. (**lăcrĭma**), *to shed tears, weep, cry; weep* or *cry for.*

lăcrĭmor (**cry**), **āri**, **ātus sum**, *dep*. (**lăcrĭma**), *weep, bewail, lament.*

lăcus, **ūs**, *m*. (§ **12**, 3, *d*), *a lake.*

lædo, **lædĕre**, **læsi**, **læsum**, *a*., *to strike, hurt, injure, damage; annoy, vex; violate.*

læt-ĭtia, **æ**, *f*. (**lætus**, § **44**, 1, *c*, 2), *joy, gladness.*

lætor, **āri**, **ātus sum**, *dep*. (**lætus**), *to feel joy, rejoice, be glad; rejoice at.*

lætus, **a**, **um**, *adj*., *joyful, rejoicing, joyous, glad; happy; pleasant, agreeable; fortunate, lucky; rich, fertile;* **pabula læta**, *rich fodder.*

læva, **æ**, *f*. (**lævus**), *the left hand.*

Lævīnus, **i**, *m*., a Roman name.

lævus, **a**, **um**, *adj*., *left, on the left hand.*

lambo, **ĕre**, **i**, **ĭtum**, *a*., *to lick, lap.*

lāmentor, **āri**, **ātus sum**, *dep*. (**lāmentum**), *to lament, weep over, bewail.*

lāmentum, i, *n., a bewailing, lamentation.*

lāmĭna, æ, *f., a plate* (of metal, wood, &c.), *leaf, layer, blade.*

lāna, æ, *f., wool, down; soft hair.*

lancea, æ, *f., a light spear; a lance.*

lān-ĭ-fĭcium, ii, *n.* (**lāna; făcio**), *wool-spinning, wool-weaving.*

lănista, æ, *m., a trainer of gladiators; an instructor in evil; a sword-master.*

lănius, ii, *m.* (**lănio,** to tear), *a butcher.*

lăpĭd-eus, a, um, *adj.* (**lăpis,** § **44,** 1, *c,* 3), *consisting of stones, stony;* **murus lapideus,** *a stone wall.*

lăpis, ĭdis, *m., a stone; a stone* (placed at the end of every 1000 paces), *a mile-stone.*

lap-sus, ūs, *m.* (**lābor,** § **44,** 1, *c,* 2), *a gliding; slip, fall.*

lăqueus, ei, *m., a noose, halter, snare.*

Lārentia (Acca), æ, *f.*, the wife of Faustulus, foster-mother of Romulus and Remus.

Lăres, um *and* **ium,** *m. pl., the Lares; household gods,* whose images were placed in a little shrine by the hearth, or in a small chapel in the interior of the house.

larg-ior, īri, ītus sum, *dep.* (**largus**), *to give bountifully, bestow, distribute; bribe.*

largī-tio, ōnis, *f.* (**largior,** § **44,** 1, *c,* 2), *a giving freely; liberality; bribery, corruption.*

largus, a, um, *adj., large, long, great; abundant, plentiful.*

lass-ĭtūdo, ĭnis, *f.* (**lassus,** § **44,** 1, *c,* 2), *faintness, weariness.*

lassus, a, um, *adj., faint, languid, weary, tired.*

lāt-ē, *adv.* (**lātus**), *widely; far and wide, broadly;* **late patere,** *to be of wide extent.*

lăt-ĕbra, æ, *f.* (**lăteo**), *a hiding-place, lurking-place.*

lăteo, ēre, ui, *no sup., n.* (§ **52,** 2, *d*), *to be* or *lie hid; to be concealed, keep concealed.*

lăter, ĕris, *m., a brick* or *tile.*

lătĕr-ĭtius (-ĭcius), a, um, *adj.* (**lăter,** § **44,** 1, *c,* 3), *made* or *consisting of bricks, brick.*

lăt-ĭbŭlum, i, *n.* (**lăteo**), *a hiding-place, covert, den.*

Lăt-īnus, i, *m.* (**Lătium**), *Latinus;* a king of the Laurentians, who entertained Æneas and gave him his daughter Lavinia in marriage.

Lăt-īnus, a, um, *adj.* (**Lătium**), *of* or *belonging to Latium; Latin.*

Lăt-īni, ōrum, *m. pl.* (**Lătium**), *the inhabitants of Latium; Latins.*

lāt-ĭtūdo, ĭnis, *f.* (**lātus,** § **44,** 1, *c,* 2), *breadth, width; extent; fullness, richness.*

Lătium, ii, *n.*, a country of Italy in which Rome was situated (now Campagna di Roma).

lātro, āre, āvi, ātum, *n.* and *a., to bark, bawl, yelp; bark at; demand.*

lătro, ōnis, *m., a robber, highwayman.*

lătrōcĭn-ium, ii, *n.* (**lătrōcĭnor**), *robbery; artifice, roguery.*

lătrō-cĭnor, āri, ātus, *dep.* (**lătro**), *to practise highway robbery; to commit piracy.*

lātus, a, um, *adj., broad, wide.*

lătus, ĕris, *n., the side, flank, body, lungs;* **lateris** *or* **laterum dolor,** *pain in the side, pleurisy.*

lā-tus, a, um, *part.* (**fĕro**), *borne, carried.*

laudā-bĭlis, e, *adj.* (**laudo**), *praiseworthy, laudable.*

laudo, āre, āvi, ātum, *a.* (**laus**), *to praise, extol, commend, eulogize.*

laurea, æ, *f., a laurel-tree; laurel-crown.*

Laurentia, *see* **Lārentia.**

laurus, i, *or* **ūs,** *f., a laurel-tree; a laurel* (wreaths of which were worn by victorious generals); *triumph, victory, success.*

laus, laudis, *f., praise, commendation; glory;* **laudes,** *fame, renown.*

laut-e, *adv.* (**lautus**), *elegantly, magnificently, splendidly, sumptuously.*

lau-tus, a, um, *part.* (**lăvo**), *elegant, splendid, sumptuous, noble, magnificent; distinguished, grand.*

Lāvīnia, æ, *f.*, daughter of Latīnus and wife of Ænēas.

Lāvīn-ium, ii, *n.* (**Lāvīnia**), a city of Latium, founded by Æneas in honor of his wife Lavinia.

lăvo, lăvāre *and* **lăvĕre, lăvāvi** *and* **lāvi, lăvātum, lautum,** *and* **lōtum,** *a.* and *n., to wash, bathe; wet, moisten; wash away, atone for, expiate.*

lax-e, *adv.* (**laxus**), *loosely, freely, widely, openly.*

lax-ĭtas, ātis, *f.* (**laxus,** § **44**, 1, *c*, 2), *width, roominess, spaciousness; laxity, looseness, slackness.*

laxo, āre, āvi, ātum, *a.* (**laxus**), *to unloose, loosen, relax, lighten, set free, relieve, open, slacken.*

lect-īca, æ, *f.* (**lectus**), *a litter, sedan; bier.*

lect-ĭto, āre, āvi, ātum, *a. frequentative* (from **lĕgo**, through the obsolete verb **lecto**), (§ **36**, *b*, and note, and **44**, 2, *b*), *to read often; read with eagerness; to read.*

lec-tor, ōris, *m.* (**lĕgo,** § **44**, 1, *c*, 1), *one who reads; a reader.*

lec-tus, a, um, *part.* (**lĕgo**), *picked out, choice, excellent.*

lec-tus, i, *m.* (**lĕgo**), *a couch, bed.*

lēgā-tio, ōnis, *f.* (**lēgo,** § **44**, 1, *c*, 2), *an embassy, legation.*

lēgā-tus, i, *m.* (**lēgo**), *an ambassador, lieutenant, messenger.*

lĕg-io, ōnis, *f.* (**lĕgo**), *a legion;* consisting of between 4200 and 6000 men.

lĕgiōn-ārius, a, um, *adj.* (**lĕgio**), *of* or *belonging to a legion; legionary.*

lēgo, āre, āvi, ātum, *a., to send, appoint, to bequeath as a legacy.*

lĕgo, lĕgĕre, lēgi, lectum, *a., to gather, collect, choose, select; read, recite.*

Lĕmannus, i, *m.*, Lake Geneva.

lēn-io, īre, īvi *or* **ii, ītum,** *a.* (**lēnis**), *to soften, assuage, render gentle, soothe, appease, pacify.*

lēnis, e, *adj., soft, smooth; moderate, gentle, easy; mild, calm.*

lēn-ĭtas, ātis, *f.* (**lēnis,** § **44**, 1, *c*, 2), *softness, gentleness, mildness, smoothness.*

lēn-ĭter, *adv.* (**lēnis**), *gently, softly, quietly.*

Lentŭlus, i, *m.*, a surname of a distinguished Roman family.

lentus, a, um, *adj., tough, slow, inactive, tedious; lasting.*

leo, ōnis, *m., a lion.*

lĕpus, ŏris, *m.* (epicene, § **6**, 4), *a hare.*

lēt-ālis, e, *adj.* (**lētum**), *deadly, fatal, mortal.*

lētum, i, *n., death, ruin, destruction.*

lĕvis, e, *adj., light, swift, quick, easy, slight, unimportant.*

lēvis, e, *adj., smooth, polished, bright, shining; fair, beautiful.*

lĕv-ĭtas, ātis, *f.* (**lĕvis,** § **44**, 1, *c*, 2), *lightness, fickleness, levity.*

lĕv-ĭter, *adv.* (**lĕvis**), *lightly; a little, not much, somewhat; mildly, gently, patiently,*

lĕvo, āre, āvi, ātum, *a.* (**lĕvis**), *to make light, lighten; ease, relieve; lessen, diminish, abate; alleviate, console, comfort.*

lex, lēgis, *f.* (**lĕgo**), *a law, precept, regulation, condition.*

lĭbel-lus, i, *m. dim.* (**lĭber,** § **44**, 1, *c*, 3), *a little book, pamphlet, journal, diary; handbill.*

lĭbens, entis, *part.* (**lĭbeo**), *willing, ready, glad.*

lĭbent-er, *adv.* (**lĭbens**), *willingly, cheerfully, gladly.*

lĭbeo, ēre, ui, ĭtum, *n., to please;* **libet,** *impers., it pleases, it is agreeable.*

lĭber, ĕra, ĕrum, *adj.*, *free, unrestricted*; in *pl.*, **lībĕri, ōrum,** *m.*, *children.*

lĭber, bri, *m.*, the inner *bark* of a tree; *a book* (since the bark of a tree was used as material for writing upon).

lībĕr-ālis, e, *adj.* (**līber**), *befitting a free man, decorous, gentlemanly, noble, generous.*

lībĕrāl-ĭtas, ātis, *f.* (**lībĕrālis,** § **44**, 1, *c*, 2), *generosity, liberality.*

lībĕrāl-ĭter, *adv.* (**lībĕrālis**), *nobly, generously; courteously, bountifully, liberally.*

lībĕr-ē, *adv.* (**līber**), *freely, frankly.*

lībĕri, ōrum, *m. pl.*, *see* **līber.**

lībĕro, āre, āvi, ātum, *a.* (**līber**), *to free, liberate, release, acquit, discharge, extricate.*

līber-tas, ātis, *f.* (**līber,** § **44**, 1, *c*, 2), *freedom, liberty; frankness, candor.*

līber-tus, i, *m.* (**lībĕro**), *a freedman.*

lĭbet, lĭbēre, lĭbuit *or* **lĭbĭtum est,** *n. impers.*, *it pleases.*

lĭb-īdo, ĭnis, *f.* (**lĭbeo**), *desire, eagerness, longing; passion, caprice, wilfulness.*

lībra, æ, *f.*, *a pair of scales, balance; a pound.*

lībro, āre, āvi, ātum, *a.* (**lībra**), *to poise, balance; brandish; hurl, dash; speed, hasten; weigh, ponder, consider*

lĭcent-ia, æ, *f.* (**lĭcens,** § **44**, 1, *c*, 2), *freedom, liberty; boldness, presumption; lawlessness, licentiousness.*

lĭceor, ēri, ĭtus sum, *dep.*, *to bid* (at an auction).

lĭcet, lĭcuit *or* **lĭcĭtum est,** *n. impers.*, *it is allowable, allowed, permitted; one may, can;* **licet venias,** *you may come.*

lĭcet, *conj.* (§ **43**, 2, *g*), *although, though, even if.*

Lĭcĭnius, ii, *m.*, a Roman name.

lic-tor, ōris, *m.* (**lĭgo,** § **44**, 1, *c*, 1), *a lictor;* an attendant granted to a magistrate, as a sign of official dignity.

lign-eus, a, um, *adj.* (**lignum,** § **44**, 1, *c*, 3), *of wood, wooden.*

lignum, i, *n.*, *wood; pl., fire-wood.*

lĭgo, āre, āvi, ātum, *a.*, *to bind, fasten, tie.*

līlium, ii, *n.*, *a lily.*

līneā-mentum, i, *n.* (**līnea,** a line), *a line; pl., drawings, designs; features, lineaments.*

Lingŏnes, um, *m.* (*acc. pl.*, **Lingŏnăs**), a people in Celtic Gaul.

lingua, æ, *f.*, *the tongue; language.*

linter, tris, *f.*, *a boat, skiff, wherry.*

lĭquĕ-făcio, făcĕre, fēci, factum, *a.*; and *pass.*, **lĭquĕ-fīo, fiĕri, factus sum** (**lĭqueo; făcio**), *to make liquid; to melt, dissolve; weaken.*

lĭqu-ĭdus, a, um, *adj.* (**lĭqueo**), *flowing, fluid, liquid.*

līs, lītis, *f.*, *a strife, dispute, quarrel; law-suit.*

Liscus, i, *m.*, an Æduan chief.

lītĭgā-tor, ōris, *m.* (**lītĭgo,** § **44**, 1, *c*, 1), *a party to a law-suit, a litigant, disputant.*

littĕra (**lītĕra**), **æ,** *f.*, *a letter* (of the alphabet); **litteræ,** *pl.*, *an epistle, literature.*

litter-ārius (**līt**), **a, um,** *adj.* (**littĕra**), *of* or *belonging* to *learning, letters;* **litterarius ludus,** *an elementary school.*

lītus (**littus**), **ŏris,** *n.*, *the seashore, shore, coast, beach.*

lŏcŭ-ples, ētis, *adj.* (**lŏcus; pleo**), *rich, wealthy, opulent.*

lŏcŭplēto, āre, āvi, ātum, *a.* (**lŏcŭples**), *to enrich, make rich; adorn, beautify, decorate.*

lŏcus, i, *m.*, *pl.*, **lŏci** *or* **lŏca,** *m.* and *n.* (§ **14**, 2, *c*), *a place, spot, region.*

lŏc-ūtus, a, um, *part.* (**lŏquor**).

long-e, *adv.* (**longus**), *far off; widely, greatly, much, by far* (*comp.*, **longius**; *superlative,* **longissime**).

long-inq-uus, a, um, *adj.* (**longus; hinc**), *far off, distant, remote; long;* **e** *or* **ex longinquo,** *from a distance, from afar.*

long-ĭtūdo, ĭnis, *f.* (**longus,** § **44,** 1, *c,* 2), *length.*

longus, a, um, *adj., long; tall; remote, distant, tedious.*

lŏqu-ax, ācis, *adj.* (**lŏquor,** § **44,** 1, *c,* 3), *prone to talk, talkative, loquacious, wordy.*

lŏquor, lŏqui, lŏcūtus sum, *dep., to speak, talk, say, tell, utter, mention; speak of.*

lōr-īca, æ, *f.* (**lōrum**), *a cuirass* or *corselet* (made of leathern thongs), *coat-of-mail.*

lōrum, i, *n., a thong, bridle.*

lŭb, *see* **lĭb.**

lūceo, lūcēre, luxi, *no sup., n., to shine, be brilliant, be conspicuous, evident.*

lūc-ĭdus, a, um, *adj.* (**lūceo**), *shining, bright, clear.*

Lūcius, ii, *m.,* a Roman name.

lŭ-crum, i, *n.* (**luo**), *gain, profit, advantage; avarice; wealth, riches.*

lucta, æ, *f.* (**luctor**), *a wrestling, wrestling-match.*

luctā-tio, ōnis, *f.* (**luctor,** § **44,** 1, *c,* 2), *a wrestling; struggle, contest, fight.*

luctor, āri, ātus sum, *dep., to seize, grasp; strive, contend, struggle; wrestle.*

luc-tus, ūs, *m.* (**lūgeo,** § **44,** 1, *c,* 2), *sorrow, mourning, lamentation, grief.*

Lūcullus, i, *m., Lucius Licinius Lucullus,* a wealthy Roman noble, commander against Mithridates.

lūcus, i, *m., grove, sacred grove; wood.*

lūd-ĭbrium, ii, *n.* (**lūdo**), *a mocking, mockery, derision; jest, scoff, sport.*

lūd-ĭcer (crus), (*nom. sing. masc.* not used), **cra, crum,** *adj.* (**lūdus**), *sportive.*

lūd-ĭcrum, i, *n., sport, jest; show, public games.*

lūd-ĭ-fĭco, āre, āvi, ātum, *a.* and *n.* (**lūdus; făcio**), *to make sport of, make a fool of; delude, deceive; mock.*

lūd-ĭ-fĭcor, āri, ātus sum, *dep.* (**lūdus; făcio**), *to make sport of; to mock, delude, deride.*

lūdo, dĕre, si, sum, *n.* and *a.* (**lūdus**), *to sport, play, delude, mock, deceive.*

lūdus, i, *m., a play, game, pastime; school;* in *pl., public games, shows.*

lūgeo, lūgēre, luxi, luctum, *n.* and *a., to lament, sorrow, bewail; mourn for.*

lū-men, ĭnis, *n.* (**lūceo**), *light, daylight, day; the eye.*

lū-na, æ, *f.* (**lūceo**), (the shining one), *the moon.*

luo, luĕre, lui, luĭtum *or* **lūtum,** *a., to wash; wash out, atone for, expiate.*

luo, luĕre, lui, luĭtum *or* **lūtum,** *a., to pay.*

lŭpa, æ, *f., a she-wolf.*

lŭpus, i, *m., a wolf.*

lustro, āre, āvi, ātum, *a.* (**lustrum**), *to purify, illumine, make clear; review; traverse.*

lu-strum, i, *n.* (**luo**), *an expiatory offering,*

lū-sus, ūs, *m.* (**lūdo,** § **44,** 1, *c,* 2), *a playing; sport, amusement, game.*

lux, lūcis, *f.* (**lūceo**), *light, splendor, brightness; the light of day, daylight;* **prima lux,** *day-break.*

luxŭria, æ, *f. luxury, excess, extravagance.*

luxus, ūs, *m., luxury, excess, extravagance.*

M.

M, as an abbreviation, denotes *Marcus.* [*Marius.*

M', as an abbreviation, denotes

Măcĕdŏnia, æ, *f.*, a country between Thessaly and Thrace.
măc-er, cra, crum, *adj.* (**măceo,** to be lean), *lean, meagre, poor, thin.*
māchĭna, æ, *f.*, *a military engine; trick, artifice.*
măc-ies, ēi, *f.* (**măceo**), *leanness, thinness, poverty.*
măcĭ-lentus, a, um, *adj.* (**măcies**), *lean, thin.*
Mæcēnas, ātis, *m.*, the friend of Augustus and patron of Horace and Virgil.
mæreo (mœr), ēre, *no perf.*, *no sup.*, *n.* and *a.*, *to grieve, mourn, lament; bemoan, mourn over.*
mær-or (mœr), ōris, *m.* (**mæreo,** § **44,** 1, *c*, 2), *a mourning, sadness, grief, lamentation.*
mæs-tus (mœs), a, um, *adj.* (**mæreo**), *sad, sorrowful, afflicted, dejected.*
măgis, *comp. adv.*, *more, rather.*
măg-ister, tri, *m.*, *a master, chief, head, director, leader.*
măgistr-ātus, ūs, *m.* (**măgister**), *a magistracy, office, magistrate.*
magnĭfĭc-e, *adv.* (**magnĭfĭcus**), *nobly, magnificently, splendidly, richly* (*comp.*, **magnificentius**; *superlative*, **magnificentissime**).
magn-ĭ-fĭcus, a, um, *adj.* (*comp.*, **magnificentior**; *superlat.*, **magnificentissimus**), (§ **17,** 1, *c*), (**magnus; făcio**), *noble, distinguished, eminent, grand.*
magn-ĭtūdo, ĭnis, *f.* (**magnus,** § **44,** 1, *c*, 2), *greatness, size, bulk.*
magn-ŏpĕre (magno opere), *adv.* (**magnus; ŏpus**), *very much, greatly, exceedingly.*
magnus, a, um, *adj.* (*comp.*, **mājor**; *superlative*, **maximus**), *great, large; abundant, numerous; powerful, loud;* **natu major,** *greater in birth, older.*
Maius, ii, *m.*, the month of *May.*
māj-estas, ātis, *f.* (**magnus**), *honor, dignity, excellence, splendor, majesty.*
majōres, rum, *m. pl.* (**mājor**), *ancestors.*
măl-e, *adv.* (*comp.*, **pējus**; *superlative*, **pessime**), (**mălus**), *badly, incorrectly, wickedly, hurtfully, unfortunately.*
mălĕ-dīco, dīcĕre, dixi, dictum, *n.*, *to speak ill of, revile, slander.*
mălĕ-dictum, i, *n.*, *a reviling, slander, curse.*
mā-lo, malle, mālui, *no sup.*, *a.*, *irreg.* (§ **37, 3**), (**măgis; vŏlo**), *to choose rather, prefer.*
mălum, i, *n.* (**mălus**), *evil, misfortune, calamity, damage.*
mălus, a, um, *adj.* (*comp.*, **pējor**; *superlative*, **pessimus**), *evil, bad, wicked, low, injurious.*
mandā-tum, i, *n.* (**mando**), *a charge, order, commission.*
man-do, āre, āvi, ātum, *a.* (**mănus; do**), *to commit into one's hands; to enjoin, order, command.*
māne, *n. indecl.*, *the morning.* As ADV., *in the morning, early in the morning.*
măneo, mănēre, mansi, mansum, *n.* and *a.*, *to stay, remain, stop, last, endure; wait for, await.*
mănĭfesto, āre, āvi, ātum, *a.* (**mănĭfestus**), *to make public, discover, show, manifest.*
mănĭfestus, a, um, *adj.*, *clear, plain, evident, manifest.*
măn-ĭ-pŭlus, i, *m.* (**mănus; pleo**), *a handful; a company, maniple; troop.*
Manlius, ii, *m.*, a Roman name.
mansuē-tūdo, ĭnis, *f.* (**mansuētus,** mild), (§ **44,** 1, *c*, 2), *mildness, gentleness, clemency.*
mănū-mitto, mittĕre, mīsi, missum, *a.* (**mănus; mitto**), *to release from one's power; set at liberty; enfranchise, emancipate.*
mănus, ūs, *f.*, *a hand; band* (of troops), *force.*
Marcus, i, *m.*, *see* **Brūtus.**
măre, is, *n.*, *the sea;* **mare internum,** *the Mediterranean.*

margo, **ĭnis**, *m.* and *f.*, *an edge, brink, border, margin.*

măr-īnus, **a**, **um**, *adj.* (**măre**), *of* or *belonging to the sea; marine.*

măr-ĭtĭmus, **a**, **um**, *adj.*, *of* or *belonging to the sea; maritime; bordering on the sea;* **copiæ maritimæ**, *naval forces.* As NOUN, **maritima**, **ōrum**, *n. pl.*, *places on the sea-coast.*

măr-īta, **æ**, *f.* (**mas**), *a married woman.*

mărīt-us, **i**, *m.* (**mărīta**), *a married man, husband.*

Mărius, **ii**, *m.*, *Caius Marius* (157–86 B.C.); the conqueror of Jugurtha, and chief of the popular party at Rome. He was consul seven times.

mar-mor, **ŏris**, *n.* (**măre**), *the sea; marble* (from its white glistening appearance).

marmŏr-eus, **a**, **um**, *adj.* (**marmor**, § **44**, 1, *c*, 3), *made of marble, consisting of marble.*

Mars, **tis**, *m.*, the fabled father of Romulus; the god of war, of husbandry, of shepherds and seers.

Martius, **a**, **um**, *adj.* (**Mars**), *of Mars; of* or *belonging to March.*

Martius, **ii**, *m.*, the month of *March.*

mās, **măris**, *m.*, *a male.* As ADJ., *male, manly.*

massa, **æ**, *f.*, *a lump, mass.*

māter, **tris**, *f.*, *a mother.*

mātĕr-ia, **æ**, *f.* (**māter**), *matter, material; timber.*

mātĕr-ies, **iēi**, *f.* (**māter**), *matter, material; timber.*

mātr-ĭ-cīda, **æ**, *com. gen.* (**māter**; **cædo**), *a mother's murderer, a matricide.*

mātrĭcīd-ium, **ii**, *n.* (**mātrĭcīda**), *the murdering of one's mother; matricide.*

mātr-ĭmōnium, **ii**, *n.* (**māter**), *wedlock, marriage;* **in matrimonium ducere**, *to marry* (used only of a man marrying a woman).

mātr-ōna, **æ**, *f.* (**māter**), *a married woman, wife, matron.*

Mātrŏna, **æ**, *m.*, a river in Gaul (now the *Marne*).

mātūr-ē, *adv.* (**mātūrus**), *early, speedily, quickly* (*comp.*, **maturius**; *superlative*, **maturrime** *and* **maturissime**).

mātūr-ĭtas, **ātis**, *f.* (**mātūrus**, § **44**, 1, *c*, 2), *perfection, ripeness, maturity; promptness, speediness.*

mātūr-o, **āre**, **āvi**, **ātum**, *a.* and *n.* (**mātūrus**), *to make ripe, ripen; make haste, hasten; to become ripe, ripen.*

mātūrus, **a**, **um**, *adj.*, *ripe, mature; excellent; early; timely, seasonable.*

maxĭm-e (**maxŭm-**), *adv.* (**maxĭmus**), *in the highest degree; very, especially, exceedingly; mostly, chiefly.*

maxĭmus, **a**, **um**, *adj.*, superlative of **magnus**, *greatest.*

Maxĭmus, **i**, *m.*, a Roman name.

mē-cum, *with me* (§ **19**, 3, *e*).

mĕdeor, **ēri**, *no perf.*, *dep.*, *to heal, cure; remedy, relieve, correct.*

mĕdĭcā-men, **ĭnis**, *n.* (**mĕdĭco**), *a drug, remedy, medicine.*

mĕdĭcā-mentum, **i**, *n.* (**mĕdĭco**), *a drug, remedy, medicine.*

mĕdĭc-īna, **æ**, *f.* (**mĕdĭcus**), *medicine, remedy.*

mĕdĭco, **āre**, **āvi**, **ātum**, *a.* (**mĕdĭcus**), *to heal, cure.*

mĕdĭcor, **āri**, **ātus sum**, *dep.* (**mĕdĭcus**), *to heal, cure.*

mĕd-ĭcus, **a**, **um**, *adj.* (**mĕdeor**), *healing, curative.* As NOUN, **mĕdĭcus**, **i**, *m.*, *a physician, surgeon.*

mĕdĭtor, **āri**, **ātus sum**, *dep.*, *to think* or *reflect upon; to muse over, consider; study; design, purpose.*

mĕdium, **ii**, *n.*, *the middle, midst; the presence* or *sight;* **e medio tollere**, *to put out of the way.*

mĕdius, **a**, **um**, *adj.*, *middle, mid;*

half-way; intervening, intermediate.

mel, mellis, *n., honey; sweetness, pleasantness.*

membrum, i, *n., a limb; part, portion, division.*

mĕmĭni, isse, *n. def.* (§ **38**, 1, *c*), *to remember, recollect.*

mĕmor, ŏris, *adj., mindful, remembering; unforgetting, vindictive, unsleeping, watchful.*

mĕmŏră-bĭlis, e, *adj.* (**mĕmŏro**), *memorable, remarkable; worthy of mention.*

mĕmŏr-ia, æ, *f.* (**mĕmor**), *memory, recollection, remembrance;* **memoriæ tradere** *or* **prodere**, *to hand down to posterity.*

mĕmŏro, āre, āvi, ātum, *a.* (**mĕmor**), *to remind of; call to mind: mention, relate, tell, narrate.*

mens, mentis, *f., the mind, understanding, intellect, reason.*

mensa, æ, *f., a table;* (that which is put on table), *food.*

mensis, is, *m., a month.*

mentio, ōnis, *f., a mentioning, calling to mind, mention.*

mentior, īri, ītus sum, *dep., to lie, cheat, deceive; pretend, imitate, counterfeit.*

meo, āre, āvi, ātum, *n., to go, to pass; to be on the march.*

mercā-tor, ōris, *m.* (**mercor**, § **44**, 1, *c*, 1), *a trader, merchant.*

mercā-tūra, æ, *f.* (**mercor**, § **44**, 1, *c*, 2), *trade, traffic, commerce.*

mer-ces, ēdis, *f.* (**merx; cēdo**), *hire, pay, wages, salary, fee, reward; bribe; price; punishment; cost, injury.*

mercor, āri, ātus sum, *dep.* (**merx**), *to trade, traffic; buy, purchase.*

mĕreo, ēre, ui, ĭtum, *a.* and *n., to get, gain, acquire; to deserve, merit.*

mĕreor, ēri, ĭtus sum, *dep., to get, gain, acquire, obtain; deserve, merit.*

mergo, mergĕre, mersi, mersum, *a., to dip, plunge, immerse; sink, overwhelm; destroy.*

mĕrī-dies, ēi, *m.* (**mĕdius; dies**), (§ **13**, 2), *midday, noon; the south.*

mĕrĭt-o, *adv.* (**mĕrĭtus**), *deservedly, justly.*

mĕr-ĭtum, i, *n.* (**mĕreo**), *a service, kindness, benefit; merit, reward.*

mĕr-ĭtus, a, um, *part.* (**mĕreor**), *deserving.*

mer-sus, a, um, *part.* (**mergo**), *plunged.*

mĕrus, a, um, *adj., pure, unmixed, unadulterated.*

mer-x, mercis, *f.* (**mĕreo**), *goods, wares, commodities.*

mes-sis, is, *f.* (**mĕto**), *a harvest.*

mĕtallum, i, *n., a mine; a metal.*

Mĕtellus, i, *m.*, a Roman general.

mētior, mētīri, mensus sum, *dep., to measure, mete, distribute by measure.*

mĕto, mĕtĕre, messui, messum, *a., to mow, reap; gather.*

mētor, āri, ātus sum, *dep., to measure, mark off.*

Mettius, ii, *m.*, a Roman name.

mĕtuo, mĕtuĕre, mĕtui, mĕtūtum, *a.* and *n.* (**mĕtus**), *to fear, dread, be afraid of; be afraid.*

mĕtus, ūs, *m., fear, dread, apprehension, anxiety.*

me-us, a, um, *pron. possessive* (**me**), (*vocative sing. masc.*, **mi**, *rarely* **meus**), *my, mine, belonging to me.*

mīgro, āre, āvi, ātum, *n., to depart, migrate, go away.*

mīles, ĭtis, *com. gen., a soldier, a foot-soldier.*

Mīlēsius, a, um, *adj., of* or *belonging to the city of Miletus; Milesian.*

Mīlētus, i, *m.*, a city of Caria in Asia Minor.

mīlia, ium, *n. pl., see* **mille.**

milies, *see* **millies.**

mīlĭt-āris, e, *adj.* (**mīles**), *of* or *belonging to a soldier* or *the* *soldiers; military;* **res militaris,** *military science.*

mīlĭt-ia, æ, *f.* (**mīlĭto**), *military service; warfare.*

mīlĭto, āre, āvi, ātum, *n.* (**mīles**), *to be a soldier; wage war.*

mille (**mīle**), *numeral adj. indecl., a thousand.* As NOUN, used only in the *nom.* and *acc. sing.* (**mille**), and in *pl. n.*, **millia, ium,** *a thousand;* followed by the *partitive gen.*, as **millia passuum,** *a thousand paces, one mile.*

mill-ies (**iens**), *adv.* (**mille**), *a thousand times.*

mīmus, i, *m., a mimic actor, mime; a farce, play.*

mĭnĭmus, a, um, *adj. superlative* (**parvus**), *least.*

mĭnister, tri, *m., an attendant, waiter, servant; helper, supporter, abettor.*

mĭnistĕr-ium, ii, *n.* (**mĭnister**), *attendance, waiting, service.*

mĭn-ĭtor, āri, ātus sum, *dep. frequentative* (**mĭnor,** § **36,** *b*, and **44,** 2, *b*), *to threaten, menace.*

mĭnor, āri, ātus sum, *dep., to jut forth, project; threaten, menace.*

mĭnor, us, *adj. comparative* (**parvus**), *less.* As NOUN, **mĭnōres, um,** *com. gen. pl., descendants.*

mĭnuo, uĕre, ui, ūtum, *a.* and *n., to lessen, diminish, lower, reduce; to grow less.*

mĭnus, *adv., less;* **si minus,** *if not* (**părum, mĭnus, mĭnĭme**).

mĭnū-tus, a, um, *part.* (**mĭnuo**), *little, small, minute.*

mīrā-bĭlis, e, *adj.* (**mīror**), *wonderful, marvellous, extraordinary.*

mīrābĭl-ĭter, *adv.* (**mīrābĭlis**), *wonderfully, astonishingly.*

mīr-ĭ-fĭcus, a, um, *adj.* (**mīrus; făcio**), *causing wonder, wonderful, extraordinary, strange* (**mirificus, mirificentior, mirificentissimus**), (§ **17,** 1, *c*).

mīror, rāri, rātus sum, *dep., to admire; to wonder at.*

mīr-us, a, um, *adj.* (**mīror**), *wonderful, marvellous, strange, extraordinary.*

misceo, miscēre, miscui, mistum *or* **mixtum,** *a., to mix, mingle, intermingle, blend.*

mĭser, ĕra, ĕrum, *adj., wretched, unfortunate, pitiable; sick, ill.*

mĭsĕrā-bĭlis, e, *adj.* (**mĭser**), *worthy of pity, pitiable, lamentable.*

mĭsĕr-eor, ēri, ĭtus sum, *dep.* (**mĭser**), (§ **50,** 4, *c, and* 1), *to pity, feel pity for, commiserate.*

mĭsĕre-sco, scĕre, *no perf., no sup., n. inch.* (**mĭsĕreo,** § **36,** *a.*, and **44,** 2, *b*), (§ **50,** 4, *c, and* 1), *to feel pity, have compassion for.*

mĭsĕret, mĭsĕrēre, mĭsĕruit, *n. impers.* (§ **50,** 4, *c*, and 2), *it distresses, stirs pity;* **miseret me,** *I pity.*

mĭsĕrĭcord-ia, æ, *f.* (**mĭsĕrĭcors,** § **44,** 1, *c*, 2), *pity, compassion, mercy.*

mĭsĕr-ĭ-cors, cordis, *adj.* (**mĭsĕreo; cor**), *having a pitying heart; tender-hearted, compassionate, merciful.*

mĭsĕr-or, āri, ātus sum, *dep.* (**mĭser**), (§ **50,** 4, *c*, 1), *to lament, deplore, bewail; pity, compassionate.*

mis-sus, a, um, *part.* (**mitto**), *sent.*

mīt-esco, escĕre, *no perf., no sup., n. inch.* (**mītis**), *to become mild, gentle.*

Mĭthrĭdātes, is, *m., Mithridates the Great,* king of Pontus, who waged war with the Romans, and, being at last conquered by Pompeius, stabbed himself.

Mĭthrĭdāt-ĭcus, a, um, *adj.* (**Mĭthrĭdātes**), *of* or *belonging to Mithridates; Mithridatic.*

mītis, e, *adj., mild, gentle; ripe, mellow.*

mitto, mittĕre, mīsi, missum, *a., to send, despatch; throw, dis-*

charge; dismiss, release; **vocem mittere**, *to speak.*

mŏdĕrā-tio, ōnis, *f.* (**mŏdĕror**, § **44**, 1, *c*, 2), *a restricting; moderation; regularity; control.*

mŏdĕrā-tus, a, um, *part.* (**mŏdĕro**), *limited, moderate.*

mŏd-ĕror, āri, ātus sum, *dep.* (**mŏdus**), *to put a limit to, set bounds; restrict; regulate, rule, govern.*

mŏd-estus, a, um, *adj.* (**mŏdus**), *modest, sober, discreet.*

mŏd-ĭcus, a, um, *adj.* (**mŏdus**), *of a moderate size, moderate; modest; temperate; small.*

mŏdŏ, *adv., only, merely; at all; just now;* **modo . . . modo,** *now . . . now, at one moment . . . at another;* **non modo . . . sed etiam,** *not only . . . but also;* **modo,** with the subjunctive mood, *if only, provided that.*

mŏdus, i, *m., a measure* or *standard; bounds, limits, end; way manner, method, mode;* **ad modum, in modum,** *with the gen., after the manner of; like;* **modo fluminis,** *like a river;* **hunc in modum,** *after this fashion;* **nullo modo,** *by no means.*

mœnia, ium, *n. pl., defensive walls, ramparts, bulwarks, city walls; fortifications, defences.*

mœreo (**mæreo**), **ēre,** *no perf., no sup., n.* and *a., to be sad; to mourn, grieve, lament; mourn over, bemoan, lament.*

mœror (**mæror**), **ōris,** *m.* (**mœreo**, § **44**, 1, *c*, 2), *a mourning, sadness, grief, lamentation.*

mœs-tus (**mæs**), **a, um,** *adj.* (**mœreo**), *sad, sorrowful.*

mōles, is, *f., a mass, heap; mole, dam, pier; difficulty, labor, trouble.*

mŏlest-ē, *adv.* (**mŏlestus**), *with trouble;* **moleste ferre,** *to be annoyed at.*

mŏlest-ia, æ, *f.* (**mŏlestus**, § **44**, 1, *c*, 2), *trouble, annoyance, vexation, disgust, dislike.*

mŏlesto, āre, āvi, ātum, *a.* (**mŏlestus**), *to trouble, annoy, molest.*

mŏlestus, a, um, *adj., troublesome, irksome, grievous, annoying.*

mōl-ior, īri, ītus sum, *dep.* (**mōles**), *to endeavor, toil, struggle; to undertake, attempt; to throw, hurl; force open; to build, erect; to fortify.*

moll-io, īre, īvi *or* **ii, ītum,** *a.* (**mollis**), *to soften, mitigate; render easy, gentle.*

mol-lis, e, *adj.* (**mŏveo**), *soft, tender, mild, agreeable, easy, weak, feeble; effeminate; timid.*

Mŏlo, ōnis, *m.*, a teacher of rhetoric.

mŏlo, ĕre, ui, ĭtum, *a., to grind, crush, bruise.*

mŏneo, ēre, ui, ĭtum, *a., to remind, admonish, advise, warn; punish; teach, tell, inform.*

mŏn-ĭtio, ōnis, *f.* (**mŏneo**, § **44**, 1, *c*, 2), *an admonishing, admonition, advice, warning.*

mŏn-ĭtus, ūs, *m.* (**mŏneo**, § **44**, 1, *c*, 2), *advice, warning.*

mon-s, montis, *m.* (**mĭneo**, to project), *a mountain.*

monstro, āre, āvi, ātum, *a.* (**monstrum**), *to show, point out.*

mon-strum, i, *n.* (**mŏneo**), *a divine omen, an omen; a monster; a terrible wonder.*

mŏn-ŭmentum, i, *n.* (**mŏneo**), (a thing serving to remind), *a memorial, monument.*

mŏra, æ, *f., a delay; obstacle.*

morbus, i, *m., a sickness, disease, disorder, illness; sorrow, grief, affliction.*

mordeo, mordēre, mŏmordi (**mĕmordi**), **morsum,** *a., to bite, eat, devour; injure, hurt.*

mŏrior, mŏri (**mŏrīri**), **mortuus sum,** *dep.* (*fut. part.*, **mŏrĭtūrus**), *to die, decay.*

mŏror, āri, ātus sum, *dep.* (**mŏra**),

to tarry, stay, delay, linger, loiter, wait; hinder.

mor-s, mortis, *f.* **(mŏrior),** *death.*

mor-tuus, a, um, *part.* **(mŏrior),** *dead.*

mos, mōris, *m., usage, custom, practice;* in *pl., character, conduct;* **ex more,** *according to custom;* **morem gerere alicui,** *to carry out one's will; to obey one.*

mō-tus, ūs, *m.* **(mŏveo,** § **44,** 1, *c,* 2), *a moving; movement; emotion; passion: commotion, tumult, revolt.*

mŏveo, mŏvēre, mōvi, mōtum, *a., to move, set in motion; stir up; cause; take away, remove; influence;* **arma movere,** *to take arms;* **bellum movere,** *to undertake war;* **risum movere,** *to excite laughter.*

mox, *adv., presently, soon, directly: afterwards, then.*

mūcro, ōnis, *m., a sharp edge; a sword; edge, point, extremity, sharpness.*

mulcto, *see* **multo.**

mŭlier, iĕris, *f., a woman, female.*

mult-ĭtūdo, ĭnis, *f.* **(multus,** § **44,** 1, *c,* 2), *a great number, multitude; a crowd.*

multo (mulcto), āre, āvi, ātum, *a.* **(multa,** a fine), *to fine; to punish.*

mult-o, *adv.* **(multus),** *much, far, greatly; by far, by much; long;* **multo post** *or* **ante,** *long after* or *before.*

mult-um, *adv.* **(multus),** *much, greatly, very much.*

multus, a, um, *adj.* (*comp.,* **plūs;** *superlative,* **plūrĭmus),** *much, many.*

mundus, i, *m., the universe; the world, the earth.*

mūnia, ōrum, *n. pl., duties, functions* (of office).

mūnĭfĭcent-ia, æ, *f.* **(mūnĭfĭcus),** *bountifulness, munificence, beneficence.*

mūnī-mentum, i, *n.* **(mūnio),** *fortification, defence, covering.*

mūn-io, īre, īvi *or* **ii, ītum,** *a.* **(mœnia),** *to fortify, build, defend.*

mūnī-tio, ōnis, *f.* **(mūnio,** § **44,** 1, *c,* 2), *a fortification, rampart.*

mūnus, ĕris, *n., an office; gift, reward, present; employment, service;* **munera,** *public shows, entertainments.*

mūræna, æ, *f., the murēna* (a fish of which the ancients were very fond).

mūrus, i, *m., a wall.*

mūs, mūris, *com. gen., a mouse.*

musca, æ, *f., a fly.*

mūtā-tio, ōnis, *f.* **(mūto,** § **44,** 1, *c,* 2), *a changing; change; interchange, exchange.*

Mŭtĭna, æ, *f.,* a city of Cisalpine Gaul (now *Modena*).

Mŭtĭn-ensis, e, *adj.* **(Mŭtĭna),** *of* or *belonging to Mutina.*

mū-to, āre, āvi, ātum, *a. intens.* **(mŏveo),** *to change, alter; exchange.*

mūtus, a, um, *adj., speechless, dumb, mute, silent.*

mūt-uus, a, um, *adj.* **(mūto),** *mutual, reciprocal.*

myrtus, i *and* **ūs,** *f.* and *m., a myrtle-tree, a myrtle.*

N.

Nac-tus, a, um, *part.* **(nanciscor),** *having obtained.*

nam, *conj.* (§ **43,** 3, *d*), *for.*

nam-que, *conj.* (§ **43,** 3, *d*), *for, for indeed, for truly.*

nanc-iscor, nancisci, nactus *or* **nanctus sum,** *dep., to get, obtain, receive; take advantage of; find.*

nans, antis, *part.* of **no.**

narro, āre, āvi, ātum, *a., to tell, relate, narrate, recount.*

nascor, nasci, nātus sum, *dep., to be born; to be descended from;*

be produced; to arise, grow, spring forth.

Nāsīca, æ, *m.* (**nāsus**, a nose), (one having a large nose), a cognomen in the Scipio family; *Publius Scipio Nasica*, slayer of Gracchus.

nāsus, **i**, *m.*, or **nāsum**, **i**, *n.*, *a nose.*

nāt-ālis, **e**, *adj.*, (**nātus**), *of* or *belonging to one's birth, natal;* **natalis dies**, *birth-day.*

nā-tio, **ōnis**, *f.* (**nascor**, § **44**, 1, *c*, 2), *a being born; a race, nation, people.*

nă-to, **āre**, **āvi**, **ātum**, *n.* and *a.* (**no**), *to swim, float; swim in, float upon.*

nā-tū, *m. def.* (used only in *abl. sing.*), (**nascor**), *by birth, in age;* **maximus natu**, *eldest;* **minimus natu**, *youngest.*

nā-tūra, æ, *f.* (**nascor**), *nature; creation; constitution, disposition, character;* **naturā**, *naturally.*

nātūr-ālis, **e**, *adj.* (**nātūra**), *natural.*

nā-tus, **a**, **um**, *part.* (**nascor**), *having been born, born, made; designed, formed, intended.*

nā-tus, **i**, *m.* (**nascor**), *a son.*

nau-frăg-ium, **ii**, *n.* (**navis**; **frango**), *a shipwreck.*

nauta (**nāvĭta**), æ, *m.*, *a sailor, seaman.*

nāv-ālis, **e**, *adj.* (**nāvis**), *naval; pertaining to ships.*

nāv-āle, **is**, *n.* (**nāvis**), *a dockyard, dock; haven, harbor.*

nāv-ĭcŭla, æ, *f. dim.* (**nāvis**, § **44**, 1, *c*, 3), *a small vessel; boat, skiff,*

nāvĭgā-tio, **ōnis**, *f.* (**nāvĭgo**, § **44**, 1, *c*, 2), *a sailing, navigation.*

nāvĭg-ium, **ii**, *n.* (**nāvĭgo**, § **44**, 1, *c*, 2), *a sailing; vessel, ship, boat.*

nāv-ĭgo, **āre**, **āvi**, **ātum**, *n.* and *a.* (**nāvis**), *to sail; swim; sail over, navigate.*

nāvis, **is**, *f.* (*acc.*, **navem** *or* **navim**; *abl.*, **nave** *or* **navi**), *a ship;* **navis longa**, *a ship of war.*

nāvĭta, *see* **nauta**.

nē, *adv.* and *conj.*, 1. *adv.*, *not, no;* **ne . . . quidem**, *not even* (the word or phrase emphasized always between the **ne** and **quidem**); 2. *conj.*, *that not, lest.*

nĕ, *interrog.* and *enclitic particle* (§ **71**, 1), *whether* (in direct questions **ne** is not to be translated, except by laying emphasis upon the word to which it is joined).

nĕbŭla, æ, *f.*, *mist, vapor; a cloud.*

nec, *see* **nĕque**.

nĕcessāri-o, *adv.* (**nĕcessārius**), *necessarily, unavoidably.*

nĕcess-ārius, **a**, **um**, *adj.* (**nĕcesse**), *unavoidable, necessary.* As NOUN, *m.*, *a relative, relation, kinsman.*

nĕ-ces-se, *neut. adj.* (found only in *nom.* and *acc. sing.*), (**ne**; **cēdo**), *unavoidable, inevitable, necessary.*

nĕcess-ĭtas, **ātis**, *f.* (**nĕcesse**, § **44**, 1, *c*, 2), *necessity; constraint, compulsion, force; need.*

nĕcess-ĭtūdo, **ĭnis**, *f.* (**nĕcesse**, § **44**, 1, *c*, 2), *necessity; connection, relationship; intimacy, friendship.*

nec-nĕ, *conj.*, *or not.*

nĕco, **āre**, **āvi**, **ātum**, *a.*, *to kill, slay, put to death.*

necto, **nectĕre**, **nexui** *and* **nexi**, **nexum**, *a.*, *to bind, fetter; imprison.*

nē-dum, *conj.*, *by no means, much less; not to say, much more.*

nĕ-fas, *n. indecl.*, *that which is unlawful, execrable, abominable; wrong, crime; a monster, wretch.*

nĕg-lĭgo, **lĭgĕre**, **lexi**, **lectum**, *a.* (**nec**; **lĕgo**), *to neglect, disregard, despise, disdain.*

nĕgo, **āre**, **āvi**, **ātum**, *n.* and *a.*, *to say no; deny, refuse.*

nĕg-ōtium, ii, *n.* **(nec; ōtium),** *a business, occupation, employment; difficulty, trouble; matter, thing;* **nullo negotio,** *without trouble;* **negotium dare alicui,** *to give the management of an affair to any one.*

nē-mo, ĭnis, *m.* and *f.* **(ne; hŏmo),** *no one, nobody;* **nemo non,** *every body, all;* **non nemo,** *some.*

nempe, *conj., for indeed, certainly, truly, surely, why!*

nĕmus, ŏris, *n., a woodland* (with meadows in it), *a grove.*

neo, nēre, nēvi, nētum, *a., to spin, weave.*

nĕpos, ōtis, *m.* and *f., a grandson, a grand-daughter, a nephew.*

neptis, is, *f., a grand-daughter.*

nēquam, *adj. indecl., worthless, good for nothing, wretched, vile, bad.*

nĕ-que *or* **nec,** *conj., and not;* **neque (nec) . . . neque (nec),** *neither . . . nor.*

nĕ-queo, quīre, quīvi *and* **quii, quĭtum,** *n.* (§ 38, 2, *g*), *to be unable;* **nequeo,** *I cannot.*

ne-quis, qua, quod *or* **quid,** *pron., lest any, that no one.*

Nervii, ōrum, *m.,* a people of Belgic Gaul.

nervus, i, *m., a sinew; string; nerve, courage.*

ne-scio, scīre, scīvi *or* **scii, scītum,** *a., not to know, to be ignorant of.*

nescius, a, um, *adj.* **(nescio),** *unknowing, ignorant, unaware.*

nē-ve (neu), *and not, nor;* **neve . . . neve,** *neither . . . nor.*

nex, nĕcis, *f.* **(nĕco),** *death, murder, slaughter.*

nī, *conj., if not, unless.*

nīdus, i, *m., a nest.*

nĭger, gra, grum, *adj., black, dark, dusky.*

nĭhil (nīl), *n. indecl., nothing, not at all;* **nihil habeo quod,** *I have no reason that;* **non nihil,** *something;* **nihilomĭnus,** *nevertheless.*

nĭhil-dum, *adv., nothing as yet.*

nĭhĭlo, *adv.* (with *comparatives*), *by nothing, no;* **nihilo major,** *no greater.*

nĭhĭlōmĭnus, *adv., see* **nĭhil.**

nīl, *see* **nĭhil.**

Nīlus, i, *m., the Nile;* a river in Egypt, celebrated for its annual overflow.

nimbus, i, *m., a rain-storm, rain-cloud, thunder-cloud, storm, tempest.*

nĭmis, *adv., too much, over much, excessively.*

nĭmium, *adv., too much, too; very much, greatly.*

nĭmius, a, um, *adj., beyond measure, excessive, too much.*

nĭ-si, *conj., if not, unless; except, only.*

nĭteo, ēre, ui, *no sup., n., to shine, glitter, glisten.*

nītor, nīti, nīsus *or* **nixus sum,** *dep., to rest upon, rely upon; to strive, endeavor.*

nix, nĭvis, *f., snow.*

nix-us, a, um, *part.* **(nītor).**

no, nāre, nāvi, *no sup., n., to swim, float.*

nō-bĭlis, e, *adj.* **(nosco),** *that can be known; famous, celebrated; high born.*

nōbĭl-ĭtas, ātis, *f.* **(nōbĭlis,** § 44, 1, *c*, 2), *celebrity, fame, renown; the nobility, nobles.*

nŏcens, entis, *part.* **(nŏceo),** *hurtful, injurious; guilty.*

nŏceo, ēre, ui, ĭtum, *n.* (with *dat.*), *to harm, hurt, injure.*

noctu, *abl.* (used adverbially), *by night.*

noct-ua, æ, *f.* **(nox),** *a night-owl, an owl.*

noct-urnus, a, um, *adj.* **(nox),** *nightly, nocturnal.*

nŏc-uus, a, um, *adj.* **(nŏceo),** *hurtful, injurious.*

nōdus, i, *m., a knot.*

Nōla, æ, *f.,* a city of Campania.

nōlo, nolle, nōlui, *irreg.* **(non; vŏlo),** (§ **37**), *to not wish, be unwilling.*

nō-men, ĭnis, *n.* **(nosco),** (§ **15**), *a name; renown;* **nomen habere,** *to be famous.*

nōmĭnā-tim, *adv.* **(nōmĭno),** *by name, expressly.*

nōmĭno, āre, āvi, ātum, *a.* **(nōmen),** *to name, call by name; nominate.*

nōn, *adv., not, no.*

Nōnæ, ārum, *f.* **(nōnus),** *the Nones;* the fifth day in every month of the year, except March, May, July, and October, in which it was the seventh. So called because it was the *ninth* day before the Ides.

non-dum, *adv., not yet.*

non-nĕ, *interrog. particle* (§ **71**, 1), *not?*

non-nullus, a, um, *adj., some, several.* As NOUN, **nonnulli, ōrum,** *m. pl., persons, several.*

non-nunquam (numquam), *adv., sometimes, occasionally.*

nō-nus, a, um, *adj.* **(nŏvem),** *the ninth.* As NOUN, **nōna, æ,** *f., the ninth hour of the day,* i. e., the third hour before sunset, at which hour business was ended at Rome.

nōs, nostrum *or* **nostri,** *pl.* of **ego,** *we.*

nosco (gnosco), noscĕre, nōvi, nōtum, *a., to become acquainted with; learn;* **nōvi,** *perf.* with *pres.* meaning, *I know;* **noveram,** *I knew.*

nos-ter, tra, trum, *possess. pron.* **(nos),** *our, our own, ours;* in *pl.,* **nostri, ōrum,** *m., our men, our troops.*

nŏta, æ, *f., a mark, note, sign.*

nŏto, āre, āvi, ātum, *a.* **(nŏta),** *to mark, indicate, denote; designate.*

nō-tus, a, um, *part.* **(nosco),** *known.*

nŏvem, *num. indecl. adj., nine.*

Nŏvem-ber, bris, *m.* **(nŏvem),** *November;* the *ninth* month of the old Roman year (which began in March).

Novembris, e, *adj., of November.*

nōvi, *see* **nosco.**

nŏv-ĭtas, ātis, *f.* **(nŏvus,** § **44**, 1, *c,* 2), *newness, novelty.*

nŏvus, a, um, *adj., new; recent, fresh, young, novel, strange;* **novæ res,** *revolution;* the comparative of this *adj.* is wanting, superlative **novissimus,** *latest, last;* **novissimum agmen,** *the rear.*

nox, noctis, *f., night; darkness.*

nūbes, is, *f., a cloud.*

nūbo, nūbĕre, nupsi, nuptum, *n.* **(nūbes),** *to veil one's self, marry* (used only of a woman marrying a man, and governs the dative), see **matrimonium.**

nūdo, āre, āvi, ātum, *a.* **(nūdus),** *to make bare, strip, uncover.*

nūdus, a, um, *adj., naked, bare, unclothed.*

nullus, a, um, *adj.* **(ne; ullus),** (§ **16**, 1, *b*), *not any, none, no.*

num, *interrog. particle* (§ **71**, 1), *whether.*

Nŭma, æ, *m. Numa Pompilius; second* king of Rome.

nū-men, ĭnis, *n.* **(nuo,** to nod), *a nod; will, might; deity, divinity, god.*

nŭmĕro, āre, āvi, ātum, *a.* **(nŭmĕrus),** *to count, reckon, number; esteem, consider.*

nŭmĕrus, i, *m., a number; a multitude.*

Nŭmĭda, æ, *m., a Numidian.*

Nŭmĭdia, æ, *f.,* a country of northern Africa (now Algeria).

Nŭmĭtor, ōris, *m.,* a king of Alba, brother of Amulius and grandfather of Romulus and Remus.

nummus (nūmus), i, *m.* (*gen. pl.,* **nummûm**), *coin, money;* as a Roman silver coin, *a sesterce;* in *pl., money, ready money.*

numquam (**nunquam**), *adv.* (**ne**; **umquam**), *at no time, never;* **non nunquam**, *sometimes.*
num-quid, *interrog. adv., whether (any).* [*time.*
nunc, *adv., now, at present, at this*
nunquam, *see* **numquam**.
nuntio (**nuncio**), **āre, āvi, ātum,** *a.* (**nuntius**), *to announce, declare.*
nuntius (**cius**), **ii**, *m., a messenger; news, tidings.*
nū-per, *adv.* (**nŏvus**), *recently, not long ago, lately; just now.*
nupt-iæ, ārum, *f.* (**nupta**, a married woman), *marriage, wedding, nuptials.*
nŭrus, ūs, *f., a daughter-in-law; a young woman.*
nusquam, *adv.* (**ne**; **usquam**), *nowhere, in no place.*
nūtrio, īre, īvi *and* **ii, ītum**, *a., to suckle, nourish, feed, foster, bring up.*
nūtrix, īcis, *f.* (**nūtrio**, § **44**, 1, *c*, 1), *a nurse.*
nux, nŭcis, *f., a nut.*
nympha, æ, *f., nymph, spouse.*

O.

Ō, *interj., O! oh!*
ob, *prep.* with *acc., on account of, for;* **quam ob rem**, *wherefore, accordingly.*
ŏb-ær-ātus, a, um, *adj.* (**ob**; **æs**), *involved in debt.* As Noun, **obærātus, i**, *m., a debtor.*
ob-dūco, dūcĕre, duxi, ductum, *a., to spread over, cover, surround.*
ŏbēdiens, entis, *part.* (**ŏbēdio**), *obedient, compliant.*
ŏbēdien-ter, *adv.* (**ŏbēdiens**), *obediently, willingly, readily.*
ŏb-ēdio, īre, īvi *or* **ii, ītum**, *n.* (**ob**; **audio**), (with *dat.*), *to give ear to; obey, be subject to.*
ŏb-eo, īre, īvi *or* **ii, ĭtum**, *n.* and *a., to go towards, meet, oppose; perish, die.*
ob-jĭcio, jĭcĕre, jēci, jectum, *a.* (**ob**; **jăcio**), *to cast in the way, oppose, expose, give over to; taunt, reproach.*
ob-jurgo, āre, āvi, ātum, *a., to chide, scold, blame, rebuke, reprove.*
ob-lecto, āre, āvi, ātum, *a.* (**ob**; **lacto**, to entice), *to delight, please, divert, entertain, amuse.*
ob-ligo, āre, āvi, ātum, *a., to bind, tie; put under obligation, oblige.*
oblīquus, a, um, *adj., sidelong, slanting, oblique; indirect; envious.*
oblī-tus, a, um, *part.* (**oblīviscor**), *having forgotten; forgetful.*
oblīv-io, ōnis, *f.* (**oblīviscor**, § **44**, 1, *c*, 2), *a forgetting; forgetfulness; oblivion.*
oblīviscor, oblīvisci, oblītus sum, *dep.* (§ **50**, 4, *a*), *to forget.*
ob-noxius, a, um, *adj.* (**ob**; **noxa**), *frail, weak; liable, subject to; submissive, obedient.*
ob-ruo, ruĕre, rui, rŭtum, *a., to overwhelm, strike down; cover; bury, conceal; oppress; overpower.*
obscūro, āre, āvi, ātum, *a.* (**obscūrus**), *to cover; render dark, obscure.*
obscūrus, a, um, *adj., dark, shady, obscure; unseen; ignoble, low, mean; secret, reserved.*
ob-sĕcro, āre, āvi, ātum, *a.* (**ob**; **săcra**), *to beseech, entreat, implore, conjure, supplicate.*
ob-sĕquor, sĕqui, sĕcūtus sum, *dep., to gratify, humor; submit, yield, comply with; indulge one's self in.*
ob-servo, āre, āvi, ātum, *a., to notice, observe, mark, watch, note; regard, respect, attend to.*
obses, ĭdis, *m.* and *f.* (**obsĭdeo**), *a hostage; security.*
ob-sĭdeo, sĭdēre, sēdi, sessum, *a.* (**ob**; **sĕdeo**), *to besiege, invest, blockade.*

obsĭd-io, **ōnis**, *f.* (**obsĭdeo**, § **44**, 1, *c*, 2), *a siege*, *blockade*.

ob-signo, **āre**, **āvi**, **ātum**, *a.*, *to seal*, *seal up*; *attest*.

ob-sisto, **sistĕre stĭti**, **stĭtum**, *n.*, *to oppose*, *hinder*, *obstruct*.

obstĭnā-tus, **a**, **um**, *part.* (**obstĭno**, to be resolved upon), *firmly resolved*, *resolute*, *determined*.

ob-sto, **stāre**, **stĭti**, **stātum**, *n.*, *to stand against*, *oppose*, *hinder*, *obstruct*, *delay*.

ob-strĕpo, **ĕre**, **ui**, **ĭtum**, *n.*, *to make a noise against*; *to drown with noise*; *to oppose with great clamor*.

ob-stringo, **stringĕre**, **strinxi**, **strictum**, *a.*, *to bind*, *tie*, *fasten*; *pledge*, *oblige*, *put under obligation*.

ob-tempĕro, **āre**, **āvi**, **ātum**, *n.*, *to comply with*, *attend to*, *conform to*, *obey*.

ob-tĭneo, **tĭnēre**, **tĭnui**, **tentum**, *a.* and *n.* (**ob**; **tĕneo**), *to hold*, *possess*, *occupy*, *maintain*, *get*; *last*, *continue*.

ob-tingo, **tingĕre**, **tĭgi**, *no sup.*, *a.* and *n.* (**ob**; **tango**), *to touch*, *strike*; *to fall to one*, *happen*, *occur*.

ob-trecto, **āre**, **āvi**, **ātum**, *n.* and *a.* (**ob**; **tracto**), *to disparage*, *underrate*, *decry*; *injure*, *thwart*.

ob-trunco, **āre**, **āvi**, **ātum**, *a.*, *to cut off*; *kill*, *slay*.

ob-tundo, **tundĕre**, **tŭdi**, **tūsum** *and* **tunsum**, *a.*, *to strike against*, *beat*, *blunt*.

obtū-sus, **a**, **um**, *part.* (**obtundo**), *blunt*, *dull*; *weak*, *powerless*.

ob-vĕnio, **vĕnīre**, **vēni**, **ventum**, *n.*, *to meet*; *to fall to one's lot*; *befall*, *happen*, *occur*.

obviam, *adv.* (**obvius**), (with *dat.*), *in the way*, *against*; **obviam ire alicui**, *to go to meet any one*.

ob-vius, **a**, **um**, *adj.* (**ob**; **via**), *meeting*, *in the way*, *so as to meet*; **obvium ire alicui**, *to meet one*.

ob-volvo, **volvĕre**, **volvi**, **vŏlūtum**, *a.*, *to wrap around*, *muffle up*; *cover*, *disguise*.

occā-sio, **ōnis**, *f.* (**occĭdo**, § **44**, 1, *c*, 2), *an occasion*, *opportunity*, *favorable moment*.

occā-sus, **ūs**, *m.* (**occĭdo**, § **44**, 1, *c*, 2), *a fall*, *downfall*; *perishing*, *end*, *death*; *overthrow*, *ruin*.

oc-cīdo, **cīdĕre**, **cīdi**, **cīsum**, *a.* (**ob**; **cædo**), *to strike down*, *cut down*, *kill*, *slay*.

oc-cĭdo, **cĭdĕre**, **cĭdi**, **cāsum**, *n.* (**ob**; **cădo**), *to fall down*; *to fall*, *perish*, *die*; *to go down*, *set*.

oc-cŭlo, **cŭlĕre**, **cŭlui**, **cultum**, *a.* (**ob**; **cŭlo**), *to cover*, *hide*, *conceal*.

occul-tus, **a**, **um**, *part.* (**occŭlo**), *hidden*, *concealed*, *secret*.

oc-cumbo, **cumbĕre**, **cŭbui**, **cŭbĭtum**, *n.* (**ob**; **cumbo**), *to fall* or *sink into* or *down*: *to perish*, *die*; *to submit*, *yield*, *succumb to*.

oc-cŭpo, **āre**, **āvi**, **ātum**, *a.* (**ob**, **căpio**), *to take*, *seize*, *lay hold of*; *occupy*, *enter*.

oc-curro, **currĕre**; **curri** (rarely **cŭcurri**), **cursum**, *n.*, *to run towards*, *run to meet*; *attack*, *oppose*; *happen*.

Ōceănus, **i**, *m.*, *the ocean*.

ōc-ior, **ius**, *comp. adj.* (*superlative*, **ōcissimus**), *quicker*, *sooner*, *earlier*.

Octāvia, **æ**, *f.*, sister of Augustus.

Octāviānus, **i**, *m.*, a cognomen of the Emperor Augustus.

Octāvius, **ii**, *m.*, name of Augustus.

oct-āvus, **a**, **um**, *adj.* (**octo**), *the eighth*.

octin-genti, **æ**, **a**, *num. adj.* (**octo**; **centum**), *eight hundred*.

octo, *num. adj. indecl.*, *eight*.

Octō-ber, **bris**, *m.* (**octo**), *October* (originally the *eighth* month of the Roman year, reckoning from March). As Adj., **Octobris**, **e**, *of October*.

octō-dĕcim, *num. adj. indecl.* (**octo**; **dĕcem**), *eighteen.*
octō-ginta, *num. adj. indecl.*, *eighty.*
ŏcŭlus, **i**, *m.*, *an eye.*
ōdi, **ōdisse**, *a. defect.* (§ **38**, 1), *to hate, dislike.*
ŏd-ium, **ii**, *n.* (**ōdi**, § **44**, 1, *c*, 2), *hatred, grudge, ill-will.*
ŏdor, **ōris**, *m.*, *a smell, scent, odor; fragrance.*
of-fendo, **fendĕre**, **fendi**, **fensum**, *a.* and *n.* (**ob**; **fendo**, obsolete), *to strike, hit; hurt, injure; offend, displease, vex; blunder, make a mistake.*
offen-sa, **æ**, *f.* (**offendo**), *an offence, affront, wrong; displeasure, disfavor.*
of-fĕro, **offerre**, **obtŭli**, **oblātum**, *a.* (**ob**; **fĕro**), *to present, produce, exhibit, show, offer, bestow.*
of-fĭcio, **fĭcĕre**, **fēci**, **fectum**, *a.* and *n.* (**ob**; **făcio**), *to impede, hinder, obstruct; injure, hurt, oppose.*
offĭci-ōsus, **a**, **um**, *adj.* (**offĭcium**, § **44**, 1, *c*, 3), *full of complaisance, obliging; dutiful.*
of-fĭc-ium, **ii**, *n.* (**ops**; **făcio**), *a kindness, favor, service; duty; employment, business.*
ŏlea, **æ**, *f.*, *an olive; olive-tree.*
ŏleum, **i**, *n.*, *oil, olive-oil.*
ōlim, *adv.*, *formerly, once; hereafter; long ago; some day, ever;* **si olim**, *if ever.*
ŏlīva, **æ**, *f.*, *an olive; olive-tree.*
ōmen, **ĭnis**, *n.*, *a sign, token, omen, portent.*
ŏ-mitto, **mittĕre**, **mīsi**, **missum**, *a.* (**ob**; **mitto**), *to let go, let loose; neglect, disregard; pass over, omit; leave off, cease.*
omn-īno, *adv.* (**omnis**), *altogether, wholly, entirely, utterly; at all; generally.*
omnis, **e**, *adj.*, *every, all.* As NOUN, **omnes**, **ium**, *com. gen.*, *all persons;* **omnes ad unum**, *all to a man.*

ŏnĕro, **āre**, **āvi**, **ātum**, *a.* (**ŏnus**), *to load, overload.*
ŏnus, **ĕris**, *n.*, *a load, burden, weight.*
ŏpĕra, **æ**, *f.* (**ŏpĕror**), *pains, exertion, work, labor;* **operā**, *by all means;* **operam dare alicui**, *to attend to, listen to, obey one;* **operæ pretium est**, *it is worth while;* **meā operā**, *by my aid, through my agency.*
ŏpĕrio, **īre**, **ui**, **ertum**, *a.*, *to cover; hide, conceal.*
ŏper-tus, **a**, **um**, *part.* (**ŏpĕrio**), *hidden, concealed, secret.*
opes, *see* **ops**.
ŏpĭ-fex, **ĭcis**, *com. gen.* (**ŏpus**; **făcio**), *a worker, framer, maker; workman, artisan, mechanic.*
ŏp-īmus, **a**, **um**, *adj.* (**opes**), *rich, abundant, copious, noble, splendid;* **spŏlia ŏpīma**, *spoils of honor*, i.e., the arms taken on the field of battle by a victorious general from the general whom he had conquered.
ŏpīn-io, **ōnis**, *f.* (**ŏpīnor**, § **44**, 1, *c*, 2), *opinion, conjecture, supposition.*
ŏpīnor, **āri**, **ātus sum**, *dep.*, *to think, suppose.*
ŏportet, **ēre**, **uit**, *n. impers.*, *it is necessary, needful, proper; I* (thou, she, &c.) *must* or *ought.*
op-pĕto, **pĕtĕre**, **pĕtīvi** *and* **pĕtii**, **pĕtītum**, *a.*, *to go to meet, encounter;* **mortem oppetere**, *to face death, die.*
oppĭd-ānus, **a**, **um**, *adj.* (**oppĭdum**), *of* or *belonging to a town.* As NOUN, **oppĭdāni**, **ōrum**, *m. pl.*, *the inhabitants of a town, townsmen, townsfolk.*
oppĭdum, **i**, *n.*, *a town* (other than *Rome*, which was called **Ŭrbs**).
op-pōno, **pōnĕre**, **pŏsui**, **pŏsĭtum**, *a.* (**ob**; **pōno**), *to place against, set opposite, oppose, allege.*
opportūn-ĭtas, **ātis**, *f.* (**opportūnus**, § **44**, 1, *c*, 2), *fitness; a*

favorable time, opportunity, advantage.

op-portūnus, a, um, *adj.* **(ob; portus),** *fit, meet, convenient, suitable, seasonable.*

op-prĭmo, prĭmĕre, pressi, pressum, *a.* **(ob; prĕmo),** *to crush, overwhelm, subdue, overcome.*

oppugnā-tio, ōnis, *f.* **(oppugno, § 44,** 1, *c*, 2), *an attack, assault, siege.*

op-pugno, āre, āvi, ātum, *a.* **(ob; pugno),** *to attack, assault, fight against, besiege, invest.*

ops, ŏpis, *f.* (*nominative* and *dat. sing.* wanting), *power, might, strength;* in *pl.*, **opes, um,** *wealth, resources, power.*

optĭmātes, um *or* **ium,** *m. pl.*, *the principal men; the aristocracy, the nobility.*

optĭm-e, *adv.* (*superl.* of **bĕnĕ**), *excellently.*

optĭmus, a, um, *adj.* (*superl.* of **bŏnus**), *best.*

opto, āre, āvi, ātum, *a.*, *to choose; wish for, desire.*

ŏpus, ĕris, *n.*, *work, labor, task.*

ŏpus, *n. indecl.* (§ **54,** 1, *d*), *that which is necessary, need.* As Adj., *needful, necessary.*

ōra, æ, *f.*, *a border, coast, shore, region, district.*

ōrā-tio, ōnis, *f.* **(ōro, § 44,** 1, *c*, 2), *a speaking, speech; oration, harangue; eloquence.*

ōrā-tor, ōris, *m.* **(ōro, § 44,** 1, *c*, 1), *a speaker, orator, ambassador.*

orbis, is, *m.*, *a circle, ring, orbit;* **orbis terrarum,** *the whole world, the globe.*

orbo, āre, āvi, ātum, *a.* **(orbus),** *to deprive, bereave.*

orbus, a, um, *adj.*, *deprived, bereft, destitute.*

ordior, ordīri, orsus sum, *dep.*, *to begin, commence, undertake.*

ordo, ĭnis, *m.* **(ordior),** *an arranging, row, rank, order, line;* **ordine, ex ordine, in ordinem,** *in order, in turn;* **extra ordinem,** *out of order, irregularly;* **ordo equester,** *the equestrian order, the knights.*

Orgĕtŏrix, ĭgis, *m.*, a Helvetian noble.

ŏri-ens, entis, *part.* **(ŏrior),** *rising.* As Noun, *m.*, *the east; the rising sun.*

ŏr-īgo, ĭnis, *f.* **(ŏrior),** *birth, origin, lineage, source.*

ŏrior, ŏri (ŏrīri), ortus sum, *dep.* (§ **35,** 1, *h*), *to arise, originate from, spring, descend from; to begin, commence.*

ŏri-undus, a, um, *adj.* **(ŏrior),** *descended, sprung from.*

ornā-mentum, i, *n.* **(orno, § 44,** 1, *c*, 2), *an ornament, decoration, equipment;* in *pl.*, *jewels.*

ornā-tus, a, um, *part.* **(orno),** *adorned, ornamented.*

orno, āre, āvi, ātum, *a.*, *to adorn, ornament, embellish; praise, commend; honor; fit out, furnish.*

ōro, āre, āvi, ātum, *a.* **(ōs),** *to pray, beg, beseech.*

or-sus, a, um, *part.* **(ordior),** *having begun.*

or-tus, ūs, *m.* **(ŏrior),** *a rising, beginning, origin, birth.*

ōs, ōris, *n.*, *the mouth, the face, countenance; speech.*

ŏs, ossis, *n.*, *a bone.*

os-cŭlum, i, *n. dim.* **(ōs, § 44,** 1, *c*, 3), *a little mouth; a kiss.*

os-tendo, tendĕre, tendi, tensum *or* **tentum,** *a.* **(ob; tendo),** *to show, exhibit, display; declare, say, make known;* **præmia ostendere,** *to offer rewards.*

osten-to, āre, āvi, ātum, *a. intens.* **(ostendo, § 36,** *b*, and **44,** 2, *b*), *to display, boast of, show off; reveal, point out.*

osten-tus, ūs, *m.* **(ostendo, § 44,** 1, *c*, 2), *a showing, display.*

ōsus, a, um, *part.* **(ōdi),** *hating, hatred.*

ōtiōs-e, *adv.* **(ōtiōsus),** *at ease, calmly, quietly; gently, gradually; fearlessly.*

ōti-ōsus, a, um, *adj.* (**ōtium,** § **44,** 1, *c*, 3), *at leisure, unoccupied; quiet; indolent.*

ōtium, ii, *n., leisure, freedom from business; ease, inactivity, idle life; rest, repose, quiet.*

ŏvis, is, *f., a sheep.*

ŏvo, āre, āvi, ātum, *n., to exult, rejoice, triumph in an ovation.*

ōvum, i, *n., an egg.*

P.

P., an abbreviation of *Publius.*

pābŭlor, āri, ātus sum, *dep.* (**pābŭlum**), *to seek for food; to forage.*

pā-bŭlum, i, *n.* (**pasco**), *food, nourishment; fodder.*

pācā-tus, a, um, *part.* (**pāco**), *pacified, calm, quiet, tranquil.*

păciscor, păcisci, pactus sum, *dep., to make a bargain, agree, stipulate.*

pāco, āre, āvi, ātum, *a.* (**pax**), *to make peaceful; to quiet, still, appease.*

pac-tio, ōnis, *f.* (**păciscor,** § **44,** 1, *c*, 2), *an agreement, covenant, contract, bargain.*

pac-tum, i, *n.* (**păciscor**), *an agreement, covenant, contract; manner, way;* **quo pacto,** *in what manner?*

pædăgōgus, i, *m., boy's attendant* (a slave who took children to and from school and had charge of them at home), *a preceptor, tutor.*

pæne, *adv., nearly, almost.*

pāg-ānus, a, um, *adj.* (**pāgus**), *rustic.* As Noun, **pāgānus, i,** *m., a countryman, peasant.*

pāgus, i, *m., a canton, village; country-district.*

pălam, *adv., openly, publicly;* as *prep.* with *abl., before, in the presence of.*

Pălātium, ii, *n.,* one of the seven hills of Rome. The emperor Augustus had his residence on the Palatium; hence it came to mean *a royal abode, palace.*

palleo, ēre, ui, *no sup., n., to be pale; be sick for a thing; eagerly desire.*

pall-or, ōris, *m.* (**palleo,** § **44,** 1, *c*, 2), *paleness, pallor; alarm, terror.*

palma, æ, *f., the palm, hand.*

pălūdāmentum, i, *n., a military cloak, soldier's cloak, general's cloak.*

pā-lus, i, *m., a stake, prop, pale.*

pălus, ūdis, *f., a swamp, marsh, bog.*

pando, pandĕre, pandi, pansum *and* **passum,** *a., to spread out, extend, throw open;* **passis crinibus,** *with dishevelled hair.*

pango, pangĕre, panxi (pēgi, pĕpĭgi), panctum (pactum), *a., to fasten, fix; determine, settle; stipulate, contract.*

pānis, is, *m., bread, loaf.*

pār, păris, *adj.* (*gen. pl.,* **părium**), *equal, equal to, a match for; suitable, fit.*

pār, păris, *n., a pair.*

pără-bĭlis, e, *adj.* (**păro**), *procurable, easy to get.*

pără-tus, a, um, *part.* (**păro**), *prepared, ready, equipped, furnished.*

parco, parcĕre, pĕperci *or* **parsi, parcĭtum** *or* **parsum,** *n.* with *dat.* (**parcus**), *to spare, refrain from, forbear, leave off, cease.*

parcus, a, um, *adj., sparing, frugal, thrifty.*

păr-ens, entis, *m.* and *f.* (*gen. pl.,* **parentum** *and* **parentium**), (**părio**), *a parent; father, mother.*

pāreo, ēre, ui, ĭtum, *n., to appear, obey, comply with.*

părio, părĕre, pĕpĕri, părĭtum *and* **partum,** *a., to bring forth, bear, lay, produce, beget, accomplish.*

păr-ĭter, *adv.* (**pār**), *equally, in like manner, as well.*

păro, āre, āvi, ātum, *a.*, *to get ready, prepare, furnish, provide, get, obtain.*

pars, partis, *f.*, *a part, piece, portion, share; party, quarter;* **ex omni parte,** *in all respects;* **nullā ex parte,** *in no respect;* **a partibus alicujus stare,** *to stand on one's side, belong to one's party.*

Parthi, ōrum, *m. pl.*, *the Parthians;* a Scythian people, famed in ancient times as roving warriors and skillful archers.

part-im, *adv.* (**partior**), *partly, in part.*

part-ior, īri, ītus sum, *dep.* (**pars**), *to part, share, divide, distribute.*

partus, ūs, *m.* (**păria**, § **44**, 1, *c*, 2), *a bearing, bringing forth, birth; offspring.*

păr-um, *adv.* (akin to **parvus**), *too little, not enough* (**părum, mīnus, mīnĭme**).

parvŭ-lus, a, um, *adj. dim.* (**parvus**, § **44**, 1, *c*, 3), *very small, petty, slight; young.* As NOUN, **parvŭlus, i,** *m.*, *a little boy;* **parvŭla, æ,** *f.*, *a little girl.*

parvus, a, um, *adj.* (*comp.* **mĭnor,** *superl.* **mĭnĭmus**), *small, little.*

pasco, pascĕre, pāvi, pastum, *a.* and *n.*, *to nourish, maintain, feed; pasture, graze.*

pascor, pasci, pastus sum, *dep.*, *to feed* or *browse upon.*

passer, ĕris, *m.*, *a sparrow.*

pas-sim, *adv.* (**pando**), *here and there, hither and thither, in all directions; promiscuously.*

pas-sus, a, um, *part.* (**pătior**), *having suffered, endured.*

pas-sus, ūs, *m.* (**pando**), *a step, pace; foot-step, track; pace* (as measure of length, consisting of *five* Roman feet); **mille passuum,** *one mile.*

pas-tor, ōris, *m.* (**pasco**, § **44**, 1, *c*, 1), *a feeder, keeper, herdsman, shepherd.*

păteo, ēre, ui, *no sup.*, *to be open; to stretch out, extend; be manifest, be free.*

păter, tris, *m.*, *a father.*

păter-fāmĭlias, patris-fāmĭlias, *m.*, *a father of a family, master of a household.*

păter-nus, a, um, *adj.* (**păter**), *of* or *belonging to a father, paternal, fatherly, hereditary.*

păti-ens, entis, *part.* (**pătior**), *suffering, allowing, bearing, patient; firm, unyielding;* **patiens oneris,** *able to bear a burden.*

pătien-ter, *adv.* (**pătiens**), *patiently.*

pătient-ia, æ, *f.* (**pătiens**, § **44**, 1, *c*, 2), *patience, forbearance, indulgence, lenity.*

pătior, păti, passus sum, *dep.*, *to bear, support, endure, suffer, allow.*

pătr-ia, æ, *f.* (**păter**), *fatherland, native country, native place.*

pătr-īcius, a, um, *adj.*, (**păter**), *patrician, noble.*

pătr-īmōnium, ii, *n.* (**păter**), *an estate inherited from a father; patrimony, inheritance; fortune, property.*

pătr-ius, a, um, *adj.* (**păter**), *of* or *belonging to one's father, paternal.*

pătrōcĭn-ium, ii, *n.* (**pătrōcĭnor**, § **44**, 1, *c*, 2), *protection, defence, patronage.*

pătrō-cĭnor, āri, ātus sum, *dep.* (**pătrōnus**), *to protect, defend, support, patronize.*

pătr-ōnus, i, *m.* (**păter**), *a protector, patron; defender, advocate; pleader.*

pătr-uus, i, *m.* (**păter**), *a father's brother, an uncle on the father's side.*

pauca, ōrum, *n. pl.*, *a few words.*

pauci, æ, a, *adj. pl.*, *few, little.*

paulo, *adv.* (**paulus**), *by a little, a little, somewhat.*

paulus (**paullus**), **a, um,** *adj.*, *little, small.*

paullātim (**paulātim**), *adv.* (**paulus**), *by degrees, gradually.*

pauper, ĕris, *adj., poor, needy, scanty, slender* (*comp.* **pauperior,** *superl.* **pauperrimus**).

pauper-tas, ātis, *f.* (**pauper,** § **44,** 1, *c*, 2), *poverty, need, want.*

păveo, păvēre, pāvi, *no sup., n.* and *a., to tremble with fear; be terrified; to fear, dread.*

păv-ĭdus, a, um, *adj.* (**păveo**), *trembling, quaking, fearful, timid; anxious, disturbed.*

pāvo, ōnis, (**pāvus, i**), *m., a peacock.*

păv-or, ōris, *m.* (**păveo,** § **44,** 1, *c*, 2), *a trembling; anxiety, fear, dread.*

pax, pācis, *f., peace; grace, favor;* **pace tua,** *with your permission.*

peccā-tum, i, *n.* (**pecco**), *a fault, error, sin.*

pecco, āre, āvi, ātum, *n., to transgress, sin, offend.*

pecto, pectĕre, pexi, pexum *and* **pectĭtum,** *a., to comb, card.*

pectus, ŏris, *n., the breast; heart, feelings; courage.*

pĕcū-nia, æ, *f.* (**pĕcus, ŭdis**), *property, riches, wealth.*

pĕcus, ŏris, *n., a herd, flock; cattle.*

pĕcus, ŭdis, *f., a beast, a sheep; an animal;* in *pl., cattle.*

pĕd-es, ĭtis, *m.* (**pes; eo**), (one that goes on foot), *a foot-soldier; infantry.*

pĕd-ester, tris, tre, *adj.* (**pes**), *on foot, pedestrian; by land, land.*

pējor, us, *adj.* (*comp.* of **mălus**), *worse.*

pellis, is, *f., a skin, hide; a garment* (made of skin).

pello, pellĕre, pĕpŭli, pulsum, *a., to drive* or *thrust out; expel, set aside; rout, put to flight; hurl, impel; move, affect.*

pendeo, pendēre, pĕpendi, *no sup., n., to hang, be suspended; overhang; float, rest upon.*

pendo, pendĕre, pĕpendi, pensum, *a., to weigh, weigh out; pay, pay out; consider, estimate; value, esteem.*

pĕnes, *prep.* with *acc., with, in the power of.*

pĕnĭtus, *adv., deeply, inwardly; thoroughly, utterly, wholly.*

penna, æ, *f., a feather, wing; an arrow.*

pēnūria, æ, *f., want, need.*

per, *prep.* with *acc., through, during, by, by means of, on account of, over, across.*

pĕr-ăgo, ăgĕre, ēgi, actum, *a., to finish, accomplish, carry through, complete.*

pĕr-ăgro, āre, āvi, ātum (**per; ăger**), *to wander about; traverse; travel through.*

per-cello, cellĕre, cŭli, culsum, *a., to strike, beat down, overthrow; discourage; ruin, destroy.*

per-cĭpio, cĭpĕre, cēpi, ceptum, *a.* (**per; căpio**), *to seize, occupy; obtain, receive; perceive, observe, learn.*

percunctā-tio (**contātio**), **ōnis,** *f.* (**percunctor,** § **44,** 1, *c*, 2), *an inquiring of; an inquiry.*

per-cunctor (**contor**), **āri, ātus sum,** *dep., to ask particularly of; to inquire, ask, interrogate; investigate.*

per-curro, currĕre, cŭcurri *or* **curri, cursum,** *a., to run through, pass through, traverse; scan briefly.*

percus-sio, ōnis, *f.* (**percŭtio,** § **44,** 1, *c*, 2), *a beating, striking.*

percus-sor, ōris, *m.* (**percŭtio,** § **44,** 1, *c*, 1), *a striker; murderer, slayer.*

per-cŭtio, cŭtĕre, cussi, cussum, *a.* (**per; quătio**), *to strike, pierce through; slay, kill; beat;* **fœdus percutere,** *to conclude a treaty.*

perd-ĭtus, a, um, *part.* (**perdo**), *destroyed, ruined, desperate, corrupt, abandoned.*

perdo, perdĕre, perdĭdi, perdĭtum, *a., to destroy, lose, ruin; squander, waste.*
per-dūco, dūcĕre, duxi, ductum, *a., to lead through, bring, conduct; prolong, lengthen out, induce; draw out, extend.*
per-eo, īre, ii (īvi), ĭtum, *n. irr., to perish, be ruined, be lost, die; be wasted, spent.*
per-fĕro, ferre, tŭli, lātum, *a. irr., to carry through, convey; accomplish; suffer, endure.*
per-fĭcio, fĭcĕre, fēci, fectum, *a.* (per; făcio), *to make, make up, form; finish, complete; accomplish, carry out; effect, cause.*
perfĭd-ia, æ, *f.* (perfĭdus, § **44**, 1, *c*, 2), *faithlessness, dishonesty, treachery, falsehood.*
per-fĭdus, a, um, *adj.* (per; fĭdes), *faithless, false, dishonest, treacherous.*
per-fŏdio, fŏdĕre, fōdi, fossum, *a., to dig through; pierce, stab, transfix.*
per-fŏro, āre, āvi, ātum, *a., to bore through, pierce, perforate.*
per-fringo, fringĕre, frēgi, fractum, *a.* (per; frango), *to break* or *dash in pieces; to shatter; violate, infringe.*
per-fruor, frui, fructus sum, *dep., to enjoy fully; fulfil, perform.*
per-fŭgio, fŭgĕre, fūgi, fŭgĭtum, *n., to flee; desert; fly* (for refuge).
per-go, pergĕre, perrexi, perrectum, *a.* and *n.* (per; rĕgo), *to commence, undertake; go on, proceed.*
pĕr-hĭbeo, hĭbēre, hĭbui, hĭbĭtum, *a.* (per; hăbeo), *to hold out, present, afford; ascribe, attribute; consider, regard.*
pĕrīcl-ĭtor, āri, ātus sum, *dep.* (pĕrīclum), *to try, prove, test; risk, venture; to be in danger.*
pĕrīcŭl-ōsus, a, um, *adj.* (pĕrīcŭlum, § **44**, 1, *c*, 3), *full of danger; dangerous, hazardous, perilous.*
pĕrī-cŭlum (-clum), i, *n.* (pĕrior, obsolete), *a trial, attempt; risk, hazard, danger.*
pĕr-ĭmo, ĭmĕre, ēmi, emptum, *a.* (per; ĕmo), *to take away; annihilate, destroy; kill, slay.*
pĕr-inde, *adv., quite, as; just as; in like manner, equally.*
pĕrī-tus, a, um, *adj.* (pĕrior, obsolete), *experienced, practised, skillful, expert.*
per-magnus, a, um, *adj., very great, very large.*
per-mitto, mittĕre, mīsi, missum, *a., to let through; let go; let loose; permit; cast, hurl; intrust.*
per-mŏveo, mŏvēre, mōvi, mōtum, *a., to move deeply, stir greatly; rouse up, excite; persuade.*
per-multus, a, um, *adj., very much, [very many.*
pernĭc-ies, iēi, *f.* (pernĕco), *destruction, ruin, overthrow.*
pernĭci-ōsus, a, um, *adj.* (pernĭcies, § **44**, 1, *c*, 3), *very destructive, ruinous, pernicious.*
per-paucus, a, um, *adj., very little, very few.*
perpĕtu-o, *adv.* (perpĕtuus), *constantly, perpetually.*
perpĕtu-um, *adv.* (perpĕtuus), *forever, perpetually.*
perpĕtuus, a, um, *adj., continuing, continuous, unbroken; constant, lasting.*
per-rumpo, rumpĕre, rūpi, ruptum, *a., to break through, force one's way through; overcome; break up.*
per-sæpe, *adv., very often, very frequently.*
per-sĕquor, sĕqui, sĕcūtus sum, *dep., to follow after, chase, pursue, proceed against, attack, hunt after, obtain.*
persĕvēro, āre, āvi, ātum, *n.* and *a.* (persĕvērus), *to persist, persevere* (in any thing).
per-sĕvērus, a, um, *adj., very strict.*

Persia, æ, *f.*, *Persia.*

Persis, ĭdis, *f.*, *Persia.*

per-sisto, sistĕre, stĭti, stĭtum, *n.*, *to continue steadfastly; to persist.*

per-solvo, solvĕre, solvi, sŏlūtum, *a.*, *to pay, give, render; solve, explain.*

per-spĭcio, spĭcĕre, spexi, spectum, *a.* (**per; spĕcio**), *to see through; view, examine, inspect.*

per-sto, stāre, stĭti, stātum, *n.*, *to stand firmly, hold out, persevere, persist.*

per-stringo, stringĕre, strinxi, strictum, *a.*, *to bind, tie, fasten; seize; wound slightly; censure, reprove.*

per-suadeo, suadēre, suasi, suasum, *a.*, *to convince, persuade, induce, prevail upon.*

per-terreo, terrēre, terrui, terrĭtum, *a.*, *to frighten* or *terrify thoroughly.*

pertĭnāc-ia, æ, *f.* (**pertĭnax**, § **44**, 1, *c*, 2), *perseverance, constancy, obstinacy.*

pertĭnāc-ĭter, *adv.* (**pertĭnax**), *firmly, stubbornly.*

per-tĭnax, ācis, *adj.* (**per; tĕnax**), *firm, constant, steadfast, persevering; stubborn, obstinate.*

per-tĭneo, tĭnēre, tĭnui, tentum, *n.* (**per; tĕneo**), *to stretch, reach, extend; belong to, relate, have reference to.*

per-trăho, trăhĕre, traxi, tractum, *a.*, *to drag, entice, allure.*

per-turbo, āre, āvi, ātum, *a.*, *to confuse utterly; to disturb, discompose, embarrass, confound.*

per-ūtĭlis, e, *adj.*, *very useful.*

per-vĕnio, vĕnīre, vēni, ventum, *n.*, *to arrive at, reach, attain to.*

per-vŏlo, āre, āvi, ātum, *n.*, *to fly through.*

pēs, pĕdis, *m.*, *a foot;* **pedibus**, *on foot.*

pessĭmus, a, um, *adj.* (*superl.* of **mălus**), *worst.*

pestis, is, *f.*, *a plague, pest, pestilence; destruction, ruin.*

pĕt-ītio, ōnis, *f.* (**pĕto**, § **44**, 1, *c*, 2), *a request, petition, candidateship.*

pĕto, pĕtĕre, pĕtīvi *and* **pĕtii, pĕtītum**, *a.*, *to attack, assail; seek; beg, ask, entreat* (§ **52**, 2, *c*, remark).

phălanx, angis, *f.*, *a band of soldiers, phalanx.*

phălĕræ, ārum, *f. pl.*, *trappings for horses, military ornaments, decorations.*

Pharnăces, is, *m.*, king of Pontus.

Pharsāl-ĭcus, a, um, *adj.* (**Pharsālus**), *of Pharsalus, Pharsalian.*

Pharsālus, i, *f.*, a city of Thessaly, where Cæsar defeated Pompey, B. C. 48.

Phĭlippi, ōrum, *m. pl.*, a city of Macedonia, on the borders of Thrace, celebrated for the battle in which Octavianus and Antony defeated Brutus and Cassius, B. C. 42.

phĭlŏsŏphia, æ, *f.*, *philosophy.*

phĭlŏsŏphor, āri, ātus sum, *dep.* (**phĭlŏsŏphus**), *to philosophize.*

phĭlŏsŏphus, i, *m.*, *a philosopher.*

pi-ĕtas, ātis, *f.* (**pius**, § **44**, 1, *c*, 2), *piety; duty, affection, love, gratitude.*

pĭger, gra, grum, *adj.*, *slow, lazy, dull, sluggish, indolent.*

pĭget, pĭgēre, pĭguit *and* **pĭgĭtum est**, *impers.* (§ **50**, 4, *c*, 2), *it vexes, annoys, troubles;* **piget me alicujus rei**, *I dislike, loathe a thing.*

pignus, ŏris *and* **ĕris**, *n.*, *a pledge, security, token, proof.*

pĭla, æ, *f.*, *a ball, playing-ball.*

pīlum, i, *n.*, *a javelin* (a heavy javelin of the Roman infantry, which they hurled at the enemy at the beginning of an action, and then used their swords).

pingo, pingĕre, pinxi, pictum, *a.*, *to paint, embroider; stain; adorn, decorate.*

pinguis, e, *adj.*, *fat, rich, fertile; dull, stupid.*

pīnus, ūs *and* i, *f.*, *a pine, pine-tree; a fir, fir-tree.*

pīrāta, æ, *m.*, *a sea-robber, pirate.*

pīrātĭcus, a, um, *adj.*, *of pirates, piratical.*

pisc-īna, æ, *f.* (**piscis**), *a fish-pond; a pond.*

piscis, is, *m.*, *a fish.*

piscor, āri, ātus sum, *dep. n.* (**piscis**), *to fish.*

pius, a, um, *adj.* (*comp.* **magis pius**, *superl.* **piissimus**), *pious, devout; tender, kind; patriotic.*

pix, pĭcis, *f.*, *pitch.*

plăcā-bĭlis, e, *adj.* (**plāco**), *easily pacified; mild, gentle.*

plăceo, ēre, ui, ĭtum, *n.*, *to please, satisfy;* **placet**, *impers.*, *it seems good, it is thought best, resolved on.*

plăc-ĭdus, a, um, *adj.* (**plăceo**), *gentle, quiet, calm, mild, peaceful.*

plāco, āre, āvi, ātum, *a.*, *to quiet, soothe, calm, appease; reconcile; pacify.*

plāga, æ, *f.*, *a blow, stroke; thrust, wound; injury.*

plăga, æ, *f.*, *a hunting net, snare; trap.*

plān-e, *adv.* (**plānus**), *simply, clearly, distinctly; wholly, entirely, completely, quite.*

plān-ĭties, iēi, *f.* (**plānus**), *level ground, plain.*

plānus, a, um, *adj.*, *even, level, flat, plain.*

plēbs, plēbis, *f.*, *the common people.*

plecto, plectĕre, plexi *and* plexui, plexum, *a.*, *to plait, braid, interweave; twist.*

plecto, plectĕre, *no perf.*, *no sup.*, *a.*, *to strike, punish* (with blows).

plē-nus, a, um, *adj.* (**pleo**, to fill), *full, filled; complete.*

plērus-que, plērăque, plērumque, *adj.*, *the larger* or *greater part of;* generally found in *pl.*, *very many, the most;* **plerumque**, as *adv.*, *for the most part, very often, frequently.*

plĭco, āre, āvi (ui), ātum *and* ĭtum, *a.*, *to fold, fold up; to coil.*

plumb-eus, a, um, *adj.* (**plumbum**, § **44**, 1, *c*, 3), *of lead, made of lead, leaden.*

plumbum, i, *n.*, *lead.*

pluo, pluĕre, plui *or* plūvi, *no sup.*, *n.*, *to rain;* **pluit**, *it rains* (§ **39**, *a*).

plū-rĭmus, a, um, *adj.* (*superl.* of **multus**), *very much; most;* as *adv.*, **plurimum**, *mostly, chiefly, exceedingly, very much.*

plūs, plūris, *adj.* (*comp.* of **multus**), (§ **16**, 3, *b*), *more.* As NOUN in *pl.*, **plūres**, ium, *m.*, *several.*

plūs, *adv.*, *more; too much.*

plŭ-via, æ, *f.* (**pluo**), *rain.*

pōcŭlum, i, *n.*, *a cup, goblet, bowl.*

pŏdăgra, æ, *f.*, *the gout* (in the feet).

poēma, ătis, *n.* (*dat.* and *abl. pl.*, **poēmătĭbus** *or* **poēmătis**), *a poem.*

pœna, æ, *f.*, *punishment, penalty;* **pœnas dare**, *to pay the penalty, be punished;* **pœnas sumere**, *to inflict punishment.*

pœn-ĭtet, pœnĭtēre, pœnĭtuit, *no sup.*, *impers.* (§ **50**, 4, *c*, 2), *it repents;* with *acc.* of person and *gen.* of the thing, or *infinitive* in place of the thing; **pœnitet me facti**, *I repent of the action;* **pœnitet me fecisse**, *I repent having done it.*

poēta, æ, *m.*, *a poet.*

pollens, entis, *part.* (**polleo**), *strong, mighty, able, powerful.*

pol-leo, ēre, ui, *no sup.*, *n.* (**pŏtis; văleo**), *to be strong; to be able; to prevail.*

poll-ex, ĭcis, *m.* (**polleo**), *the thumb; the great toe.*

pol-lĭceor, lĭcēri, lĭcĭtus sum, *dep.* (**pŏtis; lĭceor**), *to promise.*

Pollio, ōnis, *m.*, a Roman name.

pol-luo, uĕre, ui, ūtum, *a.* **(pŏtis; luo),** *to soil, defile, pollute; dishonor, violate.*

pompa, æ, *f., a procession; suite, retinue; display, parade, pomp.*

Pompēi-ānus, a, um, *adj.* **(Pompēius),** *of Pompey, Pompeian.*

Pompēius, ii, *m., Cneius Pompeius Magnus;* a Roman general and rival of Cæsar; defeated at Pharsālus, B. C. 48.

pōmum, i, *n., fruit.*

pond-us, ĕris, *n.* **(pendo),** *a weight, mass, load, burden; influence, authority.*

pōne, *adv.* and *prep.* with *acc., after, behind, back.*

pōno, pōnĕre, pŏsui, pŏsĭtum, *a., to put, place, set, lay;* **castra ponere,** *to pitch camp.*

pons, pontis, *m., a bridge.*

pontĭfex, fĭcis, *m., a high-priest, pontiff.*

Pontus, i, *m., the Black Sea* **(Pontus Euxīnus),** also a region about the Black Sea.

Popedius, ii, *m.,* a Latin chief.

pŏpŭl-āris, e, *adj.* **(pŏpŭlus),** *of* or *belonging to the people; popular; native.*

pŏpŭlor, āri, ātus sum, *dep.* **(pŏpŭlus),** *to lay waste, ravage, devastate, plunder, pillage.*

pŏpŭlus, i, *m., a people; a multitude, host, crowd.*

Porcia, æ, *f.,* wife of Brutus.

por-rĭgo, rĭgĕre, rexi, rectum, *a.* **(por = pro; rĕgo),** *to put forth, reach out, extend; offer, present.*

porro, *adv., onward, henceforth, again, moreover.*

porta, æ, *f., a gate, door.*

por-tendo, dĕre, di, tum, *a.* **(por = pro; tendo),** *to foretell, predict, portend.*

porten-tum, i, *n.* **(portendo),** *a sign, token, omen, portent; monster.*

port-ĭcus, ūs, *f.* **(porta),** *a piazza, colonnade, portico.*

porto, āre, āvi, ātum, *a., to carry, convey, bring.* [*port.*

portus, ūs, *m., a harbor, haven,*

posco, poscĕre, pŏposci, *no sup., a., to beg, demand, request, desire, ask, require.*

Pŏsīdōnius, ii, *m.,* a celebrated philosopher of Rhodes.

pŏs-ĭtus, a, um, *part.* **(pōno),** *situated, placed, lying, standing.*

posses-sio, ōnis, *f.* **(possĭdeo,** § **44,** 1, *c,* 2), *a possessing, possession; property.*

pos-sĭdeo, sĭdēre, sēdi, sessum, *a.* **(pŏtis; sĕdeo),** *to possess, have, hold.*

pos-sīdo, sīdĕre, sēdi, sessum, **(pŏtis; sīdo),** *to take possession of, occupy.*

pos-sum, posse, pŏtui, *n. irr.* **(pŏtis; sum),** *to have the power, can, be able;* **plurimum posse,** *to have very great influence.*

post, *adv.* and *prep.* with *acc., behind, back, after, beneath.*

post-eā, *adv., afterwards, hereafter.*

posteā-quam, *conj., after that, when.*

postĕrior, ius, *adj.* (*comp.* of **postĕrus**), *after, later; inferior; latter.*

post-ĕrus, a, um, *adj.* **(post),** *coming after, following, next, ensuing, future.* As Noun, **postĕri, ōrum,** *m. pl., descendants, posterity.*

post-hăbeo, hăbēre, hăbui, hăbĭtum, *a., to place after; esteem less, postpone, neglect.*

post-hac, *adv., after this, hereafter, henceforth.*

post-pōno, pōnĕre, pŏsui, pŏsĭtum, *a., to put after, postpone; to esteem less; neglect.*

post-quam, *conj., after that, after, as soon as, when.*

postrēm-o, *adv.* **(postrēmus),** *at last, lastly, finally.*

postr-ī-die, *adv.* **(postĕrus, dies),** *on the day after, on the next day.*

postŭlā-tum, **i**, *n.* (**postŭlo**), *a demand, request.*
postŭlo, **āre**, **āvi**, **ātum**, *a.* (§ **52**, 2, *c*, remark), *to ask, demand, require, request, desire.*
pŏtens, **entis**, *part.* (**possum**), *able, mighty, powerful, strong.*
pŏtent-ātus, **ūs**, *m.* (**pŏtens**), *rule, dominion, command.*
pŏten-ter, *adv.* (**pŏtens**), *strongly, mightily, powerfully, effectually.*
pŏtent-ia, **æ**, *f.* (**pŏtens**, § **44**, 1, *c*, 2), *might, force, power; efficacy; authority.*
pŏtes-tas, **ātis**, *f.* (**pŏtens**, § **44**, 1, *c*, 2), *ability, power; dominion, rule, empire; opportunity;* **potestatem facere pugnandi**, *to give* (one) *the opportunity of fighting.*
pōt-io, **ōnis**, *f.* (**pōto**, § **44**, 1, *c*, 2), *a drinking; a drink, draught.*
pŏt-ior, **īri**, **ītus sum**, *dep.* (**pŏtis**), *to take possession of, get, obtain; be master of, hold, possess* (§ **54**, 6, *d*).
pŏtis, **e**, *adj.*, *powerful; able; possible.*
pŏti-us, *adv.* (**pŏtis**), *rather, preferably, more.*
pōto, **pōtāre**, **pōtāvi**, **pōtātum** *or* **pōtum**, *a.* and *n.*, *to drink, tipple.*
præ, *adv.* and *prep.* with *abl.*, *before; in comparison with; because of; in front of;* in composition, *very, very much, too much.*
præ-beo, **bēre**, **bui**, **bĭtum**, *a.* (contracted from **præhĭbeo**; **præ**; **hăbeo**), *to reach out, proffer; give, furnish, afford; exhibit.*
præ-căveo, **căvēre**, **cāvi**, **cautum**, *a.* and *n.*, *to guard against beforehand, to seek to prevent; to take care beforehand; be on one's guard, beware.*
præ-cēdo, **cēdĕre**, **cessi**, **cessum**, *a.* and *n.*, *to go before, precede; surpass, outstrip, outdo, excel.*
præ-ceps, **cĭpĭtis**, *adj.* (**præ**; **căput**), *headforemost, headlong.*
præcep-tum, **i**, *n.* (**præcĭpio**), *a maxim, rule, precept; order, command.*
præ-cīdo, **cīdĕre**, **cīdi**, **cīsum**, *a.* (**præ**; **cædo**), *to cut off, take away; break off; refuse, deny.*
præ-cĭpio, **cĭpĕre**, **cēpi**, **ceptum**, *a.* (**præ**; **căpio**), *to take in advance, anticipate; direct, order, enjoin.*
præcĭpĭto, **āre**, **āvi**, **ātum**, *a.* and *n.* (**præceps**), *to throw headlong; precipitate; to rush down, fall to ruin.*
præcĭpu-e, *adv.* (**præcĭpuus**), *especially, chiefly; particularly, principally.*
præcĭp-uus, **a**, **um**, *adj.* (**præcĭpio**), *particular, peculiar, especial; principal, chief, foremost; distinguished.*
præclār-e, *adv.* (**præclārus**), *very clearly, excellently, admirably, very well.*
præ-clārus, **a**, **um**, *adj.*, *very clear; glorious, excellent, noble, renowned, distinguished, famous, celebrated.*
præco, **ōnis**, *m.*, *a crier, herald.*
præda, **æ**, *f.*, *booty, spoil, plunder; prey, game.*
præ-dĭco, **āre**, **āvi**, **ātum**, *a.*, *to publish, proclaim, state, declare; praise, commend, laud.*
præ-dīco, **dīcĕre**, **dixi**, **dictum**, *a.*, *to foretell, predict; admonish, warn, command.*
præ-dĭtus, **a**, **um**, *adj.* (**præ**; **do**), *gifted, endowed, provided with, possessed of.*
prædo, **ōnis**, *m.* (**prædor**), *one that plunders, a plunderer, robber.*
prædor, **āri**, **ātus sum**, *dep.* (**præda**), *to plunder, rob, pillage, despoil.*
præ-eo, **īre**, **īvi** *and* **ii**, **ĭtum**, *n.*, *to go before, precede.*
præfec-tus, **i**, *m.* (**præfĭcio**), *a governor, chief, commander, prefect.*

præ-fĕro, ferre, tŭli, lātum, *a. irr., to carry before; to prefer, choose rather; display, exhibit.*

præ-fĭcio, fĭcĕre, fēci, fectum, *a.* (præ; făcio), *to place over, set over; put in command of; appoint.*

præ-mitto, mittĕre, mīsi, missum, *a., to send before, despatch in advance.*

præ-mium, ii, *n.* (præ; ĕmo), *profit, advantage; reward, recompense.*

præpără-tio, ōnis, *f.* (præpăro, § 44, 1, *c*, 2), *a preparing, preparation.*

præ-păro, āre, āvi, ātum, *a., to get ready beforehand; prepare.*

præ-pōno, pōnĕre, pŏsui, pŏsĭtum, *a., to set over, place in charge of, appoint.*

præ-rĭpio, rĭpĕre, rĭpui, reptum, *a.* (præ; răpio), *to snatch away, forestall, anticipate.*

præ-scrībo, scrībĕre, scripsi, scriptum, *a., to appoint, direct, command, prescribe.*

præscrip-tio, ōnis, *f.* (præscrībo, § 44, 1, *c*, 2), *an inscription, title; precept, rule, law.*

præscrip-tum, i, *n.* (præscrībo), *a precept, order, rule.* [*present.*

præ-sens, entis, *adj.* (præ; sum),

præsent-ia, æ, *f.* (præsens, § 44, 1, *c*, 2), *presence; readiness;* **in præsentiā,** *at present, now.*

præ-sertim, *adv.* (præ; sĕro), *especially.*

præ-sĭdeo, sĭdēre, sēdi, sessum, *n.* and *a.* (præ; sĕdeo), *to sit before; guard, protect; direct, command.*

præsĭd-ium, ii, *n.* (præsĭdeo, § 44, 1, *c*, 2), *defence, aid, protection, help; a garrison, guard.*

præstans, antis, *part.* (præsto), *pre-eminent, excellent, distinguished, extraordinary.*

præstant-ia, æ, *f.* (præstans, § 44, 1, *c*, 2), *pre-eminence, superiority, excellence.*

præsto, *adv., at hand, ready, present, here.*

præ-sto, stāre, stĭti, stĭtum, *n.* and *a., to be superior; surpass, exceed; show, exhibit, manifest; fulfill, pay;* **præstat,** *it is better.*

præ-sum, esse, fui, *n. irr., to be over, be in command of, have charge of, govern, superintend;* **summæ rerum præesse,** *to have the supreme command.*

præ-sūmo, sūmĕre, sumpsi *and* **sumsi, sumptum** *and* **sumtum,** *a., to take before, take in advance; conceive beforehand, suppose, presume.*

præter, *adv.* and *prep.* with *acc., except, over, beyond, past, against, besides.*

prætĕr-eā, *adv., besides, moreover, beyond; henceforth, hereafter.*

prætĕr-eo, īre, īvi *and* **ii, ĭtum,** *n.* and *a., to go past; pass by, pass over, neglect, forget.*

prætĕrĭ-tus, a, um, *part.* (prætĕreo), *past, gone by, departed.* As Noun, **prætĕrĭta, ōrum,** *n. pl., the past.*

præ-texo, texĕre, texui, textum, *a., to weave before; to fringe; to furnish, provide; conceal, disguise.*

prætex-ta, æ, *f.* (prætexo), the "toga prætexta," *a mantle* (with purple border, worn by magistrates and children).

prætext-ātus, a, um, *adj.* (prætexta), *wearing the mantle;* (hence), as Noun, *m., a boy.*

præ-tor, ōris, *m.* (præ; eo), *prætor* (officer of justice), *chief, commander.*

prætōr-ium, ii, *n.* (prætor), *a general's tent.*

prætōr-ius, a, um, *adj.* (prætor), *of the prætor.*

præ-tūra, æ, *f., the office of a prætor, the prætorship.*

præ-vălĭdus, a, um, *adj., very strong.*

præ-vĕnio, vĕnīre, vēni, ventum, *n.* and *a.*, *to go before, precede; anticipate, prevent; surpass, excel.*
præ-vĭdeo, vĭdēre, vīdi, vīsum, *a.*, *to see beforehand, foresee.*
prandeo, prandēre, prandi, pransum, *n.* and *a.*, *to breakfast; to take as breakfast.*
prand-ium, ii, *n.* (**prandeo,** § **44,** 1, *c*, 2), *breakfast.*
prātum, i, *n.*, *a meadow.*
prāvus, a, um, *adj.*, *crooked; perverse, wrong, vicious, bad.*
prĕci, prĕcem, prĕce, *in pl.*, **preces, um,** *f.*, *prayer, entreaty, request.*
prĕcor, āri, ātus sum, *dep.*, *to pray, beg, entreat.*
prĕhendo, dĕre, di sum, *a.*, *to seize, catch, grasp, snatch.*
prĕmo, prĕmĕre, pressi, pressum, *a.*, *to press, press hard on, oppress; pursue, annoy.*
prendo, *see* **prehendo.**
prĕti-ōsus, a, um, *adj.* (**prĕtium,** § **44,** 1, *c*, 3), *valuable, precious; costly, expensive.*
prĕtium, ii, *n.*, *money, wealth; worth, value, price.*
prex, *see* **prĕci.**
prīdem, *adv.*, *a long time ago, long since, formerly.*
prī-die, *adv.* (**præ; dies**), *on the day before* (§ **50,** 4, *e*, remark).
prīm-o, *adv.* (**prīmus**), *at first, in the beginning, first, firstly.*
prīm-um, *adv.*, *first, in the first place, for the first time;* **quam primum,** *as soon as possible.*
prī-mus, a, um, *adj.*, *superlative* (**præ, prior, prīmus,** § **17,** 3), *first, foremost.*
prin-ceps, cĭpis, *adj.* (**prīmus; căpio**), *first.* As NOUN, *com. gen.*, *chief ruler, emperor;* **principes,** *m. pl.*, *chiefs, princes.*
princĭp-ātus, ūs, *m.* (**princeps**), *the chief place, supremacy, dominion;* **principatum tenere,** *to be at the head of.*
prior, prius, *adj. comp.* (**præ, prior, prīmus**), *former, previous, prior, first* (of two).
pristĭnus, a, um, *adj.*, *former, early, primitive, pristine.*
prius . . . quam, *conj.*, *before that, before, sooner;* **priusquam non,** *not until.*
prius, *comp. adv.*, *before, sooner.*
prīv-ātim, *adv.* (**prīvus**), *in private, privately; apart, separately.*
prīvā-tus, a, um, *part.* (**prīvo**), *private.*
prīvo, āre, āvi, ātum, *a.* (**prīvus**), *to deprive of, bereave.*
prīvus, a, um, *adj.*, *single; each, every.*
prō, *prep.* with *abl.*, *before, in front of, instead of, for, in consideration of, for the good of, in behalf of; according to, as.*
prŏb-e, *adv.* (**prŏbus**), *rightly, well, properly, fitly.*
prŏb-ĭtas, ātis, *f.* (**prŏbus,** § **44,** 1, *c*, 2), *goodness, worth, uprightness, honesty, probity.*
prōbrum, i, *n.*, *disgrace, shame, reproach; a shameful act, disgraceful deed.*
prŏ-bus, a, um, *adj.* (**prō**), *good, excellent, superior, upright, virtuous.*
prŏc-ax, ācis, *adj.* (**prŏco,** to demand), *bold, shameless, forward, pert.*
prō-cēdo, cēdĕre, cessi, cessum, *n.*, *to go forward, advance, proceed, turn out, succeed.*
prŏcella, æ, *f.*, *a hurricane, tempest, storm.*
prōcērus, a, um, *adj.*, *high, tall.*
Procillus, i, *m.*, a Roman name.
prōcinctus, a, um, *part.* (**prōcingo**), *prepared for battle, ready for action, in fighting order.*
prō-cingo, cingĕre, *no perf.*, *no sup.*, *a.*, *to gird up, prepare, equip.*
prō-clāmo, āre, āvi, ātum, *n.* and *a.*, *to call* or *cry out.*

prō-consul, ŭlis, *m.*, *a pro-consul;* one who at the close of his consulship in Rome was governor of a province, or military commander under a governor.

prŏcul, *adv.*, *afar, remote, at a distance, from afar; far, distant, remote.*

prō-cumbo, cumbĕre, cŭbui, cŭbĭtum, *n.*, *to lean* or *bend forwards; fall forward; sink; fall down.*

prō-curro, currĕre, cŭcurri *and* **curri, cursum,** *n.*, *to run forth, rush forward: go on, advance.*

prō-d-eo, īre, ii, ĭtum, *n. irr.* (**pro; eo**), *to go forth; advance, proceed; appear; project.*

prōdĭgus, a, um, *adj.* (**prōdĭgo,** to waste), *wasteful, lavish, prodigal.*

prō-do, dĕre, dĭdi, dĭtum, *a.*, *to put forth, make known, disclose, announce; give over, betray, abandon;* **memoriā proditur,** *it is handed down by memory.*

prō-dūco, dūcĕre, duxi, ductum, *a.*, *to lead forth; bring forth, produce; prolong, protract.*

prœlium, ii, *n.*, *a battle, combat, strife, contest.*

prŏfec-tio, ōnis, *f.* (**prŏfĭciscor,** § **44**, 1, *c*, 2), *a going away, setting out, departure.*

prŏ-fect-o, *adv.* (**pro; factum**), *actually, indeed, really, truly, certainly.*

prŏfec-tus, a, um, *part.* (**prŏfĭciscor**), *having set out, gone.*

prō-fĕro, ferre, tŭli, lātum, *a. irr.*, *to carry* or *bring forward; to thrust out; bring forth; bring to light, discover; reveal; pronounce, utter.*

prō-fĭcio, fĭcĕre, fēci, fectum, *n.* and *a.*, *to advance; be useful, help; effect, accomplish.*

prŏ-fĭc-iscor, fĭcisci, fectus sum, *dep. inch.* (**pro; făcio,** § **36**, *a*, and **44**, 2, *b*), *to set out, go, march, travel, depart.*

prŏ-fĭteor, fĭtēri, fessus sum, *dep.* (**pro; făteor**), *to declare publicly, confess, acknowledge, profess, promise.*

prō-flīgo, āre, āvi, ātum, *a.*, *to strike to the ground; cast down, overcome, conquer.*

prŏ-fŭgio, fŭgĕre, fūgi, fŭgĭtum, *a.* and *n.*, *to flee, fly from; run away, escape; flee for succor.*

prŏfŭgus, i, *m.* (**prŏfŭgio**), *a fugitive, exile.*

prŏ-fundo, fundĕre, fūdi, fūsum, *a.*, *to pour forth, shed; lavish, squander, dissipate;* **profundere se,** *to rush forth.*

prō-grĕdior, grĕdi, gressus sum, *dep.* (**pro; grădior**), *to go forth; go forward, go on, advance, proceed.*

prŏ-hĭbeo, ēre, ui, ĭtum, *a.* (**pro; hăbeo**), *to hold back, restrain, hinder, check, prevent, avert; forbid, prohibit; preserve, defend.*

prŏ-inde, *adv.*, *hence, therefore, just so.*

prō-jĭcio, jĭcĕre, jēci, jectum, *a.* (**pro; jăcio**), *to throw forwards; throw down, fling away, renounce, reject.*

prō-lābor, lābi, lapsus sum, *dep.*, *to slip forward, fall down; sink, decline.*

prōles, is, *f.*, *offspring, posterity.*

prōmĭnens, entis, *part.* (**prōmĭneo**), *projecting, overhanging.*

prō-mĭneo, mĭnēre, mĭnui, *no sup.*, *n.*, *to project, overhang; reach out, extend.*

prō-mitto, mittĕre, mīsi, missum, *a.*, *to send forth; promise, assure.*

prō-mŏveo, mŏvēre, mōvi, mōtum, *a.*, *to move forward, push on, advance, promote.*

prōnus, a, um, *adj.*, *turned, bent, inclined; leaning forward, stooping; favorable to, easy.*

prŏpe, *adv.* and *prep.* with *acc.* (**prŏpius, proxĭme**), *near, nigh; near by; nearly; about.*

prŏpĕro, āre, āvi, ātum, *a.* and *n.* (**prŏpĕrus**), *to hasten, quicken; prepare, make with haste; to make haste, be quick.*

prŏpĕrus, a, um, *adj., quick, speedy, hastening.*

prŏpinquo, āre, āvi, ātum, *a.* and *n.* (**prŏpinquus**), *to hasten, accelerate; come nigh, approach.*

prŏp-inquus, a, um, *adj.* (**prŏpe; hinc**), *near, neighboring; akin; similar, like.* As Noun, *m., a relative, kinsman.*

prō-pōno, pōnĕre, pŏsui, pŏsĭtum, *a., to place* or *lay before; make public, display, propose, dispose, set forth; design, determine;* **mihi propositum est,** *I have determined.*

prōpŏs-ĭtum, i, *n.* (**prōpōno**), *a statement; purpose, resolution, plan, design.*

proprius, a, um, *adj., one's own, special, peculiar.*

prop-ter, *prep.* with *acc.* (**prŏpe**), *near, close to; on account of, because.*

proptĕr-eā, *adv., therefore, for that reason, on that account;* **propterea quod,** *because that.*

prōpul-so, āre, āvi, ātum, *a. intens.* (**prōpello,** § **36,** *b,* and **44,** 2, *b*), *to drive back, keep* or *ward off, repel, repulse; avert.*

prō-rĭpio, rĭpĕre, rĭpui, reptum, *a.* (**pro; răpio**), *to drag forth, hurry away;* **proripere se,** *to leave hastily.*

prō-rumpo, rumpĕre, rūpi, ruptum, *a., to burst* or *break forth.*

prō-scindo, scindĕre, scĭdi, scissum, *a., to tear up, rend, cleave; assail; to revile, defame.*

prō-scrībo, scrībĕre, scripsi, scriptum, *a., to publish, outlaw, proscribe.*

prōscrip-tio, ōnis, *f.* (**prōscrībo,** § **44,** 1, *c,* 2), *outlawry, proscription, confiscation.*

prō-sĕquor, sĕqui, sĕcūtus sum, *dep., to accompany, attend upon, follow; pursue; attack, assail.*

prō-sĭlio, sĭlīre, sĭlui, sĭlīvi *or* **sĭlii,** *no sup., n.* (**pro; sălio**), *to leap forth; spring up, spring forth.*

prospec-tus, ūs, *m.* (**prospĭcio**), *a look-out, prospect; sight, vision.*

prospĕr-e, *adv.* (**prospĕrus**), *favorably, fortunately, luckily.*

prospĕr-ĭtas, ātis, *f.* (**prospĕrus,** § **44,** 1, *c,* 2), *good fortune, success, prosperity.*

prospĕro, āre, āvi, ātum, *a.* and *n.* (**prospĕrus**), *to make fortunate* or *happy, prosper; to give prosperity* (with *dat.*).

pro-spĕrus, a, um, *adj.* (**pro; spes**), *favorable, fortunate, prosperous.*

prō-spĭcio, spĭcĕre, spexi, spectum, *n.* and *a.* (**pro; spĕcio**), *to look out, look forth, foresee, espy, watch; to provide for* any thing (with *acc.*).

prō-sterno, sternĕre, strāvi, strātum, *a., to throw down, overthrow, prostrate.*

prō-sum, prōdesse, prōfui, *n. irr.* (§ **29,** *b*), *to be useful; to do good; to benefit, profit.*

prō-tendo, tendĕre, tendi, tensum *and* **tentum,** *a., to stretch forth* or *out, extend.*

prō-tĕro, tĕrĕre, trīvi, trītum, *a., to crush; overthrow, beat; destroy; abuse.*

prō-tĭnus (tĕnus), *adv.* (**pro; tĕnus**), *straightforward, forthwith, immediately.*

prō-vĕho, vĕhĕre, vexi, vectum, *a., to bear forward, conduct, convey;* in *pass.,* **provĕhi,** *to push forward, advance.*

prō-vĭdeo, vĭdēre, vīdi, vīsum, *n.* and *a., to foresee, provide for, take care; provide.*

prōvĭd-us, a, um, *adj.* (**prōvĭdeo**), *cautious, prudent.*

prōvincia, æ, *f., a province;* a territory out of Italy, acquired by the Romans and brought under Roman government.

prō-vŏco, **āre**, **āvi**, **ātum**, *a.* and *n.*, *to call forth, call out, challenge, summon; exasperate, rouse;* **provocare ad populum**, *to appeal to the people.*

proxĭm-e, *adv.* (**proxĭmus**), *nearest, very near, next* (**prŏpe**, **prŏpius**, **proxĭme**).

proxĭm-o, *adv.* (**proxĭmus**), *quite recently, very lately.*

proxĭmus, **a**, **um**, *adj.*, *the nearest, next;* **in proximo**, *close by, near at hand.*

prūdens, **entis** (contracted from **prōvĭdens**), *foreseeing; knowing, skilled, versed; wise, discreet; prudent; sensible.*

prūdent-ia, **æ**, *f.* (**prūdens**, § **44**, 1, *c*, 2), *foresight, sagacity, good sense, prudence, judgment.*

psittăcus, **i**, *m.*, *a parrot.*

Psylli, **ōrum**, *m. pl.*, a people of Africa.

Ptŏlĕmæus, **i**, *m.*, *Ptolemy;* king of Egypt.

pūbes, **ĕris**, *adj.*, *adult, grown up, of ripe age.* As NOUN, **pūbĕres**, **um**, *m. pl.*, *adults, men.*

pūbes, **is**, *f.*, *youth, young persons.*

publĭc-e, *adv.* (**publĭcus**), *on account of the state, at public cost; in the name of the state, publicly.*

publĭcus, **a**, **um**, *adj.* (**pŏpŭlus**), *belonging to the people* or *state, public, common.*

Publius Crassus, **i**, *m.*, a Roman name.

pŭd-or, **ōris**, *m.* (**pŭdeo**, to be ashamed, § **44**, 1, *c*, 2), *shame, sense of honor, modesty, decency, propriety.*

puel-la, **æ**, *f. dim.* (**puer**, § **44**, 1, *c*, 3), *a girl, maiden.*

puell-ŭlus, **i**, *m. dim.* (**puellus**, § **44**, 1, *c*, 3), *a little boy.*

puel-lus, **i**, *m. dim.* (**puer**, § **44**, 1, *c*, 3), *a little boy.*

puer, **ĕri**, *m.*, *a boy, child, lad* (until 17).

puĕr-īlis, **e**, *adj.* (**puer**), *boyish, childish, youthful.*

pūgio, **ōnis**, *f.*, *a dagger, dirk, poniard.*

pugna, **æ**, *f.*, *a battle, contest, dispute.*

pugn-ax, **ācis**, *adj.* (**pugno**, § **44**, 1, *c*, 3), *fond of fighting, warlike, combative; quarrelsome.*

pugno, **āre**, **āvi**, **ātum**, *n.* (**pugna**), *to fight, give battle, engage, contend.*

pulcher, **chra**, **chrum**, *adj.*, *beautiful, fair, handsome.*

pulchr-e, *adv.* (**pulcher**), *beautifully, finely, nobly.*

pul-sus, **a**, **um**, *part.* (**pello**), *having been driven, routed.*

pulvis, **ĕris**, *m.*, *dust.*

punc-tus, **ūs**, *m.* (**pungo**), *a prick, sting.*

pungo, **pungĕre**, **pŭpŭgi**, **punctum**, *a.*, *to prick, sting; trouble, disturb, annoy.*

Pūn-ĭcus (**Pœnĭcus**), **a**, **um**, *adj.* (**Pœni**, the Carthaginians), *Punic, Carthaginian.*

pūnio, **īre**, **īvi** *and* **ii**, **ītum**, *a.* (**pœna**), *to punish; avenge, revenge.*

pur-go, **āre**, **āvi**, **ātum**, *a.* (**pūrus**), *to make pure, clean, cleanse; clear, excuse, exculpate.*

purpŭra, **æ**, *f.*, *purple, a purple garment.*

purpŭr-eus, **a**, **um**, *adj.* (**purpŭra**, § **44**, 1, *c*, 3), *purple-colored, purple.*

pūrus, **a**, **um**, *adj.*, *clear, pure, clean.*

pŭter (**pŭtris**), **tris**, **tre**, *adj.*, *rotten, decaying.*

pŭto, **āre**, **āvi**, **ātum**, *a.*, *to think, consider, reckon, believe.*

Pȳrēnæi, **ōrum**, *m. pl.*, *the Pyrenees.*

Q.

Q. *or* **Qu.**, an abbreviation for *Quintus.*

quadrāg-ēsĭmus, **a**, **um**, *adj.* (**quadrāginta**), *fortieth.*

quadr-ā-ginta, *num. adj. indecl.* (**quātuor**), *forty.*

quadr-īmus, a, um, *adj.* (**quātuor**), *of four years, four years old.*

quadr-in-genti, æ, a, *num. adj.* (**quātuor; centum**), *four hundred.*

quæro, quærĕre, quæsīvi *or* **quæsii, quæsītum,** *a., to seek, ask; search, examine, inquire about, demand; look into; aim at, strive for;* **quæritur,** *the question is.*

quæso, ĕre, īvi *or* **ii,** *no sup., a., to seek, beg, pray.*

quæs-tio, ōnis, *f.* (**quæro**, § **44**, 1, *c*, 2), *a seeking, an inquiry, question.*

quæs-tor, ōris, *m.* (**quæro**, § **44**, 1, *c*, 1), *a quæstor* (treasurer or quartermaster).

quæs-tūra, æ, *f.* (**quæro**, § **44**, 1, *c*, 2), *the office of quæstor, the quæstorship.*

quālis, e, *pronominal adj., of what sort, what like; of such a kind, such as;* **tālis . . . quālis,** *such . . . as.*

quam, *adv.* (§ **17**, 5, *b*), *how, how much, as, than.*

quam-ob-rem, *adv., for what reason, wherefore, why.*

quam-quam, *conj., though, although; however, yet.*

quam-vis, *conj., however, although, albeit.*

quantus, a, um, *adj., how great; as great, as, such;* in *abl.*, **quanto** (as *adv.*), *by how much, by as much as;* **quanto magis,** *how much more.*

quā-propter, *adv., for what, why, wherefore.*

quā-re, *adv.* (**quis; res**), *from what cause, on what account, wherefore, why.*

quart-āna, æ, *f.* (**quartus**), *the quartan ague* (recurring every *fourth* day).

quar-tus, a, um, *num. adj.* (**quātuor**), *the fourth.*

quăsī, *adv., as if, just as, as it were.*

quăter, *num. adv., four times.*

quattuor, *see* **quātuor.**

quātuor, *num. adj. indecl., four.*

quattuor-dĕcim (**quātuor**), *num. adj.* (**quātuor; dĕcem**), *fourteen.*

-que, *enclitic conj., and, also.*

quĕm-ad-mŏdum, *adv., after what manner; how; as, just as.*

quercus, ūs, *f., an oak, oak-tree.*

quĕr-ēla, æ, *f.* (**quĕror**), *a complaining, a complaint.*

quĕror, quĕri, questus sum, *dep., to complain of, lament, bewail.*

ques-tus, ūs, *m.* (**quĕror**, § **44**, **1**, *c*, 2), *a complaint.*

qui, quæ, quod, *relative pron., who, which, what;* **idem qui,** *the same as.*

quia, *conj., because.*

quī-cumque, quæ-cumque, quod-cumque, *indef. relative pron.* (§ **21**, 2, *a*), *whoever, whatever, whosoever, whatsoever.*

quid, *see* **quis.**

quī-dam, quæ-dam, quod-dam, *indefinite pron., a certain one, somebody, something;* **quidam homines,** *some persons.*

quĭdem, *adv., indeed, at least;* **ne . . . quidem,** *not even* (the word or phrase that **ne . . . quidem** modifies always comes between **ne** and **quidem**).

quies, ētis, *f., rest, repose, quiet, peace.*

quie-sco, quiescĕre, quiēvi, quiētum, *n. inch.* (**quies**, § **36**, *a, and* **44**, 2, *b*), *to rest, repose, keep quiet, lie still.*

quiēt-us, a, um, *part.* (**quiesco**), *quiet, calm, tranquil, still.*

quī-lĭbet, quæ-lĭbet, quod-lĭbet, *indefinite pron., any one you please, any one.*

quīn, *conj.* (**qui; ne**), *that not, but that; why not; from* (after verbs of hindering); **quin etiam,** *moreover, nay even.*

quin-dĕcim, *num. adj. indecl.* (quinque; dĕcem), *fifteen.*
quin-genti, æ, a, *num. adj.* (quinque; centum), *five hundred.*
quin-ginti, *see* **quin-genti.**
quī-ni, æ, a, *num. distributive adj.* (quinque), *five each, by fives.*
quinqu-ā-ginta, *num. adj. indecl.* (quinque), *fifty.*
quinque, *num. adj. indecl., five.*
quinqu-ies, *adv.* (quinque), *five times.*
quinqu-iens, *see* **quinqu-ies.**
quin-tus, a, um, *num. adj.* (quinque), *the fifth.*
Quintus, i, *m.*, see **Cătŭlus.**
quippe, *adv. and conj., surely, certainly, indeed; for indeed, inasmuch as, since.*
quis, quæ, quid, *interrogative pron., who? what? which?* **si quis**, *if any one;* **ne quis**, *lest any one, that no one;* **quid** (used adverbially), *how? why? wherefore?*
quis-nam, quæ-nam, quid-nam, *interrogative pron., who, pray? which, pray? what, pray?*
quis-quam, quæ-quam, quicquam (quid-quam), *indefinite pron., any.* As Noun, *any one.*
quis-que, quæ-que, quod-que (quic-que, quid-que), *indefinite pron., each, every; each person, every one; whoever.*
quis-quis, quod-quod *or* **quicquid** *or* **quidquid**, *indef. pron., whatever, whatsoever.* As Noun, *whoever, whosoever; every one, each one.*
quī-vis, quævis, quodvis (quidvis), *indefinite pron., who* or *what you please, any whatever.*
quō, *adv.* and *conj., whither, to what place; wherefore, why; in order that* (§ **64**, 1, *a*).
quo-ad, *adv., how long; as long as, until.*
quod, *conj., that; because;* **quod** [**si**, *but if.*
quō-mĭnus, *conj.* (§ **65**, 1, *a*), *that not, from.*
quō-mŏdŏ, *adv., in what manner, how.*
quondam, *adv., formerly, once; sometimes, some day, ever.*
quŏn-iam, *adv.* (quum; jam), *since now, since, seeing that, because, whereas.*
quŏque, *conj., also, too* (placed after the word to be emphasized).
quorsum, *adv., whither; to what purpose; to what end; for what.*
quŏt, *indecl. num. adj. pl., how many; as many;* **quot . . . tot**, *as many . . . so many;* **quotannis**, *every year, yearly.*
quŏtīd-iānus, a, um, *adj.* (quŏtīdie), *every day, daily.*
quŏt-ī-die (cŏt), *adv.* (quŏt; dies), *daily, every day.*
quŏtus, a, um, *adj., one of how many, what in number;* **quŏta hōra**, *what o'clock.*
quum (cum), *conj., when, while, since, although, as;* **quum prīmum**, *as soon as;* **quum . . . tum**, *both . . . and.*

R.

răb-ĭdus, a, um, *adj.* (**răbo**, to rave), *raving, furious, savage, fierce, mad.*
rādix, īcis, *f., a root; foot* (of a hill).
rādo, rādĕre, rāsi, rāsum, *a., to scrape, shave.*
rāmus, i, *m., a branch, bow, twig.*
rāna, æ, *f., a frog.*
răp-ax, ācis, *adj.* (**răpio**, § **44**, 1, *c*, 3), *grasping, greedy, rapacious.*
răp-ĭdus, a, um, *adj.* (**răpio**), *swift, quick, rapid; violent, hasty.*
răp-īna, æ, *f.* (**răpio**), *robbery; plunder, booty.*
răpio, ĕre, ui, tum, *a., to snatch away, seize; carry off, hurry off.*
rap-tor, ōris, *m.* (**răpio**, § **44**, 1, *c*, 1), *a robber, plunderer.*

rār-o, *adv.* (**rārus**), *seldom*, *rarely*.
rārus, a, um, *adj.*, *seldom*, *rare*, *scarce*, *sparse*; in *pl.*, *few*.
ră-tio, ōnis, *f.* (**reor**, § **44**, 1, *c*, 2), *a reckoning*, *reason*, *cause*, *account*; *manner*, *plan*; *estimate*; *ground*, *consideration*.
rătis, is, *f.*, *a float*, *raft*, *vessel* (made of logs fastened together).
ră-tus, a, um, *part.* (**reor**), *having supposed*, *reckoned*, *calculated*; *established*, *settled*, *valid*.
rĕ-bello, āre, āvi, ātum, *n.*, *to wage war again*; *revolt*, *rebel*; *renew hostilities*.
rĕcens, entis, *adj.*, *fresh*, *young*, *new*, *recent*.
rĕces-sus, ūs, *m.* (**rĕcēdo**, § **44**, 1, *c*, 2), *a going back*, *receding*, *retreat*; *nook*, *recess*, *corner*, *bay*.
rĕ-cĭdo, cĭdĕre, cĭdi, cāsum, *n.*, *to fall back*, *spring back*; *recoil*; *sink down*.
rĕ-cĭpio, cĭpĕre, cēpi, ceptum, *a.* (**re**; **căpio**), *to receive back*; *take back*; *receive*, *undertake*; *recover*; **recipere se domum**, *to return home*.
rĕ-concĭlio, āre, āvi, ātum, *a.*, *to reunite*, *reconcile*.
rĕ-cordor, āri, ātus sum, *dep.* (§ **50**, 4, *a*), (**re**; **cor**), *to call to mind*, *remember*, *recollect*.
rĕ-creo, āre, āvi, ātum, *a.*, *to make anew*; *to remake*, *reproduce*, *restore*, *renew*; *revive*, *refresh*, *recruit*.
rec-tor, ōris, *m.* (**rĕgo**, § **44**, 1, *c*, 1), *a guider*, *leader*, *director*, *ruler*, *master*.
rec-tus, a, um, *part.* (**rĕgo**), *straight*, *upright*, *correct*; *just*, *virtuous*.
rĕ-cŭp-ĕro, āre, āvi, ātum, *a.* (**re**; **căpio**), *to regain*, *recover*.
rĕ-cūso, āre, āvi, ātum, *a.* (**re**; **causa**), *to decline*, *reject*, *refuse*.
red-do, dĕre, dĭdi, dĭtum, *a.*, *to give back*, *return*, *restore*, *render*; with two *accs.*, *to make*, *cause to be*. [*return*.
rĕd-eo, īre, ii, ĭtum, *n.*, *to go back*,
rĕd-ĭgo, ĭgĕre, ēgi, actum, *a.* (**red**; **ăgo**), *to drive back*, *restore*, *bring back*; *convert*; *reduce*, *compel*; **redigere in potestatem**, *to reduce to subjection*.
rĕd-ĭmo, ĭmĕre, ēmi, emptum, *a.* (**red**; **ĕmo**), *to buy back*, *redeem*, *ransom*; *buy up*; *contract for*, *farm*.
rĕd-intĕgro, āre, āvi, ātum, *a.*, *to restore*, *renew*.
rĕdĭt-io, ōnis, *f.* (**rĕdeo**, § **44**, 1, *c*, 2), *a returning*, *return*.
rĕdĭ-tus, ūs, *m.* (**rĕdeo**, § **44**, 1, *c*, 2), *a returning*, *return*.
rĕ-dūco, dūcĕre, duxi, ductum, *a.*, *to lead back*, *bring back*; **reducere in gratiam**, *to restore to favor*.
rĕ-fĕro, ferre, tŭli, lātum, *a. irr.*, *to carry back*, *bring back*; *restore*: *raise*; *transfer*, *reproduce*; *regard*; **gratiam referre**, *to show gratitude*, *repay a favor*; **referre pedem**, *to retreat*; **referre se**, *to return*.
rē-fert, ferre, tŭlit, *n. impers.* (§ **50**, 4, *d*), (**res**; **fĕro**), *it concerns*; *is of importance*.
rĕ-fĭcio, fĭcĕre, fēci, fectum, *a.* (**re**; **făcio**), *to make again*; *remake*, *restore*, *renew*, *rebuild*; *refresh*.
rĕ-fīgo, fīgĕre, fixi, fixum, *a.*, *to unfix*, *unfasten*, *unloose*; *annul*, *abolish*; *take away*, *remove*.
rĕ-flecto, flectĕre, flexi, flexum, *a.* and *n.*, *to bend back*, *turn back*, *avert*; *give way*, *yield*.
rĕ-formīdo, āre, *no perf.*, **ātum**, *a.*, *to fear greatly*, *dread*, *stand in awe of*; *shun*, *avoid*.
rĕ-fŏveo, fŏvēre, fōvi, fōtum, *a.*, *to warm again*, *cherish again*; *refresh*, *restore*, *revive*.
rĕ-fringo, fringĕre, frēgi, fractum, *a.* (**re**; **frango**), *to break down*, *break open*, *tear in pieces*.
rĕ-fŭgio, fŭgĕre, fūgi, fŭgĭtum, *n.* and *a.*, *to flee back*, *escape*, *avoid*, *shun*.

rēg-ālis, **e**, *adj.* (**rex**), *kingly, royal, regal.*
rēg-īna, **æ**, *f.* (**rĕgo**), *a queen.*
rĕg-io, **ōnis**, *f.* (**rĕgo**, § **44**, 1, *c*, 2), *a territory, district, region.*
rēg-ius, **a**, **um**, *adj.* (**rex**), *kingly, royal, regal.*
regno, **āre**, **āvi**, **ātum**, *n.* and *a.* (**regnum**), *to rule, govern, reign.*
reg-num, **i**, *n.* (**rĕgo**), *dominion, sovereignty, rule, authority, kingdom, royalty.*
rĕgo, **rĕgĕre**, **rexi**, **rectum**, *a.*, *to rule, govern, sway, control; guide, lead, direct, conduct.*
rĕ-grĕdior, **grĕdi**, **gressus sum**, *dep.* (**re**; **grădior**), *to go back, return, retire, retreat.*
rē-jĭcio, **jĭcĕre**, **jēci**, **jectum**, *a.* (**re**; **jăcio**), *to throw back; force back, repel; remove, reject; disdain, despise; defer, postpone.*
rĕ-lābor, **lābi**, **lapsus sum**, *dep.*, *to sink back; fall back; glide back, slip back.*
rĕlĭgio, **ōnis**, *f.*, *reverence* (for the gods), *piety, religion.*
rĕ-lĭgo, **āre**, **āvi**, **ātum**, *a.*, *to bind up, fasten up; bind fast; bind, fasten.*
rĕ-linquo, **linquĕre**, **līqui**, **lictum**, *a.*, *to leave behind; abandon; leave, bequeath; appoint, nominate.*
rĕlĭqu-iæ, **ārum**, *f. pl.* (**rĕlinquo**), *the remains, relics.*
rĕlĭqu-us, **a**, **um**, *adj.* (**rĕlinquo**), *remaining.* As Noun, **rĕlĭquum**, **i**, *n.*, *the rest, remainder;* reliquum est, *it remains, follows.*
rĕ-măneo, **mănēre**, **mansi**, *no sup.*, *n.*, *to stay behind, remain behind; continue, abide, endure, stay, remain.*
rĕ-mĕd-ium, **ii**, *n.* (**re**; **mĕdeor**), *a cure, remedy, medicine.*
Rēmi, **ōrum**, *m. pl.*, a people of Gaul.
rĕ-mĭn-iscor, **isci**, *no perf.*, *dep.* (re; root, men, § **50**, 4, *a*), *to recall to mind, recollect, remember.*
rĕ-mitto, **mittĕre**, **mīsi**, **missum**, *a.*, *to send back, remit, relax; remove, dismiss, resign; give back, devote.*
rēmus, **i**, *m.*, *an oar.*
Rĕmus, **i**, *m.*, the twin brother of Romulus.
rĕ-nuntio, **āre**, **āvi**, **ātum**, *a.*, *to report, give notice, declare, announce, bring back word.*
rĕ-nuo, **nuĕre**, **nui**, *no. sup.*, *n.* and *a.*, *to deny, oppose, disapprove, reject, decline, refuse.*
reor, *no inf.*, **rătus sum**, *dep.*, *to believe, think, imagine, judge, suppose, deem.*
rĕ-pello, **rĕpellĕre**, **rĕpŭli**, **rĕpulsum**, *a.*, *to drive back, push back, reject, repel, repulse.*
rĕ-pendo, **pendĕre**, **pendi**, **pensum**, *a.*, *to weigh back again; pay back, repay, requite, recompense, return, reward; redeem, ransom.*
rĕpens, **entis**, *adj.*, *sudden, hasty, unexpected, recent.*
rĕpent-e, *adv.* (**rĕpens**), *suddenly, unexpectedly.*
rĕpent-īnus, **a**, **um**, *adj.* (**rĕpens**), *sudden, hasty, unlooked-for, unexpected.*
rĕ-pĕrio, **rĕpĕrīre**, **rĕpĕri**, **rĕpertum**, *a.* (**re**; **părio**), *to find, find out, discover, learn, ascertain.*
rĕ-pĕto, **pĕtĕre**, **pĕtīvi** *or* **pĕtii**, **pĕtītum**, *a.*, *to recommence, resume, renew, repeat, demand, exact.*
rĕ-pleo, **plēre**, **plēvi**, **plētum**, *a.*, *to fill again, refill; fill up, replenish, fill full.*
rēpo, **ĕre**, **si**, **tum**, *n.*, *to creep, crawl.*
rĕ-pōno, **pōnĕre**, **pŏsui**, **pŏsĭtum**, *a.*, *to put back, place back, replace, restore; repay, requite, lay up, preserve.*
rĕ-porto, **āre**, **āvi**, **ātum**, *a.*, *to carry back, bring back; carry off, gain; report.*

rĕ-posco, poscĕre, *no perf., no sup., a., to demand back, ask for again; ask for, demand, claim.*

rĕ-prĕhendo, prĕhendĕre, prĕhendi, prĕhensum, *a., to hold back; seize; blame, censure.*

rĕ-prĭmo, prĭmĕre, pressi, pressum, *a.* (re; **prĕmo**), *to press back, keep back; check, curb, restrain.*

rĕpŭdio, āre, āvi, ātum, *a.* (**rĕpŭdium**, a separation), *to cast off, put away, divorce; reject, refuse; scorn.*

rĕ-pugno, āre, āvi, ātum, *n.* and *a., to fight against, oppose, resist.*

rĕpul-sa, æ, *f.* (**rĕpello**), *a refusal, denial, repulse.*

rĕ-pŭto, āre, āvi, ātum, *a., to count over, reckon, calculate, compute; ponder, think over, reflect upon.*

rĕ-quīro, quīrĕre, quīsīvi *or* **quīsii, quīsītum,** *a.* (**rĕ**; **quæro**), *to seek again, look after; demand, require; need, want.*

rēs, rei, *f., a thing, object, matter, event, circumstance, occurrence, condition, business;* **rē,** *in reality, in fact;* **res fămĭliāris,** *private property;* **res mīlĭtāris,** *military business, science of war;* **res gestæ,** *deeds, exploits;* **res hūmānæ,** *human affairs.*

rē-scindo, scindĕre, scĭdi, scissum, *a., to cut off, cut loose; break down; cut away; abolish, repeal, rescind.*

rĕ-sĕco, sĕcāre, sĕcui, sectum, *a., to cut loose, cut off; curtail; check, stop, restrain.*

rĕ-sĕro, āre, āvi, ātum, *a., to unlock, open, disclose, reveal.*

rĕ-servo, āre, āvi, ātum, *a., to keep back, save up; save, preserve.*

rĕ-sĭdeo, sĭdēre, sēdi, *no sup., n.* (re; **sĕdeo**), *to sit back; remain, rest, abide, reside.*

rĕ-sīdo, sīdĕre, sēdi, *no sup., n., to sit down; abate, grow calm.*

rĕ-sisto, sistĕre, stĭti, *no sup., n., to stay behind; withstand, oppose* (with dat.).

rĕ-solvo, solvĕre, solvi, sŏlūtum, *a., to untie, release, pay.*

rē-spĭcio, spĭcĕre, spexi, spectum, *n.* and *a.* (re; **spĕcio**), *to look back; to look back upon; regard, consider.*

rē-spondeo, spondēre, spondi, sponsum, *a.* and *n., to answer, reply, respond.*

rēspon-sum, i, *n.* (**rēspondeo**), *an answer, reply, response.*

res-publĭca, reī-publĭcæ, *f.* (§ **14**, 2, *d*), *the state, commonwealth, republic.*

rē-spuo, spuĕre, spui, *no sup., a., to spit back, spit out; reject, refuse, disapprove, not accept.*

rē-stinguo, stinguĕre, stinxi, stinctum, *a., to put out, quench, extinguish; annihilate, destroy.*

rē-stĭtuo, uĕre, ui, ūtum, *a.* (re; **stătuo**), *to give up, deliver up, restore, replace, renew, give back.*

rē-sto, stāre, stĭti, *no sup., n., to stand back, withstand; remain.*

rē-sūmo, sūmĕre, sumpsi, sumptum, *a., to take up again, take back, resume.*

rēte, is, *n., a net, snare.*

rĕ-tĭneo, tĭnēre, tĭnui, tentum, *a.* (re; **tĕneo**), *to keep back; detain, retain, restrain; preserve.*

rĕ-trăho, trăhĕre, traxi, tractum, *a., to draw back, withdraw, withhold, check; keep* or *drag back.*

rĕtro, *adv.* (**rĕ**), *backwards, back; before, formerly.*

rĕtro-rsum, *adv.* (**rĕtro; versum**), *back, backwards.*

re-us, i, *m.,* **rea, æ,** *f.* (**res**), *a party to an action; one who is accused* or *arraigned; a defendant, prisoner, criminal.*

rĕ-vĕho, vĕhĕre, vexi, vectum, *a., to carry back;* **rĕvĕhi,** *to go back.*

rĕvĕrent-ia, æ, *f.* (rĕvĕrens, respectful; § **44**, 1, *c*, 2), *respect, reverence, regard, fear, awe.*

rĕ-vertor, verti, versus sum, *dep., to turn back, come back, return.*

rĕ-vŏco, āre, āvi, ātum, *a., to call back, recall, revoke, recover.*

rex, rēgis, *m.* (rĕgo), *a ruler, king.*

Rhēa Sylvia, æ, *f.*, daughter of Numitor, and mother of Romulus and Remus.

rhēda, æ, *f., a four-wheeled carriage; a carriage, chariot.*

Rhēnus, i, *m., the Rhine.*

rhētor, ŏris, *m., a teacher of rhetoric; a rhetorician.*

Rhŏdănus, i, *m., the Rhone.*

Rhŏdus (os), i, *f., Rhodos;* an island near the coast of Asia Minor.

rīdeo, rīdēre, rīsi, rīsum, *n.* and *a., to laugh; smile; laugh at, ridicule.*

rĭgeo, rĭgēre, rĭgui, *no sup., n., to be stiff* or *numb, to stiffen.*

rĭg-ĭdus, a, um, *adj.* (rĭgeo), *stiff, hard, inflexible, rigid.*

rīma, æ, *f., a cleft, crack, chink, fissure, crevice.*

rīpa, æ, *f., the bank* (of a stream).

rī-sus, ūs, *m.* (rīdeo, § **44**, 1, *c*, 2), *a laughing, laughter, laugh.*

rīvus, i, *m., a brook, stream.*

rixa, æ, *f., a quarrel, dispute, contest, strife.*

rōbur, ŏris, *n., hard oak; hardness; strength, force, vigor.*

rōdo, rōdĕre, rōsi, rōsum, *a., to gnaw; eat away; waste away, corrode, consume.*

rŏgo, āre, āvi, ātum, *a., to ask, question, interrogate; propose* (a law).

Rōma, æ, *f., Rome.*

Rōm-ānus, a, um, *adj.* (**Rōma**), *Roman; of Rome.* As Noun, *m., a Roman.*

Rōm-ŭlus, i, *m.* (**Rōma**), the founder and first king of Rome (B.C. 753–717).

ros, rōris, *m., dew, moisture.*

rŏsa, æ, *f., a rose.*

ros-trum, i, *n.* (**rōdo**), *a bill, beak, snout; the curved end of a ship's prow, ship's beak.*

rŭber, bra, brum, *adj., red, ruddy.*

rŭb-or, ōris, *m.* (**rŭbeo**, to be red; § **44**, 1, *c*, 2), *redness; blush; bashfulness, modesty.*

rŭdis, e, *adj., raw, rude, rough, wild.*

rŭgio, īre, īvi *or* **ii, ītum**, *n., to roar* (as a lion).

ru-īna, æ, *f.* (ruo), *downfall, ruin, accident;* ruinæ, *pl., the ruins.*

rūmor, ōris, *m., common talk, hearsay, rumor.*

rumpo, rumpĕre, rūpi, ruptum, *a., to break, burst, tear, rend, rupture; force open; interrupt; destroy.*

ruo, ruĕre, rui, rŭtum (ruĭtum), *n.* and *a., to fall down, rush down; hasten, hurry; cast down, dash, hurl.*

rūpes, is, *f.* (**rumpo**), *a cliff, steep rock.*

rursus (sum), *adv.* (contracted from **revorsus**), *turned back; back, backwards; on the contrary, on the other hand, in turn, again.*

rus, rūris, *n.* (in *pl.* found only in *nom.* and *acc.*), *the country; lands, fields; farm, estate;* **ruri**, *in the country;* **rure**, *from the country* (§ **55**, 3, *a*, *b*, and *d*).

rus-tĭcus, a, um, *adj.* (rus), *rural, rustic.* As Noun, **rusticus, i**, *m., a countryman, rustic, peasant.*

S.

saccus, i, *m., a sack, bag.*

săcer, săcra, săcrum, *adj., holy, sacred, consecrated, venerable; accursed.* As Noun, **sacra, ōrum**, *n. pl., sacred rites, sacrifice.*

săcer-dos, ōtis, *com. gen.* (**săcer; do**), *a priest; priestess.*
săcrĭfĭc-ium, ii, *n.* (**săcrĭfĭco**; § 44, 1, *c*, 2), *a sacrifice.*
săcr-ĭ-fĭco, āre, āvi, ātum, *n.* and *a.* (**săcer; făcio**), *to sacrifice; offer in sacrifice.*
sæpe, *adv.*, *often, frequently.*
sæpĕ-nŭmĕro, *adv.*, *oftentimes, over and over again.*
sæv-io, īre, ii, ītum, *n.* (**sævus**), *to be fierce, rage, rave, be mad, violent.*
sævus, a, um, *adj.*, *raging, furious, mad, savage; fierce, cruel, severe, harsh.*
săg-ax, ācis, *adj.* (**sāgio**, to perceive quickly), *of quick perception; shrewd, keen, sagacious.*
săgīno, āre, āvi, ātum, *a.*, *to fatten; cram, stuff; pamper; nourish, feed, enrich.*
săgitta, æ, *f.*, *an arrow.*
săgitt-ārius, a, um, *adj.* (**săgitta**), *of* or *belonging to an arrow.* As Noun, **sagittarius, ii**, *m.*, *an archer, bowman.*
săgŭ-lum, i, *n. dim.* (**săgum**, § 44, 1, *c*, 3), *a small military cloak, mantle, cloak.*
săgum, i, *n.*, *a military cloak; mantle, cloak.*
sāl, sălis, *m.* (rarely *n.*), *salt;* in *pl.*, *wit.*
Sălămis, is (*acc.* **Sălămīna**), *f.*, an island near Attica.
sălio, īre, ui, tum, *n.*, *to leap, spring, bound, jump.*
saltem, *adv.*, *at least, anyhow.*
sal-tus, ūs, *m.* (**sălio**, § 44, 1, *c*, 2), *a leaping, leap, spring, bound.*
saltus, ūs, *m.*, *a forest-pasture; woodland, pasture.*
sălus, ūtis, *f.* (**salveo**, to be well), *health; welfare, property, safety.*
sălūtā-tio, ōnis, *f.* (**sălūto**, § 44, 1, *c*, 2), *a greeting, salutation.*
sălūto, āre, āvi, ātum, *a.* (**sălus**), *to greet, pay one's respects to, salute.*
salve, *see* **salveo.**
salv-eo, ēre, *no perf.*, *no sup.*, *n.* (**salvus**), *to be well, be in good health;* **salve** (*imperat.*), *heaven keep you, how are you? I hope you are well; farewell, good-by, adieu.*
salvus, a, um, *adj.*, *saved, preserved, sound, well, unhurt.*
sancio, sancīre, sanxi, sanctum, *a.*, *to render sacred; to confirm, ratify, sanction.*
sanc-tus, a, um, *part.* (**sancio**), *sacred, inviolable; august, pious, just, innocent.*
sān-e, *adv.* (**sānus**), *truly, to be sure, forsooth, certainly, however.*
sanguĭn-ŏlentus, a, um, *adj.* (**sanguis**, § 44, 1, *c*, 3), *full of blood, bloody; sanguinary.*
sanguis, ĭnis, *m.*, *blood.*
sāno, āre, āvi, ātum, *a.* (**sānus**), *to make sound, heal, cure, restore to health.*
sānus, a, um, *adj.*, *sound in body, whole, healthy, well; sound in mind, sane, rational, sober.*
săpiens, entis, *part.* (**săpio**), *wise, knowing, discreet, judicious.*
săpien-ter, *adv.* (**săpiens**), *wisely, discreetly.*
săpient-ia, æ, *f.* (**săpiens**, § 44, 1, *c*, 2), *wisdom, prudence.*
sarcĭna, æ, *f.*, *a package, bundle;* in *pl.*, *baggage.*
sătelles, ĭtis, *com. gen.*, *an attendant; accomplice, tool;* in *pl.*, *life-guards, an escort.*
sătius, *adj.* (*indecl.*) and *adv.* (*comp.* of **sătis**), *better, preferable, rather.*
sătis, *adj.* (*indecl.*) and *adv.*, *enough, sufficient, in abundance;* **satis habere**, *to deem it sufficient.*
sătis-făcio, făcĕre, fēci, factum; in *pass.*, **sătis-fīo, fiĕri, factus sum**, *n.*, *to satisfy, give satisfaction; apologize, ask pardon.*
sătur, ŭra, ŭrum, *adj.*, *sated, full; deep, strong.*

să-tus, a, um, *part.* (**sĕro**), *having been sown, planted.*

saucius, a, um, *adj.*, *wounded, hurt, injured; offended; sick, ill.*

saxum, i, *n.*, *a rock, stone.*

scando, scandĕre, scandi, scansum, *a.* and *n.*, *to climb, mount, get up; ascend, arise.*

scĕles-tus, a, um, *adj.* (**scĕlus**), *wicked, villanous, infamous, accursed.*

scĕlus, ĕris, *n.*, *a crime, sin, enormity.*

schŏla, æ, *f.*, *a school; dissertation.*

scient-ia, æ, *f.* (**sciens**, § **44**, 1, *c*, 2), *a knowing; knowledge, science, skill, expertness.*

scī-lĭcet, *adv.* (**scio**; **lĭcet**), *evidently, plainly, certainly, undoubtedly.*

scindo, scindĕre, scĭdi, scissum, *a.*, *to cut, tear, rend, split, cleave.*

scio, scīre, scīvi *or* scii, scītum, *a.*, *to know, understand, perceive.*

scīpio, ōnis, *m.*, *a staff.*

Scīpio, ōnis, *m.* (**scīpio**), the name of a celebrated family in Rome, the most famous of which were the two conquerors of the Carthaginians, *Publius Cornelius Scipio Africanus Major*, and *Publius Cornelius Scipio Æmilianus Africanus Minor.*

scrība, æ, *m.* (**scrībo**), *a clerk, secretary, scribe.*

scrībo, scrībĕre, scripsi, scriptum, *a.*, *to write, compose;* **scribere leges**, *to draw up laws.*

scurra, æ, *m.*, *a jester, buffoon.*

scūtum, i, *n.*, *a shield; defence, protection.*

se, *see* **sui**.

sē-cēdo, cēdĕre, cessi, cessum, *n.*, *to go apart, go away, separate, withdraw; secede; retire.*

sē-cerno, cernĕre, crēvi, crētum, *a.*, *to put apart; to sunder, sever, separate; distinguish, discern.*

sē-clūdo, clūdĕre, clūsi, clūsum, *a.*, *to shut off, shut up, seclude; separate; exclude.*

sĕco, āre, ui, tum, *a.*, *to cut, cut off, cut up; wound, hurt; torment.*

sēcrēt-o, *adv.* (**sēcrētus**), *apart, separately; in secret.*

sēcrē-tus, a, um, *part.* (**sēcerno**), *separate, apart; secret, private.*

sec-tor, āri, ātus, *dep. intens.* (**sĕquor**), *to follow eagerly, hunt, chase, pursue.*

sĕcund-ārius, a, um, *adj.* (**sĕcundus**), *second-rate, middling, inferior, stale.*

sĕcund-o, *adv.* (**sĕcundus**), *secondly, for the second time.*

sĕc-undus, a, um, *adj.* (**sĕquor**), *the second; favorable, fair, propitious, fortunate;* **secundo flumine**, *down stream.*

sĕcundo, āre, *no perf.*, *no sup.*, *a.* (**sĕcundus**), *to adapt, accommodate; favor, second.*

sĕd, *conj.*, *but, yet.*

sĕdeo, sĕdēre, sēdi, sessum, *n.*, *to sit, sit down, sit still; be encamped, settle.*

sēd-es, is, *f.* (**sĕdeo**), *a seat, chair; abode, residence; settlement; foundation.*

sēd-ĭ-tio, ōnis, *f.*, *dissension, civil discord, insurrection, sedition, discord.*

sēdĭti-ōsus, a, um, *adj.* (**sēdĭtio**, § **44**, 1, *c*, 3), *full of civil discord, mutinous, seditious.*

sē-dūco, dūcĕre, duxi, ductum, *a.*, *to lead aside, lead away, carry off; remove, separate.*

segnis, e, *adj.*, *slow, tardy, slack, slothful, lazy, sluggish.*

segn-ĭter, *adv.* (**segnis**), *slowly, slothfully, lazily.*

sel-la, æ, *f.* (**sĕdeo**), *a seat, chair, stool.*

sĕmel, *num. adv.*, *once, a single time, once for all;* **non semel**, *not once alone, several times;* **semel atque iterum**, *once and again, repeatedly.*

sēmen, ĭnis, *n.* (**sĕro**), *seed.*
sēmentis, is, *f.* (**sēmĭno**, to sow), *a sowing.*
semper, *adv.*, *ever*, *always*, *at all times*, *for ever.*
sĕn-ātor, ōris, *m.* (**sĕnex**), *a senator.*
sĕnātōr-ius, a, um, *adj.* (**sĕnātor**), *of a senator*, *of the senate*, *senatorial.*
sĕn-ātus, ūs, *m.* (**sĕnex**), *the senate* (*gen. sing.* sometimes **sĕnāti**).
sĕnex, sĕnis, *adj.* (*nom.* and *acc.* of the *neuter pl.* in the *positive*, and of the *neuter sing.* in the *comparative*, are wanting), *old*, *aged.* As NOUN, **sĕnex, is**, *com. gen.*, *an aged person*, *an old man*, *an old woman* (from 40 and upwards), (**sĕnex, sĕnior, maxĭmus nātu**).
sĕnior, ius, *adj.* (*comparative* of **sĕnex**), *older*, *elder.*
sēni, æ, a, *num. distributive adj.* (**sex**), *six each*, *six.*
Sĕnŏnes (**sĕnŏ**), **um**, *m. pl.*, a people of Gallia.
sentent-ia, æ, *f.* (**sentiens**), *a thinking*, *an opinion*, *sentiment;* **ex sententia**, *satisfactorily.*
sentio, tīre, si, sum, *a.*, *to discern*, *perceive*, *feel*, *think*, *observe*, *know.*
sēpărā-tim, *adv.* (**sēpăro**), *asunder*, *apart*, *separately.*
sē-păro, āre, āvi, ātum, *a.*, *to disjoin*, *sever*, *part*, *separate.*
sĕpĕlio, pĕlīre, pĕlīvi *or* **pĕlii, pultum**, *a.*, *to bury*, *inter.*
sēpes, is, *f.*, *a hedge*, *fence.*
sē-pōno, pōnĕre, pŏsui, pŏsĭtum, *a.*, *to put by*, *separate; banish.*
septem, *num. adj. indecl.*, *seven.*
Septem-trio, ōnis, *m.*, *the Great Bear; the North.*
Septem-triōnes, um, *m. pl.* (**septem; trio**), (the *seven* stars near the North Pole), *the North.*
sept-ĭmus, a, um, *num. ordinal adj.* (**septem**), *the seventh.*
septin-genti, æ, a, *num. adj.* (**septem; centum**), *seven hundred.*
septuāg-ēsĭmus, a, um, *adj.*, *num. ordinal adj.* (**septuāginta**), *the seventieth.*
septuā-ginta, *num. adj. indecl.* (**septem**), *seventy.*
sĕpul-crum (**chrum**), **i**, *n.* (**sĕpĕlio**), *a grave*, *tomb*, *sepulchre.*
sĕpul-tūra, æ, *f.* (**sĕpĕlio**, § 44, 1, *c*, 2), *a burying*, *burial*, *interment*, *funeral obsequies*, *sepulture.*
Sēquăna, æ, *f.*, *the Sequăna* (*Seine*).
Sēquăni, ōrum, *m. pl.*, a people of Gallia.
sĕquor, sĕqui, sĕcūtus sum, *dep.*, *to follow*, *go after*, *attend*, *accompany*, *pursue.*
sĕrēnus, a, um, *adj.*, *clear*, *fair*, *bright*, *serene.*
Sergius, ii, *m.*, a Roman name.
sēri-o, *adv.* (**sērius**, earnest), *in earnest*, *seriously.*
sermo, ōnis, *m.*, *talk*, *conversation*, *discourse*, *speech.*
sĕro, sĕrĕre, sēvi, sătum, *a.*, *to sow*, *plant.*
sĕro, sĕrĕre (**sĕrui**), **sertum**, *a.*, *to bind*, *plait*, *interweave*, *entwine; join*, *connect.*
sēr-o, *adv.* (**sērus**), *late*, *too late.*
serp-ens, entis, *m.* (**serpo**), *a snake*, *serpent.*
serpo, pĕre, psi, ptum, *n.*, *to creep*, *crawl; spread abroad.*
Sertōrius, ii, *m.*, a general of Marius.
ser-tum, i, *n.* (**sĕro**, to entwine), *a wreath*, *garland.*
sērus, a, um, *adj.*, *late*, *too late.*
serva, æ, *f.*, *a female slave*, *maidservant.*
Servīlia, æ, *f.*, mother of Brūtus.
serv-īlis, e, *adj.* (**servus**, § 44, 1, *c*, 3), *slavish*, *servile.*
serv-io, īre, īvi *or* **ii, ītum**, *n.* (**servus**), *to be a slave; to serve; be devoted to; comply with*, *gratify.*

serv-ĭtium, **ii**, *n.* (**servus**), *slavery*, *servitude.*
serv-ĭtūdo, **ĭnis**, *f.* (**servus**, § **44**, 1, *c*, 2), *slavery*, *servitude.*
serv-ĭtus, **ūtis**, *f.* (**servus**, § **44**, 1, *c*, 2), *slavery*, *servitude.*
Servius, **ii**, *m.*, *Servius.*
servo, **āre**, **āvi**, **ātum**, *a.*, *to save*, *deliver*, *preserve*, *protect; keep*, *observe.*
servus, **i**, *m.*, *a slave*, *servant.*
sese, reduplicated form of **se**, *acc.* of **sui**.
sestertium, **ii**, *n.* (§ **85**, **3**), one *thousand sesterces* (about $40); **decies sestertium**, 1,000,000 *sesterces* ($40,000).
sestertius, **ii**, *m.* (§ **85**, **2**), *a sesterce*, *four cents.*
seu, *see* **sive**.
sĕvēr-ĭtas, **ātis**, *f.* (**sĕvērus**, § **44**, 1, *c*, 2), *sternness*, *strictness*, *severity*, *seriousness.*
sĕvērus, **a**, **um**, *adj.*, *serious*, *grave*, *strict*, *austere.*
sex, *num. adj. indecl.*, *six.* [*sixty.*
sex-ā-ginta, *num. adj. indecl.* (**sex**),
sex-centi, **æ**, **a**, *num. adj.* (**sex**; **centum**), *six hundred.*
sex-dĕcim (**sēdĕcim**), *num. adj. indecl.*, *sixteen.*
Sext-īlis, **is**, *m.* (**sextus**), (the sixth month, March counted as the first), *August.*
Sext-īlis, **e**, *adj.* (**sextus**, § **44**, 1, *c*, 3), *of August.*
sex-tus, **a**, **um**, *num. ordinal adj.* (**sex**), *the sixth.*
si, *conj.*, *if*, *whether;* **quod si**, *but if;* **si quis**, *if any one;* **si quid**, *if any thing;* **si mĭnus**, *if not;* **si quando**, *if ever.*
sīc, *adv.*, *in this manner*, *so*, *thus.*
sīca, **æ**, *f.*, *a dagger*, *poniard.*
siccus, **a**, **um**, *adj.*, *dry*, *thirsty;* **in sicco**, *on dry land.*
Sĭcĭlia, **æ**, *f.*, *Sicily.*
Sĭcŭli, **ōrum**, *m. pl.*, *the Sicilians.*
Sĭcŭlus, **a**, **um**, *adj.*, *Sicilian.*
sīc-ut, *adv.*, *so as*, *just as*, *as; as if*, *as it were.*
sīc-ŭti, *adv.*, see **sīc-ut**.
sīdus, **ĕris**, *n.*, *a constellation*, *a star.*
sign-ĭ-fĭco, **āre**, **āvi**, **ātum**, *a.* (**signum**; **făcio**), *to show by signs*, *point out*, *make known; betoken*, *mean*, *import*, *signify.*
signo, **āre**, **āvi**, **ātum**, *a.* (**signum**), *to mark*, *mark out; point out*, *signify*, *indicate; observe*, *discover*, *find out.*
signum, **i**, *n.*, *a mark*, *token*, *sign; standard; statue*, *signal.*
sĭlent-ium, **ii**, *n.* (**sĭlens**, § **44**, **1**, *c*, 2), *silence.*
sĭlens, **entis**, *part.* (**sĭleo**, to be silent), *still*, *calm*, *quiet*, *silent.*
silva, **æ**, *f.*, *a wood*, *forest.*
silv-estris, **e**, *adj.* (**silva**), *of the forest; wooded*, *woody; wild; sylvan*, *rustic.*
Silvia, **æ**, *f.*, daughter of Numitor.
Silvius, **ii**, *m.*, an Alban king.
sīmia, **æ**, *f.*, *an ape*, *monkey.*
sĭmĭlis, **e**, *adj.*, *like*, *resembling*, *similar.*
sĭmĭl-ĭter, *adv.* (**sĭmĭlis**), *in like manner*, *similarly.*
sĭmĭl-ĭtūdo, **ĭnis**, *f.* (**sĭmĭlis**, § **44**, 1, *c*, 2), *likeness*, *resemblance*, *similitude.*
sim-plex, **ĭcis**, *adj.* (**sĕmel**; **plĭco**), *simple*, *plain; open*, *frank*, *honest*, *sincere.*
simplĭc-ĭtas, **ātis**, *f.* (**simplex**, § **44**, 1, *c*, 2), *simpleness*, *simplicity; plainness*, *frankness.*
simplĭc-ĭter, *adv.* (**simplex**), *simply*, *plainly*, *directly.*
sĭmul, *adv.*, *together*, *at once*, *at the same time;* **simul atque** *or* **ac**, *as soon as.*
sĭmŭlā-crum, **i**, *n.* (**sĭmŭlo**), *an image*, *likeness.*
sĭmŭlo, **āre**, **āvi**, **ātum**, *a.* (**sĭmĭlis**), *to pretend* (a thing is what it is not; see **dissĭmŭlo**), *to feign*, *counterfeit*, *simulate.*
sĭmul-tas, **ātis**, *f.* (*gen pl.*, **sĭmultātium**), (**sĭmul**), *dissension*,

enmity, rivalry, jealousy, grudge, hatred, animosity.

sīn, *conj.* (si; ne), *but if, if on the contrary.*

sĭne, *prep.* with *abl.*, *without.*

singŭl-āris, e, *adj.* (**singŭli**), *alone, single; singular, unique, extraordinary, remarkable.*

singŭli, æ, a, *num. distributive adj., one to each, separate, single; individual.*

sĭnister, tra, trum, *adj., left, on the left hand* or *side; awkward, perverse; unlucky, adverse;* **sub sĭnistrā**, *on the left.*

sĭnistrā, æ, *f.* (**sĭnister**), *the left hand.*

sĭno, sĭnĕre, sīvi, sĭtum, *a., to let, suffer, allow, permit.*

sĭnus, ūs, *m., the fold* (of a garment), *bosom;* **sinus maris**, *a bay.*

sī-quis *or* **sī-qui, sīqua, sīquid** *or* **sīquod**, *indef. pron., if any, if any one; if any thing.*

sisto, sistĕre, stĭti, stătum, *a.* and *n., to set, place, stand, appear, endure.*

sĭt-io, īre, īvi *or* **ii**, *no sup., n.* and *a.* (**sĭtis**), *to thirst, be thirsty; thirst for, long for, covet.*

sĭtis, is, *f.* (*acc. sing.*, **sitim**; *abl.*, **siti**), *thirst; dryness.*

sĭ-tus, a, um, *part.* (**sĭno**), *placed, set, lying, situated.*

sī-ve (seu), *conj., or if, whether, or.*

sōbrius, a, um, *adj., not drunk, sober; sensible, prudent, temperate, moderate.*

sŏcer, ĕri, *m., a father-in-law.*

sŏci-ĕtas, ātis, *f.* (**sŏcius**, § **44**, 1, *c*, 2), *fellowship, society, partnership, alliance.*

sŏcius, ii, *m., companion, comrade, partner, ally.*

sŏcius, a, um, *adj.* (**sŏcius**), *allied.*

sŏdālis, is, *com. gen., comrade, crony, boon-companion.*

sōl, sōlis, *m., the sun.*

sŏleo, sŏlēre, sŏlĭtus sum, *semi-dep.* (§ **35**, 2), *to be wont, be accustomed.*

sŏlĭdus, a, um, *adj., whole, complete; firm, solid.*

sōl-ĭtūdo, ĭnis, *f.* (**sōlus**, § **44**, 1, *c*, 2), *loneliness, solitude; a desert.*

sŏlium, ii, *n., a seat, throne.*

sollert-ia, æ, *f.* (**sollers**, clever; § **44**, 1, *c*, 2), *skill, shrewdness, dexterity, expertness.*

sollĭcĭtus, a, um, *adj., uneasy, anxious; wakeful, watchful.*

sŏlum, i, *n., the bottom, foundation; soil.*

sōlum, *adv.* (**sōlus**), *only, merely;* **non solum**, *not only.*

sōlus, a, um, *adj.* (§ **16**, 1, *b*), *alone, only, single, lonely.*

solvo, solvĕre, solvi, sŏlūtum, *a., to loose, loosen, untie, unbind; cast off* (from shore); *pay, release; dissolve, break up.*

somn-ium, ii, *n.* (**somnus**), *a dream.*

somnus, i, *m., sleep.*

sŏn-ĭtus, ūs, *m.* (**sŏno**), *a noise, sound, din.*

sŏno, āre, ui, ĭtum, *n.* and *a., to make a noise, sound, resound; to utter; cry out.*

sons, sontis, *adj., hurtful; guilty.*

sŏnus, i, *m., a noise, sound.*

sŏp-or, ōris, *m.* (**sŏpio**, to sleep; § **44**, 1, *c*, 2), *sleep.*

sordĭd-ātus, a, um, *adj.* (**sordĭdus**), *in dirty clothes, meanly* or *shabbily dressed.*

sord-ĭdus, a, um, *adj.* (**sordeo**, to be dirty), *dirty, unclean, foul, filthy, sordid.*

sŏror, ōris, *f., a sister.*

sŏrōr-ius, a, um, *adj.* (**sŏror**), *of* or *belonging to a sister.*

sors, sortis, *f., a lot, luck, fortune, fate, destiny, chance.*

sort-ior, īri, ītus sum, *dep.* (**sors**), *to cast or draw lots; allot, assign, distribute; share, divide; obtain by lot, obtain.*

spargo, spargĕre, sparsi, sparsum, *a., to scatter, sprinkle, besprinkle; disperse; spread out.*
spătium, ii, *n., room, space; interval; period.*
spĕci-es, ēi, *f.* (*gen.* and *dat. pl.* not found), (**spĕcio**), *a show, appearance, shape, form; view.*
spectā-cŭlum, i, *n.* (**specto**), *a show, sight, spectacle; public show.*
specto, āre, āvi, ātum, *a.* and *n. intens.* (**spĕcio,** to see), *to look at, observe, behold, consider, regard; aim at.*
spĕcŭlā-tor, ōris, *m.* (**spĕcŭlor**), *an explorer, spy, scout.*
spĕcŭlor, āri, ātus sum, *dep., to spy out, watch, observe, examine, explore.*
spĕc-ŭlum, i, *n.* (**spĕcio,** to see), *a looking glass, mirror.*
spĕcus, ūs (i), *m., f.,* and *n.* (§ **12,** 3, *d*), *a cave, cavern, grot, den.*
sperno, spernĕre, sprēvi, sprētum, *a., to despise, contemn, reject, scorn, spurn.*
spēro, āre, āvi, ātum, *a., to hope, expect, trust.*
spes, spĕi, *f.* (**spēro**), *hope.*
spīna, æ, *f., a thorn, prickle;* in *pl., difficulties.*
spīr-ĭtus, ūs, *m.* (**spīro**), *a breath, breeze; the breath of life, life; spirit, courage; pride.*
spīro, āre, āvi, ātum, *n.* and *a., to breathe, blow; live, breathe forth.*
splend-ĭdus, a, um, *adj.* (**splendeo,** to shine), *bright, shining; splendid, magnificent; brilliant, illustrious.*
splend-or, ōris, *m.* (**splendeo,** to shine, § **44,** 1, *c,* 2), *brightness, splendor; magnificence; honor, dignity.*
spŏlio, āre, āvi, ātum, *a.* (**spŏlium**), *to strip; rob, plunder, pillage, spoil.*
spŏlium, ii, *n., booty, prey, spoil.*
spondeo, spondēre, spŏpondi, sponsum, *a., to promise solemnly; bind, engage* or *pledge one's self; vow, betroth.*
spon-sus, i, *m.* (**spondeo**), *a betrothed, bridegroom.*
sponte, *abl.* (*gen.,* **spontis,** the only cases found), (**spondeo**), *of free will, of one's own accord.*
sprē-tus, a, um, *part.* (**sperno**), *despised.*
squāl-ĭdus, a, um, *adj.* (**squāleo,** to be filthy), *filthy, dirty, foul, neglected, squalid.*
stă-bĭlis, e, *adj.* (**sto,** § **44,** 1, *c,* 3), *that stands fast, firm, steadfast, steady, stable.*
stăbĭl-ĭtas, ātis, *f.* (**stăbĭlis**), *firmness, durability, stability.*
stă-tim, *adv.* (**sto**), *forthwith, immediately, at once.*
stă-tio, ōnis, *f.* (**sto,** § **44,** 1, *c,* 2), *a station, place, position; standing place, post.*
stătua, æ, *f.* (**stătuo**), *an image, statue.*
stătuo, stătuĕre, stătui, stătūtum, *a., to put, place, set; station; establish; believe, consider, suppose; determine.*
stă-tūra, æ, *f.* (**sto,** § **44,** 1, *c,* 2), *a standing upright; height, size, statue.*
stă-tus, ūs, *m.* (**sto,** § **44,** 1, *c,* 2), *a standing; a position, posture; condition, prosperity; state.*
stel-la, æ, *f.* (**sterno**), (the strewer of light), *a star.*
stercus, ŏris, *n., dung, excrements; filth.*
stĕrĭlis, e, *adj., unfruitful, barren, sterile.*
stĕrĭl-ĭtas, ātis, *f.* (**stĕrĭlis,** § **44,** 1, *c,* 2), *unfruitfulness, barrenness, sterility.*
sterno, sternĕre, strāvi, strātum, *a., to spread out; strew, scatter, spread; arrange, prepare; cover; prostrate.*
Sthĕrius, ii, *m.,* a chief of Sicily.
stīpendi-ārius, a, um, *adj.* (**stīpendium**), *tributary, liable to contribution.*

stīpendium, ii, *n.*, *a tax, contribution; pay; military service.*

stirps, stirpis, *f.* (rarely *m.*), *a stock, stem; race, family.*

sto, stāre, stĕti, stătum, *n.*, *to stand, stand still; persist; abide, remain, endure; to cost* (with *abl.* of *price*); **stat**, *it is a fixed purpose.*

stŏlĭdus, a, um, *adj.*, *dull, stupid, obtuse.*

stŏmăchus, i, *m.*, *the stomach; taste; distaste; displeasure; chagrin.*

strā-ges, is, *f.* (**sterno**), *a defeat, slaughter, massacre, butchery, carnage.*

strā-gŭlum, i, *n.* (**sterno**), *a bed-covering, coverlet; carpet, rug, mattress.*

strā-tus, a, um, *part.* (**sterno**), [*strown.*

strēnu-e, *adv.* (**strēnuus**), *briskly, promptly, quickly, actively, vigorously.*

strēnuus, a, um, *adj.*, *brisk, prompt, nimble, active, vigorous, strenuous.*

strĕp-ĭtus, ūs, *m.* (**strĕpo**, to make a noise; § **44**, 1, *c*, 2), *a noise, din, uproar.*

strīdeo, strīdēre, strīdi, *no sup.*, *n.*, *to creak, hiss, whizz, buzz.*

strīd-or, ōris, *m.* (**strīdeo**, § **44**, 1, *c*, 2), *a creaking, hissing, whizzing, buzzing noise.*

stringo, stringĕre, strinxi, strictum, *a.*, *to bind tight; draw together; bind, grasp;* **gladium stringere**, *to draw the sword.*

struo, struĕre, struxi, structum, *a.*, *to pile up; build, construct; arrange; contrive;* **insidias struere**, *to lay snares.*

stŭdeo, ēre, ui, *no sup.*, *n.* and *a.*, *to be eager about, strive after, be zealous for, pursue; study.*

stŭdiōs-e, *adv.* (**stŭdiōsus**), *eagerly, carefully, earnestly.*

stŭdi-ōsus, a, um, *adj.* (**stŭdium**, § **44**, 1, *c*, 3), *full of zeal; eager, zealous, fond of.*

stŭd-ium, ii, *n.* (**stŭdeo**, § **44**, 1, *c*, 2), *zeal, eagerness, fondness, desire, devotion, application to.*

stultus, a, um, *adj.*, *foolish, simple, silly.*

stŭpeo, ēre, ui, *no sup.*, *n.* and *a.*, *to be astonished, amazed; wonder at.*

stŭp-ĭdus, a, um, *adj.* (**stŭpeo**), *amazed, senseless, dull, stupid.*

suādeo, suādēre, suāsi, suāsum, *n.* and *a.*, *to advise, exhort, urge; recommend, advocate.*

suā-sor, ōris, *m.* (**suādeo**, § **44**, 1, *c*, 1), *an adviser, counsellor, persuader.*

suāvis, e, *adj.*, *sweet, pleasant, agreeable.*

suāv-ĭtas, ātis, *f.* (**suāvis**, § **44**, 1, *c*, 2), *sweetness, pleasantness, agreeableness.*

sŭb, *prep.* with *acc.* and *abl.* (§ **42**, 2, and **56**, 1, *c*), *under, below, beneath, close up to, during; just after;* **sub monte**, *at the foot of the mountain.*

sub-dūco, dūcĕre, duxi, ductum, *a.*, *to draw up* (especially *on shore*), *lift up, draw off, withdraw, remove, take away secretly.*

sŭb-eo, īre, ii, ĭtum, *n.* and *a. irr.*, *to go under, to go up; enter; advance, proceed; approach; undergo; sustain; attack; succeed; occur;* **humeris subire aliquid**, *to take up something on one's shoulders.*

sūber, ĕris, *n.*, *a cork-tree.*

sŭb-ĭgo, ĭgĕre, ēgi, actum, *a.* (**sŭb**; **ăgo**), *to bring under, get under; subdue; impel, urge on; force, constrain.*

sŭbĭt-o, *adv.* (**sŭbĭtus**), *suddenly, unexpectedly.*

sŭbĭ-tus, a, um, *part.* (**sŭbeo**), *sudden, unexpected.*

sub-jĭcio, jĭcĕre, jēci, jectum, *a.*, (**sŭb**; **jăcio**), *to bring under, subdue, subject.*

sublā-tus, a, um, *part.* (**tollo**), *elated, proud, haughty.*

sub-lĕvo, āre, āvi, ātum, *a., to raise up, hold up, support, sustain, assist, encourage, relieve.*

sublīmis, e, *adj., high, on high; lofty.*

sub-mergo, mergĕre, mersi, mersum, *a., to dip* or *plunge under; to sink, overwhelm, submerge.*

sub-mitto, mittĕre, mīsi, missum, *a., to send forth; send to one's aid; dispatch;* **submittere se,** *to submit.*

sŭb-ŏles, is, *f.* (**sŭb; ŏlesco**), *a sprout, shoot; posterity, offspring, race.*

sub-sĕquor, sĕqui, sĕcūtus sum, *dep., to follow close after; follow, succeed, ensue.*

sub-sĭd-ium, ii, *n.* (**sŭb; sĕdeo**), *a body of reserves, auxiliary forces; assistance, aid, support;* **subsidio mittere,** *to send as support.*

sub-sīdo, sīdĕre, sēdi, sessum, *n., to sit down, settle, subside; remain, abide, stay.*

sub-sisto, sistĕre, stĭti, stĭtum, *n., to stand still, stop, take a stand; hold, hold out.*

sub-stĭtuo, stĭtuĕre, stĭtui, stĭtūtum, *a.* (**sŭb; stătuo**), *to set* or *place under; substitute.*

sub-ter, *prep.* with *acc.* and *abl.* (**sŭb, § 56,** 1, *e*), *below, beneath, underneath, under; close by.*

sub-vĕho, vĕhĕre, vexi, vectum, *a., to carry up, convey, bring* (up stream).

sub-vĕnio, vĕnīre, vēni, ventum, *n., to come to one's assistance; aid, relieve, succor.*

suc-cēdo, cēdĕre, cessi, cessum, *n.* and *a.* (**sŭb; cēdo**), *to go up, mount, ascend; march on, advance; succeed to, follow; prosper.*

suc-censeo, censēre, censui, censum, *n.* and *a., to be angry, enraged; be angry at.*

succes-sor, ōris, *m.* (**succēdo, § 44,** 1, c, 1), *a follower, successor.*

suc-cīdo, cīdĕre, cīdi, cīsum, *a.* (**sŭb; cædo**), *to cut down, fell.*

suc-cingo, cingĕre, cinxi, cinctum, *a.* (**sŭb; cingo**), *to gird up, tuck up; surround, equip, furnish.*

suc-clāmo, āre, āvi, ātum, *a.* (**sŭb; clāmo**), *to call out, shout in reply.*

suc-cumbo, cumbĕre, cŭbui, cŭbĭtum, *n.* (**sŭb; cumbo**), *to yield, submit, surrender.*

suc-curro, currĕre, curri, cursum, *n.* (**sŭb; curro**), *to run under; help, assist, aid, succor.*

sūdor, ōris, *m., sweat, perspiration; toil.*

Suēvi, ōrum, *m. pl.,* a powerful Germanic people in northern Germany.

suf-fĭcio, fĭcĕre, fēci, fectum, *a.* and *n.* (**sŭb; făcio**), *to put under, put in the place of, substitute; be sufficient, suffice.*

suf-fīgo, fīgĕre, fixi, fixum, *a.* (**sŭb; fīgo**), *to fasten upon, affix.*

suf-fŏdio, fŏdĕre, fōdi, fossum, *a.* (**sŭb; fŏdio**), *to dig underneath, undermine, pierce through.*

sui, sĭbi, se *or* **sese,** *reflexive personal pron.* (for all genders and numbers), *of himself, herself, itself, themselves.*

sulcus, i, *m., a furrow.*

Sulla, æ, *m., Lucius Cornelius Sulla Felix,* the celebrated Roman Dictator, B. C. 138–78.

Sull-āni, ōrum, *m. pl.* (**Sulla**), *the followers of Sulla.*

Sull-ānus, a, um, *adj.* (**Sulla**), *of Sulla.*

sum, esse, fui, fŭtūrus, *n. irr.* (**§ 29**), *to be;* **mihi est,** &c., *I have,* &c.

summa, æ, *f.* (**summus**), *the main thing; the amount, sum, total, whole.*

sum-mergo, *see* **sub-mergo.**

sum-mitto, *see* **sub-mitto.**

summus, a, um, *adj.* (*superlative* of **sŭpĕrus**), *chief, top of.*

sūmo, sūmĕre, sumpsi, sumptum, *a.* **(sŭb; ĕmo),** *to take, assume, gather; enjoy; spend;* **bellum sumere,** *to begin war;* **pœnam sumere,** *to inflict punishment.*

sum-ptus, ūs, *m.* **(sūmo),** *expense, cost, charge.*

sŭpellex, lectĭlis, *f., furniture, household utensils.*

sŭper, *adv.* and *prep.* with *acc.* and *abl.* (§ **56**, 1, *d*), *above; moreover, besides; upon, concerning; in addition to.*

sŭperb-ia, æ, *f.* **(sŭperbus,** § **44**, 1, *c*, 2), *haughtiness, pride.*

sŭper-bus, a, um, *adj.* **(sŭper),** *haughty, proud, arrogant, insolent.*

sŭper-fundo, fundĕre, fūdi, fūsum, *a., to pour on; overflow, rush upon; extend.*

sŭpĕr-ior, ius, *adj.* (*comparative* of **sŭpĕrus**), *higher, former, past; older, superior, greater.*

sŭper-năto, āre, āvi, ātum, *n., to swim above, float on the top, swim over.*

sŭpĕro, āre, āvi, ātum, *a.* **(sŭper),** *to overcome, subdue, conquer.*

sŭper-sĕdeo, sĕdēre, sēdi, sessum, *n.* and *a., to sit upon; be superior to, surpass: forbear, omit.*

sŭper-sum, esse, fui, *n., to be left, remain, exist still; survive; be in abundance.*

sŭpĕr-us, a, um, *adj.* **(sŭper,** § **17**, 3, *a*), *upper, on high.*

sŭper-vĕnio, vĕnīre, vēni, ventum, *a.* and *n., to come upon, press upon, attack; come up, arrive; follow.*

sŭp-īnus, a, um, *adj.* **(sŭb),** *bent backwards, lying on the back, supine;* **manus supini,** *with the open palms turned upwards* (a gesture of one praying).

sup-pĕto, pĕtĕre, pĕtīvi *or* **pĕtii, pĕtītum,** *n.* **(sŭb; pĕto),** *to be at hand, be in store, be sufficient.*

sup-pleo, plēre, plēvi, plētum, *a.* **(sŭb; pleo),** *to fill up, supply, complete.*

sup-plex, ĭcis, *adj.* **(sŭb; plĭco),** *entreating, beseeching, suppliant.* As Noun, *com. gen., a suppliant.*

supplĭcā-tio, ōnis, *f.* **(supplĭco,** § **44**, 1, *c*, 2), *a public prayer* or *supplication; a day set apart for prayer.*

supplĭc-ĭter, *adv.* **(supplex),** *humbly, submissively, suppliantly.*

supplĭc-ium, ii, *n.* **(supplĭco,** § **44**, 1, *c*, 2), *a supplication; punishment;* **supplicium de aliquo sumere** *or* **aliquem supplicio afficere,** *to inflict punishment on any one.*

sup-plĭco, āre, āvi, ātum, *n.* **(sŭb; plĭco),** *to kneel down; beseech, supplicate; pray.*

sup-porto, āre, āvi, ātum, *a.* **(sŭb; porto),** *to bring up, carry, convey.*

sūpra, *adv.* and *prep.* with *acc., on the top, above; before, formerly; beyond, besides; over, above.*

sūprēmus, a, um, *adj.* (*superlative* of **sŭpĕrus**), *the highest, greatest, last.*

surdus, a, um, *adj., deaf; dull, indistinct; stupid.*

sur-go, surgĕre, surrexi, surrectum, *n.* **(sŭb; rĕgo),** *to rise.*

sur-rĭpio, rĭpĕre, rĭpui, reptum, *a.* **(sŭb; răpio),** *to snatch, steal away, pilfer, purloin.*

sūs, suis, *com. gen.* (*dat. pl.*, **suĭbus** *and* **sŭbus**), *a hog, pig, boar, sow.*

sus-cĭpio, cĭpĕre, cēpi, ceptum, *a.* **(sŭb; căpio),** *to take up, undertake; acknowledge;* **inimicitias suscipere,** *to incur enmities.*

suspec-tus, a, um, *part.* **(suspĭcio),** *mistrusted, suspected; suspicious.*

sus-pendo, pendĕre, pendi, pensum, *a.* **(sŭb; pendo),** *to hang* *up*, *suspend; keep in suspense; check*, *interrupt*.

su-spĭcio, spĭcĕre, spexi, spectum, *a*. (**sŭb; spĕcio**), *to mistrust*, *suspect*, *distrust*.

suspĭc-io, ōnis, *f*. (**suspĭcor**, § **44**, 1, *c*, 2), *mistrust*, *distrust*, *suspicion*.

suspĭcor, āri, ātus sum, *dep*. (**suspĭcio**), *to mistrust*, *suspect*.

sus-tĭneo, tĭnēre, tĭnui, tentum, *a*. (**sŭb; tĕneo**), *to hold up*, *support*, *sustain*, *endure; withstand; restrain; delay*, *put off*.

sustŭli, *perf. ind*. of **tollo**.

sū-tor, ōris, *m*. (**suo**, to sew; § **44**, 1, *c*, 1), *a shoemaker*, *cobbler*.

suus, a, um, *poss. pron*. (**sui**), *his*, *her*, *their own*, *own*.

Sȳria, æ, *f*., a country in Asia, east of the Mediterranean.

T.

T. an abbreviation for **Tĭtus**.

tăbel-la, æ, *f. dim*. (**tăbŭla**, § **44**, 1, *c*, 3), *a small board*, *tablet; a voting tablet*, *ballot; a writing tablet*.

tăberna, æ, *f*., *a hut*, *shed*, *stall*, *shop*.

tăbern-ācŭlum, i, *n*. (**tăberna**), *a tent*.

tāb-es, is, *f*. (**tābeo**, to waste away), *a wasting away; consumption*, *plague*, *pestilence*.

tăbŭla, æ, *f*., *a board*, *plank; list* (of proscribed persons); *a will; writing tablet*.

tăceo, ēre, ui, ĭtum, *n*. and *a*., *to be silent*, *to say nothing*, *hold one's peace; be still*, *quiet; pass over in silence*.

tăc-ĭtus, a, um, *part*. (**tăceo**), *silent*, *secret*.

tac-tus, a, um, *part*. (**tango**), *touched*.

tædet, tædēre, tæduit *or* **tæsum est**, *a. impers*. (§ **50**, 4, *c*, 2), *it disgusts*, *offends*, *wearies* (one); *I* (thou, he, &c.) *am disgusted*.

tæd-ium, ĭi, *n*. (**tædet**, § **44**, 1, *c*, 2), *weariness*, *loathing*, *disgust*, *tediousness*.

tæter, *see* **tēter**.

tălentum, i, *n*., *a talent;* a Greek weight, equal to about one half a hundred weight; a sum of money, equal to about $1000.

tālis, e, *adj*., *such*, *of such a kind*, *of such a nature*, *quality*, or *sort* (the relative *adj*. corresponding to **talis** is **qualis**).

tālus, i, *m*., *the ankle bone*, *ankle; a die*.

tam, *adv*., *so*, *so very;* **tam . . . quam**, *as . . . as*.

tămen, *conj*. (§ **43**, 2, *b*), *nevertheless*, *yet*, *still*.

tăm-etsi, *conj*. (**tămen; etsi**), *although*, *though*.

tam-quam, *adv*. (of comparison), *as much as*, *so as*, *like as*, *just as; as if*, *just as though*.

tan-dem, *adv*. (**tam**), *at length*, *at last*, *finally;* in interrogative clauses, *pray*, *pray now*, *now*, *then*,

tango, tangĕre, tĕtĭgi, tactum, *a*., *to touch*, *affect*.

tantī-dem, *see* **tantus-dem**.

tanto, *see* **tantus**.

tantŏpĕre, *see* **tantus**.

tant-um, *adv*. (**tantus**), *so much*, *so greatly*, *to such a degree; only*, *alone*, *merely;* **tantum non**, *almost*, *all but;* **tantum quod**, *only*, *just then*, *but just*.

tantum-mŏdo, *adv*., *only*, *merely*, *nothing but*.

tan-tus, a, um, *adj*. (**tam**), *so great;* **tantŏpĕre** (**tanto ŏpĕre**), as *adv*., *so much*, *so greatly;* **tanto** (*abl*. of degree of difference, § **54**, 6, *e*, remarks), *by so much*, *so much the*.

tantus-dem, tantădem, tantumdem, *adj*., *as large*, *as great;* **tantĭdem** (*gen*. of price, § **50**, 1, *i*, and **54**, 8, *a*), *at just so much*.

tard-e, *adv*. (**tardus**), *slowly*, *tardily*.

tardo, **āre**, **āvi**, **ātum**, *a.* and *n.* (**tardus**), *to make slow; hinder, delay, retard; to tarry, loiter, linger, delay.*
tardus, **a**, **um**, *adj.*, *slow, sluggish, tardy, late; dull, heavy, stupid.*
Tarquĭnius, **ii**, *m.*, *Tarquinius Superbus*, last king of Rome.
taurus, **i**, *m.*, *a bull, bullock, ox, steer.*
tec-tum, **i**, *n.* (**tĕgo**), (a thing that covers), *a roof; a house, dwelling, abode, shelter, quarters.*
tē-cum, *see* **tu**.
tĕgo, **tĕgĕre**, **texi**, **tectum**, *a.*, *to cover, hide, conceal; defend, protect, guard.*
tellūs, **ūris**, *f.*, *the earth; land, ground.*
tēlum, **i**, *n.*, *a dart, spear, javelin* (offensive weapon).
tĕmĕr-ārius, **a**, **um**, *adj.* (**tĕmĕre**), *rash, heedless, thoughtless, imprudent, indiscreet.*
tĕmĕre, *adv.*, *rashly, hastily, thoughtlessly, indiscreetly.*
tĕmĕr-ĭtas, **ātis**, *f.* (**tĕmĕre**, § **44**, 1, *c*, 2), *rashness, thoughtlessness, indiscretion, temerity.*
tempĕrans, **antis**, *part.* (**tempĕro**), *sober, moderate, temperate.*
tempĕrant-ia, **æ**, *f.* (**tempĕrans**, § **44**, 1, *c*, 2), *moderation, sobriety, discreetness, temperance.*
tempĕro, **āre**, **āvi**, **ātum**, *a.* and *n.*, *to rule, regulate, govern, manage; to forbear, restrain, be temperate.*
tempes-tas, **ātis**, *f.* (**tempus** *for* **temportas**, § **44**, 1, *c*, 2), *a time, season, period; storm, tempest.*
templum, **i**, *n.*, *a sanctuary, temple, shrine.*
tempus, **ŏris**, *n.*, *time;* **ad tempus**, *at a fitting time;* **ex tempore**, *off-hand, extempore;* **id temporis**, *at that time* (§ **50**, 2, *c*); in *pl.*, **tempora**, *the times, circumstances.*
tĕn-ax, **ācis**, *adj.* (**tĕneo**, § **44**, 1, *c*, 3), *holding fast, tenacious.*
tendo, **tendĕre**, **tĕtendi**, **tentum** *and* **tensum**, *a.* and *n.*, *to stretch, distend, extend, spread out; aim, tend; go, march;* **insidias tendere**, *to lay snares.*
tĕnĕbræ, **ārum**, *f. pl.*, *darkness.*
tĕneo, **ēre**, **ui**, **tum**, *a.*, *to hold, keep, have, possess; restrain, detain.*
tĕner, **ĕra**, **ĕrum**, *adj.*, *soft, delicate, tender.*
ten-to, **āre**, **āvi**, **ātum**, *a. intens.* (**tendo**, § **36**, *b*, and **44**, 2, *b*), *to handle, touch; attack, assail; attempt, try; excite, disturb.*
tentōr-ium, **ii**, *n.* (**tendo**), *a tent.*
tĕnuis, **e**, *adj.*, *thin, slim, slender; little, poor, mean.*
tĕnu-ĭtas, **ātis**, *f.* (**tĕnuis**, § **44**, 1, *c*, 2), *thinness, slenderness, smallness; poverty, indigence.*
tĕnus, *prep.* with *abl.*, *as far as, up to, down to, unto, to.*
tĕpeo, **ēre**, *no perf.*, *no sup.*, *n.*, *to be warm.*
tĕp-ĭdus, **a**, **um**, *adj.* (**tĕpeo**), *lukewarm, tepid; faint, languid.*
tĕr, *adv. num.* (**tres**), *three times, thrice.*
Tĕrentius, **ii**, *m.*, a Roman name.
tergum, **i**, *n.*, *the back;* **terga dare**, *to flee.*
termĭnus, **i**, *m.*, *a boundary, bound, limit.*
ter-ni, **æ**, **a**, *num. distributive adj.*, *three, each by threes.*
tĕro, **tĕrĕre**, **trīvi**, **trītum**, *a.*, *to rub, grind, rub away, wear, wear away.*
terra, **æ**, *f.*, *the earth, land.*
terr-ēnus, **a**, **um**, *adj.* (**terra**), *of earth, earthen.*
terreo, **ēre**, **ui**, **ĭtum**, *a.*, *to frighten, alarm, terrify.*
terr-or, **ōris**, *m.* (**terreo**, § **44**, 1, *c*, 2), *dread, alarm, terror.*
terti-o, *adv.* (**tertius**), *for the third time; thirdly.*
ter-tius, **a**, **um**, *adj.* (**tĕr**), *the third.*
testā-mentum, **i**, *n.* (**testor**, § **44**, 1, *c*, 2), *a will, testament.*

test-ĭmōnium, ii, *n.* **(testor,** § **44,** 1, *c*, 2), *witness, evidence, attestation, testimony; proof.*

testis, is, *com. gen.*, *a witness; eye-witness.*

testor, āri, ātus sum (testis), *to be a witness, to bear witness, testify, attest; prove; call to witness.*

test-ūdo, ĭnis, *f.* **(testa,** a shell), *a tortoise* (in military language, boards or shields locked together to protect a party when storming any fortified place).

tēter, tra, trum, *adj.*, *offensive, noisome, foul, hideous, loathsome.*

Teutŏnes, um, *m. pl.*, a people of Germany.

Teutŏni, ōrum, *m. pl.*, see **Teutŏnes.**

Thessălia, æ, *f.*, *Thessaly.*

Thessalŏnīca, æ, *f.*, a city of Macedonia.

Tĭbĕris, is, *m.* (*acc.* **Tiberim,** *abl.* **Tiberi),** *the Tiber.*

Tībĕrius, ii, *m.*, *Tiberius Claudius Nĕro*, emperor of Rome, A.D. 14–37.

tĭgil-lum, i, *n. dim.* **(tignum,** § **44,** 1, *c*, 3), *a little beam.*

tignum, i, *n.*, *a log, beam.*

Tīgrānes, is, *m.*, king of Armenia, son-in-law of Mithridates.

tĭgris, is *or* **ĭdis,** *com. gen.*, *a tiger, tigress.*

tĭmeo, ēre, ui, *no sup.*, *a.* and *n.*, *to fear, dread; be afraid, anxious.*

tĭmĭd-e, *adv.* **(tĭmĭdus),** *fearfully, timidly.*

tĭmĭd-ĭtas, ātis, *f.* **(tĭmĭdus,** § **44,** 1, *c*, 2), *fearfulness, cowardice, timidity.*

tĭm-ĭdus, a, um, *adj.* **(tĭmeo),** *fearful, afraid, faint-hearted, cowardly, timid.*

tĭm-or, ōris, *m.* **(tĭmeo,** § **44,** 1, *c*, 2), *fear, dread, alarm, anxiety.*

tĭtŭlus, i, *m.*, *an inscription, title, motto, epitaph.*

Tĭtus Lăbiēnus, i, *m.*, legate of Cæsar.

tŏga, æ, *f.* **(tĕgo),** *a toga* (the outer garment of a Roman citizen in time of peace), *mantle.*

tŏlĕro, āre, āvi, ātum, *a.*, *to bear, support, endure, sustain; maintain, nourish.*

tollo, tollĕre, sustŭli, sublātum, *a.*, *to lift up, elevate; carry, bear; take away, remove; do away with; kill.*

tondeo, tondēre, tŏtondi, tonsum, *a.*, *to shear, clip; cut, prune, trim; gather; crop, graze upon, feed upon.*

tŏno, āre, ui, ĭtum, *n.* and *a.*, *to thunder;* **tonat,** *impers.*, *it thunders.*

ton-sor, ōris, *m.* **(tondeo,** § **44,** 1, *c*, 1), *a shearer, clipper, shaver; barber.*

tonsōr-ius, a, um, *adj.* **(tonsor),** *of* or *belonging to shearing* or *shaving;* **culter tonsorius,** *a razor.*

torpeo, ēre, ui, *no sup.*, *n.*, *to be stiff, numb, dull, listless.*

torp-or, ōris, *m.* **(torpeo,** § **44,** 1, *c*, 2), *numbness, torpor, inactivity.*

torqueo, torquēre, torsi, tortum, *a.*, *to turn, twist, bend; whirl around; fling, hurl; wrench, rack, torture.*

torreo, torrēre, torrui, tostum, *a.*, *to burn; parch, roast, bake.*

torr-ĭdus, a, um, *adj.* **(torreo),** *dry, parched.*

tŏt, *num. adj. indecl.*, *so many.*

tŏt-ĭdem, *num. adj. indecl.* **(tŏt),** *just so many, just as many.*

tŏt-ies, *num. adv.* **(tŏt),** *so often, so many times; as often, as many times.*

tōtus, a, um, *adj.* (*gen. sing.*, **totīus),** *the whole, entire, total; all, all the.*

trabs, trăbis, *f.*, *a beam; a timber.*

trac-tus, a, um, *part.* **(trăho),** *drawn.*

trā-do, dĕre, dĭdi, dĭtum, *a.* **(trans; do),** *to give up, deliver, surrender; commit, intrust, hand* *down; teach, tell;* **traditur,** *it is said;* **traditum est,** *the tradition is.*

trā-dūco, dūcĕre, duxi, ductum, *a.* (**trans; dūco**), *to lead across, transport over, transfer, bring to an end; spend.*

trāg-ŭla, æ, *f.* (**trăho**), *a javelin* (of large size).

trăho, trăhĕre, traxi, tractum, *a., to draw, drag, drag along; collect; allure; protract; detain;* **bellum trahere,** *to prolong the war.*

trā-jĭcio, jĭcĕre, jēci, jectum, *a.* and *n.* (**trans; jăcio**), *to throw across, cast over; transport; pierce, stab; to pass over.*

tranquillus, a, um, *adj., quiet, calm, still, tranquil.*

trans, *prep.* with *acc., across, over, beyond, on the other side of.*

tran-scrībo, scrībĕre, scripsi, scriptum, *a.* (**trans; scrībo**), *to copy, transcribe; transfer, remove.*

trans-dūco, *see* **trādūco.**

trans-eo, īre, īvi *or* **ii, ĭtum,** *n.* and *a. irr., to cross over, pass over; pass by, go through; cross.*

trans-fĕro, ferre, tŭli, lātum, *a. irr., to bring over, transfer, convey.*

trans-fīgo, fīgĕre, fixi, fixum, *a., to thrust* or *pierce through; to transfix.*

trans-fŏdio, fŏdĕre, fōdi, fossum, *a., to stab through; stab, pierce.*

trans-grĕdior, grĕdi, gressus sum, *dep.* (**trans; grădior**), *to cross; to step over, go beyond, exceed.*

trans-ĭgo, ĭgĕre, ēgi, actum, *a.* (**trans; ăgo**), *to carry through, finish, complete, accomplish; settle, transact.*

tran-sĭlio *or* **trans-sĭlio, sĭlīre, sĭlīvi, sĭlii** *or* **sĭlui, sultum,** *n.* and *a.* (**trans; sălio**), *to leap* or *jump across; leap* or *spring over; go rapidly, hasten.*

trans-mitto, mittĕre, mīsi, missum, *a., to send over, throw across, send across, dispatch; traverse, cross over.*

trans-porto, āre, āvi, ātum, *a., to carry* or *convey across.*

transver-sus, a, um, *part.* (**transverto**), *lying across, crosswise, transverse, cross.*

trĕcent-ēsĭmus, a, um, *adj.* (**trĕcenti**), *three-hundredth.*

trĕ-centi, æ, a, *num. adj.* (**tres; centum**), *three hundred.*

trĕ-dĕcim, *num. adj. indecl.* (**tres; dĕcem**), *thirteen.*

trĕmo, trĕmĕre, trĕmui, *no sup., n.* and *a., to shake, tremble; tremble at.*

trĕpĭdus, a, um, *adj., restless, confused, alarmed.*

trēs, tria, *num. adj., three* (§ **18,** [**1,** *c*).

Trēvĭri, ōrum, *m. pl.,* a people of Gaul.

trĭbūn-al, ālis, *n.* (**trĭbūnus**), *a platform* (on which the seats of magistrates were placed), *judgment-seat, tribunal.*

trĭbūn-ātus, ūs, *m.* (**trĭbūnus**), *the office of a tribune, tribuneship.*

trĭb-ūnus, i, *m.* (**trĭbus,** a tribe), *a tribune.*

trĭbuo, uĕre, ui, ūtum, *a., to assign, allot, bestow, give, impart, confer; impute.*

trī-duum, ui, *n.* (**tres; dies**), *the space of three days, three days.*

trĭ-gĕmĭni, ōrum, *m. pl.* (**tres; gĕno**), *three born at a birth, three brothers.*

trī-ni, æ, a, *num. distributive adj.* (**tres**), *three each, three.*

trĭ-plex, plĭcis, *adj.* (**tres; plĭco**), *threefold, triple.*

tristis, e, *adj., sad, sorrowful, mournful.*

trī-tus, a, um, *part.* (**tĕro**), *rubbed, worn; common, familiar, trite.*

triumpho, āre, āvi, ātum, *n.* and *a.* (**triumphus**), *to triumph, exult; rejoice at.*

triumphus, **i**, *m.*, *a triumph* (solemn procession of victory).

trŭ-cīdo, **āre**, **āvi**, **ātum**, *a.* (**trux**, savage; **cædo**), *to slaughter*, *butcher*, *massacre*.

trūdo, **trūdĕre**, **trūsi**, **trūsum**, *a.*, *to thrust*, *push*, *shove; crowd; press on*, *drive*, *impel*.

truncus, **i**, *m.*, *the trunk*, *body; stem*, *stock*.

truncus, **a**, **um**, *adj.* (**trunco**, to mutilate), *maimed*, *mutilated*, *mangled*, *disfigured*.

tū, *personal pron.*, *thou*.

tŭba, **æ**, *f.*, *a trumpet*.

tueor, **tuēri**, **tuĭtus** *or* **tūtus sum**, *dep.*, *to look at*, *gaze at*, *behold; guard*, *preserve*, *defend*.

tŭli, *see* **fĕro**.

Tulingi, **ōrum**, *m. pl.*, a people of Gallia.

Tullus Hostīlius, **i**, *m.*, third king of Rome, B.C. 672–640.

tum, *adv.*, *then*, *at that time;* **cum** (**quum**) . . . **tum**, *both . . . and; not only . . . but also*.

tŭmeo, **ēre**, **ui**, *no sup.*, *n.*, *to swell; be swollen; be inflated; be puffed up*.

tŭm-ĭdus, **a**, **um**, *adj.* (**tŭmeo**), *swollen*, *tumid; elated*, *puffed up*.

tŭmultuor, **āri**, **ātus sum**, *dep.* (**tŭmultus**), *to be in an uproar*, *raise a tumult*.

tŭmultus, **ūs**, *m.*, *disturbance*, *agitation; tumult*, *insurrection*, *sedition*.

tŭm-ŭlus, **i**, *m.* (**tŭmeo**), *a mound*, *hillock*, *hill*, *a sepulchral mound*, *tomb*.

tunc, *adv.*, *then*, *at that time; immediately*.

tundo, **tundĕre**, **tŭtŭdi**, **tunsum** *or* **tūsum**, *a.*, *to beat*, *strike; pound*, *bruise*.

tŭnĭca, **æ**, *f.*, *a tunic* (an under-garment of the Romans, worn by both sexes).

turba, **æ**, *f.*, *a crowd*, *throng; a turmoil*, *hubbub*, *uproar*, *tumult*, *commotion*, *disturbance*.

turb-ĭdus, **a**, **um**, *adj.* (**turbo**), *confused*, *disordered; troubled*, *disturbed*, *perplexed*.

turbo, **āre**, **āvi**, **ātum**, *a.* (**turba**), *to disturb*, *trouble; confuse*, *confound*.

turbo, **ĭnis**, *m.*, *a whirlwind*, *tornado*, *hurricane*.

turda, **æ**, *f.*, *a thrush*.

turdus, **i**, *m.*, *a thrush*.

turgeo, **turgēre**, **tursi**, *no sup.*, *n.*, *to swell out*, *be swollen; be inflated*, *bombastic*.

turma, **æ**, *f.*, *a troop*, *squadron; band*, *body*.

turpis, **e**, *adj.*, *ugly*, *foul*, *filthy; base*, *infamous*, *dishonorable*.

turris, **is**, *f.*, *a tower; castle*.

tū-tor, **ōris**, *m.* (**tueor**, § **44**, 1, *c*, 1), *a watcher*, *protector*, *defender; guardian*, *tutor*.

tū-tus, **a**, **um**, *part.* (**tueor**), *safe*, *secure*.

tu-us, **a**, **um**, *poss. pron.* (**tu**), *thy thine*, *your*, *yours*.

tȳrannus, **i**, *m.*, *a monarch*, *ruler; despot*, *tyrant*.

U.

ūber, **ĕris**, *n.*, *a teat*, *udder*, *breast*.

ūber, **ĕris**, *adj.*, *rich*, *fruitful*, *fertile*.

ŭbi, *adv.*, *where*, *when;* **ubi primum**, *as soon as*.

ŭbĭ-cumque (**-cunque**), *adv.*, *wherever; everywhere*.

ŭbī-que, *adv.*, *wherever; anywhere*, *everywhere*.

ulciscor, **ulcisci**, **ultus sum**, *dep.*, *to revenge*, *take vengeance on*, *punish*.

ullus, **a**, **um**, *adj.* (*gen. sing.* **ullīus**, *dat.* **ulli**), *any*, *any one*.

ulmus, **i**, *f.*, *an elm*, *elm-tree*.

ultĕr-ior, **ius**, *adj.* (*comparative* of **ultra**, § **17**, 3), *further* or *the further side*, *ulterior*.

ultĭmus, **a**, **um**, *adj.* (*superl.* of **ultra**, § **17**, 3), *the furthest*, *most distant*, *most remote; last*.

ul-tio, **ōnis**, *f.* (**ulciscor**, § **44**, 1, *c*, 2), *a revenge.*

ul-tor, **ōris**, *m.* (**ulciscor**, § **44**, 1, *c*, 1), *a revenger.*

ultrā, *adv.* and *prep.* with *acc.*, *beyond, further; on the other side of, beyond, past;* **ultra fidem**, *beyond belief.*

ultro, *adv.*, *beyond; besides, moreover; of one's own accord, voluntarily.*

ul-tus, a, um, *part.* (**ulciscor**), *having avenged, punished.*

umbra, **æ**, *f.*, *a shade, shadow; an image.*

um-quam (**un-**), *adv.* (**ūnum; quam**), *at any time, ever.*

ūnā, *adv.* (**ūnus**), *together, at the same time.*

unda, **æ**, *f.*, *a wave, billow.*

unde, *adv.*, *from which place, whence; from whom, from which, from what.*

un-dĕcim, *num. adj. indecl.* (**ūnus; dĕcem**), *eleven.*

undĕcĭm-us, a, um, *num. adj.* (**undĕcim**), *the eleventh.*

un-dē-vīginti, *num. adj. indecl.* (**unus; de; vīginti**), *one from twenty; nineteen.*

und-ĭ-que, *adv. indef.* (**unde; que**), *on all sides, on every part, everywhere.*

ungo (**unguo**), **ungĕre, unxi, unctum**, *a.*, *to anoint, smear, besmear.*

unguis, is, *m.*, *a nail; talon, claw, hoof.*

ūn-ĭ-versus, a, um, *adj.* (**ūnus; versus**), *all together, whole, entire, general, universal.*

un-quam, *see* **um-quam**.

ūnus, a, um, *num. adj.* (*gen. sing.*, **unīus**; *dat.*, **uni**), *one, alone, sole, single.*

ūnus-quisque, ūnăquæque, ūnumquodque, *adj. pron.*, *each, every.*

urb-ānus, a, um, *adj.* (**urbs**), *belonging to the city, in the city; polite, courteous, refined, well-bred.*

urbs, urbis, *f.*, *a city; the city* (Rome).

urgeo, urgēre, ursi, *no sup.*, *a.*, *to press, push, force, drive, urge.*

ūrīnā-tor, ōris, *m.* (**ūrīnor**, to dive; § **44**, 1, *c*, 1), *a diver.*

ūro, ūrĕre, ussi, ustum, *a.*, *to burn; fret, chafe, vex, annoy.*

ursa, **æ**, *f.*, *a she-bear.*

ursus, i, *m.*, *a bear.*

usquam, *adv.*, *anywhere.*

usque, *adv.*, *all the way, all the while, until;* **usque ăb**, *all the way from;* **usque ad**, *even to, up to.*

ūsūra, **æ**, *f.* (**ūtor**), *use, enjoyment; interest.*

ūsu-rpo, āre, āvi, ātum, *a.* (**ūsus; răpio**), *to use, employ.*

ūsus, ūs, *m.* (**ūtor**), *use, custom, advantage, benefit, utility; experience.*

ū-sus, a, um, *part.* (**ūtor**), *having used.*

ŭt *or* **ŭti**, *adv.* and *conj.*, *how, as, so, when, since; that, so that, in order that, that not* (with words of fearing).

ut-cumque (**-cunque**), *adv.*, *in what way soever, howsoever, however, whenever.*

ūter, ūtris, *m.*, *a bag; skin.*

ŭter, ŭtra, ŭtrum, *adj. pron.* (*gen. sing.*, **ŭtrīus**; *dat.*, **ŭtri**), *which of two, which.*

ŭter-que, ŭtrăque, ŭtrumque, *adj. pron.*, *each* (of two), *both;* **ex utrāque parte**, *on either side.*

ŭti, *see* **ŭt**.

Ŭtĭca, **æ**, *f.*, a town of Africa.

ūt-ĭlis, e, *adj.* (**ūtor**), *useful, serviceable; profitable, advantageous; suitable.*

ūtĭl-ĭtas, ātis, *f.* (**ūtĭlis**, § **44**, 1, *c*, 2), *use, usefulness, utility, benefit, profit.*

ŭtĭ-nam, *adv.*, *oh that! I wish that, would that!*

ūtor, ūti, ūsus sum, *dep.*, *to use, make use of, employ, enjoy.*

ut-pŏt-e, *adv.* (**ŭt; pŏtis**), *as, namely, inasmuch as, since.*

ŭtrim-que (utrinque), *adv.* (**ŭter; que**), *on both sides, from both sides.*
ŭtrōque, *adv.* (**ŭterque**), *to both places, in both directions.*
ŭtrum, *adv.* (**ŭter**), *whether* (§ **71**, 2).
ūva, æ, *f.*, *a cluster of grapes.*
uxor, ōris, *f.*, *a wife;* **ducere uxorem**, *to marry.*

V.

văco, āre, āvi, ātum, *n.*, *to be empty, void,* or *vacant; be at leisure; be free, be free from.*
văc-uus, a, um, *adj.* (**văco**), *empty, void, free, clear.*
văd-um, i, *n.* (**vādo**, to go), *a shoal, ford* (that through which one can go).
vāgio, īre, īvi *or* **ii, ītum**, *n.*, *to cry, squall; bray.*
vāgī-tus, ūs, *m.* (**vāgio**, § **44**, 1, *c*, 2), *a crying; braying.*
văgor, āri, ātus sum, *dep.* (**văgus**), *to wander about, ramble, range, rove.*
văgus, a, um, *adj.*, *strolling about, roaming, wandering, roving; unsettled, vagrant.*
vald-e, *adv.* (**valĭdus**), *strongly, vehemently; very, very much, exceedingly.*
vălens, entis, *part.* (**văleo**), *strong, stout, vigorous.*
văleo, ēre, ui, ĭtum, *n.*, *to be strong, stout, vigorous; to be well, healthy; to have the power, be able;* **vale**, *farewell, adieu.*
Vălĕrius, ii, *m.*, a Roman name.
vălē-tūdo, ĭnis, *f.* (**văleo**), *habit, state, condition; health; sickness.*
văl-ĭdus, a, um, *adj.* (**văleo**), *strong, mighty, healthy, powerful.*
valles (is), is, *f.*, *a valley, vale.*
vallum, i, *n.*, *rampart* (earthen wall set with palisades), *wall, fortification.*
vānus, a, um, *adj.*, *empty, vacant; idle, vain, fruitless, worthless; unreasonable.*
văpor, ōris, *m.*, *steam, vapor.*
vărius, a, um, *adj.*, *diverse, changing, varying, various.*
vas, vāsis, *pl.*, **vāsa, ōrum**, *n.*, *a vessel, dish, tool;* in *pl.*, *baggage.*
vasto, āre, āvi, ātum, *a.* (**vastus**), *to lay waste, desolate, ravage; ruin, destroy.*
vastus, a, um, *adj.*, *empty, waste; huge, vast.*
vātes, is, *com. gen.* (*gen. pl.*, **vatum**), *a soothsayer, prophet, prophetess; poet, poetess.*
vātĭcĭnā-tio, ōnis, *f.* (**vātĭcĭnor**, § **44**, 1, *c*, 2), *a foretelling, prophecy, prediction.*
vāt-ĭcĭnor, āri, ātus sum, *dep.* (**vātes**), *to foretell, predict, prophesy.*
vectīgal, ālis, *n.*, *a toll, tax; revenue, income.*
vĕg-ētus, a, um, *adj.* (**vĕgeo**, to arouse), *vigorous, active, brisk, sprightly.*
vĕhĕmens, entis, *adj.*, *eager, violent, impetuous, ardent, vehement; forcible.*
vĕhĕmen-ter, *adv.* (**vĕhĕmens**), *eagerly, ardently; vigorously, forcibly, very, very much.*
vĕho, vĕhĕre, vexi, vectum, *a.*, *to bear, carry, convey;* in *pass.*, **vehi**, *to be carried, go, ride, sail.*
vĕl, *conj.*, *or;* **vel . . . vel**, *either . . . or; even, indeed, surely; the very* (with *superlatives*).
vēlā-men, ĭnis, *n.* (**vēlo**), *a covering, cover; clothing, garment.*
velle, *inf.* of **vŏlo**, *to wish.*
vello, vellĕre, vulsi, vulsum, *a.*, *to pluck, pull, pull out, tear out.*
vēl-ox, ōcis, *adj.* (**vŏlo**, to fly), *swift, fleet, rapid.*
vēlum, i, *n.*, *a sail; covering; veil.*
vĕl-ut (vĕl-ŭti), *adv.*, *just as, like as; as it were; just as if, as if, just as though.*
vēna, æ, *f.*, *a blood-vessel, vein.*
vēn-ālis, e, *adj.* (**vēnus**, a sale), *for sale, to be sold, venal.*

vēnāt-ĭcus, a, um, *adj.* **(vēnātus,** hunting), *for hunting.*
ven-do, dĕre, dĭdi, dĭtum, *a.* **(vēnum,** a sale; **do),** *to sell.*
vĕnēnum, i, *n., a poison, drug.*
vēn-eo, īre, īvi *or* **ii, ĭtum,** *n.* **(vēnum,** a sale; **eo),** *to be sold.*
vĕnĕrā-tio, ōnis, *f.* **(vĕnĕror,** to reverence; § **44,** 1, *c,* 2), *reverence, veneration.*
vĕnia, æ, *f., favor, indulgence, kindness; pardon, forgiveness.*
vĕnio, vĕnīre, vēni, ventum, *n., to come, approach, draw near.*
vēnor, āri, ātus sum, *dep., to hunt, chase, pursue.*
venter, tris, *m., the belly.*
vent-ĭto, āre, *no perf., no sup., n. intens.* **(vento,** § **36,** *b,* and **44,** 2, *b*), *to come often, be wont to come, keep coming.*
ventus, i, *m., the wind.*
verber, ĕris, *n.* (*nom., dat.,* and *acc. sing.* not found), *a lash, whip, scourge.*
verbĕro, āre, āvi, ātum, *a.* **(verber),** *to lash, whip, scourge, flog, beat.*
verbum, i, *n., a word;* **verba facere,** *to speak, discourse;* **verbi causā,** *for example.*
vĕrēcund-ia, æ, *f.* **(vĕrēcundus,** § **44,** 1, *c,* 2), *respect, veneration, reverence; bashfulness, modesty.*
vĕrē-cundus, a, um, *adj.* **(vĕreor,** § **44,** 1, *c,* 3), *bashful, modest, shy.*
vĕreor, ēri, ĭtus sum, *dep., to feel awe for, reverence, respect, revere; fear, be afraid of, dread.*
Vergĭlius, ii, *m., Publius Vergilius Maro,* the celebrated Roman poet.
vergo, vergĕre (versi), *no sup., a.* and *n., to bend, turn, lie towards, be situated.*
vēr-o, *adv.* **(vērus),** *in truth, in fact, certainly, to be sure, surely; truly, yes; but, however.*
verrūca, æ, *f., a wart.*
ver-sor, āri, ātus sum, *dep. intens.* **(verto,** § **36,** *b,* and **44,** 2, *b*), *to dwell, remain, be engaged in.*
ver-sus, ūs, *m.* **(verto,** § **44,** 1, *c,* 2), *a verse; line.*
vert-ex, ĭcis, *m.* **(verto),** *a whirl, eddy; the top, summit, peak.*
verto, vertĕre, verti, versum, *a.* and *n., to turn, change, revolve.*
vĕru, ūs, *n.* (§ **12,** 2, *d*), *a spit; dart.*
vēr-um, *adv.* **(vērus),** *truly, just so, even so, yes; but, yet.*
vērus, a, um, *adj., true, real, actual.* As Noun, **verum, i,** *n., the truth, reality.*
vescor, vesci, *no perf., dep., to feed, eat; live on.*
Vĕsontio, ōnis, *m.,* a city of Gallia, the chief town of the Sequăni (modern *Besançon*).
vesper, ĕris *and* **ĕri,** *m., the evening.*
Vesta, æ, *f.,* daughter of Saturn, goddess of flocks and herds, and of the household in general.
ves-ter, tra, trum, *possessive pron.* **(vos),** *your.*
vestīg-ium, ii, *n.* **(vestīgo,** to track; § **44,** 1, *c,* 2), *a footstep, track, trace, step.*
vestio, īre, īvi *or* **ii, ītum,** *a.* **(vestis),** *to dress, clothe, cover; adorn.*
vestis, is, *f., a garment, robe, vestment; clothing, attire.*
vĕtĕr-ānus, a, um, *adj.* **(vĕtus),** *veteran, old.*
vĕto, āre, ui, ĭtum, *a., to forbid, prohibit.*
vĕtus, ĕris, *adj., old, aged.* As Noun, **vĕtĕres, um,** *m. pl., the ancients; ancestors.*
vexillum, i, *n., a standard, banner, flag.*
vexo, āre, āvi, ātum, *a. intens.* **(veho,** § **36,** *b,* and **44,** 2, *b*), *to annoy, harass, trouble, distress, vex, abuse.*
via, æ, *f., a way, road, street; journey.*

viā-tor, ōris, *m.* (**vio**, to go; § **44**, 1, *c*, 1), *a wayfarer, traveller.*
vĭbro, āre, āvi, ātum, *a.* and *n.*, *to brandish, shake; quiver, vibrate.*
vĭc-ārius, a, um, *adj.* (**vĭcis**), *substituted.* As NOUN, *m.*, *a substitute, deputy, proxy.*
vīc-ēsĭmus, a, um, *num. adj.* (**vīginti**), *the twentieth.*
vīc-ies, *num. adv.* (**vīginti**), *twenty times.*
vīc-īnus, a, um, *adj.* (**vīcus**), *near, neighboring.*
vĭcis, vĭcem, vĭce, in *pl.*, *nom.* and *acc.* **vĭces**, *dat.* and *abl.* **vĭcĭbus**, *f.*, *change, turn;* **vicem** (followed by *gen.* or *possessive pron.*), *in the place of, instead of, on account of, for;* **in vicem**, *by turns.*
vic-tor, ōris, *m.* (**vinco**, § **44**, 1, *c*, 1), *conqueror, victor.*
victor-ia, æ, *f.* (**victor**), *victory.*
vīcus, i, *m.*, *a street; village.*
vĭdē-lĭcet, *adv.*, *it is manifest, of course, forsooth.*
vĭdeo, vĭdēre, vīdi, vīsum, *a.*, *to see, perceive, observe; look at, consider; understand;* in *pass.*, *appear, seem.*
vĭdua, æ, *f.*, *a widow.*
vĭgeo, ēre, *no perf.*, *no sup.*, *n.*, *to thrive, flourish, bloom.*
vĭg-il, ĭlis, *adj.* (**vĭgeo**), *awake, on the watch, watchful, alert.*
vĭgĭlant-ia, æ, *f.* (**vĭgĭlans**, watchful; § **44**, 1, *c*, 2), *watchfulness, vigilance, careful attention.*
vĭgĭl-ia, æ, *f.* (**vĭgĭlo**), *a watch, night-guard.*
vĭgĭlo, āre, āvi, ātum, *n.* and *a.*, *to watch, be watchful; guard.*
vīginti, *num. adj. indecl.*, *twenty.*
vĭg-or, ōris, *m.* (**vĭgeo**, § **44**, 1, *c*, 2), *liveliness, activity, force, vigor, energy.*
vīlis, e, *adj.*, *cheap, worthless; mean, base, vile.*
villa, æ, *f.*, *a country-seat, farm, villa.*

vincio, vincīre, vīnxi, vinctum, *a.*, *to bind, fetter.*
vinco, vincĕre, vīci, victum, *a.*, *to conquer, overcome, defeat, subdue, vanquish.*
vinc-ŭlum, i, *n.* (**vincio**, § **44**, 1, *c*, 2), *a bond, chain, fetter, prison.*
vindex, vindĭcis, *com. gen.* (**vindĭco**), *a defender, protector, deliverer.*
vindĭco, āre, āvi, ātum, *a.*, *to demand, claim, assume; avenge, punish, revenge.*
vīnum, i, *n.*, *wine.*
vi-ŏlens, entis, *adj.* (**vis**), *impetuous, vehement, furious, violent.*
viŏlen-ter, *adv.* (**viŏlens**), *impetuously, vehemently, violently.*
viŏlent-ia, æ, *f.* (**viŏlens**, § **44**, 1, *c*, 2), *violence, vehemence, impetuosity, ferocity.*
vi-ŏlo, āre, āvi, ātum, *a.* (**vis**), *to injure, dishonor, profane, violate.*
vir, vĭri, *m.*, *a man, husband.*
virga, æ, *f.*, *a twig, sprout; rod, switch.*
Virgĭlius, ii, *m.*, see **Vergĭlius.**
vir-go, gĭnis, *f.* (**vĭreo**, to bloom), *a maid, virgin.*
virg-ŭla, æ, *f. dim.* (**virga**, § **44**, 1, *c*, 3), *a little twig, small rod.*
virgul-tum, i, *n.* (**virgŭla**), *a bush, thicket.*
vĭr-ĭdis, e, *adj.* (**vĭreo**), *green, verdant; fresh, blooming youthful.*
vĭr-īlis, e, *adj.* (**vir**), *manly; firm, vigorous, bold, spirited.*
vĭr-ītim, *adv.* (**vir**), *man by man, singly.*
vir-tus, ūtis, *f.* (**vir**), *manliness; virtue, valor; goodness, worth.*
vīs, vis, *f.* (§ **11**, iii. 4, *d*), *strength, force, power, energy, violence;* **vi et armis**, *by armed force;* **vim facere**, *to do violence, offer violence;* in *pl.*, **vires, ium**, *forces, troops.*

vī-so, vīsĕre, vīsi, vīsum, *a. intens.* (**vĭdeo,** § **36,** *b*, and **44,** 2, *b*), *to look at attentively, view, survey; to go to see, visit.*

vī-sus, a, um, *part.* of **vĭdeo.**

vī-ta, æ, *f.* (**vīvo**), *life.*

vĭtium, ii, *n.*, *a fault; crime, offence, vice.*

vīto, āre, āvi, ātum, *a.*, *to shun, avoid.*

vīvo, vīvĕre, vixi, victum, *n.*, *to live, be alive, have life.*

vīv-us, a, um, *adj.* (**vīvo**), *alive, living.*

vix, *adv.*, *with difficulty, hardly, scarcely.*

vŏco, āre, āvi, ātum, *a.*, *to call, summon, call upon, invoke, name.*

vŏl-ĭto, āre, āvi, ātum, *n. intens.* (**vŏlo,** to fly; § **36,** *b*, and **44,** 2, *b*), *to fly to and fro, flit, fly, hover.*

vŏlo, velle, vŏlui, *no sup.*, *a. irr.* (§ **37,** 1), *to will, wish, desire.*

vŏlo, āre, āvi, ātum, *n.*, *to fly, hasten.*

Volsci, ōrum, *m. pl.*, a people of Latium.

vŏl-ŭcer, cris, cre, *adj.* (**vŏlo,** to fly), *flying, winged.* As Noun, *f.*, *a bird.*

vŏlū-men, ĭnis, *n.* (**volvo**), *a roll, volume.*

vŏlunt-ārius, a, um, *adj.* (**vŏluntas**), *voluntary, willing.*

vŏlun-tas, ātis, *f.* (**vŏlens**), *will, wish, desire, choice; good feeling, inclination;* **voluntate sua,** *of one's own accord.*

vŏluptas, ātis, *f.*, *pleasure, delight, enjoyment, gratification;* in *pl.*, *sports, pleasures.*

volvo, volvĕre, volvi, vŏlūtum, *a.*, *to roll, turn, roll along; ponder.*

vos, *pl.* of **tu.**

vŏveo, vŏvēre, vōvi, vōtum, *a.*, *to vow, dedicate, promise, wish.*

vox, vōcis, *f.* (**vŏco**), *a voice, sound, cry, speech, word.*

vulg-āris, e, *adj.* (**vulgus**), *general, common, ordinary, vulgar.*

vulg-o, *adv.* (**vulgus**), *commonly, openly, publicly.*

vulgus, i, *n.* (rarely *m.*), *the great mass; the public, people, common people, populace, mob.*

vulnĕro, āre, āvi, ātum, *a.* (**vulnus**), *to wound, hurt.*

vulnus, ĕris, *n.*, *a wound, hurt.*

vulpes, is, *f.*, *a fox.*

vultur, ŭris, *m.*, *a vulture.*

vul-tus, ūs, *m.* (**vŏlo**), *the expression* (of countenance), *countenance, face.*

Z.

zōna, æ, *f.*, *a belt, girdle, zone.*

II. ENGLISH AND LATIN.

---

a, generally untranslated; when meaning **a certain**, *quidam*.
able, be, *possum*.
about, *circiter* (ACC.)
abroad, *foris*.
absent, be, *absum*.
accuse, *accūso*, 1.
acquit, *absolvo*, 3.
across, *trans* (ACC.).
actuate, *permoveo*, 2.
admire, *admīror*, 1.
admonish, *admoneo*, 2.
advance, *progredior*, 3.
Ædui, *Ædui*, *ōrum*, M.
advantage, be, *interesse* (§ **50**, 4, *d*).
against, *in* (ACC.).
aid, *auxilium*, *i*, N.
air, *aër*, *is*, acc., *aëra*, M.
alarm, *pavor*, *ōris*, M.
all, *omnis*, *e*.
alone, *solus*, *a*, *um;* gen. *solīus*.
alongside, *præter* (ACC.).
already, *jam*.
although, *quamquam*, *ut*, *licet* (§ **61**, 2).
always, *semper*.
ambassador, *legātus*, *ī*, M.
among, *in* (ACC. or ABL.(.
and, *et*.
angry, be, *irascor*, 3
animal, *anĭmal*, *is* (§ **11**, i. 2, *c*).
another, *alius*, *a*, *ud;* gen. *īus*.
any (you wish), *quivis*, *quilibet*.
apiece, distributive numeral.
appeal, *provŏco*, 1 (*ad*).
apple, *pomum*, *i*, N.
approach, *appropinquo*, **1**; noun *adventus*, *us*, M.
army, *exercĭtus*, *ūs*, M.; (drawn up), *acies*, *ci*, F.
around, *circa* (ACC.).
art, *ars*, *artis*, F.
as, *ut*, *sicut;* (as correl. see § **22**, *b*).
ashamed, be, *pudet* (§ **50**, 4, *c*).
Asia, *Asia*, *æ*, F.
ask, *rogo*, 1 (§ **52**, 2, *c*)
assault, *oppugno*, 1.
assemble, *convenio*, 4.
assist, *sublevo*, 1.
at, *ad* (ACC.), *in* (ABL.).
Athens, *Athēnæ*, *ārum*, F. (pl.).
attack, *impĕtus*, *ūs*, M.
attempt, *tento*, 1.
attentive, *attentus*, *a*, *um*.
away from, *ab* (ABL.).

B.

bad, *malus*, *a*, *um*.
baggage, *impedimenta*, *ōrum*, N.
bank, *ripa*, *æ*, F.
bark (verb), *latro*, 1; (noun), *cortex*, M.
battle, *prœlium*, *i*, N.
beam, *trabs*, *is*, F.
bear, *fero*, (§ **37**, 4).
beautiful, *pulcher*, *chra*, *chrum*.
because, *quod*, *quia*.
become, *fio* (§ **37**, 7).
before (prep.), *ante;* (conj.), *antequam*, *priusquam*.
begin, *ineo* (§ **37**, 6), *incipio*, 3.
Belgian, *Belga*, *æ*, M.
belong, *pertineo*, 2 (*ad*).
beyond, *trans* (ACC.).
bird, *avis*, *is*, F.
black, *niger*, *gra*, *grum*.
blame, *culpo*, 1.
boat, *linter*, *tris*, F.
bond, *vincŭlum*, *i*, N.

book, *liber*, *bri*, M.
boundaries, *fines*, *ium*, M. (pl.).
born, be. *nascor*, 3.
boy, *puer*, *i*, M.
brave, *fortis*, *e*.
bravely, *fortĭter*.
bridge, *pons*, *tis*, M.
bright, *clarus*, *a*, *um*.
broad, *latus*, *a*, *um*.
brother, *frater*, *tris*, M.
build, *ædifĭco*, 1.
building, *ædificium*, *i*, N.
burden, *onus*, *ĕris*, N.
business, *negotium*, *i*, N.
but, *sed*.
by (a person after a passive verb), *ab*.

C.

Cæsar, *Cæsar*, *ăris*
call, *voco*, 1.
camp, *castra*, *ōrum*, N. (pl.).
candidly, *aperte*.
care, *cura*, *æ*, F.
carefully, *diligenter*.
carry, *porto*, 1.
Carthage, *Carthăgo*, *ĭnis*, F.
cast away, *abjicio*, 3.
cavalry, *equĭtes*, *um*, M. (pl.).
cave, *antrum*, *i*, N.
century, *centuria*, *æ*, F.
certain, *quidam*, *quædam*, *quoddam*.
chief, *princeps*, *cĭpis*, M.
children, *libĕri*, *ōrum*, M.
citizen, *civis*, *is*, M.
city, *urbs*, *is*, F.
cloak, *paludamentum*, *i*, N.
close, *claudo*, 3.
cloud, *nubes*, *is*, F.
cohort, *cohors*, *tis*, F.
column, *columna*, *æ*, F
come, *venio*, 4.
commander, *dux*, *ducis*, C.
common, *commūnis*, C.
company (in), *cum* (ABL.).
conceal, *celo*, 1 (§ **52**, 2, *d*).
concerning, *de* (ABL.).
condemn, *damno*, 1.
conquer, *vinco*, 3.
conqueror, *victor*, *ōris*.
consul, *consul*, *is*, M.
consult, *consulo*, 3 ; (one's interest, DAT.).
contend, *contendo*, 3.
contention, *contentio*, *ōnis*,
Corinth, *Corinthus*, i. F.
cottage, *casa*, *æ*, F.
country (one's own), *patria*, *æ*, F. ; *rūs* (§ **55**, iii.).
crime, *scelus*, *eris*, N. ; *crimen*, *inis*, N.
cross, *transeo*, 4 ; *transmitto*, 3.
cruel, *crudēlis*, *e*.
cultivate, *colo*, 3.
culture, *cultus*, *ūs*, M.
cut, *seco*, 1.

D.

danger, *pericŭlum*, *i*, N.
dark (of color), *niger*, *gra*, *grum*.
daughter, *filia*, *æ*, F.
day, *dies*, *ēi*, M.
death, *mors*, *mortis*, F. ; to, *capitis* (§ **50**, 4, *b*).
declare (war), *indīco*, 3 (DAT.).
deep, *altus*, *a*, *um*.
defend, *defendo*, 3.
delight, *delecto*, 1.
deliver, *trado*, 3.
demand, *postulo*, 1 (§ **52**, 2, *c*. Rem.) ; *infero*, 1 (§ **51**, 2, *c*).
dense, *densus*, *a*, *um*.
depart, *decēdo*, 3 ; (set out), *proficiscor*, 3 ; (scatter), *discēdo*.
desert, *desero*, 3.
deserter, *perfuga*, *æ*, M.
desire, *cupio*, 3.
desirous, *appetens*, *ntis* (GEN.).
destroy, *perdo*, 3.
detain, *detineo*, 2.
determine, *constituo*, 3.
dictator, *dictātor*, *ōris*, M.
differ, *differo*.

differently, *aliter*.
difficult, *difficilis*, *e* (§ **17**, 1, *b*).
diligence, *diligentia*, *æ*, F.
diligently, *diligenter*.
disorder, *confusio*, *ōnis*, F.
dissension, *dissentio*, *ōnis*, F.
distance, *spatium*, *i*, N.
distant, *longinquus*, *a*, *um;* be distant, *disto*, 1.
do, *facio*, 3.
dog, *canis*, *is*, M. (§ **11**, I. *d*, 1).
door, *janua*, *æ*, F.
draw up, *instruo*, 3.
drive, *pello*, 3.
duty, *officium*, *i*, N. (or GEN.).
dwell, *habito*, 1.

E.

each, *quisque*, *unusquisque*.
each other, *alius . . . alium*, *alter . . . alterum* (§ **47**, 9).
eager, *avidus*, *a*, *um*.
earth, *terra*, *æ*, F.
easily, *facĭle*.
easy, *facĭlis*, *e*.
educate, *edŭco*, 1.
elect, *facio*, 3, *creo*, 1.
eloquence, *eloquentia*, *æ*, F.
encompass, *cingo*, 3.
encourage, *hortor*, 1.
endure. *perfĕro* (§ **37**, 4).
enemy, *hostis*, *is*, C. the enemy (collectively), *hostes*, *ium*.
enroll, *conscrībo*, 3.
enter, *intro*, 1.
escape, *effugio*, 3.
establish, *confirmo*, 1, *statuo*, 3.
evening, *vesper*, *eri*, M.
exercise, *exerceo*, 2.
extreme, *extrēmus*, *a*, *um*.

F.

faithful, *fidēlis*, *e*.
far, *longe*.
far and wide, *late*.
farmer, *agricŏla*, *æ*, M.
farther (adj.), *ulterior*, *us*.
father, *pater*, *tris*, M.
fault, *culpa*, *æ*, F.
fear, *timeo*, 2, *metuo*, 3, *vereor*, 2 ; (noun), *timor*, *ōris*, M.
fellow-citizen, *civis*, *is*, M. with possessive.
fill, *compleo*, *repleo*, 2.
field, *ager*, *agri*, M.
fierce, *atrox*, *atrocis*.
fiercely, *acrĭter*.
fight, *dimĭco*, *pugno*, 1.
find, *reperio*, 4.
finish, *finio*, 4.
first, *primus*, *a*, *um;* adv., *primum* and *primo*.
fish, *piscis*, *is*, M.
flee, *fugio*, 3.
fleet, *classis*, *is*, F.
flight, *fuga*, *æ*, F.
flow, *fluo*, 3.
fly, *volo*, 1.
following (day), *posterus*, *a*, *um*.
folly, *stultitia*, *æ*, F.
foot-soldier, *pedes*, *ĭtis*, M.
for, *nam*, *enim*, *etĕnim*.
forces, *copiæ*, *ārum*, F. (pl.).
forest, *silva*, *æ*, F.
forget, *obliviscor*, 3.
fortify, *munio*, 4.
fortunate, *fortunātus*.
found, *condo*, 3.
friend, *amīcus*, *i*, M.
friendship, *amicitia*, *æ*, F.
from, *ab*, *ex*.
fruit, *fructus*, *ūs*, M. ; (of fields), *fruges*, *um*, F. (§ **14**, 1, *c*).
fugitive, *fugiens*, part. of *fugio*.
full, *plenus*, *a*, *um*.
further, adj., *ulterior*, *us*.
fury, *furor*, *ōris*, M.

G.

gain, *lucrum*, *i*, N.
games, *ludi*, *ōrum*, M. (pl.).
garden, *hortus*, *i*, M.
Gaul (the country), *Gallia*, *æ*, F.
Gaul (an inhabitant), *Gallus*, *i*, M.

general, *dux*, *ducis*, M., *imperātor*, *ōris*, M.
German, *Germānus*, *a*, *um*.
girl, *puella*, *æ*, F.
give, *do*, 1; give up, *dedo*, 3.
glad, *lætus*.
glory, *gloria*, *æ*, F.
go, *eo*, 4 (§ **37**, 6); go on, pass. of *gero*, 3.
god, *deus*, *i*, M. (§ **10**, 4, *f*).
going to (fut. act. part.).
gold, *aurum*, *i*, N.
good, *bonus*, *a*, *um*.
grandfather, *avus*, *i*, M.
great, *magnus*, *a*, *um*.
ground, *humus*, *i*, F.
grow weak, *languesco*, 3.
guide, *dux*, *ducis*, M.

H.

hall, *aula*, *æ*, F.
happens, it, *accidit*.
happy, *felix*, *īcis*; *beātus*, *a*, *um*.
harbor, *portus*, *ūs*, M.
hardship, *durum*, *i*, N. (§ **47**, 4).
hasten, *festīno*, *propĕro*, 1.
hatred, *odium*, *i*, N.
have, *habeo*, 2.
hear, *audio*, 4.
Helvetians, *Helvetii*, *ōrum*, M.
here, be, *adsum*.
high, *altus*, *a*, *um*.
highly, *magni* (§ **50**, 1, *i*.).
hither (adj.), *citerior*, *us*.
home (to), *domum* (§ **55**, 3, *b*); (at), *domi* (§ **55**, 3, *c*).
honor, *honor*, *ōris*, M.
hope, *spes*, *ei*, F.
horse, *equus*, *i*, M.
horseman, *eques*, *ĭtis*, M.
hostage, *obses*, *ĭdis*, C.
house, *domus*, *ūs*, F. (§ **12**, 3, *e*).
hunger, *fames*, *is*, F.

I.

immediately, *statim*, *confestim*.
immortal, *immortālis*, *e*.
in, *in* (ABL.); in company with, *cum* (ABL.); in the power of, *penes* (ACC.); in turn, *invicem*.
inform, *certum* [*certiorem*] *facio*.
inhabitant, *incŏla*, *æ*, M.
inquire, *quæro*, 3.
insist on, *flagito*, 1 (ACC.).
into, *in* (ACC.).
island, *insŭla*, *æ*, F.
Italy, *Italia*, *æ*, F.

J.

journey, *iter*, *itinĕris*, N.
judge, *judex*, *icis*, M.
just, *justus*, *a*, *um*; (time), *ipse*.

K.

keep off, *prohibeo*, 2.
kill, *interficio*, 3; *occīdo*, 3.
kind, *benignus*, *a*, *um*.
king, *rex*, *regis*, M.
kingdom, *regnum*, *i*, N.
know, *scio*, 4.

L.

Lacedæmonian, *Lacedæmonius*, *a*, *um*.
lake, *lacus*, *ūs*, M.
land, *terra*, *æ*, F.
language, *lingua*, *æ*, F.
large, *magnus*, *amplus*, *a*, *um*.
last, *proxĭmus*; (furthest), *extrēmus*, *a*, *um*.
Latin, *Latīnus*, *a*, *um*.
lay waste, *vasto*, 1.
lead, *duco*, 3.
lead out, *edūco*, 3.
leap, *salto*, 1; over, *transilio*, 4.
learn, *disco*, 3.
leave, *relinquo*, 3.
legate, *legātus*, *i*, M.

legion, *legio, ōnis,* F.
letter, *litteræ, ārum,* F. (pl.).
liberate, *lībĕro,* 1.
lie, *jaceo,* 2 ; (speak falsehood), *mentior,* 4.
lieutenant, *legātus, i.*
life, *vita, æ,* F.
light, *lux, lucis,* F. ; be light, *luceo,* 2.
light, *levis, e.*
like, *simĭlis, e* (DAT. or GEN.).
line (of battle), *acies, ēi,* F.
lion, *leo, ōnis,* M.
literature, *litteræ, ārum,* F. (pl.).
live, *vivo,* 3 ; (dwell), *habĭto,* 1.
lofty, *excelsus, a, um.*
long, *longus, a, um.*
look at, *specto,* 1.
love, *amo,* 1.

M.

make, *facio,* 3 ; (a magistrate), *creo,* 1 ; (war upon), *infero* (DAT.). ; (cloak), *conficio.*
maker, *faber, bri,* M.
man, *homo, ĭnis,* C. ; *vir, viri,* M.
maniple, *manipŭlum, i,* N.
many, *multi, æ, a.*
master (of boys), *magister, tri;* (of slaves), *dominus, i,* M.
meet (death), *obeo,* 4.
memory, *memoria, æ,* F.
messenger, *nuntius, i,* M.
midday, *meridies, ēi,* M.
midnight, *media nox* (at, ABL.).
migrate, *migro,* 1.
mile, *mille passuum* (§ **18**, 1, *e*).
Miletus, *Milētus, i,* F.
mind, *anĭmus, i,* M.
mistaken, be, *fallor* (pass.).
money, *pecunia, æ,* F.
moon, *luna, æ,* F.
more, *magis;* comp. degree, *plus, amplius.*
morrow, on the, *postero die.*
most, superl. degree.
mountain, *mons, tis,* M.
mourn, *lugeo,* 2.
move, *moveo,* 2.
music, *musice, es,* F.
must, *oportet,* or gerundive.
my, *meus, a, um.*

N.

name, *nomen, ĭnis,* N.
narrow, *angustus, a, um.*
near, *prope* (DAT. or ACC.).
nearest, *proxĭmus.*
need, *opus* (§ **54**, 1, *d*).
never, *nunquam.*
new, *novus, a, um.*
night, *nox, noctis,* F. ; by night, *noctu.*
no, not, *non.*
none, *nullus, a, um* (§ **16**, 1, *b*).
now, *nunc.*
nowhere, *nusquam.*
number, *numĕrus, i.*
Numitor, *Numĭtor, ōris,* M.

O.

obey, *pareo,* 2 (§ **52**, 2, *a*).
obtain possession, *potior,* 4 (§ **54**, 6, *d*).
of, genitive case.
often, *sæpe.*
old man, *senex, senis,* M. ; *grandĭs natu.*
on, *in* (ABL.) ; on this side, *citra* (ACC.).
one, *unus, a, um;* gen. *īus;* one . . . another, *alius . . . alius* (§ **47**, 9).
oppress, *opprimo,* 3.
orator, *orātor, ōris,* M.
order, or give orders, *jubeo,* 2 (§ **70**, 3, *a*).
other, *alius, a, ud;* gen. *īus* (§ **16**, 1, *b*).
our, *noster, tra, trum.*
out of, *ex* (ABL.).
outside of, *extra* (ACC.).
over, *super,* prep.

P.

part, *pars*, *tis*, F. (gen. case).
pass, *transeo* (summer), *exigo*, 3.
patiently, *patienter*.
peace, *pax*, *pacis*, F.
people, *populus*, *i*, M.
perish, *pereo* (§ **37**, 6).
place, *locus*, *i*, M. (§ **14**, 2, *c*); verb, *pono*, 3, place around, *circumdo*, 3 (§ **51**, 1, *c*); take place, pass. of *gero*, 3.
plain, *planities*, *ēi*, F.
plan, *consilium*, *i*, N.
play, *ludo*, 3.
pleasing, *acceptus*, *a*, *um*.
pleasure, *voluptas*, *ātis*, F.
plough, *aro*, 1.
poet, *poëta*, *æ*, M.
Pompey, *Pompeius*, *i*, M.
poor, *pauper*, *ĕris*.
possession, obtain, *potior*, 4 (§ **54**, 6, *d*).
power (in ... of), *penes* (ACC.).
powerful, *potens*, *tis*.
praise, *laus*, *laudis*, F.
praise, *laudo*, 1.
prefer, *malo* (§ **37**, 3); *antepōno*, 3.
prepare, *paro*, 1.
present, be, *adsum*.
preserve, *conservo*, 1.
pretend, *simŭlo*, 1.
prevent, *prohibeo*, 2.
prisoner, *captīvus*, *i*, M.
produce, *fruges*, *um*, F. (pl. § **14**, 1, *c*).
promissum, i, N.; verb, *promitto*, 3, *polliceor*, 2.
prosper, *secundo*, 1.
protection, *præsidium*, *i*, N.
provided, *dum*, *dummodo* (§ **6**, 1, 3).
punish, *punio*, 4.
punishment, *pœna*, *æ*, F.
pupil, *discipŭlus*, *i*, M.
put, *conjicio*, 3.

Q.

quæstor, *quæstor*, *ōris*, M.
queen, *regīna*, *æ*, F.

R.

rapacious, *rapax*, *ācis*.
rapidly, *celerĭter*.
rather (had), *malo* (§ **37**, 3).
reach, *venio* (4), *ad*.
read, *lego*, 3.
receive, *accipio*, 3.
recognize, *agnosco*, 3.
recover, *recipio* (3) *se*.
refresh, *reficio*, 3.
rejoice, *gaudeo*, 2 (§ **35**, 2).
remain, *maneo*, 2.
remind, *admoneo*, 2.
renew, *redintegro*, 1.
repent, *pœnitet* (§ **50**, 4, 2).
report, *fama*, *æ*, F.
republic, *res publica*, *æ*, F. (§ **14**, 2, *d*).
repulse, *repello*, 3.
restrain, *tempĕro*, 1 (DAT.).
return, *reverto*, 3; *redeo*, 4.
revolution, *novæ res*.
reward, *præmium*, *i*, N.
rise, *orior*, 4; *surgo*, 3.
river, *fluvius*, *i*, M.; *flumen*, *ĭnis*, N.
river-bank, *ripa*, *æ*, F.
road, *via*, *æ*, F.
rock, *saxum*, *i*, N.
roll, *volvo*, 3.
Roman, *Romānus*, *a*, *um*.
Rome, *Roma*, *æ*, F.
rugged, *asper*, *era*, *erum*.
rule (the republic), *gero*, 3.
run, *curro*, 3.

S.

sad, *tristis*, *e*.
sailor, *nauta*, *æ*, F.
sake, for the, *causā* or *gratiā* (§ **50**, 1, *i*, Rem.).

same, *idem* (§ **20**, 2).
say, *dico*, 3.
school, *ludus*, *i*, M.
scholar, *discipŭlus*, *i*, M.
sea, *mare*, *is*, N.
sea-shore, *ora*, *æ*, F.
seated, be, *consideo*, 2.
see, *video*, 2.
seek, *peto*, 3 ; *quæro*, 3.
seem, *videor*, 2.
seize, *occŭpo*, 1.
sell, *vendo*, 3.
senate, *senātus*, *us*, M.
send, *mitto*, 3.
servant, *famŭlus*, *i*, M.
serviceable, *utilis*, *e*.
sesterce, *sestertius*, *i*, M. ; **thousands**, *sestertium*, *i*, N.
set out, *proficiscor*, 3.
severely, *graviter*.
shade, *umbra*, *æ*, F.
ship, *navis*, *is*, F.
shore, *ora*, *æ*, F.
short, *brevis*, *e*.
shoulder, *humerus*, *i*, N.
show, *monstro*, 1.
show, *species*, *ēi*, F.
side, *latus*, *eris*, N. ; **on this**, *citra* (ACC.).
signal, *signum*, *i*, N.
since, *quoniam*, *cum*.
sit, *sedeo*, 2.
skilled, *perĭtus*, *a*, *um* (§ **50**, 3, *b*).
sky, *cœlum*, *i*, N.
slaughter, *clades*, *is*, F.
slave, *servus*, *i*, M.
small, *parvus*, *a*, *um*.
so, *ita*, *sic* ; (**such**), *talis*, *e*.
soldier, *miles*, *ĭtis*, C.
some, *quidam*, *aliquis*, *aliquantum* (GEN.).
some . . . other, *alius . . . alius* (§ **47**, 9).
son, *filius*, *i*, M.
soon, *mox*.
Spain, *Hispania*, *æ*, F.
spare, *pareo*, 3.
speak, *loquor*, 3 ; (of an orator), *dico*, 3.
stand, *sto*, 1.
star, *stella*, *æ*, F.
state, *civitas*, *ātis*, F.
story, *fabula*, *æ*, F.
strange, *novus*, *a*, *um*.
strive, *nitor*, 3.
strong, *valĭdus*, *a*, *um*.
study, *studeo*, 2.
subdue, *subigo*, 3.
Suessiones, *Suessiones*, *um*.
summer, *æstas*, *ātis*, F.
sun, *sol*, *solis*, M.
surrender, *deditio*, *ōnis*, F.
surround, *cingo*, 3 ; *circum-sto*, 1.
sustain, *sustineo*, 2.
swift (rivers), *rapĭdus*, *a*, *um*, (persons, &c.), *velox*, *ōcis*.
swiftness, *celerĭtas*, *ātis*, F.
swim, *nato*, 1.
sword, *ferrum*, *i*, N.

T.

take, *capio*, 3, (possession of), *occŭpo*, 1, (place), passive of *gero*, 3.
talent, *talentum*, *i*, N.
teach, *doceo*, 2.
teacher, *doctor*, *toris*, M.
tell, *narro*, 1, *dico*, 3.
temper, *anĭmus*, *i*, M.
tenacious, *tenax*, *ācis*.
territories, *fines*, *ium*, M.
than, *quam*, or abl. case (§ **54**, 5).
that, *ille*, *a*, *ud ;* (after same), *qui*.
theatre, *theatrum*, *i*, N.
there, *ibi*, *illic ;* **thither**, *eo ;* **there is**, *est*.
thick, *densus*, *a*, *um*, (wall), *latus*, *a*, *um*.
thing, neut. adj. (§ **47**, 4).
think, *puto*, 1.
thirst (noun), *sitis*, *is*, F. ; (verb), *sitio*, 4 (§ **52**, 1, *a*).
this side of, *citra* (ACC.).
through, *per* (ACC.).
throw, *jacio*, 3.
Tiber, *Tibĕris*, *is*, M. ; (ACC. *im*).
to, *ad* (ACC.), or dative case.

to-day, *hodie*.
towards, *ad* (ACC.), of time, *sub* (ACC.).
town, *oppĭdum*, *i*, N.
train, *exerceo*, 2.
treachery, *proditio*, *ōnis*, F.
tribune, *tribūnis*, *i*, M.
troublesome, *molestus*, *a*, *um*.
trust, *credo*, 3 (§ **51**, 2, *a*).
truth (true things), *vera* (n. pl.).
tumult, *tumultus*, *us*, M.
turn (verb), *verto*, 3; (noun), *invicem*.

U.

understanding, *intellectus*, *ūs*, M.
undertaking, *inceptum*, *i*, N.
unequal, *impar*.
unfriendly, *inimīcus*, *a*, *um*.
unless, *nisi*.
unlike, *dissimĭlis*, *e* (§ **17**, 1, *b*).
until, *dum*, *donec*.
unwilling, **be**, *nolo* (§ **37**, 2).
unworthy, *indignus*, *a*, *um*.
upon, *in* (ABL.).
use (verb), *utor*, 3; (noun), *usus*, *us*, M.

V.

value, *æstimo*, 1.
very, superlative degree (§ **17**, 5, *b*).
vessel, *navis*, *is*, F.
vexed (to be), *piget* (§ **50**, 4, *c*, 2).
victory, *victoria*, *æ*, F.
villa, *villa*, *æ*, F.
vulture, *vultur*, *is*, M.

W.

wait, *exspecto*, 1.
walk, *ambŭlo*, 1.
wall, *murus*, *i*, M.; (of a city), *mœnia*, *ōrum*, N. (pl.).
war, *bellum*, *i*, N.
warn, *moneo*, 2.
waste, lay, *vasto*, 1.
watch, *vigilia*, *æ*, F.
water, *aqua*, *æ*, F.
wave, *fluctus*, *ūs*, M.
way, *via*, *æ*, F.
weak, grow, *languesco*, 3.
weapon, *telum*, *i*, N.
wearied, *fessus*, *a*, *um*; **be**, *tædet* (§ **50**, 4, *c*).
well, *bene*.
what o'clock, *quota hora*.
when, *cum*, or an appositive.
where, *ubi*.
whether, *num*, *nĕ*.
which (of two), *uter* (§ **16**, 1, *b*).
white, *albus*, *a*, *um*.
wide, *latus*, *a*, *um*.
wind, *ventus*, *i*, M.
winter, *hiems*, *is*, F.
wise, *sapiens*, *ntis*.
wish, *volo* (§ **37**, 1), *cupio*, 3.
with, abl. case; (in company with), *cum* (ABL.).
within, *intra* (ACC.).
wolf, *lupus*, *i*, M.
woods, *silva*, *æ*, F.
worthy, *dignus*, *a*, *um*, with abl.
wound, *vulnĕro*, 1.
write, **scribo**, 3.

Y.

year, *annus*, *i*, M.
yes, repeat the verb.
yesterday, *heri*.
yet, *tamen*; **not yet**, *nondum*.

Z.

Zeno, *Zeno*, *ōnis*, M.

INDEX OF SYNONYMES.

BOSTON, September, 1874.

GINN BROTHERS,

Publishers,

4 Beacon Street, ... BOSTON.

Terms: Cash in Thirty Days. **Wholesale and Retail Prices.**

ENGLISH.

Wholesale. Retail.

ARNOLD'S MANUAL of ENGLISH LITERATURE. Historical and Critical. With an Appendix on English Metres. By THOMAS ARNOLD, M. A., of University College, Oxford. Third Edition, revised . . . $2.50

CRAIK'S ENGLISH OF SHAKESPEARE. Illustrated in a Philological Commentary on his Julius Cæsar, by GEORGE L. CRAIK, Queen's College, Belfast. Edited by W. J. ROLFE, Cambridge. Cloth . . . 1.40 1.75

ENGLISH OF THE XIV. CENTURY. Illustrated by Notes, Grammatical and Etymological, on Chaucer's Prologue and Knight's Tale. Designed to serve as an Introduction to the Critical Study of English. By STEPHEN H. CARPENTER, A. M., Professor of Rhetoric and English Literature in the State University of Wisconsin 1.40 1.75

This work is designed to furnish an introduction to the critical study of the English language. The selections are edited with ample Notes and a Glossary, and are intended to be studied with the care and thoroughness usually given to classical authors. An attempt has been made to elucidate English grammar, not by a set of formal rules, but by explaining idioms and difficult constructions as they arise in the course of reading.

HUDSON'S FAMILY SHAKESPEARE: Plays selected and prepared, with Notes and Introductions, for Use in Families.

Volume I., containing As You Like It, The Merchant of Venice, Twelfth Night, First and Second of King Henry the Fourth, Julius Cæsar, and Hamlet.

Volume II., containing The Tempest, The Winter's Tale, King Henry the Fifth, King Richard the Third, King Lear, Macbeth, and Antony and Cleopatra.

Volume III., containing A Midsummer Night's Dream, Much Ado about Nothing, King Henry the Eighth, Romeo and Juliet, Cymbeline, Coriolanus, and Othello.

And Hudson's Life, Art, and Characters of Shakespeare. 2 vols.

		Wholesale.	Retail.
5 vols.	Cloth	8.00	10.00
	Half morocco	12.00	15.00
	Full calf	16.00	20.00

HUDSON'S LIFE, ART, AND CHARACTERS OF SHAKESPEARE. Including an Historical Sketch of the Origin and Growth of the Drama in England, with Studies in the Poet's Dramatic Architecture, Delineation of Character, Humor, Style, and Moral Spirit, also with Critical Discourses on the following plays, — A Midsummer Night's Dream, The Merchant of Venice, The Merry Wives of Windsor, Much Ado about Nothing, As You Like It, Twelfth Night, All 's Well that Ends Well, Measure for Measure, The Tempest, The Winter's Tale, King John, King Richard the Second, King Henry the Fourth, King Henry the Fifth, King Richard the Third, King Henry the Eighth, Romeo and Juliet, Julius Cæsar, Hamlet, Macbeth, King Lear, Antony and Cleopatra, Othello, Cymbeline, and Coriolanus. In Two Volumes. Cloth, per vol., ... 3.20 4.00

HUDSON'S SERMONS. 1.40 1.75

	Wholesale.	Retail.
HUDSON'S SCHOOL SHAKESPEARE. 1st Series.	$1.60	$2.00

Containing As You Like It, The Merchant of Venice, Twelfth Night, The Two Parts of Henry IV., Julius Cæsar, Hamlet.

Selected and prepared for Use in Schools, Clubs, Classes, and Families. With Introductions and Notes. By the Rev. Henry N. Hudson.

HUDSON'S SCHOOL SHAKESPEARE. 2d Series.	1.60	2.00

Containing The Tempest, The Winter's Tale, King Henry the Fifth, King Richard the Third, King Lear, Macbeth, Antony and Cleopatra.

HUDSON'S SCHOOL SHAKESPEARE. 3d Series.	1.60	2.00

Containing A Midsummer Night's Dream, Much Ado about Nothing, King Henry VIII., Romeo and Juliet, Cymbeline, Coriolanus, Othello.

HUDSON'S SEPARATE PLAYS OF SHAKESPEARE.

THE MERCHANT OF VENICE. In Paper Cover	.32	.40
JULIUS CÆSAR. In Paper Cover	.32	.40
HAMLET. In Paper Cover	.32	.40
THE TEMPEST. In Paper Cover	.32	.40
MACBETH. In Paper Cover	.32	.40
HENRY THE EIGHTH. In Paper Cover	.32	.40
AS YOU LIKE IT	.32	.40
HENRY THE FOURTH. Part I.	.32	.40
KING LEAR	.32	.40
MUCH ADO ABOUT NOTHING	.32	.40
ROMEO AND JULIET	.32	.40
OTHELLO	.32	.40

HALSEY'S GENEALOGICAL AND CHRONOLOGICAL CHART of the Rulers of England, Scotland, France, Germany, and Spain. By C. S. Halsey. Mounted, 33 × 48 inches. Folded and Bound in 4to, 10 × 12 inches 1.50

HALSEY'S BIBLE CHART OF GENEALOGY AND CHRONOLOGY, from the Creation to A. D. 100. Prepared by C. S. Halsey 1.00 1.25

This Chart is designed to illustrate Bible History by showing on a clear and simple plan the genealogy and chronology of the principal persons mentioned in the Scriptures.

HARVARD EXAMINATION PAPERS. Collected and arranged by R. F. Leighton, A. M., Master of Melrose High School. Second Edition, containing papers of June and September, 1873 . . . . 1.25 1.56

These are all the questions (except on the subject of Geometry), in the form of papers, which have been used in the examinations for admission to Harvard College since 1860. They will furnish an excellent series of Questions in Modern, Physical, and Ancient Geography; Grecian and Roman History; Arithmetic and Algebra; Plane and Solid Geometry; Logarithms and Trigonometry; Latin and Greek Grammar and Composition; Physics and Mechanics They have been published in this form for the convenience of Teachers, classes in High Schools, and especially for pupils preparing for college.

THE LIVING WORD; or, Bible Truths and Lessons .80 1.00

The distinguishing feature of this book is the arrangement by subjects of the spiritual and moral truths of the Bible, so that all its most expressive utterances upon a given subject may be read in unbroken succession. It is believed that this will furnish what has been long needed for public and private reading in the home, the school, and the church.

OUR WORLD, No. I.; or, First Lessons in Geography. Revised edition, with new Maps, by Mary L. Hall . . . . .75 .94

Designed to give children clear and lasting impressions of the different countries and inhabitants of the earth rather than to tax the memory with mere names and details.

GREEK.

Wholesale. Retail.

GOODWIN'S GREEK GRAMMAR. By WILLIAM W. GOODWIN, Ph. D., Eliot Professor of Greek Literature in Harvard University. Half morocco $1.25 $1.56

The object of this Grammar is to state *general principles* clearly and distinctly, with special regard to those who are preparing for college. In the sections on the Moods are stated, for the first time in an elementary form, the principles which are elaborated in detail in the author's "Syntax of the Greek Moods and Tenses."

GREEK MOODS AND TENSES. The Fonrth Edition. By WILLIAM W. GOODWIN, Eliot Professor of Greek Literature in Harvard University. 1 vol. 12mo. Cloth. pp. 264 . . . . 1.40 1.75

This work was first published in 1860, and it appeared in a new form — much enlarged and in great part rewritten — in 1865. In the present edition the whole has been again revised; some sections and notes have been rewritten, and a few notes have been added. The object of the work is to give a plain statement of the principles which govern the construction of the Greek Moods and Tenses, — the most important and the most difficult part of Greek Syntax.

GOODWIN'S GREEK READER. Consisting of Extracts from Xenophon, Plato, Herodotus, and Thucydides; being a full equivalent for the seven books of the Anabasis, now required for admission at Harvard. With Maps, Notes, References to GOODWIN'S GREEK GRAMMAR, and parallel References to CROSBY'S and HADLEY'S GRAMMARS. Edited by PROFESSOR W. W. GOODWIN, of Harvard College, and J. H. ALLEN, Cambridge. Half morocco 1.60 2.00

This book contains the third and fourth books of the Anabasis (entire), the greater part of the second book of the Hellenica, and the first chapter of the Memorabilia, of Xenophon; the last part of the Apology, and the beginning and end of the Phaedo, of Plato; selections from the sixth, seventh, and eighth books of Herodotus, and from the fourth book of Thucydides.

LEIGHTON'S GREEK LESSONS. Prepared to accompany Goodwin's Greek Grammar. By R. F. LEIGHTON, Master of Melrose High School. Half morocco 1.25 1.56

This work contains about one hundred lessons, with a progressive series of exercises (both Greek and English), mainly selected from the first book of Xenophon's Anabasis. The exercises on the Moods are sufficient, it is believed, to develop the general principles as stated in the Grammar. The text of four chapters of the Anabasis is given entire, with notes and references. Full vocabularies accompany the book.

These lessons, with the additional exercises to be translated into Greek, are believed to be a sufficient preparation in Greek Composition for admission to any American College.

LIDDELL & SCOTT'S GREEK-ENGLISH LEXICON. Abridged from the new Oxford Edition. 13th Edition.

Morocco back 2.40 3.00
Sheep binding 2.80 3.50

LIDDELL & SCOTT'S GREEK-ENGLISH LEXICON. The sixth Oxford Edition unabridged. 4to. Morocco back . . 9.60 12.00
Sheep binding . 10.40 13.00

We have made arrangements with Messrs. Macmillan & Co. to publish in this country their new edition of Liddell & Scott's Greek Lexicons, and are ready to supply the trade.

The English editions of Liddell & Scott are *not stereotyped;* but each has been thoroughly revised, enlarged, and printed anew The sixth edition, just published, is larger by one eighth than the fifth, and contains 1865 pages. It is an *entirely different work* from the first edition, the whole department of etymology having been rewritten in the light of modern investigations, and the forms of the irregular verbs being given in greater detail by the aid of Veitch's Catalogue. No student of Greek can afford to dispense with this invaluable Lexicon, the price of which is now for the first time brought within the means of the great body of American scholars.

THE ŒDIPUS TYRANNUS OF SOPHOCLES. Edited, with an Introduction, Notes, and full explanation of the metres, by JOHN W. WHITE, A. M., Professor of the Greek Language and Literature in Baldwin University.

WILKIN'S MANUAL OF GREEK PROSE COMPOSITION. 1 vol. 12mo. Cloth 2.00 2.50

LATIN.

ALLEN & GREENOUGH'S LATIN GRAMMAR. Founded on Comparative Grammar. By J. H. ALLEN, Cambridge, and J. B. GREENOUGH, Instructor in Latin in Harvard College, and Lecturer on Comparative Philology in the University course. pp. 268 . . . . 1.25 1.56

"A complete Latin Grammar, to be used from the beginning of the study of Latin till the end of the college course." The forms of the language and the constructions of Syntax are fully illustrated by classical examples and by comparison with parallel forms of kindred languages.

ALLEN & GREENOUGH'S SELECT ORATIONS OF CICERO. Chronologically arranged, covering the entire period of his Public Life. Edited by J. H. & W. F. ALLEN and J. B. GREENOUGH, with References to Allen & Greenough's Latin Grammar. Containing the Defence of Roscius (abridged), Verres I., Manilian Law, Catiline, Archias, Sestius (abridged), Milo, Marcellus, Ligarius, and the Fourteenth Philippic. With Life, Introductions, Notes, and Index 1.40 1.75

ALLEN & GREENOUGH'S VIRGIL. Containing the Bucolics and six books of the Æneid 1.40 1.75

ALLEN & GREENOUGH'S SALLUST'S CATILINE. 80 1.00

ALLEN & GREENOUGH'S CICERO DE SENECTUTE (Cato Major), in uniform style with Allen & Greenough's Cicero. 1 vol. 12mo. Cloth . . . . .60 .75

ALLEN & GREENOUGH'S SHORTER COURSE OF LATIN PROSE: Consisting chiefly of the Prose Selections of Allen's Latin Reader (to p. 134), the Notes being wholly rewritten, enlarged, and adapted to Allen & Greenough's Grammar; accompanied by Six Orations of Cicero, — the Manilian, the four Catilines, and Archias, — thus forming a volume adapted to the second or shorter preparatory course at Harvard 2.00 2.50

ALLEN & GREENOUGH'S LATIN SELECTIONS. With full Notes and References to Allen & Greenough's Grammar . . . 1.25 1.56

ALLEN & GREENOUGH'S CÆSAR (Gallic War, Four Books). With very full Notes, Maps, and References to their Grammar as well as Gildersleeve's 1.25 1.56
Do. without Vocabulary 1.00 1.25

ALLEN'S LATIN READER. 12mo. 518 pages. Consisting of Selections from Cæsar, Curtius, Nepos, Sallust, Ovid, Virgil, Plautius, Terence, Cicero, Pliny, and Tacitus, with Notes, and a general Vocabulary of Latin of more than 16,000 words 2.00 2.50

ALLEN'S LATIN LEXICON. 12mo. 205 pages. (Being the Vocabulary to the Reader.) Cloth 1.00 1.25

ALLEN'S LATIN PRIMER. A First Book of Latin for Boys and Girls. By J. H. ALLEN. 155 pages. Cloth 1.00 1.25

This is designed for the use of scholars of a younger class, and consists of thirty lessons, carefully arranged (an adaptation of the Robertsonian method), so as to give a full outline of the Grammar, accompanied by Tables of Inflection, with Dialogues (Latin and English), and Selections for reading.

www.ingramcontent.com/pod-product-compliance
Lightning Source LLC
LaVergne TN
LVHW020211110826
845151LV00003B/670

* 9 7 8 1 4 2 5 5 3 4 4 2 4 *